CREATIVE NONFICTION

CREATIVE NONFICTION

A Guide to Form, Content, and Style, with Readings

Eileen Pollack
University of Michigan

Australia • Brazil • Japan • Korea • Mexico • Singapore • Spain • United Kingdom • United States

Creative Nonfiction: A Guide to Form, Content, and Style, with Readings
Eileen Pollack

Senior Publisher: Lyn Uhl
Publisher: Michael Rosenberg
Development Editor: Stephanie Pelkowski Carpenter
Assistant Editor: Megan Garvey
Editorial Assistant: Rebekah Matthews
Marketing Manager: Christina Shea
Marketing Assistant: Ryan Ahern
Marketing Communications Manager: Stacey Purviance Taylor
Senior Content Project Manager: Michael Lepera
Senior Art Director: Cate Rickard Barr
Senior Print Buyer: Betsy Donaghey
Permissions Editor: Timothy Sisler
Text Researcher: Norah Piehl
Production Service/Compositor: Graphic World Publishing Services
Text Designer: Patricia Bracken, Bracken Design
Photo Manager: Don Schlotman
Photo Researcher: Jaime Jankowski, Pre-PressPMG
Cover Designer: Patricia Bracken, Bracken Design
Cover Image: Greektown, Monroe St., Detroit; 1993, 24 × 36 oil on canvas. Courtesy of Robert Gniewek.

Library of Congress Control Number: 2008938691
ISBN-13: 978-1-4282-3105-4
ISBN-10: 1-4282-3105-6

Wadsworth
25 Thomson Place
Boston, MA 02210-1202
USA

Cengage Learning products are represented in Canada by Nelson Education, Ltd.

Printed in Canada
1 2 3 4 5 6 7 12 11 10 09 08

Brief Contents

Contents

Preface to Instructors

As you may be seeing firsthand, the demand for courses in creative nonfiction is growing, with undergraduate and graduate students in the humanities and sciences eager to take classes that will help them present factual material in ways that will be accessible and attractive to mainstream audiences. MFA programs in creative nonfiction are springing up around the country, existing programs in fiction and poetry are adding nonfiction seminars to their curricula, and such courses are being offered with increasing frequency in journalism departments at the undergraduate and graduate levels. Because the genre combines the attractions of the personal essay with the requirement that students move beyond the self to engage with other people, visit new places, and explore unfamiliar bodies of knowledge, creative nonfiction also has much to offer instructors of composition and essay-writing courses, even at the high school level.

During my twenty-seven years of teaching creative nonfiction to undergraduate and graduate students, journalists, and lay writers of all ages, I have discovered that dividing nonfiction anthologies and textbooks according to content or subject matter (i.e., "memoir," "nature writing," "travel writing," "science writing") leaves students seeking inspiration and guidance when they come to write and revise their own essays. "But where do I begin?" they ask. And: "Where do I go from there?"

In *Creative Nonfiction*, my method is to lay bare the strategies that nonfiction writers actually use to generate their ideas and to write and revise their essays and to introduce students to a dazzling array of intuitively clear and organic structures that—in combination with a compelling central question—can lend their own essays a dynamic forward motion and a pleasing sense of intentionality. In theory and in practice, the essay's central question keeps the writer focused on what he or she is supposed to be doing with the material while the structure (or *form*) provides a way for the writer to develop, organize, and present his or her line of thinking and research about that question. As a result, students find that they are able to use the strategies and structures presented in this book to generate their own pieces of creative nonfiction, *no matter the material*.

This is a method that I have developed while teaching courses in composition, essay writing, and creative nonfiction at the undergraduate and graduate levels, working as a writing coach at newspapers around the country, and offering workshops to teenagers and adults of varied backgrounds. The essays in this book consistently have proven to be effective and inspiring in these same courses, the selections having benefited from extensive feedback from scores of students, journalists, academics, and freelance writers. The book's movement from experience-based essays to more analytical- or research-based essays, from fairly simple structures to more complex (and compound) forms, from writing about the self to writing about other people, from writing about one person to writing about a group and then an entire community, from writing about an object to a collection of objects or from a small space to a much larger space, is designed to help students master nearly all aspects of generating, researching, writing, and revising nonfiction.

The Organization of *Creative Nonfiction*

Although I have organized this book so that students encounter increasingly complex and analytical forms as they read from beginning to end, the format is also flexible. The book's division into three distinct parts lends itself to customization for your course:

Part I covers the essentials of style, content, and form. Chapters 1 through 4 establish what makes creative nonfiction creative—not a disregard for the truth, but the writer's reliance on his or her own voice and eye for detail; a variety of literary styles and techniques drawn from fiction, poetry, and drama; the writer's selection of a topic that genuinely interests him or her and a question about that topic that he or she wants to explore; and the structure or *form* best suited to searching for an answer to that question and presenting the resulting discoveries to an audience of nonspecialists.

Each chapter in **Part II** then introduces a new form of creative nonfiction, with samples drawn from a diverse array of essays, followed by exercises and prompts designed to guide students as they use this form to explore their own material and structure their own essays.

Part III assists students in revising their drafts, both on their own and with the help of other writers. The questions and pointers in these final three chapters work to remind students of the fundamentals of style, content, and form discussed throughout the text.

Key Features of *Creative Nonfiction*

- **Unique form-based approach.** *Creative Nonfiction* is the only book combining an emphasis on teaching the forms of nonfiction with a fully integrated reader.
- **Fresh and diverse readings.** Diverse readings exemplify each chapter's lessons in craft. Among the 49 essays included in this book are selections both new and familiar, whether by writers whose mastery of the genre is long acknowledged or by talented newcomers. These authors include: John D'Agata, Charles Baxter, Emily Bernard, Judith Ortiz Cofer, Bernard Cooper, Annie Dillard, Barbara Ehrenreich, Jamaica Kincaid, Li-Young Lee, Primo Levi, Phillip Lopate, James Alan McPherson, Naomi Shihab Nye, George Orwell, Grace Paley, Daniel Rivas, David Sedaris, Leslie Marmon Silko, Brent Staples, and E. B. White.
- **Formal variety.** *Creative Nonfiction* begins with the personal narrative form, but quickly expands a student's repertoire to include experiments, group portraits, spatial forms, and many others. Students will find that they can apply the methods they learn in this book to many disparate writing situations, from first-year composition or service-learning courses to creative-writing workshops, feature writing, memoir writing, and so on.
- **Opportunities for practice.** The guided questions in each "Learning from Other Writers" section and the generative exercises and activities presented as "Inspirations" are designed to help students learn to think like creative writers.

In short, by capturing the elusive process by which writers turn a vague idea or assignment into a tightly focused, fully researched, well-written and well-organized essay (or book) and by presenting models and Inspirations to help students emulate this process, *Creative Nonfiction* provides a toolbox of techniques and blueprints that will allow students to generate nearly any variety of the genre they might ever want to build.

Acknowledgments

My approach to creative nonfiction owes much to my apprenticeship with one of the inventors of the genre, John Hersey. Not only was Hersey a brilliant writer and teacher, he was also a kind and generous mentor and friend, and this book would not exist without him.

I am grateful to Mike Pride and the *Concord Monitor* for hiring me when I had virtually no experience as a journalist and allowing me to put into practice Hersey's theories, both as a reporter and as a writing coach.

As a graduate student at the University of Iowa in the early 1980s, I was fortunate to study composition theory with Cleo Jones and Dennis Moore, who helped me to apply Hersey's methods to teaching undergraduates how to write.

In developing the methods of teaching embodied in this book, I profited immeasurably from the suggestions and support offered by my students and colleagues at Tufts, Harvard, Emerson, and the University of Michigan, most notably Jeremiah Chamberlain, Miles Harvey, Donovan Hohn, Laura Kasischke, Fritz Swanson, and the members of the graduate seminar I taught at Michigan during Winter Term 2008.

I also am grateful to the following instructors for their helpful feedback: Alex Albright, East Carolina University; Thomas Amorose, Seattle Pacific University; Gerri Brightwell, University of Alaska, Fairbanks; Jill C. Christman, Ball State University; Earnest Cox, University of Arkansas at Little Rock; Deb Cumberland, Winona State University; Carol DeBoer-Langworthy, Brown University; Monika Elbert, Montclair State University; Debra Gwartney, Portland State University; Alyson Hagy, University of Wyoming; Rochelle Harris, Central Michigan University; Catherine Keohane, Montclair State University; David Leach, University of Victoria; Mike Magnuson, Southern Illinois University–Carbondale; Craig Meyer, Missouri State University; Matt Oliver, Old Dominion University; Michael Pearson, Old Dominion University; Daphne Read, University of Alberta; Kathryn Rhett, Gettysburg College; Mark Sanders, Stephen F. Austin State University; Kelly Shea, Seton Hall University; Marcia Smith, University of Arkansas at Little Rock; Jerry Wemple, Bloomsburg University; and Donald Wolff, Eastern Oregon University.

My sincere and lasting appreciation to my assistant, Whitney Stubbs, who helped me decide which essays to keep and cut and who not only wrote the author bios but also managed to make them sing, and to my agent, Maria Massie, whose wisdom and devotion seem to know no bounds.

Finally, my deepest thanks and appreciation to everyone at Cengage Learning: Michael Rosenberg, Publisher, for having the foresight to appreciate a completely new approach to a still-emerging field, the courage to share my vision for this book, and the generosity to ensure that our vision would be realized; Stephanie Pelkowski Carpenter, Senior Development Editor, for her light-handed editing suggestions and her patience and good humor while guiding me through a long and complex process; Megan Garvey, Assistant Editor, and Rebekah Matthews, Editorial Assistant, for their proficient handling of the time-consuming work involved in editing and reviewing this manuscript; Laura Slown Sullivan, Production Editor at Graphic World Publishing Services, for her careful attention to detail; Michael Lepera, Senior Content Project Manager, for his wise and artistic supervision of production; Mandee Eckersley, Executive Marketing Manager, and the good people on her sales force, for their enthusiasm on my behalf; Cate Rickard Barr, Senior Art Director, for her expert eye in selecting and designing a cover; and Laura Mado, Sales Representative, for her passionate response when I approached her at the book fair in the Graduate Student Lounge and asked if she would be interested in reading the proposal for a new textbook and anthology called *Creative Nonfiction*.

How to Use This Book

Most books about creative nonfiction divide the genre according to the material covered in the essays—"memoir," "nature writing," "science writing," "travel." But focusing on what an essay is *about* doesn't provide much guidance if you are trying to figure out how to write a similar essay or hoping to discover new possibilities for your craft. If someone shows you an essay about glaciers or groundhogs and advises you to write an essay of your own about the natural world, what are you supposed to do? You might imitate the author's style. But that doesn't help you to develop an original line of thinking about your subject or solve the problem of structure, by which I mean such questions as: "Where do I begin?" and "Where do I go from there?"

The impetus for any essay needs to be your passion for what you write. But once you have found that passion, knowing that it can be categorized under "history," "science," or "art" provides little if any help in figuring out something original to say about your subject or structuring the finished piece. Over the years, I have found that a combined focus on an essay's central question and its structure or *form* is by far the most useful way to teach creative nonfiction. My method is to lay bare the strategies that most writers use to generate their ideas and to write and revise their essays, then guide you in using these strategies to generate your own essays (or books), *no matter your material.*

The aim of *Creative Nonfiction* is to provide you with a comprehensive understanding of the genre, along with the tools you need to write what you want to write and a set of engaging and well-crafted essays (grouped according to their forms rather than their subjects) that can serve as structural models for your own endeavors. (Although documentaries, blogs, and graphic narratives are beyond the scope of this book, all the discussions of form in the chapters that follow can be applied to their counterparts in other media.)

We begin by discussing the ways in which creative nonfiction is creative—not in a license to disregard the truth, but a license to use your own voice, to select a central thematic question that genuinely interests you, and to choose or invent a form that shapes your search for answers and helps you to organize what you find. Each succeeding chapter introduces a new structure or form of creative nonfiction, with samples drawn from a diverse array of essays and excerpts from longer works, followed by prompts (I call these "Inspirations") to guide you in using that form to explore and present your own material.

Although you needn't read every chapter to get a sense of my method, I suggest that you begin with Part I, which covers the essentials of style, content, and form, then read the first chapter in Part II, which uses the personal narrative to illustrate these ideas. Similarly, I would suggest that you try at least some of the Inspirations in Part I and in the first chapter of Part II because I devote much more detail there to describing how to formulate a central question and generate a rough draft of an essay than is true in later chapters. And be sure to take a look at Part III for pointers on revising your early drafts and sharing them with other writers.

After that, you can choose which chapters to read and which Inspirations to attempt based on your own inclinations and/or your teacher's assignments. Don't be intimidated by the length, complexity, or literary style of the most accomplished essays in this anthology. Just as novice tennis-players begin by practicing each stroke in isolation before moving on to combine forehands, backhands, serves, volleys, and lobs in an actual game, you can study each aspect of creative nonfiction on its own before trying to combine to produce your own versions of the genre. Rather than trying to compete with the authors in this book, use them as guides to help you formulate and carry out your own personal narratives, journeys, profiles, or experiments. If you are reading this on your own, my advice would be to work your way through the book, seizing on the two or three Inspirations that get you most excited, then concentrate on writing and revising those pieces. As for the other Inspirations, you can jot down your ideas for future essays and go back and write them later.

Nina Hauser

Eileen Pollack is the author of *Woman Walking Ahead: In Search of Catherine Weldon and Sitting Bull,* which won a 2003 WILLA Finalist Award in nonfiction; a collection of stories called *The Rabbi in the Attic;* the novel *Paradise, New York;* and, most recently, *In the Mouth: Stories & Novellas.* Her essays, stories, and reviews have appeared in many periodicals, and she is the recipient of fellowships from the National Endowment for the Arts, the Michener Foundation, and the Rona Jaffe Foundation, among others. A graduate of Yale and the University of Iowa, she has taught at Tufts, Harvard, and Emerson, and is now the Zell Director of the MFA Program in Creative Writing at the University of Michigan.

PART 

What Makes Creative Nonfiction Creative?

A Creative Presentation of the Truth

If you tell enough people that you write creative nonfiction, eventually someone will laugh and say, "What's that? Sounds as if you earn your living as a liar!" But the alternatives for describing what you do are equally fraught with misunderstanding. If you tell people that you write essays, they will probably think you spend your time writing term papers of the sort they were forced to write in college, and who would choose to do *that*? You could say you write literary nonfiction, but that has a fussy, pretentious air. ("Oh, yes, I write *literature* for a living.") On the other hand, saying you write "features" sounds as if you're eking out stories for the local advertising supplement about the lady who crochets rugs out of Wonder Bread wrappers or the pumpkin at the county fair that resembles Winston Churchill.

Rather than take offense at the confusion that ensues when I tell people I write creative nonfiction, I embrace the paradox of the term and explain that my use of the adjective *creative* doesn't imply that I am taking liberties with the noun *nonfiction*, but rather that I am trying to present the truth in such a way that most people would want to read it.

I know, I know. There is no such thing as "the truth." Everyone who witnesses or participates in an event is going to describe it from a unique perspective. History depends on who gets to write it. Once you select *this* detail rather than some other, you have fictionalized your account. Memory is so unreliable that anything you say about your childhood is open for dispute.

I grant all of the above. *But you still know when you're lying.* You know when you're stretching the truth to make a story funnier or more dramatic. You know when you're filling the gaps in your memory by making something up. Those of us who have come to creative nonfiction from careers—however brief—as reporters for daily newspapers still write as if we had an editor looking over our shoulders, ready to fire us if we spell a detective's name as "Smith" instead of "Smythe" or tell our readers that a murder victim lived—and died—at 524 Hayden Drive when the correct address is 542. Some of us won't say that it was raining on the morning we started kindergarten unless we've looked up the weather report for that day and year. Given that the largest and most prestigious magazines employ at least one person whose job is to challenge every verifiable statement in every piece of nonfiction slated to be published and contact every source to make sure he or she actually said what he or she is quoted as having said, most of us also write with a fact checker in our brains to prevent our eventual humiliation by the fact checker at *The New Yorker*.

But even poets and fiction writers who turn to nonfiction to compose a lyric essay about sandhill cranes or a memoir about growing up in a family of migrant laborers will need to formulate a set of rules that governs what they will or won't do when conveying a childhood memory, capturing dialogue on the page, or changing a name to protect a friend. Such rules differ from writer to writer. But when confronted by the temptation to exaggerate or invent, you might put yourself in your readers' place and ask whether those readers, if they could compare what you've written to what you know to be true, would feel that you had violated their trust. You might ask if the world needs even one more grain of dishonesty added to the towering mountain of lies that have been told since time began. You might ask if the dead, no matter how despicable they were when they were living, deserve to be portrayed as worse than they really were. And, if you lie about the small stuff, you might ask how anyone will believe you when you urgently want and need to be believed, especially about some fact or event that otherwise might strike your readers as unbelievable.

Face it, if your friend tells you about the time he shot and killed an elephant and you later find out that he actually killed a bunny, you will feel that you've been had. If your aunt tells you about the time she spent six months in prison for protesting the war in Vietnam, and your mother sneers, "What a crock. Auntie Grace only spent six *days* in jail," you will roll your eyes and wonder whether you can ever again believe anything Aunt Grace says. You certainly don't want to end up as your generation's James Frey, apologizing to your readers (on *Oprah*, no less) for claiming (in his memoir, *A Million Little Pieces*) that you survived eighty-seven days in jail for hitting a cop with your car, resisting arrest, and trying to incite a riot when in fact you spent *three hours* in jail, and that for drunk driving (for further examples of Frey's dishonesty, see "A Million Little Lies: Exposing James Frey's Fiction Addition," which appeared on The Smoking Gun web site on January 8, 2006[1]). On the other hand, if your friend writes about the time he saved his little sister from a charging bull by waving a bright red undershirt at the beast, you probably won't feel cheated if his sister pipes up to say that the shirt was more orange than red. And you won't lose your faith in dear Aunt Grace if she admits to having forgotten "which important year of the famous sixties" she spent six days in jail or tells you that she's not sure which act of civil disobedience earned her this penalty, but it "probably consisted of sitting down to impede or slow some military parade."

Even the draconian policy I've outlined above leaves plenty of room for humor. The sorts of spoofs and parodies you find in a "newspaper" like *The Onion* or in the "Shouts and Murmurs" column of *The New Yorker* can be as wacky as you want and entirely a product of your imagination. And most readers of humorous essays (that is, pieces of creative nonfiction that have a serious intent underlying their laughter-inducing surface) are sophisticated enough to discern an exaggeration when they hear one. If the pro basketball player who lived next door when you were growing up was six feet eleven inches tall, your readers won't mind if you describe him as nearly seven feet tall, or so tall that when you looked up at him, his body swayed like the Empire State Building and his face was hidden in the clouds hovering above the Bronx that day. You can even tell us that when this neighbor showed up at the local playground and challenged you to a friendly game of one-on-one, he crossed the court in a single step, jumped higher than your head, and let the ball drop *down* into the basket from above.

You just can't tell your readers that he was *more* than seven feet tall, or that you beat him at that game of one-on-one, or even that you scored a single point—unless you did. Your readers will let you stretch the truth—and a basketball player's height—if they know you're trying to make them laugh rather than trying to put one over on them. In reading David Sedaris's wildly funny "Six to Eight Black Men" (see Chapter 12), we wouldn't be upset to learn that the author hadn't recorded his conversation with the cab driver verbatim. But if the Michigan law he

---

[1] See www.thesmokinggun.com/jamesfrey/0104061jamesfrey1.html.

cites—or the Dutch customs he describes—turned out to be fictitious, we would feel as if our laughter hadn't been honestly earned. (If you are interested in Sedaris's work and want to find out how much of what he's written is invented, see Alex Heard's investigative piece about Sedaris in the March 19, 2007, issue of *The New Republic.* For the record, despite my disappointment in learning that Sedaris fabricated or grossly exaggerated his experiences in several essays, I remain a big fan.)

To summarize, the term *creative nonfiction* was never meant to hide or condone shoddy thinking, a paucity of research, an absence of verifiable data, or a cavalier attitude toward the facts. Reporters and scholars can use any of the techniques or approaches in this book to present their material in an appealing, engaging way to an audience of laypeople or professionals without worrying that they are violating the standards of their field. (In the first instance, the results would qualify as creative nonfiction or literary journalism, as distinct from straight or standard journalism or reporting; in the second instance, the distinction might be made between creative nonfiction and standard academic articles and books.) What's creative about creative nonfiction isn't your attitude toward the truth but the language and stylistic techniques you use to convey that truth, your choice of a general topic and an interesting central question about that topic, and your selection of a structure or form that allows you to present your meditations and discoveries about your question in a clear and organic way.

2 An Engaging Voice and Style

LANGUAGE

Rather than rely on the same tired language that most writers use to report on that day's bombings, football games, or tornadoes, or to review the latest thrillers at the Cineplex, or to analyze the learning-related impacts of below-average funding on economically deprived and under-resourced inner-city schools, those of us who write creative nonfiction try to use clear, natural language to bring alive the people, places, and events we are describing. Granted, there are times when you simply need to sit down and write a clear, straightforward, jargon-free scientific report, scholarly article, legal brief, or analysis of the relationship between spending and achievement in poor urban schools. But if you want to present the truth about people, places, and events in ways that your readers will find entertaining, moving, memorable, or poetic, you will need to speak to them in a voice that is entertaining, moving, memorable, or poetic—or better still, a voice that is entertaining, moving, memorable, *and* poetic.

Joyce Carol Oates, in her introduction to *The Best American Essays of the Century*, describes the allure of language that is fresh and alive:

> Where in life we sometimes (allegedly infrequently) fall in love at first sight, in reading we may fall in love with the special, singular qualities of another's voice; we may become mesmerized, haunted; we may be provoked, shocked, illuminated; we may be galvanized into action; we may be enraged, revulsed, and yet!—drawn irresistibly to experience this *voice* again, and again. It's a writer's unique employment of language to which we, as readers, are drawn, though we assume we admire the writer primarily for what he or she "has to say."[1]

How do you come up with a distinctive voice—without trying so hard to be distinctive that you overshoot the mark and end up with prose that is overly ornate, stiff, or forced? My advice would be to try to sound like yourself—albeit your *best* self, your most thoughtful or funniest self, your kindest or most observant or most grammatically correct self—rather than trying to sound like most other people who write about your subject. At first, this advice might seem frightening. Sound like *myself*? How could that make me a better writer? But most of us are fairly talented speakers. We know how to keep the interest of our listeners, how to moderate our tone (now serious, now funny, now thoughtful, solemn, wise, now modest and self-effacing) and vary

[1] This quote appears on p. xix of the anthology, which was edited by Oates and Robert Atwan and published by Houghton Mifflin in 2000.

our diction (now high, now low, now polite, now profane), how to quote and mimic other people ("You will never guess what he had the nerve to say next!"). We run into trouble only when we sit down to write and become someone we're not. Trying to sound like yourself on paper not only tends to produce your best prose, it allows your natural—and naturally unique—voice to come through.

Or perhaps I should say "voices." You might write one essay in your jazziest, most street-wise voice and another in the voice you use when offering advice to your beloved younger sister. You may even switch from one voice to another within a single essay; doing so can be jarring to a reader, but with practice, most of us can learn to play our voices like musical instruments, changing tempo and tone as a given song requires.

Still, it's easy to lose confidence and fall back on prefabricated language. I once worked with a sportswriter who couldn't churn out a sentence without using at least two clichés. His teams thrashed their opponents on their way to garnering trophies. His freshman quarterbacks hailed from all-American hometowns, were uniformly promising, put their noses to the grindstone, gave their teams their all, and made their families, friends, teammates, and coaches proud. When I asked this reporter why he relied so heavily on expressions that so many sportswriters before him had relied on, he said that he assumed such expressions were a sort of professional lingo he needed to learn if he was going to advance in his field!

At another newspaper, I read a stack of editorials weighed down by hackneyed allusions to football and war (the members of the city council needed *to tackle the issue of unfair taxation*, while the superintendent of schools was urged *to enter the field and annihilate the disparity in test scores between black and white students*), even though the editorial writer turned out to be a pixieish twentysomething feminist who hadn't attended a single football game or served a day in the military. "What have I done?" she moaned. "I'm the first woman to hold this job, and I guess I thought I needed to sound like one of the guys." Happily, all she needed to do to develop an original voice—and win an award for her editorials—was to stop trying to sound like all the other editorial writers she had ever read.

Not that a reliance on jargon or stale expressions is limited to sports reporters or editorial writers. In some academic disciplines, earning a PhD can seem like an exercise in stringing together whatever buzzwords are in vogue. Even in daily life, when we sit around talking about love or work or child rearing, we often fall back on pop-psychological jargon about families that are dysfunctional, significant others who refuse to communicate about their issues or commit to a relationship, and bosses who were abused as children and therefore suffer from post-traumatic stress disorder and pass along their issues and baggage to their employees. We may think we know precisely what we mean, and maybe we do, but other people don't.

Suppose I write: "When I was a child, my father had a problem with alcohol that caused him to engage in domestic abuse with the rest of our family. This impacted on me when I was young, but eventually I learned to deal with the situation." The reality behind this necklace of clichés might be that my father was a drunk who would come home from the factory, go through a case of beer, then accuse my mother of cheating on him with everyone from the letter carrier to the checkout clerk at the A&P, after which he would hurl her against the refrigerator or twist her arm behind her back until she confessed to whatever infidelity he wanted her to confess to. The "impact" of this "situation" might be that I cowered in my room with my hands pressed against my ears, wishing that I were big and strong enough to protect my mother. And my eventual ability to "deal with" my father might mean that when I hit seventh grade, I grew ten inches, put on fifty pounds, and started working out at the gym, with the result that the next time he attempted to stuff my mother's hand down the garbage disposal, I was able to yank him off her and knock out two of his teeth, after which I threw his clothes in the street and changed the locks.

Then again, my father's "problem with alcohol" might describe a dad who occasionally drank too much bourbon and called me a stupid, ugly slut. Maybe, when I was young, I believed what he said. But after my mom divorced him and sent me to see a therapist, I realized that I was neither stupid nor ugly nor any more promiscuous than other girls my age. Best of all, a few years ago, my dad joined AA and begged my forgiveness for the terrible names he used to call me.

Whatever the case, you wouldn't really know from that original description of my father's "problem with alcohol" and the "impact" of the "situation" on my ability to "deal with it" or not.

Years ago, a humorist named Frank Sullivan wrote a series of columns in which a "cliché expert" named Mr. Arbuthnot testifies on subjects as diverse as love, politics, Christmas, and nuclear energy. Ordered (under oath!) to explain the effects of the first test of the atomic bomb, Arbuthnot attests that it "ushered in the atomic age." Pressed as to whether the atomic age could have arrived by means of any other verb than "usher," Arbuthnot replies that no, "'Usher' has the priority." His questioner prods him further. Now that the atomic age has been ushered in, what will never be the same?

> A[rbuthnot]—The world.
> Q[uestioner]—Are you pleased?
> A—I don't know. The splitting of the atom could prove a boon to mankind. It could pave the way for a bright new world. On the other hand, it may spell the doom of civilization as we know it.
> Q—You mean that it has—
> A—Vast possibilities for good or evil.
> Q—At any rate, Mr. Arbuthnot, as long as the bomb had to be discovered, I am glad we got it first.
> A—If you don't mind, I will be the one to recite the clichés here. You asked me to, you know.
> Q—I'm sorry.
> A—Quite all right. I shudder to think.
> Q—What?
> A—Of what might have happened if Germany or Japan had got the bomb first.
> Q—What kind of race was it between the Allied and German scientists?
> A—A close race.
> Q—What pressed?
> A—Time pressed.
> Q—With what kind of energy did the scientists work in their race to get the bomb?
> A—Feverish energy. Had the war lasted another six months the Germans might have had the bomb. It boggles.
> Q—What boggles?
> A—This tremendous scientific discovery boggles the imagination. Also stirs the same.
> Q—Where do we stand, Mr. Arbuthnot?
> A—At the threshold of a new era.
> Q—And humanity is where?
> A—At the crossroads ....[2]

[2] "The Cliché Expert Testifies on the Atom" first appeared in the November 17, 1945, issue of *The New Yorker;* it also can be found—along with transcripts of Mr. Arbuthnot's testimony on other subjects—in *A Rock in Every Snowball,* a collection of Frank Sullivan's humor pieces published by Little, Brown and Company in 1946.

Writing in clichés not only makes your language stale, it makes your thinking stale. I once heard a fiction writer say that he tried never to use a phrase that he had heard any other writer use. Rather than describe a bruise as "black and blue," he preferred to say "blue and black." This advice struck me as useful, but it doesn't go far enough. Reversing the order of the terms in a cliché still leaves you with a clichéd way of seeing. I don't know about you, but when *I* walk into a table, I develop a lump as hard and purple as a plum, after which the bruise fades to a sickly yellowish-green puddle that spreads slowly across my skin.

The most pleasurable way of inoculating yourself against hackneyed prose is to write a column in which your own cliché expert testifies about whatever subject you intend to cover, be it computers, literature, golf, education, Abstractionism, or Existentialism. Then ban every cliché that shows up in the transcript. Finding your own language might take longer than grabbing the first cliché that raises its hand and begs to be given the job, but it's a much more effective—and enjoyable—way to write. Wouldn't you rather provide two horrifying examples of your sixth-grade gym teacher's brutality than simply dismiss him as "the gym teacher from hell"?

Nothing is wrong with using a vague generalization or a hackneyed phrase as a sort of placeholder in a rough draft. But don't forget to go back and substitute fresh, specific details or examples later. When you catch yourself using a phrase you've heard before ("black and blue" or "gym teacher from hell"), ask yourself whether the cliché actually describes what you're trying to describe (your bruises, your gym teacher) or whether some other word or words might be more accurate (or funnier or more exciting) in conveying what you saw, heard, smelled, tasted, felt, or experienced. Not only is it more enjoyable to think up a good detail, you won't find your voice as a writer—or the true subject of your essay—until you get down at least a few specific sentences. And one specific sentence usually leads to a second detailed sentence, which leads to a third and fourth, if not to an entire essay.

The exercise I like to use to illustrate this principle is to ask everyone in the class to compose a sentence that conveys something essential about one of the adults who raised him or her. Then we go around the room and read our sentences aloud. "My mother works from sun up to sun down to pay for the things we need," a student might write, or: "My aunt always makes me crack up," or: "My father is the most forgiving man in the world." But as is true with any generalization, these examples raise as many questions as they answer. Does the first student's mother wake at 4 a.m. and take the train to Manhattan, where she shouts herself hoarse on the floor of the Stock Exchange so she can buy the student and her sister thousand-dollar handbags? Or does she spend ten hours a day cleaning houses and washing laundry so she can pay the rent on the shabby bungalow the writer and his six siblings share on the outskirts of a small Kentucky mining town? Does the second writer's aunt tell knock-knock jokes until her nephew chokes on his fried chicken, or does she imitate the sermons delivered by his father, a priggish and not very successful Baptist minister?

As to the assertion that the third writer's father is the most forgiving man on the planet, doesn't it beg you to disagree? In the first class I ever taught, a student wrote a similar sentence, prompting us to ask what made *her* father any more forgiving than our own. "After all," one young man said, "I totaled my father's Porsche, and the only thing he ever said was that he was glad I didn't get hurt." Another student said that *his* father had forgiven him for getting expelled from high school for smoking pot—three times. Then the student who wrote the sentence explained that her grandfather used to berate her father for being lazy and stupid and beat her father so badly that he broke both of her father's legs, yet her father now worked two jobs so that he could support the old man in a private nursing home rather than let him live out his days in the dilapidated and poorly run institution financed by the state. Not only did we concede that her father was forgiving, we wanted to read an essay about his deeper motives in working so hard to support a man who had beaten and berated him when he was young.

Most writers don't need long to figure out that a detailed sentence is more memorable and convincing than an unproven generalization. ("My father rarely laughs," one of my students wrote. After a quick revision, the same description read: "My father's laughter is a beautiful silver fish that leaps from a quiet stream." Another student told us that her father was "an asshole," a description she revised to read: "My mother doesn't appreciate my father's habit of showing our dinner guests photos of his mistresses.") But some writers become so enamored of using details that they don't know when to stop. A simple sentence meant to convey the fresh smell and silky feel of the spring air on prom night in a small Ohio town might become so overstuffed with sensory detail that the description becomes laughably fussy and overloaded, slowing us to the point that we never make it to the Holiday Inn for the actual event.

In "Finding a Focus" (Chapter 3), we will discuss how to figure out which details to keep and which to cut. For now, let's just say that most such decisions are a matter of asking yourself whether a detail is relevant to what you are trying to do in a given sentence, paragraph, or scene and whether you are putting in so many details that your readers will become impatient to move ahead to what happens next. If you can't answer these questions, try coming back to what you've written a few days later and seeing if the prose strikes you as cluttered or overwritten, or give your manuscript to a trusted reader and ask him or her which details should stay or go. (For most writers, a paucity of details is the more common problem than an overload of the same.)

EXPOSITION AND SCENE

Three basic modes of discourse tend to be employed in writing creative nonfiction: exposition; dramatic or scenic writing; and meditation. Let's leave the last of those three modes, meditation, for Chapter 3, on how to find and develop a central question for your essay, and Chapter 16, on meditative and argumentative essays. Here, we will confine ourselves to understanding exposition and scene.

Knowing how to compose an effective expository sentence—that is, a sentence that conveys an opinion or a fact—is an essential skill for any writer. Sometimes, you need to come right out and tell us that copals are "fossil resins of vegetable origin, with a rather high melting point, and in the state in which they are found and sold in commerce are insoluble in oil" (see Primo Levi's essay "Chromium," in Chapter 7) or that when you were fourteen, your family moved to Northbrook, Illinois, where "life is good. The average home costs $340,00; 97 percent of the kids go to college; and when you buy groceries at Sunset Foods, crimson-vested valets scurry to load your car" (as Robert Kurson informs us in "My Favorite Teacher," also in Chapter 7).

But few writers of contemporary creative nonfiction rely solely on exposition; rather, they supplement their stylistic choices with techniques borrowed from fiction, poetry, drama, and film. In addition to using exposition to tell their readers *about* a subject, writers of creative nonfiction use literary devices such as dialogue, gesture, and setting to *re-create* their subjects for their readers. To phrase this in the language of fiction-writing workshops, writers of creative nonfiction don't confine themselves to either "showing" or "telling"; they tend to show *and* tell. (One difference between standard journalism and literary journalism or creative nonfiction is that writers of the former tend to rely almost exclusively on expository prose, whereas writers of the latter use expository *and* scenic writing.) When you write creative nonfiction, you don't merely tell your readers about the animals at the zoo; you take your readers to the zoo to watch the monkeys swinging around their cage and the hippos wallowing in their stagnant, shallow pond. Better yet, you take your readers on a safari so they can see the animals in the wild.

Given the prevalence of movies in our culture, writing in a scenic or dramatic mode comes more naturally for most of us than it did for our predecessors. Even if you've never studied filmmaking, you probably are familiar with the way a director uses the camera to establish a setting and then show a character or characters carrying out a specific action in that place before fading to black and cutting to a different place and time. (Playwrights indicate their scene changes by dimming and raising the lights or by bringing down the curtain, changing the scenery, and then bringing the curtain back up.) If you think of expository prose as a sort of narrative voice-over that introduces or concludes a scene, and if you understand that writers use white space, chapter headings, and simple verbal transitions ("A few days later, in Chicago ...") to mark the beginnings and ends of their scenes, you can understand how great a debt creative nonfiction owes to drama and film.

A few years ago, when my niece was trying to describe the last time she visited her father in the hospital before he died, she told me that she was frustrated because she knew she had a lot to say but somehow had managed to say it all in two pages. Guessing that she had used exposition to summarize her experience, I told her to try again, this time pretending that she was entering her father's hospital room while using a video camera to record everything she saw or heard, except that her camera also could record whatever she tasted, smelled, or touched ... along with whatever emotions or thoughts she experienced in response to what she saw, tasted, smelled, or touched. She went back to her room, emerging the next morning to tell me that she now had twenty pages ... and could keep going and write a book.

How do you know which mode to use for a given passage? Keep asking yourself whether you want to tell your readers something straight out, in which case you will use expository prose to convey a fact or summarize an event, or whether your best strategy would be to bring alive your subject by re-creating the scene for your readers so they can experience it for themselves. If you are writing about a bank robbery, you might *tell* your readers where the criminals were born, how old they were at the time of the robbery, whether this was the first bank they tried to rob or whether they had been pulling off similar heists for years. You might *show* what the bank looked like and use dialogue to let us hear exactly what the robbers said during the holdup. You might *tell* us what you were thinking as you lay on the floor listening to the robbers argue about whether to kill you or let you go. You might use description to *show* the gun battle that raged above your head when the SWAT team stampeded in. You might *tell* us which of your fellow hostages were wounded in the fray, who did or didn't survive. You might use *scenic* writing to re-create the robbers' trials, then sum up the prison sentences the judge meted out in a brief *expository* epilogue at the end.

Most of us let intuition be our guide, choosing to employ exposition at the start of an essay or a chapter to establish the context for a scene, then slipping into the scene itself, then weaving in background information on a need-to-know basis, then returning to scenic mode when the exposition has gone on too long and readers are longing to hear another voice (through dialogue) or to witness an event directly. Then we give that initial draft to a trusted reader to see if our intuition was correct.

To supplement this trial-and-error method, keep in mind that you shouldn't use exposition to explain what you've already shown. If you've done your job in describing that bank robbery, you won't need to tell your readers how grateful you were when the SWAT team burst in and saved you. On the other hand, if you were disappointed that your ordeal didn't last a few days longer and garner you a spot on the national news—or a contract for a book about your captivity—you probably will need to tell us that.

To gain a bit of practice juggling exposition and scene, go back and try the exercise in which you write one specific sentence about someone who raised you. Then write another five or six detailed expository sentences about that person. Finally, close your eyes and bring to mind a memory in which your subject is acting in such a way that he or she reveals something essential about his or her character. Let the memory play itself out in your head. Where is this person? What is he or she doing or saying? How does he look? Is she interacting with other people? What do you see? Hear? Smell? Without losing your mental movie of that scene, try to get everything down on paper.

Now compare this scene with the expository sentences you wrote earlier. Which tactic is more effective? Are there aspects of the scene that couldn't be conveyed by exposition? Which expository sentences convey information that couldn't be conveyed through scene?

Once you understand the basic characteristics of expository and scenic writing and the relative advantages of each mode, you will need to consider how to regulate the flow of the information that you dispense to your readers via exposition and the length and pacing of each scene. In reality, much of a writer's skill in both arenas—rate of revelation and dramatic pacing—is acquired naturally through reading other people's prose and by workshopping and revising early drafts of a given manuscript. As you will see when you read the essays in this anthology, few writers begin their essays with pages and pages of exposition whose purpose is to provide readers with the background necessary to understand the main action; instead, we get a paragraph or two of crucial information at the start, then learn more as we go on reading, a paragraph here, a sentence there, on a need-to-know basis.

On the other hand, you rarely encounter a writer who withholds crucial facts in a misguided effort to create suspense. Real suspense comes from what readers *know* rather than what they don't know; to follow a mystery or a thriller, we need to have a clear idea what the mystery or conspiracy *is*. Instead of withholding information, mystery writers dole out clues as the narrative progresses. The resolution of a mystery shouldn't come as a complete shock; rather, the surprise of the final revelation gives way to a satisfying sense that the writer has been preparing us for that ending all along.

As to pacing, no one wants to read pages and pages of exposition about the months a soldier spends hanging around the barracks, only to rush through a two-paragraph scene in which he comes under attack in his first gun battle in Iraq. Again, most of us have watched enough movies that we have acquired an intuitive feel for pacing. We know that subjecting an audience to twenty minutes of expository voice-over is a clumsy way to start a film, or that asking viewers to read chapter after chapter of historical background scrolling across a screen begs them to draw unfavorable parallels to the opening moments of *Star Wars*. And most of us are familiar with the way directors use quickly cut scenes or montages to convey the passing of empty time, only to watch the pacing slow dramatically as the two main characters are finally reunited and find themselves alone in a motel room.

All these references to movies might make you consider taking up screenwriting instead of creative nonfiction. Certainly, a prose writer can find it frustrating to spend twenty pages describing the visual and aural details a camera can reveal in an instant. But writers of creative nonfiction enjoy several significant advantages over filmmakers: we can convey to our readers the way something smells, tastes, or feels; we can provide important background information without resorting to stilted dialogue whose only purpose is to clue in the audience rather than the other members of the conversation; we can create the impression of habitual (rather than one-time) action simply by changing our verb tenses; we can reveal what's going on inside our characters' heads; and we can work on our own, with equipment that is easy to obtain and operate, on an extremely modest budget.

No writer has ever been more alive to the cinematic possibilities of written prose than James Agee, who was not only a master of fiction and creative nonfiction but also one of the first and finest movie critics our culture has produced. Yet as Agee demonstrates in the essay that follows, written prose can hypnotize us with the aural and visual poetry of everyday life in ways that movies cannot hope to accomplish. In "Knoxville: Summer of 1915," Agee renders for his readers a typical summer evening from his youth. Read the essay once for enjoyment. Then go back and see if you can identify the passages in which the author uses exposition to tell us something essential about the rituals he remembers from his childhood, as opposed to the passages in which he uses scenic writing to re-create those rituals for his readers. See if you can figure out how he manages to convey that this is a *typical* summer evening rather than one specific night, even as he uses very specific details to bring alive the sights and sounds and smells he experienced as a boy.

JAMES AGEE

KNOXVILLE: SUMMER OF 1915

We are talking now of summer evenings in Knoxville, Tennessee, in the time that I lived there so successfully disguised to myself as a child. It was a little bit mixed sort of block, fairly solidly lower middle class, with one or two juts apiece on either side of that. The houses corresponded: middle-sized gracefully fretted wood houses built in the late nineties and early nineteen hundreds, with small front and side and more spacious back yards, and trees in the yard, and porches. These were softwooded trees, poplars, tulip trees, cottonwoods. There were fences around one or two of the houses, but mainly the yards ran into each other with only now and then a low hedge that wasn't doing very well. There were few good friends among the grown people, and they were not poor enough for the other sort of intimate acquaintance, but everyone nodded and spoke, and even might talk short times, trivially, and at the two extremes of the general or the particular, and ordinarily nextdoor neighbors talked quite a bit when they happened to run into each other, and never paid calls. The men were mostly small businessmen, one or two very modestly executives, one or two worked with their hands, most of them clerical, and most of them between thirty and forty-five.

But it is of these evenings, I speak.

Supper was at six and was over by half past. There was still daylight, shining softly and with a tarnish, like the lining of a shell; and the carbon lamps lifted at the corners were on in the light, and the locusts were started, and the fire flies were out, and a few frogs were flopping in the dewy grass, by the time the fathers and the children came out. The children ran out first hell bent and yelling those names by which they were known; then the fathers sank out leisurely in crossed suspenders, their collars removed and their necks looking tall and shy. The mothers stayed back in the kitchen washing and drying, putting things away, recrossing their traceless footsteps like the lifetime journeys of bees, measuring out the dry cocoa for breakfast. When they came out they had taken off their aprons and their skirts were dampened and they sat in rockers on their porches quietly.

It is not of the games children play in the evening that I want to speak now, it is of a contemporaneous atmosphere that has little to do with them: that of the fathers of families, each in his space of lawn, his shirt fishlike pale in the unnatural light and his face nearly anonymous, hosing their lawns. The hoses were attached at spiggots that stood out of the brick foundations of the houses. The nozzles were variously set but usually so there was a long sweet stream of spray, the nozzle wet in the hand, the water trickling the right forearm and the peeled-back cuff, and the water whishing out a long loose and low-curved cone, and so gentle a sound. First an insane noise of violence in the nozzle, then the still irregular sound of adjustment, then the smoothing into steadiness and a pitch as accurately tuned to the size and style of stream as any violin. So many qualities of sound out of one hose: so many choral differences out of those several hoses that were in earshot. Out of any one hose, the almost dead silence of the release, and the short still arch of the separate big drops, silent as a held breath, and the only noise the flattering noise on leaves and the slapped grass at the fall of each big drop. That, and the intense hiss with the intense stream; that, and that same intensity not growing less but growing more quiet and delicate with the turn of the nozzle, up to that extreme tender whisper when the water was just a wide bell of film. Chiefly, though, the hoses were set much alike, in a compromise between distance and tenderness of spray (and quite surely a sense of art behind this compromise, and a quiet deep joy, too real to recognize itself), and the sounds therefore were pitched much alike; pointed by the snorting start of a new hose; decorated by some man playful with the nozzle; left empty, like God by the sparrow's fall, when any single one of them desists: and all, though near alike, of various pitch; and in this unison. These sweet pale streamings in the light lift out their pallors and their voices all together, mothers hushing their children, the hushing unnaturally prolonged, the men gentle and silent and each snail-like withdrawn into the quietude of what he singly is doing, the urination of huge children stood loosely military against an invisible wall, and gentle happy and peaceful, tasting the mean goodness of their living like the last of their suppers in their mouths; while the locusts carry on this noise of hoses on their much higher and sharper key. The noise of the locust is dry, and it seems not to be rasped or vibrated but urged from him as if through a small orifice by a breath that can never give out. Also there is never one locust but an illusion of at least a thousand. The noise of each locust is pitched in some classic locust range out of which none of them varies more than two full tones: and yet you seem to hear each locust discrete from all the rest, and there is a long, slow, pulse in their noise, like the scarcely defined arch of a long and high set bridge. They are all around in every tree, so that the noise seems to come from nowhere and everywhere at once, from the whole shell heaven, shivering in your flesh and teasing your eardrums, the boldest of all the sounds of night. And yet it is habitual to summer nights, and is of the great order of noises, like the noises of the sea and of the blood her precocious grandchild, which you realize you are hearing only when you catch yourself listening. Meantime from low in the dark, just outside the swaying horizons of the hoses, conveying always grass in the damp of dew and its strong green-black smear of smell, the regular yet spaced noises of the crickets, each a sweet cold silver noise three-noted, like the slipping each time of three matched links of a small chain.

But the men by now, one by one, have silenced their hoses and drained and coiled them. Now only two, and now only one, is left, and you see only ghostlike shirt with the sleeve garters, and sober mystery of his mild face like the lifted face of large cattle enquiring of your presence in a pitchdark pool of meadow; and now he too is gone; and it has become that time of evening when people sit on their porches, rocking gently and talking gently and watching the street and the standing up into their sphere of possession of the trees, of birds hung havens, hangars. People go by; things go by. A horse, drawing a buggy, breaking his hollow iron music on the asphalt; a loud auto; a quiet auto; people in pairs, not in a hurry, scuffling, switching their weight of aestival body, talking casually, the taste hovering over them of vanilla, strawberry, pasteboard and starched milk, the image upon them of lovers and horsemen, squared with clowns in hueless amber. A street car raising its iron moan; stopping, belling and starting; stertorous; rousing and raising again its iron increasing moan and swimming its gold windows and straw seats on past and past and past, the bleak spark crackling and cursing above it like a small malignant spirit set to dog its tracks; the iron whine rises on rising speed; still risen, faints; halts; the faint stinging bell; rises again, still fainter, fainting, lifting, lifts, faints forgone: forgotten. Now is the night one blue dew.

Now is the night one blue dew, my father has drained, he has coiled the hose.
Low on the length of lawns, a frailing of fire who breathes.
Content, silver, like peeps of light, each cricket makes his comment over and over in the drowned grass.
A cold toad thumpily flounders.
Within the edges of damp shadows of side yards are hovering children nearly sick with joy of fear, who watch the unguarding of a telephone pole.

Around white carbon corner lamps bugs of all sizes are lifted elliptic, solar systems. Big hardshells bruise themselves, assailant: he is fallen on his back, legs squiggling.
Parents on porches: rock and rock: From damp strings morning glories: hang their ancient faces.
The dry and exalted noise of the locusts from all the air at once enchants my eardrums.

On the rough wet grass of the back yard my father and mother have spread quilts. We all lie there, my mother, my father, my uncle, my aunt, and I too am lying there. First we were sitting up, then one of us lay down, and then we all lay down, on our stomachs, or on our sides, or on our backs, and they have kept on talking. They are not talking much, and the talk is quiet, of nothing in particular, of nothing at all in particular, of nothing at all. The stars are wide and alive, they seem each like a smile of great sweetness, and they seem very near. All my people are larger bodies than mine, quiet, with voices gentle and meaningless like the voices of sleeping birds. One is an artist, he is living at home. One is a musician, she is living at home. One is my mother who is good to me. One is my father who is good to me. By some chance, here they are, all on this earth; and who shall ever tell the sorrow of being on this earth, lying, on quilts, on the grass, in a summer evening, among the sounds of night. May God bless my people, my uncle, my aunt, my mother, my good father, oh, remember them kindly in their time of trouble; and in the hour of their taking away.

After a little I am taken in and put to bed. Sleep, soft smiling, draws me unto her: and those receive me, who quietly treat me, as one familiar and well-beloved in that home: but will not, oh, will not, not now, not ever; but will not ever tell me who I am.

—1938

INSPIRATIONS: BEING THERE

1. Think of a ritual that is as important to you as the lawn-watering ritual seems to be to Agee.
2. Close your eyes and bring to mind a specific time and place this ritual was performed (Mardi Gras in New Orleans in 1995, or the first Passover Seder at which you were old enough to ask the Four Questions), or a typical occurrence of this ritual (any one of a hundred high-school band practices, or one of the many times your father took you to the city to help him sell the vegetables from your farm). Let the ritual play itself out in your mind until you know where the action is taking place, the sights, sounds, and smells the ritual entails, who is doing and saying what.
3. Without losing your mental movie of this ritual (you might imagine it to be projected on the computer or page before you), try to get the ritual down on paper. Don't worry about grammar or mechanics. You don't even need to write in complete sentences. If you want to tell us what you are thinking or feeling as you observe or participate in the ritual, that's fine, but you often can convey what you think or feel about an event through the words you choose to re-create it.

IMAGERY

Reading Agee's evocation of a summer night in Knoxville, you probably noticed the poetry of his prose. In some places, Agee chooses his words so their sound and rhythm will match the sense of what he is describing. ("Out of any one hose, the almost dead silence of release, and the short still arch of the separate big drops, silent as a held breath, and the only noise the flattering noise on leaves and the slapped grass at the fall of each big drop.") In other passages, he uses simile and metaphor to make his descriptions more vivid and convey a certain mood. For instance, he tells us that the waning light "[shines] softly and with a tarnish, like the lining of a shell." The mothers tidy up their kitchens, "recrossing their traceless footsteps like the lifetime journeys of bees." The water from a hose forms "a wide bell of film," while the men stand "gentle and silent and each snail-like withdrawn into the quietude of what he singly is doing, the urination of huge children stood loosely military against an invisible wall."

Some writers of creative nonfiction are as lyrical as Agee (see Annie Dillard's essay "The Stunt Pilot" in Chapter 9), while other writers' voices are more straightforward (see Joseph Mitchell's "Evening with a Gifted Child" in the same chapter). But even the most literal and down-to-earth writers rely to some extent on imagery, as is true when Philip Weiss (in "How to Get Out of a Locked Trunk" in Chapter 8) explains that the lock on the trunk of his friend's Grand Marquis "closed in much the same way that a lobster might clamp on to a pencil," while the latch plate on a Skylark the author rented "had a perfect hole, a square in which the edge of the lock's jaw appeared like a face in a window."

INSPIRATIONS: DON'T BE SO LITERAL

1. Go back to the passage in which you re-created an important ritual for your readers and find at least one image or action that you could make more vivid—or richer in connotation—by using a metaphor or simile to describe it. Try to choose imagery that isn't obvious or clichéd (Agee *doesn't* say that the mothers in their kitchens are as busy as beavers), although you don't have to make your metaphors outlandishly eccentric (it's perfectly acceptable to say that the spray from a hose is shaped like a bell).
2. Even the best metaphor or simile needs to work in concert with the other elements of the essay in which it finds itself, so make sure your imagery seems relevant to the world you're describing. (Look at those reluctantly domesticated fathers and the ways in which Agee makes them seem like little boys—or soldiers—competing to find out who can pee the farthest.)

DIALOGUE

In his description of a typical Knoxville evening in 1915, James Agee is trying to recreate what he saw and heard as a child. At that age, Agee reminds us, the voices of adults are "gentle and meaningless like the voices of sleeping birds," which relieves him of the need to reproduce their actual words. But the actual words of the cautionary tales that Judith Ortiz Cofer's grandmother, mother, and sisters related in her presence most afternoons while sipping *café con leche* were vital to the lessons these women intended to teach Judith and her cousin about what it was like to be a Puerto Rican woman. As she renders one of her grandmother's favorite *cuentos*, Ortiz Cofer conveys not only *how* Mamá spoke ("I remember the rise and fall of her voice, the sighs, and her constantly gesturing hands, like two birds swooping through her words") but also the flavor of Mamá's speech (in this case, in translation) and her masterful control of suspense and humor.

Capturing the way people talk is an important skill for any writer. Later, in the chapter on profiles, we will discuss interviewing techniques and the mechanics of transcribing dialogue on the page. For now, with Ortiz Cofer's essay as a model, use the following prompts and your memories of the best storytellers in your family to develop your ear for the varieties of human speech.

JUDITH ORTIZ COFER

CASA: A PARTIAL REMEMBRANCE OF A PUERTO RICAN CHILDHOOD

At three or four o'clock in the afternoon, the hour of *café con leche,* the women of my family gathered in Mamá's living room to speak of important things and retell familiar stories meant to be overheard by us young girls, their daughters. In Mamá's house (everyone called my grandmother Mamá) was a large parlor built by my grandfather to his wife's exact specifications so that it was always cool, facing away from the sun. The doorway was on the side of the house so no one could walk directly into her living room. First they had to take a little stroll through and around her beautiful garden where prize-winning orchids grew in the trunk of an ancient tree she had hollowed out for that purpose. This room was furnished with several mahogany rocking chairs, acquired at the births of her children, and one intricately carved rocker that had passed down to Mamá at the death of her own mother.

It was on these rockers that my mother, her sisters, and my grandmother sat on these afternoons of my childhood to tell their stories, teaching each other, and my cousin and me, what it was like to be a woman, more specifically, a Puerto Rican woman. They talked about life on the island, and life in *Los Nueva Yores,* their way of referring to the United States from New York City to California: the other place, not home, all the same. They told real-life stories though, as I later learned, always embellishing them with a little or a lot of dramatic detail. And they told *cuentos,* the morality and cautionary tales told by the women in our family for generations: stories that became a part of my subconscious as I grew up in two worlds, the tropical island and the cold city, and that would later surface in my dreams and in my poetry.

One of these tales was about the woman who was left at the altar. Mamá liked to tell that one with histrionic intensity. I remember the rise and fall of her voice, the sighs, and her constantly gesturing hands, like two birds swooping through her words. This particular story usually would come up in a conversation as a result of someone mentioning a forthcoming engagement or wedding. The first time I remember hearing it, I was sitting on the floor at Mamá's feet, pretending to read a comic book. I may have been eleven or twelve years old, at that difficult age when a girl was no longer a child who could be ordered to leave the room if the women wanted freedom to take their talk into forbidden zones, nor really old enough to be considered a part of their conclave. I could only sit quietly, pretending to be in another world, while absorbing it all in a sort of unspoken agreement of my status as silent auditor. On this day, Mamá had taken my long, tangled mane of hair into her ever-busy hands. Without looking down at me and with no interruption of her flow of words, she began braiding my hair, working at it with the quickness and determination that characterized all her actions. My mother was watching us impassively from her rocker across the room. On her lips played a little ironic smile. I would never sit still for *her* ministrations, but even then, I instinctively knew that she did not possess Mamá's matriarchal power to command and keep everyone's attention. This was never more evident than in the spell she cast when telling a story.

"It is not like it used to be when I was a girl," Mamá announced. "Then, a man could leave a girl standing at the church altar with a bouquet of fresh flowers in her hands and disappear off the face of the earth. No way to track him down if he was from another town. He could be a married man, with maybe even two or three families all over the island. There was no way to know. And there were men who did this. Hombres with the devil in their flesh who would come to a pueblo, like this one, take a job at one of the haciendas, never meaning to stay, only to have a good time and to seduce the women."

The whole time she was speaking, Mamá would be weaving my hair into a flat plait that required pulling apart the two sections of hair with little jerks that made my eyes water; but knowing how grandmother detested whining and *boba* (sissy) tears, as she called them, I just sat up as straight and stiff as I did at La Escuela San Jose, where the nuns enforced good posture with a flexible plastic ruler they bounced off of slumped shoulders and heads. As Mamá's story progressed, I noticed how my young Aunt Laura lowered her eyes, refusing to meet Mamá's meaningful gaze. Laura was seventeen, in her last year of high school, and already engaged to a boy from another town who had staked his claim with a tiny diamond ring, then left for Los Nueva Yores to make his fortune. They were planning to get married in a year. Mamá had expressed serious doubts that the wedding would ever take place. In Mamá's eyes, a man set free without a legal contract was a man lost. She believed that marriage was not something men desired, but simply the price they had to pay for the privilege of children and, of course, for what no decent (synonymous with "smart") woman would give away for free.

"María La Loca was only seventeen when *it* happened to her." I listened closely at the mention of this name. María was a town character, a fat middle-aged woman who lived with her old mother on the outskirts of town. She was to be seen around the pueblo delivering the meat pies the two women made for a living. The most peculiar thing about María, in my eyes, was that she walked and moved like a little girl though she had the thick body and wrinkled face of an old woman. She would swing her hips in an exaggerated, clownish way, and sometimes even hop and skip up to someone's house. She spoke to no one. Even if you asked her a question, she would just look at you and smile, showing her yellow teeth. But I had heard that if you got close enough, you could hear her humming a tune without words. The kids yelled out nasty things at her, calling her *La Loca,* and the men who hung out at the bodega playing dominoes sometimes whistled mockingly as she passed by with her funny, outlandish walk. But María seemed impervious to it all, carrying her basket of *pasteles* like a grotesque Little Red Riding Hood through the forest.

María La Loca interested me, as did all the eccentrics and crazies of our pueblo. Their weirdness was a measuring stick I used in my serious quest for a definition of normal. As a Navy brat shuttling between New Jersey and the pueblo, I was constantly made to feel like an oddball by my peers, who made fun of my two-way accent: a Spanish accent when I spoke English, and when I spoke Spanish I was told that I sounded like a *Gringa*. Being the outsider had already turned my brother and me into cultural chameleons. We developed early on the ability to blend into a crowd, to sit and read quietly in a fifth story apartment building for days and days when it was too bitterly cold to play outside, or, set free, to run wild in Mamá's realm, where she took charge of our lives, releasing Mother for a while from the intense fear for our safety that our father's absences instilled in her. In order to keep us from harm when Father was away, Mother kept us under strict surveillance. She even walked us to and from Public School No. 11, which we attended during the months we lived in Paterson, New Jersey, our home base in the states. Mamá freed all three of us like pigeons from a cage. I saw her as my liberator and my model. Her stories were parables from which to glean the *Truth*.

"María La Loca was once a beautiful girl. Everyone thought she would marry the Méndez boy." As everyone knew, Rogelio Méndez was the richest man in town. "But," Mamá continued, knitting my hair with the same intensity she was putting into her story, "this *macho* made a fool out of her and ruined her life." She paused for the effect of her use of the word "macho," which at that time had not yet become a popular epithet for an unliberated man. This word had for us the crude and comical connotation of "male of the species," stud; a *macho* was what you put in a pen to increase your stock.

I peeked over my comic book at my mother. She too was under Mamá's spell, smiling conspiratorially at this little swipe at men. She was safe from Mamá's contempt in this area. Married at an early age, an unspotted lamb, she had been accepted by a good family of strict Spaniards whose name was old and respected, though their fortune had been lost long before my birth. In a rocker Papá had painted sky blue sat Mamá's oldest child, Aunt Nena. Mother of three children, stepmother of two more, she was a quiet woman who liked books but had married an ignorant and abusive widower whose main interest in life was accumulating wealth. He too was in the mainland working on his dream of returning home rich and triumphant to but the *finca* of his dreams. She was waiting for him to send for her. She would leave her children with Mamá for several years while the two of them slaved away in factories. He would one day be a rich man, and she a sadder woman. Even now her life-light was dimming. She spoke little, an aberration in Mamá's house, and she read avidly, as if storing up spiritual food for the long winters that awaited her in Los Nueva Yores without her family. But even Aunt Nena came alive to Mamá's words, rocking gently, her hands over a thick book in her lap.

Her daughter, my cousin Sara, played jacks by herself on the tile porch outside the room where we sat. She was a year older than I. We shared a bed and all our family's secrets. Collaborators in search of answers, Sara and I discussed everything we heard the women say, trying to fit it all together like a puzzle that, once assembled, would reveal life's mysteries to us. Though she and I still enjoyed taking part in boys' games—chase, volleyball, and even *vaqueros,* the island version of cowboys and Indians involving cap-gun battles and violent shoot-outs under the mango tree in Mamá's backyard—we loved best the quiet hours in the afternoon when the men were still at work, and the boys had gone to play serious baseball at the park. Then Mamá's house belonged only to us women. The aroma of coffee perking in the kitchen, the mesmerizing creaks and groans of the rockers, and the women telling their lives in *cuentos* are forever woven into the fabric of my imagination, braided like my hair that day I felt my grandmother's hands teaching me about strength, her voice convincing me of the power of storytelling.

That day Mamá told how the beautiful María had fallen prey to a man whose name was never the same in subsequent versions of the story; it was Juan one time, José, Rafael, Diego, another. We understood that neither the name nor any of the *facts* were important, only that a woman had allowed love to defeat her. Mamá put each of us in María's place by describing her wedding dress in loving detail: how she looked like a princess in her lace as she waited at the altar. Then, as Mamá approached the tragic denouement of her story, I was distracted by the sound of my Aunt Laura's violent rocking. She seemed on the verge of tears. She knew the fable was intended for her. That week she was going to have her wedding gown fitted, though no firm date had been set for the marriage. Mamá ignored Laura's obvious discomfort, digging out a ribbon from the sewing basket she kept by her rocker while describing María's long illness, "a fever that would not break for days." She spoke of a mother's despair: "that woman climbed the church steps on her knees every morning, wore only black as a *promesa* to the Holy Virgin in exchange for her daughter's health." By the time María returned from her honeymoon with death, she was ravished, no longer young or sane. "As you can see, she is almost as old as her mother already," Mamá lamented while tying the ribbon to the ends of my hair, pulling it back with such force that I just knew I would never be able to close my eyes completely again.

"That María's getting crazier every day." Mamá's voice would take a lighter tone now, expressing satisfaction, either for the perfection of my braid, or for a story well told—it was hard to tell. "You know that tune María is always humming?" Carried away by her enthusiasm, I tried to nod, but Mamá still had me pinned between her knees.

"Well that's the wedding march." Surprising us all, Mamá sang out, "Da, da, dara ... da, da, dara." Then lifting me off the floor by my skinny shoulders, she would lead me around the room in an impromptu waltz—another session ending with the laughter of women, all of us caught up in the infectious joke of our lives.

—1989

INSPIRATIONS: WHAT DID YOU SAY?

1. Ask a relative or a friend (preferably, someone older than forty) to tell you about his or her most important romance. How did this person meet his or her beloved? Who asked whom out on the first date? What happened on that date? Try to jot down as much of your subject's story as possible, then use your notes to write a monologue that conveys the sense of the speaker's story as well as his or her voice.
2. Think of the best storyteller you know. From memory, try to get down this person's best story in his or her own words.
3. Think of the most disturbing (or funniest) conversation you've ever had and transcribe it on the page.
4. Go back to the earlier Inspiration in which you described an important ritual; this time, try to weave in the voices of the participants. Or start over from scratch and daydream your way back to another ritual that seems equally rich in meaning. Whose voices do you hear? What are those voices saying? Can you convey their unique texture and variety on the page?

An Interesting Central Question

FINDING A FOCUS

As we have seen in the previous chapter, details, whether literal or metaphoric, are the building blocks of effective exposition and vivid scenes. But how do you know which details to leave out or include? The answer is: You often don't. The first time you describe something, you might not know *why* you're describing it. But that's why God created rough drafts. If you freewrite a description of a person, place, or thing, or a memory of an experience, and then you go back and reread what you've written, you will see patterns and recurring themes. Again and again, your conscious or unconscious mind will have returned to some aspect of your subject that seems troubling or important. In the next draft, you can focus your description more closely around this pattern or theme and develop its significance.

Look at the following excerpt from Barbara Ehrenreich's essay "Nickel-and-Dimed: On (Not) Getting By in America." (Ehrenreich went on to write a book with this title; the original essay, which first appeared in *Harper's*, appears in its entirety in Chapter 8.) Earlier in this essay, the author has told us about her job waiting tables at the Hearthside, where, if nothing else, she is able to derive some satisfaction from the companionship of her coworkers and her ability to talk to and please her customers. But her description of Jerry's, the no-frills restaurant where she takes a second job to supplement the less-than-livable wages she earns at the Hearthside, serves another goal. As you read, ask yourself why Ehrenreich might have chosen to include *these* details while omitting others—for instance, descriptions of her coworkers and conversations with her customers. What is the overall point to this description of Jerry's? What does it reveal about how Jerry's compares to the slightly classier Hearthside?

> Picture a fat person's hell, and I don't mean a place with no food. Instead there is everything you might eat if eating had no bodily consequences—cheese fries, chicken-fried steaks, fudge-laden desserts—only here every bite must be paid for, one way or another, in human discomfort. The kitchen is a cavern, a stomach leading to the lower intestine that is the garbage and dishwashing area, from which issue bizarre smells combining the edible and the offal: creamy carrion, pizza barf, and that unique and enigmatic Jerry's scent—citrus fart. The floor is slick with spills, forcing us to walk through the kitchen with tiny steps, like Susan McDougal in leg irons. Sinks everywhere are clogged with scraps of lettuce, decomposing lemon wedges, waterlogged toast crusts. Put your hand down on any counter and you risk being stuck to it by the film of ancient syrup spills, and this is unfortunate, because hands are utensils here,

used for scooping up lettuce onto salad plates, lifting out pie slices, and even moving hash browns from one plate to another. The regulation poster in the single unisex restroom admonishes us to wash our hands thoroughly and even offers instructions for doing so, but there is always some vital substance missing—soap, paper towels, toilet paper—and I never find all three at once. You learn to stuff your pockets with napkins before going in there, and too bad about the customers, who must eat, though they don't realize this, almost literally out of our hands.

The break room typifies the whole situation: there is none, because there are no breaks at Jerry's. For six to eight hours in a row, you never sit except to pee. Actually, there are three folding chairs at a table immediately adjacent to the bathroom, but hardly anyone ever sits here, in the very rectum of the gastro-architectural system. Rather, the function of the peri-toilet area is to house the ashtrays in which servers and dishwashers leave their cigarettes burning at all times, like votive candles, so that they don't have to waste time lighting up again when they dash back for a puff. Almost everyone smokes as if his or her pulmonary well-being depended on it—the multinational mélange of cooks, the Czech dishwashers, the servers, who are all American natives—creating an atmosphere in which oxygen is only an occasional pollutant. My first morning at Jerry's, when the hypoglycemic shakes set in, I complain to one of my fellow servers that I don't understand how she can go so long without food. "Well, I don't understand how you can go so long without a cigarette," she responds in a tone of reproach—because work is what you do for others; smoking is what you do for yourself. I don't know why the antismoking crusaders have never grasped the element of defiant self-nurturance that makes the habit so endearing to its victims—as if, in the American workplace, the only thing people have to call their own is the tumors they are nourishing and the spare moments they devote to feeding them.

Now, the Industrial Revolution is not an easy transition, especially when you have to zip through it in just a couple of days. I have gone from craft work straight into the factory, from the air-conditioned morgue of the Hearthside directly into the flames. Customers arrive in human waves, sometimes disgorged fifty at a time from their tour buses, peckish and whiny. Instead of two "girls" on the floor at once, there can be as many as six of us running around in our brilliant pink-and-orange Hawaiian shirts. Conversations, either with customers or fellow employees, seldom last more than twenty seconds at a time. On my first day, in fact, I am hurt by my sister servers' coldness. My mentor for the day is an emotionally uninflected twenty-three-year-old, and the others, who gossip a little among themselves about the real reason someone is out sick today and the size of the bail bond someone else has had to pay, ignore me completely. On my second day, I find out why. "Well, it's good to see you again," one of them says in greeting. "Hardly anyone comes back after the first day." I feel powerfully vindicated—a survivor—but it would take a long time, probably months, before I could hope to be accepted into this sorority.

INSPIRATIONS: NINE TO FIVE

1. Think of the first job you ever held (even if it was as a babysitter or newspaper carrier). Close your eyes and picture a typical day at that job. Then, without losing the memory, describe what you see, hear, smell, taste, feel, say, and think.
2. Look back at what you've written. Do you notice any common threads that connect two or more observations? Were you stunned by how spoiled the campers in your bunkhouse tended to be—and baffled as to how you might make them behave? Were you surprised at

the honesty—or dishonesty—of your fellow employees at Wal-Mart? Were you confused by the rules on the assembly line that first day at the Ford plant? Were you proud of how your body withstood the pain as you spread gravel on a new road in the hot sun, hour after hour?

3. Once you've figured out what point you were trying to make about your job, go back and write a new version of the scene, keeping the details that relate to your overall purpose, cutting the details that don't, adding descriptions or events or dialogue that help you convey your point.
4. Repeat the exercise, this time writing about the worst day you experienced at some job. Or the best day.

ASKING THE QUESTIONS YOU TRULY WANT TO ASK

Just as a passage of exposition or a scene needs a purpose, so your essay as a whole needs a reason to exist. This is the second way that creative nonfiction is creative: your selection of a topic—and a question about that topic—that you genuinely want to explore.

Why a question? Because it's hard to be creative if you're writing an essay to prove a point that you already understand or believe to be true. If you know what you know and believe what you believe before you sit down to write, all you need to do is to list the evidence that supports your opinion and be done with the whole damn thing. For such a piece of writing, the only form you need is the standard five-paragraph essay. *Here's what I believe. Here are three reasons that I believe it. And, in conclusion, here's what I proved that I believe.* But a question... a question implies movement. You start in ignorance and end in knowledge (or in partial enlightenment, or in slightly less ignorance than when you began). And the process by which you move from ignorance to knowledge provides the structural backbone of your essay.

At first, the freedom to choose your own topic—and a question about that topic—might seem more frightening than exciting. Most of us are accustomed to receiving an assignment from a teacher, an editor, or a boss. Topic in hand, we visit the library, perform an Internet search, or call an expert. Then we write up what we've learned. Even if we don't experience the thrill of thinking creatively about the topic or discovering something new, at least we don't risk returning to our teacher or boss or editor with nothing to show for a long day's work. In lieu of the adventure of the hunt, we can take comfort in knowing where the berry bushes are, visiting them with a pail, and bringing the berries home.

But even when your topic is assigned, fulfilling that assignment is more meaningful and enjoyable if you can discover something new about your topic rather than rehash what other people think. As much as libraries, Internet sites, and experts are storehouses of information that any writer is going to need and want to consult, there are other sources of enlightenment in this world, including a writer's own wisdom and experience.

If you still feel nervous about coming up with a question for an essay, if you hear voices in your head insisting that the question you've come up with is stupid, naïve, or obvious or assuring you that someone smarter or more qualified already has asked that question and answered it more effectively or intelligently than you could ever do, try to figure out whose voices you are hearing. Is that your father telling you that you're stupid or naïve? Or the sixth-grade teacher who never liked you because you weren't as polite or studious as your older brother? Talk to this person—nicely. Tell him or her that you have every right to ask whatever questions you want to ask and are perfectly capable of finding answers to those questions. If all else fails, think of the Scarecrow in *The Wizard of Oz* and how all the Wizard needed to do was to hand the Scarecrow a piece of sheepskin labeled "A Diploma" to make him understand how brilliant he already was. By virtue of the fact that I have never run across a single soul who couldn't come up with an interesting question and try to answer it, I hereby grant each and every person reading this book a Diploma in Thinkology.

Skeptical? I guarantee that by the time you were ten or twelve, you had asked enough interesting questions about the world to provide you with material for a lifetime. Another hundred questions go flitting through your mind every day. The trick is to catch these questions by the tail—or remember the questions that puzzled you as a child—and trust that most such questions would make an exciting focus for an essay. As Phillip Lopate puts it in "Writing Personal Essays: On the Necessity of Turning Oneself into a Character,"[1] what makes an essay dynamic "is the need to work out some problem, especially a problem that is not easily resolved. Fortunately, human beings are conflicted animals, so there is no shortage of tensions that won't go away."

At first, your question might seem too narrow to interest anyone beyond yourself. Suppose you get up with a hangover after yet another Friday night drinking far too much alcohol at a party and wonder why you can't keep your repeated vow to confine yourself to no more than two beers. To turn this into a question that might interest other people, all you need to do is ask yourself why so many other students at your university seem to feel the same need to drink to excess. Or you're shopping for shoes for your kids and find yourself wondering how anyone expects you to make ends meet on the crappy wages you earn working full time at the local grocery store. All you need to do is broaden your question to include other parents who are trying to feed their families on similarly crappy wages. Not everyone will care about the answer. There are people on this planet who have never held a minimum-wage job and don't give a fig about anyone who does. But even a billionaire might pause to wonder how her employees can pay the rent or provide dental care for their kids.

Of course, you will want to avoid taking on a question that no one could possibly answer, at least not in a ten-page essay. "What is consciousness?" and "What caused the present conflict in the Middle East?" are terrific questions, but as Lopate goes on to caution, "If you take on a problem that is too philosophically large or historically convoluted, you may choke on the details and give up." Finding a question that's the right size for the essay you're trying to write—not so small that discovering the answer is trivial, not so large that you don't have the time or resources to get it done in time, or at all—is a matter of common sense and practice.

To prove that you're qualified to be an essayist, carry around a notebook and write down every question that passes through your mind, not bothering to ask if it's a good question or a silly one. Maybe winter vacation is coming up and you're curious as to who invented Kwanzaa and whether you might find the celebration meaningful. Or you wonder how Jews came up with the tradition of eating potato pancakes on Hanukah and whether there's any historical truth to the legend that one small vial of oil fueled a lamp for eight days and nights. Or, like David Sedaris in "Six to Eight Black Men," you wonder whether our holiday traditions seem natural to us only because we've grown up hearing them.

Then again, maybe it's an ordinary August day, you're opening a can of dog food, and you can't stifle your impulse to find out if that beef or chicken really tastes as good as the label claims. Or you wonder why you can't stop thinking about the Hoover Dam, or why you keep obsessing about how you would get out of the trunk of your Camaro if someone were to lock you in.

My bet is that if you jot down the questions flitting around your mind, by the end of the second day, you will have filled an entire notebook and need to go buy a new one. Which isn't to say that writers always know exactly what question they're trying to answer before they sit

---

[1] From *Writing Creative Nonfiction: Instruction and Insights from Teachers of the Associated Writing Programs*, first published by Story Press in 2001 and reprinted in *Contemporary Creative Nonfiction: I & Eye*, edited by Bich Minh Nguyen and Porter Shreve, Pearson Longman, 2005.

down to write. One writer might start with a question that's fairly vague, then focus the question more tightly as he conducts his initial research and writes and revises draft after draft. Another writer might begin with the question she thinks she *ought* to ask, then realize that the question she actually cares about is altogether different. In most cases, there's a back-and-forth interaction between the writer's initial question, which allows him or her to start the project, and the demands and revelations that present themselves at later stages of the process. Ever since Montaigne invented the essay, with its roots in the verb *to try*, the challenge to its practitioners has been to discover what they want to say while they are trying to say it. Sometimes, you can't quite articulate your central thematic question until days or weeks into a project. Even then, the question might seem too eccentric or disturbing to pursue. And no matter how much you argue with those voices in your head, you might continue to worry that you lack the right credentials or expertise to answer it.

Luckily, the very process by which you acquire the courage or expertise to answer your question might be included in your essay. That's one of the beauties of creative nonfiction. Academics tend to hide the obstacles to their research. When they sit down to write, they put the answer to their question right at the beginning, followed by a series of logical propositions that attempts to convince the reader to accept that premise as true. All the false starts, spilled beakers, failed experiments, and futile trips to the archives are omitted. In creative nonfiction, the process of discovery, with all its frustration and suspense, often provides the very backbone of the essay.

4

A Natural, Organic Form

With their imposing Roman numerals and alphabetical subpoints, the logical outlines most of us learned to use in elementary school can help a writer organize a wealth of information. But logical outlines rarely correspond to anything we experience outside our heads. Nothing about such a structure draws the writer through his or her material in a natural way, and nothing pulls the reader through the finished product.

Think of the generations of reporters who learned to structure their articles in that famous inverted pyramid, or the legions of science students who were taught the proper protocol for writing up their experiments, or the cadres of PhDs tutored in the only acceptable form for a dissertation, or all the law students schooled in the appropriate structure of a brief. These hand-me-down structures provide writers with a means to organize what they know but don't provide a mechanism by which they can generate or develop new ideas.

In contrast, creative nonfiction is creative precisely because it encourages its practitioners to choose—or invent—the form that seems best suited to exploring the material they wish to explore. If you're not sure what I mean by "form," think of an essay's structure or organization. How do you know where to start your essay? In what order do you string together the expository passages and scenes? How do you weave these expository passages and scenes with meditations on the thematic question you are attempting to answer? Finally, how do you know when to stop?

The interplay between the central question that guides your research and the structure or form that helps you organize what you learn is at the living, breathing heart of creative nonfiction. Take the most common form of contemporary creative nonfiction, the personal narrative. As you move forward in time, the friction between the story you are telling and the question you are trying to answer throws up meditative sparks. The narrative provides a chronological road for the essay to follow. At any point at which your readers might need a bit of background to understand what's going on, you weave in that information, then move on to the next action or event. No matter how interesting a fact or scene, unless it elucidates an important aspect of the narrative or helps to answer the central question, you force yourself to leave it out. (Well, some facts and scenes are just too good to cut, but beware the digression that spawns the digression that destroys the last shred of an essay's coherence; you can console yourself with the knowledge that a fact or scene that doesn't fit in one essay may become the cornerstone or foundation of an essay all its own.) Finally, you go back and revise the essay to give your readers the impression that you knew what story you were telling and what question you were exploring all along.

As vital as structure is, it rarely gets discussed, and when it does, the emphasis tends to fall on the personal narrative as the primary—or only—form that creative nonfiction is allowed to take. This isn't surprising, given that a narrative (by which I mean a story told in roughly the order in which it happened) is the most comfortable way that human beings have devised to organize their experience. *First this happened, then that, then that.* But the forms of creative nonfiction aren't confined to narratives. As we will see in Part II, they are as wonderful and various as the fishes in the sea. And finding the perfect form for the material you are trying to shape is the most important factor in determining whether that material will advance from a one- or two-page beginning to a promising initial draft to a polished—and publishable—essay or book.

As a writing coach at various newspapers, I used to watch talented reporters amass notebooks full of research, then sweat and smoke their way to a massive first draft of the investigative series or the multipart feature they were trying to produce, then weep in frustration as editor after editor called up this beast on a computer screen and pronounced it "lacking in focus" or "disorganized." Each editor would cut and paste some paragraphs, give the reporter a few suggestions for revision, then pass the article to the next editor, who would move around a few more paragraphs and make the creature even more ungainly. The story would swim for months in the murky depths of cyberspace, surfacing now and then on an editor's desk but never appearing in print. *Sharks*, I began to call them. Mutant, disfigured sharks, circling and circling, searching for their proper form.

The dangers are even worse for books. Although an experienced writer might focus a book around two or more related questions and employ more than one form to organize this material, novices who start a book with neither a basic structure nor a single well-focused question are almost guaranteed to grow overwhelmed and lose their way.

What, then, are the forms available to nonfiction writers? As mentioned earlier, a first-person narrative is by far the most common; the writer describes a life-changing event that happened to him or her as that story unfolds in time. But you don't need to remain confined by the boundaries of what you already know or what you already have experienced when you write. In trying to answer your central question, you will want to do more than consult your memories; you will want to visit places you've never gone, speak to people you've never met, inspect new objects, dissect new organisms, solve a mystery, or conduct experiments. Even better, these adventures or explorations can provide you with the structure for the essay (or book) you eventually sit down to write.

In a similar way, you might want to spend time with an interesting person and describe whatever activity makes him or her a likely candidate for a profile, or structure your essay or book around the activities of a *group* of interesting people, or conduct fieldwork in a community whose rituals and codes you hope to understand and translate for your readers.

Nor do you have to confine yourself to organizational structures that move your readers through the chronology of some event. You can move your audience through *space* instead of time, taking them on a tour of your baseball glove or your body, your favorite painting or a map of Paris, your grandfather's will or your housemate's grocery list, your bedroom or a museum or the battlefield at Bunker Hill. Or you might use a variation of the aforementioned forms to structure a meditative journey through the nooks and crannies of your mind.

In the chapters that follow, you will encounter myriad forms that enable you to move beyond what you know and organize what you discover as you answer whatever questions interest or perplex you. Each set of essays will provide examples of a given form, questions to help you recognize and assimilate various techniques and tools appropriate to that form, and a series of "Inspirations" designed to guide you as you use your own material to produce an original example of the form. Along the way, I offer additional considerations relevant to the practice and craft of creative nonfiction, including how to write about your family and friends without ending up alone, divorced, or in a courtroom, how to carry out research, and how to conduct an interview. Although each chapter will assist you in developing and refining your work, the material in Part III is intended to provide additional guidance for revision, whether on your own or in a workshop.

If all this seems overwhelming, don't worry. No one starts out knowing exactly what question he or she wants to answer, along with the perfect form to structure the resulting essay. You might find yourself daydreaming about the cottage on the lake where your family spent two weeks every August, then remember the tales your father told about the town that flourished in the valley before the river was dammed and the village flooded by the lake, at which you might ask what gives any government the right to take away someone's home for the greater good—especially if the "greater good" consists of a reservoir on which a few lucky families can water ski, sail, and fish. Armed with this central question, you might then decide to interview five of the elderly residents who lost their houses in the valley and still live year-round on the reservoir's shores.

Or you might find yourself wondering if there's any point in issuing a curfew for your kids, given that they would only break it anyway, as you used to break *your* curfew when you were their age. You might try to answer this question by allowing your kids to come home as late as they please, then write an essay in which you describe your experiment ... and its results.

Rarely does a writer begin with a form, but I once had a student who attended a wedding at which the bride and groom proclaimed their fidelity not only to each other, but also to Ayn Rand and her Objectivist philosophy. My student wasn't sure what she wanted to say about Objectivism, but she knew that she was going to use the structure of the wedding ceremony to shape her meditations on Rand's philosophy and why it irked her.

Writing an essay is like any artistic endeavor: you begin with what you have—a memory, a voice, a question, or a form—and go wherever you can go from there.

PART II

The Forms of Creative Nonfiction

5

Personal (and Not-So-Personal) Narratives

Not only has the personal narrative come to be the most common form of creative nonfiction (at least in this country), it seems the easiest to define: a writer's first-person account of something he or she has experienced, told in roughly chronological order, as a story. But as is true of most definitions, this one is clear only until you consider it more closely. A writer's experiences, observations, and use of the pronoun "I" may play a significant role in an essay that isn't primarily about the writer. And an essay based on the writer's life might assume a shape other than chronological.

Nonetheless, our basic definition of a personal narrative will allow us to study its ingredients. A narrative is a story, and as any good storyteller knows, good stories start where the action heats up rather than so far back in time that the audience is asleep before the baby disappears or the team arrives in Beijing for the long-anticipated Olympic diving competition. As we've seen in Part I, once you've gained your audience's attention, you will need to maintain it by providing details that bring alive the people and events that figure in your narrative and the location where the events are set. You might mimic the way the characters talk or convey what they were thinking when they realized that their airplane was low on gas. You will need to fill in just enough background to allow everyone in the audience to understand what's going on without slowing the action so much that your listeners lose interest. You will need to use drama and suspense, humor, evocative descriptions, and startling turns of phrase to keep your readers enthralled. And you will need to keep your story going until your audience's expectations and curiosity have been satisfied ... but not so long that you've continued past the point where the excitement ends.

Most of us understand these elements well enough that we can tell an amusing anecdote. And usually that's enough. If you tell your friends about the day you got lost in Yellowstone, then tumbled off a cliff and looked up to see a bear, no doubt they will stick around to find out what happened next. And anyone with a sense of humor will enjoy your account of walking in a classroom, teaching your best-ever lecture on *Pride and Prejudice*, becoming more and more perplexed by your students' unwillingness or inability to answer even the most basic questions about the text, then figuring out that you had wandered into the wrong classroom and spent half an hour lecturing about Jane Austen to a bunch of computer engineers.

But the most memorable stories do more than entertain. Like the best movies, the best personal narratives keep us thinking about the questions they raise long after the lights have gone up or we've put down the book. You can't just describe something funny or upsetting.

If your audience doesn't know you, they won't care that your father humiliated you when you were a kid because you couldn't hit a baseball. When a stranger on a plane starts to tell you about her husband's infidelities or her own inability to stay out of bars, you want to move to another seat. *Why do I need to know this? Why would you think I care?*

What distinguishes the very best storytellers from those who are mediocre (or worse) is their ability to make a good story not only from a brush with death or a meeting with the pope but from something as trivial as getting cheated at a card game or being pressured by a friend into smoking a cigarette. Which generally means that the storyteller is using the card game or cigarette to explore some larger question about what it means to be human. Which *doesn't* mean that the storyteller is trying to teach us a lesson about honesty being the best policy or peer pressure being an evil force that causes young people to smoke and use drugs and fornicate indiscriminately. (An essay *testing* one of those clichés might be worth writing. *Is* honesty the best policy? Always? Can't peer pressure sometimes be a *helpful* part of growing up?) If you know the significance of a story before you commit it to paper, why bother to tell it? What are you going to discover in the writing? How can you not be bored? And if *you're* bored, how can you hope not to bore your audience? How can you prevent your readers from thinking: "*So what?*"

If you're a college student, you've probably fielded questions as to why you would want to learn to write creative nonfiction instead of the sorts of academic essays, research papers, or dissertations you will be required to turn in for your other courses. These critics have a point. A narrow emphasis on the personal narrative encourages writers to stick to what they know rather than leading them to explore the world beyond the self. And a shaky grasp of the essentials of the genre might leave students with the faulty impression that they can write about an experience without developing an original and focused line of inquiry *about* that experience.

What most opponents of courses in creative nonfiction oppose is not that students learn to use details and dialogue or evocative, fresh, clear language, or even that they employ the pronoun "I," but that they tend to be applauded for writing essays that merely *describe* their experiences without trying to convey the *significance* of those experiences or using research and analysis to place those experiences within a larger societal (or historical, literary, psychological, or scientific) context. No matter whether you're writing about your love for deer hunting or the hardships your family suffered during and after Hurricane Katrina, you will need to formulate an interesting question about your topic, develop at least a partial answer to that question, and present your findings and discoveries in a comprehensible and compelling way.

GO WITH WHAT YOU KNOW, THEN GO FURTHER

A willingness to write about what you *don't* know rather than what you do know is the difference between a raconteur's breezy and oft-recited anecdote and an essay in which a memoirist revisits an important incident from his childhood or early adulthood armed with a question that genuinely troubles him or her about that incident. In George Orwell's justifiably famous essay "Shooting an Elephant," the synergy between content and form is preserved in the finished product. The essay matters as it does because Orwell feels compelled to figure out why he shot an elephant that didn't need to be shot. He doesn't tell the story as a predigested anecdote, a bloody good yarn to entertain the officers at the club. Rather, he reconsiders an experience that he didn't fully understand when it happened, an experience that *still* disturbs him. The news that a rampaging elephant has killed a poor coolie propels the younger Orwell out the door. And yet, when he finds the elephant, he knows with "perfect certainty" that he ought not to shoot.

> It is a serious matter to shoot a working elephant—it is comparable to destroying a huge and costly piece of machinery—and obviously one ought not to do it if it can possibly be avoided.... I thought then and I think now that his attack of "must" was already passing off; in which case he would merely wander harmlessly about until the mahout came back and caught him.... I decided that I would watch him for a while to make sure that he did not turn savage again, and then go home.

There Orwell stands, surrounded by a mob silently willing him to shoot the elephant for the spectacle of the thing, and there, at that moment, he grasps "the futility of the white man's dominion in the East."

> Here was I, the white man with his gun, standing in the front of the unarmed native crowd—seemingly the leading actor of the piece; but in reality I was only an absurd puppet pushed to and fro by the will of those yellow faces behind. I perceived in this moment that when the white man turns tyrant it is his own freedom that he destroys.... For it is the condition of his rule that he shall spend his life in trying to impress the "natives," and so in every crisis he has got to do what the "natives" expect of him.... I had got to shoot the elephant.... To come all that way, rifle in hand, with two thousand people marching at my heels, and then to trail feebly away, having done nothing—no, that was impossible. The crowd would laugh at me. And my whole life, every white man's life in the East, was one long struggle not to be laughed at.

As Orwell answers the question of why he shot the elephant, he also partially answers the more universal question in which his conundrum nests: Why do imperialists act in ways that are not in their own best interests or the interests of the people they hope to rule? "Shooting an Elephant" is a marvelous example of the manner in which a compelling narrative and a sincere question about that narrative work together to produce an essay imbued not only with the suspense of "what will happen next" but the deeper suspense as to what the experience will end up meaning. The thesis isn't presented at the start, with the rest of the essay proving it true. Rather, the reader watches the narrator struggling to reach his conclusion at every point along the way.

That's how most narratives work. The writer replays the events of a story while comparing those events at every point to the question that troubles him or her. If the writer thinks that his or her task is to describe an unusually dramatic or comic incident, he or she will be tempted to put in every detail, provoking the reader to ask—even for a story about a near-death experience or a horrifying instance of abuse—why are you telling me all this? On the other hand, if a writer sits down to ponder an abstract question (Why do imperialists act in ways that run counter to their own best interests?), the meditation will likely stall after the first five minutes (nothing makes a mind wander more quickly to what's for lunch than an abstract question).

A writer need not have served the Raj to come up with an experience worth describing or a question that's worth exploring. In "A Clack of Tiny Sparks," Bernard Cooper revisits the fall and winter of his typical ninth-grade—gay—boyhood to figure out why, when the girl who sat beside him in algebra class asked, "Are you a fag?," he lied and said no. From the safety of adulthood, happily coupled with his male partner of seven years, Cooper recounts a series of highly charged events from his adolescence in an attempt to understand how his life might have turned out differently if he hadn't been so intent on hiding from his parents and classmates his knowledge that he loved and desired men. Although Cooper's essay doesn't tell us anything earthshakingly new about what it means to grow up gay, the author allows his audience to experience from the inside the struggle to figure out whether a young person chooses his sexual preference or whether it chooses him. The accuracy and honesty of Cooper's observations, his eye and ear for the perfect detail, remind us of not only how ninth grade smelled and how it tasted, what people said and did and wore, but also what ninth grade *felt* like. Taken as a whole, Cooper's scenic depiction of his sexual turmoil, combined with his meditations on the causes of that turmoil, raise "A Clack of Tiny Sparks" to the level of art.

Similarly, Andre Dubus III uses sensory detail and a keen sense of time and place to recreate for his readers a typical winter day in 1974, when he and his younger brother and their best friend skipped school and wandered the dying mill town where all three boys grew up. All three are obsessed with sex and violence. All three are surrounded by poverty, unemployment, alcohol, and drugs. Yet only one of the boys grows up to beat his wife and die a violent and premature death.

Although Dubus at fifteen is too immature—and too close to his subject—to ponder much more than how to stay warm, in later years he finds himself haunted by questions about the ties that once bound him to his friend and the forces that eventually led their tracks to diverge so radically. Why was the friend shunted off to trade school, while Dubus, who hated gym and was failing algebra, managed to go to college? How did the author evade the lure of drugs that even his sister sold? How and why did that "hawny" fourteen-year-old grow up to be a wife-beater, while Dubus grew up to be a man who pulls on his boots and jacket and goes for a walk rather than risk an argument with his girlfriend? Who or what was responsible for the friend's brutality toward his wife? When Dubus runs into his friend in a convenience store, when he receives an invitation to the friend's wedding, when he hears about the friend's death, when he reads in the newspaper about the friend's wife serving time for what turns out to be a fairly common crime—killing an abusive spouse—he meditates on what might have led the two of them to follow such wildly different paths, despite their shared childhood in their "economically depressed" hometown. Perhaps the friend's alcoholic mother was to blame. And yet, if this was so, how to explain the time Dubus stopped by unexpectedly at his friend's house and witnessed a startling display of maternal—and filial—affection that in no easy way could have predicted the growth of a violent, woman-hating son?

As the essays by Dubus and Orwell demonstrate, one secret to writing a personal narrative is to achieve enough distance from the events you are describing to see them in a new way and formulate a question that you might not have been able to articulate, let alone answer, when you witnessed or experienced them. Sometimes, you can achieve such distance by stepping back from the accident or crime in which you were involved, catching your breath, sitting on a bench, and drinking a cup of coffee. At other times, you might need to move to another state, marry, have children of your own, and wait until those children are the age you were when you got arrested for shoplifting or setting fire to an abandoned shack. You might be spurred to remember an incident from long ago by an obituary that appears in your local paper, an e-mail from an old girlfriend, a whiff of cigar smoke in a crowd. Or you might find yourself thinking about the events from an earlier time simply because you are now living in such different circumstances, as Bernard Cooper finds himself moved to write about the agonies of his gay boyhood from the astonishing safety and contentment of his adult (male) lover's arms.

If you have lived a long life, you shouldn't have much trouble achieving the necessary distance to look back on incidents from your childhood, or even your adolescence. But if you're still in your teens or twenties, or if you're trying to write about events that happened last week or last month, you might need to imagine or project a certain distance from the incidents you describe. This isn't as hard as it sounds; one trick is simply to imagine that you're a few years older than you are, or that you've grown beyond the self you were when you experienced what you experienced. When I was twenty-four and working my first job as a reporter, I begged my editor to let me write a column. "A column?" he said. "You have to be pretty wise to write a column. Why would our readers care what someone in her early twenties thinks?" Despite the editor's sarcasm, I could see the truth in what he said. After wheedling his promise that I could write six columns on a trial basis, I sat at my computer and—pretending that I was ten years older than I was—wrote an essay about the yard sales I had visited that past weekend in a neighboring town, where people seemed to be trading their junk for someone else's junk in a frenzy whose purpose eluded me until I figured out that they were actually affirming their connections with one another—and the town. The column wasn't exactly a candidate for a Pulitzer Prize, but my editor—and my readers—seemed sufficiently impressed by my simulated wisdom (which, by the third or fourth column, began to feel real) that the six weeks I had been allotted for my experiment turned into six months. (I would have kept going, but turning out a weekly column in addition to fulfilling my daily assignments was making me feel ninety rather than thirty-five.)

What's tricky is achieving the necessary intellectual distance from an incident without robbing your narrative of emotion. You wouldn't want to achieve so much distance on your grandmother's death that you describe her funeral with complete detachment. But neither can you expect your readers to cry simply because you describe the tears you shed for a generically sweet old woman. That's the technique used by advertising executives and greeting-card manufacturers who want to manipulate us into believing that *our* grandma is the generically sweet old lady sitting in that rocker on the porch, *our* daughter or niece is the chubby-cheeked infant in that cradle, *our* shabby, smelly mutt is that adorable big-eyed basset hound looking up from the laundry basket, and *we* are one half of that handsome and fit (if slightly blurry) couple walking along the beach. The paradox is that the vivid, eccentric details you use to characterize *your* grandmother (or baby, mutt, or boyfriend) will cause your readers to bring to mind the vivid, eccentric details that characterize their own. The particular question you choose to ask about your particular grandmother will lead the rest of us to read what you write with interest, even if our grandma is nothing like yours.

In "No Burden to Bear," Marcie Hershman focuses not on her beloved grandmother's death, or even her own grief at that loss, but on the question of what it means to be a pallbearer. Rather than trying to describe everything about her grandmother, Hershman presents us with a single characteristic scene (a lovely example of the exercise in Chapter 2 in which you were asked to show a person performing the action most indicative of who she is). Rather than engage in a harangue designed to convince us that women should be pallbearers, the author simply presents two brief stories—one about her childhood dance sessions with her grandmother and the other a scene from her grandmother's funeral—linked by the question of what it means for one person to carry, literally and metaphorically, someone she loves. When we reach the final passage, in which the author describes what she thought and felt when she lifted her grandmother's coffin, we grant that she has earned the right to express these particular emotions and ideas.

No one would equate the death of a grandparent with the death of a pet, but in both cases, writing about the loss of someone or something you love is difficult without slipping into sentimentality. (*Sentiment* is a person's honest emotional response to an event, whereas *sentimentality* is the expression of an unearned, generic, wildly excessive, or insincere emotion.) In "Death of a Pig," E. B. White avoids this danger by presenting his eponymous pig in all its warty individuality and trying to deny just how badly shaken he was by the suffering of this nameless animal.

DISCOVERING SYMBOLS

From scene to scene, White's central question as to why he did, in fact, care so deeply about his pig, especially because he was raising the pig to kill it, not only gives rise to his meditations on mortality, both porcine and human, it also bestows a profound significance on the humblest objects that figure in the telling. When White gives his pig an enema, he muses that the pig's lot and his own "were inextricably bound now, as though the rubber tube were the silver cord." If not for the central question, that rubber tube would remain a tube.

As you revisit an experience while trying to answer a question that intrigues you about that experience, certain aspects of the story—objects, images, gestures, or snatches of dialogue—will gradually assume a greater thematic weight than they might have otherwise attained. Early in "Tracks and Ties," the author's friend uses a "black-handled Buck knife" to carve a peace sign into the back of a bus seat as he and the narrator and the narrator's brother aimlessly ride around and around the cold, economically depressed town in which they live. Years later, the author learns that his friend has been stabbed to death with this same black-handled Buck knife. The quiet irony of a young man expressing his desire for peace by defacing public property with a knife and later being murdered with this same weapon is beautifully conveyed by the recurrent list of adjectives used to describe the knife, just as the idea that most young people who grow up in this working-class town face constricted lives is subtly reinforced by the image of the bus going around and around the same loop, "all the way through town, along the river, up to the Westgate shopping center, then back again."

I doubt that the author of "Tracks and Ties" set out to *create* these symbols. Setting out to create symbols, whether in fiction, nonfiction, or poetry, tends to result in heavy-handed or overly obvious imagery. Like most of us, he probably just noticed as he wrote that certain objects, ideas, or images seemed more important than others, more emotionally charged, more relevant to his central question, and as he moved from draft to draft, he highlighted these motifs (i.e., by using the same phrase to describe the knife both times it appears in the story and by using constricted, repetitive clauses to describe the loop the bus repeatedly makes through the town).

MAKING THE PERSONAL UNIVERSAL

Depending on the writer's inclination, the personal can become political (as in the essays by Orwell, Cooper, Dubus, and Hershman) or philosophical (as in "Death of a Pig"). In either case, the trick is to ask what you don't understand about a given experience and see if you can phrase that question in a slightly more general way so at least a few people (other than your family and friends) will be interested in the answer. That doesn't mean your question needs to interest everyone in the world. An essay in which you try to figure out why your immigrant Chinese father never seemed satisfied with your accomplishments will interest other sons of Chinese fathers, not to mention the sons of Korean and Japanese fathers. It also might interest the daughters of such fathers, along with the sons and daughters of Russian and Kenyan immigrants. It might even interest readers who don't seem able to satisfy their American-born parents, or who teach in schools with a substantial population of immigrant children, or who are married to the offspring of immigrants, or who simply want to learn more about the tribulations faced by immigrants and their kids.

Although most of us feel comfortable telling stories about our experiences, analyzing these same experiences in an original way requires surprising confidence. Often, the writer simply gives up and says, "I don't know why I did what I did," or "I don't know why my father did what he did," at which I earn my salary by writing in the margin: "This is the whole essay right here! Go deeper. *Think* about why you did what you did (or why your father did what he did). Then put that meditation on the page!" We rarely are encouraged to think about our lives in anything but clichéd terms. (*What doesn't kill you makes you stronger. Everything works out for the best. You made your bed, now lie in it.*) Using your experience to prove what most people already know (or think they know) is easy and safe. It also tends to be tedious—and dishonest.

Most middle-aged women don't get arrested and thrown in jail for sitting down in front of a police horse during an antiwar protest. The rare middle-aged woman to whom this does happen might discover that jail is not a pleasant place or that acting on her political convictions harms her kids. The former discovery would hardly be surprising (compared to the discovery that a week in jail can be a pleasant or useful interlude in one's life). The latter discovery (with a debate as to whether shortchanging one's kids in the service of a larger political belief is justifiable) is more promising material for an essay. But in "Six Days: Some Rememberings," Grace Paley trusts her instincts and makes a discovery about her time in jail that few of us would have made. Although she finds her incarceration unpleasant and feels so guilty about her inability to send her son to camp that she bursts out crying ("real running-down-the-cheek tears"), what she discovers about her six days in the Women's House of Detention in Greenwich Village is that

> if there are prisons, they ought to be in the neighborhood, near a subway—not way out in distant suburbs, where families have to take cars, buses, ferries, trains, and the population that considers itself innocent forgets, denies, chooses to never know that there is a whole huge country of the bad and the unlucky and the self-hurters, a country with a population greater than that of many nations in our world.

What proof does Paley offer in support of this recommendation? Nothing but what she sees and hears while she's in jail. Nothing but her pain at being separated from her family and friends and the comfort she takes in seeing her children pass the jail "on their way to music lessons or Greenwich House pottery." Nothing but her delight in hearing her good friend Myrt calling up to her from the street before a cop shoos Myrt away, mistakenly thinking that Grace would be ashamed to hear her presence in jail advertised in such a way. Nothing but her own memories of the times that she and her children walked past the jail and needed to thread her way

> through whole families calling up—bellowing, screaming to the third, seventh, tenth floor, to figures, shadows behind bars and screened windows—How you feeling? Here's Glena. She got big. Mami, mami you like my dress? We gettin you out baby. New lawyer come by.
>
> And the replies, among which I was privileged to live for a few days—shouted down.—You lookin beautiful. What he say? Fuck you, James. I got a chance? Bye bye. Come next week.

Paley supports her opinions in subtle ways. She knows (from her involvement in the feminist and antiwar movements and her questioning of her fellow prisoners) that because "a young woman named Andrea Dworkin" was arrested for protesting the war in front of the U.S. Mission to the U.N. and refused to allow the guards to subject her to a painful and embarrassing search of her bodily cavities, the physical examinations to which Grace and her cellmates are subjected are less sadistic than otherwise might be the case. She knows that the Women's House of Detention used to be fourteen stories tall, that after her stay there the building was torn down and replaced by a garden, that New York officials have since moved most of the city's prisons to more remote locations, and that the prison population in the United States is now greater than the population of many countries.

As journalists who take my class love to point out, Paley relies largely on her own experiences and common sense to support her assertion that we ought to keep prisons in the communities whose populations they serve. "If I handed in something like this, my editors would fire me," one reporter said. "Does she really think that politicians are going to make policy decisions based on one woman's observations about the six days she spent in a house of detention?" But that's one of the differences between straight journalism and literary essays or journalistic pieces that qualify as creative nonfiction. Not that Paley is allowed to make things up. If we were to find out that she had never been to jail or that she had never seen and heard children calling up to their mothers and mothers calling down to their children from the barred windows of their cells, we would feel that our contract with the writer had been violated. Nor can Paley ignore her obligation to persuade us of the validity of her opinion that jails should remain in town. But she doesn't need to prove her case as strenuously as an investigative journalist (or a political scientist or a municipal planner) would need to do. She need only convince us that such a case *might in fact be proved*.

In service of this goal, Paley is permitted to use her own experience, supplemented by research as needed, rather than being forced to rely solely on information provided by experts. No mayor in his or her right mind would decide where to locate a prison based on nothing but Paley's essay. But the essay might give that mayor pause before knocking down a prison and moving it out of sight or prod a politician to appoint a commission to ascertain if keeping jails downtown might benefit the community. Citizens might be less inclined to yell "Not in my backyard!" in response to a proposal to build a prison in their neighborhood if they had read Paley's essay first. Or another writer might be inspired by "Six Days in Jail" to conduct an exhaustive investigation into the effects of moving prisons out of town or take to heart the author's plea that regular people ought to spend a few nights in jail now and then to see how the inmates are being treated, who they are, and how they ended up in prison in the first place. (Ted Conover spent a year as a guard at Sing Sing and wrote a remarkably evenhanded account of that harrowing experience; see *Newjack: Guarding Sing Sing*, Vintage Books, 2001.)

Again, the difference between standard journalism and creative nonfiction has little to do with content and everything to do with style, central question, and form. Even reporters on daily beats can use the forms and styles of creative nonfiction to turn out engaging, well-researched, and influential articles for their newspapers or magazines. Randy Shilts, the first openly gay reporter to cover a gay beat for a major American newspaper, used the mystery form (Chapter 7) to document the earliest attempts of the medical and political establishments to figure out what was killing gay men. Shilts's book *And the Band Played On: Politics, People, and the AIDS Epidemic (1980–1985)*, which was published in 1987 by St. Martins Press/Stonewall Inn Editions, not only is a magnificent example of investigative reporting, but the narrative is so engrossing that it later was turned into a movie. Although Shilts was diagnosed as HIV positive in 1987, he managed to travel the talk-show circuit for a few years, promoting his book and educating the public about the still-taboo subject of AIDS. In his award-winning personal narrative "Talking AIDS to Death," which you can find in *The Best American Essays 1990*, Shilts uses his experiences as "the world's first AIDS celebrity," along with his wry humor, his barely restrained anger, a wealth of hard-core statistics, and a brilliant sense of structure, to try to figure out why the country's public response to the AIDS epidemic has been so much slower and less compassionate than would seem warranted by people's private fears of catching the disease and their compassion for friends and relatives who are dying of AIDS.

GEORGE ORWELL

SHOOTING AN ELEPHANT

In Moulmein, in lower Burma, I was hated by large numbers of people—the only time in my life that I have been important enough for this to happen to me. I was sub-divisional police officer of the town, and in an aimless, petty kind of way anti-European feeling was very bitter. No one had the guts to raise a riot, but if a European woman went through the bazaars alone somebody would probably spit betel juice over her dress. As a police officer I was an obvious target and was baited whenever it seemed safe to do so. When a nimble Burman tripped me up on the football field and the referee (another Burman) looked the other way, the crowd yelled with hideous laughter. This happened more than once. In the end the sneering yellow faces of young men that met me everywhere, the insults hooted after me when I was at a safe distance, got badly on my nerves. The young Buddhist priests were the worst of all. There were several thousands of them in the town and none of them seemed to have anything to do except stand on street corners and jeer at Europeans.

All this was perplexing and upsetting. For at that time I had already made up my mind that imperialism was an evil thing and the sooner I chucked up my job and got out of it the better. Theoretically—and secretly, of course—I was all for the Burmese and all against their oppressors, the British. As for the job I was doing, I hated it more bitterly than I can perhaps make clear. In a job like that you see the dirty work of Empire at close quarters. The wretched prisoners huddling in the stinking cages of the lock-ups, the gray, cowed faces of the long-term convicts, the scarred buttocks of the men who had been flogged with bamboos—all these oppressed me with an intolerable sense of guilt. But I could get nothing into perspective. I was young and ill educated and I had had to think out my problems in the utter silence that is imposed on every Englishman in the East. I did not even know that the British Empire is dying, still less did I know that it is a great deal better than the younger empires that are going to supplant it. All I knew was that I was stuck between my hatred of the empire I served and my rage against the evil-spirited little beasts who tried to make my job impossible. With one part of my mind I thought of the British Raj as an unbreakable tyranny, as something clamped down, in *saecula saeculorum,* upon the will of prostrate peoples; with another part I thought that the greatest joy in the world would be to drive a bayonet into a Buddhist priest's guts. Feelings like these are the normal by-products of imperialism; ask any Anglo-Indian official, if you can catch him off duty.

One day something happened which in a roundabout way was enlightening. It was a tiny incident in itself; but it gave me a better glimpse than I had had before of the real nature of imperialism—the real motives for which despotic governments act. Early one morning the sub-inspector at a police station the other end of the town rang me up on the 'phone and said that an elephant was ravaging the bazaar. Would I please come and do something about it? I did not know what I could do, but I wanted to see what was happening and I got on to a pony and started out. I took my rifle, an old .44 Winchester and much too small to kill an elephant, but I thought the noise might be useful *in terrorem.* Various Burmans stopped me on the way and told me about the elephant's doings. It was not, of course, a wild elephant, but a tame one which had gone "must." It had been chained up, as tame elephants always are when their attack of "must" is due, but on the previous night it had broken its chain and escaped. Its mahout, the only person who could manage it when it was in that state, had set out in pursuit, but had taken the wrong direction and was now twelve hours' journey away, and in the morning the elephant had suddenly reappeared in the town. The Burmese population had no weapons and were quite helpless against it. It had already destroyed somebody's bamboo hut, killed a cow and raided some fruit-stalls and devoured the stock; also it had met the municipal rubbish van and, when the driver jumped out and took to his heels, had turned the van over and inflicted violences upon it.

The Burmese sub-inspector and some Indian constables were waiting for me in the quarter where the elephant had been seen. It was a very poor quarter, a labyrinth of squalid bamboo huts, thatched with palm-leaf, winding all over a steep hillside. I remember that it was a cloudy, stuffy morning at the beginning of the rains. We began questioning the people as to where the elephant had gone and, as usual, failed to get any definite information. That is invariably the case in the East; a story always sounds clear enough at a distance, but the nearer you get to the scene of events the vaguer it becomes. Some of the people said that the elephant had gone in one direction, some said that he had gone in another, some professed not even to have heard of any elephant. I had almost made up my mind that the whole story was a pack of lies, when we heard yells a little distance away. There was a loud, scandalized cry of "Go away, child! Go away this instant!" and an old woman with a switch in her hand came round the corner of a hut, violently shooing away a crowd of naked children. Some more women followed, clicking their tongues and exclaiming; evidently there was something that the children ought not to have seen. I rounded the hut and saw a man's dead body sprawling in the mud. He was an Indian, a black Dravidian coolie, almost naked, and he could not have been dead many minutes. The people said that the elephant had come suddenly upon him round the corner of the hut, caught him with its trunk, put its foot on his back and ground him into the earth. This was the rainy season and the ground was soft, and his face had scored a trench a foot deep and a couple of yards long. He was lying on his belly with arms crucified and head sharply twisted to one side. His face was coated with mud, the eyes wide open, the teeth bared and grinning with an expression of unendurable agony. (Never tell me, by the way, that the dead look peaceful. Most of the corpses I have seen looked devilish.) The friction of the great beast's foot had stripped the skin from his back as neatly as one skins a rabbit. As soon as I saw the dead man I sent an orderly to a friend's house nearby to borrow an elephant rifle. I had already sent back the pony, not wanting it to go mad with fright and throw me if it smelt the elephant.

The orderly came back in a few minutes with a rifle and five cartridges, and meanwhile some Burmans had arrived and told us that the elephant was in the paddy fields below, only a few hundred yards away. As I started forward practically the whole population of the quarter flocked out of the houses and followed me. They had seen the rifle and were all shouting excitedly that I was going to shoot the elephant. They had not shown much interest in the elephant when he was merely ravaging their homes, but it was different now that he was going to be shot. It was a bit of fun to them, as it would be to an English crowd; besides they wanted the meat. It made me vaguely uneasy. I had no intention of shooting the elephant—I had merely sent for the rifle to defend myself if necessary—and it is always unnerving to have a crowd following you. I marched down the hill, looking and feeling a fool, with the rifle over my shoulder and an ever-growing army of people jostling at my heels. At the bottom, when you got away from the huts, there was a metalled road and beyond that a miry waste of paddy fields a thousand yards across, not yet ploughed but soggy from the first rains and dotted with coarse grass. The elephant was standing eight yards from the road, his left side toward us. He took not the slightest notice of the crowd's approach. He was tearing up bunches of grass, beating them against his knees to clean them, and stuffing them into his mouth.

I had halted on the road. As soon as I saw the elephant I knew with perfect certainty that I ought not to shoot him. It is a serious matter to shoot a working elephant—it is comparable to destroying a huge and costly piece of machinery—and obviously one ought not to do it if it can possibly be avoided. And at that distance, peacefully eating, the elephant looked no more dangerous than a cow. I thought then and I think now that his attack of "must" was already passing off; in which case he would merely wander harmlessly about until the mahout came back and caught him. Moreover, I did not in the least want to shoot him. I decided that I would watch him for a little while to make sure that he did not turn savage again, and then go home.

But at that moment I glanced round at the crowd that had followed me. It was an immense crowd, two thousand at the least and growing every minute. It blocked the road for a long distance on either side. I looked at the sea of yellow faces above the garish clothes—faces all happy and excited over this bit of fun, all certain that the elephant was going to be shot. They were watching me as they would watch a conjurer about to perform a trick. They did not like me, but with the magical rifle in my hands I was momentarily worth watching. And suddenly I realized that I should have to shoot the elephant after all. The people expected it of me and I had got to do it; I could feel their two thousand wills pressing me forward, irresistibly. And it was at this moment, as I stood there with the rifle in my hands, that I first grasped the hollowness, the futility of the white man's dominion in the East. Here was I, the white man with his gun, standing in front of the unarmed native crowd—seemingly the leading actor of the piece; but in reality I was only an absurd puppet pushed to and fro by the will of those yellow faces behind. I perceived in this moment that when the white man turns tyrant it is his own freedom that he destroys. He becomes a sort of hollow, posing dummy, the conventionalized figure of a sahib. For it is the condition of his rule that he shall spend his life in trying to impress the "natives," and so in every crisis he has got to do what the "natives" expect of him. He wears a mask, and his face grows to fit it. I had got to shoot the elephant. I had committed myself to doing it when I sent for the rifle. A sahib has got to act like a sahib; he has got to appear resolute, to know his own mind and do definite things. To come all that way, rifle in hand, with two thousand people marching at my heels, and then to trail feebly away, having done nothing—no, that was impossible. The crowd would laugh at me. And my whole life, every white man's life in the East, was one long struggle not to be laughed at.

But I did not want to shoot the elephant. I watched him beating his bunch of grass against his knees with that preoccupied grandmotherly air that elephants have. It seemed to me that it would be murder to shoot him. At that age I was not squeamish about killing animals, but I had never shot an elephant and never wanted to. (Somehow it always seems worse to kill a *large* animal.) Besides, there was the beast's owner to be considered. Alive, the elephant was worth at least a hundred pounds; dead, he would only be worth the value of his tusks, five pounds, possibly. But I had got to act quickly. I turned to some experienced-looking Burmans who had been there when we arrived, and asked them how the elephant had been behaving. They all said the same thing: he took no notice of you if you left him alone, but he might charge if you went too close to him.

It was perfectly clear to me what I ought to do. I ought to walk up to within, say, twenty-five yards of the elephant and test his behavior. If he charged, I could shoot; if he took no notice of me, it would be safe to leave him until the mahout came back. But also I knew that I was going to do no such thing. I was a poor shot with a rifle and the ground was soft mud into which one would sink at every step. If the elephant charged and I missed him, I should have about as much chance as a toad under a steam-roller. But even then I was not thinking particularly of my own skin, only of the watchful yellow faces behind. For at that moment, with the crowd watching me, I was not afraid in the ordinary sense, as I would have been if I had been alone. A white man mustn't be frightened in front of "natives"; and so, in general, he isn't frightened. The sole thought in my mind was that if anything went wrong those two thousand Burmans would see me pursued, caught, trampled on, and reduced to a grinning corpse like that Indian up the hill. And if that happened it was quite probable that some of them would laugh. That would never do. There was only one alternative. I shoved the cartridges into the magazine and lay down on the road to get a better aim.

The crowd grew very still, and a deep, low, happy sigh, as of people who see the theater curtain go up at last, breathed from innumerable throats. They were going to have their bit of fun after all. The rifle was a beautiful German thing with cross-hair sights. I did not then know that in shooting an elephant one would shoot to cut an imaginary bar running from ear-hole to ear-hole. I ought, therefore, as the elephant was sideways on, to have aimed straight at his ear-hole; actually I aimed several inches of front of this, thinking the brain would be further forward.

When I pulled the trigger I did not hear the bang or feel the kick—one never does when a shot goes home—but I heard the devillish roar of glee that went up from the crowd. In that instant, in too short a time, one would have thought, even for the bullet to get there, a mysterious, terrible change had come over the elephant. He neither stirred, nor fell, but every line of his body had altered. He looked suddenly stricken, shrunken, immensely old, as though the frightful impact of the bullet had paralyzed him without knocking him down. At last, after what seemed a long time—it might have been five seconds, I dare say—he sagged flabbily to his knees. His mouth slobbered. An enormous senility seemed to have settled upon him. One could have imagined him thousands of years old. I fired again into the same spot. At the second shot he did not collapse but climbed with desperate slowness to his feet and stood weakly upright, with legs sagging and head drooping. I fired a third time. That was the shot that did for him. You could see the agony of it jolt his whole body and knock the last remnant of strength from his legs. But in falling he seemed for a moment to rise, for as his hind legs collapsed beneath him he seemed to tower upward like a huge rock toppling, his trunk reaching skyward like a tree. He trumpeted, for the first and only time. And then down he came, his belly toward me, with a crash that seemed to shake the ground even where I lay.

I got up. The Burmans were already racing past me across the mud. It was obvious that the elephant would never rise again, but he was not dead. He was breathing very rhythmically with long rattling gasps, his great mound of a side painfully rising and falling. His mouth was wide open—I could see far down into caverns of pale pink throat. I waited a long time for him to die, but his breathing did not weaken. Finally I fired my two remaining shots into the spot where I thought his heart must be. The thick blood welled out of him like red velvet, but still he did not die. His body did not even jerk when the shots hit him, the tortured breathing continued without a pause. He was dying, very slowly and in great agony, but in some world remote from me where not even a bullet could damage him further. I felt that I had got to put an end to that dreadful noise. It seemed dreadful to see the great beast lying there, powerless to move and yet powerless to die, and not even to be able to finish him. I sent back for my small rifle and poured shot after shot into his heart and down his throat. They seemed to make no impression. The tortured gasps continued as steadily as the ticking of a clock.

In the end I could not stand it any longer and went away. I heard later that it took him half an hour to die. Burmans were bringing dahs and baskets even before I left, and I was told they had stripped his body almost to the bones by the afternoon.

Afterward, of course, there were endless discussions about the shooting of the elephant. The owner was furious, but he was only an Indian and could do nothing. Besides, legally I had done the right thing, for a mad elephant has to be killed, like a mad dog, if its owner fails to control it. Among the Europeans opinion was divided. The older men said I was right, the younger men said it was a damn shame to shoot an elephant for killing a coolie, because an elephant was worth more than any damn Coringhee coolie. And afterward I was very glad that the coolie had been killed; it put me legally in the right and it gave me a sufficient pretext for shooting the elephant. I often wondered whether any of the others grasped that I had done it solely to avoid looking a fool.

—1936

Learning from Other Writers

1. What is the effect of Orwell's decision to open his essay with two paragraphs of background information rather than the appearance of the elephant? Given that these opening paragraphs are written in expository rather than scenic prose, how does Orwell keep them interesting?
2. Much of Orwell's essay illustrates the racism at the heart of British imperialism. Why doesn't Orwell make this racism the point of his essay?
3. Where and how does Orwell employ the perspective of the young, ignorant policeman he was at the time he shot the elephant? Where does he speak from the perspective of the older, wiser man he is at the time he writes his essay?
4. Orwell asserts that his feelings of ambivalence about the Raj and the people it oppresses "are the normal by-products of imperialism." He also claims that it is "invariably the case in the East" that "a story always sounds clear enough at a distance, but the nearer you get to the scene of events the vaguer it becomes." What—if anything—gives him the right to make such sweeping generalizations?
5. What are the most memorable details that Orwell uses to bring alive his story?
6. Can you find the passages in which Orwell tries to develop an answer to his central question? How does he use repetition to signpost these meditations?
7. Some readers think the elephant symbolizes British rule in India. Do you agree or disagree?
8. What is the effect of concluding the essay not with the elephant's death but with the general debate as to whether the author was right to kill it?

BERNARD COOPER

A CLACK OF TINY SPARKS: REMEMBRANCES OF A GAY BOYHOOD

Theresa Sanchez sat behind me in ninth-grade algebra. When Mr. Hubbley faced the blackboard, I'd turn around to see what she was reading; each week a new book was wedged inside her copy of *Today's Equations*. The deception worked; from Mr. Hubbley's point of view, Theresa was engrossed in the value of X, but I knew otherwise. One week she perused *The Wisdom of the Orient,* and I could tell from Theresa's contemplative expression that the book contained exotic thoughts, guidelines handed down from high. Another week it was a paperback novel whose title, *Let Me Live My Life,* appeared in bold print atop every page, and whose cover, a gauzy photograph of a woman biting a strand of pearls, head thrown back in an attitude of ecstasy, confirmed my suspicion that Theresa Sanchez was mature beyond her years. She was the tallest girl in school. Her bouffant hairdo, streaked with blond, was higher than the flaccid bouffants of other girls. Her smooth skin, plucked eyebrows, and painted fingernails suggested hours of pampering, a worldly and sensual vanity that placed her within the domain of adults. Smiling dimly, steeped in daydreams, Theresa moved through the crowded halls with a languid, self-satisfied indifference to those around her. "You are merely children," her posture seemed to say. "I can't be bothered." The week Theresa hid *101 Ways to Cook Hamburger* behind her algebra book, I could stand it no longer and, after the bell rang, ventured a question.

"Because I'm having a dinner party," said Theresa. "Just a couple of intimate friends."

No fourteen-year-old I knew had ever given a dinner party, let alone used the word "intimate" in conversation. "Don't you have a mother?" I asked.

Theresa sighed a weary sigh, suffered my strange inquiry. "Don't be so naive," she said. "Everyone has a mother." She waved her hand to indicate the brick school buildings outside the window. "A higher education should have taught you that." Theresa draped an angora sweater over her shoulders, scooped her books from the graffiti-covered desk, and just as she was about to walk away, she turned and asked me, "Are you a fag?"

There wasn't the slightest hint of rancor or condescension in her voice. The tone was direct, casual. Still I was stunned, giving a sidelong glance to make sure no one had heard. "No," I said. Blurted really, with too much defensiveness, too much transparent fear in my response. Octaves lower than usual, I tried a "Why?"

Theresa shrugged. "Oh, I don't know. I have lots of friends who are fags. You remind me of them." Seeing me bristle, Theresa added, "It was just a guess." I watched her erect, angora back as she sauntered out the classroom door.

She had made an incisive and timely guess. Only days before, I'd invited Grady Rogers to my house after school to go swimming. The instant Grady shot from the pool, shaking water from his orange hair, freckled shoulders shining, my attraction to members of my own sex became a matter I could no longer suppress or rationalize. Sturdy and boisterous and gap-toothed, Grady was an inveterate backslapper, a formidable arm wrestler, a wizard at basketball. Grady was a boy at home in his body.

My body was a marvel I hadn't gotten used to; my arms and legs would sometimes act of their own accord, knocking over a glass at dinner or flinching at an oncoming pitch. I was never singled out as a sissy, but I could have been just as easily as Bobby Keagan, a gentle, intelligent, and introverted boy reviled by my classmates. And although I had always been aware of a tacit rapport with Bobby, a suspicion that I might find with him a rich friendship, I stayed away. Instead, I emulated Grady in the belief that being seen with him, being like him, would somehow vanquish my self-doubt, would make me normal by association.

Apart from his athletic prowess, Grady had been gifted with all the trappings of what I imagined to be a charmed life: a fastidious, aproned mother who radiated calm, maternal concern; a ruddy, stoic father with a knack for home repairs. Even the Rogerses' small suburban house in Hollywood, with its spindly Colonial furniture and chintz curtains, was a testament to normalcy.

Grady and his family bore little resemblance to my clan of Eastern European Jews, a dark and vociferous people who ate with abandon—matzo and halvah and gefilte fish; foods the goyim couldn't pronounce—who cajoled one another during endless games of canasta, making the simplest remark about the weather into a lengthy philosophical discourse on the sun and the seasons and the passage of time. My mother was a chain-smoker, a dervish in a frowsy housedress. She showed her love in the most peculiar and obsessive ways, like spending hours extracting every seed from a watermelon before she served it in perfectly bite-sized, geometric pieces. Preoccupied and perpetually frantic, my mother succumbed to bouts of absentmindedness so profound she'd forget what she was saying midsentence, smile and blush and walk away. A divorce attorney, my father wore roomy, iridescent suits, and the intricacies, the deceits inherent in his profession, had the effect of making him forever tense and vigilant. He was "all wound up," as my mother put it. But when he relaxed, his laughter was explosive, his disposition prankish: "Walk this way," a waitress would say, leading us to our table, and my father would mimic the way she walked, arms akimbo, hips liquid, while my mother and I were wracked with laughter. Buoyant or brooding, my parents' moods were unpredictable, and in a household fraught with extravagant emotion it was odd and awful to keep my longing secret.

One day I made the mistake of asking my mother what a "fag" was. I knew exactly what Theresa had meant but hoped against hope it was not what I thought; maybe "fag" was some French word, a harmless term like "naive." My mother turned from the stove, flew at me, and grabbed me by the shoulders. "Did someone call you that?" she cried.

"Not me," I said. "Bobby Keagan."

"Oh," she said, loosening her grip. She was visibly relieved. And didn't answer. The answer was unthinkable.

For weeks after, I shook with the reverberations from that afternoon in the kitchen with my mother, pained by the memory of her shocked expression and, most of all, her silence. My longing was wrong in the eyes of my mother, whose hazel eyes were the eyes of the world, and if that longing continued unchecked, the unwieldy shape of my fate would be cast, and I'd be subjected to a lifetime of scorn.

During the remainder of the semester, I became the scientist of my own desire, plotting ways to change my yearning for boys into a yearning for girls. I had enough evidence to believe that any habit, regardless of how compulsive, how deeply ingrained, could be broken once and for all: The plastic cigarette my mother purchased at the Thrifty pharmacy—one end was red to approximate an ember, the other tan like a filtered tip—was designed to wean her from the real thing. To change a behavior required self-analysis, cold resolve, and the substitution of one thing for another: plastic, say, for tobacco. Could I also find a substitute for Grady? What I needed to do, I figured, was kiss a girl and learn to like it.

This conclusion was affirmed one Sunday morning when my father, seeing me wrinkle my nose at the pink slabs of lox he layered on a bagel, tried to convince me of its salty appeal. "You should try some," he said. "You don't know what you're missing."

"It's loaded with protein," added my mother, slapping a platter of sliced onions onto the dinette table. She hovered above us, cinching her housedress, eyes wet from onion fumes, the mock cigarette dangling from her lips.

My father sat there chomping with gusto, emitting a couple of hearty grunts to dramatize his satisfaction. And still I was not convinced. After a loud and labored swallow, he told me I may not be fond of lox today, but sooner or later I'd learn to like it. One's tastes, he assured me, are destined to change.

"Live," shouted my mother over the rumble of the Mixmaster. "Expand your horizons. Try new things." And the room grew fragrant with the batter of a spice cake.

The opportunity to put their advice into practice, and try out my plan to adapt to girls, came the following week when Debbie Coburn, a member of Mr. Hubbley's algebra class, invited me to a party. She cornered me in the hall, furtive as a spy, telling me her parents would be gone for the evening and slipping into my palm a wrinkled sheet of notebook paper. On it were her address and telephone number, the lavender ink in a tidy cursive. "Wear cologne," she advised, wary eyes darting back and forth. "It's a make-out party. Anything can happen."

The Santa Ana wind blew relentlessly the night of Debbie's party, careening down the slopes of the Hollywood hills, shaking the road signs and stoplights in its path. As I walked down Beachwood Avenue, trees thrashed, surrendered their leaves, and carob pods bombarded the pavement. The sky was a deep but luminous blue, the air hot, abrasive, electric. I had to squint in order to check the number of the Coburns' apartment, a three-story building with glitter embedded in its stucco walls. Above the honeycombed balconies was a sign that read BEACHWOOD TERRACE in lavender script resembling Debbie's.

From down the hall, I could hear the plaintive strains of Little Anthony's "I Think I'm Going Out of My Head." Debbie answered the door bedecked in an Empire dress, the bodice blue and orange polka dots, the rest a sheath of black and white stripes. "Op art," proclaimed Debbie. She turned in a circle, then proudly announced that she'd rolled her hair in orange juice cans. She patted the huge unmoving curls and dragged me inside. Reflections from the swimming pool in the courtyard, its surface ruffled by wind, shuddered over the ceiling and walls. A dozen of my classmates were seated on the sofa or huddled together in corners, their whispers full of excited imminence, their bodies barely discernible in the dim light. Drapes flanking the sliding glass doors bowed out with every gust of wind, and it seemed that the room might lurch from its foundations and sail with its cargo of silhouettes into the hot October night.

Grady was the last to arrive. He tossed a six-pack of beer into Debbie's arms, barreled toward me, and slapped my back. His hair was slicked back with Vitalis, lacquered furrows left by the comb. The wind hadn't shifted a single hair. "Ya ready?" he asked, flashing the gap between his front teeth and leering into the darkened room. "You bet," I lied.

Once the beers had been passed around, Debbie provoked everyone's attention by flicking on the overhead light. "Okay," she called. "Find a partner." This was the blunt command of a hostess determined to have her guests aroused in an orderly fashion. Everyone blinked, shuffled about, and grabbed a member of the opposite sex. Sheila Garabedian landed beside me—entirely at random, though I wanted to believe she was driven by passion—her timid smile giving way to plain fear as the light went out. Nothing for a moment but the heave of the wind and the distant banter of dogs. I caught a whiff of Sheila's perfume, tangy and sweet as Hawaiian Punch. I probed her face with my own, grazing the small scallop of an ear, a velvety temple, and though Sheila's trembling made me want to stop, I persisted with my mission until I found her lips, tightly sealed as a private letter. I held my mouth over hers and gathered her shoulders closer, resigned to the possibility that, no matter how long we stood there, Sheila would be too scared to kiss me back. Still, she exhaled through her nose, and I listened to the squeak of every breath as though it were a sigh of inordinate pleasure. Diving within myself, I monitored my heartbeat and respiration, trying to will stimulation into being, and all the while an image intruded, an image of Grady erupting from our pool, rivulets of water sliding down his chest. "Change," shouted Debbie, switching on the light. Sheila thanked me, pulled away, and continued her routine of gracious terror with every boy throughout the evening. It didn't matter whom I held—Margaret Sims, Betty Vernon, Elizabeth Lee—my experiment was a failure; I continued to picture Grady's wet chest, and Debbie would bellow "change" with such fervor, it could have been my own voice, my own incessant reprimand.

Our hostess commandeered the light switch for nearly half an hour. Whenever the light came on, I watched Grady pivot his head toward the newest prospect, his eyebrows arched in expectation, his neck blooming with hickeys, his hair, at last, in disarray. All that shuffling across the carpet charged everyone's arms and lips with static, and eventually, between low moans and soft osculations, I could hear the clack of tiny sparks and see them flare here and there in the dark like meager, short-lived stars.

I saw Theresa, sultry and aloof as ever, read three more books—*North American Reptiles, Bonjour Tristesse,* and *MGM: A Pictorial History*—before she vanished early in December. Rumors of her fate abounded. Debbie Coburn swore that Theresa had been "knocked up" by an older man, a traffic cop, she thought, or a grocer. Nearly quivering with relish, Debbie told me and Grady about the home for unwed mothers in the San Fernando Valley, a compound teeming with pregnant girls who had nothing to do but touch their stomachs and contemplate their mistake. Even Bobby Keagan, who took Theresa's place behind me in algebra, had a theory regarding her disappearance colored by his own wish for escape; he imagined that Theresa, disillusioned with society, booked passage to a tropical island, there to live out the rest of her days without restrictions or ridicule. "No wonder she flunked out of school," I overheard Mr. Hubbley tell a fellow teacher one afternoon. "Her head was always in a book."

Along with Theresa went my secret, or at least the dread that she might divulge it, and I felt, for a while, exempt from suspicion. I was, however, to run across Theresa one last time. It happened during a period of torrential rain that, according to reports on the six o'clock news, washed houses from the hillsides and flooded the downtown streets. The halls of Joseph Le Conte Junior High were festooned with Christmas decorations: crepe-paper garlands, wreaths studded with plastic berries, and one requisite Star of David twirling above the attendance desk. In Arts and Crafts, our teacher, Gerald (he was the only teacher who allowed us—*required* us—to call him by his first name), handed out blocks of balsa wood and instructed us to carve them into bugs. We would paint eyes and antennae with tempera and hang them on a Christmas tree he'd made the previous night. "Voilà," he crooned, unveiling his creation from a burlap sack. Before us sat a tortured scrub, a wardrobe-worth of wire hangers that were bent like branches and soldered together. Gerald credited his inspiration to a Charles Addams cartoon he's seen in which Morticia, grimly preparing for the holidays, hangs vampire bats on a withered pine. "All that red and green," said Gerald. "So predictable. So *boring.*"

As I chiseled a beetle and listened to rain pummel the earth, Gerald handed me an envelope and asked me to take it to Mr. Kendrick, the drama teacher. I would have thought nothing of his request if I hadn't seen Theresa on my way down the hall. She was cleaning out her locker, blithely dropping the sum of its contents—pens and textbooks and mimeographs—into a trash can. "Have a nice life," she sang as I passed. I mustered the courage to ask her what had happened. We stood alone in the silent hall, the reflections of wreaths and garlands submerged in brown linoleum.

"I transferred to another school. They don't have grades or bells, and you get to study whatever you want." Theresa was quick to sense my incredulity. "Honest," she said. "The school is progressive." She gazed into a glass cabinet that held the trophies of track meets and intramural spelling bees. "God," she sighed, "this place is so ... barbaric." I was still trying to decide whether or not to believe her story when she asked me where I was headed. "Dear," she said, her exclamation pooling in the silence, "that's no ordinary note, if you catch my drift." The envelope was blank and white; I looked up at Theresa, baffled. "Don't be so naive," she muttered, tossing an empty bottle of nail polish into the trash can. It struck bottom with a resolute thud. "Well," she said, closing her locker and breathing deeply, "bon voyage." Theresa swept through the double doors and in seconds her figure was obscured by rain.

As I walked toward Mr. Kendrick's room, I could feel Theresa's insinuation burrow in. I stood for a moment and watched Mr. Kendrick through the pane in the door. He paced intently in front of the class, handsome in his shirt and tie, reading from a thick book. Chalked on the blackboard behind him was THE ODYSSEY BY HOMER. I have no recollection of how Mr. Kendrick reacted to the note, whether he accepted it with pleasure or embarrassment, slipped it into his desk drawer or the pocket of his shirt. I have scavenged that day in retrospect, trying to see Mr. Kendrick's expression, wondering if he acknowledged me in any way as his liaison. All I recall is the sight of his mime through a pane of glass, a lone man mouthing an epic, his gestures ardent in empty air.

Had I delivered a declaration of love? I was haunted by the need to know. In fantasy, a kettle shot steam, the glue released its grip, and I read the letter with impunity. But how would such a letter begin? Did the common endearments apply? This was a message between two men, a message for which I had no precedent, and when I tried to envision the contents, apart from a hasty, impassioned scrawl, my imagination faltered.

Once or twice I witnessed Gerald and Mr. Kendrick walk together into the faculty lounge or say hello at the water fountain, but there was nothing especially clandestine or flirtatious in their manner. Besides, no matter how acute my scrutiny, I wasn't sure, short of a kiss, exactly what to look for—what semaphore of gesture, what encoded word. I suspected there were signs, covert signs that would give them away, just as I'd unwittingly given myself away to Theresa.

In the school library, a *Webster's* unabridged dictionary lay on a wooden podium, and I padded toward it with apprehension; along with clues to the bond between my teachers, I risked discovering information that might incriminate me as well. I had decided to consult the dictionary during lunch period, when most of the students would be on the playground. I clutched my notebook, moving in such a way as to appear both studious and nonchalant, actually believing that, unless I took precautions, someone would see me and guess what I was up to. The closer I came to the podium, the more obvious, I thought, was my endeavor; I felt like the model of The Visible Man in our science class, my heart's undulations, my overwrought nerves legible through transparent skin. A couple of kids riffled through the card catalogue. The librarian, a skinny woman whose perpetual whisper and rubber-soled shoes caused her to drift through the room like a phantom, didn't seem to register my presence. Though I'd looked up dozens of words before, the pages felt strange beneath my fingers. *Homer* was the first word I saw. *Hominid. Homogenize.* I feigned interest and skirted other words before I found the word I was after. Under the heading HO·MO·SEX·U·AL was the terse definition: *adj. Pertaining to, characteristic of, or exhibiting homosexuality.—n. A homosexual person.* I read the definition again and again, hoping the words would yield more than they could. I shut the dictionary, swallowed hard, and, none the wiser, hurried away.

As for Gerald and Mr. Kendrick, I never discovered evidence to prove or dispute Theresa's claim. By the following summer, however, I had overheard from my peers a confounding amount about homosexuals: They wore green on Thursday, couldn't whistle, hypnotized boys with a piercing glance. To this lore, Grady added a surefire test to ferret them out.

"A test?" I said.

"You ask a guy to look at his fingernails, and if he looks at them like this"—Grady closed his fingers into a fist and examined his nails with manly detachment—"then he's okay. But if he does this"—he held out his hands at arm's length, splayed his fingers, and coyly cocked his head—"you'd better watch out." Once he'd completed his demonstration, Grady peeled off his shirt and plunged into our pool. I dove in after. It was early June, the sky immense, glassy, placid. My father was cooking spareribs on the barbecue, an artist with a basting brush. His apron bore the caricature of a frazzled French chef. Mother curled on a chaise lounge, plumes of smoke wafting from her nostrils. In a stupor of contentment she took another drag, closed her eyes, and arched her face toward the sun.

Grady dog-paddled through the deep end, spouting a fountain of chlorinated water. Despite shame and confusion, my longing for him hadn't diminished; it continued to thrive without air and light, like a luminous fish in the dregs of the sea. In the name of play, I swam up behind him, encircled his shoulders, astonished by his taut flesh. The two of us flailed, pretended to drown. Beneath the heavy press of water, Grady's orange hair wavered, a flame that couldn't be doused.

I've lived with a man for seven years. Some nights, when I'm half-asleep and the room is suffused with blue light, I reach out to touch the expanse of his back, and it seems as if my fingers sink into his skin, and I feel the pleasure a diver feels the instant he enters a body of water.

I have few regrets. But one is that I hadn't said to Theresa, "Of course I'm a fag." Maybe I'd have met her friends. Or become friends with her. Imagine the meals we might have concocted: hamburger Stroganoff, Swedish meatballs in a sweet translucent sauce, steaming slabs of Salisbury steak.

—1991

Learning from Other Writers

1. Cooper opens his essay with a scene involving Theresa Sanchez. Can you find the *end* of that scene? What is it about that ending that prompts the combination of exposition and meditation that follows? How does Cooper manage to make that second section (his meditation on whether or not he is "a fag") so vivid and revealing? Why does the author include *this* information about his parents and not some other set of facts?
2. How does Cooper use the exposition in the first three paragraphs after the space break to move us through time? What is the function of the scenic passage after that (in which Cooper's parents urge him to try the lox)?
3. After a brief bit of exposition ("The opportunity to put their advice into practice, and try out my plan to adapt to girls ..."), Cooper launches into the main section of his narrative. How would you describe the experiment the teenage Cooper carries out at Debbie Coburn's party? What are your favorite details? Bits of dialogue?
4. What is the role of the final section, in which Cooper narrates his final encounter with Theresa? Can you highlight the expository bridge between that scene and the next, in which the adolescent narrator looks up "homosexual" in the dictionary? And the expository bridge from there to the final scene, in which the narrator and Grady are talking about homosexuals while swimming in the Coopers' pool?
5. What structural and thematic roles does Theresa play in this essay? What is the function of the final two paragraphs, in which Cooper jumps forward in time to the present day?

ANDRE DUBUS III

TRACKS AND TIES

Years later, when I was twenty-six, she said in the *New York Times* you would tie her naked and spread-eagled on the bed, that you would take a bat to her. She said you'd hit her for any reason. But in Haverhill, Massachusetts, you were my best friend, my brother's too. I was fifteen and you two were fourteen and in 1974 we walked the avenues on cold gray days picking through dumpsters for something to beat off to. We'd beat off to anything, though I was shy about it and couldn't do it just anywhere.

One February morning we skipped school and went downtown. It was ten or eleven degrees and the dirty snow piled along both sides of River Street had become ice; the air made my lungs hurt and our noses, ears, and fingers felt burned, but you wore your faded blue jean jacket with the green magic marker peace signs drawn all over it. You wore sneakers and thin fake denim pants that looked more purple than blue. It was so cold I pulled the rubber band from my ponytail and let my hair down around my neck and leather-jacketed shoulders. Your hair was long too, brown and stringy. My brother, barely fourteen, needed a shave.

We had a dollar between us so we sat in a booth at Vahally's Diner and drank coffee with so much milk and sugar in it you couldn't call it coffee anymore. The Greek man behind the counter hated us; he folded his black hairy forearms across his chest and watched us take our free refills until we were giddy with caffeine. You went for your seventh cup and he yelled something at you in Greek. On the way out you stole two dollars someone had left on their check under a sugar shaker.

You paid our way on the city bus that was heated and made a loop all the way through town, along the river, up to the Westgate shopping center, then back again. We stayed on it for two hours, taking the loop six times. In the far rear, away from the driver, you took out your black-handled Buck knife and carved a peace sign into the aluminum-backed seat in front of you. For a while I looked out the window at all the red brick factory buildings, the store-fronts with their dusty windows, bright neon price deals taped to the bottom and top. Barrooms on every block. I probably thought of the high school algebra I was flunking, the gym class I hated, the brown mescaline and crystal meth and THC my sister was selling. The bus was warm, too warm, and more crowded than before. A woman our mothers' age sat in her overcoat and scarf in the seat in front of you both. Her back was to you and I'm sure she heard you laughing but she didn't see my brother hunched forward in his seat, jerking back and forth on his penis and coming in no time, catching it all in his hand. I think I looked away and I don't remember what he did with it.

After the bus, we made our way through the narrow factory streets, most of the buildings' windows covered with gray plywood, though your mother still worked at Schwartz's Shoe, on the fifth floor, when she wasn't drinking. We walked along the railroad tracks, its silver rails flush with the packed snow, the wooden ties gone under. And we laughed about the summer before when we three built a barricade for the train, a wall of broken creosote ties, an upside-down shopping cart, cinder blocks, and a rusted oil drum. We covered it with brush, then you siphoned gas from a Duster behind Schwartz's and poured it on. My brother and I lit it, air sucked by us in a whoosh, and we ran down the bank across the parking lot into the abandoned brewery to the second floor to watch our fire, to wait for the Boston & Maine, to hear the screaming brakes as it rounded the blind curve just off the trestle over the river. But a fat man in a good shirt and tie showed up at the tracks, then a cop, and we ran laughing to the first floor where we turned on the keg conveyor belt, lay on it belly-first, and rode it up through its trap door over and over.

As we made our way through town it began to snow. My brother and I were hungry, but you were never hungry; you were hawny, you said. One morning, as we sat in the basement of your house and passed a homemade pipe between us, your mother upstairs drunk on Kappy's vodka and Pepsi, singing to herself, you said: "I'm always hawny in the mawnin'."

My brother and I laughed and you didn't know why, then you inhaled resin on your next hit and said, "Shit man, the screem's broken."

"The *what?*"

"The screem. You know, the screem. Like a *screem* door?"

By the time we reached the avenues the snow had blanketed the streets. There were two sisters on Seventh who lived in the projects that always had motorcycles in front of them, and trash, and bright-colored babies' toys. Trish and Terry were older, sixteen and seventeen and so skinny their breasts looked like prunes beneath their shirts, but they had dark skin and long hair and sometimes, if they were high, they'd suck you. But there was a day party on the first floor of their building, and it had only been two weeks since Harry Wright and Kevin McConigle, rent collectors for Fat Billy, both twenty-three or -four, beat us up, you and me, just walked us out of a pot party we were both quiet at, walked us off the front porch into the mud then kicked and punched us until they were through. So we kept walking, heading for a street close to the highway where we knew three girls who would fuck if you had wine and rubbers, though after the wine they didn't mention the rubbers.

On Cedar Street, cars spun out snow as they drove from the curb or the corner store. You let out a yelp and a holler and went running after a Chevy that had just pulled away, skidding slightly as it went. You ran low, bent over so the driver wouldn't see you, and when you reached the back bumper you grabbed it and squatted on your sneakers, your butt an inch or two from the road. And you skied away, just like that, the snow shooting out from under the wheels of the car, out from under your Zayre Department Store sneakers, blue exhaust coughing out its pipe beside you.

In the spring and summer we hopped trucks. A mile from the highway was a crosswalk on Main with a push-button traffic signal pole that we three leaned against until a truck came along and one of us pressed the button to turn red. I was the decoy that day, for a white refrigerator truck from Shoe City Beef. It stopped at the line, and I crossed the street jerking my head like a chicken to keep his attention from the mirrors while you two ran around to the back and climbed up on the foot-wide iron ledge at the bottom of its rear doors. As soon as I got to the sidewalk I heard the driver shift from neutral to first, heard him give it the gas. I waited for a car to drive by from the opposite direction, then I ran out into the street behind the truck, which was only shifting up to second. You and my brother stood on the ledge waiting, smiling, nodding your heads for me to hurry. I reached the ledge just as the truck moved into higher gear and I grabbed the bolt lock on its back doors and pulled myself up, the truck going faster now, shifting again, dipping and rattling through a low spot in the road. You both held an iron handle on opposite sides of the door so I stayed down, gripping the bolt lock with both hands, sitting on the ledge.

A car horn behind us honked and the driver, some man who combed his hair to the side like a teacher, shook his head and honked his horn again. You gave him the finger and we laughed but it was a scared laugh because the truck wasn't slowing down as it got to the gas stations and Kappy's Liquor near the highway, it was speeding up. Before, we'd jumped off into the grass of the highway ramp, but now we couldn't; he took the turn without leaving third gear and you yelled: "He *knows!* He friggin' *knows!*" My brother wasn't smiling anymore, and he stuck his head around the corner and let the growing wind hit him in the face, run through the hair on his cheeks as he squeezed the handle with both hands and I wanted to stand, to get my feet on something solid, but there was no room and now the driver was in fourth gear, heading north on 495, going fifty, then sixty, then sixty-five. He moved to the middle lane and I tried not to look down at the zip of the asphalt a foot beneath my dangling boots, but it was worse looking out at the cars, at the drivers looking at us like we might be a circus act they should catch sometime. Some honked as they passed so I looked up at you, at the side of your face as you looked around the corner, the June wind snapping your hair back past your forehead and ears, your mouth open in a scream I could barely hear. You smiled and shook your head at my brother then down at me, your brown eyes wet from the wind, your cheeks flushed in a satisfaction so deep I had to look back at the cars behind us, at the six or seven I was convinced would run me over one after the other, after my fingers failed. Miles later, at the tollbooths of the New Hampshire line, the truck slowed to a stop and we jumped off exhausted, our fingers stiff, and thumbed home.

That fall you went to the trade school, my brother joined me at the high school, and I saw you six years later in an all-night store in Monument Square. I was buying cigarettes for my college girl-friend. She waited in the car. It was winter. The floor was dirty with people's slush and mud tracks, the overhead light was fluorescent and too bright, and I was waiting my turn at the register when I saw you, watching me, smiling as you walked up. You carried a carton of ice cream and a quart of Coke. I had on a sweater and a jacket but you wore only a T-shirt, green Dickie work pants, and sneakers. You were taller than me, lean, and your young black mustache and goatee made you look sinister until you started talking in that high voice that hadn't changed since you'd told us you were hawny in the mawnin'. You said you were living down on the avenues, that you were getting married soon. I said congratulations, then I was at the counter asking for a pack of Parliaments and you touched me on the shoulder, said to say hi to my brother. I said I would. At the door I glanced back at you and watched you dig into your front pocket for crumpled bills. You nodded and smiled at me, winked even, and as I left the store, the cold tightening the skin on my face, I remembered the time your mother went to visit her sister in Nebraska for a whole month. I could never understand why she went alone, why she'd leave her family like that to go off for a visit. Then my mother told me it was detox she went to, some twenty-eight-day program in Boston. When I told you I knew, you laughed and said, "Nah," but you swallowed twice and walked away to do nothing in particular.

Six months after I saw you in the store my brother and I got invitations to your wedding. We didn't go.

Four more years and you were dead.

I heard about it after you were buried. They said your wife stabbed you in the back. That was it; she stabbed you. But a year later I was behind the bar at McMino's Lounge and Fat Billy's son, Bill Jr., told me what really happened, that you were cooked, always thinking your wife was cheating on you, always beating her up. That night you ran outside off the porch to go kill the guy you thought she was fucking. This was down on one of the avenues, behind the projects, and you took the trail in back of your house. But your wife opened your black-handled Buck knife and chased after you, screaming. She was short and small, barely five feet, and just as you reached the weeds she got to you and drove it in low, sinking the blade into your liver, snipping something called the portal artery. You went down without a sound. You curled up in a heap. But your wife spent four hours at a neighbor's house crying before they called anyone, and then it was the cops, and you were gone.

I served Bill Jr. another White Russian and for a second I felt sure it was him she went to that night, and I thought about hitting him for not making a faster call, but I felt no heat in my hands, no pull inside me. And I've always hated woman beaters. Part of me thought you got what you deserved. I left Bill Jr. to finish his too-sweet drink.

The following winter I was living in New York City, in a one-room studio with my girlfriend. It was late on a Sunday morning and we both sat with our feet up on the couch reading the *New York Times*. Outside our barred window snow fell on parked cars, on the sidewalk and street. I got tired of the movie section and picked up a story about three women in prison, all there for the same reason, for killing the husbands who beat them. And your wife was one of them; they gave her full name, *your* name. They wrote how she chased you outside and stabbed you. They described the town you both lived in as economically depressed, once a thriving textile town but no more. I lowered the paper and started to tell my girlfriend all about you, but she and I weren't doing so well, both past wanting to hear anything extra about each other, so I pulled on my boots and jacket and went walking. I crossed Third Avenue and Second and First. A car alarm went off in front of some Chinese laundry. I stuck my hands in my pockets and wished I'd worn a hat. I passed an empty basketball court, then I waited for the traffic on FDR Drive and walked the last block to the East River. To my right and left were bridges over to Queens. Though from where I stood I could see only the backs of warehouses, dry weeds five feet tall, then the gray river, swirling by fast.

The snow had stopped and I started walking along the cobblestone walk. One morning I skipped school and cut through back yards to your house. I didn't know your mother was home from Nebraska and I almost stepped back when she answered the door. She'd dyed her brown hair black, she wore sweatpants and a sweater, she had a cold sore on her bottom lip, and she'd gained weight, but she smiled and kissed me on the cheek and invited me in. The small kitchen was clean and warm. It smelled like coffee and cinnamon rolls. She put one on a napkin and handed it to me. I thanked her, and while I chewed the sweet buttery bread, she lit up a cigarette and asked about my mother. Then you came downstairs in just your jeans, no shirt, your chest pale and thin, your nipples pink, and your mother rushed over and kissed and hugged you like you'd been gone and just gotten home. And you didn't pull away, you hugged her back, and when your eyes caught mine, you lowered your face into the hair at her shoulder, and kept hugging.

—1993

Learning from Other Writers

1. Who is the "you" to whom the author addresses his essay? Is that "you" the essay's real audience? Why might Dubus have selected this unusual form of address?
2. The main narrative describes the three boys' journey around Haverhill in a single winter's day in February 1974. What details does the author use to bring alive the various characters in this story, especially his friend? What is the function of dialogue in this story? Which details help create a picture of the story's setting? Does Dubus use exposition to insert any background information into this narrative, or does he mostly stick to the events of that February day?
3. After a brief use of expository prose to move us forward in time ("That fall you went to the trade school, my brother joined me at the high school, and I saw you six years later in an all-night store in Monument Square"), Dubus presents a second (shorter) scene. What purpose seems to govern his selection of details to present in the scene in the convenience store?
4. After a few more expository sentences that move us forward in time, Dubus presents the scene at McMino's Lounge. What is the function of this scene? Why doesn't Dubus let Bill Jr. tell the story of the friend's murder in his own words?
5. What is the function of the scene in New York City? What causes the narrator to remember the time he visited his friend and was surprised to find the friend's mother at the door?

MARCIE HERSHMAN

NO BURDEN TO BEAR

"Put your foot right on top of mine," she'd say. "That's good, *mamelah*. Now come stand on me with the other one."

"But doesn't it hurt you, Nanny?"

"Hurt me?" With a laugh, she smoothed the loose strands of blond hair back into my ponytail. "Why, you're so light, you weigh nothing. You're like a pinch of air. Other foot on top, come on—*up!* That's good: balance on me. And put an arm around my waist so no one falls." Playfully, my grandmother took hold of my free hand and wove her fingers with mine. Her fingers were thick and wrinkled; mine so thin and smooth and squirmy they seemed a different species entirely—kin to the freshly struck No. 2 pencils I was learning to write with in school.

"Don't be afraid; let what happens happen. But don't let me slip out from under," she warned.

"I won't."

"So?" Her square chin lifted even higher. She was smiling over the top of my head to whoever was watching. "Oh, how we are going to dance!" Taking a deep breath, she took a first simple step sideways, and my foot stepped, too, with hers. Then she took a bigger step; my whole leg was lifting.

"Oh!" I exclaimed.

"See how easy?" Nanny said. "Easy as pie."

Clinging to her wide, warm, familiar body, giggling and gasping. I spun with my grandmother in giant circles across the dark parquet floor of the living room. Occasionally I slid off her feet (my anklet socks wouldn't hold), but I always scrambled right back. We danced on and on, unequal partners who in those moments absolutely loved all the inequalities about us, the jokiness, the seriousness. My grandmother was singing: her voice was loud and clear. She spun me for a long time. Our heads thrown back, legs stepping, arms pumping, our fingers intertwined.

"Now," said the funeral director, with a nod. And at that signal we lifted the casket. It was—she was—so light. She weighed nothing, like a pinch of air. I'd been afraid that I wouldn't be able to hold her up. I'd feared that I wouldn't be able to balance the casket and that it would tilt and my grandmother's body would fall out at my feet. But, really, she was so light, held by the six of us. I had no idea it would feel like this to be a pallbearer. Gentle. Cradling. Maternal.

We'd slid the plain wooden box out of the back of the hearse and started up a path of icy snow that wound among the standing gravestones to where the rabbi waited by a deeply dark grave. I wanted to carry her safely. Carrying now was a responsibility given over to me—it was completion and connection.

The Hebrew phrase associated with pallbearing is *hesed shel emeth*, an act of truthful and pure loving kindness. It is pure because the giver can have no expectation of reciprocity. Watching from the sidelines of the burial processions of others I'd loved in the past, I'd never known how the loving kindness in the act overflowed, how it returned to fill the hearts of those who raised the casket and carried it to its measure of earth.

I'd thought of pallbearing as gloom, oppressiveness, darkness, a struggle to remain upright under both a physical and atmospheric—an impossible—weight. That narrow box of a word with all light extinguished, all weight given over, yielded only effort and loss. Pallbearing was connected to destruction. And like war in its soldiering, it traditionally has been shouldered by men. Men, who it seemed could bear up under the burden where women would not.

When my grandfather died, I'd just turned 16. I recall standing with my three younger brothers as his casket was carried past. What I wanted most to do for Papa then was to keep my chin high and not let any tears fall, because three years earlier I'd watched Jackie Kennedy grieving that way during J.F.K.'s televised funeral. The image of a woman who stood erectly, quietly, sadly, was rebroadcast countless times—and gradually it became embedded in the culture itself. The First Lady's stillness and bearing showed us a way we, too, might act to pay our last respects.

My mother doesn't like to think of herself as radical or unconventional, but on that sad morning her mother was to be buried it was she who broke first with tradition. I was writing a eulogy when she came quietly into the room. She waited a moment, then suddenly asked if I'd like to serve as one of the pallbearers.

"Mom?" I looked up at her, my eyes wide. The possibility had never entered my mind.

Months later, I asked if she'd ever seen a woman serve as a pallbearer before. Mom said, "Come to think of it, no."

"Then why did you think I could be one?"

"I guess I was upset and wasn't thinking clearly right then," she said distractedly. Then she caught herself. "No, not true. I really thought, well, this is the last honor someone can do for a person they love. And I knew you loved Nanny. You loved her as much as anyone did."

I stood up with my brothers and two of our cousins and went to an alcove off the main chapel of the funeral parlor. A man waiting there for us held out a basket filled with black cloth gloves. Along with the others, I selected a pair, the smallest they had. Gloves for pallbearing are made for a man's hands. I pulled them on; they fit. Two male assistants wheeled Nanny's bier into the room. The six of us positioned ourselves around it. The funeral director went over to the double doors that led to the parking lot. Family and friends would gather out there; I knew the aisle they'd make by standing on the sidelines would guide Anna Weiss's casket to the back of the hearse. The director opened the doors. The December wind blew right in.

"Ready?" he asked. We each grasped a side handle.

"Okay," he said, waving us forward. "Lift."

Lift.

"Now," said one of my brothers. "Together."

We lifted—and my arm was pulled downward, but that was all. As we slowly moved into the wind, I didn't buckle. For how absolutely steady Nanny's last weight was; how perfectly still. How little it asked of me. Only that I carry her gently. As so many times she had on her own carried me.

—1992

Learning from Other Writers

1. The first third of Hershman's essay (up to the space break) consists of a single scene, with virtually no exposition or meditation. What is the effect of this stylistic choice?
2. After the first space-break, Hershman skips directly to a second (much later) scene, without using any exposition to bridge the gap. What effect does this produce?
3. After giving us a bit of information about the origins of the Hebrew phrase associated with pallbearing, Hershman offers a few paragraphs of meditation. What spurs her to these particular feelings and thoughts?
4. Why does she skip backward in time to describe her grandfather's funeral? And why the skip from there to the scene before her grandmother's funeral, when her mother asked her if she wanted to help carry her grandmother's coffin? How does the author keep you from getting confused as she jumps back and forth in time?
5. What details does Hershman choose to bring alive the final scene (the five paragraphs after the second space-break)? What spurs her to come up with the meditation in the final paragraph?

E.B. WHITE

DEATH OF A PIG

I spent several days and nights in mid-September with an ailing pig and I feel driven to account for this stretch of time, more particularly since the pig died at last, and I lived, and things might easily have gone the other way round and none left to do the accounting. Even now, so close to the event, I cannot recall the hours sharply and am not ready to say whether death came on the third night or the fourth night. This uncertainty afflicts me with a sense of personal deterioration; if I were in decent health I would know how many nights I had sat up with a pig.

The scheme of buying a spring pig in blossomtime, feeding it through summer and fall, and butchering it when the solid cold weather arrives, is a familiar scheme to me and follows an antique pattern. It is a tragedy enacted on most farms with perfect fidelity to the original script. The murder, being premeditated, is in the first degree but is quick and skillful, and the smoked bacon and ham provide a ceremonial ending whose fitness is seldom questioned.

Once in a while something slips—one of the actors goes up in his lines and the whole performance stumbles and halts. My pig simply failed to show up for a meal. The alarm spread rapidly. The classic outline of the tragedy was lost. I found myself cast suddenly in the role of pig's friend and physician—a farcical character with an enema bag for a prop. I had a presentiment, the very first afternoon, that the play would never regain its balance and that my sympathies were now wholly with the pig. This was slapstick—the sort of dramatic treatment that instantly appealed to my old dachshund, Fred, who joined the vigil, held the bag, and, when all was over, presided at the interment. When we slid the body into the grave, we both were shaken to the core. The loss we felt was not the loss of ham but the loss of pig. He had evidently become precious to me, not that he represented a distant nourishment in a hungry time, but that he had suffered in a suffering world. But I'm running ahead of my story and shall have to go back.

My pigpen is at the bottom of an old orchard below the house. The pigs I have raised have lived in a faded building that once was an icehouse. There is a pleasant yard to move about in, shaded by an apple tree that overhangs the low rail fence. A pig couldn't ask for anything better—or none has, at any rate. The sawdust in the icehouse makes a comfortable bottom in which to root, and a warm bed. This sawdust, however, came under suspicion when the pig took sick. One of my neighbors said he thought the pig would have done better on new ground—the same principle that applies in planting potatoes. He said there might be something unhealthy about that sawdust, that he never thought well of sawdust.

It was about four o'clock in the afternoon when I first noticed that there was something wrong with the pig. He failed to appear at the trough for his supper, and when a pig (or a child) refuses supper a chill wave of fear runs through any household, or icehousehold. After examining my pig, who was stretched out in the sawdust inside the building, I went to the phone and cranked it four times. Mr. Dameron answered. "What's good for a sick pig?" I asked. (There is never any identification needed on a country phone; the person on the other end knows who is talking by the sound of the voice and by the character of the question.)

"I don't know, I never had a sick pig," said Mr. Dameron, "but I can find out quick enough. You hang up and I'll call Henry."

Mr. Dameron was back on the line again in five minutes. "Henry says roll him over on his back and give him two ounces of castor oil or sweet oil, and if that doesn't do the trick give him an injection of soapy water. He says he's almost sure the pig's plugged up, and even if he's wrong, it can't do any harm."

I thanked Mr. Dameron. I didn't go right down to the pig, though. I sank into a chair and sat still for a few minutes to think about my troubles, and then I got up and went to the barn, catching up on some odds and ends that needed tending to. Unconsciously I held off, for an hour, the deed by which I would officially recognize the collapse of the performance of raising a pig; I wanted no interruption in the regularity of feeding, the steadiness of growth, the even succession of days. I wanted no interruption, wanted no oil, no deviation. I just wanted to keep on raising a pig, full meal after full meal, spring into summer into fall. I didn't even know whether there were two ounces of castor oil on the place.

Shortly after five o'clock I remembered that we had been invited out to dinner that night and realized that if I were to dose a pig there was no time to lose. The dinner date seemed a familiar conflict: I move in a desultory society and often a week or two will roll by without my going to anybody's house to dinner or anyone's coming to mine, but when an occasion does arise, and I am summoned, something usually turns up (an hour or two in advance) to make all human intercourse seem vastly inappropriate. I have come to believe that there is in hostesses a special power of divination, and that they deliberately arrange dinners to coincide with pig failure or some other sort of failure. At any rate, it was after five o'clock and I knew I could put off no longer the evil hour.

When my son and I arrived at the pigyard, armed with a small bottle of castor oil and a length of clothesline, the pig had emerged from his house and was standing in the middle of his yard, listlessly. He gave us a slim greeting. I could see that he felt uncomfortable and uncertain. I had brought the clothesline thinking I'd have to tie him (the pig weighed more than a hundred pounds) but we never used it. My son reached down, grabbed both front legs, upset him quickly, and when he opened his mouth to scream I turned the oil into his throat—a pink, corrugated area I had never seen before. I had just time to read the label while the neck of the bottle was in his mouth. It said Puretest. The screams, slightly muffled by oil, were pitched in the hysterically high range of pigsound, as though torture were being carried out, but they didn't last long: it was all over rather suddenly, and, his legs released, the pig righted himself.

In the upset position the corners of his mouth had been turned down, giving him a frowning expression. Back on his feet again, he regained the set smile that a pig wears even in sickness. He stood his ground, sucking slightly at the residue of oil; a few drops leaked out of his lips while his wicked eyes, shaded by their coy little lashes, turned on me in disgust and hatred. I scratched him gently with oily fingers and he remained quiet, as though trying to recall the satisfaction of being scratched when in health, and seeming to rehearse in his mind the indignity to which he had just been subjected. I noticed, as I stood there, four or five small dark spots on his back near the tail end, reddish brown in color, each about the size of a housefly. I could not make out what they were. They did not look troublesome but at the same time they did not look like mere surface bruises or chafe marks. Rather they seemed blemishes of internal origin. His stiff white bristles almost completely hid them and I had to part the bristles with my fingers to get a good look.

Several hours later, a few minutes before midnight, having dined well and at someone else's expense, I returned to the pighouse with a flashlight. The patient was asleep. Kneeling, I felt his ears (as you might put your hand on the forehead of a child) and they seemed cool, and then with the light made a careful examination of the yard and the house for a sign that the oil had worked. I found none and went to bed.

We had been having an unseasonable spell of weather—hot, close days, with the fog shutting in every night, scaling for a few hours in midday, then creeping back again at dark, drifting in first over the trees on the point, then suddenly blowing across the fields, blotting out the world and taking possession of houses, men, and animals. Everyone kept hoping for a break, but the break failed to come. Next day was another hot one. I visited the pig before breakfast and tried to tempt him with a little milk in his trough. He just stared at it, while I made a sucking sound through my teeth to remind him of past pleasures of the feast. With very small, timid pigs, weanlings, this ruse is often quite successful and will encourage them to eat; but with a large, sick pig the ruse is senseless and the sound I made must have made him feel, if anything, more miserable. He not only did not crave food, he felt a positive revulsion to it. I found a place under the apple tree where he had vomited in the night.

At this point, although a depression had settled over me, I didn't suppose that I was going to lose my pig. From the lustiness of a healthy pig a man derives a feeling of personal lustiness; the stuff that goes into the trough and is received with such enthusiasm is an earnest of some later feast of his own, and when this suddenly comes to an end and the food lies stale and untouched, souring in the sun, the pig's imbalance becomes the man's vicariously, and life seems insecure, displaced, transitory.

As my own spirits declined, along with the pig's, the spirits of my vile old dachshund rose. The frequency of our trips down the footpath through the orchard to the pigyard delighted him, although he suffers greatly from arthritis, moves with difficulty, and would be bedridden if he could find anyone willing to serve him meals on a tray.

He never missed a chance to visit the pig with me, and he made many professional calls on his own. You could see him down there at all hours, his white face parting the grass along the fence as he wobbled and stumbled about, his stethoscope dangling—a happy quack, writing his villainous prescriptions and grinning his corrosive grin. When the enema bag appeared, and the bucket of warm suds, his happiness was complete, and he managed to squeeze his enormous body between the two lowest rails of the yard and then assumed full charge of the irrigation. Once, when I lowered the bag to check the flow, he reached in and hurriedly drank a few mouthfuls of the suds to test their potency. I have noticed that Fred will feverishly consume any substance that is associated with trouble—the bitter flavor is to his liking. When the bag was above reach, he concentrated on the pig and was everywhere at once, a tower of strength and inconvenience. The pig, curiously enough, stood rather quietly through this colonic carnival, and the enema, though ineffective, was not as difficult as I had anticipated.

I discovered, though, that once having given a pig an enema there is no turning back, no chance of resuming one of life's more stereotyped roles. The pig's lot and mine were inextricably bound now, as though the rubber tube were the silver cord. From then until the time of his death I held the pig steadily in the bowl of my mind; the task of trying to deliver him from his misery became a strong obsession. His suffering soon became the embodiment of all earthly wretchedness. Along toward the end of the afternoon, defeated in physicking, I phoned the veterinary twenty miles away and placed the case formally in his hands. He was full of questions, and when I casually mentioned the dark spots on the pig's back, his voice changed its tone.

"I don't want to scare you," he said, "but when there are spots, erysipelas has to be considered."

Together we considered erysipelas, with frequent interruptions from the telephone operator, who wasn't sure the connection had been established.

"If a pig has erysipelas can he give it to a person?" I asked.

"Yes, he can," replied the vet.

"Have they answered?" asked the operator.

"Yes, they have," I said. Then I addressed the vet again. "You better come over here and examine this pig right away."

"I can't come myself," said the vet, "But McFarland can come this evening if that's all right. Mac knows more about pigs than I do anyway. You needn't worry too much about the spots. To indicate erysipelas they would have to be deep hemorrhagic infarcts."

"Deep hemorrhagic what?" I asked.

"Infarcts," said the vet.

"Have they answered?" asked the operator.

"Well," I said, "I don't know what you'd call these spots, except they're about the size of a housefly. If the pig has erysipelas I guess I have it, too, by this time, because we've been very close lately."

"McFarland will be over," said the vet.

I hung up. My throat felt dry and I went to the cupboard and got a bottle of whiskey. Deep hemorrhagic infarcts—the phrase began fastening its hooks in my head. I had assumed that there could be nothing much wrong with a pig during the months it was being groomed for murder; my confidence in the essential health and endurance of pigs had been strong and deep, particularly in the health of pigs that belonged to me and that were part of my proud scheme. The awakening had been violent and I minded it all the more because I knew that what could be true of my pig could be true also of the rest of my tidy world. I tried to put this distasteful idea from me, but it kept recurring. I took a short drink of the whiskey and then, although I wanted to go down to the yard and look for fresh signs, I was scared to. I was certain I had erysipelas.

It was long after dark and the supper dishes had been put away when a car drove in and McFarland got out. He had a girl with him. I could just make her out in the darkness—she seemed young and pretty. "This is Miss Owen," he said. "We've been having a picnic supper on the shore, that's why I'm late."

McFarland stood in the driveway and stripped off his jacket, then his shirt. His stocky arms and capable hands showed up in my flashlight's gleam as I helped him find his coverall and get zipped up. The rear seat of his car contained an astonishing amount of paraphernalia, which he soon overhauled, selecting a chain, a syringe, a bottle of oil, a rubber tube, and some other things I couldn't identify. Miss Owen said she'd go along with us and see the pig. I led the way down the warm slope of the orchard, my light picking out the path for them, and we all three climbed the fence, entered the pighouse, and squatted by the pig while McFarland took a rectal reading. My flashlight picked up the glitter of an engagement ring on the girl's hand.

"No elevation," said McFarland, twisting the thermometer in the light. "You needn't worry about erysipelas." He ran his hand slowly over the pig's stomach and at one point the pig cried out in pain.

"Poor piggledy-wiggledy!" said Miss Owen.

The treatment I had been giving the pig for two days was then repeated, somewhat more expertly, by the doctor, Miss Owen and I handing him things as he needed them—holding the chain that he had looped around the pig's upper jaw, holding the syringe, holding the bottle stopper, the end of the tube, all of us working in darkness and in comfort, working with the instinctive teamwork induced by emergency conditions, the pig unprotesting, the house shadowy, protecting, intimate. I went to bed tired but with a feeling of relief that

I had turned over part of the responsibility of the case to a licensed doctor. I was beginning to think, though, that the pig was not going to live.

He died twenty-four hours later, or it might have been forty-eight—there is a blur in time here, and I may have lost or picked up a day in the telling and the pig one in the dying. At intervals during the last day I took cool fresh water down to him and at such times as he found the strength to get to his feet he would stand with head in the pail and snuffle his snout around. He drank a few sips but no more; yet it seemed to comfort him to dip his nose in water and bobble it about, sucking in and blowing out through his teeth. Much of the time, now, he lay indoors half buried in sawdust. Once, near the last, while I was attending him I saw him try to make a bed for himself but he lacked the strength, and when he set his snout into the dust he was unable to plow even the little furrow he needed to lie down in.

He came out of the house to die. When I went down, before going to bed, he lay stretched in the yard a few feet from the door. I knelt, saw that he was dead, and left him there: his face had a mild look, expressive neither of deep peace nor of deep suffering, although I think he had suffered a good deal. I went back up to the house and to bed, and cried internally—deep hemorrhagic intears. I didn't wake till nearly eight the next morning, and when I looked out the open window the grave was already being dug, down beyond the dump under a wild apple. I could hear the spade strike against the small rocks that blocked the way. Never send to know for whom the grave is dug, I said to myself, it's dug for thee. Fred, I well knew, was supervising the work of digging, so I ate breakfast slowly.

It was a Saturday morning. The thicket in which I found the gravediggers at work was dark and warm, the sky overcast. Here, among alders and young hackmatacks, at the foot of the apple tree, Lennie had dug a beautiful hole, five feet long, three feet wide, three feet deep. He was standing in it, removing the last spadefuls of earth while Fred patrolled the brink in simple but impressive circles, disturbing the loose earth of the mound so that it trickled back in. There had been no rain in weeks and the soil, even three feet down, was dry and powdery. As I stood and stared, an enormous earthworm which had been partially exposed by the spade at the bottom dug itself deeper and made a slow withdrawal, seeking even remoter moistures at even lonelier depths. And just as Lennie stepped out and rested his spade against the tree and lit a cigarette, a small green apple separated itself from a branch overhead and fell into the hole. Everything about this last scene seemed over-written—the dismal sky, the shabby woods, the imminence of rain, the worm (legendary bedfellow of the dead), the apple (conventional garnish of a pig).

But even so, there was a directness and dispatch about animal burial, I thought, that made it a more decent affair than human burial: there was no stopover in the undertaker's foul parlor, no wreath nor spray; and when we hitched a line to the pig's hind legs and dragged him swiftly from his yard, throwing our weight into the harness and leaving a wake of crushed grass and smoothed rubble over the dump, ours was a businesslike procession, with Fred, the dishonorable pallbearer, staggering along in the rear, his perverse bereavement showing in every seam in his face; and the post mortem performed handily and swiftly right at the edge of the grave, so that the innards that had caused the pig's death preceded him into the ground and he lay at last resting squarely on the cause of his own undoing.

I threw in the first shovelful, and then we worked rapidly and without talk, until the job was complete. I picked up the rope, made it fast to Fred's collar (he is a notorious ghoul), and we all three filed back up the path to the house, Fred bringing up the rear and holding back every inch of the way, feigning unusual stiffness. I noticed that although he weighed far less than the pig, he was harder to drag, being possessed of the vital spark.

The news of the death of my pig traveled fast and far, and I received many expressions of sympathy from friends and neighbors, for no one took the event lightly and the premature expiration of a pig is, I soon discovered, a departure which the community marks solemnly on its calendar, a sorrow in which it feels fully involved. I have written this account in penitence and in grief, as a man who failed to raise his pig, and to explain my deviation from the classic course of so many raised pigs. The grave in the woods is unmarked, but Fred can direct the mourner to it unerringly and with immense good will, and I know he and I shall often revisit it, singly and together, in seasons of reflection and despair, on flagless memorial days of our own choosing.

—1948

Learning from Other Writers

1. What is the author's small, personal question about the death of his pig? What is the larger thematic question that might interest a reader who has never had to care for a dying pig?
2. What does the author understand about his pig's death at the time he writes his essay that he didn't understand while the pig was dying?
3. What details does White offer to describe the pig house and farm where the story takes place? Why these details and not others?
4. What role does Fred play in the narrative? The author's son?
5. Find the scenes in which White uses dialogue. Surely this wasn't all that anyone said during the pig's illness. Why might the author have chosen to include these lines and not others?
6. How and why does White use humor?
7. How and why does he use allusions to other literary works?
8. How does White avoid the pitfall of sentimentality?
9. Does the author ever answer his initial question about why he cares so deeply about the death of a pig that he intended to slaughter anyway?
10. Why does White (like Orwell) choose to end his essay with the community's (and Fred's) reaction to the news of an animal's death rather than his own meditations on that death?

GRACE PALEY

SIX DAYS: SOME REMEMBERINGS

I was in jail. I had been sentenced to six days in the Women's House of Detention, a fourteen-story prison right in the middle of Greenwich Village, my own neighborhood. This happened during the American War in Vietnam, I have forgotten which important year of the famous sixties. The civil disobedience for which I was paying a small penalty probably consisted of sitting down to impede or slow some military parade.

I was surprised at the sentence. Others had been given two days or dismissed. I think the judge was particularly angry with me. After all, I was not a kid. He thought I was old enough to know better, a forty-five-year-old woman, a mother and teacher. I ought to be too busy to waste time on causes I couldn't possibly understand.

I was herded with about twenty other women, about 90 percent black and Puerto Rican, into the bullpen, an odd name for a women's holding facility. There, through someone else's lawyer, I received a note from home, telling me that since I'd chosen to spend the first week of July in jail, my son would probably not go to summer camp, because I had neglected to raise the money I'd promised. I read this note and burst into tears, real running-down-the-cheek tears. It was true: thinking about other people's grown boys, I had betrayed my little son. The summer, starting that day, July 1, stood up before me day after day, steaming the city streets, the after-work crowded city pool.

I guess I attracted some attention. You—you white girl you—you never been arrested before? A black woman about a head taller than I put her arm on my shoulder.—It ain't so bad. What's your time sugar? I gotta do three years. You huh?

Six days.

Six days? What the fuck for?

I explained, sniffling, embarrassed.

You got six days for sitting down front of a horse? Cop on the horse? Horse step on you? Jesus in hell, cops gettin crazier and stupider and meaner. Maybe we get you out.

No, no, I said. I wasn't crying because of that. I didn't want her to think I was scared. I wasn't. She paid no attention. Shoving a couple of women aside—Don't stand in front of me, bitch. Move over. What you looking at?—she took hold of the bars of our cage, commenced to bang on them, shook them mightily, screaming—Hear me now, you motherfuckers, you grotty pigs, get this housewife out of here! She returned to comfort me.—Six days in this low-down hole for sitting front of a horse!

Before we were distributed among our cells, we were dressed in a kind of nurse's aide scrub uniform, blue or green, a little too large or a little too small. We had had to submit to a physical in which all our hiding places were investigated for drugs. These examinations were not too difficult, mostly because a young woman named Andrea Dworkin had fought them, refused a grosser, more painful examination some months earlier. She had been arrested protesting the war in front of the U.S. Mission to the UN. I had been there too, but I don't think I was arrested that day. She was mocked for that determined struggle at the Women's House, as she had been for other braveries, but according to the women I questioned, certain humiliating, perhaps sadistic customs had ended—for that period at least.

My cellmate was a beautiful young woman, twenty-three years old, a prostitute who'd never been arrested before. She was nervous, but she had been given the name of an important long-termer. She explained in a businesslike way that she *was* beautiful, and would need protection. She'd be O.K. once she found that woman. In the two days we spent together, she tried *not* to talk to the other women on our cell block. She said they were mostly street whores and addicts. She would never be on the street. Her man wouldn't allow it anyway.

I slept well for some reason, probably the hard mattress. I don't seem to mind where I am. Also I must tell you, I could look out the window at the end of our corridor and see my children or their friends, on their way to music lessons or Greenwich House pottery. Looking slantwise I could see right into Sutter's Bakery, then on the corner of Tenth Street. These were my neighbors at coffee and cake.

Sometimes the cell block was open, but not our twelve cells. Other times the reverse. Visitors came by: they were prisoners, detainees not yet sentenced. They seemed to have a strolling freedom, though several, unsentenced, unable to make bail, had been there for months. One woman peering into the cells stopped when she saw me. Grace! Hi! I knew her from the neighborhood, maybe the park, couldn't really remember her name.

What are you in for? I asked.

Oh nothing—well a stupid drug bust. I don't even use—oh well forget it. I've been here six weeks. They keep putting the trial off. Are you O.K.?

Then I complained. I had planned not to complain about anything while living among people who'd be here in these clanging cells a long time; it didn't seem right. But I said, I don't have anything to read and they took away my pen and I don't have paper.

Oh you'll get all that eventually, she said. Keep asking.

Well they have all my hairpins. I'm a mess.

No no she said, you're O.K. You look nice.

(A couple of years later, the war continuing, I was arrested in Washington. My hair was still quite long. I wore it in a kind of bun on top of my head. My hairpins gone, my hair straggled wildly every which way. Muriel Rukeyser, arrested that day along with about thirty other women, made the same generous sisterly remark. No no Grace, love you with your hair down, you really ought to always wear it this way.)

The very next morning, my friend brought me *The Collected Stories of William Carlos Williams.*—These O.K.?

God! O.K.—Yes!

My trial is coming up tomorrow, she said. I think I'm getting off with time already done. Over done. See you around?

That afternoon, my cellmate came for her things—I'm moving to the fourth floor. Working in the kitchen. Couldn't be better. We were sitting outside our cells, she wanted me to know something. She'd already told me, but said it again.—I still can't believe it. This creep, this guy, this cop, he waits he just waits till he's fucked and fine, pulls his pants up, pays me, and arrests me. It's not legal. It's not. My man's so mad, he like to kill *me,* but he's not that kind of—he's not a criminal type, *my* man. She never said the word pimp. Maybe no one did. Maybe that was our word.

I had made friends with some of the women in the cells across the aisle. How can I say "made friends." I just sat and spoke when spoken to, I was at school. I answered questions—simple ones. Why I would do such a fool thing on purpose? How old were my children? My man any good? Then, you live around the corner? That was a good idea, Evelyn said, to have a prison in your own neighborhood, so you could keep in touch, yelling out the window. As in fact we were able to do right here and now, calling and being called from Sixth Avenue, by mothers, children, boyfriends.

About the children: One woman took me aside. Her daughter was brilliant, she was in Hunter High School, had taken a test. No she hardly ever saw her, but she wasn't a whore—it was the drugs. Her daughter was ashamed, the grandmother, the father's mother made the child ashamed. When she got out in six months it would be different. This made Evelyn and Rita, right across from my cell, laugh. Different, I swear. Different. Laughing. But she *could* make it, I said. Then they really laughed. Their first laugh was a bare giggle compared to these convulsive roars. Change her ways? That dumb bitch Ha!!

Another woman, Helen, the only other white woman on the cell block, wanted to talk to me. She wanted me to know that she was not only white but Jewish. She came from Brighton Beach. Her father, he should rest in peace, thank God, was dead. Her arms were covered with puncture marks almost like sleeve patterns. But she needed to talk to me, because I was Jewish (I'd been asked by Rita and Evelyn—was I Irish? No, Jewish. Oh, they answered). She walked me to the barred window at the end of the corridor, the window that looked down on West Tenth Street. She said, How come you so friends with those black whores? You don't hardly talk to me. I said I liked them, but I liked her too. She said, If you knew them for true, you wouldn't like them. They nothing but street whores. You know, once I was friends with them. We done a lot of things together, I knew them fifteen years Evy and Rita maybe twenty, I been in the streets with them, side by side, Amsterdam, Lenox, West Harlem; in bad weather we covered each other. Then one day along come Malcolm X and they don't know me no more, they ain't talking to me. You too white. I ain't all that white. Twenty years. They ain't talking.

My friend Myrt called one day, that is called from the street, called—Grace Grace. I heard and ran to the window. A policeman, the regular beat cop, was addressing her. She looked up, then walked away before I could yell my answer. Later on she told me that he'd said, I don't think Grace would appreciate you calling her name out like that.

What a mistake! For years, going to the park with my children, or simply walking down Sixth Avenue on a summer night past the Women's House, we would often have to thread our way through whole families calling up—bellowing, screaming to the third, seventh, tenth floor, to figures, shadows behind bars and screened windows—How you feeling? Here's Glena. She got big. Mami mami you like my dress? We gettin you out baby. New lawyer come by.

And the replies, among which I was privileged to live for a few days—shouted down.—You lookin beautiful. What he say? Fuck you James. I got a chance? Bye bye. Come next week.

Then the guards, the heavy clanking of cell doors. Keys. Night.

I still had no pen or paper despite the great history of prison literature. I was suffering a kind of frustration, a sickness in the way claustrophobia is a sickness—this paper-and-penlessness was a terrible pain in the area of my heart, a nausea. I was surprised.

In the evening, at lights out (a little like the army or on good days a strict, unpleasant camp), women called softly from their cells. Rita hey Rita sing that song—Come on sister sing. A few more importunings and then Rita in the cell diagonal to mine would begin with a ballad. A song about two women and a man. It was familiar to everyone but me. The two women were prison sweethearts. The man was her outside lover. One woman, the singer, was being paroled. The ballad told her sorrow about having been parted from him when she was sentenced, now she would leave her loved woman after three years. There were about twenty stanzas of joy and grief.

Well, I was so angry not to have pen and paper to get some of it down that I lost it all—all but the sorrowful plot. Of course she had this long song in her head, and in the next few nights she sang and chanted others, sometimes with a small chorus.

Which is how I finally understood that I didn't lack pen and paper but my own memorizing mind. It had been given away with a hundred poems, called rote learning, old-fashioned, backward, an enemy of creative thinking, a great human gift, disowned.

Now there's a garden where the Women's House of Detention once stood. A green place, safely fenced in, with protected daffodils and tulips; roses bloom in it too, sometimes into November.

The big women's warehouse and its barred blind windows have been removed from Greenwich Village's affluent throat. I was sorry when it happened; the bricks came roaring down, great trucks carried them away.

I have always agreed with Rita and Evelyn that if there are prisons, they ought to be in the neighborhood, near a subway—not way out in distant suburbs, where families have to take cars, buses, ferries, trains, and the population that considers itself innocent forgets, denies, chooses to never know that there is a whole huge country of the bad and the unlucky and the self-hurters, a country with a population greater than that of many nations in our world.

—1994

Learning from Other Writers

1. Paley doesn't start her essay with the sort of historical or philosophical overview that Orwell and White choose for their opening paragraphs. What does she do instead? If she's going to start with a scene rather than with exposition, why not a description of the protest that got her arrested?

2. Paley casts doubt on her ability to remember the details of her experience. Does this make you more or less inclined to believe her story?
3. List all the arguments, subtle or explicit, that Paley presents in favor of keeping jails in city neighborhoods.
4. How and why does Paley use dialogue? Why doesn't she put the dialogue in quotation marks?
5. Do you think Paley needs to specify the race of the inmate who accosts her in the fourth paragraph? What is the effect of including the scene in which the author talks to Helen, "the only other white woman on the cell block," who is "not only white but Jewish"?
6. List the lines that strike you as funny. Can you figure out what makes these lines funny? List all the phrases that grab your attention or please your ear. Can you figure out what Paley does to make each such phrase seem noteworthy or poetic?

INSPIRATIONS: WHY DID I DO THAT?

1. Think of the most interesting, upsetting, funny, or odd event that ever happened to you. Or think of the time that (like Orwell) you were important enough to be hated (or loved, admired, feared, or just plain noticed) by more than the usual number of people.
2. What ***don't*** you understand about the experience you've chosen? What genuinely puzzles you about the event? Is there a question that you've never had the time, inclination, or courage to ask about this period in your life? In one sentence (and no more than one sentence!), write the question on an index card or a Post-it.
3. Using exposition and scenic writing, re-create your experience for your readers while trying to answer the question you've posed.

ADDITIONAL CONSIDERATIONS: HOW PERSONAL IS TOO PERSONAL?

Most of us are comfortable with the "narrative" part of a personal narrative. What could be more natural than coming home after a long day at work or school and telling a friend or relative what happened? And some of us have little if any problem with the "personal" part of a personal narrative. We love to write about ourselves; the more personal, the better.

But some writers squirm at the idea of any sort of personal revelation; they dislike even those first few moments of a new class in which the teacher asks students to introduce themselves and say a few words about where they're from and what they're studying. Anything but that! To those writers I say: Relax. In writing a personal narrative, the term *personal* implies only that you write from your own perspective, in your own voice, about something that happened to you or someone you know, not necessarily that you write about an event you found to be traumatic or embarrassing.

In "On the Necessity of Turning Oneself into a Character," Phillip Lopate notes that most young essayists are "torn between two contrasting extremes," the first being the idea that "I am so weird that I could never tell on the page what is really, secretly going on in my mind" and the second that "I am so boring, nothing ever happens to me out of the ordinary, so who would want to read about me?" Lopate speculates that both extremes "are rooted in shame, and both reflect a lack of worldliness," the first exaggerating "how isolated one is in one's 'wicked' thoughts, instead of recognizing that everyone has strange, surreal, immoral notions," and the second requiring a "reeducation" so the essayist can acknowledge "the charm of the ordinary" in his or her loves and friendships, brushes with history, and interactions with the natural world and thereby "recognize that life remains a mystery—even one's own so-called boring life."

Which isn't to say that you won't be troubled by the repercussions of telling the truth about your life ... and the lives of others. Although a personal narrative needn't be confessional, the very difficulty or scariness of writing about certain events or topics is often a sign that the topic or event demands to be written about. Unless you intend to whip off a shallow, slick piece, deciding what to say about yourself and others is as much a part of writing a good essay as developing a natural, clear, original voice, selecting an interesting topic and central question, and finding a useful, effective form. Will your grandmother's feelings be hurt if you write about the time your grandfather stole a neighbor's cow and got shot by the animal's irate owner? If you describe the roaches in the basement of the steakhouse where you worked, will you risk putting the owner out of business? If your narrative casts certain members of your community in an unfavorable light, might members of that community be angry?

As is the case when you decide what—if any—liberties you are willing to take with the truth before you have violated your contract with your readers, you will need to formulate your own guidelines as to what facts you are willing to include, leave out, or change to protect your subjects. When Annie Dillard wrote her best-selling memoir *An American Childhood* (Harper & Row, 1987), she decided to omit anything that might disturb her family. As she tells us in "To Fashion a Text" (which can be found in *Inventing the Truth: The Art and Craft of Memoir*, Houghton Mifflin, 1987), everyone she was writing about was "alive and well, in full possession of his faculties, and possibly willing to sue." Things were simpler when she wrote about nature rather than about herself, Dillard says. Muskrats can't hire lawyers.

Although leaving out anything that might trouble anyone in your family might seem extreme, Dillard's advice serves as an antidote to the equally extreme impulse to use autobiographical writing to get even with anyone who ever hurt us. "Writing in the first person can trap the writer into airing grievances," Dillard warns. Literature is an art, but "it's not a martial art," and the pages of a story or an essay "are no place to defend yourself from an attack, real or imagined, and no place from which to launch an attack, particularly against the very people who painstakingly reared you to your present omniscience." Taking on powerful public figures might be fair sport, Dillard writes, but it isn't fair to kick around people who can't defend themselves or fight back because they "don't have access to a printing press."

Surprisingly, most people don't mind seeing their names in print. Parents tend to be proud of their children getting published, even at the risk that their own unattractive habits might be revealed to the reading public. We live in a culture in which celebrity of any kind is better than anonymity: think of all the revealing or humiliating stunts that people are willing—if not eager—to perform on TV. If you simply present a scene and don't editorialize about what the characters are doing, if you don't disparage them with a mocking tone or treat them in a condescending way, the participants are likely to see themselves in a much more favorable light than your readers will see them. Most readers of Joseph Mitchell's profile of Philippa Duke Schuyler ("Evening with a Gifted Child" in Chapter 9) are taken aback by Mrs. Schuyler's insistence that her daughter eat only raw food. But Mrs. Schuyler probably wouldn't object to being portrayed in such a way. After all, she considers this regimen to be beneficial. Rather than criticize the Schuylers for the way they raise Philippa, the author uses scenic writing and objective exposition to present the Schuylers as they are and leaves the judgments to us.

Of course, seeing yourself portrayed in print is like seeing a photo of yourself or hearing your voice on an answering machine: Few of us like the way we appear or sound. I once wrote a highly complimentary profile of a police officer who had devoted her life to rescuing juvenile delinquents. I practically nominated her for sainthood. But after the profile appeared, she called and chewed me out. Why? In one scene, I described her leaping a fence to chase a juvie who ought to have been in school. Leaping this fence was a feat that could impress the reader only if I mentioned that the officer was barely five feet tall and anything but svelte. Apparently, the other officers at the station were riding her because I'd called her "stocky." The moral? It's difficult to predict who will take offense at what. Even when your subjects protest that you've misquoted or offended them, they might only be defending themselves from ribbing by the people with whom they work (my guess is that the subject of my profile needed to pretend to be offended at the single pejorative word in my story to distract her fellow officers from feeling jealous at all that praise).

Some writers—Dillard among them—protect themselves from the hostility of their subjects by letting them preview any passages or quotes that pertain to them. Although newspapers reporters generally are prohibited from showing a story to a subject before it appears in print, the rules for freelancers and memoirists tend to be more fluid. At the very least, showing your subjects the most important passages or quotes that concern them will allow you to correct any mistakes you've made before your essay or book sees print. (If you write for a commercial publication, the fact checkers are going to contact your subjects and do this anyway.) Asking your subjects to present their side of a story, even if it conflicts with *your* side of that story, usually results in a more complex view of that event. At worst, your subjects might ask you to change or omit a passage you don't want to omit or change. But nothing says you must do what your subjects ask—or even demand—you do.

Strictly speaking, you can use anything that has ever happened to you as your material. If someone knows that you're a writer, you are allowed to publish whatever you see and hear in that person's presence, even if he or she tells you later that what you saw or heard was off the record. (Technically, a subject must tell you *before* he says or does something that what *follows* will be off the record, but more on this question in Chapter 9.) You can be sued for libel only if you know that what you're writing isn't true and go ahead and write it anyway, with intent to harm your subject.

Other strategies for protecting people who might be hurt by what you write include changing their names and identifying characteristics or (in very rare cases) combining several subjects into one composite figure, *provided you inform your readers that you're doing this*. Again, it might help if you think of your contract with your reader. No one is going to complain if you call your first-grade teacher Mrs. Green when her name was Mrs. Jones. Nor will your readers feel betrayed if you tell them that for obvious reasons you've changed the names of the friends with whom you used to break into houses, or for reasons of economy—or self-protection—you've combined all your former drug suppliers into one composite kingpin. But if I tell you that my first-grade teacher's name was Mrs. Prettyman, and if I use that name as a metaphor for the confusion I felt as to what made a man a man or a woman a woman or what made a person pretty or desirable, and if you later find out that my first-grade teacher's name was Mrs. Smith, you probably will feel betrayed. (The truth? Mrs. Smith was my teacher in *fifth* grade, and yes, Mrs. Prettyman was my teacher in first.)

In the end, most of us simply ask if the benefits of what we write—not in terms of the money or fame that might accrue to us but the benefits to our readers—are likely to outweigh the physical, emotional, or financial damages that our essay or book might cause. Writing about your sister's rape might bring shame to your family, but bringing such rapes to the attention of a wider public might help to change the laws and attitudes that currently prevent the arrest and prosecution of white people who commit such crimes against Indians on reservations.

You don't want to ruin someone's life without giving your obligations a second thought. But neither do you want to water down the truth. Charles Baxter, whose fearless essay "Dysfunctional Narratives: or: 'Mistakes Were Made'" appears in Chapter 16, once told me that no one was going to pay twenty-five dollars for the book I was writing if I was afraid to take risks. If you're loathe to say that a person is overweight or bald or clumsy or that she can't reach for a high note without veering off pitch, you might be better off writing press releases or advertising copy than creative nonfiction. You could confine yourself to writing about muskrats instead of people. But you would be surprised at how controversial a muskrat can be among readers who devote their lives to studying, saving, or hunting such creatures.

Journeys, Pilgrimages, and Quests

One of the joys of creative nonfiction is leaving your house and discovering something you never could have invented. Your journey might lead you to the North Pole by dogsled or to the rain forest by canoe, but even if you are constrained by a paltry budget, limited free time, and a modest means of transportation, you can plan and carry out an essay-worthy trip. A bicycle ride through the farmland beyond your campus, a pilgrimage to the grave of the first female graduate of your college, or a quest to the town dump for the perfect sofa might provide you with more than enough material to create an impressive example of this form. If you look back at "Tracks and Ties" in the previous chapter, you will see that three teenage boys with no more than a dollar among them and an afternoon to kill were able to undertake an adventure as risky and memorable as a trek up Mt. Kilimanjaro.

WHY YOU ARE LEAVING HOME

Although an account of a journey is in some sense a narrative, an essay of the former type moves through space as well as time and is directed toward a physical goal or destination that doesn't necessarily shape a more stationary narrative. You might travel with the intention of reporting on whatever noteworthy sights or sites you encounter along the way, or make a pilgrimage to pay homage to a person or a place, or set out on a quest to find something of value that only can be attained in a certain place or from a specific person.

Yet a destination is not enough. Without a reason to undertake such a trek, the pilgrim might feel compelled to take notes about every single thing that happens along the way, then dump all these observations in his essay. In "Walden," E. B. White takes us on a pilgrimage to Henry David Thoreau's cabin at Walden Pond with the purpose of ascertaining whether or not Thoreau's account of the year he spent living simply on its shores might still be relevant to White's contemporaries (the essay was published in 1939) and—by extension—to us. Right at the outset, the author sees a sight that rubs up against his central question and strikes a spark. As White glimpses a woman cutting her grass with a "motorized lawn mower," he can't help but think that she is having such a hard time handling the machine that it appears as if "the lawn [is] mowing the lady." All along the way, other such sparks are struck, as when the author reads a sign warning of the "cotton surface" of the road ahead without having the faintest idea what a cotton surface is, or when he catches himself undertaking the elaborate ritual of locking all four doors of his car to protect a lap robe he never uses.

For most of his journey, White finds support for his hypothesis that Thoreau's isolation at Walden Pond can serve as a model for how we live today. But when he reaches the pond and finds it crowded with townies cooling off on a scorching summer afternoon, the model seems less relevant. Rather than disparage the bathers for ruining this pristine site, White meditates on the swimmers' camaraderie and the more democratic use to which they put the beach:

> ... bodies plunged vigorously into the water and emerged wet and beautiful in the bright air. As I left, a boatload of town boys were splashing about in mid-pond, kidding and fooling, the young fellows singing at the tops of their lungs in a wild chorus:
>
> *Amer-ica, Amer-ica, God shed his grace on thee,*
> *And crown thy good with brotherhood*
> *From sea to shi-ning sea!*

Nor can the author emulate his hero's disavowal of material goods. Although he admits that the money he has spent on shelter and food reveals "a meanness and grossness in my nature which you would find contemptible," he cannot so easily dismiss the baseball bat he has bought his son. After all, he reminds Thoreau, "You must remember that the house where you practiced the sort of economy which I respect was haunted only by mice and squirrels. You never had to cope with a shortstop."

Just as E. B. White set off on a pilgrimage to Walden Pond to pay homage to Thoreau and answer his central question concerning the continuing relevance or validity of his idol's writings in our own time, so Alice Walker traveled to Eatonville, Florida, in 1973 to see what she could learn about Zora Neale Hurston's life and death and the way that Hurston is—or is not—remembered in her own hometown. Although Walker is knowledgeable about Hurston's life and work and uses her journey to Eatonville as an excuse to talk about both, the discoveries that Walker makes about her literary aunt couldn't have been made in Walker's living room—or even in the Beinecke archives at Yale. A pilgrimage of the type undertaken by White or Walker not only provides the essayist or biographer with an excuse to tell us what he or she already knows about the subject; the pilgrimage allows the writer to make discoveries about the relationship between the subject's character and surroundings, to stumble on material the writer wouldn't otherwise have known existed, and to interview informants other biographers might have overlooked. (See also Richard Holmes's entertaining and enlightening quartet of essays about Robert Lewis Stevenson, Mary Wollstonecraft, Percy Shelley, and Gerard de Nerval in *Footsteps: Adventures of a Romantic Biographer*, published by Vintage in 1996.)

Not that such a pilgrimage is the exclusive domain of biographers who are paying tribute to famous writers or searching for information about dead artists or celebrities. The form also lends itself to paying homage to one's own ancestors and beginnings. What better way to understand the effects of the Vietnam War on a generation of reluctant soldiers than by accompanying your father to the Memorial on the Mall in Washington, D.C., or the village in Vietnam where he was stationed in his teens? How else to comprehend what life on the farm was like for your grandparents before they lost their land to drought and debt in the 1930s than to visit your family's long-abandoned homestead in Oklahoma?

Years ago, in planning a book about a white artist and activist named Catherine Weldon, who lived with Sitting Bull and his family during the last years of his life, I was stymied by a paucity of information that prevented me from recording Weldon's life in simple chronological order. Instead, I structured each chapter as a quest to find an artifact of this forgotten woman's life—the apartment she rented in Brooklyn before she set out for the Dakotas; the remote cabin on the reservation where she and Sitting Bull and their families lived; the portraits Weldon painted of Sitting Bull the summer before he was killed; the stretch of the Missouri River where her steamboat ran aground and her adolescent son, Christie, died of lockjaw; the cemetery in Kansas City where she buried Christie's body; and, finally, the grave in which Weldon herself lies buried. Not only did this structure provide a way to do justice to a woman about whom so little was known, it also meshed with the thematic question that concerned me most: How can we unearth evidence of the lives of women and men who were lied about or ignored in their own time and forgotten or erased from history after they were dead?[1]

The Pulitzer-prize-winning author James Alan McPherson (who taught me a great deal of what I know about creative nonfiction and gave me the idea of writing my book about Catherine Weldon) uses a circuitous trip to Baltimore on his quest for the perfect crab cakes as the structural core of his brilliant book of essays, deliciously titled (what else?) *Crabcakes*.[2] In "Umbilicus," which appears in modified form as a chapter in *Crabcakes*, McPherson describes a trip he undertook to break free of his safe but reclusive habits in Iowa City, driving northeast on country roads in search of "the sources of the Mississippi," which he "had always wanted to see."

At first, the expedition brings him a sense of renewal. Driving "very slowly and very carefully from one rural town to the next," McPherson sees

> the light brown beauty of harvested fields, when soybeans and corn and wheat had given up their energy to entropy, to the enigma of renewal, for the risk of winter and the promise of spring. I saw that life, my own life, too, *all life*, lay under the promise of an agreement with something outside, and far, far beyond, the little roles we play on the surface of things. I am saying that the slow drive along the back roads reawakened my spirits. I began to reconsider the essential importance of risk to the enterprise of life.

Pleased with his renewed courage, McPherson drives north as far as he thinks necessary, then turns around and drives home, reaching the outskirts of Cedar Rapids, about thirty miles north of his home in Iowa City. Alas, his engine catches fire and he has to pull over, believing the burning engine to be "God's punishment" for his abandonment of the "simple rituals" that had become his life. As he begins the long walk toward Cedar Rapids, a truck pulls over, and the driver and his passenger ask if McPherson needs help.

The men are white, McPherson is black, and even though the two men in the pickup appear to mean well ("'We saw your car smoking back there, brother,' the man in the passenger seat said to me. 'Can we give you a ride?'"), and even though they don't speak in the accents of the author's youth in the Jim Crow South, the truck they drive and the gun rack across its rear window take McPherson's memories "back to the terror of that long road I had traveled to this place. There was the truck, the gun rack, the white faces, the road."

Despite his terror, McPherson struggles to move beyond the long, brutal history of blacks and whites in this country, particularly the history of rural white farmers and lone black men walking along the road. As the men hook McPherson's car to the back of their truck, he tries to see the rope between the vehicles as an umbilicus connecting the fate of whites and blacks in this country and giving birth to a new era of friendship and trust between them ... even as the reader sees the rope as a reminder of the more sinister uses that white men have found for ropes where black men are concerned (most recently, in Texas, tying a black man to the back of their pickup and dragging him down the road).

Although McPherson eventually calls a halt to the two men's efforts to help him get his car to a service station (an ending that disappoints most of my white students but causes many of my black students to exclaim, "He was crazy to trust them in the first place!"), his quest to

---

[1] As immodest as it seems to provide a footnote for one's own work, the book is *Woman Walking Ahead: In Search of Catherine Weldon and Sitting Bull*, published in 2002 by University of New Mexico Press.

[2] Simon & Schuster, 1998.

find the wellsprings of courage and trust, despite his fearful history as a black man in America, has provided us with an image of what it would mean for the lynching rope to become an umbilicus joining blacks and whites.

Another type of quest involves the search for answers to nagging questions.

In Sue Hubbell's "The Vicksburg Ghost," the author describes her journey to a small Michigan town to tease out the motives behind the first reported sighting of Elvis Presley after he was dead, an event that allegedly occurred in September 1987 when a housewife named Louise Welling saw Elvis at Felpausch's Supermarket buying "something little—fuses, I think, not groceries." Each person Hubbell encounters sparks a new variation on this question. Are those who say they've sighted Elvis crazy? Are they playing a trick on the rest of us—or having a trick played on *them*? Are they trying to relieve the boredom of life in the middle of nowhere? Hoping to sell newspapers or attract tourists to their town? Or are they simply victims of unrequited love and faulty logic? And if this last hypothesis is the case, why does this particular entertainer continue to exert such a hold on so many of us so long after he died (if he *did* die, that is)?

In his thought-provoking article "Trucking through the AIDS Belt," which appeared in the August 16, 1993, issue of *The New Yorker* and was reprinted in the 1994 edition of *Best American Essays* (I omit it from this chapter only because of length), Ted Conover reverses the black-and-white imagery of McPherson's essay and hitches a ride with a convoy of long-distance truckers driving through eastern Africa in his attempt to understand why such men continue to have unprotected sex with prostitutes despite the dangers of contracting HIV. Given the high rate of infection among long-distance truckers in Africa—fifty-one percent—and their role in spreading AIDS, Conover's question is vitally important to millions of people and raises a host of related questions about the best ways to educate Africans on how to prevent the spread of the disease, not to mention a disturbing subtext directed at the essay's Western audience, namely: Are Africans so unlike Americans and Europeans that they would disregard their safety in ways that few of us would ever do? Ordinarily, a middle-class reporter's responses to the discomforts and frustrations of such a journey would be irrelevant in light of the horrifying dimensions of the epidemic facing Africa, yet Conover weaves his own perspective in and around the experiences of the truckers, subtly conveying his discovery that given the same circumstances, even a highly educated and scientifically minded Westerner might behave in life-endangering ways.

THE SHAPE OF YOUR JOURNEY

As you read the essays in this section, you will find that some of the authors (White and Walker) don't tell us anything about their preparations for their trips, while others (McPherson and Hubbell) offer brief explanations of their motives before they set out. As tempting as it is to regale your readers with your dawning realization that you must cross Death Valley on foot, your frustrating acquisition of the necessary supplies, and your heroic struggle to stuff these supplies in the trunk of your SUV, you probably are better off beginning your essay with that first footstep you took into the burning sands with your full-to-bursting backpack weighing heavily on your shoulders; after that, you can pause to reveal what we need to know about your motives or preparations when you sit down to take a break in the shade of a skinny cactus, nibble your high-energy beef jerky, and sip a carefully measured ounce of water from your super-light reservoir and filtration system.

E.B. WHITE

WALDEN

Miss Nims, take a letter to Henry David Thoreau. Dear Henry: I thought of you the other afternoon as I was approaching Concord doing fifty on Route 62. That is a high speed at which to hold a philosopher in one's mind, but in this century we are a nimble bunch.

On one of the lawns in the outskirts of the village a woman was cutting the grass with a motorized lawn mower. What made me think of you was that the machine had rather got away from her, although she was game enough, and in the brief glimpse I had of the scene it appeared to me that the lawn was mowing the lady. She kept a tight grip on the handles, which throbbed violently with every explosion of the one-cylinder motor, and as she sheered around bushes and lurched along at a reluctant trot behind her impetuous servant, she looked like a puppy who had grabbed something that was too much for him. Concord hasn't changed much, Henry; the farm implements and the animals still have the upper hand.

I may as well admit that I was journeying to Concord with the deliberate intention of visiting your woods; for although I have never knelt at the grave of a philosopher nor placed wreaths on moldy poets, and have often gone a mile out of my way to avoid some place of historical interest, I have always wanted to see Walden Pond. The account which you left of your sojourn there is, you will be amused to learn, a document of increasing pertinence; each year it seems to gain a little headway, as the world loses ground. We may all be transcendental yet, whether we like it or not. As our common complexities increase, any tale of individual simplicity (and yours is the best written and the cockiest) acquires a new fascination; as our goods accumulate, but not our well-being, your report of an existence without material adornment takes on a certain awkward credibility.

My purpose in going to Walden Pond, like yours, was not to live cheaply or to live dearly there, but to transact some private business with the fewest obstacles. Approaching Concord, doing forty, doing forty-five, doing fifty, the steering wheel held snug in my palms, the highway held grimly in my vision, the crown of the road now serving me (on the righthand curves), now defeating me (on the lefthand curves), I began to rouse myself from the stupefaction which a day's motor journey induces. It was a delicious evening, Henry, when the whole body is one sense, and imbibes delight through every pore, if I may coin a phrase. Fields were richly brown where the harrow, drawn by the stripped Ford, had lately sunk its teeth; pastures were green; and overhead the sky had that same everlasting great look which you will find on Page 144 of the Oxford pocket edition. I could feel the road entering me, through tire, wheel, spring, and cushion; shall I not have intelligence with earth too? Am I not partly leaves and vegetable mold myself?—a man of infinite horsepower, yet partly leaves.

Stay with me on 62 and it will take you into Concord. As I say, it was a delicious evening. The snake had come forth to die in a bloody S on the highway, the wheel upon its head, its bowels flat now and exposed. The turtle had come up too to cross the road and die in the attempt, its hard shell smashed under the rubber blow, its intestinal yearning (for the other side of the road) forever squashed. There was a sign by the wayside which announced that the road had a "cotton surface." You wouldn't know what that is, but neither, for that matter, did I. There is a cryptic ingredient in many of our modern improvements—we are awed and pleased without knowing quite what we are enjoying. It is something to be traveling on a road with a cotton surface.

The civilization round Concord today is an odd distillation of city, village, farm, and manor. The houses, yards, fields look not quite suburban, not quite rural. Under the bronze beech and the blue spruce of the departed baron grazes the milch goat of the heirs. Under the porte-cochère stands the reconditioned station wagon; under the grape arbor sit the puppies for sale. (But why do men degenerate ever? What makes families run out?)

It was June and everywhere June was publishing her immemorial stanza; in the lilacs, in the syringa, in the freshly edged paths and the sweetness of moist beloved gardens, and the little wire wickets that preserve the tulips' front. Farmers were already moving the fruits of their toil into their yards, arranging the rhubarb, the asparagus, the strictly fresh eggs on the painted stands under the little shed roofs with the patent shingles. And though it was almost a hundred years since you had taken your ax and started cutting out your home on Walden Pond, I was interested to observe that the philosophical spirit was still alive in Massachusetts: in the center of a vacant lot some boys were assembling the framework of the rude shelter, their whole mind and skill concentrated in the rather inauspicious helter-skeleton of studs and rafters. They too were escaping from town, to live naturally, in a rich blend of savagery and philosophy.

That evening, after supper at the inn, I strolled out into the twilight to dream my shapeless transcendental dreams and see that the car was locked up for the night (first open the right front door, then reach over, straining, and pull up the handles of the left rear and the left front till you hear the click, then the handle of the right rear, then shut the right front but open it again remembering that the key is still in the ignition switch, remove the key, shut the right front again with a bang, push the tiny keyhole cover to one side, insert key, turn, and withdraw). It is what we all do, Henry. It is called locking the car. It is said to confuse thieves and keep them from making off with the laprobe. Four doors to lock behind one robe. The driver himself never uses a laprobe, the free movement of his legs being vital to the operation of the vehicle; so that when he locks the car it is a pure and unselfish act. I have in my life gained very little essential heat from laprobes, yet I have ever been at pains to lock them up.

The evening was full of sounds, some of which would have stirred your memory. The robins still love the elms of New England villages at sundown. There is enough of the thrush in them to make song inevitable at the end of the day, and enough of the tramp to make them hang round the dwellings of men. A robin, like many another American, dearly loves a white house with green blinds. Concord is still full of them.

Your fellow-townsmen were stirring abroad—not many afoot, most of them in their cars; and the sound which they made in Concord at evening was a rustling and a whispering. The sound lacks steadfastness and is wholly unlike that of a train. A train, as you know who lived so near the Fitchburg line, whistles once or twice sadly and is gone, trailing a memory in smoke, soothing to ear and mind. Automobiles, skirting a village green, are like flies that have gained the inner ear—they buzz, cease, pause, start, shift, stop, halt, brake, and the whole effect is a nervous polytone curiously disturbing.

As I wandered along, the toc toc of ping pong balls drifted from an attic window. In front of the Reuben Brown house a Buick was drawn up. At the wheel, motionless, his hat upon his head, a man sat, listening to Amos and Andy on the radio (it is a drama of many scenes and without an end). The deep voice of Andrew Brown, emerging from the car, although it originated more than two hundred miles away, was unstrained by distance. When you used to sit on the shore of your pond on Sunday morning, listening to the church bells of Acton and Concord, you were aware of the excellent filter of the intervening atmosphere. Science has attended to that, and sound now maintains its intensity without regard for distance. Properly sponsored, it goes on forever.

A fire engine, out for a trial spin, roared past Emerson's house, hot with readiness for public duty. Over the barn roofs the martins dipped and chittered. A swarthy daughter of an asparagus grower, in culottes, shirt, and bandanna, pedalled past on her bicycle. It was indeed a delicious evening, and I returned to the inn (I believe it was your house once) to rock with the old ladies on the concrete veranda.

Next morning early I started afoot for Walden, out Main Street and down Thoreau, past the depot and the Minuteman Chevrolet Company. The morning was fresh, and in a bean field along the way I flushed an agriculturalist, quietly studying his beans. Thoreau Street soon joined Number 126, an artery of the State. We number our highways nowadays, our speed being so great we can remember little of their quality or character and are lucky to remember their number. (Men have an indistinct notion that if they keep up this activity long enough all will at length ride somewhere, in next to no time.) Your pond is on 126.

I knew I must be nearing your woodland retreat when the Golden Pheasant lunchroom came into view—Sealtest ice cream, toasted sandwiches, hot frankfurters, waffles, tonics, and lunches. Were I the proprietor, I should add rice, Indian meal, and molasses—just for old time's sake. The Pheasant, incidentally, is for sale: a chance for some nature lover who wishes to set himself up beside a pond in the Concord atmosphere and live deliberately, fronting only the essential facts of life on Number 126. Beyond the Pheasant was a place called Walden Breezes, an oasis whose porch pillars were made of old green shutters sawed into lengths. On the porch was a distorting mirror, to give the traveler a comical image of himself, who had miraculously learned to gaze in an ordinary glass without smiling. Behind the Breezes, in a sun-parched clearing, dwelt your philosophical descendants in their trailers, each trailer the size of your hut, but all grouped together for the sake of congeniality. Trailer people leave the city, as you did, to discover solitude and in any weather, at any hour of the day or night, to improve the nick of time; but they soon collect in villages and get bogged deeper in the mud than ever. The camp behind Walden Breezes was just rousing itself to the morning. The ground was packed hard under the heel, and the sun came through the clearing to bake the soil and enlarge the wry smell of cramped housekeeping. Cushman's bakery truck had stopped to deliver an early basket of rolls. A camp dog, seeing me in the road, barked petulantly. A man emerged from one of the trailers and set forth with a bucket to draw water from some forest tap.

Leaving the highway I turned off into the woods toward the pond, which was apparent through the foliage. The floor of the forest was strewn with dried old oak leaves and *Transcripts*. From beneath the flattened popcorn wrapper *(granum explosum)* peeped the frail violet. I followed a footpath and descended to the water's edge. The pond lay clear and blue in the morning light, as you have seen it so many times. In the shallows a man's waterlogged shirt undulated gently. A few flies came out to greet me and convoy me to your cove, past the No Bathing signs on which the fellows and the girls had scrawled their names. I felt strangely excited suddenly to be snooping around your premises, tiptoeing along watchfully, as though not to tread by mistake upon the intervening century. Before I got to the cove I heard something which seemed to me quite wonderful: I heard your frog, a full, clear *troonk,* guiding me, still hoarse and solemn, bridging the years as the robins had bridged them in the sweetness of the village evening. But he soon quit, and I came on a couple of young boys throwing stones at him.

Your front yard is marked by a bronze tablet set in a stone. Four small granite posts, a few feet away, show where the house was. On top of the tablet was a pair of faded blue bathing trunks with a white stripe. Back of it is a pile of stones, a sort of cairn, left by your visitors as a tribute I suppose. It is a rather ugly little heap of stones, Henry. In fact the hillside itself seems faded, browbeaten; a few tall skinny pines, bare of lower limbs, a smattering of young maples in suitable green, some birches and oaks, and a number of trees felled by the last big wind. It was from the bole of one of these fallen pines, torn up by the roots, that I extracted the stone which I added to the cairn—a sentimental act in which I was interrupted by a small terrier from a nearby picnic group, who confronted me and wanted to know about the stone.

I sat down for a while on one of the posts of your house to listen to the bluebottles and the dragonflies. The invaded glade sprawled shabby and mean at my feet, but the flies were tuned to the old vibration. There were the remains of a fire in your ruins, but I doubt that it was yours; also two beer bottles trodden into the soil and become part of earth. A young oak had taken root in your house, and two or three ferns, unrolling like the ticklers at a banquet. The only other furnishings were a DuBarry pattern sheet, a page torn from a picture magazine, and some crusts in wax paper.

Before I quit I walked clear round the pond and found the place where you used to sit on the northeast side to get the sun in the fall, and the beach where you got sand for scrubbing your floor. On the eastern side of the pond, where the highway borders it, the State has built dressing rooms for swimmers, a float with diving towers, drinking fountains of porcelain, and rowboats for hire. The pond is in fact a State Preserve, and carries a twenty-dollar fine for picking wild flowers, a decree signed in all solemnity by your fellow-citizens Walter C. Wardwell, Erson B. Barlow, and Nathaniel I. Bowditch. There was a smell of creosote where they had been building a wide wooden stairway to the road and the parking area. Swimmers and boaters were arriving; bodies plunged vigorously into the water and emerged wet and beautiful in the bright air. As I left, a boatload of town boys were splashing about in mid-pond, kidding and fooling, the young fellows singing at the tops of their lungs in a wild chorus:

Amer-ica, Amer-ica, God shed his grace on thee,
And crown thy good with brotherhood
From sea to shi-ning sea!

I walked back to town along the railroad, following your custom. The rails were expanding noisily in the hot sun, and on the slope of the roadbed the wild grape and the blackberry sent up their creepers to the track.

The expense of my brief sojourn in Concord was:

Canvas shoes	$1.95	
Baseball bat	.25	} gifts to take back to a boy
Left-handed fielder's glove	1.25	}
Hotel and meals	4.25	
In all	$7.70	

As you see, this amount was almost what you spent for food for eight months. I cannot defend the shoes or the expenditure for shelter and food: they reveal a meanness and grossness in my nature which you would find contemptible. The baseball equipment, however, is the kind of impediment with which you were never on even terms. You must remember that the house where you practiced the sort of economy which I respect was haunted only by mice and squirrels. You never had to cope with a shortstop.

—1939

Learning from Other Writers

1. Does Miss Nims exist? What does the author gain or lose by pretending that Thoreau is the audience for his "letter"?
2. Highlight the passages in which White meditates on his central question. In each case, can you identify what specific aspect of his journey inspired this particular meditation?

3. What effect does White create with his many allusions to Thoreau's original text (see, for example, paragraph four of White's essay)?
4. What is the relevance of the passage on Walden Breezes? Trailer parks tend to be objects of ridicule in American culture. What is White's tone in describing Walden Breezes?
5. What effect is produced by the details White uses to describe the site of Thoreau's cabin at Walden Pond?
6. One common source of humor in written prose is the contrast between high and low culture or high and low diction. Can you find examples of this stylistic technique in White's essay?

ALICE WALKER

LOOKING FOR ZORA

> On January 16, 1959, Zora Neale Hurston, suffering from the effects of a stroke and writing painfully in longhand, composed a letter to the "editorial department" of Harper & Brothers inquiring if they would be interested in seeing "the book I am laboring upon at present—a life of Herod the Great." One year and twelve days later, Zora Neale Hurston died without funds to provide for her burial, a resident of the St. Lucie County, Florida, Welfare Home. She lies today in an unmarked grave in a segregated cemetery in Fort Pierce, Florida, a resting place generally symbolic of the black writer's fate in America.
>
> Zora Neale Hurston is one of the most significant unread authors in America, the author of two minor classics and four other major books.
>
> —Robert Hemenway, "Zora Hurston and the Eatonville Anthropology," in *The Harlem Renaissance Remembered*

On August 15, 1973, I wake up just as the plane is lowering over Sanford, Florida, which means I am also looking down on Eatonville, Zora Neale Hurston's birthplace. I recognize it from Zora's description in *Mules and Men:* "the city of five lakes, three croquet courts, three hundred brown skins, three hundred good swimmers, plenty guavas, two schools, and no jailhouse." Of course I cannot see the guavas, but the five lakes are still there, and it is the lakes I count as the plane prepares to land in Orlando.

From the air, Florida looks completely flat, and as we near the ground this impression does not change. This is the first time I have seen the interior of the state, which Zora wrote about so well, but there are the acres of orange groves, the sand, mangrove trees, and scrub pine that I know from her books. Getting off the plane I walk through the humid air of midday into the tacky but air-conditioned airport. I search for Charlotte Hunt, my companion on the Zora Hurston expedition. She lives in Winter Park, Florida, very near Eatonville, and is writing her graduate dissertation on Zora. I see her waving—a large, pleasant-faced white woman in dark glasses. We have written to each other for several weeks, swapping our latest finds (mostly hers) on Zora, and trying to make sense out of the mass of information obtained (often erroneous or simply confusing) from Zora herself—through her stories and autobiography—and from people who wrote about her.

Eatonville has lived for such a long time in my imagination that I can hardly believe it will be found existing in its own right. But after twenty minutes on the expressway, Charlotte turns off and I see a small settlement of houses and stores set with no particular pattern in the sandy soil off the road. We stop in front of a neat gray building that has two fascinating signs: EATONVILLE POST OFFICE and EATONVILLE CITY HALL.

Inside the Eatonville City Hall half of the building, a slender, dark-brown-skin woman sits looking through letters on a desk. When she hears we are searching for anyone who might have known Zora Neale Hurston, she leans back in thought. Because I don't wish to inspire foot-dragging in people who might know something about Zora they're not sure they should tell, I have decided on a simple, but I feel profoundly *useful,* lie.

"I am Miss Hurston's niece," I prompt the young woman, who brings her head down with a smile.

"I think Mrs. Moseley is about the only one still living who might remember her," she says.

"Do you mean *Mathilda* Moseley, the woman who tells those 'woman-is-smarter-than-man' lies in Zora's book?"

"Yes," says the young woman. "Mrs. Moseley is real old now, of course. But this time of day, she should be at home."

I stand at the counter looking down on her, the first Eatonville resident I have spoken to. Because of Zora's books, I feel I know something about her; at least I know what the town she grew up in was like years before she was born.

"Tell me something," I say. "Do the schools teach Zora's books here?"

"No," she says, "they don't. I don't think most people know anything about Zora Neale Hurston, or know about any of the great things she did. She was a fine lady. I've read all of her books myself, but I don't think many other folks in Eatonville have."

"Many of the church people around here, as I understand it," says Charlotte in a murmured aside, "thought Zora was pretty loose. I don't think they appreciated her writing about them."

"Well," I say to the young woman, "thank you for your help." She clarifies her directions to Mrs. Moseley's house and smiles as Charlotte and I turn to go.

> The letter to Harper's does not expose a publisher's rejection of an unknown masterpiece, but it does reveal how the bright promise of the Harlem Renaissance deteriorated for many of the writers who shared in its exuberance. It also indicates the personal tragedy of Zora Neale Hurston: Barnard graduate, author of four novels, two books of folklore, one volume of autobiography, the most important collector of Afro-American folklore in America, reduced by poverty and circumstance to seek a publisher by unsolicited mail.
>
> —Robert Hemenway

> Zora Hurston was born in 1901, 1902, or 1903—depending on how old she felt herself to be at the time someone asked.
>
> —Librarian, Beinecke Library, Yale University

The Moseley house is small and white and snug, its tiny yard nearly swallowed up by oleanders and hibiscus bushes. Charlotte and I knock on the door. I call out. But there is no answer. This strikes us as peculiar. We have had time to figure out an age for Mrs. Moseley—not dates or a number, just old. I am thinking of a quivery, bedridden invalid when we hear the car. We look behind us to see an old black and white Buick—paint peeling and grillwork rusty—pulling into the drive. A neat old lady in a purple dress and with white hair is straining at the wheel. She is frowning because Charlotte's car is in the way.

Mrs. Moseley looks at us suspiciously. "Yes, I knew Zora Neale," she says, unsmilingly and with a rather cold stare at Charlotte (who, I imagine, feels very *white* at that moment), "but that was a long time ago, and I don't want to talk about it."

"Yes, ma'am," I murmur, bringing all my sympathy to bear on the situation.

"Not only that," Mrs. Moseley continues. "I've been sick. Been in the hospital for an operation. Ruptured artery. The doctors didn't believe I was going to live, but you see me alive, don't you?"

"Looking well, too," I comment.

Mrs. Moseley is out of her car. A thin, sprightly woman with nice gold-studded false teeth, uppers and lowers. I like her because she stands there *straight* beside her car, with a hand on her hip and her straw pocketbook on her arm. She wears white T-strap shoes with heels that show off her well-shaped legs.

"I'm eighty-two years old, you know," she says. "And I just can't remember things the way I used to. Anyhow, Zora Neale left here to go to school and she never really came back to live. She'd come here for material for her books, but that was all. She spent most of her time down in South Florida."

"You know, Mrs. Moseley, I saw your name in one of Zora's books."

"You did?" She looks at me with only slightly more interest. "I read some of her books a long time ago, but then people got to borrowing and borrowing and they borrowed them all away."

"I could send you a copy of everything that's been reprinted," I offer. "Would you like me to do that?"

"No," says Mrs. Moseley promptly. "I don't read much any more. Besides, all of that was so long ago...."

Charlotte and I settle back against the car in the sun. Mrs. Moseley tells us at length and with exact recall every step in her recent operation, ending with: "What those doctors didn't know—when they were expecting me to die (and they didn't even think I'd live long enough for them to have to take out my stitches!)—is that Jesus is the best doctor, and if *He* says for you to get well, that's all that counts."

With this philosophy, Charlotte and I murmur quick assent: being Southerners and church bred, we have heard that belief before. But what we learn from Mrs. Moseley is that she does not remember much beyond the year 1938. She shows us a picture of her father and mother and says that her father was Joe Clarke's brother. Joe Clarke, as every Zora Hurston reader knows, was the first mayor of Eatonville; his fictional counterpart is Jody Starks of *Their Eyes Were Watching God.* We also get directions to where Joe Clarke's store *was*—where Club Eaton is now. Club Eaton, a long orange-beige nightspot we had seen on the main road, is apparently famous for the good times in it regularly had by all. It is, perhaps, the modern equivalent of the store porch, where all the men of Zora's childhood came to tell "lies," that is, black folk tales, that were "made and used on the spot," to take a line from Zora. As for Zora's exact birthplace, Mrs. Moseley has no idea.

After I have commented on the healthy growth of her hibiscus bushes, she becomes more talkative. She mentions how much she *loved* to dance, when she was a young woman, and talks about how good her husband was. When he was alive, she says, she was completely happy because he allowed her to be completely free. "I was so free I had to pinch myself sometimes to tell if I was a married woman."

Relaxed now, she tells us about going to school with Zora. "Zora and I went to the same school. It's called Hungerford High now. It *was* only to the eighth grade. But our teachers were so good that by the time you left you knew college subjects. When I went to Morris Brown in Atlanta, the teachers there were just teaching me the same things I had already learned right in Eatonville. I wrote Mama and told her I was going to come home and help her with her babies. I wasn't learning anything new."

"Tell me something, Mrs. Moseley," I ask. "Why do you suppose Zora was against integration? I read somewhere that she was against school desegregation because she felt it was an insult to black teachers."

"Oh, one of them [white people] came around asking me about integration. One day I was doing my shopping. I heard 'em over there talking about it in the store, about the schools. And I got on out of the way because I knew if they asked me, they wouldn't like what I was going to tell 'em. But they came up and asked me anyhow. 'What do you think about this integration?' one of them said. I acted like I thought I had heard wrong. 'You're asking *me* what *I* think about integration?' I said. 'Well, as you can see, I'm just an old colored woman'—I was seventy-five or seventy-six then—'and this is the first time anybody ever asked me about integration. And nobody asked my grandmother what she thought, either, but her daddy was one of you all.'" Mrs. Moseley seems satisfied with this memory of her rejoinder. She looks at Charlotte. "I have the blood of three races in my veins," she says belligerently, "white, black, and Indian, and nobody asked me *anything* before."

"Do you think living in Eatonville made integration less appealing to you?"

"Well, I can tell you this: I have lived in Eatonville all my life, and I've been in the governing of this town. I've been everything but mayor and I've been *assistant* mayor. Eatonville was and is an all-black town. We have our own police department, post office, and town hall. Our own school and good teachers. Do I need integration?

"They took over Goldsboro, because the black people who lived there never incorporated, like we did. And now I don't even know if any black folks live there. They built big houses up there around the lakes. But we didn't let that happen in Eatonville, and we don't sell land to just anybody. And you see, we're still here."

When we leave, Mrs. Moseley is standing by her car, waving. I think of the letter Roy Wilkins wrote to a black newspaper blasting Zora Neale for her lack of enthusiasm about the integration of schools. I wonder if he knew the experience of Eatonville she was coming from. Not many black people in America have come from a self-contained, all-black community where loyalty and unity are taken for granted. A place where black pride is nothing new.

There is, however, one thing Mrs. Moseley said that bothered me.

"Tell me, Mrs. Moseley," I had asked, "why is it that thirteen years after Zora's death, no marker has been put on her grave?"

And Mrs. Moseley answered: "The reason she doesn't have a stone is because she wasn't buried here. She was buried down in South Florida somewhere. I don't think anybody really knew where she was."

> Only to reach a wider audience, need she ever write books—because she is a perfect book of entertainment in herself. In her youth she was always getting scholarships and things from wealthy white people, some of whom simply paid her just to sit around and represent the Negro race for them, she did it in such a racy fashion. She was full of sidesplitting anecdotes, humorous tales, and tragicomic stories, remembered out of her life in the South as a daughter of a traveling minister of God. She could make you laugh one minute and cry the next. To many of her white friends, no doubt, she was a perfect "darkie," in the nice meaning they give the term—that is, a naïve, childlike, sweet, humorous, and highly colored Negro.
>
> But Miss Hurston was clever, too—a student who didn't let college give her a broad "a" and who had great scorn for all pretensions, academic or otherwise. That is why she was such a fine folklore collector, able to go among the people and never act as if she had been to school at all. Almost nobody else could stop the average Harlemite on Lenox Avenue and measure his head with a strange-looking, anthropological device and not get bawled out for the attempt, except Zora, who used to stop anyone whose head looked interesting, and measure it.
>
> —Langston Hughes, *The Big Sea*

> What does it matter what white folks must have thought about her?
>
> —Student, black women writers' class, Wellesley College

Mrs. Sarah Peek Patterson is a handsome, red-haired woman in her late forties, wearing orange slacks and gold earrings. She is the director of Lee-Peek Mortuary in Fort Pierce, the establishment that handled Zora's burial. Unlike most black funeral homes in Southern towns that sit like palaces among the general poverty, Lee-Peek has a run-down, *small* look. Perhaps this is because it is painted purple and white, as are its Cadillac chariots. These colors do not age well. The rooms are cluttered and grimy, and the bathroom is a tiny, stale-smelling prison, with a bottle of black hair dye (apparently used to touch up the hair of the corpses) dripping into the face bowl. Two pine burial boxes are resting in the bathtub.

Mrs. Patterson herself is pleasant and helpful.

"As I told you over the phone, Mrs. Patterson," I begin, shaking her hand and looking into her penny-brown eyes, "I am Zora Neale Hurston's niece, and I would like to have a marker put on her grave. You said, when I called you last week, that you could tell me where the grave is."

By this time I am, of course, completely into being Zora's niece, and the lie comes with perfect naturalness to my lips. Besides, as far as I'm concerned, she *is* my aunt—and that of all black people as well.

"She was buried in 1960," exclaims Mrs. Patterson. "That was when my father was running this funeral home. He's sick now or I'd let you talk to him. But I know where she's buried. She's in the old cemetery, the Garden of the Heavenly Rest, on Seventeenth Street. Just when you go in the gate there's a circle, and she's buried right in the middle of it. Hers is the only grave in that circle—because people don't bury in that cemetery any more."

She turns to a stocky, black-skinned woman in her thirties, wearing a green polo shirt and white jeans cut off at the knee. "This lady will show you where it is," she says.

"I can't tell you how much I appreciate this," I say to Mrs. Patterson, as I rise to go. "And could you tell me something else? You see, I never met my aunt. When she died, I was still a junior in high school. But could you tell me what she died of, and what kind of funeral she had?"

"I don't know exactly what she died of," Mrs. Patterson says. "I know she didn't have any money. Folks took up a collection to bury her.... I believe she died of malnutrition."

"*Malnutrition?*"

Outside, in the blistering sun, I lean my head against Charlotte's even more blistering car top. The sting of the hot metal only intensifies my anger. "*Malnutrition,*" I manage to mutter. "Hell, our condition hasn't changed *any* since Phillis Wheatley's time. *She* died of malnutrition!"

"Really?" says Charlotte. "I didn't know that."

> One cannot overemphasize the extent of her commitment. It was so great that her marriage in the spring of 1927 to Herbert Sheen was short-lived. Although divorce did not come officially until 1931, the two separated amicably after only a few months, Hurston to continue her collecting, Sheen to attend Medical School. Hurston never married again.
>
> —Robert Hemenway

"What is your name?" I ask the woman who has climbed into the back seat.

"Rosalee," she says. She has a rough, pleasant voice, as if she is a singer who also smokes a lot. She is homely, and has an air of ready indifference.

"Another woman came by here wanting to see the grave," she says, lighting up a cigarette. "She was a little short, dumpty white lady from one of these Florida schools.

Orlando or Daytona. But let me tell you something before we gets started. All I know is where the cemetery is. I don't know one thing about that grave. You better go back in and ask her to draw you a map."

A few moments later, with Mrs. Patterson's diagram of where the grave is, we head for the cemetery.

We drive past blocks of small, pastel-colored houses and turn right onto Seventeenth Street. At the very end, we reach a tall curving gate, with the words "Garden of the Heavenly Rest" fading into the stone. I expected, from Mrs. Patterson's small drawing, to find a small circle—which would have placed Zora's grave five or ten paces from the road. But the "circle" is over an acre large and looks more like an abandoned field. Tall weeds choke the dirt road and scrape against the sides of the car. It doesn't help either that I step out into an active ant hill.

"I don't know about y'all," I say, "but I don't even believe this." I am used to the haphazard cemetery-keeping that is traditional in most Southern black communities, but this neglect is staggering. As far as I can see there is nothing but bushes and weeds, some as tall as my waist. One grave is near the road, and Charlotte elects to investigate it. It is fairly clean, and belongs to someone who died in 1963.

Rosalee and I plunge into the weeds; I pull my long dress up to my hips. The weeds scratch my knees, and the insects have a feast. Looking back, I see Charlotte standing resolutely near the road.

"Aren't you coming?" I call.

"No," she calls back. "I'm from these parts and I know what's out there." She means snakes.

"Shit," I say, my whole life and the people I love flashing melodramatically before my eyes. Rosalee is a few yards to my right.

"How're you going to find anything out here?" she asks. And I stand still a few seconds, looking at the weeds. Some of them are quite pretty, with tiny yellow flowers. They are thick and healthy, but dead weeds under them have formed a thick gray carpet on the ground. A snake could be lying six inches from my big toe and I wouldn't see it. We move slowly, very slowly, our eyes alert, our legs trembly. It is hard to tell where the center of the circle is since the circle is not really round, but more like half of something round. There are things crackling and hissing in the grass. Sandspurs are sticking to the inside of my skirt. Sand and ants cover my feet. I look toward the road and notice that there are, indeed, *two* large curving stones, making an entrance and exit to the cemetery. I take my bearings from them and try to navigate to exact center. But the center of anything can be very large, and a grave is not a pinpoint. Finding the grave seems positively hopeless. There is only one thing to do:

"Zora!" I yell, as loud as I can (causing Rosalee to jump). "Are you out here?"

"If she is, I sho hope she don't answer you. If she do, I'm gone."

"Zora!" I call again. "I'm here. Are you?"

"If she is," grumbles Rosalee, "I hope she'll keep it to herself."

"Zora!" Then I start fussing with her. "I hope you don't think I'm going to stand out here all day, with these snakes watching me and these ants having a field day. In fact, I'm going to call you just one or two more times." On a clump of dried grass, near a small bushy tree, my eye falls on one of the largest bugs I have ever seen. It is on its back, and is as large as three of my fingers. I walk toward it, and yell "Zo-ra!" and my foot sinks into a hole. I look down. I am standing in a sunken rectangle that is about six feet long and about three or four feet wide. I look up to see where the two gates are.

"Well," I say, "this is the center, or approximately anyhow. It's also the only sunken spot we've found. Doesn't this look like a grave to you?"

"For the sake of not going no farther through these bushes," Rosalee growls, "yes, it do."

"Wait a minute," I say, "I have to look around some more to be sure this is the only spot that resembles a grave. But you don't have to come."

Rosalee smiles—a grin, really—beautiful and tough.

"Naw," she says, "I feels sorry for you. If one of these snakes got ahold of you out here by yourself I'd feel *real* bad." She laughs. "I done come this far, I'll go on with you."

"Thank you, Rosalee," I say. "Zora thanks you too."

"Just as long as she don't try to tell me in person," she says, and together we walk down the field.

> The gusto and flavor of Zora Neal[e] Hurston's storytelling, for example, long before the yarns were published in "Mules and Men" and other books, became a local legend which might... have spread further under different conditions. A tiny shift in the center of gravity could have made them best-sellers.
>
> —Arna Bontemps, *Personals*

> Bitter over the rejection of her folklore's value, especially in the black community, frustrated by what she felt was her failure to convert the Afro-American world view into the forms of prose fiction, Hurston finally gave up.
>
> —Robert Hemenway

When Charlotte and I drive up to the Merritt Monument Company, I immediately see the headstone I want.

"How much is this one?" I ask the young woman in charge, pointing to a tall black stone. It looks as majestic as Zora herself must have been when she was learning voodoo from those root doctors down in New Orleans.

"Oh, *that* one," she says, "that's our finest. That's Ebony Mist."

"Well, how much is it?"

"I don't know. But wait," she says, looking around in relief, "here comes somebody who'll know."

A small, sunburned man with squinty green eyes comes up. He must be the engraver, I think, because his eyes are contracted into slits, as if he has been keeping stone dust out of them for years.

"That's Ebony Mist," he says. "That's our best."

"How much is it?" I ask, beginning to realize I probably *can't* afford it.

He gives me a price that would feed a dozen Sahelian drought victims for three years. I realize I must honor the dead, but between the dead great and the living starving, there is no choice.

"I have a lot of letters to be engraved," I say, standing by the plain gray marker I have chosen. It is pale and ordinary, not at all like Zora, and makes me momentarily angry that I am not rich.

We go into his office and I hand him a sheet of paper that has:

ZORA NEALE HURSTON
"A GENIUS OF THE SOUTH"
NOVELIST FOLKLORIST
ANTHROPOLOGIST
1901 1960

"A genius of the South" is from one of Jean Toomer's poems.

"Where is this grave?" the monument man asks. "If it's in a new cemetery, the stone has to be flat."

"Well, it's not a new cemetery and Zora—my aunt—doesn't need anything flat, because with the weeds out there, you'd never be able to see it. You'll have to go out there with me."

He grunts.

"And take a long pole and 'sound' the spot," I add. "Because there's no way of telling it's a grave, except that it's sunken."

"Well," he says, after taking my money and writing up a receipt, in the full awareness that he's the only monument dealer for miles, "you take this flag" (he hands me a four-foot-long pole with a red-metal marker on top) "and take it out to the cemetery and put it where you think the grave is. It'll take us about three weeks to get the stone out there."

I wonder if he knows he is sending me to another confrontation with the snakes. He probably does. Charlotte has told me she will cut my leg and suck out the blood if I am bit.

"At least send me a photograph when it's done, won't you?"

He says he will.

> Hurston's return to her folklore-collecting in December of 1927 was made possible by Mrs. R. Osgood Mason, an elderly white patron of the arts, who at various times also helped Langston Hughes, Alain Locke, Richmond Barthe, and Miguel Covarrubias. Hurston apparently came to her attention through the intercession of Locke, who frequently served as a kind of liaison between the young black talent and Mrs. Mason. The entire relationship between this woman and the Harlem Renaissance deserves extended study, for it represents much of the ambiguity involved in white patronage of black artists. All her artists were instructed to call her "Godmother"; there was a decided emphasis on the "primitive" aspects of black culture, apparently a holdover from Mrs. Mason's interest in the Plains Indians. In Hurston's case there were special restrictions imposed by her patron: although she was to be paid a handsome salary for her folklore collecting, she was to limit her correspondence and publish nothing of her research without prior approval.
>
> —Robert Hemenway

> You have to read the chapters Zora *left out* of her autobiography.
>
> —Student, Special Collections Room, Beinecke Library, Yale University

Dr. Benton, a friend of Zora's and a practicing M.D. in Fort Pierce, is one of those old, good-looking men whom I always have trouble not liking. (It no longer bothers me that I may be constantly searching for father figures; by this time, I have found several and dearly enjoyed knowing them all.) He is shrewd, with steady brown eyes under hair that is almost white. He is probably in his seventies, but doesn't look it. He carries himself with dignity, and has cause to be proud of the new clinic where he now practices medicine. His nurse looks at us with suspicion, but Dr. Benton's eyes have the penetration of a scalpel cutting through skin. I guess right away that if he knows anything at all about Zora Hurston, he will not believe I am her niece. "Eatonville?" Dr. Benton says, leaning forward in his chair, looking first at me, then at Charlotte. "Yes, I know Eatonville; I grew up not far from there. I knew the whole bunch of Zora's family." (He looks at the shape of my cheekbones, the size of my eyes, and the nappiness of my hair.) "I knew her daddy. The old man. He was a hard-working, Christian man. Did the best he could for his family. He was the mayor of Eatonville for a while, you know.

"My father was the mayor of Goldsboro. You probably never heard of it. It never incorporated like Eatonville did, and has just about disappeared. But Eatonville is still all black."

He pauses and looks at me. "And you're Zora's niece," he says wonderingly.

"Well," I say with shy dignity, yet with some tinge, I hope, of a nineteenth-century blush, "I'm illegitimate. That's why I never knew Aunt Zora."

I love him for the way he comes to my rescue. "You're *not* illegitimate!" he cries, his eyes resting on me fondly. "All of us are God's children! Don't you even *think* such a thing!"

And I hate myself for lying to him. Still, I ask myself, would I have gotten this far toward getting the headstone and finding out about Zora Hurston's last days without telling my lie? Actually, I probably would have. But I don't like taking chances that could get me stranded in central Florida.

"Zora didn't get along with her family. I don't know why. Did you read her autobiography, *Dust Tracks on a Road?*"

"Yes, I did," I say. "It pained me to see Zora pretending to be naïve and grateful about the old white 'Godmother' who helped finance her research, but I loved the part where she ran off from home after falling out with her brother's wife."

Dr. Benton nods. "When she got sick, I tried to get her to go back to her family, but she refused. There wasn't any real hatred; they just never had gotten along and Zora wouldn't go to them. She didn't want to go to the county home, either, but she had to, because she couldn't do a thing for herself."

"I was surprised to learn she died of malnutrition."

Dr. Benton seems startled. "Zora *didn't* die of malnutrition," he says indignantly. "Where did you get that story from? She had a stroke and she died in the welfare home." He seems peculiarly upset, distressed, but sits back reflectively in his chair. "She was an incredible woman," he muses. "Sometimes when I closed my office, I'd go by her house and just talk to her for an hour or two. She was a well-read, well-traveled woman and always had her own ideas about what was going on...."

"I never knew her, you know. Only some of Carl Van Vechten's photographs and some newspaper photographs ... What did she look like?"

"When I knew her, in the fifties, she was a big woman, *erect*. Not quite as light as I am [Dr. Benton is dark beige], and about five foot seven inches, and she weighed about two hundred pounds. Probably more. She..."

"What! Zora was *fat!* She wasn't, in Van Vechten's pictures!"

"Zora loved to eat," Dr. Benton says complacently. "She could sit down with a mound of ice cream and just eat and talk till it was all gone."

While Dr. Benton is talking, I recall that the Van Vechten pictures were taken when Zora was still a young woman. In them she appears tall, tan, and healthy. In later newspaper photographs—when she was in her forties—I remembered that she seemed heavier and several shades lighter. I reasoned that the earlier photographs were taken while she was busy collecting folklore materials in the hot Florida sun.

"She had high blood pressure. Her health wasn't good... She used to live in one of my houses—on School Court Street. It's a block house.... I don't recall the number. But my wife and I used to invite her over to the house for dinner. *She always ate well,*" he says emphatically.

"That's comforting to know," I say, wondering where Zora ate when she wasn't with the Bentons.

"Sometimes she would run out of groceries—after she got sick—and she'd call me. 'Come over here and see 'bout me,' she'd say. And I'd take her shopping and buy her groceries.

"She was always studying. Her mind—before the stroke—just worked all the time. She was always going somewhere, too. She once went to Honduras to study something. And when she died, she was working on that book about Herod the Great. She was so intelligent! And really had perfect expressions. Her English was beautiful." (I suspect this is a clever way to let me know Zora herself didn't speak in the "black English" her characters used.)

"I used to read all of her books," Dr. Benton continues, "but it was a long time ago. I remember one about... it was called, I think, 'The Children of God' [*Their Eyes Were Watching God*], and I remember Janie and Teapot [Teacake] and the mad dog riding on the cow in that hurricane and bit old Teapot on the cheek...."

I am delighted that he remembers even this much of the story, even if the names are wrong, but seeing his affection for Zora I feel I must ask him about her burial. "Did she *really* have a pauper's funeral?"

"She *didn't* have a pauper's funeral!" he says with great heat. "Everybody around here *loved* Zora."

"We just came back from ordering a headstone," I say quietly, because he *is* an old man and the color is coming and going on his face, "but to tell the truth, I can't be positive what I found is the grave. All I know is the spot I found was the only grave-size hole in the area."

"I remember it wasn't near the road," says Dr. Benton, more calmly. "Some other lady came by here and we went out looking for the grave and I took a long iron stick and poked all over that part of the cemetery but we didn't find anything. She took some pictures of the general area. Do the weeds still come up to your knees?"

"And beyond," I murmur. This time there isn't any doubt. Dr. Benton feels ashamed.

As he walks us to our car, he continues to talk about Zora. "She couldn't really write much near the end. She had the stroke and it left her weak; her mind was affected. She couldn't think about anything for long.

"She came here from Daytona, I think. She owned a houseboat over there. When she came here, she sold it. She lived on that money, then she worked as a maid—for an article on maids she was writing—and she worked for the *Chronicle* writing the horoscope column.

"I think black people here in Florida got mad at her because she was for some politician they were against. She said this politician *built* schools for blacks while the one they wanted just talked about it. And although Zora wasn't egotistical, what she thought, she thought; and generally what she thought, she said."

When we leave Dr. Benton's office, I realize I have missed my plane back home to Jackson, Mississippi. That being so, Charlotte and I decide to find the house Zora lived in before she was taken to the county welfare home to die. From among her many notes, Charlotte locates a letter of Zora's she has copied that carries the address: 1734 School Court Street. We ask several people for directions. Finally, two old gentlemen in a dusty gray Plymouth offer to lead us there. School Court Street is not paved, and the road is full of mud puddles. It is dismal and squalid, redeemed only by the brightness of the late afternoon sun. Now I can understand what a "block" house is. It is a house shaped like a block, for one thing, surrounded by others just like it. Some houses are blue and some are green or yellow. Zora's is light green. They are tiny—about fifty by fifty feet, squatty with flat roofs. The house Zora lived in looks worse than the others, but that is its only distinction. It also has three ragged and dirty children sitting on the steps.

"Is this where y'all live?" I ask, aiming my camera.

"No, ma'am" they say in unison, looking at me earnestly. "We live over yonder. This Miss So-and-So's house; but she in the hospital."

We chatter inconsequentially while I take more pictures. A car drives up with a young black couple in it. They scowl fiercely at Charlotte and don't look at me with friendliness, either. They get out and stand in their doorway across the street. I go up to them to explain. "Did you know Zora Hurston used to live right across from you?" I ask.

"Who?" They stare at me blankly, then become curiously attentive, as if they think I made the name up. They are both Afroed and he is somberly dashikied.

I suddenly feel frail and exhausted. "It's too long a story," I say, "but tell me something: is there anybody on this street who's lived here for more than thirteen years?"

"That old man down there," the young man says, pointing. Sure enough, there is a man sitting on his steps three houses down. He has graying hair and is very neat, but there is a weakness about him. He reminds me of Mrs. Turner's husband in *Their Eyes Were Watching God.* He's rather "vanishing" looking, as if his features have been sanded down. In the old days, before black was beautiful, he was probably considered attractive, because he has wavy hair and light-brown skin; but now, well, light skin has ceased to be its own reward.

After the preliminaries, there is only one thing I want to know: "Tell me something," I begin, looking down at Zora's house. "Did Zora like flowers?"

He looks at me queerly. "As a matter of fact," he says, looking regretfully at the bare, rough yard that surrounds her former house, "she was crazy about them. And she was a great gardener. She loved azaleas, and that running and blooming vine [morning-glories], and she really loved that night-smelling flower [gardenia]. She kept a vegetable garden year-round, too. She raised collards and tomatoes and things like that.

"Everyone in this community thought well of Miss Hurston. When she died, people all up and down this street took up a collection for her burial. We put her away nice."

"Why didn't somebody put up a headstone?"

"Well, you know, one was never requested. Her and her family didn't get along. They didn't even come to the funeral."

"And did she live down there by herself?"

"Yes, until they took her away. She lived with—just her and her companion, Sport."

My ears perk up. "Who?"

"Sport, you know, her dog. He was her only companion. He was a big brown and white dog."

When I walk back to the car, Charlotte is talking to the young couple on their porch. They are relaxed and smiling.

"I told them about the famous lady who used to live across the street from them," says Charlotte as we drive off. "Of course they had no idea Zora ever lived, let alone that she lived across the street. I think I'll send some of her books to them."

"That's real kind of you," I say.

> I am not tragically colored. There is no great sorrow dammed up in my soul, nor lurking behind my eyes. I do not mind at all. I do not belong to the sobbing school of Negrohood who hold that nature somehow has given them a lowdown dirty deal and whose feelings are all hurt about it.... No, I do not weep at the world—I am too busy sharpening my oyster knife.
>
> —Zora Neale Hurston, "How It Feels to Be Colored Me," *World Tomorrow,* 1928

There are times—and finding Zora Hurston's grave was one of them—when normal responses of grief, horror, and so on do not make sense because they bear no real relation to the depth of the emotion one feels. It was impossible for me to cry when I saw the field full of weeds where Zora is. Partly this is because I have come to know Zora through her books and she was not a teary sort of person herself; but partly, too, it is because there is a point at which even grief feels absurd. And at this point, laughter gushes up to retrieve sanity.

It is only later, when the pain is not so direct a threat to one's own existence, that what was learned in that moment of comical lunacy is understood. Such moments rob us of both youth and vanity. But perhaps they are also times when greater disciplines are born.

—1975

Learning from Other Writers

1. What is Alice Walker's personal reason for making a pilgrimage to the towns where Zora Neale Hurston lived and died? Is there a larger, more general question that Walker is trying to answer in making her pilgrimage to Eatonville?
2. What discoveries does Walker make about Hurston that she couldn't have made if she had stayed at home? Does Walker make any discoveries that aren't directly related to Hurston? If so, why might Walker have included these discoveries in an essay about "looking for Zora"?
3. How does Walker reproduce or portray the speaking patterns of the people she quotes in her essay? What do you think of her portrayal of Rosalee?
4. Highlight the overt discussions of racism and integration that Walker includes in her essay. Now highlight the passages or scenes that pertain to racism and integration but aren't directly commented on as such by Walker.
5. What do you think about Walker's lie that she is Hurston's niece?
6. What is the effect of Walker's decision to include quotations from experts? Can you find any guiding principle that governs which quotes she includes and where she places them in the essay?
7. What is the condition of Hurston's gravesite today? Do you think that Walker's essay played any role in raising the public's awareness of Hurston's contribution to American literature? Do you think Walker's essay qualifies as scholarly? Why or why not?

JAMES ALAN MCPHERSON

UMBILICUS

In the late fall of that first year, when I was growing secure in my solitude, a friend, an Englishman, came to this house and offered what he believed was an act of compassion: "Now look here," he told me, "you are becoming a recluse. Why don't you go out once in a while? At least go out into your own backyard and see how delightful the fall is. I'm told that way north of here, along the Minnesota border, it is even more beautiful. Why don't you at least take a drive up there before winter comes?" His was a call back to the more complex rituals of life. After some serious reflection, I accepted it as such. I had always wanted to see the northeastern part of the state, the sources of the Mississippi. And so, on a Saturday morning, a golden and blue fall day, I pulled away from the security of this house. I drove northeasterly on county roads. I drove very slowly and very carefully from one rural town to the next. I saw the light brown beauty of harvested fields, when soybeans and corn and wheat had given up their energy to entropy, to the enigma of renewal, for the risk of winter and the promise of spring. I saw that life, my own life, too, *all life,* lay under the promise of an agreement with something outside, and far, far beyond, the little roles we play on the surface of things. I am saying that the slow drive along the backroads reawakened my spirits. I began to reconsider the essential importance of risk to the enterprise of life. I mustered sufficient courage to stop several times along the road, once for lunch, and again for gasoline and oil. I drove as far north as I thought was necessary, and then I turned around and drove back toward home. But in the late afternoon, on the far side of Cedar Rapids, the engine of my car began to smoke and burn. By the time I had parked on the narrow road bank, the engine was on fire. It was here that the old sickness began to reclaim its place in my emotions. I began to feel that the burning engine was God's punishment for my abandoning the simple rituals that had become my life. I felt that, because I had left the refuge of my house, I had *earned* this fate. I abandoned the car. I steeled myself to walk back home, or at least to walk as far as the outskirts of Cedar Rapids, many miles down that county road, as a form of self-punishment. I focused my mind on my house, my bed, my table, and I began walking toward these three things, and *only* these three things.

But several miles along that road, approaching dusk, a truck with two men in it stopped just ahead of me. The two men, both white, sat in the truck and waited for me to approach it. "We saw your car smoking back there, brother," the man in the passenger seat said to me. "Can we give you a ride?" The two of them seemed to be laborers, or at least farmers. The gun rack stretched across the rear window took my memories back to the terror of that long road I had traveled to this place. There was the truck, the gun rack, the white faces, the road. But they did not have the oily Southern accent. I accepted their offer, and the passenger moved over and allowed me to take his seat. Now the three of us were squeezed together on the high seat. They gave me a beer, from the remains of a case of beer on the floor, and we drove toward Cedar Rapids. "A lot of our friends don't like the colored," the driver, who seemed the older of the two, announced to me. "But, hell, me and my brother here, we got colored neighbors. We go over to their houses sometimes for parties. They ain't exactly like us, but we like them all the same." We toasted with our beer and talked of the need for more brotherhood in the world, and of the house parties given by their black neighbors in Cedar Rapids. But at the first service station we reached, just on the outskirts of Cedar Rapids, we were informed that no tow truck was available. The attendant advised us to continue on into Cedar Rapids, toward a station where a tow truck could be available.

Now the older of the two men, in the proximity of safety and social gradation seeming to look more and more "poor white," used this opportunity to offer a radical plan. "Now look," he told me. "I already told you that we *like* the colored. We go over to their house parties in Cedar. You know that some colored are our neighbors. Now here's what I'm gonna do. There's a rope on the back of this truck. We can drive on back and tie that rope to the front bumper of your car. Then we'll just tow her on in to Cedar. You can pay us what you were gonna pay the tow truck, plus we'll do it for less money."

The cool fall evening was closing in. I hesitated, but the desperation of the situation caused me to risk some trust. I accepted their offer. With the bargain struck, with the night closing around us, we drove back to the dead car. We drank more beer in celebration of brotherhood, and we even made some jokes. At the car, after the ropes had been tied to link my own wreck to the back end of their truck, the connection, the *umbilicus,* was tightened until my car could be raised so that only its back wheels were grounded. The two brothers cautioned me to take my former place behind the wheel and manage my car as best I could while they drove the truck. I was handed another beer, for toasting our newly struck brotherhood, while we steered in unison toward the distant lights of Cedar Rapids. And so we started out, slowly and jerkily at first, but then with more and more speed.

Legend has it that all the "I" states are flat. This is not so. There are reasons why the Mississippi River begins in Minnesota, and why its tributaries contribute every drop of water in its meandering and then rapid flow down to the Gulf of Mexico. There are hills in this landscape, and hillocks and dales and rills. The expression *from here to there,* with its promise of fixed purpose, is found in the engineering of straight roadways. But, in contradiction to this illusion of purposeful will, nature itself still has something else to say. Nature will not cede an inch, without struggle, to *any* expression of fixed purpose. Something mysterious in nature, or in the restless growing edge of life itself, imposes a counterintention on all illusion of control. The Great River overflows its banks, flows and ebbs, crests and slackens, rushes and lingers, dies, and then is mighty and waterful again, according to its own instincts. So also the straightest of roads are forced to acknowledge the rhythms of the lands that lap under them. Such rhythms are gentle under the four wheels of a tractioned car. But under only two wheels, these same rhythms are foreboding. They speak waywardly of the tenuous nature of life. And in the fall, after harvest time, the uniform brownness of the field, or perhaps it is the withdrawal of the subtle shades of green, keeps one close to the recognition that *death* is the very next season *after* life. You must also add to this the horror of the peculiar angle of a windshield looking *up* into the dark, evening sky, closing down on the emptiness all around the roadbed, and over the top of a truck ahead that you cannot really see. And add also the swaying of the elevated car, first leftward, toward possibly oncoming traffic you cannot see, then rightward, toward sharp and narrow embankments, black-dirted and brown-coated and deathly deep. Imagine also the unsteady stretching of the ropes, the *umbilicus,* connecting the two vehicles. It stretches close to breaking when the truck moves uphill; it relaxes, and the weight of the towed car pushes forward freely and crazily, when the towing truck goes down a dale. Such a haphazardly improvised *umbilical* cord cares nothing for *verbal* affirmations of brotherhood. It encourages very bad manners. It permits the front of the towed car to bump the back of the towing truck, and when the towed car brakes—because its driver tries to steady it when it bumps the rear of the truck ahead, and releases the brake when the rope becomes too tight—both car and towing truck begin to sway dangerously. And add more to it. Add to it the fading illusion of rescue, and the more sharply focused recognition that these are two *white men,* blood brothers, both drunk on beer, who are pulling off the rescue. Add also to it the fact that you have had two beers yourself, and that there is a third beer, open but untouched, on the seat beside you. An additional inducement for fear is that, while these two white men say that they like the colored, and while the three of you raised two toasts to *abstract* brotherhood, the world you live in, especially now, does not perceive things in this same idealized light.

Now, in the entire history of this country there has developed absolutely no substantial body of evidence to support either the authenticity, the genuineness, or the practicality of such a web of self-extension, such an *umbilicus,* extending from either extreme of this great psychological divide. There has been no *real* trust between black and white, especially in such life-risking circumstances. With each sway of the car, within every pull and slack of the rope, the improvised *umbilical* cord—up dale and down dale, inching and then swaying toward the evening lights of Cedar Rapids, the old life lessons came back. *There has never been a life-affirming umbilicus between black and white.* And if this is true, then something else must follow. If the rope should break and the car should crash, no one will really care or even attempt to understand just how this failed and sloppily improvised community of purpose had first come into existence. On the evening news, if even there, it will be dismissed as just another road-kill. *I will never be able to reclaim my bed, my table, or the simple, little, self-protective rituals—sleeping and eating and reading and being reclusive—that I had created to protect what remained of my life.*

I braked my car and both vehicles, my car and their truck, went off the road.

But the rope, the *umbilicus, held,* while the car and truck swerved into the ditch at the edge of the roadside.

The two vehicles, the three of us, went into the ditch together. There was no moon over the brown harvested fields that evening. There was no magnetic field, no spiritual center.

There was only the spilled can of beer, and its acrid scent mingled with the smell of burning oil, inside my car. Death was announcing itself all around.

I had no trust left in me.

But the three of us were unhurt. The two brothers, after inspecting their truck, dismissed the incident as no more than a joke played on the three of us by the rhythm of the road. "Now we told you we like the colored," the older brother announced. "See, the rope is still tight. We can just push our truck out of the ditch and then hook you up again to it. We'll still drive you on in to Cedar."

I paid the brothers much more than I had promised them, and I began walking down the road toward the lights of Cedar Rapids, toward my bed, my window looking out on my backyard, my table, and toward the simple rituals I had worked out for my life. These things still resided on the far side of Cedar Rapids. I walked away from the urgings of my brothers that we could very easily rescue both truck and car from the ditch, that we had only a few more miles to go before hitting Cedar, that they had always been good neighbors to the colored who lived next door. I kept walking away from them. In my own reduced frame of reference, my two rescuers, my brothers, had become two drunk white men, who, through uncaring, had put my life at risk. I walked away, while behind me they pleaded for the unimportance of money and for the practicality of their plan.

I left it to them to cut the rope, the *umbilicus,* connecting my dead car to their truck.

—1997

Learning from Other Writers

1. In "Umbilicus," McPherson tells us (in paragraph one) that his concrete goal is a desire to see the "sources of the Mississippi." What is his larger, more universal goal in taking this trip?
2. What does McPherson tell you about his life prior to undertaking this quest? What can you surmise by reading between the lines?
3. What role does the terrain play in this essay? What does McPherson mean by "the rhythm of the road"?
4. Why does the author bother to tell us that he left it to the two white men to cut the rope that connects his dead car to their truck?

SUE HUBBELL

THE VICKSBURG GHOST

> The human predicament is typically so complex that it is not altogether clear which lies are vital and what truths beg for discovery.
>
> —"Vital Lies, Simple Truths: The Psychology of Self-Deception," by Daniel Coleman

I guess most people found it hard to believe that Elvis Presley didn't die after all but instead is alive and well and shopping at Felpausch's Supermarket, in Vicksburg, Michigan. I know I did when I read about it in the *New York Times* last fall. The *Times* wasn't on record as saying "The King Lives," or anything like that, but it did report that a Vicksburg woman named Louise Welling had said she'd seen him the year before, in the supermarket's checkout line. Her sighting encouraged Elvins everywhere, many of whom believe that Presley faked his death. It also added an extra fillip to Elvismania, which is part nostalgia and part industry, the industry part consisting of the production of Elvis memorabilia, books, articles, tours, and prime-time TV "docudramas." Fans have made periodic demands for an Elvis postage stamp, and a multimedia musical, *Elvis: A Rockin' Remembrance,* had an off-Broadway run this summer.

Promotion was what made Elvis Presley. In 1977, the year of his death, his likeness was more widely reproduced than any other save that of Mickey Mouse, and it has been reported that the news of his demise was greeted by one cynic with the words "Good career move!" According to Albert Goldman, the biographer who tells this story, Presley was by then a porky, aging, drug-befuddled Las Vegas entertainer and was getting to be a hard personality to promote. The Presley image shorn of the troublesome real man was easier to market. For example, after the King's death, Presley's manager, Colonel Thomas A. Parker, contracted with a vineyard in Paw Paw, Michigan—a town not far from Vicksburg—to produce a wine called Always Elvis. Its label bears a head shot of the entertainer, in a high-collared spangled white shirt, singing into a handheld microphone. Colonel Parker's own four-stanza poem appears on the back of the bottle. Goldman has computed that the poem earned Parker $28,000 in royalties, "making him, line for line, the best-paid poet in the world." Although the wine is no longer produced, I was able to find a dusty old bottle in my local liquor store. In the interests of journalism, I sampled it. It was an adequate companion to the poem, which closes with the couplet

> We will play your songs from day to day
> For you really never went away.

In its year-end double issue, *People* ran a story featuring recent photographs of Elvis purportedly taken by readers around the country, each picture as vague and tantalizing as snapshots of the Loch Ness monster. While debate mounted over whether or not Elvis Presley was still alive, I got stuck back there in the part of the *Times* story which said that he was shopping at Felpausch's. By the latter part of the 1950s, when Elvis arrived to sweep away the dreariness of the Eisenhower years, I was too old to respond to the Dionysian sexual appeal that he had for his teenage maenads; consequently, I was also unmoved by retro-Elvis. But I did grow up near Vicksburg. My family lived in Kalamazoo, a bigger town (in which Elvis was also said to have appeared) twelve miles to the north, and we spent our summers at a lake near Vicksburg. My widowed mother now lives at the lake the year round, and when I visit her I often shop at Felpausch's myself. I know Vicksburg tolerably well, so when I read the account in the *Times* I strongly suspected that the reporter had been snookered by a group of the guys over at Mar-Jo's Café on Main Street, half a block from Felpausch's, which is on Prairie Street, the town's other commercial thoroughfare. Last June, while I was visiting my mother, I decided to drive into Vicksburg and find out what I could about the Elvis Presley story.

Vicksburg is a pretty village of two thousand people, more or less. A hundred and fifty years ago, when it was first settled by white people, the land was prairie and oak forest. James Fenimore Cooper, who lived for a time in the nearby town of Schoolcraft, wrote about the area in his book *Oak Openings*. It is in southern Michigan, where the winters are long and gray, and even the earliest settlers complained of the ferocity of the summertime mosquitoes. Vicksburg's one-block commercial section has been spruced up in recent years. There are beds of petunias at the curb edges, and new facades on the nineteenth-century buildings. The carefully maintained Victorian houses on the side streets are shaded by maples big enough to make you think elm. A paper mill, built near a dam that the eponymous John Vickers constructed on Portage Creek for his flour mill, has long provided employment for the local people, but today the village has become something of a bedroom community for commuters to Kalamazoo. Still, it seems very like the place I knew when I used to come to band concerts on Wednesday evenings at the corner of Main and Prairie during the summers of the 1930s and 1940s. The band concerts are a thing of the past, but there are other homegrown entertainments, such as one going on the week I was there—the annual Vicksburg Old Car Festival, which is run by Skip Knowles, a local insurance man. The festival has a fifties theme, and last year, inspired by the commotion that Louise Welling's sighting of Elvis had produced, Knowles added an Elvis-look-alike contest to the roster of events. Knowles has his office in a storefront on Main Street that used to be Matz's Confectionery, where I first discovered lime phosphates (known locally as "green rivers").

And the teenagers are still bored. While I was in the library going through back issues of local newspapers, two high school girls introduced themselves to me, saying that they had lived in Vicksburg all their lives and would be happy to talk to me about it. I asked them what they thought about Elvis Presley. They smiled patronizingly and informed me that no one they knew paid any attention to him. "But *everything* just stands still in Vicksburg," one of them confided. "We go to Kalamazoo on Saturday nights. I can't wait to get out of here and go to college."

Mar-Jo's has stayed the same, too. It has been in the same place for forty years. It was named after Marge Leitner and her partner, Josephine, whose last name no one at the café can remember. It is your basic tan place: tan floor, tan walls, tan tables, tan counter. The sign taped to the cash register was new to me. It said:

THIS IS NOT
BURGER KING
YOU GET IT
MY WAY
OR YOU DON'T
GET IT
AT ALL

But the men having coffee together at the big round table near the front windows could have been the same ones sitting there the last time I was in, which was a couple of years ago.

"How's you-know-who?" gray crew cut asks feed-store cap. "Don't see her anymore."

The others guffaw, and one says, "He's taken her clothes."

"What clothes?" feed-store cap shoots back. A ripple of caffeine-fueled laughter circles the table.

Shirley White, a small, wiry woman, has been a waitress at Mar-Jo's for eleven years. Her hair is dark and tightly curled. She is efficient and cheerful. She knows virtually all her customers by name and how they like their coffee, and she banters with all of them. She gets to work at 4:45 every morning, so she is usually way ahead of the best of the town wits, giving as good as she gets. The coffee-club boys once arranged the kind of prank on her that made me suspect them of the Elvis Presley caper. One of the regulars was a big man whom she could deftly unsettle with a clever phrase or two. His invariable riposte was a mumbled "Paybacks are hell." A few years ago, he was on vacation in Florida when her birthday came around, and she had nearly forgotten about him. Mar-Jo's was jammed that day, and no one would tell her why. "Just as I was busiest, this really big monkey walked in," she told me. "At least, it was a big guy dressed in a monkey costume, and he kept following me around, getting in my way. I was real embarrassed, and everyone kept laughing. Then a messenger handed me something called an Ape-O-Gram. It had just three words: 'Paybacks are hell.'"

Nearly all the coffee drinkers thought that the Elvis Presley sighting was as funny as the Ape-O-Gram, but no one would own up to having had a hand in making up the story. Louise Welling, it seemed, was a real person, and well known in town. She lived to the east, a few miles outside the village, they told me. "She's different, that's for sure," one of the coffee drinkers said. "No one believes her about Elvis Presley, but we all enjoyed it. Kind of put Vicksburg on the map. Isn't it funny? Elvis Presley wasn't even a very good singer. But I don't think Louise thinks it's funny." They referred me to a woman in town who knew Louise Welling better than they did and lived not far from her.

I went over to see the woman, who had an office in town, and talked to her with the understanding that her name would not be used. "Yes," she said. "I guess you could say that Louise is different. Her whole family is different, except for her husband, who works at General Motors. He's real quiet. But she's not crazy or anything. In fact, I think she's real bright. I don't know what to make of her claim that she saw Elvis Presley. She was a big Elvis fan from way back, but she doesn't bring him up or talk about this stuff unless someone asks her. She's a kind woman. She's reliable, too, and I wouldn't hesitate to call her if I had trouble. I'm afraid that after the story came out a lot of people played jokes on her. Made Elvis phone calls. Sent her Elvis letters. I'm pretty sure she's not in it for money. She just seems to think it's an interesting story, and it makes her mad when people don't believe her. Of course, none of us do. I don't know anyone in this town who thinks she really saw Elvis Presley. She was furious with the Vicksburg newspaper because they wouldn't run her story."

It seemed odd to me that the *Vicksburg Commercial* had not used Louise Welling's story—a story that had made the *New York Times*—so I called up Jackie Lawrence, the owner of the *Commercial,* and asked her to meet me for lunch at Mar-Jo's. Jackie Lawrence, a former nurse, is a big woman with curly brown hair, and she smiles a lot when she talks about Vicksburg, her adopted town. There are, she said, perhaps a dozen loyal Elvis fans in town—people who make pilgrimages to Graceland and would *like* to believe Louise Welling even if they don't.

We studied the daily specials, which were posted on the wall, and I decided to order Ken's Homemade Goulash. Next to the list of specials were snapshots of Ken Fowler, a cheerful young man with a fine brushy mustache, who bought Mar-Jo's two years ago and does a lot of the café's cooking. Shortly after he bought the place, he had a birthday, and the regulars, the waitresses, and Ken's wife conspired to bring in a belly dancer. The event was captured on film, and the posted snapshots show Ken, in apparent embarrassment, on a chair in one corner of the café, surrounded by laughing customers as a woman in gold draperies writhes in front of him.

Jackie Lawrence told me that she remembered Louise Welling coming into the newspaper office, which is a few doors down from Mar-Jo's, in March 1988, six months after the sighting at Felpausch's. At the time of her visit, Mrs. Welling knew that her story would soon be printed nationally, in the *Weekly World News*—and so it was, three months later. (According to Jim Leggett, who is the dean of freelance tabloid photojournalists and once schemed to drill a hole in Howard Hughes's coffin in order to photograph his face, the *Weekly World News* is not exactly esteemed in the trade. "It prints the flotsam left by the better tabloids," he told me.) Mrs. Welling had wanted the *Commercial* to run her story first, Lawrence said. "She stood right by my desk, trying to tell me all about it. I said to her, 'I'm sorry, I don't have time for this,' and showed her out the door. And if she came in again, I'd say the same thing."

There was only one mention in the *Commercial* of the stir caused by Louise Welling's encounter with Elvis. The winner of Skip Knowles's 1988 Elvis-look-alike contest, a truck driver named Ray Kajkowski, came into the newspaper office a few days after the event to ask for prints of any pictures that might have been taken. While he was there, he kissed Jean Delahanty, one of the *Commercial's* reporters, and she wrote a column about it, which concluded, "Some days are better than others!"

There is no chamber of commerce, as such, in Vicksburg. The town doesn't need one; it has Skip Knowles. I had telephoned Knowles before coming to Vicksburg. "Give me a jingle when you get in," he said. "Maybe we can do lunch." He is a handsome, trim, dark-haired man, and at our lunch a gold chain showed through the open collar of his shirt. There was another gold chain around his wrist. He was born in Atchison, Kansas, he told me, but spent his teenage years—from 1962 to 1968—near Detroit, where he developed a passion for cars and for cruising, that cool, arm-on-the-window, slow patrolling of city streets which was favored by the young in those days. His dark eyes sparkled at the memory.

"We had what we called the Woodward Timing Association," he said. "It was made up of the guys that cruised Woodward Avenue. The Elias Big Boy at Thirteen Mile Road and Woodward was the place we'd go. But you know how the grass is always greener somewhere else? Well, my ultimate dream was to cruise the Sunset Strip. It wasn't until I got married, in 1969, and went out to California that I got to do that. And I talked to those guys cruising the Strip, and you know what they told me? It was *their* dream to cruise Woodward." He shook his head and laughed. "My wife and I still cruise when we go to a city." He hoped the local people had got cruising down pat for this year's festival, he said, handing me a packet of publicity material and a schedule of festival events. "I had to *teach* them how to cruise last year, which was the first time we closed off the streets for it."

The second annual Elvis-look-alike contest would be held at 9 P.M. Saturday over on Prairie Street, in the parking lot of the Filling Station, a fast-food restaurant across the street from Felpausch's. Skip Knowles knew a good thing when he had it. Before last summer, he said, the festival had been drawing several thousand people, but each year he had had more trouble getting good publicity. "I can't understand the way they handled the Elvis business over at Felpausch's," he told me. "They even refused an interview with the *New York Times*. But I decided to play it for whatever it was worth."

After the first Elvis-look-alike contest, Knowles received a lot of calls from Louise Welling, who wanted to talk about Elvis Presley with him. "I put her off," he said. "She's *really* different. I think she really believes Presley never died." He also received other phone calls and visits. When his secretary told him last fall that a reporter from the *Times* was in his outer office waiting to talk to him, he thought it was just a hoax—a joke like the ones dreamed up at Mar-Jo's. But when he came out the man introduced himself as the paper's Chicago bureau chief and interviewed him about the Elvis contest. Then a producer from Charles Kuralt's show, *Sunday Morning*, called and said he was interested in doing a segment for the show on the impact of the Elvis sighting in Vicksburg, and would anything be going on in Vicksburg around Thanksgiving time? "I told him, 'Look, I'll do *anything* to get you here,'" Knowles recalled. "'If you want me to rent Cadillac limos and parade them up and down Main Street for you to film, I'll get them.' But the TV people never came."

I decided that it was time to talk to Louise Welling herself. I couldn't make an appointment with her by telephone because she had recently obtained an unlisted number, but one midweek morning I took a chance on finding her at home and drove out to see her. The Wellings live in the country, in a modest splitlevel house on non-split-level terrain; this is the sandy, flat part of Michigan, too far south for the ice-age glaciers to have sculpted it. Mrs. Welling sometimes works as a babysitter, but this morning she was home, along with four of her five children—all of them grown—and Nathan, her four-year-old grandson. Mrs. Welling is a heavyset woman with closely cropped dark hair and a pleasant face. Her eyes stay sad when she smiles. She touched my arm frequently as we talked, and often interrupted herself to digress as she told me her story. She said that she grew up in Kalamazoo and for a time attended St. Mary's, a Catholic grammar school there. When she turned sixteen, she was given a special present—a ticket to a Presley concert in Detroit. "Somehow, the fellow who took tickets didn't take mine, so after the first show I was able to move up, and I sat in front during the second," she said. "And then, toward the end, Elvis got down on his knee right in front of me and spread his arms wide open. Well, you can imagine what *that* would be like for a sixteen-year-old girl." Her voice trailed off, and she fell silent, smiling.

I asked her if she had continued to follow his career.

"When I got married, I started having children, and I never thought much about Elvis," she said. "After all, I had problems of my own." But then, in 1973, she saw a notice in a throwaway shopping newspaper from Galesburg, a nearby town, saying that Presley would be in Kalamazoo and, although he would not be performing, would stay at the Columbia Hotel there.

"I didn't try to get in touch with him," Mrs. Welling said, adding, with a womanly smile, "I had a husband, and you know how that is." Three years later, however, Presley appeared in concert in Kalamazoo, and she sent flowers to him at the Columbia Hotel, because she assumed that he would be staying there again. She went to the concert, too, and as she remembers it, Elvis announced in the course of it that he had a relative living in Vicksburg. "He said he liked this area," she recalled. "Kalamazoo is a peaceful place. He'd like that. And I think he's living at the Columbia right now, under another name. But they won't admit it there. Every time I call, I get a runaround. You know what I think? I think he has become an undercover agent. He was interested in that sort of thing."

"What year was it that you saw him in concert in Detroit?" I asked. I had read somewhere that Presley had not started touring outside the South until 1956.

"Oh, I don't remember," Mrs. Welling said, "I'm fifty-one now, and I just had turned sixteen—you figure it out."

The arithmetic doesn't work out—nor, for someone who grew up in Kalamazoo, does the Columbia Hotel. The Columbia had its days of glory between the First World War and Prohibition, and it was growing seedy by the forties, when I used to ride by it on my way to school. Its decline continued after I left Kalamazoo, until—according to Dan Carter, one of the partners in a development company that remodeled the hotel to create an office complex called Columbia Plaza—it became "a fleabag flophouse and, for a while, a brothel." Carter also told me that in the mid-eighties a rumor arose that Elvis Presley was living there, behind the grand pink double doors on the mezzanine, which open into what was once a ballroom. The doors have been locked for years—the empty ballroom, its paint peeling, belongs to the man who owns Bimbo's Pizza on the floor below—but that didn't deter Elvins here and abroad from making pilgrimages to Columbia Plaza. "You'd hear foreign voices out in the hallway almost every day," he said. "Then there was a visit from some people from Graceland—at least, they told us they were from Graceland, and they looked the part—who came by to see if we were making any money off this." They weren't, he said, and today the building's management denies that Elvis Presley, under any name, lives anywhere on the premises.

Mrs. Welling's next good look at Elvis Presley came at Felpausch's in September, 1987. There had been, she told me, earlier hints. In 1979, she had seen a man in the back of the county sheriff's car when the police came to her house to check on the family's dog, which had nipped a jogger. "The man in the back seat was all slouched down, and he didn't look well," she said. "I'm sure it was Elvis." A few years later, black limousines began to appear occasionally on the road where she lives. "Now, who around here would have a limo?" she asked. Then she began seeing a man she believes was Elvis in disguise. "He looked real fake," she recalled. "He was wearing new bib overalls, an Amish hat, and a beard that didn't look real. I talked to a woman who had seen the same man, and she said he sometimes wore a false nose. Now, why does he have to bother with disguises? Why couldn't he have said that he needed a rest, and gone off to some island to get better?"

A note of exasperation had crept into Mrs. Welling's voice. She showed me a cassette that she said contained a tape that Presley made after he was supposed to have died; in it, she said, he explained why he had faked his death. But when she played it the sound was blurred and rumbly, and I couldn't make out the words. The tape had been issued in 1988, to accompany a book by a woman—with whom Mrs. Welling has corresponded—who put forward the theory that the body buried as Presley's was not his own. The book and another by the same author, which Welling said was a fictional account of a rock star who fakes his death, were lovingly inscribed ("It's hard to take the heat") to Mrs. Welling.

Here is what Mrs. Welling said happened to her in September 1987. She had just been to eleven o'clock Sunday Mass at St. Martin's Church. With grandson Nathan, she stopped at Felpausch's to pick up a few groceries. Having just celebrated one publicly accepted miracle, she saw nothing strange in the private miracle at the supermarket.

"The store was just about deserted," she said. "There wasn't even anyone at the checkout register when I went in. But back in the aisles I felt and heard someone behind me. It must have been Elvis. I didn't turn around, though. And then, when I got up to the checkout, a girl was there waiting on Elvis. He seemed kind of nervous. He was wearing a white motorcycle suit and carrying a helmet. He bought something little—fuses, I think, not groceries. I was so startled I just looked at him. I knew it was Elvis. When you see someone, you know who he is. I didn't say anything, because I'm kind of shy and I don't speak to people unless they speak first. After I paid for the groceries, I went out to the parking lot, but no one was there."

I asked Mrs. Welling if she had told anyone at the time what she had seen. She replied that she had told no one except the author of the Elvis-isn't-dead book, who was "very supportive." After that, she and her daughter Linda started seeing Elvis in Kalamazoo—once at a Burger King, once at the Crossroads Shopping Mall, and once driving a red Ferrari. And she said that just recently, while she was babysitting and filling her time by listening to the police scanner, she heard a man's voice ask, "Can you give me a time for the return of Elvis?" and heard Presley reply, "I'm here now."

I asked her what her family thought about her experiences. Linda, a pale, blond woman who was sitting off to one side in a dining alcove smoking cigarettes while I talked to her mother, was obviously a believer, and occasionally she interjected reports of various Elvis contacts of her own. "But *my* mother thinks it's all nutty," Mrs. Welling said, laughing. "She says I should forget about it. My husband doesn't say much—he's real quiet—but he knows I'm not crazy."

It wasn't until the spring of 1988, Mrs. Welling said, that she started getting in touch with the media. She claims that she didn't bother talking to the people at the Vicksburg newspaper (although Jackie Lawrence remembers otherwise), because "it wasn't an important newspaper." Instead, she tried to tell her story to the *Kalamazoo Gazette* and people at the television station there. No one would take her seriously—except, of course, the author of the Elvis book. After Mrs. Welling had written to her and talked to her on the telephone, a writer for the *Weekly World News* phoned for an interview. Mrs. Welling asked him how he knew about her, but he declined to reveal his sources. In early May, the tabloid prepared the ground for Mrs. Welling's story by running one that took note of the rumor that Presley was living in Columbia Plaza, and gave Mrs. Welling's friend a nice plug for her book. Shortly after that, the syndicated columnist Bob Greene gave the rumor a push. By that time, the *Kalamazoo Gazette* realized that it could no longer ignore Mrs. Welling's phone calls, and in its May 15 issue Tom Haroldson, a staff writer, wrote a front-page story headlined "'Elvis Alive' in Kalamazoo, Say Area Woman and News Tabloid." That was the beginning of

Mrs. Welling's fame, but it was not until June 28 that the *Weekly World News* told her whole story. In thousands of supermarkets, the issue appeared with a big front-page picture of Mrs. Welling and a headline in type an inch and a half high proclaiming, "I've Seen Elvis in the Flesh!" The story began to be picked up by newspapers around the country as a brightener to the increasingly monotonous accounts of the preconvention presidential campaigns. CBS investigated it for possible production on *60 Minutes.* Radio stations from coast to coast and as far away as Australia called to interview Louise Welling and anyone else they could find. Kalamazoo's mayor, Edward Annen, reacted to all this by announcing to a *Gazette* reporter, "I've told them that everyone knows this is where he lives and that they should send their residents here to spend tourist dollars to find him."

Funny signs sprouted throughout Kalamazoo and Vicksburg in places of commerce. A rival market of Felpausch's posted one that said, "Jimmy Hoffa Shops Here." A dentist boasted, "Elvis Has His Teeth Cleaned Here." At Mar-Jo's, the sign read, "Elvis Eats Our Meatloaf." The folks at Felpausch's, however, were not amused. Cecil Bagwell, then the store's manager, told the *Gazette,* "The cashier who supposedly checked out Elvis that day cannot remember anything about it," and characterized Mrs. Welling as "an Elvis fanatic." Bagwell no longer works at Felpausch's, but I spoke with Jack Mayhew, the assistant manager, who scowled when I brought up the subject. "I won't comment," he said, adding, nonetheless, "We've never given the story to anyone, and we're not going to. All I'll say is that the woman is totally—" and he rotated an extended finger beside his head.

Before I left Mrs. Welling that morning, I asked her why she thought it was that *she* had seen Elvis, when others had not—did not even believe her.

"I don't know, but the Lord does," she answered. "I'm a religious woman, and when things like this happen—that we don't understand—it just proves that the Lord has a plan."

The next day, a friend who had heard about my investigations telephoned to tell me that there had been an Elvis sighting just a week or so earlier, in Kalamazoo, at the delivery bay of the Fader Construction Company, which is owned by her family. She hadn't seen the man herself, she said, but the women in the office had insisted that the truck driver making the delivery was Elvis Presley. I suspected that it might have been Ray Kajkowski, winner of the Elvis-look-alike contest and kisser of Jean Delahanty. This turned out to be true. On Friday evening, at a runthrough for the Old Car Festival's cruising event, I was introduced to Kajkowski by Skip Knowles, and Kajkowski confirmed that he had made quite a stir while delivering a shipment of concrete forms to Fader. He gave me his card—he has apparently made a second career for himself as an Elvis impersonator at parties and night clubs—and then he whipped out a pair of mirrored sunglasses, put them on, and kissed me, too. "Young, old, fat, skinny, black, white, good looking, not so good looking, I kiss them all," he said. "I'm a pretty affectionate fellow. I was raised in a family that hugged a lot."

Ray Kajkowski lives in Gobles, not far from Vicksburg. At forty-one, he is thick-featured, a bit on the heavy side, and looks like—well, he looks like Elvis Presley. He has big sideburns and dyed black hair, which he wears in a pompadour. He went down to Graceland recently with his wife and his two teenage sons to study the Presley scene and recalls that while he was in the mansion's poolroom a couple came in and the wife took one look at him and collapsed on the floor in a faint.

"When I was growing up, I felt like an outsider," he told me. "I didn't think I was as good as other people, because my dad wasn't a doctor or a lawyer. We were just common folks. I knew about Elvis even when I was a little kid. I didn't pay much attention, though, except that some of my buddies had pictures of Elvis, so we'd trade those to our older sisters and their friends for baseball cards." He laughed.

"I felt like we were invaded when the Beatles came over," he continued. By that time—1963—he was at Central High School in Kalamazoo, and had begun to appreciate Presley's music and to defend it against foreign stars. "I mean, Elvis was a small-town boy who made good. He was just ordinary, and, sure, he made some mistakes, just like me or you or any of us. But he went from zero to sixty. He had charisma with a capital *C*, and somehow people still know it."

After Presley's death, Kajkowski said, he felt sad and started reading about Elvis and studying his old movies. "Then, in September or October 1987, right around then, I was at a 1950s dance in Gobles. My hair was different then, and I had a beard, but there was a fifty-dollar prize for the best Elvis imitator. Fifty bucks sounded pretty good to me, and I watched this one guy do an imitation, and he didn't move or anything, and I thought to myself, I can do better than that, so I got up and entered and won, beard and all. After that, I shaved off my beard, dyed my hair, and started building my act. I do lip-synch to Elvis tapes. I've got three suits now, one black, one white, one blue. My wife does my setups for me and runs the strobe lights. Evenings when we don't have anything else to do, we sit around and make scarves for me to give away. I cut them, and she hems them. When I'm performing, I sweat real easy, and I mop off the sweat with the scarves and throw them out to the gals. They go crazy over them. And the gals proposition me. They don't make it easy. Sometimes they rub up against me, and when I kiss them they stick their tongues halfway down my throat. Once, I went over to shake the guys' hands, because I figured it was better to have them on my side. But one big guy wouldn't shake my hand, and later he came over and grabbed me like a grizzly bear and told me to quit it. 'You don't sound like Elvis Presley. You don't look like Elvis Presley. Stop it.' I told him, 'Hey, it's all lip-synch! it's just an act! It's entertainment!' But I try to keep it under control. My wife's the woman I have to go home with after the act."

I asked Kajkowski if he had ever been in Felpausch's. As a truck driver, he said, he had made deliveries there; occasionally, he even shopped there. But although he owned a motorcycle, he said, he rarely drove it, and he never wore a white motorcycle suit.

I asked him what he made of Mrs. Welling's story.

"Well," he said thoughtfully, "when someone puts another person at the center of their life, they read about him, they think about him, I'm not surprised that he becomes real for that person."

Saturday night at nine o'clock Louise Welling is standing next to me in the Filling Station's parking lot—it is built on the site of John Vickers's flour mill—in a crowd that has just seen prizes awarded in the fifties dance concert and is waiting for the beginning of the second annual Elvis-look-alike contest. She is neatly dressed in a blue-and-white checked overblouse and dark pants. Her hair is fluffed up, and she is wearing pretty pink lipstick. She invited me to come to the contest, and told me that although many of the entrants in such affairs didn't come close to Elvis she was hoping that this one would draw the real Elvis Presley out from hiding. "If he came to me in the past, I believe he'll come again," she said. "I hope it will be before I die. If he comes, I'm going to grab him and hold on to him and ask him why he couldn't just be honest about needing to get away for a rest. Why couldn't he just tell the truth? Look at all the trouble he's caused those who love him."

Earlier in the day, I stopped in at Mar-Jo's for coffee. There were lots of extra visitors in the café. Ken Fowler had turned on the radio to WHEZ, a Kalamazoo station, which was broadcasting live from out on the street, acting as the festival's musical host. Rock music filled the café. Patrons were beating time on their knees, and the waitresses had begun to boogie up and down behind the counter. I asked one of them—a girl named Laurie, who was decked out fifties style with a white floaty scarf around her ponytail—what she made of Mrs. Welling's story. "I think it's kind of fun," she said. "I haven't met the lady, but, you know, maybe she's right. After all, if Elvis Presley never died he has to be someplace."

Mrs. Welling is subdued as she stands next to me, but all attention—scanning the people, anticipatory. We are at the very back of the good-natured crowd, which has enjoyed the nostalgia, the slick cars, the dances, the poodle skirts, and the ponytails. She spots Kajkowski and says to me that he's not Elvis but "so far he's the only one here who even looks anything like him."

Skip Knowles is up on the stage, in charge of what has turned out to be a successful event. There have been record-breaking crowds. Six hundred and fifty cars were entered. He has had plenty of media coverage, and he seems to be having a very good time. He calls for the Elvis contest to begin. Ray Kajkowski's act is so good now that he has no competition—he is the only one to enter. I watch him play the crowd. He had told me, "When I first started, I really liked the attention, but now it's just fun to do the show, and, yeah, I do get caught up in it. I like the holding power I have over people. I know how it is to feel left out, so I play to everyone. But I like people in their mid-thirties or older best. I don't like to entertain for these kids in their twenties. The gals back off when I try to drape a scarf around them. I think that's an insult." Now he is dancing around the edge of the crowd, reaching out to kiss the women, who respond to him with delight and good humor, and then he launches into what Mrs. Welling tells me is "You're a Devil in Disguise." I look at her, and she seems near tears. Her shoulders slump. "I don't like to watch," she says softly, and walks away to gather her family together for the trip home.

On my own way home, on the morning after the festival, I made one final stop in Vicksburg, on the south side of town, at what is left of Fraser's Grove. For about forty years—up until the early 1920s—Fraser's Grove was one of this country's premier spiritualist centers. In 1883, Mrs. John Fraser, the wife of a well-to-do Vicksburg merchant, turned the twenty-acre woodland into a camp and gathering place for mediums, believers in mediums, and the curious. She had been inspired by a lecture on spiritualism given in a hall on Prairie Street by one Mrs. R. S. Lily, of Cassadaga, New York, a town in the spiritually fervent "burned-over" district of that state. In the years that followed, Mrs. Fraser became a national figure in séance circles, and another resident of Vicksburg, C. E. Dent, was elected president of something called the Mediums' Protection Union. A group calling itself the Vicksburg Spiritualists was formed shortly after Mrs. Lily's visit, and it met each Sunday. Its Ladies' Auxiliary held monthly chicken dinners (fifteen cents a plate, two for a quarter). On summer Sunday afternoons, people from around this country and abroad packed the campground at Fraser's Grove to talk of materialization and reincarnation and watch mediums go into trances to contact the dead. According to a 1909 issue of the *Vicksburg Commercial,* they debated subjects such as "Is the planet on which we live approaching final destruction, or is it becoming more permanent?" (A follow-up article reports that the Spiritualists opted for permanency.)

Trees still stand in much of Fraser's Grove, although some of them have been cut down to make room for a small housing development. The campground itself has been taken over by the Christian Tabernacle, which makes use of the old camp buildings. Tazzie, my German shepherd, was with me, and I parked at the edge of the grove to let her out for a run before we drove onto the interstate highway. We headed down a dim path, where events passing strange are said to have taken place. The grove produced no Elvis, no John Vickers, not even a phantom band concert or the apparition of Mr. Matz—no spirits at all. But Tazzie did scare up a rabbit, and the oaks were still there, and, untamed through a hundred and fifty generations, so were the mosquitoes.

—1989

Learning from Other Writers

1. It is easy to mock people who believe that they have seen flying saucers, the Loch Ness Monster ... or Elvis. What tone does Hubbell take toward Louise Welling? The other citizens of Vicksburg?
2. What background information does Hubbell choose to include about Vicksburg and the surrounding area? What purpose does this information serve?
3. Why doesn't Hubbell interview Louise Welling as soon as she gets to Vicksburg? To whom does she speak before she visits Welling? What does each person add to Hubbell's investigation?
4. "Cecil Bagwell" is a wonderfully Dickensian name for the manager of a grocery store. How would you react if you were to learn that Hubbell had invented the name?
5. Find the statements that Welling and her neighbors employ to bolster the claim that Elvis never died and has in fact visited Vicksburg, Michigan. Does Hubbell analyze the logic behind these reasons? Why or why not?
6. What is Ray Kajkowski's role in Hubbell's essay?
7. What is the effect of ending the essay not with Welling's tearful remarks about Kajkowski's performance but with the scene at Fraser's Grover?

INSPIRATIONS: HITTING THE ROAD

1. Plan a pilgrimage to a site that holds some special meaning for you, or a quest to find or bring back some special object, or a journey to a place where you might find someone or something that will clear up a mystery whose resolution strikes you as important. (Your destination might be far away or around the corner; your journey might take an hour, a day, or all of Thanksgiving vacation.)
2. Jot down a tentative version of the question you hope to answer by going on this pilgrimage, quest, or journey.
3. Carry out your trip while taking notes on what you observe or experience along the way and meditations on possible answers to your question.
4. If necessary, refocus your essay's central question. Supplement any research you carried out on your journey with any further research you might need to do to answer your question.
5. Write an initial draft of your essay, using the pilgrimage, quest, or journey to structure your observations, discoveries, and meditations. Unless your preparations for your trip are somehow important, try to start as close as possible to the actual beginning of the journey; once you're underway, you can weave in background information if and when it seems relevant.

Beware the impulse to use this as an excuse to tell us about everything you did on spring break or during your junior year abroad. You probably didn't go to Cancun to answer a specific question, so your memories or diary entries won't lend themselves to answering such a question. And narrating a journey that's safely in the past won't allow you to convey an authentic sense of discovery. That said, if you are going to be traveling abroad in the near future, you certainly can use that trip as an opportunity to carry out the sort of journey, pilgrimage, or quest described in this Inspiration.

Mysteries and Investigations

As we saw in the previous chapter, one way to find the answer to a question is to go on a journey and conduct research along the way. Direct that journey toward a crime scene, take as your purpose investigating a murder, add a few side trips to interview witnesses and forensics experts, and the resulting piece of nonfiction might then steal its form from the mystery or detective novel (the classic example being Truman Capote's *In Cold Blood*, which was serialized in *The New Yorker* in 1965 and published by Random House as a book the following year).

Not feeling qualified to solve a murder? In his disturbing but insightful essay "My Favorite Teacher," Robert Kurson demonstrates that you can use the detective model to investigate other mysteries in your life—in Kurson's case, the author attempts to understand why he still admires a teacher who abducted, raped, and murdered several other teenage boys. As my colleague Miles Harvey put it, "My Favorite Teacher" is not a who-dunnit, but a why-dunnit, exhibiting a portrayal of teenage angst and self-loathing with which many of us can identify, as well as a masterfully drawn profile of the author and title character. (Miles's own book, *The Island of Lost Maps: A True Story of Cartographic Crime*, is a why-dunnit that keeps its readers turning pages to figure out what kind of person would devote his life to stealing rare maps ... and what kind of author would devote so much time to tracking down such a thief.)

Then there are the mysteries that don't involve a crime. An essay might describe a scientist's trip to the lab to search for a cure for a disease, or, as is true of the quirky case studies that comprise Oliver Sacks's *The Man Who Mistook His Wife for a Hat*, a doctor's attempts to unravel the conundrums of human consciousness. Although Sacks isn't the sort of doctor you would want to call in to operate on your brain—these days, he is more of a philosopher than a practitioner—his willingness to ponder and probe previously incomprehensible enigmas of medical science has deepened our understanding of what it means to be human.

And what's to stop a writer from turning his or her investigative skills toward the annoying little mysteries of everyday life, such as what happens to an e-mail message when it fails to reach its intended recipient (see "Your Mail Has Vanished" by Michael Specter in the December 6, 1999, issue of *The New Yorker*) or the age at which our taste in music or food becomes cemented forever ("Open Season" by Robert M. Sapolsky in the March 30, 1998, issue of the same magazine). In "Chromium," Primo Levi (who was a practicing chemist as well as a writer) uses a dinner debate as to the reasons that people are supposed to eat red wine with meat and white wine with fish as the impetus to inquire why so many of us ignore our common sense—and, at times, our basic decency—to follow traditions, rules, and orders, even though the consequences threaten to be disastrous.

Years ago, a freshman of mine at Iowa handed in an essay in which he attempted to figure out how he might increase the yield of soybeans on the few acres of land his father had allowed him to divert from the other crops on the family farm, the larger question being whether the author's insistence on attending college in the first place was a waste of money and time, as his father seemed to believe, or whether his education might yet turn out to be an asset in the family's struggle to save their farm. And in 2003, a record collector named Dori Hadar was sifting through boxes at a flea market when he came across a set of fake cardboard LPs with hand-painted covers, each album "intricately crafted with gatefold interiors, extensive liner notes, and grooves drawn into the 'vinyl.'" The albums seemed to be the work of a self-invented "soul superstar" named Mingering Mike. But who *was* Mingering Mike? And what inspired him to create not only a false identity as a musical genius who had "recorded over fifty albums, managed thirty five of his own record labels, and starred in nine of his own motion pictures" but also the physical documents and paraphernalia that such a career would leave behind? If you want to learn the answer, you can consult *Mingering Mike: The Amazing Career of an Imaginary Superstar*, the book that Hadar ended up writing about his discovery of the albums and his solution to the mystery of who had created them—and why.[1]

Sometimes, you don't even need to leave your house to find a mystery worth investigating. I grew up hearing my father's oft-repeated claim—which had been passed along to him by his best friend and tent mate in Calcutta during World War II—that the first Pahlavi Shah of Iran started life as a Russian Jew. When my father was in his eighties, I decided to press him for the details, then check the validity of the facts that might prove—or disprove—his claim and try to solve the mystery of what had happened to my father's friend after the war was over and the two men were shipped home to New York. Although I wasn't able to verify my father's theory, neither could I disprove it, and everything that I learned about the value of family legends more than justified my investigation. (The resulting essay, "The Jewish Shah," was published in the fall 2004 issue of *Fourth Genre*.)

Often, as was the case with my essay about my father, a writer's family history turns out to be entwined with the history of a larger group or a whole society. In "Fire," which was included in *The Best American Essays 2002*, Amy Kolen tries to reconcile her memories of the sweet, attentive grandma who served her soft-boiled eggs "in elegant porcelain heart-shaped egg cups" and praised her for using words like "magenta" or "irresistible" with the unrepentant apologist for the family's connection to the Triangle Shirtwaist Company, where the management's brutal disregard for the welfare of its workers led to the deaths of 146 people, most of them young immigrant women; in doing so, Kolen writes not only about her family but also about the relationship between immigration and labor in America.

[1] For the source of these quotations—and examples of the album covers—see www.mingeringmike.com, "the home of all things Mingering."

ROBERT KURSON

MY FAVORITE TEACHER

One night twenty years ago, my biology teacher picked up a seventeen-year-old hitchhiker named Jefferson Wesley.

Hitchhikers were rare on Chicago's exclusive North Shore, where kids owned Camaros and carried plenty of taxi cash. Even rarer were high school teachers who picked them up. It was midnight. Mr. Lindwall pulled over his yellow Toyota Land Cruiser and told Wesley to hop in.

Down the road, Mr. Lindwall stopped the Land Cruiser and asked Wesley to wait a second, the spare tire was rattling in back. Wesley said cool.

Mr. Lindwall shut off the headlights, exited the vehicle, and popped open the back hatch. Among a pile of tools, he found his hunting knife, which he unsheathed and poked at Wesley's back. He ordered the boy to bend over and locate the hangman's noose by his feet. Wesley found it and tightened it around his neck in the way Mr. Lindwall instructed.

My teacher climbed back into the driver's seat and explained: The seat belts in this jeep don't unfasten. Put your head between your legs. I'm going to tape your hands behind your back. This noose is attached to a series of pulleys. If you struggle, I can pull tight from here and control you.

Wesley now had good reason to believe he'd be killed. The son of a Chicago cop, he'd heard his share of stories, and in those stories kids wearing nooses didn't live.

2

Recently, I wrote a letter to Mr. Lindwall. It's been twenty years since we've seen each other, I said, but I remember you. I'd like to visit, to catch up and talk about our lives.

What I didn't tell Mr. Lindwall was that I'd never stopped thinking about him. While his name had become a sick punch line to anyone who had known him, I still admired him. And I needed to figure out why.

3

Northbrook, Illinois, happens to a person when life is good. The average home costs $340,000; 97 percent of the kids go to college; and when you buy groceries at Sunset Foods, crimson-vested valets scurry to load your car. Northbrook offers gazebos to its picnickers and electronic scoreboards to its Little Leaguers. Seniors who stroll the downtown's winding lanes enjoy handsome discounts on hand-dipped ice cream.

My family moved to Northbrook when I was fourteen. Fashionable welcome ladies helped me pronounce the name of my new street—Michelline Lane—and instructed me to celebrate my lucky transplant into Glenbrook North High School, the crown jewel in this gilded community and one of the top high schools in the country. My personal high school guidance counselor raved about Glenbrook North's high SAT scores and swimming-pool wing and plans for the multimillion-dollar Center for the Performing Arts. Kids who attend GBN, he said, turn out to be doctors, lawyers, CEOs; in short, adults worthy of living in Northbrook.

You've seen Glenbrook North before. Perhaps not in person but in near-documentary form in The Breakfast Club, Sixteen Candles, and Ferris Bueller's Day Off, the films based on the high school by director and Northbrook favorite son John Hughes (Glenbrook North, '68). Show up at Glenbrook North with the wrong folder, the wrong parents, the wrong nose, and you didn't just amuse students, you sickened them.

Feeling like an alien in high school of course did not make me unique, but it felt so at the time. Looking back, it seems like Glenbrook North decided up front to hate me. My

Afro was fucked. My voice was fucked. My clothes were fucked. Even my name—Rob, the most innocuous name on the planet—somehow was fucked. In class, on the bus, in Sunset Foods with my mom on Saturday, just the sight of me offended important students—and at Glenbrook North they were all important. They took to blurting "Rob!" into the air whenever I was around, turning the word into the latest euphemism for asshole. "You're such a Rob!" one girl squealed to another in the participation-counts algebra class I was flunking for fear of making a peep.

I would have given my life to become invisible at Glenbrook North, but at six three, with my gangly limbs and towering Dr. J. Afro sprawling in all directions, that was impossible.

And soon enough, I came around to Glenbrook North's way of thinking. At home, I'd pound the crap out of my little brother because he still thought my hair looked cool or because he continued to dub himself "the Kurs Jr.," in honor of my nickname from the days in the old neighborhood, where people had liked me. I told my mom to go to hell in front of frail relatives when she remarked at a family wedding that I looked handsome, because who can deal with a parent who's too stupid to see what a hundred rich kids can see so clearly every day in school—that I was as ugly as they came?

Against this backdrop appeared Mr. Lindwall, perhaps the only individual at Glenbrook North more out of place than I was. A giant, bearded bear of a man, Mr. Lindwall lived in a trailer, adored the outdoors, and walked apologetically, with shoulders hunched in, as I did. His potbelly was proof that he didn't belong to any of the many area health clubs, and his baggy pants made him look like a kid whose mom shopped outlet and never knew enough to iron. By all rights, GBN students should have eaten this science teacher alive, sent him and his rusty jeep and corny sweater-vests whimpering back to whatever the hell Yosemite National Redwood Sherwood Forest he crawled out from.

Instead, they embraced him, sensed something safe about him. Mr. Lindwall had an intuition about kids. Before learning names, he divined who required extra attention, who was hurting at home, who needed to call him Rick. He listened for underlying messages, and he understood that sometimes a question about amoebas was really a question about alienation.

Almost immediately, an impressed administration asked him to devote time to the school's "alternatives" program, Northbrook code for the outsider-druggie-loser program. To most teachers, it would have been a baby-sitting sentence. To Mr. Lindwall, it was a calling. In weeks, kids who had been thrown away by mom, by life, by Northbrook, were learning science for "Rick" and calling him the greatest teacher they'd ever had.

My first contact with Mr. Lindwall came in the training room during football season, where he taped athletes' ankles and worked out their aches after school. When I needed treatment, he taught me how to stretch to avoid shinsplints as if I actually fit in at Glenbrook North. And he did this despite my football teammates' obvious and noisy disdain for me—made it seem as if he didn't even hear them blurt out "Rob!" when I climbed onto the training table. Other athletes probably figured Mr. Lindwall's lack of eye contact to be his need to concentrate on their ailments. But I knew that downward stare. This was a man who ached with shame on the inside, who prayed that if he couldn't see you, you couldn't see him. That other people adored Mr. Lindwall made him my favorite teacher in the school, because if Mr. Lindwall could still be liked despite not liking himself, there was hope for me, too.

4

Able to manipulate the noose around Jefferson Wesley's neck from the driver's seat, Mr. Lindwall turned on the Land Cruiser's headlights, adjusted the AM radio, and pulled onto Route 120. His trailer home near Northbrook was just twenty miles away, but he zigzagged along side roads for more than an hour in order to disorient the boy.

Perhaps Wesley thought of his mother during this ride. He had hung up on her earlier that evening when she told him to stay where he was, not to walk home, she'd come get him. Or maybe he thought of his girlfriend, Donna, whom he'd seen that night. The couple had planned to attend her turnabout dance next week. They were in love.

The Land Cruiser pulled into the trailer park near Northbrook after 1:00 A.M., and Mr. Lindwall parked it flush against his unit's screen door. He stepped around to Wesley's side, opened the door, removed the noose, and placed a hood over his head. Using a screwdriver, he jimmied the rigged seat-belt buckle until the mechanism clicked. It took only moments to drag the boy backward, heels scraping, into the trailer home.

In the living room, Mr. Lindwall laid Wesley on his back, bound the boy's ankles with athletic tape, removed the hood, and taped his eyes shut. Then he asked Wesley questions. Do you have a girlfriend? Do you poke this girlfriend? Do you masturbate? Does it shoot out? Then Mr. Lindwall went into another room to find a screwdriver and some Vaseline.

5

During class one day in my sophomore year, Mr. Popular strutted into my face, preened for his sporto buddies, then announced in front of teachers and students that he'd received an "awesome" blow job from my sister. I punched him in the face and knocked him down. I was 210 pounds, he was no more than 130, and he was clearly beat. But I wasn't done. I kicked him in the face with my boot, not once, not twice, but maybe ten, twelve times while his hysterical friends screamed, "Uncool!" and he was bleeding and begging and microscopes were shattering. In this fog of fury and resentment, I might have killed the kid, but teachers locked on to my arms and pulled me off. Only later, in the dean's office, would I realize that I had been sobbing myself while administering this beating.

Mr. Lindwall, who had been teaching in an adjacent room, rushed over, settled a hand on my shoulder, and used his back to shield me from the jeering students; he couldn't abide them watching me cry.

"You're better than that," he said in a low voice. "You're better than them."

I was stunned. Here was an adult, a man everyone loved, whose instinct was to rush past the kid with the broken face to comfort the kid with the broken feelings. I was right about Mr. Lindwall, I thought as I was led away to the dean's office. He and I come from the same place. We recognize each other.

6

Mr. Lindwall undid Wesley's brown corduroys and pushed them to his ankles, then did the same with his own pants. He ordered Wesley to open his mouth, placed his penis inside, and told Wesley to fellate him. Wesley complied, but Mr. Lindwall could not climax; he withdrew his penis and began masturbating. Near climax, he put his penis back into Wesley's mouth and ejaculated. That done, Wesley pleaded, "That's enough, that's enough, please, no more, that's enough."

An hour passed. Mr. Lindwall tied a knot in a sock, stuffed it into Wesley's mouth, and taped the boy's lips shut. Mr. Lindwall rolled the boy onto his stomach and said, "I'm going to do anal intercourse to you now," but found that he could not maintain an erection, a disaster because Wesley might think him a neuter. Mr. Lindwall scooped out some Vaseline, smoothed it over the screwdriver handle, and dragged the tool over Wesley's buttocks, telling him, "Now I'm going to do it to you." He pushed the tip of the handle inside Wesley's anus and said, "Now I'm doing it to you." A moment later, he removed the tool and told Wesley he had changed his mind.

Mr. Lindwall pulled up the boy's pants and dragged him back into the Land Cruiser, where he fastened the seat belt and reaffixed the noose. All the while, he assured Wesley that he would be dropped off near home. Wesley trembled and shook. Mr. Lindwall put the hood over the boy's head and pulled the noose tight until Wesley's head was down between his knees. Mr. Lindwall started the Land Cruiser and zigzagged back toward Wesley's town.

Near Wesley's home, the boy began to mumble and struggle again. Mr. Lindwall pulled the noose tighter and told him to relax, they were almost there. But the mumbling continued, so Mr. Lindwall turned up the radio because the groans were disturbing him. Near Route 120, he pulled off the road to let the boy out. After removing Wesley's hood, Mr. Lindwall saw that the boy wasn't moving. He loosened the noose and heard the boy gurgle, but he knew the sounds were not words. Wesley was dead.

Mr. Lindwall executed a U-turn and drove back to his home, where he lugged Wesley's corpse to the rear bedroom, undressed and unbound it, then bent it into the fetal position before rigor mortis could set in. He bathed the body, covered it with a blanket, waited until daylight, then drove to the hardware store to buy heavy-duty garbage bags. When he returned, he stuffed the naked body into two of those bags until no skin showed, pushed the heap into the Land Cruiser, and set out for a Wisconsin campground. He dumped the body next to a tree. By Monday morning, he was back at Glenbrook North, teaching sophomores about mitosis.

7

A few weeks after Mr. Lindwall shielded me and told me that I was "better than them," he was charged with the kidnapping, sexual assault, and murder of Jefferson Wesley. He also was being investigated, newspapers said, for the kidnappings and sexual assaults of two other young men nearby. Rumors swirled about more possible victims, ten of them even, about foster children he'd molested and maybe other dead Lindwall bodies out there. "Mr. Lindwall has a toothache," teachers and administrators told students who showed up for his class the morning after his arrest. Then, eventually, they assured the dumbfounded kids that Mr. Lindwall was not anything like what he appeared. He was nothing like us.

8

After a few days, Mr. Lindwall answered my letter:

"I'll be happy to visit with you, Bob. Send me some of your recent writings so I can get a feel for the kind of man you turned out to be. Let's get together in a week. I look forward to it very much."

I shove the letter under a pile of bills in a bottom drawer. What am I looking for from this guy? Do I want him to tell me I'm a good boy? Do I need him to tell me that I wasn't as much of an asshole as all those kids in high school said I was? If so, I need more help than Mr. Lindwall can give me.

The letter stays buried in my drawer for a few days. Then I write back. "Dear Mr. Lindwall, tell me when and where to go. I look forward to seeing you, too."

9

To visit an inmate at the Joliet Correctional Center, that inmate must add your name to an approved visitors list. The process takes a few days. I spent those days investigating Mr. Lindwall's case. After all these years, I still didn't really know what had happened, whom he had killed and whom he hadn't, what was rumor and what was fact. I called classmates and teachers, some of whom I still despised, who told me about "Rick" as teacher and colleague. I read newspaper accounts and the lengthy trial transcript, including Mr. Lindwall's detailed confession and speech to the court before sentencing. For the first time since 1979, Mr. Lindwall returned to my life in three dimensions.

10

Rick Lindwall loved being a kid. If other ten-year-olds in suburban north Chicago in 1954 tempered their play with a rich-kid demurral, Rick was balls-out rough-and-tumble, a jumping bean with permanent scrapes on his elbows and knees who capped two-hour games of cowboys and Indians with mile-long swims.

Rick Lindwall loved being a kid until he was ten, when he contracted rheumatic fever and his life changed. The disease, which affects the heart, forced the boy to bed for a summer and caused him to miss eight weeks of sixth grade. For a cowboy who had slain thousands of Indians, this wasn't too much to handle. But soon after, other parts of his body betrayed him.

At age twelve, Rick developed breasts. Not just the folds of flesh you find on a fat kid, which he wasn't, but boobs, tits, the real thing. Around the same time, his penis began to shrink and his pubic hair stopped growing, until the horrified child began to wonder if he was still a boy. Rick ached to tell his parents but said nothing; he sensed that these developments had something to do with sex, and sex was taboo in the Lindwall home.

Rick managed to agonize silently for a time, but when his shame turned to despair he had to tell his parents. His father was unapproachable, a Milquetoast of a man too timid even to select a restaurant, so he confided in his mother, a domineering pants-wearer in a June Cleaver era. He begged her for help and told her he hated himself. She declared it a "general" problem and urged as much to the family doctor, who complied by treating the boy with shots and a pat on the back. When the breasts grew larger, Mom and Doc shrugged their shoulders; sure, there were still "bumps" under his sweaters, but listen, kids grow out of things, why ever bring it up again?

Nobody knew in 1956 that Rick Lindwall likely had something called Klinefelter's syndrome. People with this condition have an extra X chromosome and a jumble of sexual characteristics and are sexually sterile. A few injections of testosterone would have made Rick feel like a boy again, might have restored his masculine appearance, at least might have helped him withstand what was to come.

At school, Rick became choice locker-room fodder for boys whose own fresh pubic hair had infused them with newfound bravado. "Where's your bra?" "You're in the wrong class," they sing-songed in falsetto, pointing him to the girl's bathroom. It was in the locker room that Rick began to consider himself "God's mistake."

Through junior high and high school, Rick kept no friends and managed just a single date. Consumed by shame, he didn't dare allow anyone to know him, because you don't come across a neuter every day. He kept himself close to sports, which he loved, by becoming the high school's athletic trainer, the guy who tapes the football players. Inside the training room, he found himself captivated by physiques, and, here's the curious thing, not in a sexual way, because Rick still didn't know what sexual feelings were, didn't know they existed. He stared at the jocks to gather information about what he should have been.

At Ripon College in Wisconsin, Mr. Lindwall rushed Delta Upsilon. He hadn't made a friend since he was ten, but these guys liked him, actually wanted him. When he discovered that initiation included a Hell Week during which pledges removed their shirts, he quit. For the remainder of college and into the Air Force, peers ridiculed him mercilessly with the familiar "Where's your bra?" Had he not lucked into a medical discharge, he might have turned suicide in the Air Force. Instead, Mr. Lindwall became a teacher.

Northbrook Junior High was thrilled to get Mr. Lindwall. He was smart, knew his science, and didn't take himself too seriously. The administration believed him ideal for that toughest of junior high classes, sex education. Mr. Lindwall accepted the assignment with equanimity, then dashed to the bookstore to cram the basics. He was twenty-seven years old and had never even masturbated.

Kids at the junior high loved Mr. Lindwall, loved that he dug science the way they dug Led Zeppelin, loved the scientific but silly pictures he drew on their notebooks and arms.

They told their parents about him, sometimes so fervently that mom or dad would schedule an appointment just to thank him in person. All the while, he knew little about his subject. If a kid asked a technical question, he'd chuckle and suggest, "Let's check the book for that one!" If a student used sexual slang, he'd approach another teacher after school and ask, "How would you answer a kid who wants to know if you can get VD from eating a girl out?" caring little about the VD part but desperate to know what "eating out" meant.

Mr. Lindwall spent seven years teaching sex ed and science at Northbrook Junior High before getting the call to the big leagues, Glenbrook North High School. There, he impressed the administration as he had at the junior high, and soon he was teaching the bad kids in the "alternatives" program and prompting those freaks to issue their ultimate compliment, He's cool, but I actually learn shit. He also settled in as GBN's athletic trainer. Coaches loved the guy because he'd give anything for the team; they called him "Lindoo Can-Do," because what better nickname could you hang on a great guy who always said yes? After victories on the road, the coaches would invite Mr. Lindwall out to Tonelli's for pizza and beer, their treat, but he always took the rain check. In the hallways at Glenbrook North, students, staff, and janitors felt good about themselves when Mr. Lindwall smiled at them. But when they invited him to parties, Mr. Lindwall declined, because who knew if it might require removing your shirt? Or discussing dating. Folks got the message. In the nearly ten years Mr. Lindwall taught in Northbrook, only three people, family included, ever visited him at home.

II

A year and three weeks after Mr. Lindwall disposed of Jefferson Wesley, he picked up another late-night hitchhiker. Kelly Smith, eighteen, needed a lift to a tavern.

Mr. Lindwall's method was consistent—rattling tire, hunting knife, noose, tape, hood. His application this time, however, was unthorough. He taped Smith's wrists loosely, allowing the young man to stretch the binds during the circuitous ride back to the trailer.

Once inside, Mr. Lindwall didn't tape Smith's ankles. He forced him down face-first on the carpet, then exited the room, saying he needed to move his Land Cruiser. Smith, believing his execution to be imminent, worked a hand free from behind his back and flung off the hood and noose. He could now make out the figure of his captor outside the front door, so he scrambled for a rear exit. When he could find none, he rushed the front door and came face-to-face with Mr. Lindwall, who ordered him to stop.

Smith hurtled past him and into the trailer park's common area, banging on doors and shrieking, "Help! Help! Police!" Moments later, a squad car arrived and took the teenager to the Glenview police station, just two miles from Glenbrook North High School.

When Smith arrived at the station, he was startled to see Mr. Lindwall parking his Land Cruiser. Officers questioned Smith in the basement and made note of his appearance—white athletic tape around one sleeve of his blue windbreaker, inflamed wrists, three punctures in the back of the jacket. Smith told police his story.

Upstairs, Mr. Lindwall told a different version. He calmly explained that after he had picked up Smith, the two had decided to hit the bars and needed to return to the trailer for money. Inside, he had observed Smith stealing various items and naturally had chased the young man away.

When officers asked if they could search the Land Cruiser and the trailer home, Mr. Lindwall said, Of course—I am a respected member of the community and a teacher at Glenbrook North and I have nothing to hide. At his trailer home, Mr. Lindwall urged the police to look around and said, I want to get to the bottom of this as much as you do and I am a good person and a foster parent who takes in wayward boys.

The two officers worked from front to back. In the bedroom, one found a roll of film marked BOYS, which Mr. Lindwall said had been taken during a high school camping trip, and hundreds of snapshots of boys, which Mr. Lindwall said showed the same. On a kitchen chair, one officer found a rope inside a hood. The rope is for camping, Mr. Lindwall told them. Outside, with dawn breaking, one officer spotted a noose, a knife, and three rolls of athletic tape and asked Mr. Lindwall if he'd like to tell them what really happened.

12

By the time Mr. Lindwall reached trial in the summer of 1980, he was suicidal and had done everything in his power to convince the state to execute him. His confessions were detailed, his memory sharp, and his despair complete as he informed investigators of nine to twelve hitchhikers abducted and molested over the past three years. He advised his lawyers, "Don't work too hard for me; I just want to die."

The state charged Mr. Lindwall with the murder, aggravated kidnapping, and deviate sexual assault of Jefferson Wesley, plus the aggravated kidnappings of Kelly Smith and another young man. Dozens of other charges were put on hold to make the trial manageable.

Reporters shoved for position when opening arguments began Wednesday morning, July 16. Mr. Lindwall's mother and brother had visited with him before the proceedings, visited so loudly in fact that a sheriff's deputy found Judge James M. Bailey in chambers and told him, Sad story, Judge, I just overheard that man's family ask him why he doesn't do everyone a favor and just kill himself.

Mr. Lindwall drooped into court wearing a V-neck sweater-vest, the same style he'd worn countless times to cover his breasts at Glenbrook North, even during sweltering Indian-summer days. During the weeklong trial, witnesses would continue to identify Mr. Lindwall in court by pointing to "the man over there in the tan sweater-vest." For his part, Mr. Lindwall would spend most of the trial with his head in his hands.

The state's case was cinematic and lurid. The other young man told of trick seat belts and nooses and an abduction in which he was masturbated by Mr. Lindwall four times over twelve hours, with respite only when Mr. Lindwall retired to another room to watch the Bears game on TV. Prosecutors dragged the seat from Mr. Lindwall's Land Cruiser into the courtroom, and Kelly Smith climbed in, fastened the inescapable seat belt, slipped the noose around his neck, and allowed lawyers to poke at him with a knife the way Mr. Lindwall had. Smith identified for the jury the athletic tape, the hood, the noose that still bore his gnaw marks. The state's psychiatrist swore Mr. Lindwall was sane.

The public defender called Mr. Lindwall's mother, who testified to her son's boyhood days and his loose-fitting shirts and get-out-of-gym notes. Among the character witnesses from the Glenbrook North faculty was the head of the science department, who averred his teacher's sterling character and reputation. The defense psychiatrist declared Mr. Lindwall insane.

Mr. Lindwall testified, too. He swore that he molested boys not for sexual thrills but to process what they "had," to watch their penises "get real hard and point up toward their heads" while his wouldn't, to watch theirs "spurt out" because his didn't. He claimed to abduct boys only on weekends because he didn't want to upset their weekly routine, they were in school. He insisted that he had never been homosexual and never meant to kill Jefferson Wesley. Such claims were routine and always false inside the Cook County Courthouse, but from the melancholy and self-incriminating Mr. Lindwall, they rang true. Medical witnesses agreed that Wesley's death was most likely accidental.

The jury took two hours to convict Mr. Lindwall on all counts. The next morning, headlines blared from the Chicago daily newspapers, and the city wanted blood. Sensing that the judge had been moved by Mr. Lindwall's story, his lawyer opted to have Bailey decide the sentence rather than the jury. Mr. Lindwall would be allowed to address the court first.

"I have the life of Jefferson Wesley on my conscience, and that's something that will stay there until I die. I would publicly like to apologize to his parents for the terror and grief, the suffering I've put them through. And to the other young men who have had the misfortune of crossing my path, I also apologize and hope that the scars that may remain will soon disappear.

"I am not looking for sympathy, nor am I offering excuses. I believe those of you who knew me deserve an explanation. I also believe there is something to be learned from all that has occurred."

Mr. Lindwall described his boyhood, the cruelty he endured as his body changed, and the impossibility of living as a neuter, as God's mistake. He expressed relief that he had been stopped when he had.

"In closing, if any of you have a problem which hurts you to the point of altering how you feel about yourselves, for God's sake don't keep it to yourself. Don't get trapped into believing that no one can help. If the first person you go to does not ease your concerns, then try someone else. Whatever you do, don't surrender to your problem.

"Nothing I say can bring back Jefferson Wesley, or get rid of all the pain and suffering I've caused. But, God, don't let it happen to somebody else."

While Mr. Lindwall spoke, Judge Bailey scratched these notes into his oversized notebook: "He lived a good life." "No prior criminal record." "Bizarre case." Then he announced to the courtroom, "I must say, the defendant is a very unusual one as far as this court is concerned. In ten years as a judge here and four years as a federal prosecutor, you come across very few defendants like this one. ... Considering the factors involved here, I have no alternative but to sentence the defendant to the Illinois penitentiary on the murder charge for natural life without parole, and sixty years on the other charges, all to run concurrent. That's it."

Expressionless, Mr. Lindwall gathered his papers just as he had after biology class, waited a moment to make sure no one needed him, then disappeared into the Illinois penal system. He was thirty-six years old.

13

I'm thirty-six years old. Today, I go to see Mr. Lindwall.

The mustard stone walls at the Joliet Correctional Center have stood sentry over 140 years of broken men. The prison, landscaped in pillowy bales of barbed wire, will hold Mr. Lindwall until he dies.

At the sign-in counter, a guard checks a list for my name and informs me that, whoa, the dude I'm here to see never gets any visitors. He points me to a locker for my belongings, then searches me in a no-man's holding zone to make sure I'm not stashing anything in my hair or between my toes—visitors are not allowed to bring anything, not even a pencil, into a visit. I'm moved to a waiting area that sells ice cream sandwiches and Joliet Correctional Center T-shirts, then stamped on the hand with an ultraviolet blotch and led through two sets of iron doors and into the visiting room.

I search for the bushy-bearded, 240-pound teacher, but he's not among the tattooed convicts, their weary-faced women, or yelping kids. Only one man sits alone in this room, but he's got a neatly trimmed gray beard and weighs no more than 160 pounds. He wears his prison-issue blue shirt looser than the other prisoners, and he has kind eyes. Mr. Lindwall and I shake hands.

He apologizes for not remembering me. I'm nervous and can only muster a dopey "Wow, you look great." He says he's in the best shape of his life, jogs every day and lifts weights like this, he says, hoisting two invisible dumbbells and grinning. We sit on bolted-down stools at opposite ends of a pizza-sized table. He fills me in on the incidentals of his everyday life. His day always begins with a hot chocolate, then six hours of laundry folding before working crossword puzzles, the harder the better. He resents Oprah for asking guests, "How did that make you feel?" since he's discovered that nothing "makes" you feel any way—you decide how to feel.

Mr. Lindwall is polite and gracious, but then he turns to me. Why are you interested in me? he asks. For a moment, I strain to recapture the sophisticated explanations I'd rehearsed in the car. Instead, I blurt out, "Was I wrong to like you?"

"You weren't wrong," he says after long consideration. "I was a good teacher and sometimes I was a good person. I did a lot of good things. But I led two separate lives."

"Why did you do it?" I ask.

And then he begins telling me about his crimes.

"I'm not homosexual. These weren't sex crimes. I did them to ... satisfy my curiosity," he says. "The newspapers said that I never touched any of my foster children. Well, that's not true. And I did other ... things ..., that didn't, let's say, come out completely. If you think someone like me starts committing crimes when he's thirty-one, you're wrong. These things go back a long, long way.

"Did you know I had already resigned from Glenbrook North before I got caught? I did that because I was going to hurt my own students. The things I was doing weren't satisfying me anymore. I knew I was going to take things to... another level. If I hadn't been caught, I would have turned into another Gacy. No. I was going to live as a hermit, and I would have been worse than Gacy."

Mr. Lindwall asks if I remember his trial. I tell him that I'd read the papers and, like everyone else, admired his speech to the court.

"That speech was bullshit," Mr. Lindwall says softly. "I remember believing it at the time—I'm not saying I purposely lied. But I had no feeling for my victims, nothing. It took me years in here before I felt anything for victims, mine or anyone else's.

"Remember Sporto Hall? I remember once, this very sensitive kid walked down Sporto Hall and the jocks were merciless, teasing him, and when this guy came back he was in tears. I embraced him, tried to comfort him. I felt so bad for the kid, I just wanted to ease his pain. But even then, at the very moment I was comforting him, I also wanted to hurt him."

After a while, a guard pokes me and says time's up. Mr. Lindwall apologizes for focusing so much on his crimes and says that he'd like me to come back, so perhaps we can get to know each other better. I am a little disoriented and react by trying to buy him a Mountain Dew for the road. He smiles and says, No thanks, it's not allowed. Mr. Lindwall shakes my hand as I leave. "I feel like you came here for a reason," he says. "I'm not very religious, so I don't mean this religiously. But I feel like you showed up, I mean right now, at this time, for a purpose. I don't know the purpose, but I appreciate it."

In the parking lot, I scribble out notes:

"Smart. Articulate. Soft voice. Honest."

"Was about to hurt own students."

"Says he was ready to become serial killer, worse than Gacy."

"Other crimes no one knows about."

"Remembers wanting to comfort—but also hurt—'sensitive' kid in GBN hallway."

"Still a good guy."

I'm numb as I pull onto the snowy expressway, back to Northbrook, the place I despised, so of course it's where I now live, and I'm wondering what I have discovered about

Mr. Lindwall. Wondering if this is finally over for me. My mind is full and racing, skimming across the surface of the experience like a smooth stone. Is it possible to reconcile fond feelings for someone who had been such a positive influence yet had turned out to be capable of such evil? It happens all the time, I suppose—adults in positions of responsibility betraying impressionable children, sometimes much worse. How is a kid supposed to process that? And I'm driving and thinking about our conversation, about his laundry detail and Oprah and undiscovered crimes and crimes that had been planned and not executed, combing, combing for clues. And then suddenly, halfway between prison and home, I take my foot off the accelerator and the car drifts slowly over to the icy shoulder.

"Still a good guy."

Eighteen-wheelers blast by, sending up the snow in a dirty swirl, as I sit there staring straight ahead, engine running. I'm thinking about the sensitive student Mr. Lindwall had comforted yet wanted to hurt.

And I know that Mr. Lindwall was talking about me.

—2000

Learning from Other Writers

1. What are the effects of Kurson's choice to open his essay with an account of Mr. Lindwall's abduction of Jefferson Wesley? Why start there, rather than with a scene that depicts his own relationship with his teacher?
2. Where does the author present the reasons he decided to investigate his former teacher's crimes?
3. From section 4 onward, what is the basic structure of Kurson's essay?
4. The details of Lindwall's crimes against Jefferson Wesley are gruesome and disturbing. Could the author have omitted some or all of these details? What can you say about the language and tone Kurson uses to describe Wesley's ordeal? How do you think Kurson learned of these details, given that the victim died?
5. What role does the detailed description of Lindwall's childhood and adolescence play in this essay? How might Kurson have learned so much about his teacher's life before Lindwall came to teach at Glenbrook North?
6. How might you have responded to this essay if the author hadn't visited his former teacher at the Joliet Correctional Center? Why does Kurson include his scribbled notes?
7. Look at the author's meditations in the last four paragraphs of the essay. Has he figured out why his teacher committed the crimes he committed? Has he figured out why he continued to admire his teacher for so many years, despite his knowledge of Lindwall's crimes? Does Kurson *still* admire Mr. Lindwall? Why or why not?

OLIVER SACKS

THE MAN WHO MISTOOK HIS WIFE FOR A HAT

Dr P. was a musician of distinction, well-known for many years as a singer, and then, at the local School of Music, as a teacher. It was here, in relation to his students, that certain strange problems were first observed. Sometimes a student would present himself, and Dr P. would not recognise him; or, specifically, would not recognise his face. The moment the student spoke, he would be recognised by his voice. Such incidents multiplied, causing embarrassment, perplexity, fear—and, sometimes, comedy. For not only did Dr P. increasingly fail to see faces, but he saw faces when there were no faces to see: genially, Magoo-like, when in the street he might pat the heads of water hydrants and parking meters, taking these to be the heads of children; he would amiably address carved knobs on the furniture and be astounded when they did not reply. At first these odd mistakes were laughed off as jokes, not least by Dr P. himself. Had he not always had a quirky sense of humour and been given to Zen-like paradoxes and jests? His musical powers were as dazzling as ever; he did not feel ill—he had never felt better; and the mistakes were so ludicrous—and so ingenious—that they could hardly be serious or betoken anything serious. The notion of there being 'something the matter' did not emerge until some three years later, when diabetes developed. Well aware that diabetes could affect his eyes, Dr P. consulted an ophthalmologist, who took a careful history and examined his eyes closely. 'There's nothing the matter with your eyes,' the doctor concluded. 'But there is trouble with the visual parts of your brain. You don't need my help, you must see a neurologist.' And so, as a result of this referral, Dr P. came to me.

It was obvious within a few seconds of meeting him that there was no trace of dementia in the ordinary sense. He was a man of great cultivation and charm who talked well and fluently, with imagination and humour. I couldn't think why he had been referred to our clinic.

And yet there *was* something a bit odd. He faced me as he spoke, was oriented towards me, and yet there was something the matter—it was difficult to formulate. He faced me with his *ears*, I came to think, but not with his eyes. These, instead of looking, gazing, at me, 'taking me in', in the normal way, made sudden strange fixations—on my nose, on my right ear, down to my chin, up to my right eye—as if noting (even studying) these individual features, but not seeing my whole face, its changing expressions, 'me', as a whole. I am not sure that I fully realised this at the time—there was just a teasing strangeness, some failure in the normal interplay of gaze and expression. He saw me, he *scanned* me, and yet...

'What seems to be the matter?' I asked him at length.

'Nothing that I know of,' he replied with a smile, 'but people seem to think there's something wrong with my eyes.'

'But *you* don't recognise any visual problems?'

'No, not directly, but I occasionally make mistakes.'

I left the room briefly to talk to his wife. When I came back, Dr P. was sitting placidly by the window, attentive, listening rather than looking out. 'Traffic,' he said, 'street sounds, distant trains—they make a sort of symphony, do they not? You know Honegger's *Pacific 234*?'

What a lovely man, I thought to myself. How can there be anything seriously the matter? Would he permit me to examine him?

'Yes, of course, Dr Sacks.'

I stilled my disquiet, his perhaps, too, in the soothing routine of a neurological exam—muscle strength, coordination, reflexes, tone.... It was while examining his reflexes—a trifle abnormal on the left side—that the first bizarre experience occurred. I had taken off his left shoe and scratched the sole of his foot with a key—a frivolous-seeming but essential test of a reflex—and then, excusing myself to screw my ophthalmoscope together, left him to put on the shoe himself. To my surprise, a minute later, he had not done this.

'Can I help?' I asked.

'Help what? Help whom?'

'Help you put on your shoe.'

'Ach,' he said, 'I had forgotten the shoe,' adding, *sotto voce*. 'The shoe? The shoe?' He seemed baffled.

'Your shoe,' I repeated. 'Perhaps you'd put it on.'

He continued to look downwards, though not at the shoe, with an intense but misplaced concentration. Finally his gaze settled on his foot: 'That is my shoe, yes?'

Did I mis-hear? Did he mis-see?

'My eyes,' he explained, and put a hand to his foot. '*This* is my shoe, no?'

'No, it is not. That is your foot. *There* is your shoe.'

'Ah! I thought that was my foot.'

Was he joking? Was he mad? Was he blind? If this was one of his 'strange mistakes', it was the strangest mistake I had ever come across.

I helped him on with his shoe (his foot), to avoid further complication. Dr P. himself seemed untroubled, indifferent, maybe amused. I resumed my examination. His visual acuity was good: he had no difficulty seeing a pin on the floor, though sometimes he missed it if it was placed to his left.

He saw all right, but what did he see? I opened out a copy of the *National Geographic Magazine* and asked him to describe some pictures in it.

His responses here were very curious. His eyes would dart from one thing to another, picking up tiny features, individual features, as they had done with my face. A striking brightness, a colour, a shape would arrest his attention and elicit comment—but in no case did he get the scene-as-a-whole. He failed to see the whole, seeing only details, which he spotted like blips on a radar screen. He never entered into relation with the picture as a whole—never faced, so to speak, *its* physiognomy. He had no sense whatever of a landscape or scene.

I showed him the cover, an unbroken expanse of Sahara dunes.

'What do you see here?' I asked.

'I see a river,' he said. 'And a little guest-house with its terrace on the water. People are dining out on the terrace. I see coloured parasols here and there.' He was looking, if it was 'looking', right off the cover into mid-air and confabulating nonexistent features, as if the absence of features in the actual picture had driven him to imagine the river and the terrace and the coloured parasols.

I must have looked aghast, but he seemed to think he had done rather well. There was a hint of a smile on his face. He also appeared to have decided that the examination was over and started to look around for his hat. He reached out his hand and took hold of his wife's head, tried to lift it off, to put it on. He had apparently mistaken his wife for a hat! His wife looked as if she was used to such things.

I could make no sense of what had occurred in terms of conventional neurology (or neuropsychology). In some ways he seemed perfectly preserved, and in others absolutely, incomprehensibly devastated. How could he, on the one hand, mistake his wife for a hat and, on the other, function, as apparently he still did, as a teacher at the Music School?

I had to think, to see him again—and to see him in his own familiar habitat, at home.

A few days later I called on Dr P. and his wife at home, with the score of the *Dichterliebe* in my briefcase (I knew he liked Schumann), and a variety of odd objects for the testing of perception. Mrs P. showed me into a lofty apartment, which recalled fin-de-siècle Berlin. A magnificent old Bösendorfer stood in state in the centre of the room, and all around it were music stands, instruments, scores.... There were books, there were paintings, but the music was central. Dr P. came in, a little bowed, and, distracted, advanced with outstretched hand to the grandfather clock, but, hearing my voice, corrected himself, and shook hands with me. We exchanged greetings and chatted a little of current concerts and performances. Diffidently, I asked him if he would sing.

'The *Dichterliebe!*' he exclaimed. 'But I can no longer read music. You will play them, yes?'

I said I would try. On that wonderful old piano even my playing sounded right, and Dr P. was an aged but infinitely mellow Fischer-Dieskau, combining a perfect ear and voice with the most incisive musical intelligence. It was clear that the Music School was not keeping him on out of charity.

Dr P.'s temporal lobes were obviously intact: he had a wonderful musical cortex. What, I wondered, was going on in his parietal and occipital lobes, especially in those areas where visual processing occurred? I carry the Platonic solids in my neurological kit and decided to start with these.

'What is this?' I asked, drawing out the first one.

'A cube, of course.'

'Now this?' I asked, brandishing another.

He asked if he might examine it, which he did swiftly and systematically: 'A dodecahedron, of course. And don't bother with the others—I'll get the icosahedron, too.'

Abstract shapes clearly presented no problems. What about faces? I took out a pack of cards. All of these he identified instantly, including the jacks, queens, kings, and the joker. But these, after all, are stylised designs, and it was impossible to tell whether he saw faces or merely patterns. I decided I would show him a volume of cartoons which I had in my briefcase. Here, again, for the most part, he did well. Churchill's cigar, Schnozzle's nose: as soon as he had picked out a key feature he could identify the face. But cartoons, again, are formal and schematic. It remained to be seen how he would do with real faces, realistically represented.

I turned on the television, keeping the sound off, and found an early Bette Davis film. A love scene was in progress. Dr P. failed to identify the actress—but this could have been because she had never entered his world. What was more striking was that he failed to identify the expressions on her face or her partner's, though in the course of a single torrid scene these passed from sultry yearning through passion, surprise, disgust, and fury to a melting reconciliation. Dr P. could make nothing of any of this. He was very unclear as to what was going on, or who was who or even what sex they were. His comments on the scene were positively Martian.

It was just possible that some of his difficulties were associated with the unreality of a celluloid, Hollywood world; and it occurred to me that he might be more successful in identifying faces from his own life. On the walls of the apartment there were photographs of his family, his colleagues, his pupils, himself. I gathered a pile of these together and, with some misgivings, presented them to him. What had been funny, or farcical, in relation to the movie, was tragic in relation to real life. By and large, he recognised nobody: neither his family, nor his colleagues, nor his pupils, nor himself. He recognised a portrait of Einstein because he picked up the characteristic hair and moustache; and the same thing happened with one or two other people. 'Ach, Paul!' he said, when shown a portrait of his brother. 'That square jaw, those big teeth—I would know Paul anywhere!' But was it Paul he recognised, or one or two of his features, on the basis of which he could make a reasonable guess as to the subject's identity? In the absence of obvious 'markers', he was utterly lost. But it was not merely the cognition, the *gnosis*, at fault; there was something radically wrong with the whole way he proceeded. For he approached these faces—even of those near and dear—as if they were abstract puzzles or tests. He did not relate to them, he did not behold. No face was familiar to him, seen as a 'thou', being just identified as a set of features, an 'it'. Thus, there was formal, but no trace of personal, gnosis. And with this went his indifference, or blindness, to expression. A face, to us, is a person looking out—we see, as it were, the person through his *persona*, his face. But for Dr P. there was no *persona* in this sense—no outward *persona*, and no person within.

I had stopped at a florist on my way to his apartment and bought myself an extravagant red rose for my buttonhole. Now I removed this and handed it to him. He took it like a botanist or morphologist given a specimen, not like a person given a flower.

'About six inches in length,' he commented. 'A convoluted red form with a linear green attachment.'

'Yes,' I said encouragingly, 'and what do you think it *is*, Dr P.?'

'Not easy to say.' He seemed perplexed. 'It lacks the simple symmetry of the Platonic solids, although it may have a higher symmetry of its own.... I think this could be an inflorescence or flower.'

'Could be?' I queried.

'Could be,' he confirmed.

'Smell it,' I suggested, and he again looked somewhat puzzled, as if I had asked him to smell a higher symmetry. But he complied courteously, and took it to his nose. Now, suddenly, he came to life.

'Beautiful!' he exclaimed. 'An early rose. What a heavenly smell!' He started to hum '*Die Rose, die Lillie...*' Reality, it seemed, might be conveyed by smell, not by sight.

I tried one final test. It was still a cold day, in early spring, and I had thrown my coat and gloves on the sofa.

'What is this?' I asked, holding up a glove.

'May I examine it?' he asked, and, taking it from me, he proceeded to examine it as he had examined the geometrical shapes.

'A continuous surface,' he announced at last, 'infolded on itself. It appears to have'—he hesitated—'five outpouchings, if this is the word.'

'Yes,' I said cautiously. 'You have given me a description. Now tell me what it is.'

'A container of some sort?'

'Yes,' I said, 'and what would it contain?'

'It would contain its contents!' said Dr P., with a laugh. There are many possibilities. It could be a change purse, for example, for coins of five sizes. It could...'

I interrupted the barmy flow. 'Does it not look familiar? Do you think it might contain, might fit, a part of your body?'

No light of recognition dawned on his face.*

No child would have the power to see and speak of 'a continuous surface ... infolded on itself,' but any child, any infant, would immediately know a glove as a glove, see it as familiar, as going with a hand. Dr P. didn't. He saw nothing as familiar. Visually, he was lost in a world of lifeless abstractions. Indeed, he did not have a real visual world, as he did not have a real visual self. He could speak about things, but did not see them face-to-face. Hughlings Jackson, discussing patients with aphasia and left-hemisphere lesions, says they have lost 'abstract' and 'propositional' thought—and compares them with dogs (or, rather, he compares dogs to patients with aphasia). Dr P., on the other hand, functioned precisely as a machine functions. It wasn't merely that he displayed the same indifference to the visual world as a computer but—even more strikingly—he construed the world as a computer construes it, by means of key features and schematic relationships. The scheme might be identified—in an 'identi-kit' way—without the reality being grasped at all.

The testing I had done so far told me nothing about Dr P.'s inner world. Was it possible that his visual memory and imagination were still intact? I asked him to imagine

---

* Later, by accident, he got it on, and exclaimed, 'My God. It's a glove!' This was reminiscent of Kurt Goldstein's patient 'Lanuti', who could only recognise objects by trying to use them in action.

entering one of our local squares from the north side, to walk through it, in imagination or in memory, and tell me the buildings he might pass as he walked. He listed the buildings on his right side, but none of those on his left. I then asked him to imagine entering the square from the south. Again he mentioned only those buildings that were on the right side, although these were the very buildings he had omitted before. Those he had 'seen' internally before were not mentioned now; presumably, they were no longer 'seen'. It was evident that his difficulties with leftness, his visual field deficits, were as much internal as external, bisecting his visual memory and imagination.

What, at a higher level, of his internal visualisation? Thinking of the almost hallucinatory intensity with which Tolstoy visualises and animates his characters, I questioned Dr P. about *Anna Karenina*. He could remember incidents without difficulty, had an undiminished grasp of the plot, but completely omitted visual characteristics, visual narrative, and scenes. He remembered the words of the characters but not their faces; and though, when asked, he could quote, with his remarkable and almost verbatim memory, the original visual descriptions, these were, it became apparent, quite empty for him and lacked sensorial, imaginal, or emotional reality. Thus, there was an internal agnosia as well.[†]

But this was only the case, it became clear, with certain sorts of visualisation. The visualisation of faces and scenes, of visual narrative and drama—this was profoundly impaired, almost absent. But the visualisation of *schemata* was preserved, perhaps enhanced. Thus, when I engaged him in a game of mental chess, he had no difficulty visualising the chessboard or the moves—indeed, no difficulty in beating me soundly.

Luria said of Zazetsky that he had entirely lost his capacity to play games but that his 'vivid imagination' was unimpaired. Zazetsky and Dr P. lived in worlds which were mirror images of each other. But the saddest difference between them was that Zazetsky, as Luria said, 'fought to regain his lost faculties with the indomitable tenacity of the damned,' whereas Dr P. was not fighting, did not know what was lost, did not indeed know that anything was lost. But who was more tragic, or who was more damned—the man who knew it, or the man who did not?

When the examination was over, Mrs P. called us to the table, where there was coffee and a delicious spread of little cakes. Hungrily, hummingly, Dr P. started on the cakes. Swiftly, fluently, unthinkingly, melodiously, he pulled the plates towards him and took this and that in a great gurgling stream, an edible song of food, until, suddenly, there came an interruption: a loud, peremptory rat-tat-tat at the door. Startled, taken aback, arrested by the interruption, Dr P. stopped eating and sat frozen, motionless, at the table, with an indifferent, blind bewilderment on his face. He saw, but no longer saw, the table; no longer perceived it as a table laden with cakes. His wife poured him some coffee: the smell titillated his nose and brought him back to reality. The melody of eating resumed.

How does he do anything? I wondered to myself. What happens when he's dressing, goes to the lavatory, has a bath? I followed his wife into the kitchen and asked her how, for instance, he managed to dress himself. 'It's just like the eating,' she explained. 'I put his usual clothes out, in all the usual places, and he dresses without difficulty, singing to himself. He does everything singing to himself. But if he is interrupted and loses the thread, he comes to a complete

† I have often wondered about Helen Keller's visual descriptions, whether these, for all their eloquence, are somehow empty as well? Or whether, by the transference of images from the tactile to the visual, or, yet more extraordinarily, from the verbal and the metaphorical to the sensorial and the visual, she *did* achieve a power of visual imagery, even though her visual cortex had never been stimulated, directly, by the eyes? But in Dr P.'s case it is precisely the cortex that was damaged, the organic prerequisite of all pictorial imagery. Interestingly and typically he no longer dreamed pictorially—the 'message' of the dream being conveyed in nonvisual terms.

stop, doesn't know his clothes—or his own body. He sings all the time—eating songs, dressing songs, bathing songs, everything. He can't do anything unless he makes it a song.'

While we were talking my attention was caught by the pictures on the walls.

'Yes,' Mrs P. said, 'he was a gifted painter as well as a singer. The School exhibited his pictures every year.'

I strolled past them curiously—they were in chronological order. All his earlier work was naturalistic and realistic, with vivid mood and atmosphere, but finely detailed and concrete. Then, years later, they became less vivid, less concrete, less realistic and naturalistic, but far more abstract, even geometrical and cubist. Finally, in the last paintings, the canvasses became nonsense, or nonsense to me—mere chaotic lines and blotches of paint. I commented on this to Mrs P.

'Ach, you doctors, you're such Philistines!' she exclaimed. 'Can you not see *artistic development*—how he renounced the realism of his earlier years, and advanced into abstract, nonrepresentational art?'

'No, that's not it,' I said to myself (but forbore to say it to poor Mrs P.). He had indeed moved from realism to nonrepresentation to the abstract, yet this was not the artist, but the pathology, advancing—advancing towards a profound visual agnosia, in which all powers of representation and imagery, all sense of the concrete, all sense of reality, were being destroyed. This wall of paintings was a tragic pathological exhibit, which belonged to neurology, not art.

And yet, I wondered, was she not partly right? For there is often a struggle, and sometimes, even more interestingly, a collusion between the powers of pathology and creation. Perhaps, in his cubist period, there might have been both artistic and pathological development, colluding to engender an original form; for as he lost the concrete, so he might have gained in the abstract, developing a greater sensitivity to all the structural elements of line, boundary, contour—an almost Picasso-like power to see, and equally depict, those abstract organisations embedded in, and normally lost in, the concrete.... Though in the final pictures, I feared, there was only chaos and agnosia.

We returned to the great music room, with the Bösendorfer in the centre, and Dr P. humming the last torte.

'Well, Dr Sacks,' he said to me. 'You find me an interesting case, I perceive. Can you tell me what you find wrong, make recommendations?'

'I can't tell you what I find wrong,' I replied, 'but I'll say what I find right. You are a wonderful musician, and music is your life. What I would prescribe, in a case such as yours, is a life which consists entirely of music. Music has been the centre, now make it the whole, of your life.'

This was four years ago—I never saw him again, but I often wondered about how he apprehended the world, given his strange loss of image, visuality, and the perfect preservation of a great musicality. I think that music, for him, had taken the place of image. He had no body-image, he had body-music: this is why he could move and act as fluently as he did, but came to a total confused stop if the 'inner music' stopped. And equally with the outside, the world...‡

In *The World as Representation and Will*, Schopenhauer speaks of music as 'pure will'. How fascinated he would have been by Dr P., a man who had wholly lost the world as representation, but wholly preserved it as music or will.

‡ Thus, as I learned later from his wife, though he could not recognise his students if they sat still, if they were merely 'images', he might suddenly recognise them if they *moved*. 'That's Karl,' he would cry. 'I know his movements, his body-music.'

And this, mercifully, held to the end—for despite the gradual advance of his disease (a massive tumour or degenerative process in the visual parts of his brain) Dr P. lived and taught music to the last days of his life.

Postscript

How should one interpret Dr P.'s peculiar inability to interpret, to judge, a glove as a glove? Manifestly, here, he could not make a cognitive judgment, though he was prolific in the production of cognitive hypotheses. A judgment is intuitive, personal, comprehensive, and concrete—we 'see' how things stand, in relation to one another and oneself. It was precisely this setting, this relating, that Dr P. lacked (though his judging, in all other spheres, was prompt and normal). Was this due to lack of visual information, or faulty processing of visual information? (This would be the explanation given by a classical, schematic neurology.) Or was there something amiss in Dr P.'s attitude, so that he could not relate what he saw to himself?

These explanations, or modes of explanation, are not mutually exclusive—being in different modes they could coexist and both be true. And this is acknowledged, implicitly or explicitly, in classical neurology: implicitly, by Macrae, when he finds the explanation of defective schemata, or defective visual processing and integration, inadequate; explicitly, by Goldstein, when he speaks of 'abstract attitude'. But abstract attitude, which allows 'categorisation', also misses the mark with Dr P.—and, perhaps, with the concept of 'judgment' in general. For Dr P. *had* abstract attitude—indeed, nothing else. And it was precisely this, his absurd abstractness of attitude—absurd because unleavened with anything else—which rendered him incapable of perceiving identity, or particulars, rendered him incapable of judgment.

Neurology and psychology, curiously, though they talk of everything else, almost never talk of 'judgment'—and yet it is precisely the downfall of judgment (whether in specific realms, as with Dr P., or more generally, as in patients with Korsakov's or frontal-lobe syndromes—see below, Chapters Twelve and Thirteen) which constitutes the essence of so many neuropsychological disorders. Judgment and identity may be casualties—but neuropsychology never speaks of them.

And yet, whether in a philosophic sense (Kant's sense), or an empirical and evolutionary sense, judgment is the most important faculty we have. An animal, or a man, may get on very well without 'abstract attitude' but will speedily perish if deprived of judgment. Judgment must be the *first* faculty of higher life or mind—yet it is ignored, or misinterpreted, by classical (computational) neurology. And if we wonder how such an absurdity can arise, we find it in the assumptions, or the evolution, of neurology itself. For classical neurology (like classical physics) has always been mechanical—from Hughlings Jackson's mechanical analogies to the computer analogies of today.

Of course, the brain *is* a machine and a computer—everything in classical neurology is correct. But our mental processes, which constitute our being and life, are not just abstract and mechanical, but personal, as well—and, as such, involve not just classifying and categorising, but continual judging and feeling also. If this is missing, we become computer-like, as Dr P. was. And, by the same token, if we delete feeling and judging, the personal, from the cognitive sciences, we reduce *them* to something as defective as Dr P.—and we reduce *our* apprehension of the concrete and real.

By a sort of comic and awful analogy, our current cognitive neurology and psychology resemble nothing so much as poor Dr P.! We need the concrete and real, as he did; and we fail to see this, as he failed to see it. Our cognitive sciences are themselves suffering from an agnosia essentially similar to Dr P.'s. Dr P. may therefore serve as a warning and parable—of what happens to a science which eschews the judgmental, the particular, the personal, and becomes entirely abstract and computational.

It was always a matter of great regret to me that, owing to circumstances beyond my control, I was not able to follow his case further, either in the sort of observations and investigations described, or in ascertaining the actual disease pathology.

One always fears that a case is 'unique', especially if it has such extraordinary features as those of Dr P. It was, therefore, with a sense of great interest and delight, not unmixed with relief, that I found, quite by chance—looking through the periodical *Brain* for 1956—a detailed description of an almost comically similar case, similar (indeed identical) neuropsychologically and phenomenologically, though the underlying pathology (an acute head injury) and all personal circumstances were wholly different. The authors speak of their case as 'unique in the documented history of this disorder'—and evidently experienced, as I did, amazement at their own findings.[§] The interested reader is referred to the original paper, Macrae and Trolle (1956), of which I here subjoin a brief paraphrase, with quotations from the original.

Their patient was a young man of 32, who, following a severe automobile accident, with unconsciousness for three weeks, '... complained, exclusively, of an inability to recognise faces, even those of his wife and children'. Not a single face was 'familiar' to him, but there were three he could identify; these were workmates: one with an eye-blinking tic, one with a large mole on his cheek, and a third 'because he was so tall and thin that no one else was like him'. Each of these, Macrae and Trolle bring out, was 'recognised solely by the single prominent feature mentioned'. In general (like Dr P.) he recognised familiars only by their voices.

He had difficulty even recognising himself in a mirror, as Macrae and Trolle describe in detail: 'In the early convalescent phase he frequently, especially when shaving, questioned whether the face gazing at him was really his own, and even though he knew it could physically be none other, on several occasions grimaced or stuck out his tongue "just to make sure." By carefully studying his face in the mirror he slowly began to recognise it, but "not in a flash" as in the past—he relied on the hair and facial outline, and on two small moles on his left cheek.'

In general he could not recognise objects 'at a glance', but would have to seek out, and guess from, one or two features—occasionally his guesses were absurdly wrong. In particular, the authors note, there was difficulty with the *animate*.

On the other hand, simple schematic objects—scissors; watch, key, etc.—presented no difficulties. Macrae and Trolle also note that: 'His *topographical memory* was strange: the seeming paradox existed that he could find his way from home to hospital and around the hospital, but yet could not name streets *en route* [unlike Dr P., he also had some aphasia] or appear to visualize the topography.'

It was also evident that visual memories of people, even from long before the accident, were severely impaired—there was memory of conduct, or perhaps a mannerism, but not of visual appearance or face. Similarly, it appeared, when he was questioned closely, that he no longer had visual images in his *dreams*. Thus, as with Dr P., it was not just visual

§ Only since the completion of this book have I found that there is, in fact, a rather extensive litrature on visual agnosia in general, and prosopagnosia in particular. In particular I had the great pleasure recently of meeting Dr Andrew Kertesz, who has himself published some extremely detailed studies of patients with such agnosias (see, for example, his paper on visual agnosia, Kertesz 1979). Dr Kertesz mentioned to me a case known to him of a farmer who had developed prosopagnosia and in consequence could no longer distinguish (the faces of) his *cows*, and of another such patient, an attendant in a Natural History Museum, who mistook his own reflection for the diorama of an *ape*. As with Dr P., and as with Macrae and Trolle's patient, it is especially the animate which is so absurdly misperceived. The most important studies of such agnosias, and of visual processing in general, are now being undertaken by A. R. and H. Damasio (see article in Mesulam [1985], pp. 259–288; or see p. 79 below).

perception, but visual imagination and memory, the fundamental powers of visual representation, which were essentially damaged in this patient—at least those powers insofar as they pertained to the personal, the familiar, the concrete.

A final, humorous point. Where Dr P. might mistake his wife for a hat, Macrae's patient, also unable to recognise his wife, needed her to identify herself by a visual *marker*, by '... a conspicuous article of clothing, such as a large hat'.

—1985

Learning from Other Writers

1. What steps does Oliver Sacks take toward solving the mystery regarding Dr. P.'s condition?
2. Does Sacks ever solve this mystery? What, if anything, does he learn along the way?
3. Why does Sacks think that anyone other than Dr. P. and his wife would be interested in reading about Dr. P.'s illness?
4. What sort of scientific information does Sacks include in his essay? Where and how does he weave this information into his discussion of Dr. P.'s case? How does he credit his sources?
5. How would you describe the audience for this essay? Is the language appropriate to that audience? Do you think an audience of neurologists would consider this essay to be worthy of publication in a scientific journal or suitable only for lay readers?
6. Does Sacks offer Dr. P. any cure for his condition? Do you find the last section before the postscript to be satisfying? Troubling?
7. What purpose—if any—does the postscript serve?

PRIMO LEVI

CHROMIUM

The entrée was fish, but the wine was red. Versino, head of maintenance, said that it was all a lot of nonsense, provided the wine and fish were good; he was certain that the majority of those who upheld the orthodox view could not, blindfolded, have distinguished a glass of white wine from a glass of red. Bruni, from the Nitro Department, asked whether somebody knew why fish goes with white wine: various joking remarks were made but nobody was able to answer properly. Old man Cometto added that life is full of customs whose roots can no longer be traced: the color of sugar paper, the buttoning from different sides for men and women, the shape of a gondola's prow, and the innumerable alimentary compatibilities and incompatibilities, of which in fact the one in question was a particular case: but in any event, why were pig's feet obligatory with lentils, and cheese on macaroni.

I made a rapid mental review to be sure that none of those present had as yet heard it, then I started to tell the story of the onion in the boiled linseed oil. This, in fact, was a dining room for a company of varnish manufacturers, and it is well known that boiled linseed oil has for many centuries constituted the fundamental raw material of our art. It is an ancient art and therefore noble: its most remote testimony is in Genesis 6:14, where it is told how, in conformity with a precise specification of the Almighty, Noah coated (probably with a brush) the Ark's interior and exterior with melted pitch. But it is also a subtly fraudulent art, like that which aims at concealing the substratum by conferring on it the color and appearance of what it is not: from this point of view it is related to cosmetics and adornment, which are equally ambiguous and almost equally ancient arts (Isaiah 3:16). Given therefore its pluri-millenial origins, it is not so strange that the trade of manufacturing varnishes retains in its crannies (despite the innumerable solicitations it modernly receives from kindred techniques) rudiments of customs and procedures abandoned for a long time now.

So, returning to boiled linseed oil, I told my companions at table that in a prescription book published about 1942 I had found the advice to introduce into the oil, toward the end of the boiling, two slices of onion, without any comment on the purpose of this curious additive. I had spoken about it in 1949 with Signor Giacomasso Olindo, my predecessor and teacher, who was then more than seventy and had been making varnishes for fifty years, and he, smiling benevolently behind his thick white mustache, had explained to me that in actual fact, when he was young and boiled the oil personally, thermometers had not yet come into use: one judged the temperature of the batch by observing the smoke, or spitting into it, or, more efficiently, immersing a slice of onion in the oil on the point of a skewer; when the onion began to fry, the boiling was finished. Evidently, with the passing of the years, what had been a crude measuring operation had lost its significance and was transformed into a mysterious and magical practice.

Old Cometto told of an analogous episode. Not without nostalgia he recalled his good old times, the times of copal gum: he told how once boiled linseed oil was combined with these legendary resins to make fabulously durable and gleaming varnishes. Their fame and name survive now only in the locution "copal shoes," which alludes precisely to a varnish for leather at one time very widespread that has been out of fashion for at least the last half century. Today the locution itself is almost extinct. Copals were imported by the British from the most distant and savage countries, and bore their names, which in fact distinguished one kind from another: copal of Madagascar or Sierra Leone or Kauri (whose deposits, let it be said parenthetically, were exhausted along about 1967), and the very well known and noble Congo copal. They are fossil resins of vegetable origin, with a rather high melting point, and in the state in which they are found and sold in commerce are insoluble in oil: to render them soluble and compatible they were subjected to a violent, semi-destructive boiling, in the course of which their acidity diminished (they decarboxylated) and also the melting point was lowered. The operation was carried out in a semi-industrial manner by direct fire in modest, mobile kettles of four or six hundred pounds; during the boiling they were weighed at intervals, and when the resin had lost 16 percent of its weight in smoke, water vapor, and carbon dioxide, the solubility in oil was judged to have been reached. Along about 1940, the archaic copals, expensive and difficult to supply during the war, were supplanted by phenolic and maleic resins, both suitably modified, which, besides costing less, were directly compatible with the oils. Very well: Cometto told us how, in a factory whose name shall not be uttered, until 1953 a phenolic resin, which took the place of the Congo copal in a formula, was treated exactly like copal itself—that is, by consuming 16 percent of it on the fire, amid pestilential phenolic exhalations—until it had reached that solubility in oil which the resin already possessed.

Here at this point I remembered that all languages are full of images and metaphors whose origin is being lost, together with the art from which they were drawn: horsemanship having declined to the level of an expensive sport, such expressions as "belly to the ground" and "taking the bit in one's teeth" are unintelligible and sound odd; since mills with superimposed stones have disappeared, which were also called millstones, and in which for centuries wheat (and varnishes) were ground, such a phrase as "to eat like four millstones" sounds odd and even mysterious today. In the same way, since Nature too is conservative, we carry in our coccyx what remains of a vanished tail.

Bruni told us about an episode in which he himself had been involved, and as he told the story, I felt myself invaded by sweet and tenuous sensations which later I will try to explain. I must say first of all that Bruni worked from 1955 to 1965 in a large factory on the shores of a lake, the same one in which I had learned the rudiments of the varnish-making trade during the years 1946–47. So he told us that, when he was down there in charge of the Synthetic Varnishes Department, there fell into his hands a formula of a chromate-based anti-rust paint that contained an absurd component: nothing less than ammonium chloride, the old, alchemical sal ammoniac of the temple of Ammon, much more apt to corrode iron than preserve it from rust. He had asked his superiors and the veterans in the department about it: surprised and a bit shocked, they had replied that in that formulation, which corresponded to at least twenty or thirty tons of the product a month and had been in force for at least ten years, that salt "had always been in it," and that he had his nerve, so young in years and new on the job, criticizing the factory's experience, and looking for trouble by asking silly hows and whys. If ammonium chloride was in the formula, it was evident that it had some sort of use. What use it had nobody any longer knew, but one should be very careful about taking it out because "one never knows." Bruni is a rationalist, and he took all this very badly; but he is a prudent man, and so he accepted the advice, according to which in that formulation and in that lakeshore factory, unless there have been further developments, ammonium chloride is still being put in; and yet today it is completely useless, as I can state from firsthand experience because it was I who introduced it into the formula.

The episode cited by Bruni, the rustproof formula with chromates and ammonium chloride, flung me back in time, all the way to the freezing cold January of 1946, when meat and coal were still rationed, nobody had a car, and never in Italy had people breathed so much hope and so much freedom.

But I had returned from captivity three months before and was living badly. The things I had seen and suffered were burning inside of me; I felt closer to the dead than the living, and felt guilty at being a man, because men had built Auschwitz, and Auschwitz had gulped down millions of human beings, and many of my friends, and a woman who was dear to my heart. It seemed to me that I would be purified if I told its story, and I felt like Coleridge's Ancient Mariner, who waylays on the street the wedding guests going to the feast, inflicting on them the story of his misfortune. I was writing concise and bloody poems, telling the story at breakneck speed, either by talking to people or by writing it down, so much so that gradually a book was later born: by writing I found peace for a while and felt myself become a man again, a person like everyone else, neither a martyr nor debased nor a saint: one of those people who form a family and look to the future rather than the past.

Since one can't live on poetry and stories, I looked feverishly for work and found it in the big lakeshore factory, still damaged from the war, and during those months besieged by mud and ice. Nobody was much concerned with me: colleagues, the director, and workers had other things to think about—the son who wasn't returning from Russia, the stove without wood, the shoes without soles, the warehouses without supplies, the windows without panes, the freezing cold which split the pipes, inflation, famine, and the virulent local feuds. I had been benignly granted a lame-legged desk in the lab, in a corner full of crashing noise, drafts, and people coming and going carrying rags and large cans, and I had not been assigned a specific task. I, unoccupied as a chemist and in a state of utter alienation (but then it wasn't called that), was writing in a haphazard fashion page after page of the memories which were poisoning me, and my colleagues watched me stealthily as a harmless nut. The book grew under my hands, almost spontaneously, without plan or system, as intricate and crowded as an anthill. Every so often, impelled by a feeling of professional conscience, I would ask to see the director and request some work, but he was much too busy to worry about my scruples. I should read and study; when it came to paints and varnishes I was still, if I didn't mind his saying so, an illiterate. I didn't have anything to do? Well, I should praise God and sit in the library; if I really had the itch to do something useful, well, look, there were articles to translate from German.

One day he sent for me and with an oblique glint in his eyes announced that he had a little job for me. He took me to a corner of the factory's yard, near a retaining wall: piled up at random, the lowest crushed by the highest, were thousands of square blocks of a bright orange color. He told me to touch them: they were gelatinous and softish; they had the disagreeable consistency of slaughtered tripes. I told the director that, apart from the color, they seemed to me to be livers, and he praised me: that's just how it was described in the paint manuals! He explained that the phenomenon which had produced them was called just that in English, "livering"; under certain conditions certain paints turned from liquids into solids, with the consistency precisely of the liver or lungs, and must be thrown out. These parallelepiped shapes had been cans of paint: the paint had livered, the cans had been cut away, and the contents had been thrown on the garbage dump.

That paint, he told me, had been produced during the war and immediately after; it contained a basic chromate and alkyd resin. Perhaps the chromate was too basic or the resin too acidic: these were exactly the conditions under which a "livering" can take place. All right, he made me the gift of that pile of old sins; I should think about it, make tests and examinations, and try to say with precision why the trouble had occurred, what should be done so that it was not repeated, and if it were possible to reclaim the damaged goods.

Thus set forth, half chemistry and half police work, the problem attracted me: I was reconsidering it that evening (it was Saturday evening) as one of the sooty, freezing freight trains of that period lugged me to Turin. Now it happened that the next day destiny reserved for me a different and unique gift: the encounter with a woman, young and made of flesh and blood, warm against my side through our overcoats, gay in the humid mist of the avenues, patient, wise and sure as we were walking down streets still bordered with ruins. In a few hours we knew that we belonged to each other, not for one meeting but for life, as in fact has been the case. In a few hours I felt reborn and replete with new powers, washed clean and cured of a long sickness, finally ready to enter life with joy and vigor; equally cured was suddenly the world around me, and exorcized the name and face of the woman who had gone down into the lower depths with me and had not returned. My very writing became a different adventure, no longer the dolorous itinerary of a convalescent, no longer a begging for compassion and friendly faces, but a lucid building, which now was no longer solitary: the work of a chemist who weighs and divides, measures and judges on the basis of assured proofs, and strives to answer questions. Alongside the liberating relief of the veteran who tells his story, I now felt in the writing a complex, intense, and new pleasure, similar to that I felt as a student when penetrating the solemn order of differential calculus. It was exalting to search and find, or create, the right word, that is, commensurate, concise, and strong; to dredge up events from my memory and describe them with the greatest rigor and the least clutter. Paradoxically, my baggage of atrocious memories became a wealth, a seed; it seemed to me that, by writing, I was growing like a plant.

In the freight train of the following Monday, squeezed in a sleepy crowd bundled in scarfs, I felt full of joy and alert as never before or after. I was ready to challenge everything and everyone, in the same way that I had challenged and defeated Auschwitz and loneliness: disposed, especially, to engage in joyous battle with the clumsy pyramid of orange livers that awaited me on the lakeshore.

It is the spirit that dominates matter, is that not so? Was it not this that they had hammered into my head in the Fascist and Gentile *liceo*? I threw myself into the work with the same intensity that, at not so distant a period, we had attacked a rock wall; and the adversary was still the same, the not-I, the Button Molder,* the *hyle*: stupid matter, slothfully hostile as human stupidity is hostile, and like it strong because of its obtuse passivity. Our trade is to conduct and win this interminable battle: a livered paint is much more rebellious, more refractory to your will than a lion in its mad pounce; but, let's admit it, it's also less dangerous.

The first skirmish took place in the archives. The two partners, the two fornicators from whose embrace had sprung our orange-colored monsters, were the chromate and the resin. The resin was fabricated on the spot: I found the birth certificate of all the batches, and they did not offer anything suspicious; the acidity was variable, but always inferior to 6, as prescribed. One batch that was found to have a pH of 6.2 had been dutifully discarded by an inspector with a flowery signature. In the first instance the resin could not be faulted.

The chromate had been purchased from different suppliers, and it too had been duly inspected batch by batch. According to Purchase Specification 480/0 it should have contained not less than 28 percent of chromium oxide in all; and now here, right before my eyes I had the interminable list of tests from January 1942 until today (one of the least exciting forms of reading imaginable), and all the values satisfied the specification, indeed were equal among themselves: 29.5 percent, not one percent more, not one less. I felt my inner being as a chemist writhe, confronted by that abomination; in fact, one should know that the natural oscillations in the method of preparation of such a chromate, added to the inevitable analytical errors, make it extremely improbable that the many values found in different batches and on different days could coincide so exactly. How come nobody had gotten suspicious? But in fact at that time I did not yet know the frightening anesthetic power of company papers, their capacity to hobble, douse, and dull every leap of intuition and every spark of talent. It is well known to the scholarly that all secretions can be harmful or toxic: now under pathological conditions it is not rare that the paper, a company secretion, is reabsorbed to an excessive degree, and puts to sleep, paralyzes, or actually kills the organism from which it has been exuded.

The story of what had happened began to take shape. For some reason, some analyst had been betrayed by a defective method, or an impure reagent, or an incorrect habit; he had diligently totted up those so obviously suspicious but formally blameless results; he had punctiliously signed each analysis, and his signature, swelling like an avalanche, had been consolidated by the signatures of the lab chief, the technical director, and the general director. I could see him, the poor wretch, against the background of those difficult years: no longer young, since all the young men were in the military services; perhaps chivied by the Fascists, perhaps himself a Fascist being looked for by the partisans; certainly frustrated, because being an analyst is a young man's job; on guard in his lab within the fortress of his minuscule specialty, since the analyst is by definition infallible; and derided and regarded with a hostile eye outside the lab just because of his virtues as an incorruptible guardian, a severe, pedantic, unimaginative little judge, a stick poked in the wheels of production. To judge from the anonymous, neat handwriting, his trade must have exhausted him and at the same time brought him to a crude perfection, like a pebble in a mountain stream that has been twirled over and over all the way to the stream's mouth. It was not surprising that, with time, he had developed a certain insensitivity to the real significance of the operations he was performing and the notes he was writing. I planned to look into his particular case but nobody knew anything more about him; my questions were met with discourteous or absentminded

* A character in Ibsen's *Peer Gynt*.

replies. Moreover, I was beginning to feel around me and my work a mocking and malevolent curiosity: who was this Johnny-come-lately, this pipsqueak earning 7,000 lire a month, this maniac scribbler who was disturbing the nights of the guest quarters typing away at God knows what, and sticking his nose into past mistakes and washing a generation's dirty linen? I even had the suspicion that the job that had been assigned me had the secret purpose of getting me to bump into something or somebody; but by now this matter of the livering absorbed me body and soul, *tripes et boyaux*—in short, I was enamored of it almost as of that aforementioned girl, who in fact was a little jealous of it

It was not hard for me to procure, besides the Purchase Specification (the PS), also the equally inviolable CS, the Checking Specifications: in a drawer in the lab there was a packet of greasy file cards, typewritten and corrected several times by hand, each of which contained the way to carry out a check of a specific raw material. The file card on prussian blue was stained with blue, the file card on glycerine was sticky, and the file card on fish oil smelled like sardines. I took out the file card on chromate, which due to long use had become the color of a sunrise, and read it carefully. It was all rather sensible and in keeping with my not-so-far-off scholastic notions; only one point seemed strange to me. Having achieved the disintegration of the pigment, it prescribed adding twenty-three drops of a certain reagent. Now, a drop is not so definite a unit as to entail so definite a numerical coefficient; and besides, when all is said and done, the prescribed dose was absurdly high: it would have flooded the analysis, leading in any case to a result in keeping with the specification. I looked at the back of the file card: it bore the date of the last review, January 4, 1944; the birth certificate of the first livered batch was on the succeeding February 22.

At this point I began to see the light. In a dusty archive I found the CS collection no longer in use, and there, lo and behold, the preceding edition of the chromate file card bore the direction to add "2 or 3" drops, and not "23": the fundamental "or" was half erased and in the next transcription had gotten lost. The events meshed perfectly: the revision of the file card had caused a mistake in transcription, and the mistake had falsified all succeeding analyses, concealing the results on the basis of a fictitious value due to the reagent's enormous excess and thus bringing about the acceptance of shipments of pigment which should have been discarded; these, being too basic, had brought about the livering.

But there is trouble in store for anyone who surrenders to the temptation of mistaking an elegant hypothesis for a certainty: the readers of detective stories know this quite well. I got hold of the sleepy man in charge of the storeroom, requested from him all the samples of all the shipments of chromate from January 1944 on, and barricaded myself behind a workbench for three days in order to analyze them according to the incorrect and correct methods. Gradually, as the results lined up in a column on the register, the boredom of repetitious work was being transformed into nervous gaiety, as when as children you play hide and seek and discover your opponent clumsily squatting behind a hedge. With the mistaken method you constantly found the fateful 29.5 percent; with the correct method, the results were widely dispersed, and a good quarter, being inferior to the prescribed minimum, corresponded to the shipments which should have been rejected. The diagnosis was confirmed, the pathogenesis discovered: it was now a matter of defining the therapy.

This was found pretty soon, drawing on good inorganic chemistry, that distant Cartesian island, a lost paradise, for us organic chemists, bunglers, "students of gunks": it was necessary to neutralize in some way, within the sick body of that varnish, the excess of basicity due to free lead oxide. The acids were shown to be noxious from other aspects: I thought of ammonium chloride, capable of combining stably with lead oxide, producing an insoluble and inert chloride and freeing the ammonia. Tests on a small scale gave promising results: now quick, find the chloride, come to an agreement with the head of the Milling Department, slip into a small ball mill two of the livers disgusting to see and touch, add a weighed quantity of the presumed medicine, start the mill under the skeptical eyes of the onlookers. The mill, usually so noisy, started almost grudgingly, in a silence of bad omen, impeded by the gelatinous mass which stuck to the balls. All that was left was to go back to Turin to wait for Monday, telling the patient girl in whirlwind style the hypotheses arrived at, the things understood at the lakeshore, the spasmodic waiting for the sentence that the facts would pronounce.

The following Monday the mill had regained its voice: it was in fact crunching away gaily with a full, continuous tone, without that rhythmic roaring that in a ball mill indicates bad maintenance or bad health. I stopped it and cautiously loosened the bolts on the manhole; there spurted out with a hiss an ammoniacal puff, as it should. Then I took off the cover. Angels and ministers of grace!—the paint was fluid and smooth, completely normal, born again from its ashes like the Phoenix. I wrote out a report in good company jargon and the management increased my salary. Besides, as a form of recognition, I received the assignment of two tires for my bike.

Since the storeroom contained several shipments of perilously basic chromate, which must also be utilized because they had been accepted by the inspection and could not be returned to the supplier, the chloride was officially introduced as an anti-livering preventive in the formula of that varnish. Then I quit my job: ten years went by, the postwar years were over, the deleterious, too basic chromates disappeared from the market, and my report went the way of all flesh: but formulas are as holy as prayers, decree-laws, and dead languages, and not an iota in them can be changed. And so my ammonium chloride, the twin of a happy love and a liberating book, by now completely useless and probably a bit harmful, is religiously ground into the chromate anti-rust paint on the shore of that lake, and nobody knows why anymore.

—1984

Learning from Other Writers

1. What is the effect of the opening sentence of "Chromium"?
2. List the customs that Levi mentions or describes before he reaches the main section of the essay (i.e., the passage that begins "The episode cited by Bruni"). What is the effect of including so many examples of meaningless customs before introducing the main narrative?
3. Does Levi make his examples accessible to readers who aren't chemists? If so, how does he accomplish this?
4. The author waits until late in his essay to tell us that he survived Auschwitz, then barely mentions the experience again. Can you find any *indirect* references to the author's experiences in the concentration camps (or to the Holocaust in general)? Why doesn't Levi meditate more overtly on the connections between his ordeal during the war and his later experiences at the paint factory?
5. What is the effect of the final paragraph of the essay? The last five words?

INSPIRATIONS: THAT'S A MYSTERY TO ME

1. Think of a mystery that perplexes you. (If you've been keeping a notebook of questions, as suggested in Chapter 3, you may find several mysteries lurking there.) If nothing occurs to you, visit a museum (of any kind) or a place where interesting objects tend to accumulate (a junk shop, for instance, or a grandparent's basement or attic) and try to come up with a question about something you find.

2. At the start, your mystery might seem too narrow to be worth investigating. You might find yourself wondering how your mother's brother really died, or why none of the nude statues in a museum have hair on their bodies, or how a Navaho sheepherder like your grandfather ended up with a Japanese bayonet on the wall of his *hogan*. If that's the case, try to broaden the question so other people might care about the answer. What was it really like to be a gay man teaching music in a rural town in West Virginia in the early 1970s? How have societal and cultural attitudes toward body hair changed—or not changed—over the past few centuries? Who were the code talkers, and what was their role in World War II? What was it like to go from being a poor, neglected Indian on a remote reservation in New Mexico to a hero in the Marines?
3. Conduct whatever research seems necessary to solve your mystery. (For assistance, see the following section, "A Footnote on Research.")
4. Write an essay in which you present your initial question and describe the steps you took to answer it. You might or might not choose to meditate directly on the larger thematic significance of this mystery as you write, but make sure that your readers know what that question is and the ways in which your essay contributes to solving it.

ADDITIONAL CONSIDERATIONS: A FOOTNOTE ON RESEARCH

Most people who write creative nonfiction share a love of research. In fact, most of us find it difficult to stop researching our questions and actually sit down to write. Those of you who dislike the sort of research you're required to do for school might consider this a sign of our insanity. But trying to answer a genuine question that you've come up with on your own—especially if it's a question whose exploration takes you over previously untraveled ground and leads you to a discovery no one else has made—tends to be more exciting than hunting down the answer to someone else's question, especially if it's a question whose answer is already known.

As you've seen, conducting research for an essay might involve a pilgrimage to Walden Pond or to the town in which your family used to spend summer vacations. You might need to visit your tenth-grade teacher (whether in prison or somewhere else), scrounge through record bins at a flea market, or, as we'll see in the next chapter, figure out how to open the trunk of a car—from inside the trunk.

How do you know what you need to know? As we've already seen, you start with what you have and go wherever you can go from there. You might begin with a general topic, then carry out enough research so you can formulate a question about that topic, then travel from place to place and expert to expert until you've arrived at an answer. Or you might begin with some fragmentary memories of a significant event from your childhood, write a first draft of a narrative based on those recollections, leaving blank spaces to indicate the gaps in your knowledge, then consult people and periodicals that might enable you to fill in those lacunae.

Usually, once you get started on your research, the problem is how to stop, given that the first person to whom you speak will refer you to another, and the first book you read will mention another book, and the curator of one archive or museum will refer you to another archive or museum, which you absolutely *must* visit if you hope to solve the mystery you're attempting to solve. You don't need to be an expert on any particular topic; you simply need to be persistent enough to find someone who is.

These days, most of us start our research by consulting the Internet. And most of us are aware that we need to be careful when evaluating the accuracy of whatever we find online. Consulting Wikipedia might be useful, but you often need to check another source to determine whether the "facts" you find there are *facts*. As is true with any source—but doubly true on the

Web—be sure to note the complete address of any information you find so you can go back and locate it later and so interested readers can track down the source. Because Internet sites tend to be evanescent, you probably will want to print out what you've found in case you need it later and the site has disappeared. And whether you are consulting an online site, a library book, or the mayor of your city, keep good notes so you can remember which thoughts and quotes are yours and which belong to someone else.

Oh, and here's one final word of caution: viewing a page on the Internet can't provide an accurate replacement for viewing an actual three-dimensional painting or sculpture, a fragment of papyrus, or a street scene from Istanbul. Most of what's interesting in the world hasn't been put online. Libraries, as old-fashioned as they seem, hold treasures that haven't yet been digitized, not only books, but newspapers, diaries, letters, and magazines (you would be amazed at the sorts of interesting and important details that get lost when hard copies of periodicals are turned into digital images, let alone copied onto microfiche), as well as collections of musical instruments, campaign buttons, pin cushions, and bat skulls. Most useful of all: libraries come equipped with librarians, who delight in helping writers find answers to their questions.

Nor can you write a vivid scene if you haven't witnessed something vivid happening; you can't describe a place in all its glorious sensory detail unless you've visited that place yourself; and you can't describe a person's face, let alone her mannerisms, if you have read nothing but her biography and a few choice quotations on the Web. As you will see in Chapter 9, if you want to know what it's really like to be an aerialist, you need to go up in the plane and ask the pilot to do a barrel roll. If you want to figure out whether a child prodigy is truly gifted or merely a product of her overly ambitious, eccentric parents, you need to visit that child at home.

Although the standards for proving your assertions and hypotheses when writing a creative essay tend to be more lax than when you are writing a scholarly article or a doctoral dissertation, you will need to verify any important, controversial, or potentially libelous information you include. If you fulfill a class assignment by interviewing your neighbor about her experiences as a soldier in Iraq, you probably won't have the time or resources to verify everything she tells you. But if you intend to publish the resulting essay in a magazine, you will need to check that everything she has said is true, starting with her claim that she enlisted in the army and served in Iraq.

Similarly, the requirements for documenting your sources in a piece of creative nonfiction are more flexible than is true in a thesis or dissertation. But you are no more entitled to take other people's thoughts, language, or discoveries as your own than is ethical or allowable in any genre. Here, your contract with your readers demands that you provide them with a sense of how reliable your sources are and the ability to verify what you've written or learn more about a topic for which you've piqued their curiosity. The trick is to cite your sources in such a way that the citations don't interfere with the casual feel of your essay or the fluidity of your prose. As you can see from the selections in this anthology, the solution might involve mentioning a source informally within the text (or in an artfully placed parentheses). Some writers use footnotes, while others wait to place their references at the end, often in a brief discussion of sources and acknowledgments. For elegant models of a how to cite your sources, look at the essays in this anthology by Alice Walker, Oliver Sacks, and Jane Brox.

8 Experiments

Sometimes, the questions that pop up in your mind when you think about writing an essay lead you to consider performing an experiment to figure out the answer. "What would happen if . . . ?" "What's it really like to . . . ?" "Could that urban legend be based in fact?" Carrying out such an experiment usually requires no advanced degree in science. Often, it requires little more than owning a pet. In the essays in this chapter, Ann Hodgman samples various kinds of dog food to determine if the advertising claims surrounding them are true ("No Wonder They Call Me a Bitch"), and Richard Feynman (who was indeed a scientist—and a genius) demonstrates the amazing range of talents most human beings possess but don't put to use ("Testing Bloodhounds"); in a third commonly anthologized example of the experiment form, Elizabeth Marshall Thomas follows a friend's husky on the animal's nocturnal rounds to gain insights into "The Hidden Life of Dogs."[1]

The experiment form isn't new. George Orwell's first novel, *Down and Out in Paris and London*, which he published in 1933, is deeply rooted in the experiment he undertook to shake off his upper-class British childhood by washing dishes in the kitchen of a fancy French restaurant and living in British slums among paupers, tramps, and beggars. Starting in the mid 1960s, George Plimpton risked serious injury to his body and his pride in a series of exercises in what he called *immersion journalism*, trying out as a rookie quarterback for the Detroit Lions, tending goal for the Boston Bruins, pitching against some of baseball's all-time greats, and playing professional golf for a month on the PGA tour (see, in order, Plimpton's *Paper Lion*, *Open Net*, *Out of My League*, and *Bogey Man*, all from Lyons Press). But the form seems to have assumed a recent upsurge in popularity, perhaps because it is the literary and intellectual equivalent of a reality TV show, with writers stripping onstage in men's clubs or trying to live for a year on food that comes from within a hundred-mile radius of their houses, presumably for the greater public good.

On the surface, such experiments are designed to answer factual questions. But the answers also need to matter for deeper thematic reasons. In "How to Get Out of a Locked Trunk" (which I include for those of you who don't own a dog), Philip Weiss not only figures out how to perform the mechanical act indicated by his title, he also comes to understand why the threat of a living burial haunts him, especially on the eve of his marriage to a woman he thinks he loves.

Like Weiss's essay, many examples of this form turn out to be both serious and hilarious. I once had a student go a month without a bath to see if his fraternity brothers would notice

[1] In 1993, Houghton Mifflin published a book-length version of Thomas's observations of her dogs, with the same title.

his stink amid the general reek of where they lived (no surprise, they didn't). Mike Paterniti's "1957 Man,"[2] an account of the weeks the author spent living by the rules of male behavior circa 1957, certainly evokes a laugh even as it induces fear, loathing, gratitude, and nausea in most of its female readers. And A. J. Jacobs's decision to spend a year adhering to the rules set out in the Bible as literally as possible not only allows him to test "the relevance of faith in our modern world" and "make you see history's most influential book with new eyes," as the jacket copy claims, but also provides an occasion for some wildly funny asides and observations (which you can find in his aptly titled *The Year of Living Biblically*).

Other examples of essays in which the writer carries out an experiment are far more serious, as evidenced by Lawrence Otis Graham's decision to take a leave of absence from his midtown Manhattan law firm, get a job as a busboy at an exclusive Connecticut country club that he wouldn't have been allowed to join by virtue of his skin color, and write a searing chronicle of the humiliation to which he was subjected and the racist and anti-Semitic conversations he overheard (see "Invisible Man," which was published in *New York Magazine* in 1992 and later reprinted in Graham's collection of essays, *A Member of the Club*[3]), and Barbara Ehrenreich's attempt to survive on the pittance she earned working several jobs that paid the minimum wage (see the essay version of her book, *Nickel and Dimed: On (Not) Getting By in America*, which is included in this chapter).

As is true with the journey form, you will need to decide how much time to spend telling your readers how and why you came to formulate this experiment and what was entailed in your preparations. (In the book that Barbara Ehrenreich came to write about trying to survive on minimum-wage jobs, she devotes an entire introductory chapter to explaining her methodology and addressing her readers' possible objections to her project.) You might choose to meditate on your findings along the way, or save such meditations for the end, where you analyze your discoveries in the sort of "results" section you are required to include in the write-up for a lab in physics or biology. Just be careful to take the literary equivalent of wearing gloves and goggles, by which I mean that you need to take precautions so your experiment doesn't land you in the hospital or in jail.

---

[2] In the October 2007 issue of *GQ*.

[3] HarperCollins, 1996.

ANN HODGMAN

NO WONDER THEY CALL ME A BITCH

I've always wondered about dog food. Is a Gaines-burger really like a hamburger? Can you fry it? Does dog food "cheese" taste like real cheese? Does Gravy Train actually make gravy in the dog's bowl, or is that brown liquid just dissolved crumbs? And exactly what *are* by-products?

Having spent the better part of a week eating dog food, I'm sorry to say that I now know the answers to these questions. While my dachshund, Shortie, watched in agonies of yearning, I gagged my way through can after can of stinky, white-flecked mush and bag after bag of stinky, fat-drenched nuggets. And now I understand exactly why Shortie's breath is so bad.

Of course, Gaines-burgers are neither mush nor nuggets. They are, rather, a miracle of beauty and packaging—or at least that's what I thought when I was little. I used to beg my mother to get them for our dogs, but she always said they were too expensive. When I finally bought a box of cheese-flavored Gaines-burgers—after 20 years of longing—I felt deliciously wicked.

"Dogs love real beef," the back of the box proclaimed proudly. "That's why Gaines-burgers is the only beef burger for dogs with real beef and no meal by-products!" The copy was accurate: meat by-products did not appear in the list of ingredients. Poultry by-products did, though—right there next to preserved animal fat.

One Purina spokesman told me that poultry by-products consist of necks, intestines, undeveloped eggs and other "carcass remnants," but not feathers, heads or feet. When I told him I'd been eating dog food, he said, "Oh, you're kidding! Oh no!" (I came to share his alarm when, weeks later, a second Purina spokesman said that Gaines-burgers *do* contain poultry heads and feet—but *not* undeveloped eggs.)

Up close my Gaines-burger didn't much resemble chopped beef. Rather, it looked—and felt—like a single long, extruded piece of redness that had been chopped into segments and formed into a patty. You could make one at home if you had a Play-Doh Fun Factory.

I turned on the skillet. While I waited for it to heat up I pulled out a shred of cheese-colored material and palpated it. Again, like Play-Doh, it was quite malleable. I made a little cheese bird out of it; then I counted to three and ate the bird.

There was a horrifying rush of cheddar taste, followed immediately by the dull tang of soybean flour—the main ingredient in Gaines-burgers. Next I tried a piece of red extrusion. The main difference between the meat-flavored and cheese-flavored extrusions is one of texture. The "cheese" chews like fresh Play-Doh, whereas the "meat" chews like Play-Doh that's been sitting out on a rug for a couple of hours.

Frying only turned the Gaines-burger black. There was no melting, no sizzling, no warm meat smells. A cherished childhood illusion was gone. I flipped the patty into the sink, where it immediately began leaking rivulets of red dye.

As alarming as the Gaines-burgers were, their soy meal began to seem like an old friend when the time came to try some *canned* dog foods. I decided to try the Cycle foods first. When I opened them, I thought about how rarely I use can openers these days, and I was suddenly visited by a long-forgotten sensation of can-opener distaste. *This* is the kind of unsavory place can openers spend their time when you're not watching! Every time you open a can of, say, Italian plum tomatoes, you infect them with invisible particles of by-product.

I had been expecting to see the usual homogeneous scrapple inside, but each can of Cycle was packed with smooth, round, oily nuggets. As if someone at Gaines had been tipped off that a human would be tasting the stuff, the four Cycles really were different from one another. Cycle-1, for puppies, is wet and soyish. Cycle-2, for adults, glistens nastily with fat, but it's passably edible—a lot like some canned Swedish meatballs I once got in a care package at college. Cycle-3, the "lite" one, for fatties, had no specific flavor; it just tasted like dog food. But at least it didn't make me fat.

Cycle-4, for senior dogs, had the smallest nuggets. Maybe old dogs can't open their mouths as wide. This kind was far sweeter than the other three Cycles—almost like baked beans. It was also the only one to contain "dried beef digest," a mysterious substance that the Purina spokesman defined as "enzymes" and my dictionary defined as "the products of digestion."

Next on the menu was a can of Kal-Kan Pedigree with Chunky Chicken. Chunky chicken? There were chunks in the can, certainly—big, purplish-brown chunks. I forked one chunk out (by now I was becoming more callous) and found that while it had no discernible chicken flavor, it wasn't bad except for its texture—like meat loaf with ground-up chicken bones.

In the world of canned dog food, a smooth consistency is a sign of low quality—lots of cereal. A lumpy, frightening, bloody, stringy horror is a sign of high quality—lots of meat. Nowhere in the world of wet dog foods was this demonstrated better than in the fanciest I tried—Kal Kan's Pedigree Select Dinners. These came not in a can but in a tiny foil packet with a picture of an imperious Yorkie. When I pulled open the container, juice spurted all over my hand, and the first chunk I speared was trailing a long gray vein. I shrieked and went instead for a plain chunk, which I was able to swallow only after taking a break to read some suddenly fascinating office equipment catalogs. Once again, though, it tasted no more alarming than, say, canned hash.

Still, how pleasant it was to turn to *dry* dog food! Gravy Train was the first I tried, and I'm happy to report that it really does make a "thick, rich, real beef gravy" when you mix it with water. Thick and rich, anyway. Except for a lingering rancid-fat flavor, the gravy wasn't beefy, but since it tasted primarily like tap water, it wasn't nauseating either.

My poor dachshund just gets plain old Purina Dog Chow, but Purina also makes a dry food called Butcher's Blend that comes in Beef, Bacon & Chicken flavor. Here we see dog food's arcane semiotics at its best: a red triangle with a *T* stamped into it is supposed to suggest beef: a tan curl, chicken; and a brown *S*, a piece of bacon. Only dogs understand these messages. But Butcher's Blend does have an endearing slogan: "Great Meaty Tastes—without bothering the Butcher!" *You know, I wanted to buy some meat, but I just couldn't bring myself to bother the butcher. . . .*

Purina O.N.E. ("Optimum Nutritional Effectiveness") is targeted at people who are unlikely ever to worry about bothering a tradesperson. "We chose chicken as a primary ingredient in Purina O.N.E. for several reasonings," the long, long essay on the back of the bag announces. Chief among these reasonings, I'd guess, is the fact that chicken appeals to people who are—you know—*like us.* Although our dogs do nothing but spend 18-hour days alone in the apartment, we still want them to be *premium* dogs. We want them to cut down on red meat, too. We also want dog food that comes in a bag with an attractive design, a subtle type-face and no kitschy pictures of slobbering golden retrievers.

Besides that, we want a list of the Nutritional Benefits of our dog food—and we get it on O.N.E. One thing I especially like about this list is its constant references to a dog's "hair coat," as in "Beef tallow is good for the dog's skin and hair coat." (On the other hand, beef fallow merely provides palatability, while the dried beef digest in Cycle provides palatability *enhancement.*)

I hate to say it, but O.N.E. was pretty palatable. Maybe that's because it has about 100 percent more fat than, say, Butcher's Blend. Or maybe I'd been duped by the packaging; that's been known to happen before.

As with people food, dog snacks taste much better than dog meals. They're better-looking too. Take Milk-Bone Flavor Snacks. The loving-hands-at-home prose describing each flavor is colorful; the writers practically choke on their own exuberance. Of bacon they say, "It's so good, your dog will think it's hot off the frying pan." Of liver: "The only taste your dog wants more than liver—is even more liver!" Of poultry: "All those farm fresh flavors deliciously mixed in one biscuit. Your dog will bark with delight!" And of vegetable: "Gardens of taste! Specially blended to give your dog that vegetable flavor he wants—but can rarely get!"

Well, I may be a sucker, but advertising *this* emphatic just doesn't convince me. I lined up all seven flavors of Milk-Bone Flavor Snacks on the floor. Unless my dog's palate is a lot more sensitive than mine—and considering that she steals dirty diapers out of the trash and eats them, I'm loath to think it is—she doesn't detect any more difference in the seven flavors than I did when I tried them.

I much preferred Bonz, the hard-baked, bone-shaped snack stuffed with simulated marrow. I liked the bone part, that is: it tasted almost exactly like the cornmeal it was made of. The mock-marrow inside was a bit more problematic: in addition to looking like the sludge that collects in the treads of my running shoes, it was bursting with tiny hairs.

I'm sure you have a few dog food questions of your own. To save us time, I've answered them in advance.

Q. Are those little cans of Mighty Dog actually branded with the sizzling word BEEF, the way they show in the commercials?
A. You should know by now that that kind of thing never happens.
Q. Does chicken-flavored dog food taste like chicken-flavored cat food?
A. To my surprise, chicken cat food was actually a little better—more chickeny. It tasted like inferior canned pâté.
Q. Was there any dog food that you just couldn't bring yourself to try?
A. Alas, it was a can of Mighty Dog called Prime Entree with Bone Marrow. The meat was dark, dark brown, and it was surrounded by gelatin that was almost black. I knew I would die if I tasted it, so I put it outside for the raccoons.

—1989

Learning from Other Writers

1. Did Ann Hodgman really eat dog food for this experiment? Is there any way you can tell? How would you respond if you found out that she hadn't eaten any of the products she describes having eaten? Some? Most?
2. What is the concrete factual question Hodgman is trying to answer? Is there any larger cultural or psychological significance to this question? Does Hodgman's experiment answer her original question? What (if anything) is the larger significance to this discovery?
3. What is the role of humor in this essay? Find the lines that make you laugh. Can you figure out exactly what makes those lines funny?
4. Describing how something tastes or smells is difficult, in part because translating sensory experiences into words is difficult, in part because it's hard to find new ways to describe familiar tastes and smells. Look closely at Hodgman's descriptions of each product in terms of appearance, taste, smell, texture (and sound, if any of the foods make a sound). Do her descriptions strike you as effective? If so, what does she do to achieve this effect?

RICHARD P. FEYNMAN

TESTING BLOODHOUNDS

When I was at Los Alamos and would get a little time off, I would often go visit my wife, who was in a hospital in Albuquerque, a few hours away. One time I went to visit her and couldn't go in right away, so I went to the hospital library to read.

I read an article in *Science* about bloodhounds, and how they could smell so very well. The authors described the various experiments that they did—the bloodhounds could identify which items had been touched by people, and so on—and I began to think: It *is* very remarkable how good bloodhounds are at smelling, being able to follow trails of people, and so forth, but how good are *we*, actually?

When the time came that I could visit my wife, I went to see her, and I said, "We're gonna do an experiment. Those Coke bottles over there (she had a six-pack of empty Coke bottles that she was saving to send out)—now you haven't touched them in a couple of days, right?"

"That's right."

I took the six-pack over to her without touching the bottles, and said, "OK. Now I'll go out, and you take out one of the bottles, handle it for about two minutes, and then put it back. Then I'll come in, and try to tell which bottle it was."

So I went out, and she took out one of the bottles and handled it for quite a while—lots of time, because I'm no bloodhound! According to the article, they could tell if you just touched it.

Then I came back, and it was absolutely obvious! I didn't even have to smell the damn thing, because, of course, the temperature was different. And it was also obvious from the smell. As soon as you put it up near your face, you could smell it was dampish and warmer. So that experiment didn't work because it was too obvious.

Then I looked at the bookshelf and said, "Those books you haven't looked at for a while, right? This time, when I go out, take one book off the shelf, and just open it—that's all—and close it again; then put it back."

So I went out again, she took a book, opened it and closed it, and put it back. I came in—and nothing *to* it! It was easy. You just smell the books. It's hard to explain, because we're not used to saying things about it. You put each book up to your nose and sniff a few times, and you can tell. It's very different. A book that's been standing there a while has a dry, uninteresting kind of smell. But when a hand has touched it, there's a dampness and a smell that's very distinct.

We did a few more experiments, and I discovered that while bloodhounds are indeed quite capable, humans are not as *in*capable as they think they are: it's just that they carry their nose so high off the ground!

(I've noticed that my dog can correctly tell which way I've gone in the house, especially if I'm barefoot, by smelling my footprints. So I tried to do that: I crawled around the rug on my hands and knees, sniffing, to see if I could tell the difference between where I walked and where I didn't, and I found it impossible. So the dog *is* much better than I am.)

Many years later, when I was first at Caltech, there was a party at Professor Bacher's house, and there were a lot of people from Caltech. I don't know how it came up, but I was telling them this story about smelling the bottles and the books. They didn't believe a word, naturally, because they always thought I was a faker. I had to demonstrate it.

We carefully took eight or nine books off the shelf without touching them directly with our hands, and then I went out. Three different people touched three different books: they picked one up, opened it, closed it, and put it back.

Then I came back, and smelled everybody's hands, and smelled all the books—I don't remember which I did first—and found all three books correctly; I got one person wrong.

They still didn't believe me; they thought it was some sort of magic trick. They kept trying to figure out how I did it. There's a famous trick of this kind, where you have a confederate in the group who gives you signals as to what it is, and they were trying to figure out who the confederate was. Since then I've often thought that it would be a good card trick to take a deck of cards and tell someone to pick a card and put it back, while you're in the other room. *You say*, "Now I'm going to tell you which card it is, because I'm a bloodhound: I'm going to *smell* all these cards and tell you which card you picked." Of course, with that kind of patter, people wouldn't believe for a minute that that's what you were actually doing!

People's hands smell very different—that's why dogs can identify people; you have to *try* it! All hands have a sort of moist smell, and a person who smokes has a very different smell on his hands from a person who doesn't; ladies often have different kinds of perfumes, and so on. If somebody happened to have some coins in his pocket and happened to be handling them, you can smell that.

—1985

Learning from Other Writers

1. "Testing Bloodhounds" is an excerpt from Richard Feynman's autobiography, a book structured as a collection of anecdotes from the author's life. As we discussed in the Introduction, an anecdote is a narrative that might be entertaining but has no larger thematic significance. Does "Testing Bloodhounds" rise above the level of pure anecdote? Does it qualify as an essay?
2. Feynman barely mentions that at the time he carried out these experiments, he also was working at Los Alamos to develop the atomic bomb, and his young wife was dying of cancer in a hospital in Albuquerque "a few hours away." Do these facts change your reading of this piece? Why doesn't Feynman make more of the dramatic circumstances surrounding his experiments?
3. Feynman had a degree in physics. Does this make him more qualified than the average person to carry out the experiments he describes?
4. You probably won't be surprised to learn that Feynman was a terrific teacher. Throughout his life, he tried to convey to his students—and the general public—that it's more important to learn by understanding than by memorization, that even the most difficult problems are solvable (given enough patience, clear thinking, and perseverance) and that we all should make a habit of testing fancy theories against reality and common sense. Are any of these principles illustrated in "Testing Bloodhounds"?

PHILIP WEISS

HOW TO GET OUT OF A LOCKED TRUNK

On a hot Sunday last summer my friend Tony and I drove my rental car, a '91 Buick, from St. Paul to the small town of Waconia, Minnesota, forty miles southwest. We each had a project. Waconia is Tony's boyhood home, and his sister had recently given him a panoramic postcard of Lake Waconia as seen from a high point in the town early in the century. He wanted to duplicate the photograph's vantage point, then hang the two pictures together in his house in Frogtown. I was hoping to see Tony's father, Emmett, a retired mechanic, in order to settle a question that had been nagging me: Is it possible to get out of a locked car trunk?

We tried to call ahead to Emmett twice, but he wasn't home. Tony thought he was probably golfing but that there was a good chance he'd be back by the time we got there. So we set out.

I parked the Buick, which was a silver sedan with a red interior, by the graveyard near where Tony thought the picture had been taken. He took his picture and I wandered among the headstones, reading the epitaphs. One of them was chillingly anti-individualist. It said, "Not to do my will, but thine."

Trunk lockings had been on my mind for a few weeks. It seemed to me that the fear of being locked in a car trunk had a particular hold on the American imagination. Trunk lockings occur in many movies and books—from *Goodfellas* to *Thelma and Louise* to *Humboldt's Gift*. And while the highbrow national newspapers generally shy away from trunk lockings, the attention they receive in local papers suggests a widespread anxiety surrounding the subject. In an afternoon at the New York Public Library I found numerous stories about trunk lockings. A Los Angeles man is discovered, bloodshot, banging the trunk of his white Eldorado following a night and a day trapped inside; he says his captors went on joyrides and picked up women. A forty-eight-year-old Houston doctor is forced into her trunk at a bank ATM and then the car is abandoned, parked near the Astrodome. A New Orleans woman tells police she gave birth in a trunk while being abducted to Texas. Tests undermine her story, the police drop the investigation. But so what if it's a fantasy? That only shows the idea's hold on us.

Every culture comes up with tests of a person's ability to get out of a sticky situation. The English plant mazes. Tropical resorts market those straw finger-grabbers that tighten their grip the harder you pull on them, and Viennese intellectuals gave us the concept of childhood sexuality—figure it out, or remain neurotic for life.

At least you could puzzle your way out of those predicaments. When they slam the trunk, though, you're helpless unless someone finds you. You would think that such a common worry should have a ready fix, and that the secret of getting out of a locked trunk is something we should all know about.

I phoned experts but they were very discouraging.

"You cannot get out. If you got a pair of pliers and bat's eyes, yes. But you have to have a lot of knowledge of the lock," said James Foote at Automotive Locksmiths in New York City.

Jim Frens, whom I reached at the technical section of *Car and Driver* in Detroit, told me the magazine had not dealt with this question. But he echoed the opinion of experts elsewhere when he said that the best hope for escape would be to try and kick out the panel between the trunk and the backseat. That angle didn't seem worth pursuing. What if your enemies were in the car, crumpling beer cans and laughing at your fate? It didn't make sense to join them.

The people who deal with rules on auto design were uncomfortable with my scenarios. Debra Barclay of the Center for Auto Safety, an organization founded by Ralph Nader, had certainly heard of cases, but she was not aware of any regulations on the matter. "Now, if there was a defect involved —" she said, her voice trailing off, implying that trunk locking was all phobia. This must be one of the few issues on which she and the auto industry agree. Ann Carlson of the Motor Vehicle Manufacturing Association became alarmed at the thought that I was going to play up a nonproblem: "In reality this very rarely happens. As you say, in the movies it's a wonderful plot device," she said. "But in reality apparently this is not that frequent an occurrence. So they have not designed that feature into vehicles in a specific way."

When we got to Emmett's one-story house it was full of people. Tony's sister. Carol, was on the floor with her two small children. Her husband, Charlie, had one eye on the golf tournament on TV, and Emmett was at the kitchen counter, trimming fat from meat for lunch. I have known Emmett for fifteen years. He looked better than ever. In his retirement he had sharply changed his diet and lost a lot of weight. He had on shorts. His legs were tanned and muscular. As always, his manner was humorous, if opaque.

Tony told his family my news: I was getting married in three weeks. Charlie wanted to know where my fiancée was. Back East, getting everything ready. A big-time hatter was fitting her for a new hat.

Emmett sat on the couch, watching me. "Do you want my advice?"

"Sure."

He just grinned. A gold tooth glinted. Carol and Charlie pressed him to yield his wisdom.

Finally he said, "Once you get to be thirty, you make your own mistakes."

He got out several cans of beer, and then I brought up what was on my mind.

Emmett nodded and took off his glasses, then cleaned them and put them back on.

We went out to his car, a Mercury Grand Marquis, and Emmett opened the trunk. His golf clubs were sitting on top of the spare tire in a green golf bag. Next to them was a toolbox and what he called his "burglar tools," a set of elbowed rods with red plastic handles he used to open door locks when people locked their keys inside.

Tony and Charlie stood watching. Charlie is a banker in Minneapolis. He enjoys gizmos and is extremely practical. I would describe his as unflappable. That's a word I always wanted to apply to myself, but my fiancée had recently informed me that I am high-strung. Though that surprised me, I didn't quarrel with her.

For a while we studied the latch assembly. The lock closed in much the same way that a lobster might clamp on to a pencil. The claw portion, the jaws of the lock, was mounted inside the trunk lid. When you shut the lid, the jaws locked on to the bend of a U-shaped piece of metal mounted on the body of the car. Emmett said my best bet would be to unscrew the bolts. That way the U-shaped piece would come loose and the lock's jaws would swing up with it still in their grasp.

"But you'd need a wrench," he said.

It was already getting too technical. Emmett had an air of endless patience, but I felt defeated. I could only imagine bloodied fingers, cracked teeth. I had hoped for a simple trick.

Charlie stepped forward. He reached out and squeezed the lock's jaws. They clicked shut in the air, bound together by heavy springs. Charlie now prodded the upper part of the left-hand jaw, the thicker part. With a rough flick of his thumb, he was able to force the jaws to snap open. Great.

Unfortunately, the jaws were mounted behind a steel plate the size of your palm in such a way that while they were accessible to us, standing outside the car, had we been inside the trunk the plate would be in our way, blocking the jaws.

This time Emmett saw the way out. He fingered a hole in the plate. It was no bigger than the tip of your little finger. But the hole was close enough to the latch itself that it might be possible to angle something through the hole from inside the trunk and nudge the jaws apart. We tried with one of my keys. The lock jumped open.

It was time for a full-dress test. Emmett swung the clubs out of the trunk, and I set my can of Schmidt's on the rear bumper and climbed in. Everyone gathered around, and Emmett lowered the trunk on me, then pressed it shut with his meaty hands. Total darkness. I couldn't hear the people outside. I thought I was going to panic. But the big trunk felt comfortable. I was pressed against a sort of black carpet that softened the angles against my back.

I could almost stretch out in the trunk, and it seemed to me I could make them sweat if I took my time. Even Emmett, that sphinx, would give way to curiosity. Once I was out he'd ask how it had been and I'd just grin. There were some things you could only learn by doing.

It took a while to find the hole. I slipped the key in and angled it to one side. The trunk gasped open.

Emmett motioned the others away, then levered me out with his big right forearm. Though I'd only been inside for a minute, I was disoriented—as much as anything because someone had moved my beer while I was gone, setting it down on the cement floor of the garage. It was just a little thing, but I could not be entirely sure I had gotten my own beer back.

Charlie was now raring to try other cars. We examined the latch on his Toyota, which was entirely shielded to the trunk occupant (i.e., no hole in the plate), and on the neighbor's Honda (ditto). But a 1991 Dodge Dynasty was doable. The trunk was tight, but its lock had a feature one of the mechanics I'd phoned described as a "tailpiece": a finger-like extension of the lock mechanism itself that stuck out a half inch into the trunk cavity: simply by twisting the tailpiece I could free the lock. I was even faster on a 1984 Subaru that had a little lever device on the latch.

We went out to my rental on Oak Street. The Skylark was in direct sun and the trunk was hot to the touch, but when we got it open we could see that its latch plate had a perfect hole, a square in which the edge of the lock's jaw appeared like a face in a window.

The trunk was shallow and hot. Emmett had to push my knees down before he could close the lid. This one was a little suffocating. I imagined being trapped for hours, and even before he had got it closed I regretted the decision with a slightly nauseous feeling. I thought of Edgar Allan Poe's live burials, and then about something my fiancée had said more than a year and a half before. I had been on her case to get married. She was divorced, and at every opportunity I would reissue my proposal—even during a commercial. She'd interrupted one of these chirps to tell me, in a cold, throaty voice, that she had no intention of ever going through another divorce: "This time, it's death out." I'd carried those words around like a lump of wet clay.

As it happened, the Skylark trunk was the easiest of all. The hole was right where it was supposed to be. The trunk popped open, and I felt great satisfaction that we'd been able to figure out a rule that seemed to apply about 60 percent of the time. If we publicized our success, it might get the attention it deserved. All trunks would be fitted with such a hole. Kids would learn about it in school. The grip of the fear would relax. Before long a successful trunk-locking scene would date a movie like a fedora dates one today.

When I got back East I was caught up in wedding preparations. I live in New York, and the wedding was to take place in Philadelphia. We set up camp there with five days to go. A friend had lent my fiancée her BMW, and we drove it south with all our things. I unloaded the car in my parents' driveway. The last thing I pulled out of the trunk was my fiancée's hat in its heavy cardboard shipping box. She'd warned me I was not allowed to look. The lid was free but I didn't open it. I was willing to be surprised.

When the trunk was empty it occurred to me I might hop in and give it a try. First I looked over the mechanism. The jaws of the BMW's lock were shielded, but there seemed to be some kind of cable coming off it that you might be able to manipulate so as to cause the lock to open. The same cable that allowed the driver to open the trunk remotely...

I fingered it for a moment or two but decided I didn't need to test out the theory.

—1992

Learning from Other Writers

1. Weiss states his central question at the end of the first paragraph of his essay. What is the purpose of each of the eight paragraphs that follow the first? How is the remainder of the essay structured?
2. Given that most of us *aren't* obsessed with how to get out of a locked trunk, why should we care about Weiss's fears?
3. Why doesn't the author feel the need to test his ability to get out of the trunk of his fiancée's BMW?
4. As is true for many of the essays in this book, "How to Get Out of a Locked Trunk" could have been included in other chapters. After all, Weiss sets out on a journey (from St. Paul to Waconia) with the aim of answering a question ("Is it possible to get out of a locked car trunk?"). The essay is a personal narrative, told more or less in chronological order. And, as we'll see in Chapter 13, the "how-to guide" is a subset of the spatial form. Was I right in classifying Weiss's essay as an experiment, or would you have placed it in a different chapter?

BARBARA EHRENREICH

NICKEL-AND-DIMED: ON (NOT) GETTING BY IN AMERICA

At the beginning of June 1998 I leave behind everything that normally soothes the ego and sustains the body—home, career, companion, reputation, ATM card—for a plunge into the low-wage workforce. There, I become another, occupationally much diminished "Barbara Ehrenreich"—depicted on job-application forms as a divorced homemaker whose sole work experience consists of housekeeping in a few private homes. I am terrified, at the beginning, of being unmasked for what I am: a middle-class journalist setting out to explore the world that welfare mothers are entering, at the rate of approximately 50,000 a month, as welfare reform kicks in. Happily, though, my fears turn out to be entirely unwarranted: during a month of poverty and toil, my name goes unnoticed and for the most part unuttered. In this parallel universe where my father never got out of the mines and I never got through college, I am "baby," "honey," "blondie," and, most commonly, "girl."

My first task is to find a place to live. I figure that if I can earn $7 an hour—which, from the want ads, seems doable—I can afford to spend $500 on rent, or maybe, with severe economies, $600. In the Key West area, where I live, this pretty much confines me to flophouses and trailer homes—like the one, a pleasing fifteen-minute drive from town, that has no air-conditioning, no screens, no fans, no television, and, by way of diversion, only the challenge of evading the landlord's Doberman pinscher. The big problem with this place, though, is the rent, which at $675 a month is well beyond my reach. All right, Key West is expensive. But so is New York City, or the Bay Area, or Jackson Hole, or Telluride, or Boston, or any other place where tourists and the wealthy compete for living space with the people who clean their toilets and fry their hash browns.[1] Still, it is a shock to realize that "trailer trash" has become, for me, a demographic category to aspire to.

1 According to the Department of Housing and Urban Development, the "fair-market rent" for an efficiency is $551 here in Monroe County, Florida. A comparable rent in the five boroughs of New York City is $704; in San Francisco, $713; and in the heart of Silicon Valley, $808. The fair-market rent for an area is defined as the amount that would be needed to pay rent plus utilities for "privately owned, decent, safe, and sanitary rental housing of a modest (non-luxury) nature with suitable amenities."

So I decide to make the common trade-off between affordability and convenience, and go for a $500-a-month efficiency thirty miles up a two lane highway from the employment opportunities of Key West, meaning forty-five minutes if there's no road construction and I don't get caught behind some sun-dazed Canadian tourists. I hate the drive, along a roadside studded with white crosses commemorating the more effective head-on collisions, but it's a sweet little place—a cabin, more or less, set in the swampy back yard of the converted mobile home where my landlord, an affable TV repairman, lives with his bartender girlfriend. Anthropologically speaking, a bustling trailer park would be preferable, but here I have a gleaming white floor and a firm mattress, and the few resident bugs are easily vanquished.

Besides, I am not doing this for the anthropology. My aim is nothing so mistily subjective as to "experience poverty" or find out how it "really feels" to be a long-term low-wage worker. I've had enough unchosen encounters with poverty and the world of low-wage work to know it's not a place you want to visit for touristic purposes; it just smells too much like fear. And with all my real-life assets—bank account, IRA, health insurance, multiroom home—waiting indulgently in the background, I am, of course, thoroughly insulated from the terrors that afflict the genuinely poor.

No, this is a purely objective, scientific sort of mission. The humanitarian rationale for welfare reform—as opposed to the more punitive and stingy impulses that may actually have motivated it—is that work will lift poor women out of poverty while simultaneously inflating their self-esteem and hence their future value in the labor market. Thus, whatever the hassles involved in finding child care, transportation, etc., the transition from welfare to work will end happily, in greater prosperity for all. Now there are many problems with this comforting prediction, such as the fact that the economy will inevitably undergo a downturn, eliminating many jobs. Even without a downturn, the influx of a million former welfare recipients into the low-wage labor market could depress wages by as much as 11.9 percent, according to the Economic Policy Institute (EPI) in Washington, D.C.

But is it really possible to make a living on the kinds of jobs currently available to unskilled people? Mathematically, the answer is no, as can be shown by taking $6 to $7 an hour, perhaps subtracting a dollar or two an hour for child care, multiplying by 160 hours a month, and comparing the result to the prevailing rents. According to the National Coalition for the Homeless, for example, in 1998 it took, on average nationwide, an hourly wage of $8.89 to afford a one-bedroom apartment, and the Preamble Center for Public Policy estimates that the odds against a typical welfare recipient's landing a job at such a "living wage" are about 97 to 1. If these numbers are right, low-wage work is not a solution to poverty and possibly not even to homelessness.

It may seem excessive to put this proposition to an experimental test. As certain family members keep unhelpfully reminding me, the viability of low-wage work could be tested, after a fashion, without ever leaving my study. I could just pay myself $7 an hour for eight hours a day, charge myself for room and board, and total up the numbers after a month. Why leave the people and work that I love? But I am an experimental scientist by training. In that business, you don't just sit at a desk and theorize; you plunge into the everyday chaos of nature, where surprises lurk in the most mundane measurements. Maybe, when I got into it, I would discover some hidden economies in the world of the low-wage worker. After all, if 30 percent of the workforce toils for less than $8 an hour, according to the EPI, they may have found some tricks as yet unknown to me. Maybe—who knows?—I would even be able to detect in myself the bracing psychological effects of getting out of the house, as promised by the welfare wonks at places like the Heritage Foundation. Or, on the other hand, maybe there would be unexpected costs—physical, mental, or financial—to throw off all my calculations. Ideally, I should do this with two small children in tow, that being the welfare average, but mine are grown and no one is willing to lend me theirs for a month-long vacation in penury. So this is not the perfect experiment, just a test of the best possible case: an unencumbered woman, smart and even strong, attempting to live more or less off the land.

On the morning of my first full day of job searching, I take a red pen to the want ads, which are auspiciously numerous. Everyone in Key West's booming "hospitality industry" seems to be looking for someone like me—trainable, flexible, and with suitably humble expectations as to pay. I know I possess certain traits that might be advantageous—I'm white and, I like to think, well-spoken and poised—but I decide on two rules: One, I cannot use any skills derived from my education or usual work—not that there are a lot of want ads for satirical essayists anyway. Two, I have to take the best-paid job that is offered me and of course do my best to hold it, no Marxist rants or sneaking off to read novels in the ladies' room. In addition, I rule out various occupations for one reason or another: Hotel front-desk clerk, for example, which to my surprise is regarded as unskilled and pays around $7 an hour, gets eliminated because it involves standing in one spot for eight hours a day. Waitressing is similarly something I'd like to avoid, because I remember it leaving me bone tired when I was eighteen, and I'm decades of varicosities and back pain beyond that now. Telemarketing, one of the first refuges of the suddenly indigent, can be dismissed on grounds of personality. This leaves certain supermarket jobs, such as deli clerk, or housekeeping in Key West's thousands of hotel and guest rooms. Housekeeping is especially appealing, for reasons both atavistic and practical: it's what my mother did before I came along, and it can't be too different from what I've been doing part-time, in my own home, all my life.

So I put on what I take to be a respectful-looking outfit of ironed Bermuda shorts and scooped-neck T-shirt and set out for a tour of the local hotels and supermarkets. Best Western, Econo Lodge, and Hojo's all let me fill out application forms, and these are, to my relief, interested in little more than whether I am a legal resident of the United States and have committed any felonies. My next stop is Winn-Dixie, the supermarket, which turns out to have a particularly onerous application process, featuring a fifteen-minute "interview" by computer since, apparently, no human on the premises is deemed capable of representing the corporate point of view. I am conducted to a large room decorated with posters illustrating how to look "professional" (it helps to be white and, if female, permed) and warning of the slick promises that union organizers might try to tempt me with. The interview is multiple choice: Do I have anything, such as child-care problems, that might make it hard for me to get to work on time? Do I think safety on the job is the responsibility of management? Then, popping up cunningly out of the blue: How many dollars' worth of stolen goods have I purchased in the last year? Would I turn in a fellow employee if I caught him stealing? Finally, "Are you an honest person?"

Apparently, I ace the interview, because I am told that all I have to do is show up in some doctor's office tomorrow for a urine test. This seems to be a fairly general rule: if you want to stack Cheerio boxes or vacuum hotel rooms in chemically fascist America, you have to be willing to squat down and pee in front of some health worker (who has no doubt had to do the same thing herself). The wages Winn-Dixie is offering—$6 and a couple of dimes to start with—are not enough, I decide, to compensate for this indignity.[2]

---

[2] According to the Monthly Labor Review (November 1996), 28 percent of work sites surveyed in the service industry conduct drug tests (corporate workplaces have much higher rates), and the incidence of testing has risen markedly since the Eighties. The rate of testing is highest in the South (56 percent of work sites polled), with the Midwest in second place (50 percent). The drug most likely to be detected—marijuana, which can be detected in urine for weeks—is also the most innocuous, while heroin and cocaine are generally undetectable three days after use. Prospective employees sometimes try to cheat the tests by consuming excessive amounts of liquids and taking diuretics and even masking substances available through the Internet.

I lunch at Wendy's, where $4.99 gets you unlimited refills at the Mexican part of the Superbar, a comforting surfeit of refried beans and "cheese sauce." A teenage employee, seeing me studying the want ads, kindly offers me an application form, which I fill out, though here, too, the pay is just $6 and change an hour. Then it's off for a round of the locally owned inns and guesthouses. At "The Palms," let's call it, a bouncy manager actually takes me around to see the rooms and meet the existing housekeepers, who, I note with satisfaction, look pretty much like me—faded ex-hippie types in shorts with long hair pulled back in braids. Mostly, though, no one speaks to me or even looks at me except to proffer an application form. At my last stop, a palatial B&B, I wait twenty minutes to meet "Max," only to be told that there are no jobs now but there should be one soon, since "nobody lasts more than a couple weeks." (Because none of the people I talked to knew I was a reporter, I have changed their names to protect their privacy and, in some cases perhaps, their jobs.)

Three days go by like this, and, to my chagrin, no one out of the approximately twenty places I've applied calls me for an interview. I had been vain enough to worry about coming across as too educated for the jobs I sought, but no one even seems interested in finding out how overqualified I am. Only later will I realize that the want ads are not a reliable measure of the actual jobs available at any particular time. They are, as I should have guessed from Max's comment, the employers' insurance policy against the relentless turnover of the low-wage workforce. Most of the big hotels run ads almost continually, just to build a supply of applicants to replace the current workers as they drift away or are fired, so finding a job is just a matter of being at the right place at the right time and flexible enough to take whatever is being offered that day. This finally happens to me at a one of the big discount hotel chains, where I go, as usual, for housekeeping and am sent, instead, to try out as a waitress at the attached "family restaurant," a dismal spot with a counter and about thirty tables that looks out on a parking garage and features such tempting fare as "Pollish [sic] sausage and BBQ sauce" on 95-degree days. Phillip, the dapper young West Indian who introduces himself as the manager, interviews me with about as much enthusiasm as if he were a clerk processing me for Medicare, the principal questions being what shifts can I work and when can I start. I mutter something about being woefully out of practice as a waitress, but he's already on to the uniform: I'm to show up tomorrow wearing black slacks and black shoes; he'll provide the rust-colored polo shirt with HEARTHSIDE embroidered on it, though I might want to wear my own shirt to get to work, ha ha. At the word "tomorrow," something between fear and indignation rises in my chest. I want to say, "Thank you for your time, sir, but this is just an experiment, you know, not my actual life."

So begins my career at the Hearthside, I shall call it, one small profit center within a global discount hotel chain, where for two weeks I work from 2:00 till 10:00 P.M. for $2.43 an hour plus tips.[3] In some futile bid for gentility, the management has barred employees from using the front door, so my first day I enter through the kitchen, where a red-faced man with shoulder-length blond hair is throwing frozen steaks against the wall and yelling, "Fuck this shit!" "That's just Jack," explains Gail, the wiry middle-aged waitress who is assigned to train me. "He's on the rag again"—a condition occasioned, in this instance, by the fact that the cook on the morning shift had forgotten to thaw out the steaks. For the next

3 According to the Fair Labor Standards Act, employers are not required to pay "tipped employees," such as restaurant servers, more than $2.13 an hour in direct wages. However, if the sum of tips plus $2.13 an hour falls below the minimum wage, or $5.15 an hour, the employer is required to make up the difference. This fact was not mentioned by managers or otherwise publicized at either of the restaurants where I worked.

eight hours, I run after the agile Gail, absorbing bits of instruction along with fragments of personal tragedy. All food must be trayed, and the reason she's so tired today is that she woke up in a cold sweat thinking of her boyfriend, who killed himself recently in an upstate prison. No refills on lemonade. And the reason he was in prison is that a few DUIs caught up with him, that's all, could have happened to anyone. Carry the creamers to the table in a monkey bowl, never in your hand. And after he was gone she spent several months living in her truck, peeing in a plastic pee bottle and reading by candlelight at night, but you can't live in a truck in the summer, since you need to have the windows down, which means anything can get in, from mosquitoes on up.

At least Gail puts to rest any fears I had of appearing overqualified. From the first day on, I find that of all the things I have left behind, such as home and identity, what I miss the most is competence. Not that I have ever felt utterly competent in the writing business, in which one day's success augurs nothing at all for the next. But in my writing life, I at least have some notion of procedure: do the research, make the outline, rough out a draft, etc. As a server, though, I am beset by requests like bees: more iced tea here, ketchup over there, a to-go box for table fourteen, and where are the high chairs, anyway? Of the twenty-seven tables, up to six are usually mine at any time, though on slow afternoons or if Gail is off, I sometimes have the whole place to myself. There is the touch-screen computer-ordering system to master, which is, I suppose, meant to minimize server-cook contact, but in practice requires constant verbal fine-tuning: "That's gravy on the mashed, okay? None on the meatloaf," and so forth—while the cook scowls as if I were inventing these refinements just to torment him. Plus, something I had forgotten in the years since I was eighteen: about a third of a server's job is "side work" that's invisible to customers—sweeping, scrubbing, slicing, refilling, and restocking. If it isn't all done, every little bit of it, you're going to face the 6:00 P.M. dinner rush defenseless and probably go down in flames. I screw up dozens of times at the beginning, sustained in my shame entirely by Gail's support—"It's okay, baby, everyone does that sometime"—because, to my total surprise and despite the scientific detachment I am doing my best to maintain, I care.

The whole thing would be a lot easier if I could just skate through it as Lily Tomlin in one of her waitress skits, but I was raised by the absurd Booker T. Washingtonian precept that says: If you're going to do something, do it well. In fact, "well" isn't good enough by half. Do it better than anyone has ever done it before. Or so said my father, who must have known what he was talking about because he managed to pull himself, and us with him, up from the mile-deep copper mines of Butte to the leafy suburbs of the Northeast, ascending from boilermakers to martinis before booze beat out ambition. As in most endeavors I have encountered in my life, doing it "better than anyone" is not a reasonable goal. Still, when I wake up at 4:00 A.M. in my own cold sweat, I am not thinking about the writing deadlines I'm neglecting; I'm thinking about the table whose order I screwed up so that one of the boys didn't get his kiddie meal until the rest of the family had moved on to their Key Lime pies. That's the other powerful motivation I hadn't expected—the customers, or "patients," as I can't help thinking of them on account of the mysterious vulnerability that seems to have left them temporarily unable to feed themselves. After a few days at the Hearthside, I feel the service ethic kick in like a shot of oxytocin, the nurturance hormone. The plurality of my customers are hardworking locals—truck drivers, construction workers, even housekeepers from the attached hotel—and I want them to have the closest to a "fine dining" experience that the grubby circumstances will allow. No "you guys" for me; everyone over twelve is "sir" or "ma'am." I ply them with iced tea and coffee refills; I return, mid-meal, to inquire how everything is; I doll up their salads with chopped raw mushrooms, summer squash slices, or whatever bits of produce I can find that have survived their sojourn in the cold-storage room mold-free.

There is Benny, for example, a short, tight-muscled sewer repairman, who cannot even think of eating until he has absorbed a half hour of air-conditioning and ice water. We chat about hyperthermia and electrolytes until he is ready to order some finicky combination like soup of the day, garden salad, and a side of grits. There are the German tourists who are so touched by my pidgin "Willkommen" and "Ist alles gut?" that they actually tip. (Europeans, spoiled by their trade-union-ridden, high-wage welfare states, generally do not know that they are supposed to tip. Some restaurants, the Hearthside included, allow servers to "grat" their foreign customers, or add a tip to the bill. Since this amount is added before the customers have a chance to tip or not tip, the practice amounts to an automatic penalty for imperfect English.) There are the two dirt-smudged lesbians, just off their construction shift, who are impressed enough by my suave handling of the fly in the piña colada that they take the time to praise me to Stu, the assistant manager. There's Sam, the kindly retired cop, who has to plug up his tracheotomy hole with one finger in order to force the cigarette smoke into his lungs.

Sometimes I play with the fantasy that I am a princess who, in penance for some tiny transgression, has undertaken to feed each of her subjects by hand. But the non-princesses working with me are just as indulgent, even when this means flouting management rules—concerning, for example, the number of croutons that can go on a salad (six). "Put on all you want," Gail whispers, "as long as Stu isn't looking." She dips into her own tip money to buy biscuits and gravy for an out-of-work mechanic who's used up all his money on dental surgery, inspiring me to pick up the tab for his milk and pie. Maybe the same high levels of agape can be found throughout the "hospitality industry." I remember the poster decorating one of the apartments I looked at, which said "If you seek happiness for yourself you will never find it. Only when you seek happiness for others will it come to you," or words to that effect—an odd sentiment, it seemed to me at the time, to find in the dank one-room basement apartment of a bellhop at the Best Western. At the Hearthside, we utilize whatever bits of autonomy we have to ply our customers with the illicit calories that signal our love. It is our job as servers to assemble the salads and desserts, pouring the dressings and squirting the whipped cream. We also control the number of butter patties our customers get and the amount of sour cream on their baked potatoes. So if you wonder why Americans are so obese, consider the fact that waitresses both express their humanity and earn their tips through the covert distribution of fats.

Ten days into it, this is beginning to look like a livable lifestyle. I like Gail, who is "looking at fifty" but moves so fast she can alight in one place and then another without apparently being anywhere between them. I clown around with Lionel, the teenage Haitian busboy, and catch a few fragments of conversation with Joan, the svelte fortyish hostess and militant feminist who is the only one of us who dares to tell Jack to shut the fuck up. I even warm up to Jack when, on a slow night and to make up for a particularly unwarranted attack on my abilities, or so I imagine, he tells me about his glory days as a young man at "coronary school"—or do you say "culinary"?—in Brooklyn, where he dated a knock-out Puerto Rican chick and learned everything there is to know about food. I finish up at 10:00 or 10:30, depending on how much side work I've been able to get done during the shift, and cruise home to the tapes I snatched up at random when I left my real home—Marianne Faithfull, Tracy Chapman, Enigma, King Sunny Ade, the Violent Femmes—just drained enough for the music to set my cranium resonating but hardly dead. Midnight snack is Wheat Thins and Monterey Jack, accompanied by cheap white wine on ice and whatever AMC has to offer. To bed by 1:30 or 2:00, up at 9:00 or 10:00, read for an hour while my uniform whirls around in the landlord's washing machine, and then it's another eight hours spent following Mao's central instruction, as laid out in the Little Red Book, which was: Serve the people.

I could drift along like this, in some dreamy proletarian idyll, except for two things. One is management. If I have kept this subject on the margins thus far it is because I still flinch to think that I spent all those weeks under the surveillance of men (and later women) whose job it was to monitor my behavior for signs of sloth, theft, drug abuse, or worse. Not that managers and especially "assistant managers" in low-wage settings like this are exactly the class enemy. In the restaurant business, they are mostly former cooks or servers, still capable of pinch-hitting in the kitchen or on the floor, just as in hotels they are likely to be former clerks, and paid a salary of only about $400 a week. But everyone knows they have crossed over to the other side, which is, crudely put, corporate as opposed to human. Cooks want to prepare tasty meals; servers want to serve them graciously; but managers are there for only one reason—to make sure that money is made for some theoretical entity that exists far away in Chicago or New York, if a corporation can be said to have a physical existence at all. Reflecting on her career, Gail tells me ruefully that she had sworn, years ago, never to work for a corporation again. "They don't cut you no slack. You give and you give, and they take."

Managers can sit—for hours at a time if they want—but it's their job to see that no one else ever does, even when there's nothing to do, and this is why, for servers, slow times can be as exhausting as rushes. You start dragging out each little chore, because if the manager on duty catches you in an idle moment, he will give you something far nastier to do. So I wipe, I clean, I consolidate ketchup bottles and recheck the cheesecake supply, even tour the tables to make sure the customer evaluation forms are all standing perkily in their places—wondering all the time how many calories I burn in these strictly theatrical exercises. When, on a particularly dead afternoon, Stu finds me glancing at a *USA Today* a customer has left behind, he assigns me to vacuum the entire floor with the broken vacuum cleaner that has a handle only two feet long, and the only way to do that without incurring orthopedic damage is to proceed from spot to spot on your knees.

On my first Friday at the Hearthside there is a "mandatory meeting for all restaurant employees," which I attend, eager for insight into our overall marketing strategy and the niche (your basic Ohio cuisine with a tropical twist?) we aim to inhabit. But there is no "we" at this meeting. Phillip, our top manager except for an occasional "consultant" sent out by corporate headquarters, opens it with a sneer: "The break room—it's disgusting. Butts in the ashtrays, newspapers lying around, crumbs." This windowless little room, which also houses the time clock for the entire hotel, is where we stash our bags and civilian clothes and take our half-hour meal breaks. But a break room is not a right, he tells us. It can be taken away. We should also know that the lockers in the break room and whatever is in them can be searched at any time. Then comes gossip; there has been gossip; gossip (which seems to mean employees talking among themselves) must stop. Off-duty employees are henceforth barred from eating at the restaurant, because "other servers gather around them and gossip." When Phillip has exhausted his agenda of rebukes, Joan complains about the condition of the ladies' room and I throw in my two bits about the vacuum cleaner. But I don't see any backup coming from my fellow servers, each of whom has subsided into her own personal funk; Gail, my role model, stares sorrowfully at a point six inches from her nose. The meeting ends when Andy, one of the cooks, gets up, muttering about breaking up his day off for this almighty bullshit.

Just four days later we are suddenly summoned into the kitchen at 3:30 P.M., even though there are live tables on the floor. We all—about ten of us—stand around

Phillip, who announces grimly that there has been a report of some "drug activity" on the night shift and that, as a result, we are now to be a "drug-free" workplace, meaning that all new hires will be tested, as will possibly current employees on a random basis. I am glad that this part of the kitchen is so dark, because I find myself blushing as hard as if I had been caught toking up in the ladies' room myself: I haven't been treated this way—lined up in the corridor, threatened with locker searches, peppered with carelessly aimed accusations—since junior high school. Back on the floor, Joan cracks, "Next they'll be telling us we can't have sex on the job." When I ask Stu what happened to inspire the crackdown, he just mutters about "management decisions" and takes the opportunity to upbraid Gail and me for being too generous with the rolls. From now on there's to be only one per customer, and it goes out with the dinner, not with the salad. He's also been riding the cooks, prompting Andy to come out of the kitchen and observe—with the serenity of a man whose customary implement is a butcher knife—that "Stu has a death wish today."

Later in the evening, the gossip crystallizes around the theory that Stu is himself the drug culprit, that he uses the restaurant phone to order up marijuana and sends one of the late servers out to fetch it for him. The server was caught, and she may have ratted Stu out or at least said enough to cast some suspicion on him, thus accounting for his pissy behavior. Who knows? Lionel, the busboy, entertains us for the rest of the shift by standing just behind Stu's back and sucking deliriously on an imaginary joint.

The other problem, in addition to the less-than-nurturing management style, is that this job shows no sign of being financially viable. You might imagine, from a comfortable distance, that people who live, year in and year out, on $6 to $10 an hour have discovered some survival stratagems unknown to the middle class. But no. It's not hard to get my co-workers to talk about their living situations, because housing, in almost every case, is the principal source of disruption in their lives, the first thing they fill you in on when they arrive for their shifts. After a week, I have compiled the following survey:

- Gail is sharing a room in a well-known downtown flophouse for which she and a roommate pay about $250 a week. Her roommate, a male friend, has begun hitting on her, driving her nuts, but the rent would be impossible alone.
- Claude, the Haitian cook, is desperate to get out of the two-room apartment he shares with his girlfriend and two other, unrelated, people. As far as I can determine, the other Haitian men (most of whom only speak Creole) live in similarly crowded situations.
- Annette, a twenty-year-old server who is six months pregnant and has been abandoned by her boyfriend, lives with her mother, a postal clerk.
- Marianne and her boyfriend are paying $170 a week for a one-person trailer.
- Jack, who is, at $10 an hour, the wealthiest of us, lives in the trailer he owns, paying only the $400-a-month lot fee.
- The other white cook, Andy, lives on his dry-docked boat, which, as far as I can tell from his loving descriptions, can't be more than twenty feet long. He offers to take me out on it, once it's repaired, but the offer comes with inquiries as to my marital status, so I do not follow up on it.
- Tina and her husband are paying $60 a night for a double room in a Days Inn. This is because they have no car and the Days Inn is within walking distance of the Hearthside.
- When Marianne, one of the breakfast servers, is tossed out of her trailer for subletting (which is against the trailer-park rules), she leaves her boyfriend and moves in with Tina and her husband.

- Joan, who had fooled me with her numerous and tasteful outfits (hostesses wear their own clothes), lives in a van she parks behind a shopping center at night and showers in Tina's motel room. The clothes are from thrift shops.[4]

It strikes me, in my middle-class solipsism, that there is gross improvidence in some of these arrangements. When Gail and I are wrapping silverware in napkins—the only task for which we are permitted to sit—she tells me she is thinking of escaping from her roommate by moving into the Days Inn herself. I am astounded: How can she even think of paying between $40 and $60 a day? But if I was afraid of sounding like a social worker, I come out just sounding like a fool. She squints at me in disbelief, "And where am I supposed to get a month's rent and a month's deposit for an apartment?" I'd been feeling pretty smug about my $500 efficiency, but of course it was made possible only by the $1,300 I had allotted myself for start-up costs when I began my low-wage life: $1,000 for the first month's rent and deposit, $100 for initial groceries and cash in my pocket, $200 stuffed away for emergencies. In poverty, as in certain propositions in physics, starting conditions are everything.

There are no secret economies that nourish the poor; on the contrary, there are a host of special costs. If you can't put up the two months' rent you need to secure an apartment, you end up paying through the nose for a room by the week. If you have only a room, with a hot plate at best, you can't save by cooking up huge lentil stews that can be frozen for the week ahead. You eat fast food, or the hot dogs and styrofoam cups of soup that can be microwaved in a convenience store. If you have no money for health insurance—and the Hearthside's niggardly plan kicks in only after three months—you go without routine care or prescription drugs and end up paying the price. Gail, for example, was fine until she ran out of money for estrogen pills. She is supposed to be on the company plan by now, but they claim to have lost her application form and need to begin the paperwork all over again. So she spends $9 per migraine pill to control the headaches she wouldn't have, she insists, if her estrogen supplements were covered. Similarly, Marianne's boyfriend lost his job as a roofer because he missed so much time after getting a cut on his foot for which he couldn't afford the prescribed antibiotic.

My own situation, when I sit down to assess it after two weeks of work, would not be much better if this were my actual life. The seductive thing about waitressing is that you don't have to wait for payday to feel a few bills in your pocket, and my tips usually cover meals and gas, plus something left over to stuff into the kitchen drawer I use as a bank. But as the tourist business slows in the summer heat, I sometimes leave work with only $20 in tips (the gross is higher, but servers share about 15 percent of their tips with the busboys and bartenders). With wages included, this amounts to about the minimum wage of $5.15 an hour. Although the sum in the drawer is piling up, at the present rate of accumulation it will be more than a hundred dollars short of my rent when the end of the month comes around. Nor can I see any expenses to cut. True, I haven't gone the lentil-stew route yet, but that's because I don't have a large cooking pot, pot holders, or a ladle to stir with (which cost about $30 at Kmart, less at thrift stores), not to mention onions, carrots, and the indispensable bay leaf. I do make my lunch almost every day—usually some slow-burning, high-protein combo like frozen chicken patties with melted cheese on top and canned pinto beans on the side. Dinner is at the Hearthside, which offers its employees a choice of BLT,

4 I could find no statistics on the number of employed people living in cars or vans, but according to the National Coalition for the Homeless's 1997 report "Myths and Facts About Homelessness," nearly one in five homeless people (in twenty-nine cities across the nation) is employed in a full- or part-time job.

fish sandwich, or hamburger for only $2. The burger lasts longest, especially if it's heaped with gut-puckering jalapeños, but by midnight my stomach is growling again.

So unless I want to start using my car as a residence, I have to find a second, or alternative, job. I call all the hotels where I filled out housekeeping applications weeks ago—the Hyatt, Holiday Inn, Econo Lodge, HoJo's, Best Western, plus a half dozen or so locally run guesthouses. Nothing. Then I start making the rounds again, wasting whole mornings waiting for some assistant manager to show up, even dipping into places so creepy that the front-desk clerk greets you from behind bulletproof glass and sells pints of liquor over the counter. But either someone has exposed my real-life housekeeping habits—which are, shall we say, mellow—or I am at the wrong end of some infallible ethnic equation: most, but by no means all, of the working housekeepers I see on my job searches are African Americans, Spanish-speaking, or immigrants from the Central European post-Communist world, whereas servers are almost invariably white and monolingually English-speaking. When I finally get a positive response, I have been identified once again as server material. Jerry's, which is part of a well-known national family restaurant chain and physically attached here to another budget hotel chain, is ready to use me at once. The prospect is both exciting and terrifying, because, with about the same number of tables and counter seats, Jerry's attracts three or four times the volume of customers as the gloomy old Hearthside.

Picture a fat person's hell, and I don't mean a place with no food. Instead there is everything you might eat if eating had no bodily consequences—cheese fries, chicken-fried steaks, fudge-laden desserts—only here every bite must be paid for, one way or another, in human discomfort. The kitchen is a cavern, a stomach leading to the lower intestine that is the garbage and dishwashing area, from which issue bizarre smells combining the edible and the offal: creamy carrion, pizza barf, and that unique and enigmatic Jerry's scent—citrus fart. The floor is slick with spills, forcing us to walk through the kitchen with tiny steps, like Susan McDougal in leg irons. Sinks everywhere are clogged with scraps of lettuce, decomposing lemon wedges, waterlogged toast crusts. Put your hand down on any counter and you risk being stuck to it by the film of ancient syrup spills, and this is unfortunate, because hands are utensils here, used for scooping up lettuce onto salad plates, lifting out pie slices, and even moving hash browns from one plate to another. The regulation poster in the single unisex restroom admonishes us to wash our hands thoroughly and even offers instructions for doing so, but there is always some vital substance missing—soap, paper towels, toilet paper—and I never find all three at once. You learn to stuff your pockets with napkins before going in there, and too bad about the customers, who must eat, though they don't realize this, almost literally out of our hands.

The break room typifies the whole situation: there is none, because there are no breaks at Jerry's. For six to eight hours in a row, you never sit except to pee. Actually, there are three folding chairs at a table immediately adjacent to the bathroom, but hardly anyone ever sits here, in the very rectum of the gastro-architectural system. Rather, the function of the peri-toilet area is to house the ashtrays in which servers and dishwashers leave their cigarettes burning at all times, like votive candles, so that they don't have to waste time lighting up again when they dash back for a puff. Almost everyone smokes as if his or her pulmonary well-being depended on it—the multinational mélange of cooks, the Czech dishwashers, the servers, who are all American natives—creating an atmosphere in which oxygen is only an occasional pollutant. My first morning at Jerry's, when the hypoglycemic shakes set in, I complain to one of my fellow servers that I don't understand how she can go so long without food. "Well, I don't understand how you can go so long without a cigarette," she responds in a tone of reproach—because work is what you do for others; smoking is what you do for yourself. I don't know why the antismoking crusaders have never grasped the element of defiant self-nurturance that makes the habit so endearing to its victims—as if, in the American workplace, the only thing people have to call their own is the tumors they are nourishing and the spare moments they devote to feeding them.

Now, the Industrial Revolution is not an easy transition, especially when you have to zip through it in just a couple of days. I have gone from craft work straight into the factory, from the air-conditioned morgue of the Hearthside directly into the flames. Customers arrive in human waves, sometimes disgorged fifty at a time from their tour buses, peckish and whiny. Instead of two "girls" on the floor at once, there can be as many as six of us running around in our brilliant pink-and-orange Hawaiian shirts. Conversations, either with customers or fellow employees, seldom last more than twenty seconds at a time. On my first day, in fact, I am hurt by my sister servers' coldness. My mentor for the day is an emotionally uninflected twenty-three-year-old, and the others, who gossip a little among themselves about the real reason someone is out sick today and the size of the bail bond someone else has had to pay, ignore me completely. On my second day, I find out why. "Well, it's good to see you again," one of them says in greeting. "Hardly anyone comes back after the first day." I feel powerfully vindicated—a survivor—but it would take a long time, probably months, before I could hope to be accepted into this sorority.

I start out with the beautiful, heroic idea of handling the two jobs at once, and for two days I almost do it: the breakfast/lunch shift at Jerry's, which goes till 2:00, arriving at the Hearthside at 2:10, and attempting to hold out until 10:00. In the ten minutes between jobs, I pick up a spicy chicken sandwich at the Wendy's drive-through window, gobble it down in the car, and change from khaki slacks to black, from Hawaiian to rust polo. There is a problem, though. When during the 3:00 to 4:00 P.M. dead time I finally sit down to wrap silver, my flesh seems to bond to the seat. I try to refuel with a purloined cup of soup, as I've seen Gail and Joan do dozens of times, but a manager catches me and hisses "No eating!" though there's not a customer around to be offended by the sight of food making contact with a server's lips. So I tell Gail I'm going to quit, and she hugs me and says she might just follow me to Jerry's herself.

But the chances of this are minuscule. She has left the flophouse and her annoying roommate and is back to living in her beat-up old truck. But guess what? she reports to me excitedly later that evening: Phillip has given her permission to park overnight in the hotel parking lot, as long as she keeps out of sight, and the parking lot should be totally safe, since it's patrolled by a hotel security guard! With the Hearthside offering benefits like that, how could anyone think of leaving?

Gail would have triumphed at Jerry's, I'm sure, but for me it's a crash course in exhaustion management. Years ago, the kindly fry cook who trained me to waitress at a Los Angeles truck stop used to say: Never make an unnecessary trip; if you don't have to walk fast, walk slow; if you don't have to walk, stand. But at Jerry's the effort of distinguishing necessary from unnecessary and urgent from whenever would itself be too much of an energy drain. The only thing to do is to treat each shift as a one-time-only emergency: you've got fifty starving people out there, lying scattered on the battlefield, so get out there and feed them! Forget that you will have to do this again tomorrow, forget that you will have to be alert enough to dodge the drunks on the drive home tonight—just burn, burn, burn! Ideally, at some point you enter what servers call "a rhythm" and psychologists term a "flow state," in which signals pass from the sense organs directly to the muscles, bypassing the cerebral cortex, and a Zen-like emptiness sets in. A male server from the Hearthside's morning shift tells me about the time he "pulled a triple"—three shifts in a row, all the way around the clock—and then got off and had a drink and met this girl, and maybe he shouldn't tell me this, but they had sex right then and there, and it was like, beautiful.

But there's another capacity of the neuromuscular system, which is pain. I start tossing back drugstore-brand ibuprofen pills as if they were vitamin C, four before each shift, because an old mouse-related repetitive-stress injury in my upper back has come back to full-spasm strength, thanks to the tray carrying. In my ordinary life, this level of disability might justify a day of ice packs and stretching. Here I comfort myself with the Aleve commercial in which the cute blue-collar guy asks: If you quit after working four hours, what would your boss say? And the not-so-cute blue-collar guy, who's lugging a metal beam on his back, answers: He'd fire me, that's what. But fortunately, the commercial tells us, we workers can exert the same kind of authority over our painkillers that our bosses exert over us. If Tylenol doesn't want to work for more than four hours, you just fire its ass and switch to Aleve.

True, I take occasional breaks from this life, going home now and then to catch up on e-mail and for conjugal visits (though I am careful to "pay" for anything I eat there), seeing *The Truman Show* with friends and letting them buy my ticket. And I still have those what-am-I-doing-here moments at work, when I get so homesick for the printed word that I obsessively reread the six-page menu. But as the days go by, my old life is beginning to look exceedingly strange. The e-mails and phone messages addressed to my former self come from a distant race of people with exotic concerns and far too much time on their hands. The neighborly market I used to cruise for produce now looks forbiddingly like a Manhattan yuppie emporium. And when I sit down one morning in my real home to pay bills from my past life, I am dazzled at the two- and three-figure sums owed to outfits like Club Body Tech and Amazon.com.

Management at Jerry's is generally calmer and more "professional" than at the Hearthside, with two exceptions. One is Joy, a plump, blowsy woman in her early thirties, who once kindly devoted several minutes to instructing me in the correct one-handed method of carrying trays but whose moods change disconcertingly from shift to shift and even within one. Then there's B.J., a.k.a. B.J.-the-bitch, whose contribution is to stand by the kitchen counter and yell, "Nita, your order's up, move it!" or, "Barbara, didn't you see you've got another table out there? Come on, girl!" Among other things, she is hated for having replaced the whipped-cream squirt cans with big plastic whipped-cream-filled baggies that have to be squeezed with both hands—because, reportedly, she saw or thought she saw employees trying to inhale the propellant gas from the squirt cans, in the hope that it might be nitrous oxide. On my third night, she pulls me aside abruptly and brings her face so close that it looks as if she's planning to butt me with her forehead. But instead of saying, "You're fired," she says, "You're doing fine." The only trouble is I'm spending time chatting with customers: "That's how they're getting you." Furthermore I am letting them "run me," which means harassment by sequential demands: you bring the ketchup and they decide they want extra Thousand Island; you bring that and they announce they now need a side of fries; and so on into distraction. Finally she tells me not to take her wrong. She tries to say things in a nice way, but you get into a mode, you know, because everything has to move so fast.[5]

I mumble thanks for the advice, feeling like I've just been stripped naked by the crazed enforcer of some ancient sumptuary law: No chatting for you, girl. No fancy service ethic

5 In *Workers in a Lean World: Unions in the International Economy* (Verso, 1997), Kim Moody cites studies finding an increase in stress-related workplace injuries and illness between the mid-1980s and the early 1990s. He argues that rising stress levels reflect a new system of "management by stress," in which workers in a variety of industries are being squeezed to extract maximum productivity, to the detriment of their health.

allowed for the serfs. Chatting with customers is for the beautiful young college-educated servers in the downtown carpaccio joints, the kids who can make $70 to $100 a night. What had I been thinking? My job is to move orders from tables to kitchen and then trays from kitchen to tables. Customers are, in fact, the major obstacle to the smooth transformation of information into food and food into money—they are, in short, the enemy. And the painful thing is that I'm beginning to see it this way myself. There are the traditional asshole types—frat boys who down multiple Buds and then make a fuss because the steaks are so emaciated and the fries so sparse—as well as the variously impaired—due to age, diabetes, or literacy issues—who require patient nutritional counseling. The worst, for some reason, are the Visible Christians—like the ten-person table, all jolly and sanctified after Sunday-night service, who run me mercilessly and then leave me $1 on a $92 bill. Or the guy with the crucifixion T-shirt (SOMEONE TO LOOK UP TO) who complains that his baked potato is too hard and his iced tea too icy (I cheerfully fix both) and leaves no tip. As a general rule, people wearing crosses or WWJD? (What Would Jesus Do?) buttons look at us disapprovingly no matter what we do, as if they were confusing waitressing with Mary Magdalene's original profession.

I make friends, over time, with the other "girls" who work my shift: Nita, the tattooed twenty-something who taunts us by going around saying brightly, "Have we started making money yet?" Ellen, whose teenage son cooks on the graveyard shift and who once managed a restaurant in Massachusetts but won't try out for management here because she prefers being a "common worker" and not "ordering people around." Easy-going fiftyish Lucy, with the raucous laugh, who limps toward the end of the shift because of something that has gone wrong with her leg, the exact nature of which cannot be determined without health insurance. We talk about the usual girl things—men, children, and the sinister allure of Jerry's chocolate peanut-butter cream pie—though no one, I notice, ever brings up anything potentially expensive, like shopping or movies. As at the Hearthside, the only recreation ever referred to is partying, which requires little more than some beer, a joint, and a few close friends. Still, no one here is homeless, or cops to it anyway, thanks usually to a working husband or boyfriend. All in all, we form a reliable mutual-support group: If one of us is feeling sick or overwhelmed, another one will "bev" a table or even carry trays for her. If one of us is off sneaking a cigarette or a pee,[6] the others will do their best to conceal her absence from the enforcers of corporate rationality.

But my saving human connection—my oxytocin receptor, as it were—is George, the nineteen-year-old, fresh-off-the-boat Czech dishwasher. We get to talking when he asks me, tortuously, how much cigarettes cost at Jerry's. I do my best to explain that they cost over a dollar more here than at a regular store and suggest that he just take one from the half-filled packs that are always lying around on the break table. But that would be unthinkable. Except for the one tiny earring signaling his allegiance to some vaguely alternative point of view, George is a perfect straight arrow—crew-cut, hardworking, and hungry for eye contact. "Czech Republic," I ask, "or Slovakia?" and he seems delighted that I know the

6 Until April 1998, there was no federally mandated right to bathroom breaks. According to Marc Linder and Ingrid Nygaard, authors of *Void Where Prohibited: Rest Breaks and the Right to Urinate on Company Time* (Cornell University Press, 1997), "The right to rest and void at work is not high on the list of social or political causes supported by professional or executive employees, who enjoy personal workplace liberties that millions of factory workers can only daydream about.... While we were dismayed to discover that workers lacked an acknowledged legal right to void at work, [the workers] were amazed by outsiders' naive belief that their employers would permit them to perform this basic bodily function when necessary.... A factory worker, not allowed a break for six-hour stretches, voided into pads worn inside her uniform; and a kindergarten teacher in a school without aides had to take all twenty children with her to the bathroom and line them up outside the stall door when she voided."

difference. "Václav Havel," I try. "Velvet Revolution, Frank Zappa?" "Yes, yes, 1989," he says, and I realize we are talking about history.

My project is to teach George English. "How are you today, George?" I say at the start of each shift. "I am good, and how are you today, Barbara?" I learn that he is not paid by Jerry's but by the "agent" who shipped him over—$5 an hour, with the agent getting the dollar or so difference between that and what Jerry's pays dishwashers. I learn also that he shares an apartment with a crowd of other Czech "dishers," as he calls them, and that he cannot sleep until one of them goes off for his shift, leaving a vacant bed. We are having one of our ESL sessions late one afternoon when B.J. catches us at it and orders "Joseph" to take up the rubber mats on the floor near the dishwashing sinks and mop underneath. "I thought your name was George," I say loud enough for B.J. to hear as she strides off back to the counter. Is she embarrassed? Maybe a little, because she greets me back at the counter with "George, Joseph—there are so many of them!" I say nothing, neither nodding nor smiling, and for this I am punished later when I think I am ready to go and she announces that I need to roll fifty more sets of silverware and isn't it time I mixed up a fresh four-gallon batch of blue-cheese dressing? May you grow old in this place, B.J., is the curse I beam out at her when I am finally permitted to leave. May the syrup spills glue your feet to the floor.

I make the decision to move closer to Key West. First, because of the drive. Second and third, also because of the drive: gas is eating up $4 to $5 a day, and although Jerry's is as high-volume as you can get, the tips average only 10 percent, and not just for a newbie like me. Between the base pay of $2.15 an hour and the obligation to share tips with the busboys and dishwashers, we're averaging only about $7.50 an hour. Then there is the $30 I had to spend on the regulation tan slacks worn by Jerry's servers—a setback it could take weeks to absorb. (I had combed the town's two downscale department stores hoping for something cheaper but decided in the end that these marked-down Dockers, originally $49, were more likely to survive a daily washing.) Of my fellow servers, everyone who lacks a working husband or boyfriend seems to have a second job: Nita does something at a computer eight hours a day; another welds. Without the forty-five-minute commute, I can picture myself working two jobs and having the time to shower between them.

So I take the $500 deposit I have coming from my landlord, the $400 I have earned toward the next month's rent, plus the $200 reserved for emergencies, and use the $1,100 to pay the rent and deposit on trailer number 46 in the Overseas Trailer Park, a mile from the cluster of budget hotels that constitute Key West's version of an industrial park. Number 46 is about eight feet in width and shaped like a barbell inside, with a narrow region—because of the sink and the stove—separating the bedroom from what might optimistically be called the "living" area, with its two-person table and half-sized couch. The bathroom is so small my knees rub against the shower stall when I sit on the toilet, and you can't just leap out of the bed, you have to climb down to the foot of it in order to find a patch of floor space to stand on. Outside, I am within a few yards of a liquor store, a bar that advertises "free beer tomorrow," a convenience store, and a Burger King—but no supermarket or, alas, laundromat. By reputation, the Overseas park is a nest of crime and crack, and I am hoping at least for some vibrant, multicultural street life. But desolation rules night and day, except for a thin stream of pedestrian traffic heading for their jobs at the Sheraton or 7-Eleven. There are not exactly people here but what amounts to canned labor, being preserved from the heat between shifts.

In line with my reduced living conditions, a new form of ugliness arises at Jerry's. First we are confronted—via an announcement on the computers through which we input orders—with the new rule that the hotel bar is henceforth off-limits to restaurant employees.

The culprit, I learn through the grapevine, is the ultra-efficient gal who trained me—another trailer-home dweller and a mother of three. Something had set her off one morning, so she slipped out for a nip and returned to the floor impaired. This mostly hurts Ellen, whose habit it is to free her hair from its rubber band and drop by the bar for a couple of Zins before heading home at the end of the shift, but all of us feel the chill. Then the next day, when I go for straws, for the first time I find the dry-storage room locked. Ted, the portly assistant manager who opens it for me, explains that he caught one of the dishwashers attempting to steal something, and, unfortunately, the miscreant will be with us until a replacement can be found—hence the locked door. I neglect to ask what he had been trying to steal, but Ted tells me who he is—the kid with the buzz cut and the earring. You know, he's back there right now.

I wish I could say I rushed back and confronted George to get his side of the story. I wish I could say I stood up to Ted and insisted that George be given a translator and allowed to defend himself, or announced that I'd find a lawyer who'd handle the case pro bono. The mystery to me is that there's not much worth stealing in the dry-storage room, at least not in any fenceable quantity: "Is Gyorgi here, and am having 200—maybe 250—ketchup packets. What do you say?" My guess is that he had taken—if he had taken anything at all—some Saltines or a can of cherry-pie mix, and that the motive for taking it was hunger.

So why didn't I intervene? Certainly not because I was held back by the kind of moral paralysis that can pass as journalistic objectivity. On the contrary, something new—something loathsome and servile—had infected me, along with the kitchen odors that I could still sniff on my bra when I finally undressed at night. In real life I am moderately brave, but plenty of brave people shed their courage in concentration camps, and maybe something similar goes on in the infinitely more congenial milieu of the low-wage American workplace. Maybe, in a month or two more at Jerry's, I might have regained my crusading spirit. Then again, in a month or two I might have turned into a different person altogether—say, the kind of person who would have turned George in.

But this is not something I am slated to find out. When my month-long plunge into poverty is almost over, I finally land my dream job—housekeeping. I do this by walking into the personnel office of the only place I figure I might have some credibility, the hotel attached to Jerry's, and confiding urgently that I have to have a second job if I am to pay my rent and, no, it couldn't be front-desk clerk. "All right," the personnel lady fairly spits, "So it's housekeeping," and she marches me back to meet Maria, the housekeeping manager, a tiny, frenetic Hispanic woman who greets me as "babe" and hands me a pamphlet emphasizing the need for a positive attitude. The hours are nine in the morning till whenever, the pay is $6.10 an hour, and there's one week of vacation a year. I don't have to ask about health insurance once I meet Carlotta, the middle-aged African-American woman who will be training me. Carla, as she tells me to call her, is missing all of her top front teeth.

On that first day of housekeeping and last day of my entire project—although I don't yet know it's the last—Carla is in a foul mood. We have been given nineteen rooms to clean, most of them "checkouts," as opposed to "stay-overs," that require the whole enchilada of bed-stripping, vacuuming, and bathroom-scrubbing. When one of the rooms that had been listed as a stay-over turns out to be a checkout, Carla calls Maria to complain, but of course to no avail. "So make up the motherfucker," Carla orders me, and I do the beds while she sloshes around the bathroom. For four hours without a break I strip and remake beds, taking about four and a half minutes per queen-sized bed, which I could get down to three if there were any reason to. We try to avoid vacuuming by picking up the larger specks by hand, but often there is nothing to do but drag the monstrous vacuum cleaner—it weighs about thirty pounds—off our cart and try to wrestle it around the floor. Sometimes Carla hands me the squirt bottle of "BAM" (an acronym for something that begins, ominously, with "butyric"; the rest has been worn off the label) and lets me do the bathrooms. No service ethic challenges me here to new heights of performance. I just concentrate on removing the pubic hairs from the bathtubs, or at least the dark ones that I can see.

I had looked forward to the breaking-and-entering aspect of cleaning the stay-overs, the chance to examine the secret, physical existence of strangers. But the contents of the rooms are always banal and surprisingly neat—zipped up shaving kits, shoes lined up against the wall (there are no closets), flyers for snorkeling trips, maybe an empty wine bottle or two. It is the TV that keeps us going, from *Jerry* to *Sally* to *Hawaii Five-O* and then on to the soaps. If there's something especially arresting, like "Won't Take No for an Answer" on *Jerry*, we sit down on the edge of a bed and giggle for a moment as if this were a pajama party instead of a terminally dead-end job. The soaps are the best, and Carla turns the volume up full blast so that she won't miss anything from the bathroom or while the vacuum is on. In room 503, Marcia confronts Jeff about Lauren. In 505, Lauren taunts poor cuckolded Marcia. In 511, Helen offers Amanda $10,000 to stop seeing Eric, prompting Carla to emerge from the bathroom to study Amanda's troubled face. "You take it, girl," she advises. "I would for sure."

The tourists' rooms that we clean and, beyond them, the far more expensively appointed interiors in the soaps, begin after a while to merge. We have entered a better world—a world of comfort where every day is a day off, waiting to be filled up with sexual intrigue. We, however, are only gatecrashers in this fantasy, forced to pay for our presence with backaches and perpetual thirst. The mirrors, and there are far too many of them in hotel rooms, contain the kind of person you would normally find pushing a shopping cart down a city street—bedraggled, dressed in a damp hotel polo shirt two sizes too large, and with sweat dribbling down her chin like drool. I am enormously relieved when Carla announces a half-hour meal break, but my appetite fades when I see that the bag of hot-dog rolls she has been carrying around on our cart is not trash salvaged from a checkout but what she has brought for her lunch.

When I request permission to leave at about 3:30, another housekeeper warns me that no one has so far succeeded in combining housekeeping at the hotel with serving at Jerry's: "Some kid did it once for five days, and you're no kid." With that helpful information in mind, I rush back to number 46, down four Advils (the name brand this time), shower, stooping to fit into the stall, and attempt to compose myself for the oncoming shift. So much for what Marx termed the "reproduction of labor power," meaning the things a worker has to do just so she'll be ready to work again. The only unforeseen obstacle to the smooth transition from job to job is that my tan Jerry's slacks, which had looked reasonably clean by 40-watt bulb last night when I handwashed my Hawaiian shirt, prove by daylight to be mottled with ketchup and ranch-dressing stains. I spend most of my hour-long break between jobs attempting to remove the edible portions with a sponge and then drying the slacks over the hood of my car in the sun.

I can do this two-job thing, is my theory, if I can drink enough caffeine and avoid getting distracted by George's ever more obvious suffering.[7] The first few days after being caught he seemed not to understand the trouble he was in, and our chirpy little conversations had

7 In 1996, the number of persons holding two or more jobs averaged 7.8 million, or 6.2 percent of the workforce. It was about the same rate for men and for women (6.1 versus 6.2), though the kinds of jobs differ by gender. About two thirds of multiple jobholders work one job full-time and the other part-time. Only a heroic minority—4 percent of men and 2 percent of women—work two full-time jobs simultaneously. (From John F. Stinson Jr., "New Data on Multiple Jobholding Available from the CPS," in the *Monthly Labor Review*, March 1997.)

continued. But the last couple of shifts he's been listless and unshaven, and tonight he looks like the ghost we all know him to be, with dark half-moons hanging from his eyes. At one point, when I am briefly immobilized by the task of filling little paper cups with sour cream for baked potatoes, he comes over and looks as if he'd like to explore the limits of our shared vocabulary, but I am called to the floor for a table. I resolve to give him all my tips that night and to hell with the experiment in low-wage money management. At eight, Ellen and I grab a snack together standing at the mephitic end of the kitchen counter, but I can only manage two or three mozzarella sticks and lunch had been a mere handful of McNuggets. I am not tired at all, I assure myself, though it may be that there is simply no more "I" left to do the tiredness monitoring. What I would see, if I were more alert to the situation, is that the forces of destruction are already massing against me. There is only one cook on duty, a young man named Jesus ("Hay-Sue," that is) and he is new to the job. And there is Joy, who shows up to take over in the middle of the shift, wearing high heels and a long, clingy white dress and fuming as if she'd just been stood up in some cocktail bar.

Then it comes, the perfect storm. Four of my tables fill up at once. Four tables is nothing for me now, but only so long as they are obligingly staggered. As I bev table 27, tables 25, 28, and 24 are watching enviously. As I bev 25, 24 glowers because their bevs haven't even been ordered. Twenty-eight is four yuppyish types, meaning everything on the side and agonizing instructions as to the chicken Caesars. Twenty-five is a middle-aged black couple, who complain, with some justice, that the iced tea isn't fresh and the tabletop is sticky. But table 24 is the meteorological event of the century: ten British tourists who seem to have made the decision to absorb the American experience entirely by mouth. Here everyone has at least two drinks—iced tea and milk shake, Michelob and water (with lemon slice, please)—and a huge promiscuous orgy of breakfast specials, mozz sticks, chicken strips, quesadillas, burgers with cheese and without, sides of hash browns with cheddar, with onions, with gravy, seasoned fries, plain fries, banana splits. Poor Jesus! Poor me! Because when I arrive with their first tray of food—after three prior trips just to refill bevs—Princess Di refuses to eat her chicken strips with her pancake-and-sausage special, since, as she now reveals, the strips were meant to be an appetizer. Maybe the others would have accepted their meals, but Di, who is deep into her third Michelob, insists that everything else go back while they work on their "starters." Meanwhile, the yuppies are waving me down for more decaf and the black couple looks ready to summon the NAACP.

Much of what happened next is lost in the fog of war. Jesus starts going under. The little printer on the counter in front of him is spewing out orders faster than he can rip them off, much less produce the meals. Even the invincible Ellen is ashen from stress. I bring table 24 their reheated main courses, which they immediately reject as either too cold or fossilized by the microwave. When I return to the kitchen with their trays (three trays in three trips), Joy confronts me with arms akimbo: "What is this?" She means the food—the plates of rejected pancakes, hash browns in assorted flavors, toasts, burgers, sausages, eggs. "Uh, scrambled with cheddar," I try, "and that's . . . " "NO," she screams in my face. "Is it a traditional, a super-scramble, an eye-opener?" I pretend to study my check for a clue, but entropy has been up to its tricks, not only on the plates but in my head, and I have to admit that the original order is beyond reconstruction. "You don't know an eye-opener from a traditional?" she demands in outrage. All I know, in fact, is that my legs have lost interest in the current venture and have announced their intention to fold. I am saved by a yuppie (mercifully not one of mine) who chooses this moment to charge into the kitchen to bellow that his food is twenty-five minutes late. Joy screams at him to get the hell out of her kitchen, please, and then turns on Jesus in a fury, hurling an empty tray across the room for emphasis.

I leave. I don't walk out, I just leave. I don't finish my side work or pick up my credit-card tips, if any, at the cash register or, of course, ask Joy's permission to go. And the surprising thing is that you can walk out without permission, that the door opens, that the thick tropical night air parts to let me pass, that my car is still parked where I left it. There is no vindication in this exit, no fuck-you surge of relief, just an overwhelming, dank sense of failure pressing down on me and the entire parking lot. I had gone into this venture in the spirit of science, to test a mathematical proposition, but somewhere along the line, in the tunnel vision imposed by long shifts and relentless concentration, it became a test of myself, and clearly I have failed. Not only had I flamed out as a housekeeper/server, I had even forgotten to give George my tips, and, for reasons perhaps best known to hardworking, generous people like Gail and Ellen, this hurts. I don't cry, but I am in a position to realize, for the first time in many years, that the tear ducts are still there, and still capable of doing their job.

When I moved out of the trailer park, I gave the key to number 46 to Gail and arranged for my deposit to be transferred to her. She told me that Joan is still living in her van and that Stu had been fired from the Hearthside. I never found out what happened to George.

In one month, I had earned approximately $1,040 and spent $517 on food, gas, toiletries, laundry, phone, and utilities. If I had remained in my $500 efficiency, I would have been able to pay the rent and have $22 left over (which is $78 less than the cash I had in my pocket at the start of the month). During this time I bought no clothing except for the required slacks and no prescription drugs or medical care (I did finally buy some vitamin B to compensate for the lack of vegetables in my diet). Perhaps I could have saved a little on food if I had gotten to a supermarket more often, instead of convenience stores, but it should be noted that I lost almost four pounds in four weeks, on a diet weighted heavily toward burgers and fries.

How former welfare recipients and single mothers will (and do) survive in the low-wage workforce, I cannot imagine. Maybe they will figure out how to condense their lives—including child-raising, laundry, romance, and meals—into the couple of hours between full-time jobs. Maybe they will take up residence in their vehicles, if they have one. All I know is that I couldn't hold two jobs and I couldn't make enough money to live on with one. And I had advantages unthinkable to many of the long-term poor—health, stamina, a working car, and no children to care for and support. Certainly nothing in my experience contradicts the conclusion of Kathryn Edin and Laura Lein, in their recent book *Making Ends Meet: How Single Mothers Survive Welfare and Low-Wage Work,* that low-wage work actually involves more hardship and deprivation than life at the mercy of the welfare state. In the coming months and years, economic conditions for the working poor are bound to worsen, even without the almost inevitable recession. As mentioned earlier, the influx of former welfare recipients into the low-skilled workforce will have a depressing effect on both wages and the number of jobs available. A general economic downturn will only enhance these effects, and the working poor will of course be facing it without the slight, but nonetheless often saving, protection of welfare as a backup.

The thinking behind welfare reform was that even the humblest jobs are morally uplifting and psychologically buoying. In reality they are likely to be fraught with insult and stress. But I did discover one redeeming feature of the most abject low-wage work—the camaraderie of people who are, in almost all cases, far too smart and funny and caring for the work they do and the wages they're paid. The hope, of course, is that someday these people will come to know what they're worth, and take appropriate action.

—1999

Learning from Other Writers

1. As Ehrenreich tells us in the first paragraph of her essay, her experiment involves subterfuge. Does that make her experiment unethical? Why or why not?
2. How does Ehrenreich anticipate her readers' objections to the terms of her experiment and/or her reasons for carrying it out? Is she successful in heading off or countering such objections?
3. What are Ehrenreich's qualifications for writing this essay? What research does she do to supplement her own experiences as a waitress and housekeeper? How does she integrate this research into her essay? Is this approach successful or intrusive?
4. Where and how does Ehrenreich use scenic (as opposed to expository) writing? Does she incorporate typical scenes from her jobs or specific events? How and where does she use dialogue? To what effect?
5. What are some of the discoveries that Ehrenreich makes about work? Poverty? Human behavior? Economics?
6. What can you say about the author's intended audience? What (if anything) might this essay persuade an economist, business owner, or politician to change or do?
7. What does Ehrenreich do to protect the people with whom she worked? Might she have asked them to reflect on their experiences in a more direct way (rather than merely quoting what she overheard)? Why or why not?
8. In another essay in this chapter, Richard Feynman recommends that ordinary people test fancy theories against their experience of reality and common sense. What theory is Ehrenreich testing?

INSPIRATIONS: WE ARE ALL MAD SCIENTISTS

1. Come up with a question whose answer requires that you carry out an experiment.
2. Design and carry out your experiment.
3. Write an essay in which you present your factual question to your readers, then describe the experiment you carried out and your findings or results. Make sure your readers understand the larger thematic significance of your question and your experiment.
4. Alternatively, think of a statement whose truth you've always doubted. (Urban legends, Internet myths, family stories, proverbs, and other bits of conventional wisdom are a good place to start.) Is there any way for you to test the validity of this claim?
5. Or think of a theory of human behavior you've often heard bandied about (perhaps this theory has to do with education, economics, psychology, government, or law). Is there any way you might conduct some sort of research or experiment that would allow you to check this theory against reality?

9 Profiles in Action

The set of first-person forms described in the previous chapters lead to a parallel set of forms describing someone else's narrative, journey, search for answers, or experiment. Obviously, you can create an engrossing narrative by describing the adventures of a person who barely survived an extreme ordeal (for a hair-raising third-person narrative of a young New Yorker's escape from a burning building, see "Werner" by Jo Ann Beard in *The Best American Essays 2007*). But the everyday experiences of ordinary people also can yield fascinating material for an essay.

Despite the torrent of words published every week, most of us have little idea what other people do to earn a living or how the mundane objects we buy are produced, distributed, sold, or disposed of. Structuring a piece of creative nonfiction around a day in the life of a zookeeper, air-traffic controller, or trash collector, or the process by which a computer—or a hammer or a surfboard—is designed and manufactured, affords insights into lives we otherwise might never witness or understand, while the activity or process you are recounting provides your essay with a pleasing movement and flow. Certainly, you will end up with more interesting profiles if you can persuade your subjects to get up from behind their desks and observe them as they do whatever it is that makes them worth writing about.

YOUR PLACE IN THE PROFILE

As is true in any piece of creative nonfiction, you will need to formulate a central question so your readers will know why the subject of your profile merits their attention and so you won't feel compelled to put in every detail about how your subject embalmed that corpse or pieced together that violin. What don't you understand about the person you want to profile, the job she performs, or the role he plays in your family, culture, or community? Once you have settled on a structure and central question, you still retain a great deal of latitude in deciding whether to leave yourself out of the piece entirely, establish your presence only when necessary, or make yourself nearly as important as your subject. If you keep calling attention to yourself, you might annoy your readers, especially if the ostensible subject of your profile is someone who is more important, wittier, smarter, or more compassionate than you are. But comparing the three profiles in this chapter reveals just how much freedom remains to the writer as far as subject and style.

EXTERNAL AND INTERNAL WORLDS

Re-creating the experiences of other people usually requires that you describe not only places and events—the *external world* of your subjects—but also your subjects' *internal reactions* to those events. In "The Winged Seed," an essay that comprises one stanza of his poetic book-length memoir by that same name, Li-Young Lee re-creates his mother's privileged but terrible girlhood in China—from his mother's point of view. The piece seems nearly supernatural in the author's ability to re-create experiences that took place long ago in another land. Yet what appears to be clairvoyance or omniscience turns out to be explicable in terms of research. As you can see if you read Li-Young Lee's essay, in his effort to understand the ways in which his mother's history continues to haunt them both, he consulted her diary and pestered her to tell him stories about her life in China. Most likely, he also visited the sites where his mother spent her girlhood, talked to members of her family, and read books about that period in Chinese history.

Some of what Li-Young Lee tells us about his subject springs from his dreams and imagination. Usually, he lets us know which descriptions are based on fact and which descriptions are invented. When he blends the two, we might accuse him of violating his contract with his readers, except that the liberties Li-Young Lee takes aren't with historic facts or anything that might place his family in a better light, but rather with his poetic impressions of his ancestors' internal lives.

Writing about the dead is less likely to get a writer sued than re-creating the experiences and internal lives of living people. In *The Perfect Storm,* Sebastian Junger undertakes to tell the tale of men who didn't live to tell their own stories. This makes his job easier in the respect that no one can testify that his account is in error; on the other hand, it presents challenges that would have daunted a less energetic and confident writer. In the foreword to his book, Junger explains how he pulled off this feat ... and why he never gave in to the temptation to make things up. I reproduce that foreword here because it speaks so elegantly not only to the methods a writer might employ in re-creating the lives—and deaths—of other people, but the integrity that leads to an authentic and convincing narrative and prevents the author from having to appear on talk shows to apologize for writing lies disguised as truth.

FOREWORD

Recreating the last days of six men who disappeared at sea presented some obvious problems for me. On the one hand, I wanted to write a completely factual book that would stand on its own as a piece of journalism. On the other hand, I didn't want the narrative to asphyxiate under a mass of technical detail and conjecture. I toyed with the idea of fictionalizing minor parts of the story—conversations, personal thoughts, day-to-day routines—to make it more readable, but that risked diminishing the value of whatever facts I *was* able to determine. In the end I wound up sticking strictly to the facts, but in as wide-ranging a way as possible. If I didn't know exactly what happened aboard the doomed boat, for example, I would interview people who had been through similar situations, and survived. Their experiences, I felt, would provide a fairly good description of what the six men on the *Andrea Gail* had gone through, and said, and perhaps even felt.

As a result, there are varying kinds of information in the book. Anything in direct quotes was recorded by me in a formal interview, either in person or on the telephone, and was altered as little as possible for grammar and clarity. All dialogue is based on the recollection of people who are still alive, and appears in dialogue form without quotation marks. *No* dialogue was made up. Radio conversations are also based on people's recollections, and appear in italics in the text. Quotes from published material are in italics, and have occasionally been condensed to better fit the text. Technical discussions of meteorology, wave motion, ship stability, etc., are based on my own library research and are generally not referenced, but I feel compelled to recommend William Van Dorn's *The Oceanography of Seamanship* as a comprehensive and immensely readable text on ships and the sea.

In short, I've written as complete an account as possible of something that can never be fully known. It is exactly that unknowable element, however, that has made it an interesting book to write and, I hope, to read. I had some misgivings about calling it *The Perfect Storm,* but in the end I decided that the intent was sufficiently clear. I use *perfect* in the meteorological sense: a storm that could not possibly have been worse. I certainly mean no disrespect to the men who died at sea or the people who still grieve for them.

My own experience in the storm was limited to standing on Gloucester's Back Shore watching thirty-foot swells advance on Cape Ann, but that was all it took. The next day I read in the paper that a Gloucester boat was feared lost at sea, and I clipped the article and stuck it in a drawer. Without even knowing it, I had begun to write *The Perfect Storm.*

Re-creating your subject's external world can be accomplished by visiting the locations where key events took place or by consulting written accounts of the events in question, photographs of the people and places you describe, and documents that might reveal the weather on a given day, the price of beef or coal, or the tasks a cowboy in Montana might have been required to perform during a typical day in the 1880s, while re-creating your subject's interior world can be accomplished by acquiring access to his or her diaries, journals, and correspondence. If your subjects are still alive, you can supplement all of the above by talking directly to your sources, asking what they witnessed or experienced and what they thought and felt as they lived through those events. Best of all, you can shadow your subjects as new events unfold and add your observations to theirs.

In a newspaper series called "Inside the Mind" that I wrote in my early twenties,[1] I used the third-person point of view to tell the story of a high school teacher who, rather than travel to Boston to have his brain tumor removed, decided to trust the surgeon at the much smaller and more humble hospital near his hometown in New Hampshire. Many writers have published first-person accounts of their own illnesses and operations, but I was still healthy enough that I had no material for such a narrative. And I wanted to be able to provide a contrast between the patient's version of his ordeal and what was going on around him as I attempted to figure out what would make a man trust the doctors and nurses at such a modest hospital to drill a hole in his skull and remove a tumor—and whether such trust was warranted.

In preparing my narrative, I talked to my subject at length, then used his language wherever possible to describe his observations. To provide background that the subject couldn't provide, I interviewed the members of his medical team, boned up on neurology, and stood beside the surgeon through the seven tense, awe-inspiring, and often nauseating hours of my subject's operation. Then I tried to weave together everything I had learned to provide a narrative of my subject's ordeal, beginning with the following passage, in which I describe Alex Glass's first intimation that something might be wrong in his brain.[2]

---

1 The series appear in the *Concord Monitor* on May 11, 12, 13, and 14, 1981.

2 Because I would be writing—and publishing—my account day by day as these events unfolded, my subject wasn't sure if he would survive, and, if he did, whether he would be "the same person." If the operation went terribly wrong, he didn't want to be viewed as an object of pity by everyone who read the series, so he asked that I change his name. Given that I was allowed to use the real names of everyone else, I figured that whatever I wrote about "Alex Glass" could be verified as a fact, so I agreed. Still, it seems disingenuous to claim to portray the deepest thoughts of an actual human being while shielding him behind a pseudonym. If I had been older and more confident, I would have pressed my subject to allow me to use his name, or pressed my editors to wait to run the series until we were sure that "Alex" would survive.

> Alexander Glass fell on the ice, but he didn't know that he had bitten the inside of his cheek until he spat in his hand and saw blood. The left side of his face had been going numb for months. It seemed to belong to someone else.
>
> The numbness hardly bothered Alex. Sometimes it came in handy. If the cheese on a pizza was too hot, he could slide it to the left side of his mouth and not feel the burn. Alex's left ear wasn't working well either, but that wasn't much of a problem. He just told his students to direct their questions to his right ear.
>
> Okay, maybe the numbness and the deafness did gnaw a little at Alex's peace of mind. While spending Thanksgiving with his in-laws, he saw a television commercial. It said that cancer's strongest ally is ignorance. The phrase kept pricking its way into Alex's thoughts.
>
> "And the numbness didn't go away, and it didn't go away, and it didn't go away. And I said, 'That's what I've got. I've got cancer.'"

Note that I don't keep reminding readers that Glass *told me* what he had experienced or thought. Verifying a subject's statements is important if those statements are indeed verifiable facts that might influence other people's lives or reputations or our understanding of historical events. But in most other cases, saying that someone *told you* something implies that what the person told you might not be the truth. (Consider the difference between "Melinda Jackson never lets her toddlers stay home alone" and "Melinda Jackson says that she never lets her toddlers stay home alone.")

To see how this technique works, here's a section of the narrative in which we eavesdrop on Glass's anxieties as he lies in the hospital the afternoon before the surgery. Listen for the passages in which I try to inflect my presentation of Glass's inner turmoil with his own language, both directly (in quotes) and indirectly (via third-person interior monologues):

> He lay there wondering what he was, what was essential to Alexander Glass, so that if he awoke on the next afternoon and found part of his being gone, he would know he was no longer himself, if he knew anything at all, if there was such a thing as *self.*
>
> And he came up with this answer: "This is Alexander Glass, the way I treat people, the way people can expect to be treated by me. I would like people to get to know me as I would like to be known."
>
> He reacted to people intellectually. That was Alexander Glass. He always thought before he acted. His wife accused him of lacking spontaneity. "But that's a sign of maturity," he said. "A child doesn't think first."
>
> He didn't want to be pitied. He didn't want visitors because they would look at him the way his little daughter looked at unfortunate people on the street.
>
> He didn't care what he looked like after the operation. "I'm not vain cosmetically," he said. "I never took care of how I dressed. It didn't bother me if my socks didn't match. I have a sagging face, that doesn't disturb me. If I'm deaf in one ear, that doesn't disturb me." He didn't care if he wobbled when he walked. He'd been a teacher for 10 years, but he didn't care if he had to find a new profession.
>
> He didn't care about material things. Blue Cross and Blue Shield were paying for the operation, he said, "but I'd start over again in my birthday suit in the woods if I didn't have this tumor."
>
> The first thing he would do when he woke up after the operation would be to try to wiggle his toes, to move his legs, his fingers, his arms. Then he would try to recite poetry.
>
> "I just want to be able to function independently again," he said. He just wanted to be able to pick up his life at the same point where he had left off. As the same Alexander Glass.

VARYING YOUR DISTANCE

In "The Stunt Pilot," Annie Dillard portrays her stoic, close-mouthed subject, Dave Rahm, first from a distance (literal and metaphoric) as she watches his aerial maneuvers from the ground, then from a much closer perspective—the seat behind him in his plane. The profile contains as much of Dillard's art as Rahm's, not only in terms of elegant discursive prose that mimics the looping arcs and curves of Rahm's acrobatic flights, but the author's elaborate meditations on Art.

My former student, Daniel Rivas, takes a more self-effacing approach to his portrait of his father, but that portrait would be far less revealing if Rivas had omitted his shifting visions of his father throughout his own childhood and young adulthood. And if Rivas hadn't structured his essay around the process by which his father manufactured tortillas, he probably wouldn't have hit upon the central analogy between his father's talent for fixing machines and his helplessness when it came to fixing his marriage, his body, or his life.

Finally, we arrive at Joseph Mitchell's wonderfully measured account of the evening he spent with a child prodigy named Philippa Duke Schulyer and her eccentric parents. While trying to ascertain if Philippa is naturally gifted or whether she has been pressured to perform by her mother, Mitchell keeps his opinions to himself. Philippa serenades the author with her piano compositions and engages him in a discussion of her favorite books and comic strips, but Mitchell remains unmoved. Only when Philippa's mother shows the author a poem that Philippa wrote when she was five does Mitchell break down and provide the judgment that "this was a wonderful poem." This is the extent of the meditation in the piece, yet Mitchell is such a master of the form that he shapes his impressions around the question of Philippa's natural talent (or lack thereof) so carefully that the profile itself becomes a meditation on the proper parental response to a prodigiously gifted child.

LI-YOUNG LEE

THE WINGED SEED

When my mother, Jiaying, is a girl in China, she loves the summers in the mountains. The rest of the year, she lives in the city below, in the haunted mansion ruled by her father's mother, a woman as cruel as she is small and desiccated, and as selfish as her feet are twisted to fit into tiny hoof-shaped shoes of brocade. It is because of this woman, my mother insists, that drafty ghosts inhabit the countless rooms and myriad corridors of the old house, whose ceilings and rafters are so high that light never reaches them, giving Jiaying the feeling of living perpetually under a great, dark, impenetrable hood. It was from the rafters in the sewing hall, the darkest room in the entire complex, that a maid, fourteen and newly hired, hung herself after only three months of waiting on the old woman.

The sewing hall is a building whose front face is wood and whose other three walls are windowless brick. Two double-door front entrances lead into a cavernous room of stone floors and two rows of three pillars each, painted thickly red, and spaced ten feet apart. Lined with tables at which thirty women sit behind mounds of various fabrics of any color, the room whines and rings with the rapid pounding of several hand-operated sewing machines. Forbidden to wear against their bodies any piece of cloth cut or sewn by men, all the female members of the nine households have their clothes made by women in the sewing hall. Thirty seamstresses, every day all year round making and mending the clothes of births and deaths for every female Yuan, cutting and sewing from patterns handed down generation to generation without mutation for nearly a century, so that almost everyone in Tientsin knows that the less fashionable you are, the older the money you come from. Thirty indentured workers, bought or born into bondage of cloth, sew in the great hall, drinking little cups of tea that amount to green seas, gossiping and telling stories. All day long, necks bent and fingers crooked to meticulous mending or making, by machine and by hand, embroidering, and weaving, and stitching, threading endless miles of spooled thread of all different colors and thicknesses. All different ages, the workers sit according to years of servitude and age, the oldest, having been there the longest, and whose eyes see the least after years of strain, sit at the front of the room where there is the most light from the windows and doorways, while behind them in progressive densities of shadow sit the younger and younger ones less and less blind. Deepest, where the sunlight never reaches, sit the youngest ones, twelve and thirteen, the newly arrived, the tenderest with their sharp, clear eyes, sewing in shadow. Soon enough, though, they'll get to move forward more and more as the very oldest grow so blind they have to quit, just as they themselves, the younger ones, will see less and less, even as they move nearer and nearer the sunlight. By the windows sit a few women old and almost completely blind and whose hands are so twisted as to be not recognizable as hands anymore. Useless and used up by years of service, they tend to the countless cats that live in the sewing hall. Cats of all different sizes and shapes and colors, living on a gruel of rice and fish, or mice, or sometimes their own litters, they far outnumber their keepers, none of whom knows how they came to live there in the first place. Nameless and nondescript, they endlessly prowl along the walls and the legs of the tables, so that the workers sense a constant motion at their feet, a continual brushing past of fur.

Jiaying hates the sewing hall because of the cats. She hates the smell and the hundreds of little eyes behind the tables and in the shadows. She hates the countless tails curling and brushing past her when she is there on an errand. There are so many of them they can hardly be called pets. The ones who have the job of tending the brood sit by the windows sipping tea, chewing their gums, and squinting. The oldest of them, who swears she remembers having sewed the President's scholar's robe for graduation, sits absently grinning to her toothless self. Whether she is recalling better days, or smiling in the knowledge of the fate of all those young pretty girls in the back, no one can tell.

It was here one morning someone looked up into the ceiling and there, where the swallows build their high unseen nests in the dark of the rafters and brackets, was one white sock dangling in midair. It was the white-stockinged foot of someone hanging from the rafters. Screaming and turning over chairs, the women cleared the sewing hall like frantic birds sprung from a box. Members of the nine households assembled in the yard and someone took the body down. The fifth wife's new maid had hung herself. Judging by all signs, she'd done it early in the morning. It must have been just light when she climbed up on a chair set on a table and scaled the rafters and scaffolding. Everyone speculated on what insanity made her go to so much trouble to hang herself from the highest ceiling in the whole complex. For days afterward everyone kept looking into the ceilings of whatever room or corridor they were in. And then people began to see the girl walking around. Even Jiaying's grandmother, who used to make the girl stay awake entire nights rubbing her feet, and beat her pitilessly if she fell asleep, claimed to have seen her once, but just once. She said she woke from a restful afternoon nap and had the feeling someone was in the room. Furious to have an uninvited guest, she opened her eyes to find the Little Ugly, as she was fond of calling her because of her pocked face, sitting next to her. *What did you do, Nai Nai?* the granddaughters gasped who were listening to the story. *What do you think I did?* she gloated. *I told her if she didn't behave I'd make her mother who sold her to me my maid as well.* The girl never visited the old lady again, although others continued to see her.

But, *Let's not talk about old things,* is my mother's response most of the time I ask her about her childhood. *Don't make me go back there. Like those evil-smelling, greenish black potions the servants cooked and served hot to me in winter for coughs and headaches as a child, the past is all one bitter draft to me,* she says as my sister combs my mother's hair in the morning, by the window looking onto her garden. When I press her, she says, *I can't tell if your head is an empty house, or a pot of boiling glue,* and then inserts the alabaster comb into her loosely piled-up hair, a black nest, and waves a silver stray back with her hand summarily, as though to dispel so much cobweb or smoke. *Now let's go buy some fish.*

At the Beautiful Asia Market in Chicago, the refugee grocer is a bent, brown-colored man with a big black mole on his right jaw, and the fish tank is empty, except for some filthy water. The only fish I see are two carp afloat in a bucket propping a mop in it. So we'll buy the gnarled man's perfectly trimmed napa cabbages, but have to get our fish elsewhere. *Elsewhere,* my mother says, *your head is always elsewhere, in the past or in the future. Why can't you be here?* I wonder about an answer while I push a tinny cart with a crazy wheel down the fragrant lanes of tea, aisles of lemon grass and sandalwood, musty narrows of spices and medicinal herbs, rows of shelves, and shelves of jars of chopped pickled mudfish and shrimp ferment, soybean paste and preserved monkfish, eel eyes staring out from brine, sealed stacks of biscuits and cocoa from Belgium and England, and cartons of instant noodles stacked to the ceiling. I browse with my mother, each of us keeping the same things we need for dinner as different lists, Chinese and English, in our heads, and my mother, because her eyes are bad, inspecting the goods with a spyglass.

In my mother's dreams, she wanders that old ground, the family compound, and it's evening, and becoming more evening. She's on an errand to the sewing hall, and the cloth in her hands is poorly folded. And I know by her description that it's the same path I walk in my own dream. In my mother's dream, she walks in the general direction of the sewing hall, but avoids it. In mine, I'm sitting on the steps and the doors are locked. In my dream, I sometimes stand among trees the way I stood three summers ago on Fragrant Mountain, and look across the valley to another mountain face, where my wife leads our children up a winding path. Below, my grandfather's bones scattered by the People's Army.

In my mother's dream, she is again a girl of sixteen in China, where she spends summer with her family on Fragrant Mountain, making the final two-day leg of the serpentine ascent through dense forests on muleback, in a train of twenty-five mules bearing her father, her mother, her father's concubine, three aunties, one brother (the other having been banished by the grandmother), two of her sisters, fourteen and thirteen years old (the other two attending boarding school in France), her favorite cousin, the same age as her and recently orphaned, two of her brother's friends whom he met in New York while attending school there in the fall at Columbia University, three bodyguards armed with rifles and pistols, four household servants, one cook, three dogs, and various equipment and supplies. On the trip up the narrow path, while one of her sisters reads aloud from Zola or Balzac, Jiaying nibbles on fresh lychees, which they carry up the mountain. The mule bearing the burden of Jiaying's favorite fruit can't tell as that burden imperceptibly and gradually lightens, as Jiaying fills her mouth with its sweetness.

When she is a little girl in China, Jiaying's favorite food is lychee. For one brief season a year, the markets are full of that globose, hard-skinned fruit tied in pink string at the bundled stems, and her father sends the servants to buy them for her each morning. Unlike all the other fruits that smell and taste of sunlight compacted, then mellowed to sugar, lychee yields to her tongue a darker perfume, a heavy redolence damp with the mild edge of fermentation. How wonderfully fitting it seems to her that such milky, soft meat should be surrounded by a rough, brown reptilian leather of a slightly red cast when ripe, and made almost impenetrable by being covered in tiny rivets and studs. Summertime, she grows thin on nothing but lychee flesh. She waits each morning for the servants to bring bundles of it home, and rather than have the fruit peeled and served to her in a porcelain bowl that fits precisely the bowl of her hand, she prefers to peel for herself the tough skin, rough to her fingers. Using her fingernails to puncture the exterior, she splits it open and takes with her teeth the white meat slippery with nectar, the whole plump bulb of it in her mouth, and eats it to the smooth pit, which she spits out, leaving on the verandah each morning a scattering of black stones and empty husks, sticky with sugar and swarming with bees. A servant sweeps the verandah, scolding her.

Ordinarily forbidden to go out beyond the confines of their home, a complex of nine mansions and attendant satellite buildings housing the families of the nine wives of Jiaying's grandfather, Jiaying and her sisters' only contact with the rest of the world has been for years through the private school they attend, where they make friends with girls who, while their families can afford the cost of private school, do not belong to titled households of rank, and who, as a result, are not bound to traditional ways and attitudes the same way Jiaying and her sisters are so strictly bound at home. When each of the Yuan sisters distinguishes herself in her studies, and is encouraged by her parents and her grandmother to continue her education after middle school, naturally, each of them takes advantage of the opportunity by enrolling in fashionable French and British boarding schools. All five of them except Jiaying, the oldest, who decided to stay home, where everything that surrounded her was so old, she was certain it must be permanent. The poems she read were thousands of years old, the calligraphy she practiced was practiced by smart refined girls like her thousands of years ago, the house she lived in and the grounds surrounding it looked to be as old as anything else in the whole country, and as half buried. During the summer sand storms, when all the tiles, the latticed windows, the carved railings and figured eaves were packed with sand, and little dunes formed against the buildings, she knew it was sand broken off eternal mountains and then driven the whole way from the Gobi, that old fabled desert, and was on its way to that most ancient of bodies, the sea. And her grandmother, only forty-five but already walking with the aid of a cane and three or four servants, seemed to be some eternal fixture in the universe with her medicinal odors and old ways. How could she conceive of a future when everything around her felt like the end of things, the world's very culmination.

Of all the things packed onto the sweating mules, Jiaying writes in her diary dated June 6, 1939, *an individual lychee is probably the lightest. Or else the calligraphy brushes. Only the little bamboo-handled goldfish nets are as light as the brushes. Next would certainly be the butterfly nets. Then Auntie's opium in its beautiful paper wrappings. Then the pipes. The weight of the rest of the things is distributed as evenly as possible: Zithers and lutes, flutes, Ba's typewriter, and tea, mirrors, telescopes, fishing poles, and jars of embalming fluids, empty bird cages, dictionaries and books in Chinese, English, and French, subjects ranging from poetry and astronomy to* The Art of War, *and magnifying glasses, boxing gloves, chess and mahjong sets, bows and arrows, slabs of salt- and sugar-cured meats, squat clay pots sealed in wax holding assorted preserved fruits and vegetables, and pages of rice paper bound in boards, ink blocks, and a monkey to grind the ink.*

They ride slowly through increasingly clearer air, making frequent stops to picnic, shoot small game, and take photographs. The cool, immense night they spend at a rest station manned by servants they sent ahead days ago to prepare for their arrival. By candlelight, Jiaying writes in her diary, which she reads to her cousin: *Miles up from the city. Many more miles to go. Here a place to rest. Ahead, another. And farther, another.*

Their last stop before reaching the summit is the ancestral graveyard. An acre of meadow bounded on three sides by woods and on the fourth by the gravekeeper's small farm, on it stand the twelve-foot-high marble headstones of various shapes. The cemetery gate is a huge nail-studded crossbeam set by wedges into twin two-story posts hewn from whole trees, the entire thing tooled and painted with patterns, symbols, and signs resembling eyes or flowers or clouds, and flanked by a set of stone mythical beasts. Half dog, half lion, half scowling, half grinning, standing on their platforms taller than the gravekeeper's house, both guardians look as though they were peering over his roof.

Once at the site, Jiaying and her family burn incense and paper money, and pray to a long line of illustrious men and women whose severe portraits hang huge and forbidding in the tall, gloomy corridors of their home in Tientsin, a city far below them now as they stand in high meadow in the mountains.

In the whirring and clicking of grasshoppers, they walk at the feet of the white marble stele. On each is carved a poem commemorating the one who lies underground shrouded in countless layers of silk and enclosed in a box filled with money and precious jewels. As well as flowers, birds, and animals, human figures are etched in various depictions of filial piety. Even as Jiaying stands bowed at the foot of a stone slab two and a half times her height and wide as a double door, above her eternally is the figure of a young girl not unlike herself clothed in a style hundreds of years old, paying her dutiful respects to the unanswering dead.

While Jiaying and her family linger over the names and poems, no one thinks that Jiaying's father and grandmother will be put in this ground soon. Even less would any of them believe that on an afternoon years from now, a group of student revolutionaries will casually pass through the gates of this place, and dig up the graves and rob them, dragging up the corpses of her father and grandmother to strip and tie them naked to a tree. Jiaying, who will have left the country by then, will have to hear about it almost half a century after the fact, from the gravekeeper himself, who after so many years still recognizes her, and falls to his knees to bow to her, calling her by her title, when she comes back here a woman. She'll have arrived by car then, accompanied by her own children, her husband dead, to be greeted by the man who has lived on this farm ever since the one day he climbed up the mountain to work for her family and never came down again. He'll walk with her over the ground, which has been turned into a pig farm. A few feet behind one of the sties, he'll take her through shoulder-high cannabis plants to see the few smashed and overturned monuments that haven't yet been removed. She'll stand in the glare of afternoon and squint to make out the pieces of names and poems in stone. She'll walk ahead a few feet and suddenly find herself standing dumbfounded at the gaping pits of concrete vaults of defiled graves. Then the old man will show her where he buried her father and grandmother after he untied them from the trees. He'll point to a strip of ground under three feeding troughs, apologizing that he can't remember who is under which trough. *But they've all been punished by heaven,* he assures her. One by one, he says, the looters died from wearing the silks they stripped off the corpses.

—1995

Learning from Other Writers

1. How might the author know the layout of the sewing hall in his mother's childhood home? The details about the cats? The servants' response to seeing the young girl hanging from the rafters?
2. What is the effect of the author's use of the present tense?
3. What role (if any) does the author play in this essay?
4. Why would the author think that anyone would care about his mother's experiences as a young girl in China, or as an older woman in Chicago, or as an exile returning to her family's graveyard?
5. Does the author seem to be writing for any particular audience? If so, does this choice of audience affect the details or information he chooses to include or leave out? What tone or attitude does the author take toward his ancestors' wealth and privilege?
6. The author is an acclaimed poet as well as an essayist and memoirist. In what (specific) ways might his background as a poet have influenced the structure of this essay? The rhythms and imagery of the prose?

ANNIE DILLARD

THE STUNT PILOT

Dave Rahm lived in Bellingham, Washington, north of Seattle. Bellingham, a harbor town, lies between the alpine North Cascade Mountains and the San Juan Islands in Haro Strait above Puget Sound. The latitude is that of Newfoundland. Dave Rahm was a stunt pilot, the air's own genius.

In 1975, with a newcomer's willingness to try anything once, I attended the Bellingham Air Show. The Bellingham airport was a wide clearing in a forest of tall Douglas firs; its runways suited small planes. It was June. People wearing blue or tan zipped jackets stood loosely on the concrete walkways and runways outside the coffee shop. At that latitude in June, you stayed outside because you could, even most of the night, if you could think up something to do. The sky did not darken until ten o'clock or so, and it never got very dark. Your life parted and opened in the sunlight. You tossed your dark winter routines, thought up mad projects, and improvised everything from hour to hour. Being a stunt pilot seemed the most reasonable thing in the world; you could wave your arms in the air all day and night, and sleep next winter.

I saw from the ground a dozen stunt pilots; the air show scheduled them one after the other, for an hour of acrobatics. Each pilot took up his or her plane and performed a batch of tricks. They were precise and impressive. They flew upside down, and straightened out; they did barrel rolls, and straightened out; they drilled through dives and spins, and landed gently on a far runway.

For the end of the day, separated from all other performances of every sort, the air show director had scheduled a program titled "Dave Rahm." The leaflet said that Rahm was a geologist who taught at Western Washington University. He had flown for King Hussein in Jordan. A tall man in the crowd told me Hussein had seen Rahm fly on a visit the king made to the United States; he had invited him to Jordan to perform at ceremonies. Hussein was a pilot, too. "Hussein thought he was the greatest thing in the world."

Idly, paying scant attention. I saw a medium-sized, rugged man dressed in brown leather, all begoggled, climb in a black biplane's open cockpit. The plane was a Bücker Jungman, built in the thirties. I saw a tall, dark-haired woman seize a propeller tip at the plane's nose and yank it down till the engine caught. He was off; he climbed high over the airport in his biplane, very high until he was barely visible as a mote, and then seemed to fall down the air, diving headlong, and streaming beauty in spirals behind him.

The black plane dropped spinning, and flattened out spinning the other way; it began to carve the air into forms that built wildly and musically on each other and never ended. Reluctantly, I started paying attention. Rahm drew high above the world an inexhaustibly glorious line; it piled over our heads in loops and arabesques. It was like a Saul Steinberg fantasy; the plane was the pen. Like Steinberg's contracting and billowing pen line, the line Rahm spun moved to form new, punning shapes from the edges of the old. Like a Klee line, it smattered the sky with landscapes and systems.

The air show announcer hushed. He had been squawking all day, and now he quit. The crowd stilled. Even the children watched dumbstruck as the slow, black biplane buzzed its way around the air. Rahm made beauty with his whole body; it was pure pattern, and you could watch it happen. The plane moved every way a line can move, and it controlled three dimensions, so the line carved massive and subtle slits in the air like sculptures. The plane looped the loop, seeming to arch its back like a gymnast; it stalled, dropped, and spun out of it climbing; it spiraled and knifed west on one side's wings and back east on another; it turned cartwheels, which must be physically impossible; it played with its own line like a cat with yarn. How did the pilot know where in the air he was? If he got lost, the ground would swat him.

Rahm did everything his plane could do: tailspins, four-point rolls, flat spins, figure eights, snap rolls, and hammerheads. He did pirouettes on the plane's tail. The other pilots could do these stunts too, skillfully, one at a time. But Rahm used the plane inexhaustibly, like a brush marking thin air.

His was pure energy and naked spirit. I have thought about it for years. Rahm's line unrolled in time. Like music, it split the bulging rim of the future along its seam. It pried out the present. We watchers waited for the split-second curve of beauty in the present to reveal itself. The human pilot, Dave Rahm, worked in the cockpit right at the plane's nose; his very body tore into the future for us and reeled it down upon us like a curling peel.

Like any fine artist, he controlled the tension of the audience's longing. You desired, unwittingly, a certain kind of roll or climb, or a return to a certain portion of the air, and he fulfilled your hope slantingly, like a poet, or evaded it untill you thought you would burst, and then fulfilled it surprisingly, so you gasped and cried out.

The oddest, most exhilarating and exhausting thing was this: he never quit. The music had no periods, no rests or endings; the poetry's beautiful sentence never ended; the line had no finish; the sculptured forms piled overhead, one into another without surcease. Who could breathe, in a world where rhythm itself had no periods?

It had taken me several minutes to understand what an extraordinary thing I was seeing. Rahm kept all that embellished space in mind at once. For another twenty minutes I watched the beauty unroll and grow more fantastic and unlikely before my eyes. Now Rahm brought the plane down slidingly, and just in time, for I thought I would snap from the effort to compass and remember the line's long intelligence; I could not add another curve. He brought the plane down on a far runway. After a pause, I saw him step out, an ordinary man, and make his way back to the terminal.

The show was over. It was late. Just as I turned from the runway, something caught my eye and made me laugh. It was a swallow, a blue-green swallow, having its own air show, apparently inspired by Rahm. The swallow climbed high over the runway, held its wings oddly, tipped them, and rolled down the air in loops. The inspired swallow. I always want to paint, too, after I see the Rembrandts. The blue-green swallow tumbled precisely, and caught itself and flew up again as if excited, and looped down again, the way swallows do, but tensely, holding its body carefully still. It was a stunt swallow.

I went home and thought about Rahm's performance that night, and the next day, and the next.

I had thought I knew my way around beauty a little bit. I knew I had devoted a good part of my life to it, memorizing poetry and focusing my attention on complexity of rhythm in particular, on force, movement, repetition, and surprise, in both poetry and prose. Now I had stood among dandelions between two asphalt runways in Bellingham, Washington, and begun learning about beauty. Even the Boston Museum of Fine Arts was never more inspiriting than this small northwestern airport on this time-killing Sunday afternoon in June. Nothing on earth is more gladdening than knowing we must roll up our sleeves and move back the boundaries of the humanly possible once more.

Later I flew with Dave Rahm; he took me up. A generous geographer, Dick Smith, at Western Washington University, arranged it, and came along. Rahm and Dick Smith were colleagues at the university. In geology, Rahm had published two books and many articles. Rahm was handsome in a dull sort of way, blunt-featured, wide-jawed, wind-burned, keen-eyed, and taciturn. As anyone would expect. He was forty. He wanted to show me the Cascade Mountains; these enormous peaks, only fifty miles from the coast, rise over nine thousand feet; they are heavily glaciated. Whatcom County has more glaciers than the lower forty-eight states combined; the Cascades make the Rocky Mountains look like hills. Mount Baker is volcanic, like most Cascade peaks. That year, Mount Baker was acting up. Even from my house at the shore I could see, early in the morning on clear days, volcanic vapor rise near its peak. Often the vapor made a cloud that swelled all morning and hid the snows. Every day the newspapers reported on Baker's activity: Would it blow? (A few years later, Mount St. Helens did blow.)

Rahm was not flying his trick biplane that day, but a faster enclosed plane, a single-engine Cessna. We flew from a bumpy grass airstrip near my house, out over the coast and inland. There was coastal plain down there, but we could not see it for clouds. We were over the clouds at five hundred feet and inside them too, heading for an abrupt line of peaks we could not see. I gave up on everything, the way you do in airplanes; it was out of my hands. Every once in a while Rahm saw a peephole in the clouds and buzzed over for a look. "That's Larsen's pea farm," he said, or "That's Nooksack Road," and he changed our course with a heave.

When we got to the mountains, he slid us along Mount Baker's flanks sideways.

Our plane swiped at the mountain with a roar. I glimpsed a windshield view of dirty snow traveling fast. Our shaking, swooping belly seemed to graze the snow. The wings shuddered; we peeled away and the mountain fell back and the engines whined. We felt flung, because we were in fact flung; parts of our faces and internal organs trailed pressingly behind on the curves. We came back for another pass at the mountain, and another. We dove at the snow headlong like suicides; we jerked up, down, or away at the last second, so late we left our hearts, stomachs, and lungs behind. If I forced myself to hold my heavy head up against the G's, and to raise my eyelids, heavy as barbells, and to notice what I saw, I could see the wrinkled green crevasses cracking the glaciers' snow.

Pitching snow filled all the windows, and shapes of dark rock. I had no notion which way was up. Everything was black or gray or white except the fatal crevasses; everything made noise and shook. I felt my face smashed sideways and saw rushing abstractions of snow in the windshield. Patches of cloud obscured the snow fleetingly. We straightened out, turned, and dashed at the mountainside for another pass, which we made, apparently, on our ear, an inch or two away from the slope. Icefalls and cornices jumbled and fell away. If a commercial plane's black box, such as the FAA painstakingly recovers from crash sites, could store videotapes as well as pilots' last words, some videotapes would look like this: a mountainside coming up at the windows from all directions, ice and snow and rock filling the screen up close and screaming by.

Rahm was just being polite. His geographer colleague wanted to see the fissure on Mount Baker from which steam escaped. Everybody in Bellingham wanted to see that sooty fissure, as did every geologist in the country; no one on earth could fly so close to it as Rahm. He knew the mountain by familiar love and feel, like a face; he knew what the plane could do and what he dared to do.

When Mount Baker inexplicably let us go, he jammed us into cloud again and soon tilted. "The Sisters!" someone shouted, and I saw the windshield fill with red rock. This mountain looked infernal, a drear and sheer plane of lifeless rock. It was red and sharp; its gritty blades cut through the clouds at random. The mountain was quiet. It was in shade. Careening, we made sideways passes at these brittle peaks too steep for snow. Their rock was full of iron, somebody shouted at me then or later; the iron had rusted, so they were red. Later, when I was back on the ground, I recalled that, from a distance, the two jagged peaks called the Twin Sisters looked translucent against the sky; they were sharp, tapered, and fragile as arrowheads.

I talked to Rahm. He was flying us out to the islands now. The islands were fifty or sixty miles away. Like many other people, I had picked Bellingham, Washington, by looking at an atlas. It was clear from the atlas that you could row in the salt water and see snow-covered mountains; you could scale a glaciated mountainside with an ice ax in August, skirting green crevasses two hundred feet deep, and look out on the islands in the sea. Now, in the air, the clouds had risen over us; dark forms lay on the glinting water. There was almost no color to the day, just blackened green and some yellow. I knew the islands were forested in dark Douglas firs the size of skyscrapers. Bald eagles scavenged on the beaches; robins the size of herring gulls sang in the clearings. We made our way out to the islands through the layer of air between the curving planet and its held, thick clouds.

"When I started trying to figure out what I was going to do with my life, I decided to become an expert on mountains. It wasn't much to be, it wasn't everything, but it was something. I was going to know everything about mountains from every point of view. So

I started out in geography." Geography proved too pedestrian for Rahm, too concerned with "how many bushels of wheat an acre." So he ended up in geology. Smith had told me that geology departments throughout the country used Rahm's photographic slides—close-ups of geologic features from the air.

"I used to climb mountains. But you know, you can get a better feel for a mountain's power flying around it, flying all around it, then you can from climbing it tied to its side like a flea."

He talked about his flying performances. He thought of the air as a line, he said. "This end of the line, that end of the line—like a rope." He improvised. "I get a rhythm going and stick with it." While he was performing in a show, he paid attention, he said, to the lighting. He didn't play against the sun. That was all he said about what he did.

In aerobatic maneuvers, pilots pull about seven positive G's on some stunts and six negative G's on others. Some gyrations push; others pull. Pilots alternate the pressures carefully, so they do not gray out or black out.

Later I learned that some stunt pilots tune up by wearing gravity boots. These are boots made to hook over a doorway; wearing them, you hang in the doorway upside down. It must startle a pilot's children to run into their father or mother in the course of their home wanderings—the parents hanging wide-eyed, upside down in the doorway like a bat.

We were landing; here was the airstrip on Stuart Island—that island to which Ferrar Burn was dragged by the tide. We put down, climbed out of the plane, and walked. We wandered a dirt track through fields to a lee shore where yellow sandstone ledges slid into the sea. The salt chuck, people there called salt water. The sun came out. I caught a snake in the salt chuck; the snake, eighteen inches long, was swimming in the green shallows.

I had a survivor's elation. Rahm had found Mount Baker in the clouds before Mount Baker found the plane. He had wiped it with the fast plane like a cloth and we had lived. When we took off from Stuart Island and gained altitude, I asked if we could turn over—could we do a barrel roll? The plane was making a lot of noise, and Dick Smith did not hear any of this, I learned later. "Why not?" Rahm said, and added surprisingly, "It won't hurt the plane." Without ado he leaned on the wheel and the wing went down and we went somersaulting over it. We upended with a roar. We stuck to the plane's sides like flung paint. All the blood in my body bulged on my face; it piled between my skull and skin. Vaguely I could see the chrome sea twirling over Rahm's head like a baton, and the dark islands sliding down the skies like rain.

The G's slammed me into my seat like thugs and pinned me while my heart pounded and the plane turned over slowly and compacted each organ in turn. My eyeballs were newly spherical and full of heartbeats. I seemed to hear a crescendo; the wing rolled shuddering down the last 90 degrees and settled on the flat. There were the islands, admirably below us, and the clouds, admirably above. When I could breathe, I asked if we could do it again, and we did. He rolled the other way. The brilliant line of the sea slid up the side window bearing its heavy islands. Through the shriek of my blood and the plane's shakes I glimpsed the line of the sea over the windshield, thin as a spear. How in performance did Rahm keep track while his brain blurred and blood roared in his ears without ceasing? Every performance was a tour de force and a show of will, a *Machtspruch*. I had seen the other stunt pilots straighten out after a trick or two: their blood could drop back and the planet simmer down. An Olympic gymnast, at peak form, strings out a line of spins ten stunts long across a mat, and is hard put to keep his footing at the end. Rahm endured much greater pressure on his faster spins using the plane's power, and he could spin in three dimensions and keep twirling till he ran out of sky room or luck.

When we straightened out, and had flown straightforwardly for ten minutes toward home, Dick Smith, clearing his throat, brought himself to speak. "What was that we did out there?"

"The barrel rolls?" Rahm said. "They were barrel rolls." He said nothing else. I looked at the back of his head; I could see the serious line of his check and jaw. He was in shirtsleeves, tanned, strong-wristed. I could not imagine loving him under any circumstance; he was alien to me, unfazed. He looked like GI Joe. He flew with that matter-of-fact, bored gesture pilots use. They click overhead switches and turn dials as if only their magnificent strength makes such dullness endurable. The half circle of wheel in their big hands looks like a toy they plan to crush in a minute; the wiggly stick the wheel mounts seems barely attached.

A crop-duster pilot in Wyoming told me the life expectancy of a crop-duster pilot is five years. They fly too low. They hit buildings and power lines. They have no space to fly out of trouble, and no space to recover from a stall. We were in Cody, Wyoming, out on the north fork of the Shoshone River. The crop duster had wakened me that morning flying over the ranch house and clearing my bedroom roof by half an inch. I saw the bolts on the wheel assembly a few feet from my face. He was spraying with pesticide the plain old grass. Over breakfast I asked him how long he had been dusting crops. "Four years," he said, and the figure stalled in the air between us for a moment. "You know you're going to die at it someday," he added. "We all know it. We accept that; it's part of it." I think now that, since the crop duster was in his twenties, he accepted only that he had to say such stuff; privately he counted on skewing the curve.

I suppose Rahm knew the fact too. I do not know how he felt about it. "It's worth it," said the early French aviator Mermoz. He was Antoine de Saint-Exupéry's friend. "It's worth the final smashup."

Rahm smashed up in front of King Hussein, in Jordan, during a performance. The plane spun down and never came out of it; it nosedived into the ground and exploded. He bought the farm. I was living then with my husband out on that remote island in the San Juans, cut off from everything. Battery radios picked up the Canadian Broadcasting Company out of Toronto, half a continent away; island people would, in theory, learn if the United States blew up, but not much else. There were no newspapers. One friend got the Sunday *New York Times* by mail boat on the following Friday. He saved it until Sunday and had a party, every week; we all read the Sunday *Times* and no one mentioned that it was last week's.

One day, Paul Glenn's brother flew out from Bellingham to visit; he had a seaplane. He landed in the water in front of the cabin and tied up to our mooring. He came in for coffee, and he gave out news of this and that, and—Say, did we know that stunt pilot Dave Rahm had cracked up? In Jordan, during a performance: he never came out of a dive. He just dove right down into the ground, and his wife was there watching. "I saw it on CBS News last night." And then—with a sudden sharp look at my filling eyes—"What, did you know him?" But no, I did not know him. He took me up once. Several years ago. I admired his flying. I had thought that danger was the safest thing in the world, if you went about it right.

Later, I found a newspaper. Rahm was living in Jordan that year. King Hussein invited him to train the aerobatics team, the Royal Jordanian Falcons. He was also visiting professor of geology at the University of Jordan. In Amman that day he had been flying a Pitt Special, a plane he knew well. Katy Rahm, his wife of six months, was sitting beside Hussein in the viewing stands, with her daughter. Rahm died performing a Lomcevak combined with a tail slide and hammerhead.

In a Lomcevak, the pilot brings the plane up on a slant and pirouettes. I had seen Rahm do this: the falling plane twirled slowly like a leaf. Like a ballerina, the plane seemed to hold its head back stiff in concentration at the music's slow, painful beauty. It was one of Rahm's favorite routines. Next the pilot flies straight up, stalls the plane, and slides down the air on his tail. He brings the nose down—the hammerhead—kicks the engine, and finishes with a low loop.

It is a dangerous maneuver at any altitude, and Rahm was doing it low. He hit the ground on the loop: the tail slide had left him no height. When Rahm went down, King Hussein dashed to the burning plane to pull him out, but he was already dead.

A few months after the air show, and a month after I had flown with Rahm, I was working at my desk near Bellingham, where I lived, when I heard a sound so odd it finally penetrated my concentration. It was the buzz of an airplane, but it rose and fell musically, and it never quit; the plane never flew out of earshot. I walked out on the porch and looked up: it was Rahm in the black and gold biplane, looping all over the air. I had been wondering about his performance flight: could it really have been so beautiful? It was, for here it was again. The little plane twisted all over the air like a vine. It trailed a line like a very long mathematical proof you could follow only so far, and then it lost you in its complexity. I saw Rahm flying high over the Douglas firs, and out over the water, and back over farms. The air was a fluid, and Rahm was an eel.

It was as if Mozart could move his body through his notes, and you could walk out on the porch, look up, and see him in periwig and breeches, flying around in the sky. You could hear the music as he dove through it: it streamed after him like a contrail.

I lost myself; standing on the firm porch, I lost my direction and reeled. My neck and spine rose and turned, so I followed the plane's line kinesthetically. In his open-cockpit black plane, Rahm demonstrated curved space. He slid down ramps of air, he vaulted and wheeled. He piled loops in heaps and praised height. He unrolled the scroll of air, extended it, and bent it into Möbius strips; he furled line in a thousand new ways, as if he were inventing a script and writing it in one infinitely recurving utterance until I thought the bounds of beauty must break.

From inside, the looping plane had sounded tinny, like a kazoo. Outside, the buzz rose and fell to the Doppler effect as the plane looped near or away. Rahm cleaved the sky like a prow and tossed out time left and right in his wake. He performed for forty minutes; then he headed the plane, as small as a wasp, back to the airport inland. Later I learned Rahm often practiced acrobatic flights over this shore. His idea was that if he lost control and was going to go down, he could ditch in the salt chuck, where no one else would get hurt.

If I had not turned two barrel rolls in an airplane, I might have fancied Rahm felt good up there, and playful. Maybe Jackson Pollock felt a sort of playfulness, in addition to the artist's usual deliberate and intelligent care. In my limited experience, painting, unlike writing, pleases the senses while you do it, and more while you do it than after it is done. Drawing lines with an airplane, unfortunately, tortures the senses. Jet bomber pilots black out. I knew Rahm felt as if his brain were bursting his eardrums, felt that if he let his jaws close as tight as centrifugal force pressed them, he would bite through his lungs.

"All virtue is a form of acting," Yeats said. Rahm deliberately turned himself into a figure. Sitting invisible at the controls of a distant airplane, he became the agent and the instrument of art and invention. He did not tell me how he felt when we spoke of his performance flying; he told me instead that he paid attention to how his plane and its line looked to the audience against the lighted sky. If he had noticed how he felt, he could not have done the work. Robed in his airplane, he was as featureless as a priest. He was lost in his figural aspect like an actor or a king. Of his flying, he had said only, "I get a rhythm and stick with it." In its reticence, this statement reminded me of Veronese's "Given a large canvas, I enhanced it as I saw fit." But Veronese was ironic, and Rahm was not; he was as literal as an astronaut; the machine gave him tongue.

When Rahm flew, he sat down in the middle of art and strapped himself in. He spun it all around him. He could not see it himself. If he never saw it on film, he never saw it at all—as if Beethoven could not hear his final symphonies not because he was deaf but because he was inside the paper on which he wrote. Rahm must have felt it happen, that fusion of vision and metal, motion and idea. I think of this man as a figure, a college professor with a Ph.D. upside down in the loud band of beauty. What are we here for? *Propter chorum*, the monks say: for the sake of the choir.

"Purity does not lie in separation from but in deeper penetration into the universe," Teilhard de Chardin wrote. It is hard to imagine a deeper penetration into the universe than Rahm's last dive in his plane, or than his inexpressible wordless selfless line's inscribing the air and dissolving. Any other art may be permanent. I cannot recall one Rahm sequence. He improvised. If Christo wraps a building or dyes a harbor, we join his poignant and fierce awareness that the work will be gone in days. Rahm's plane shed a ribbon in space, a ribbon whose end unraveled in memory while its beginning unfurled as surprise. He may have acknowledged that what he did could be called art, but it would have been, I think, only in the common misusage, which holds art to be the last extreme of skill. Rahm rode the point of the line to the possible; he discovered it and wound it down to show. He made his dazzling probe on the run. "The world is filled, and filled with the Absolute," Teilhard de Chardin wrote. "To see this is to be made free."

—1989

Learning from Other Writers

1. What are the advantages and disadvantages of the sort of slow, offhand introduction that Dillard offers to her subject?
2. Look at the passage in which Dillard describes Rahm's aerial acrobatics (starting with paragraph six, "The black plane dropped spinning ..."). What do you notice about Dillard's use of nouns and verbs? Adjectives and adverbs? See if you can cross out any words without changing the meaning or sense of those passages.
3. Why does Dillard seem to think that Rahm is worth a profile? What is the central question she explores in this essay?
4. Do you believe Dillard's assertion that the swallow in paragraph thirteen is imitating Rahm? What purpose does this passage serve in the profile as a whole?
5. What, if anything, does Dillard learn about Rahm and his art by going up with him in his plane?
6. What is the effect of Dillard telling her readers "I could not imagine loving [Rahm] under any circumstances; he was alien to me, unfazed. He looked like GI Joe"?
7. Which sections of the profile are *not* placed in chronological order? Why? What is the occasion that causes Dillard to write this profile of Rahm?
8. What purpose is served by the long meditative section at the very end of the essay (i.e., the last four paragraphs)?

DANIEL RIVAS

THE MASTER OF MACHINES

This was my father: he turns on the gas, lights his paper-sack torch, and carries it to the six-foot-long tub where he cooks corn. Leaves of glowing ash abscise behind him as he extends the torch toward the rows of burners, a rush of air preceding the blue flames. I warm myself there—the mornings were cold, even in summer—careful not to get too close, while he stirs with a lime-crusted two-by-four.

He dips a metal basket deep into the tub with his bare hand. Most of the small squares of the once-porous sieve are filled with petrified kernels (to extract them would require a good hammer, chisel, and at least an hour). He has to shake it a few times to get most of the water out, but even then, corn juice runs down his arm and onto the floor as he carries the basket to the stainless-steel grinder that conceals a stone wheel at its centre. From the ceiling hangs a thin black hose that drops a dribbling stream of water into the grinder to give the ground corn the right consistency. Almost instantly, golden flecks begin clinging to the sides of a rectangular steel bin, and within moments, those flecks become sticky lumps, then one mass—*masa*. The cavernous *tortilleta* begins to fill with a bodily smell I sometimes encounter in alleys after rain or on towels left wet on the bathroom floor.

While masa collects in viscid lumps, he prepares the machines. He lights the oven first, again taking up his paper torch; a thousand tiny flames pop into being, glow blue in neat rows. The conveyor squeaks into motion.

Masa goes into the wide-open top of the machine that slowly metes it out in the shape of a fan, my father reaching up and into the mouth to help push masa through to the two rolling presses that flatten it before it reaches the die that cuts either oblong tortillas or chips.

Through the oven, over and through again, the tortillas cook three times before they emerge the colour and texture of baked sand. They travel again on another conveyor—fifty feet long and canted up and at a right angle to the oven—cooling as they bounce left to right, right to left, back again; the purpose is to take them a long way but not far, like the lines at Disneyland. And when they become cool enough to touch, I wait with the women who count tortillas with practised speed, then bag the stack to start again.

It has been more than eleven years since this ritual ended, since my father's factory closed. It feels like the end of a particular history, one both uniquely American and outside of America's vision.

With seven hundred dollars and a house full of working children, my grandparents left the ghettos of Denver, the fields of Greeley, Toppenish, and the Skagit Valley behind and opened the Mexico Cafe in 1965. It was the first Mexican restaurant in northwestern Washington State. Within a few years, my grandfather decided they needed to make their own tortillas because those from El Ranchito in Toppenish often arrived mouldy after a long journey across the Cascades in the warm belly of a Greyhound bus. In the late sixties, my father and grandfather went down to California where they bought a tub to cook corn, a grinder, an oven, and a conveyor belt and brought them back to the long, cinder-block building beside my grandmother's house.

For more than twenty years, my father made tortillas, at first with his father, who could never cook the corn right, then alone, as a business after his father died of a heart attack in 1970. My parents met in the restaurant. My mother was a cook. In April of 1978, they eloped to Hawaii—the only way my mother's Pentecostal Christian parents would allow her to marry this Mexican man who was twelve years her senior and who did not even go to church. In 1981, my father built a large yellow house on a mound of fill dirt in the middle of a field used to grow hay and test motorcycles. My grandmother died in 1988 and made my uncle Adolph, who still runs the restaurant, the sole owner.

In 1992, when I was in eighth grade, health inspectors closed the tortilleta. My father blamed the dinginess of the building and the ignorance of the inspectors, and for the next month or two, drove my mother, sister, and me past a number of buildings for lease, none of which he could afford and none of which had the proper drainage. Soon after, he suffered a cerebral hemorrhage—a stroke—the first in a litany of illness and loss I cannot help but confuse in number and sequence: heart attack (maybe two), broken left foot, house sold due to bankruptcy, amputated right foot, diabetes.

My mother took care of him as best she could, but once he began to ease into the convalescent life, and she could think of herself again, she wanted out. By my own estimate, it took her five years and another man before she found the courage to leave him.

My sister and I were made to work in our father's factory. We were poor workers and hated the place. In fog or darkness, we pulled on clothes we could dirty and followed slowly behind our mother who was always late to work but who usually would drop us off at the tortilleta on her way.

We did not earn money, but we did earn school clothes and maybe a week-long sports camp—baseball for me, tennis for my sister—though clothes and camps were not why we were there. My father and his machines were our babysitters when school was not in session because real babysitters were often too expensive. We viewed the place as a kind of prison complex with a work element. My sister would sit obstinate, refusing to count or stack, playing instead with whatever she could find, which was not much: a pen, her hair, the flaps on a cardboard box. Though I worked harder, I would sometimes escape for long stretches, walking around the imposing concrete box that also housed a cheese factory and Skagit Valley Hospital's laundry services.

This was my father: he can leave the machines only for a few moments; too often they break down when he is on a delivery or errand, and there is no one to fix them until he returns. He comes out looking for me, and when he finds me, says, "*Get* in there," a broad, forceful sweep of his arm gesturing toward the "in," the "there." He hurries back, and I follow, the noise of the creaking machines echoing so loudly between those concrete walls that a stranger might think some kind of doomsday device were housed within. It is nearly impossible to speak to him, even if he is near. By the time I enter the factory, he is already feeding the masa into the die, his whole arm deep within the mouth of the machine.

He learned early in life that machines could be a living. His father used to take him and his brother Frankie out in their Ford pickup to collect newspapers, bottles, and scrap metal. But the real treasures, for they were rare and infinitely valuable, were the machines they would find or be given by white people who enjoyed charity. They once salvaged an 8 mm projector and reels of cartoons. They found or received Victrolas, toasters, radios, and cameras, which they spent their afternoons fixing. My grandfather taught his son, my father, to see the worth in old, broken, or disused objects.

My father still collected machines when I was a kid, though he had little time or need for them by then. We had a pachinko machine my father had picked up at some swap meet or flea market; the launching device never worked right, so my sister and I used to roll the metal balls across the basement floor or stick them up our noses. He had a Rototiller, automatic garage door, chainsaw, cars no one drove because they were broken—a Mazda RX-7 and at least one van in addition to the two or three my mother and father did drive—four-wheel motorcycle, hydraulic jack, rock polisher, electric sander. In the house my father built, he installed the infrastructure for a central vacuuming system and windows that cranked open.

My father's machines were always a source of conflict between him and my mother. She found the machines unsightly and useless, especially when they were in the yard or at the side of the house. Even in the years when I was young and they seemed happy, his machines were driving them apart.

Now that he is alone, the lessons he learned from his junk-man father keep him going still. He makes furniture from salvaged wood. Garage sales and handiwork helped him fill his house with appliances after my mother left. He recently received a broken-down Dodge van for free and fixed it, drives it now nearly every day.

Once, my father brought home a gigantic piece of blue canvas and laid it out along the wide stretch of sloping lawn at the side of the house. I remember puzzling over this stretch of fabric, walking on it and finding frogs in the pools that gathered in its thick folds after the rain. I had no concept of it until my father attached a fan and I watched it grow, shedding the water and frogs slowly, like a resurfacing submarine. When it was full of air, my sister and I unzipped the doorway and ran around in the breezy half-light feeling a sense of space and freedom we had never felt when this patch of grass had been surrounded by open air. It was for a swimming pool, he told us. We knew he did not mean *our* swimming pool, but a hypothetical pool, the purpose for this invention. Where it went I'm not certain, probably to the soggy field behind my uncle Steve's tool repair shop, but what remained for months afterwards was a long rectangle of mud and yellow grass.

In the time between the closing of my father's tortilla factory and the beginning of his litany of illness, he and I alone moved iron and steel. Though he had nowhere to take them, no factory where he could begin anew, his machines had to go. We used jacks, dollies, and hand trucks to get each one, piece by piece, onto the box truck he used for deliveries. Conveyor belts; ovens; grinder with stone wheel; the vacuum sealer I used to run just to hear the release of air, just to see the bags seize instantly; mixer with hooked arm to knead flour tortilla dough; machine to roll the dough into balls to be flattened and stretched; fryer for chips—we wheeled them out, a procession of now useless parts.

My father tested my strength and my trust in him. He rigged a series of cranks and pulleys, suspended these tons of metal, then swung them into the truck, easing them down. We drove them over to the site of the first tortilleta, a decaying, rat-infested building. The machines that had been there before, returned. The newer machines, the ones that my father had made payments on for years and that had forced him to declare bankruptcy, joined them. It became a machine cemetery. And like gravestones in remote cemeteries of former mill or gold-rush towns, my father's machines were forgotten and left to nature. Grasses grew tall around the building, obscuring entrances and glassless windows. Weeds sprouted on the mossy roof and inside, between the cracks. Pigeon or crow shit encrusted every surface. Owl pellets mixed among the dust. Rats nested in the belly of the oven and finches lodged in the exhaust pipe. Spiders saw infinite points of connection and wove long filaments.

During my junior or senior year of high school, he took me again to that weather-beaten shed, cleared the grass and weeds, and began scrubbing the machines clean. He said someone wanted to buy them and he had to get them ready. It took him weeks before he could get the masa right, keep the tortillas from falling apart. He made a batch and I ate one. It had a hollow, dirty aftertaste, but I told him it was good. I do not know what happened to that buyer. The machines were not sold.

"Jack of all trades, master of none," my father says about the handiwork he does to get by. Yet, he did know tortillas and the machines that made them. Of these alone, he was a master. His father sloughed off the responsibility soon after they started the factory, left it for my father, who came home from Weyerhaeuser after an eight-hour shift to nap until Adolph and Natalie—his youngest brother and niece—came home from school to stack and bag tortillas. Sometimes, when the machines were not running well, the kids would go inside to sleep or do homework, and my father would be left alone to make sure the corn had been cooked, ground, pressed flat, cut, and baked. He'd stay alone all night if he had to. In a short time, he built a business that delivered tortillas as far south as Tacoma and as far north as Vancouver, British Columbia.

I'm sure my father felt gratitude that the tortilleta was his own, but now he tells me he feels "left out." He explains it as begrudging glances he gets from Adolph's wife when he pours himself a cup of coffee or a soda in their restaurant, but I know he means to say he feels excluded from all his family's class climbing, feels left out of their collective success. While his brothers and sisters buy nice cars and pay off their homes, my father pays the mortgage on his small, poorly built tract house with his social security cheque. To pay bills and buy food, he rents out the rooms vacated by my sister and me to a young Mexican girl, who works at the restaurant, and her boyfriend, who is still in high school. My father spends his mornings and afternoons at the restaurant, putting chips into baskets for the bus kids, unpacking groceries from Food Service, or fixing the cooler or the plumbing, not only for the few dollars my uncle gives him, but also because he has no other way to fill his day, no job to go to. When I am back home, and we arrange to meet for lunch, I usually find him sitting at one of the tables off to the side where he can watch the customers come and go.

This is my father:

– *Hey Daaaan-el. How are things? Okay? How's school?*

– *I'm thinking about opening up a Mexican deli. All prepared stuff. For lunch, you know. And then we'll sell tortillas, fresh. There are a lot of Mexican people. I think it would be real good.*

– *Hey, I think I got someone to buy those machines. We're going to be partners.*

– *You know those machines, well this guy who lives across the street has a brother who's interested.*

– *I'm going to open up a little* carneceria *like in Mexico and then we'll sell corn tortillas too.*

– *Hey, I'm going to take those chip bins over to El Cazador. The owner maybe wants to buy one.*

Over the years, I have heard too many of his plans to distinguish one from another. He waffles between going into business again for himself and selling the machines with the stipulation that he be hired to run them, at least for a while. His plans always include the machines, which is practical in its way. In a very real sense, these machines are all the capital he has. He cannot lend his body—two bad feet, a bad heart, too much weight—to Weyerhaeuser or Norm Nelson Potatoes the way he did when he was young, the way the men of his generation were taught to do. Nor can he conjure money out of the capital of his mind in offices the way men who have been to college seem able to do. Yet, I cannot help but think the machines are about something more.

Even when machines are mysterious, when they won't run, if you continue to turn bolts, disassemble parts, grease or oil what ought to move, tighten what ought to remain firm, if you replace what is broken with a part, new or refurbished, then you can continue as before; and if the machine runs well, you will soon forget it was ever broken.

Much that has happened to my father must seem to him to be out of his control. Of course, he did have some control, and in fact, his doctors, family, my mother, and even I have placed most of the blame on him, on his inattention to sanitation, his wilful ignorance of his own health, his stubbornly bad business sense, and his workaholism. But my father sees different causes. To him, a bureaucracy closed his business; a stroke kept him from working and caused him to lose his tortilleta and the home he had built; diabetes, a disease, took his foot; all this and more caused my mother to leave, caused his loneliness. Infirmity and poverty have excluded him from climbing in class as his brothers and sisters have done. He feels helpless.

Life is not a machine. It cannot be fixed. He knows this better than I do, yet he still believes in machines. He believes in the power of machines to save him—*deus ex machina* descending to put his life improbably back in order.

Until recently, my father has relied most heavily on his prosthetic foot. It is a simple machine—hard plastic shin, Velcro straps to keep it tight around the bulbous nub where his leg ends, a joint where two plastics meet to form an ankle. The doctors at the VA hospital in Seattle have put him in a purple cast because his foot does not fit well. After a long day of walking or standing, he always has a bloody sore where flesh and plastic meet. The cast embarrasses him because now it is plain to everyone that he is missing this part. The doctors have advised him that if the sores do not heal, they will have to amputate a few more inches. They tell him that after the procedure, he would have a newer, more flexible limb. He is not convinced.

"Those doctors," he says to me as I drive him out of the parking lot. "They cut off a little, then a little more, pretty soon they want the whole leg. They don't know when to stop."

After I return to school, I call him and ask about his foot. "It's just about healed," he tells me. "I've only got a little bit left. And when it heals I can get that business started."

He says no more about the business or his machines, and I don't ask. A few minutes later, he asks if I have heard from my mother. I tell him no.

"I sometimes think about her.... It's a sad thing being alone," he says.

I sit in silence. I want so badly to find the words, but nothing comes to me. Instead I retreat into imagination. I know he will likely never run another business, will likely end his days as he began them—with nothing to his name but family. And for this reason, I decide to believe with him in the power of machines to save him. I forget his infirmities, his trouble managing a business, the rusty volatility of his machines, and think only of him examining the tortillas on two good feet, running things again, the master of machines.

—2004

Learning from Other Writers

1. What is the effect of Rivas's decision to begin his profile with a description of his father making tortillas? Why might he have decided to use the present tense in this section?
2. How do you interpret the author's statement that the tortilla-making ritual feels to him "like the end of a particular history, one both uniquely American and outside of America's vision"?
3. What sorts of details from his family's history does Rivas choose to include in the second main movement of his essay? Why these details and not others?
4. What is the function of the section in which Rivas describes the hours he and his sister were made to work in their father's tortilla factory?
5. What are the effects of Rivas's decision to examine his father's life through his relationship to machines? How has this opinion changed over time?

6. What is the function of the list of italicized bits of the author's father's speech (in the section that begins "This is my father")?
7. Why and how does Rivas compare his father's body to a machine?
8. At what point does the author seem to understand the central thematic question at the heart of his profile? Highlight his closing meditations on this question. How do these meditations relate to his earlier statement that his father's story is both "uniquely American and outside of America's vision"? If the author seems to discover his true thematic question only toward the end of his profile, how do you think he managed to produce such a coherent and well-organized essay?

JOSEPH MITCHELL

EVENING WITH A GIFTED CHILD

Philippa Duke Schuyler is probably the best example in New York City of what psychologists call a gifted child. She is nine years old. Her mental age, according to the Clinic for Gifted Children at New York University, which tests her periodically, is sixteen. She has an I.Q. of 185. Phillipa reads Plutarch on train trips, eats steaks raw, writes poems in honor of her dolls, plays poker, and is the composer of more than sixty pieces for the piano. Most of these compositions are descriptive, with such titles as "Spanish Harlem," "Men at Work," "The Cockroach Ballet," and "At the Circus." She began composing before she was four, and has been playing the piano in public, often for money, since she was six. She has an agreement with the National Broadcasting Company by which she plays new compositions for the first time in public on a Sunday-morning broadcast called "Coast to Coast on a Bus," and she frequently plays on other radio and television programs. A Schuyler album, "Five Little Pieces," has been published. She has gone on tour several times, playing compositions by Bach, Rimsky-Korsakoff, Debussy, Schumann, and herself in Grand Rapids, Cincinnati, Indianapolis, Columbus, Youngstown, Atlantic City, Trenton, and other cities. On one tour she averaged $175 an engagement, plus all expenses. Philippa is often called a genius by admiring strangers, and her parents find this displeasing. To them, her development is explained not by genius but by diet. They believe that humans should live on uncooked meats, fruits, vegetables, and nuts, and are convinced that the food Philippa has eaten most of her life is largely responsible for her precocity. She particularly likes raw green peas, raw corn on the cob, raw yams, and raw sirloin steaks.

Philippa's father, George S. Schuyler, whom she calls by his first name, is a Negro essayist and novelist, the son of a dining-car chef on the New York Central. He writes an influential column on national and world affairs for the Pittsburgh *Courier*, a weekly Negro newspaper, and is business manager of the *Crisis*, which is the official organ of the National Association for the Advancement of Colored People. He wrote often for the *American Mercury* when H. L. Mencken edited it. Mr. Schuyler's skin is jet black. He comes from one of the oldest Negro families in New York; long before the Revolutionary War, ancestors of his in Albany began using Schuyler as a surname. Since then, Negro Schuylers have occasionally also used the Christian names of distinguished white Schuylers. Philippa is named for Philip John Schuyler, the Revolutionary general. Philippa's mother, Mrs. Josephine Schuyler, is white. She is, in fact, a golden-haired blonde. She is a member of a pioneer west Texas ranching and banking family, and speaks with a Southern accent. When she was in her teens, she ran away from home and went to California; since then she has considered herself "a rebel." Before she and Mr. Schuyler were married in 1928, she had been, successively, a Mack Sennett bathing beauty, a ballet dancer in a San Francisco opera company, a painter, a poet, and a writer for the Negro press. She met Mr. Schuyler in New York when she visited the office of a magazine of which he was an editor and to which she had contributed poems and articles. This magazine was the *Messenger,* the official organ of the Brotherhood of Sleeping Car Porters. Mrs. Schuyler acquired her dietary convictions in California years ago; her husband is a more recent convert and is not quite as dead set. Mrs. Schuyler feels that both alcohol and tobacco are utterly unnecessary; her husband, however, drinks beer and smokes cigars. Mrs. Schuyler still writes occasionally for Negro newspapers under various names, but devotes most of her time to painting and Philippa. On tour, she serves as Philippa's manager. Philippa calls her Jody. The Schuylers live in a larger apartment house on Convent Avenue. This house, which is tenanted by both white and Negro families, is on a hill overlooking the western fringe of Harlem, and is several blocks from the Convent of the Sacred Heart, where Philippa is in Grade 6A.

The Schuylers recently invited me to come and hear Philippa play. I went up one evening around eight o'clock. Mrs. Schuyler met me at the door and said that Philippa was in her own room transcribing a composition called "Caprice No. 2," which she had finished just before dinner. We went into the living room, where Mr. Schuyler, in shirtsleeves, was hunched over a desk. At his elbow was a stack of clippings about Philippa from newspapers in the cities in which she had played. He was pasting these in a large scrapbook. "We have nine scrapbooks full of stuff about Philippa, one for each year," he said. "She's never seen them. In fact, so far as we know, she's never seen a clipping about herself. We're afraid it might make her self-conscious. When she gets to be a young woman, we'll bring out all her scrapbooks and say, 'Here are some things you might find interesting.'"

There were paintings, chiefly nudes, on two walls of the living room. I noticed Mrs. Schuyler's signature in the corner of one. Bookcases lined another wall, and arranged on their top shelves were a number of pieces of African sculpture. Mrs. Schuyler pointed to one, a female fetish. "George brought that back from Africa in 1931," she said. "He was down there getting material for a book. Most of these things, however, belong to Philippa. They were sent to her by people in Liberia, Nigeria, and the Ivory Coast who heard her play on the radio. They listen in on short-wave. They write to her, and she answers their letters. They know that part of her background is African, and are proud of her. Their presents to Philippa are brought here by Africans who work on ships plying between New York and various West African ports. She has a slew of medals and prizes she won in tournaments held by the New York Philharmonic, the National Guild of Piano Teachers, and similar organizations, and she keeps them in a fancy inlaid chest that was sent to her by a craftsman in Africa. Philippa is extremely proud of her Negro blood."

Mr. Schuyler looked up from the scrapbook. "She has radio fans all over the world, not only in Africa," he said. "On her last birthday she received six sable skins and a black pearl from Alaska, a scarf from Portugal, and a doll from the Virgin Islands. However, most of her presents did come from Africa."

While we were looking at an ebony elephant, Philippa came into the room. Mr. Schuyler unobtrusively closed the scrapbook and put it in a drawer of the desk. Then he introduced me to Philippa. She shook hands, not awkwardly, as most children do, but with assurance. She is slender, erect, and exquisitely boned. Her face is oval, and she has serious black eyes, black curls, and perfect teeth. Her skin is light brown. She is a beautiful child.

"Did you get through with the piece?" her mother asked her.

"Oh, yes," Philippa said. "Half an hour ago. Look, Jody, do you remember that silly little riddle book I bought at the newsstand in the station at Cincinnati and never got a chance to look at?"

"Yes, I remember."

"Well, I've just been looking through it, and some of the riddles are funny. May I ask one, please?"

Mrs. Schuyler nodded, and Philippa asked, "What has four wheels and flies?"

We were silent a minute, and then Philippa said impatiently, "Give up, please, so I can tell you."

"We give up," Mrs. Schuyler said.

"A garbage wagon," Philippa said.

Mr. Schuyler groaned, and Philippa looked at him and burst out laughing.

"Was it that bad, George?" she asked. "Wait until you hear some of the others."

"Not now, Philippa," Mrs. Schuyler said, rather hastily. "Instead, maybe you'd like to play for us in your room."

"I'd like to very much," Philippa said.

Mr. Schuyler said that he would stay in the living room and listen. Mrs. Schuyler and I followed Philippa down the hall. A large red balloon was tethered by a string to the doorknob of Philippa's room. "I like balloons," she said, spanking it into the air with the heel of her hand. "They remind me of the circus."

The Schuylers have a four-room apartment. I noticed that Philippa's room was the largest. In it there was a grand piano, a bed, an adult-size dressing table, two small chairs, and a cabinet. Mrs. Schuyler opened the doors of the cabinet. "Philippa keeps her music and dolls in here," she said. "She made this doll house. She knitted the little rug herself and sewed dresses for the dolls. She sews very well. She made me an apron the other day." On top of Philippa's piano there was a Modern Library giant edition of Plutarch, a peach kernel, a mystery novel called "The Corpse with the Floating Foot," a copy of the New York *Post* opened to the comic-strip page, a teacup half full of raw green peas, a train made of adhesive-tape spools and cardboard, a Stravinsky sonata, a pack of playing cards, a photograph of Lily Pons clipped from a magazine, and an uninflated balloon. I was standing beside the piano, examining this rather surrealistic group of objects, when Mrs. Schuyler suddenly snapped her fingers and said, "I forgot the peaches!" She started out of the room, then paused at the door and said, "It's a kind of ice cream I make. We're going to have some later on, and I forgot to put the peaches in the icebox. I'll leave you two alone for a few minutes. Philippa, don't start playing until I get back." I took one of the chairs and Philippa sat on the piano bench. Left alone with her, I felt ill at ease. I didn't know how to go about making small talk with a gifted child.

"Do you mind if I smoke in here?" I asked her.

"Of course not," Philippa said. "I'll go get you an ashtray."

When she returned, I asked her if she had been reading the Plutarch on the piano.

"Yes," she said. "I've read most of it. I got it to read on trains."

"Don't you find it rather dry?"

"Not at all. I like biography. I particularly like the sections called the comparisons. Best of all I liked Theseus and Romulus, and Solon and Poplicola. Plutarch is anything but dry. I'm very interested in the Romans. I want to get 'The Decline and Fall' next. It's in the Modern Library, too."

"What are some other books you like?"

Philippa laughed. "Lately I've been reading a Sherlock Holmes omnibus and some mystery books by Ellery Queen."

"What book do you like best of all?"

"Oh, that's almost impossible to answer. You can't just pick out one book and say you like it better than all others. I bet you can't."

"I certainly can," I said. I was not bothered any longer by the difference in our ages, and had completely got over feeling ill at ease.

"What book?"

"Mark Twain's 'Life on the Mississippi,'" I said.

"Oh, I like Mark Twain," Philippa said, clapping her hands excitedly. "I like him very much. What other writers do you like?"

"The ones I like best," I said, "are Mark Twain, Dostoevski, and James Joyce."

Philippa deliberated for a few moments.

"I guess you're right," she said. "I *can* say that there's one book I like best of all. That's the 'Arabian Nights.' George has an eight-volume set. It's an unexpurgated edition. I read it first when I was three, and at least four times since. I based my longest composition on it. I called it 'Arabian Nights Suite.' Oh, the stories in that book are absolutely wonderful!" She laughed. "Goodness!" she said. "I didn't mean to get so"—she paused and appeared to be searching for a word—"impassioned."

Mrs. Schuyler returned, and sat down.

"Look," Philippa said to me, "do you like funnies?"

"You mean comic strips?" I asked.

"Yes," she said. "Funnies."

"Of course I do," I said. "The best comic strip is 'Moon Mullins' in the *News*."

"Oh, no, it isn't," she said. "The best funny is 'Dixie Dugan' in the *Post,* and the next best is the full-page 'Katzenjammer Kids' in the Sunday *Journal*. The *Post* has the best funnies. I like 'Dixie Dugan,' 'Superman,' 'Tarzan,' 'Abbie an' Slats,' and 'The Mountain Boys,' and they're all in the *Post*. You know, I'm almost ready to write a composition about the funnies. I'm going to call it 'The Katzenjammer Kids.' I read a lot of mystery stories, and I've already written a composition called 'Mystery Story.'"

"Philippa tries to describe places and experiences in her music," Mrs. Schuyler said. "We used to live in Spanish Harlem, and she put some of the things she saw and heard in that neighborhood into a composition. She wrote 'Men at Work' while the WPA was digging a sewer in front of our apartment house. She likes the playground at Sacred Heart very much, and she described it in a piece called 'In a Convent Garden.' Once she had a canary, and it died. For its funeral she wrote a sad little piece called 'Death of the Nightingale.' Philippa, you're getting fidgety. Are you ready to play for us?"

"Yes, Jody," Philippa said, getting to her feet. She turned to me, curtsied, and said, "Think about cockroaches while I'm playing this piece. It's 'The Cockroach Ballet.' This is the story: Some cockroaches are feasting on a kitchen floor. A human comes in and kills some of them. He thinks he has killed them all. But after he leaves, one little cockroach peeps out, then another, and another. They dance a sad little dance for their dead comrades. But they aren't very sad because they know that cockroaches will go on forever and ever. Unfortunately."

Mrs. Schuyler laughed. "Philippa took that piece to Mother Stevens at Sacred Heart the afternoon she wrote it," she said. "Mother Stevens is head of the music department. She asked Philippa why she didn't write about angels instead of cockroaches. 'But dear Mother,' Philippa said, 'I've never seen an angel, but I've seen many cockroaches.'"

Philippa sat down at the piano, and began playing. I thought it was a nice piece.

Next she played a composition called "Impressions of the World's Fair, 1939." In it the sound of the tractor-train horn—that wornout phrase from "The Sidewalks of New York"—was recurrent. Then she played "Men at Work." When she finished it she asked me to enumerate the noises I had recognized. I told her I thought I had recognized an air drill, the sound of trowels knocking the tar off paving blocks, and the sound of a chisel being hammered into rock. "You're very good," Philippa said, and I felt pleased. "Here's one called 'The Jolly Pig,'" she said. In the middle of it she turned to me and asked, "Hear him laughing?" I didn't, but I said I did. After that came the "Caprice" she had finished that day. Then she played some pieces by other composers. They included Rimsky-Korsakoff's "Flight of the Bumble Bee" and Johann Sebastian Bach's "Two Part Invention No. 1." After she had played for at least an hour without any sign of weariness, she said, "I'll play just one more, one I composed a long time ago, when I was four years old. It's 'The Goldfish.' A little goldfish thinks the sky is water. He tries to jump into it, only to fall upon the floor and die."

"I'll go get the ice cream," Mrs. Schuyler said as Philippa began "The Goldfish." Just as Philippa finished playing, Mrs. Schuyler returned, bringing a tray with four saucers. She called Mr. Schuyler and he came in and sat down on the bed.

"I liked your new piece, Philippa," he said. Philippa smiled proudly.

"Thanks, George," she said. "I'm going to do a little more work on it tomorrow."

"It isn't really ice cream, and you might not like it," Mrs. Schuyler said to me as she distributed the saucers. "It's just fresh peaches and cream sweetened with honey and chilled. In this house we use almost no sugar. In her entire life, Philippa has never eaten a piece of candy. Her taste hasn't been perverted by sweets. Instead, she has a passion for lemons. She eats them the way most people eat oranges, pulp and all. Don't you, Philippa?"

"Yes, Jody," Philippa said. She was eating with gusto.

"We seldom have cooked food of any kind," Mrs. Schuyler continued. "Once in a while I broil a steak very lightly, but usually we eat meat raw. We also eat raw fish that has been soaked in lemon juice. When we're travelling, Philippa and I amaze, waiters. You have to argue with most waiters before they'll bring you raw meat. Then they stare at you while you eat. I guess it *is* rather unusual to see a little girl eating a raw steak. Philippa drinks a lot of milk, and she gets quite a large daily ration of cod-liver oil. About the only cooked thing she really likes is a hardboiled egg. She mashes the yolk and squeezes a lemon over it. When she goes to the movies she sometimes takes along an ear of corn. That's better than peanuts. She always fills her pockets with green peas before she goes to school. The other children at Sacred Heart used to stare at her, but now they think nothing of it."

"Jody makes me big birthday cakes," Philippa said. "They're made of ground-up cashew nuts. Once I had one that weighed twenty pounds. It was shaped like a white piano. This year it was shaped like the map of South America. The different countries were colored with berry and vegetable juices. It was a swell cake."

"We eat all kinds of nuts, just so they're raw," Mrs. Schuyler said. "Each year my father sends me all the pecans off one big tree on his ranch in Texas. Some people think we're peculiar, but the best proof that our diet theory is sensible is Philippa's health. She's extremely healthy, mentally and physically. Her teeth, for example, are absolutely perfect. She's never had even a tiny cavity."

Mr. Schuyler looked at his watch. "It's nine-thirty, Philippa," he said.

"May I ask another riddle before I go to bed?"

"Just one," her father said.

"All right. What's smaller than a flea's mouth?"

"Oh, I know that one," Mrs. Schuyler said.

"So do I," said Mr. Schuyler.

"All right, all right," Philippa said. "Wait until tomorrow. I'll ask you some you couldn't guess in fifteen years."

We said good night to Philippa. Mrs. Schuyler went into the kitchen and Mr. Schuyler and I went into the living room. I asked him how many hours a day Philippa studies. He said that during school months she gets up at seven-thirty, has a bath and breakfast, and starts practicing on the piano at eight. She practices for two hours. Then for half an hour she plays anything she likes. At ten-thirty her music supervisor arrives. The supervisor, a young piano teacher named Pauline Apanowitz, is with her an hour and a half. Shortly before one, Philippa walks to Sacred Heart, eating green peas on the way. She spends two afternoon hours a day at the convent, attending history, geography, and English classes. She misses arithmetic, spelling, and reading, which are morning classes. However, her examination grades for these subjects are always good. "There wouldn't be much point in Philippa going to a spelling class," Mr. Schuyler said. "When she was twenty-nine months old she could spell five hundred and fifty words. She has an enormous vocabulary. She likes jawbreakers. At four, she discovered the scientific word for silicosis, which is pneumonoultramicroscopicsilicovolcanoniosis, and she spelled it morning and night. It fascinated her. We certainly got tired of that word." Once a week, Mr. Schuyler said, she goes to Antonia Brico's studio for lessons in score-reading and conducting; William Harms, an assistant of Josef Hofmann, also gives her a weekly piano lesson. Most afternoons she spends an hour in the convent playground; rope-skipping is her favorite exercise. "Philippa isn't a Catholic, and we have no religious affiliations," Mr. Schuyler told me. "My parents were Catholics, however, and Philippa will become one if she so desires. Most of the other children at the convent are Irish Catholics. She gets along with them wonderfully."

Mrs. Schuyler came into the room, bringing several small books. "When Philippa was very little I kept a careful account of the stories and poems she wrote, the words she invented, the questions she asked, and such things," she said. "I wrote them down in the form of letters to her, letters for her to read when she becomes a young woman. The people at the gifted-child clinic saw the books and had the notations transcribed for their files. Perhaps you'd like to look through some of the books."

I opened one. At the top of the page was written "Three years, seven months." Beneath this was the following notation:

> You are very interested to know why some people are good and some bad. "What do they do with bad people?" you ask. "If they are very bad, they put them in jail," I say. "What is a jail?" you inquire. "A jail is a building full of little rooms with barred doors." "What do they do to bad people in jail?" "They don't have nice things to eat or wear," I explain. Several days later you heard about how poor most people are in Georgia, and you asked, "The poor people in Georgia who have nothing nice to eat or wear, are they bad?" "No," I said. "They are not bad. They are unlucky. Later, I will explain more fully." That afternoon you laughed and asked, archly, "Jody, when the weather is bad, do they put it in jail?" The same day you asked if flowers get white hair when they are old. And you asked if people who sleep on cots say at night, "I am going to cot." And you asked if mothers ever say to their children, "You must go crooked to bed." Walking along the street you said. "Jody, trees stand on one leg." Yesterday you began to giggle. "There's no Mr. Lady or Mrs. Man," you said, and enjoyed the humor of the idea very much. Today you made up a poem.
>
> *"Pipes are steel,*
> *But bones are real."*
>
> Tonight you sat on the floor and made up a long story. You said, "Varnetida, a little girl, and her mother, Armarnia, went to see Slowbow, a brother who lived with his father,

Solom, in a big house in Channa. They met the grandmother, Branlea, and another little girl, Jolumbow, who had a kitten named Lilgay, and a dog named Cherro. They all sat down in a chilbensian room and ate dishes of wallaga and thaga ..." and so on, as long as I would listen. If you were at a loss for a word you simply invented one with a perfectly solemn face.

I picked up another book. In it I found a poem Philippa wrote when she was five. She wrote it on Easter morning while sitting in the bathtub:

The sun is lifting his lid.
The sun is leaving his crib.
The sun is a waking baby
Who will bring the Spring maybe
Thump, thump, thump! out of the earth.

I thought that this was a wonderful poem. It was followed by this notation:

Tonight a red light flashed to green while we were walking across Fifth Avenue. The automobiles were whizzing by us. Suddenly you looked up and said, "Jody, will you please name for me all the diseases in the world?"

"Philippa must be hard to deal with at times," I said.

"She is indeed," Mrs. Schuyler said. "Women often tell me, 'You mustn't push her!' Their sympathy is misplaced. If there's any pushing done, she's the one that does it."

A few minutes later, I said good night to the Schuylers. At the door I asked Mrs. Schuyler to tell me the answer to the riddle Philippa had propounded just before she went to bed; it had been on my mind ever since. "That riddle about what's smaller than a flea's mouth?" she said. "That's an old, old nursery riddle. I guess it's the only one I know. The answer is, 'What goes in it.' I'm very sorry she got hold of that riddle book. Tomorrow at breakfast she'll have the drop on us. She'll ask us two dozen, and we probably won't know a single answer."

—1940

Learning from Other Writers

1. What is the effect of Mitchell's decision to start his profile with a list of Philippa's accomplishments, followed by her parents' claim that her achievements are explained not by genius but by a diet of raw food?
2. Taking into account that the profile was published in 1940, what is the effect of including the details about Mr. and Mrs. Schuyler's racial characteristics and family backgrounds?
3. Like Annie Dillard in her profile of David Rahm, Joseph Mitchell approaches his subject slowly and from an emotional distance. What is the effect of this strategy on Mitchell's essay?
4. Reread "Evening with a Gifted Child" and highlight those sentences in which Mitchell offers a judgment about Philippa or her parents as opposed to objective statements or descriptions. Why *these* judgments and no others?
5. What question does Mitchell set out to answer in profiling Philippa Duke Schuyler? What conclusion does he reach? Do you agree with that conclusion?
6. Writers often get ideas for essays or books by reading other people's essays or books. Does Mitchell's profile of Philippa Duke Schuyler give you any ideas for essays of your own? If so, list the possibilities. How would you find out if anyone else has already written an essay or a book on your topic?

ADDITIONAL CONSIDERATIONS: THE ART OF THE INTERVIEW

As any reporter will tell you, the more you prepare for an interview, the more likely you will be to use that time wisely. After all, how can you know what to ask if you haven't done any research? Although you might not be sure of your central question before you get a chance to spend time with your subject, you will need to develop a preliminary focus so you can draw up a list of questions to ask and suggest an activity or a location that might provide the narrative backbone or physical backdrop for your interview and resulting profile.

Nor do you want to waste time by asking your subjects obvious questions. If your subject is a public figure, you can figure out from published sources when he was born or where she went to college. But even if you are interviewing a taxidermist who lives in a secluded shack ten miles out of town, you can read up on the basics of taxidermy before you get there. In many cases, you can save your factual questions for a preliminary or follow-up e-mail. ("Just to make sure I have my facts right, do you mind telling me what year you graduated from Harvard Business School? And how many months, exactly, did you work for Enron before you got fired?")

Not only will your preliminary research guide you as to a possible focus for your interview, but you can also use this information to set your subject at ease. "So," you might begin, "what was it like to train under Anna Freud?" Or: "Your aunt says that when you were a little girl you were terrified of the water. But here you are, swimming across Lake Michigan. What were you so afraid of when you were a kid? How did you overcome that fear? Do you remember the first time you swam in water over your head? Oh, really? *Your mother just threw you in?"*

Then sit back and listen to what your subject says. Don't jump ahead to the next question on your list if your subject has just told you something that begs to be pursued. Rather than asking yes-or-no questions, try to provide your subject with more open-ended prompts. Asking a plastic surgeon if he likes his job might elicit little more than "yes." Asking him *why* he likes his job, what aspect of the job he dislikes, what his favorite (or least favorite) type of surgical procedure might be is likely to produce lengthier and more revealing answers. The same is true for questions that your subject doesn't usually get asked. Does the physicist you're interviewing ever read her horoscope? What *does* frighten the otherwise fearless member of the SWAT team you want to profile? And no matter what question you ask, give your subject a chance to answer it. A nice *long* chance. Silence makes most people so ill at ease that they eventually will begin to speak.

As you can see from the essays in this chapter, dialogue plays a large role even in profiles whose subjects are as tight-lipped as David Rahm. How do you capture or record the way your subjects speak? You can take a journalism course and listen to endless discussions as to whether to use a notebook or a tape recorder or rely primarily on your memory, but the decision will vary from reporter to reporter and subject to subject.

If the person with whom you are spending time is an important political figure or his or her statements might be controversial—or the basis for a lawsuit—you will want to get that subject's words on tape. (A reporter's dated notes constitute a legal record of a conversation, but a tape recording is better evidence if a lawsuit goes to court.) But in most instances, your decision as to whether to record an interview or rely on your ability to take notes depends on which method will increase your chances of coming away with good material. Early in my career, I found that I didn't like to spend time fussing with a tape recorder or worrying that a set of batteries might die in the middle of an interview or that the recording might come out garbled. My mind wandered if I knew that whatever my subject said would be recorded by a machine. And I hated to spend days, if not weeks, transcribing an interview from a recording, then try to knit together everything my subject said into a coherent profile. If I *didn't* rely on a recorder, I listened more closely to what my subject said ... and only wrote down his or her most interesting quotes, along with surreptitious observations about the person's mannerisms, appearance, dress, and taste in home décor. (Most reporters develop their own incomprehensible shorthand, or tiny indecipherable writing a subject can't read, especially upside down.)

I know writers who swear that relying on a recorder frees them to focus on what a subject says and that most people forget the recorder's presence in a way they never can forget the notebook and pen in a reporter's hands. But my experience is that recorders make people nervous, implying that whatever the person says can and will be used against him, whereas a notebook seems more innocuous, especially if the writer holds it off to one side or slightly beneath the subject's line of sight. (I also rely on memory, rushing to my car or the first bathroom I see to jot down what I recall.)

No matter how you gather your material, when it comes time to write up what you have, feel free to paraphrase or summarize long passages, especially passages in which the subject's voice doesn't seem to be particularly revealing or distinctive. But you will want to include quotations in which your subject lets your readers hear how he or she actually sounds. Part of what makes one speaker sound distinct from any other is that person's use of dialect, which includes his or her diction and choice of syntax, difficulty or facility with grammar, and reliance on profanity, humor, or clichés. Although you rarely if ever will want to mock your subject, neither is it necessary to make everyone sound alike. If a rancher tells you, "It just roasts my liver to think some asshole in D.C. would tell me what kind of cattle I can or can't raise on my own goddamn land. There ain't no way in hell I'm going to let myself get shoved around by some egghead behind a desk who wouldn't know cow shit if he stepped in it," little is to be gained from tidying up his quote so he seems to have said that he deplores federal intervention in his affairs and refuses to be pushed around by his own government.

On the other hand, if your subject says "aks" instead of "ask," should you indicate that on the page? Should you use repeated misspellings to indicate that a poor black or Hispanic woman drops her final g's, especially since many well-educated white professionals drop their final g's, too? As you study the use of dialect in this book, you will notice that some writers use deliberate misspellings to convey the sounds of their subjects' speech, while others capture a speaker's idiosyncrasies solely through his or her diction, syntax, and vocabulary. Similarly, as you read the essays in this book, you can see how few verbs the authors use in the tags on their quotes, how rarely they rely on any verb other than "said" or "asked."

As you might expect, you shouldn't put anything controversial or historically important in quotation marks unless you can be sure that your subject actually said it. If your material *isn't* controversial, if the nature of what you're quoting strikes you as personal rather than historical, and if you recall what your subject said reasonably well, you might feel comfortable putting at least some of the dialogue in quotation marks. (I didn't use a tape recorder when I interviewed Alexander Glass, but he never rebuked me for quoting him inaccurately.) If all else fails—if your memory as to the exact wording of a quotation is blurry or you're relying on secondhand sources for a conversation—you might be able to get away with using dialogue but not putting it in quotation marks. Although every writer and reporter can tell you stories of the time he blew an interview because his tape recorder didn't work or she wasn't adept at taking notes, most people eventually master the mechanics of the interview. What doesn't get easier is navigating your relationship to your subject. I used to think I was the only writer who felt ill at the prospect of calling a stranger to set up an interview, or even to ask for information. Then I read the preface to *Slouching to Bethlehem,* in which Joan Didion, one of the boldest and most successful writers in the country, makes the following admission:

> I am bad at interviewing people. I avoid situations in which I have to talk to anyone's press agent. (This precludes doing pieces on most actors, a bonus in itself.) I do not like to make telephone calls, and would not like to count the mornings I have sat on some Best Western motel bed somewhere and tried to force myself to put through the call to the assistant district attorney.

I can't speak for Didion, but my dread of calling strangers stems from the fear that I will need to ask that person difficult questions, the fear that, in the end, the person who was kind enough to let me tag along and interrupt and pry will feel outraged by the essay or book I write about him or her. You can warn people not to say or do anything they wouldn't want to see in print. You can remind them that unless they specify that something they are about to say or do must be kept off the record, you are legally allowed to publish it, and that specifying that something is off the record *after* they've said or done it does not legally oblige you to leave it out. But no matter how careful you are, whatever you write is likely to strike your subject as a betrayal, if for no other reason than your purpose in writing about a person's life is going to be different from his purpose in living that life or allowing you to watch.

This is true even if you have the best intentions. I once wrote a profile of a crotchety junk-dealer who was being forced to clean up his junkyard because the residents of the new condo development across the road didn't appreciate the view. Because the junk dealer was ill, his friends helped him haul away the junk. Thinking I was shining a light on their generosity, I mentioned a few such friends by name, only to receive a panicked call from a woman who said that unless I printed a retraction to the effect that I hadn't actually seen her hefting around some junk, she was going to lose her disability checks.

Few reporters set out to betray their subjects. As Joan Didion tells us at the end of her preface, it's just that she is "so physically small, so temperamentally unobtrusive, and so neurotically inarticulate that people tend to forget that [her] presence runs counter to their best interests. And it always does. That is one last thing to remember: *writers are always selling somebody out.*"

Which doesn't mean that you shouldn't write about other people. Most of us make our peace with the proposition that what we write will bring about more good than harm, especially if we remain aware of our obligations to our readers as well as to our subjects. If not for Didion's willingness to pick up that phone and dial that assistant district attorney, we wouldn't now be able to reach up and pull down from our shelves her invaluable chronicles of two very important and tumultuous decades in American history.[3]

INSPIRATIONS: GETTING INSIDE SOMEONE ELSE'S HEAD

1. Think of a friend or relative who has lived through an event of larger social or historical significance. Spend some time with that person, getting down his or her description of that event and what he or she was thinking and feeling as the event unfolded.
2. If necessary, supplement your interview(s) with other forms of research.

---

[3] *Slouching Towards Bethlehem* was published by Farrar, Straus and Giroux in 1968; *The White Album,* published by Simon and Schuster, appeared in 1979.

3. Re-create your subject's experiences for your readers. Be sure that you convey the flavor of your subject's language and a sense of his or her interior world, as well as the larger historical or cultural significance of the events he or she lived through.

INSPIRATIONS: A DAY IN THE LIFE

1. Choose someone whose work or hobby interests you. Prepare to spend time with that person as he or she engages in that activity.
2. Write a profile in which you describe your subject performing the activity you observed while you try to answer a larger thematic question about the person and his/her activity.

Group Portraits

When your subject concerns the behavior or characteristics of a group of people rather than an individual, you will want to consider the nonfiction form known as a group portrait. The form is malleable enough to serve as the structure for a personal essay, as in "Going to the Movies," in which Susan Allen Toth uses the movie-going habits of three men she dates to compare the complexities of real-life relationships to the romantic fantasies in the movies she likes to see, or an essay in which one of my undergraduates profiled the child psychologists to whom her parents sent her when she was a mildly rebellious adolescent, each therapist so peculiar as to raise the question of why we expect children to conform to stringent definitions of normality when the professionals to whom we send them don't meet those same standards.

Yet the group portrait also can serve to personalize the largest and most far-reaching historical events. In *Hiroshima*, John Hersey's groundbreaking portrayal of six survivors of the atomic blast that ended World War II, the author not only tells the stories of these six victims of the bomb but also quietly poses the question of who does or doesn't survive a nuclear catastrophe—and why. Before Hersey received his assignment (from William Shawn, the editor of *The New Yorker*) to visit Hiroshima, accounts of the bombing had focused almost exclusively on the physical devastation the bomb had wreaked. Hersey could have taken the same approach and described the wreckage, starting a mile or two from the epicenter of the explosion and moving inward to Ground Zero. Instead, he chose to focus on the bomb's effects on six inhabitants of the city, five of them Japanese civilians and one a German priest who had been living and working in Japan, a radical decision given that the Japanese and German people (civilians as well as soldiers) had been demonized and dehumanized by Allied propaganda.

If Hersey's approach seems familiar to us now, that's because nearly every disaster movie—and every spoof of every disaster movie—takes the shape of a group portrait of the lucky or unlucky victims who did or didn't survive a malfunctioning airline engine, an earthquake, a political uprising, a shipwreck, an avalanche, an alien invasion, or an outbreak of an epidemic. (In fact, the novelistic group portrait already was well worn when Hersey borrowed it from *The Bridge at San Luis Rey* by Thornton Wilder.) Yet the form has lost none of its power in structuring successful movies, novels, and works of creative nonfiction (as you will see for yourself if you read the opening chapter of Hersey's book, which is reproduced in this chapter). If anything, the form's popularity has increased, as it has become the dominant structure for documentaries.

The group portrait is especially well suited to exploring the effects of a political event or law, the best example being *Common Ground: A Turbulent Decade in the Lives of Three*

American Families, J. Anthony Lukas's award-winning book about the busing riots that erupted in Boston in 1974.[1] My former student, Mike Vitez, a reporter for the *Philadelphia Inquirer*, won a Pulitzer in 1997 for a group portrait that examines the very different ways in which human beings choose to face their deaths (see "Final Choices, Seeking the Good Death," at www.pulitzer.org). Later, Vitez used the same form to profile people who, for widely varying reasons, come to Philadelphia to run up the steps of the art museum, pump their fists in the air, and "do a Rocky." (A collection of these profiles, accompanied by photos of the subjects, ran in the *Inquirer* and was published in 2006 by Paul Dry Books as *Rocky Stories: Tales of Love, Hope, and Happiness at America's Famous Steps*.)

As you will see if you read Toth's portraits of her movie-going partners, a writer can present her subjects on their own, with no connecting material, almost as if she were showing you photos in an album. In most group portraits, however, a second level of organization is needed to allow the writer to move smoothly among the various members of the group. Journalists and academics often use traditional forms to structure their analyses of social or public policy, illustrating or supporting their arguments with case histories or miniprofiles of people whom the policies help or hurt; think of a Jell-O salad in which the analytical prose is the bowl of gelatin and the case histories or miniprofiles are the cherries, grapes, and pineapple bits. In creative nonfiction, the ratio tends to be reversed and there is far more fruit than gelatin, but the profiles still need some larger matrix to hold them together.

In *Hiroshima*, Hersey cuts from character to character as he moves along a timeline from the moments before the atomic blast to the hours and weeks that follow. This is much the same scheme Sebastian Junger employs in *The Perfect Storm* when presenting his profiles of the crew of the *Andrea Gail*. But other organizational plans are possible. If Junger had wanted to write about life on a naval destroyer rather than a fishing vessel, he might have arranged his profiles according to the sailors' functions, from the lowest swabbie to the captain.

As we saw in chapter 9, you might choose to keep yourself out of a profile, or put yourself in on every page. Susan Allen Toth could not have profiled her movie-going partners in a purely objective way. But one of the beauties of *Hiroshima* is how few editorial comments Hersey offers, despite the horrific ordeal that his characters endure. The author's every choice directs his readers' eyes and hearts and minds toward the deeply moral questions he wants us to consider; even his decision to weight his subjects so heavily toward the helping professions creates a sense that far fewer people are likely to survive an atomic blast than government officials tend to predict, if only because the people we rely on in a catastrophe might be too shattered by their own injuries and despair to do anything more than wander the rubble in a bloody daze.

More than sixty years after *Hiroshima* first appeared, the group portrait remains a highly viable tool for analyzing contemporary society. So versatile is the form it can be expanded to structure an ethnographic or sociological study; all you have to do is add a few members to the group, some rules for initiation, and a definition as to who belongs and who doesn't, and you have an essay or book that explores the nature of a culture or a community. On the surface, this might seem to describe the essay's subject rather than its structure, but as is usually true in creative nonfiction, subject and structure go hand-in-hand.

In the opening chapters of his bestselling book *The Right Stuff*,[2] Tom Wolfe profiles a group of top test-pilots by following the steps of the initiation that causes the candidates who apparently do not have the magic qualities alluded to by his title to wash out of

---

1 Vintage, 1985.

2 Farrar, Straus and Giroux, 1979.

their training program or crash their planes and die. By the time we are left with such elite members of the community as Chuck Yeager, Alan Shepard, Gus Grissom, and John Glenn, we understand that the selection process has created a cadre of pilots with sufficient moxie to beat the Russians into space, even as these same pilots feel disdain for the tiny civilians on the ground.

A similar initiation causes Elwood Reid to "do bad things for football" so his teammates and coaches will accept him as "one of the fellas." While Wolfe provides access to a community to which he doesn't belong, Reid explores the workings of a community in which he is both an insider and an outsider (before he turned to writing, Reid played as a lineman on the football team at Michigan), an uncomfortable position to occupy in real life but an extremely useful vantage from which to write an essay.

Finally, in "The Unwanted," William Finnegan takes us inside a community whose membership requires no initiation except to have been born in a certain neighborhood at a certain period in the history of California. Moving from a discussion of the factors that created a suburb "where schools and parents faltered [and] the American Dream was replaced by drugs, neo-Nazism, and despair," to an account of the groups and gangs to which one teenager in this community belongs, to the aftermath of a party at which one gang member kills another, Finnegan raises the question of what happens to young people when their parents—by necessity or choice—allow them to grow up unsupervised.

SUSAN ALLEN TOTH

GOING TO THE MOVIES

I

Aaron takes me only to art films. That's what I call them, anyway: strange movies with vague poetic images I don't understand, long dreamy movies about a distant Technicolor past, even longer black-and-white movies about the general meaninglessness of life. We do not go unless at least one reputable critic has found the cinematography superb. We went to *The Devil's Eye*, and Aaron turned to me in the middle and said, "My God, this is *funny*." I do not think he was pleased.

When Aaron and I go to the movies, we drive our cars separately and meet by the box office. Inside the theater he sits tentatively in his seat, ready to move if he can't see well, poised to leave if the film is disappointing. He leans away from me, careful not to touch the bare flesh of his arm against the bare flesh of mine. Sometimes he leans so far I am afraid he may be touching the woman on his other side instead. If the movie is very good, he leans forward too, peering between the heads of the couple in front of us. The light from the screen bounces off his glasses; he gleams with intensity, sitting there on the edge of his seat, watching the screen. Once I tapped him on the arm so I could whisper a comment in his ear. He jumped.

After *Belle de Jour*, Aaron said he wanted to ask me if he could stay overnight. "But I can't," he shook his head mournfully before I had a chance to answer, "because I know I never sleep well in strange beds." Then he apologized for asking. "It's just that after a film like that," he said, "I feel the need to assert myself."

II

Bob takes me only to movies that he thinks have a redeeming social conscience. He doesn't call them films. They tend to be about poverty, war, injustice, political corruption, struggling unions in the 1930s, and the military-industrial complex. Bob doesn't like propaganda movies, though, and he doesn't like to be too depressed either. We stayed away from *The Sorrow and the Pity*; it would be, he said, too much. Besides, he assured me, things are never that hopeless. So most of the movies we see are made in Hollywood. Because they are always very topical, these movies offer what Bob calls "food for thought." When we saw *Coming Home*, Bob's jaw set so firmly with the first half that I knew we would end up at Poppin's Fresh Pies afterward.

When Bob and I go to the movies, we take turns driving so no one owes anyone else anything. We park far away from the theater so we don't have to pay for a space. If it's raining or snowing, Bob offers to let me off at the door, but I can tell he'll feel better if I go with him while he parks, so we share the walk too. Inside the theater Bob will hold my hand when I get scared if I ask him. He puts my hand firmly on his knee and covers it completely with his own hand. His knee never twitches. After a while, when the scary part is past, he loosens his hand slightly and I know that is a signal to take mine away. He sits companionably close, letting his jacket just touch my sweater, but he does not infringe. He thinks I ought to know he is there if I need him.

One night after *The China Syndrome* I asked Bob if he wouldn't like to stay for a second drink, even though it was past midnight. He thought awhile about that, considering my offer from all possible angles, but finally he said no. Relationships today, he said, have a tendency to move too quickly.

III

Sam likes movies that are entertaining. By that he means movies that Will Jones of the *Minneapolis Tribune* loved and either *Time* or *Newsweek* rather liked; also movies that do not have sappy love stories, are not musicals, do not have subtitles, and will not force him to think. He does not go to movies to think. He liked *California Suite* and *The Seduction of Joe Tynan*, though the plots, he said, could have been zippier. He saw it all coming too far in advance, and that took the fun out. He doesn't like to know what is going to happen. "I just want my brain to be tickled," he says. It is very hard for me to pick out movies for Sam.

When Sam takes me to the movies, he pays for everything. He thinks that's what a man ought to do. But I buy my own popcorn, because he doesn't approve of it; the grease might smear his flannel slacks. Inside the theater, Sam makes himself comfortable. He takes off his jacket, puts one arm around me, and all during the movie he plays with my hand, stroking my palm, beating a small tattoo on my wrist. Although he watches the movie intently, his body operates on instinct. Once I inclined my head and kissed him lightly just behind his ear. He beat a faster tattoo on my wrist, quick and musical, but he didn't look away from the screen.

When Sam takes me home from the movies, he stands outside my door and kisses me long and hard. He would like to come in, he says regretfully, but his steady girlfriend in Duluth wouldn't like it. When the *Tribune* gives a movie four stars, he has to save it to see with her. Otherwise her feelings might be hurt.

IV

I go to some movies by myself. On rainy Sunday afternoons I often sneak into a revival house or a college auditorium for old Technicolor musicals, *Kiss Me Kate, Seven Brides for Seven Brothers, Calamity Jane*, even, once, *The Sound of Music*. Wearing saggy jeans so I can prop my feet on the seat in front, I sit toward the rear where no one will see me. I eat large handfuls of popcorn with double butter. Once the movie starts, I feel completely at home. Howard Keel and I are old friends; I grin back at him on the screen, admiring all his teeth. I know the sound tracks by heart. Sometimes when I get really carried away I hum along with Kathryn Grayson, remembering how I once thought I would fill out a formal like that. Skirts whirl, feet tap, acrobatic young men perform impossible feats, and then the camera dissolves into a dream sequence I know I can comfortably follow. It is not, thank God, Bergman.

If I can't find an old musical, I settle for Hepburn and Tracy, vintage Grant or Gable, on adventurous days Claudette Colbert or James Stewart. Before I buy my ticket I make sure it will all end happily. If necessary, I ask the girl at the box office. I have never seen *Stella Dallas* or *Intermezzo*. Over the years I have developed other peccadilloes: I will, for example, see anything that is redeemed by Thelma Ritter. At the end of *Daddy Long Legs* I wait happily for the scene where Fred Clark, no longer angry, at last pours Thelma a convivial drink. They smile at each other, I smile at them, I feel they are smiling at me. In the movies I go to by myself, the men and women always like each other.

—1988

Learning from Other Writers

1. Why doesn't Toth reveal anything about her three subjects other than their movie-going preferences and habits?
2. What function does the fourth section serve in the essay as a whole?

3. Do you think this group portrait explores a question of interest to anyone other than the author and her immediate family and friends?
4. Have you seen the movies Toth mentions in the essay? Does it matter? Why or why not?

JOHN HERSEY

FROM: *HIROSHIMA*

A NOISELESS FLASH

At exactly fifteen minutes past eight in the morning, on August 6, 1945, Japanese time, at the moment when the atomic bomb flashed above Hiroshima, Miss Toshiko Sasaki, a clerk in the personnel department of the East Asia Tin Works, had just sat down at her place in the plant office and was turning her head to speak to the girl at the next desk. At that same moment, Dr. Masakazu Fujii was settling down cross-legged to read the Osaka *Asahi* on the porch of his private hospital, overhanging one of the seven deltaic rivers which divide Hiroshima; Mrs. Hatsuyo Nakamura, a tailor's widow, stood by the window of her kitchen, watching a neighbor tearing down his house because it lay in the path of an air-raid-defense fire lane; Father Wilhelm Kleinsorge, a German priest of the Society of Jesus, reclined in his underwear on a cot on the top floor of his order's three-story mission house, reading a Jesuit magazine, *Stimmen der Zeit*; Dr. Terufumi Sasaki, a young member of the surgical staff of the city's large, modern Red Cross Hospital, walked along one of the hospital corridors with a blood specimen for a Wassermann test in his hand; and the Reverend Mr. Kiyoshi Tanimoto, pastor of the Hiroshima Methodist Church, paused at the door of a rich man's house in Koi, the city's western suburb, and prepared to unload a handcart full of things he had evacuated from town in fear of the massive B-29 raid which everyone expected Hiroshima to suffer. A hundred thousand people were killed by the atomic bomb, and these six were among the survivors. They still wonder why they lived when so many others died. Each of them counts many small items of chance or volition—a step taken in time, a decision to go indoors, catching one streetcar instead of the next—that spared him. And now each knows that in the act of survival he lived a dozen lives and saw more death than he ever thought he would see. At the time, none of them knew anything.

The Reverend Mr. Tanimoto got up at five o'clock that morning. He was alone in the parsonage, because for some time his wife had been commuting with their year-old baby to spend nights with a friend in Ushida, a suburb to the north. Of all the important cities of Japan, only two, Kyoto and Hiroshima, had not been visited in strength by *B-san,* or Mr. B, as the Japanese, with a mixture of respect and unhappy familiarity, called the B-29; and Mr. Tanimoto, like all his neighbors and friends, was almost sick with anxiety. He had heard uncomfortably detailed accounts of mass raids on Kure, Iwakuni, Tokuyama, and other nearby towns; he was sure Hiroshima's turn would come soon. He had slept badly the night before, because there had been several air-raid warnings. Hiroshima had been getting such warnings almost every night for weeks, for at that time the B-29s were using Lake Biwa, northeast of Hiroshima, as a rendezvous point, and no matter what city the Americans planned to hit, the Superfortresses streamed in over the coast near Hiroshima. The frequency of the warnings and the continued abstinence of Mr. B with respect to Hiroshima had made its citizens jittery; a rumor was going around that the Americans were saving something special for the city.

Mr. Tanimoto was a small man, quick to talk, laugh, and cry. He wore his black hair parted in the middle and rather long; the prominence of the frontal bones just above his eyebrows and the smallness of his mustache, mouth, and chin gave him a strange, old-young look, boyish and yet wise, weak and yet fiery. He moved nervously and fast, but with a restraint which suggested that he was a cautious, thoughtful man. He showed, indeed, just those qualities in the uneasy days before the bomb fell. Besides having his wife spend the nights in Ushida, Mr. Tanimoto had been carrying all the portable things from his church, in the close-packed residential district called Nagaragawa, to a house that belonged to a rayon manufacturer in Koi, two miles from the center of town. The rayon man, a Mr. Matsui, had opened his then unoccupied estate to a large number of his friends and acquaintances, so that they might evacuate whatever they wished to a safe distance from the probable target area. Mr. Tanimoto had had no difficulty in moving chairs, hymnals, Bibles, altar gear, and church records by pushcart himself, but the organ console and an upright piano required some aid. A friend of his named Matsuo had, the day before, helped him get the piano out to Koi; in return, he had promised this day to assist Mr. Matsuo in hauling out a daughter's belongings. That is why he had risen so early.

Mr. Tanimoto cooked his own breakfast. He felt awfully tired. The effort of moving the piano the day before, a sleepless night, weeks of worry and unbalanced diet, the cares of his parish—all combined to make him feel hardly adequate to the new day's work. There was another thing, too: Mr. Tanimoto had studied theology at Emory College, in Atlanta, Georgia; he had graduated in 1940; he spoke excellent English; he dressed in American clothes; he had corresponded with many American friends right up to the time the war began; and among a people obsessed with a fear of being spied upon—perhaps almost obsessed himself—he found himself growing increasingly uneasy. The police had questioned him several times, and just a few days before, he had heard that an influential acquaintance, a Mr. Tanaka, a retired officer of the Toyo Kisen Kaisha steamship line, an anti-Christian, a man famous in Hiroshima for his showy philanthropies and notorious for his personal tyrannies, had been telling people that Tanimoto should not be trusted. In compensation, to show himself publicly a good Japanese, Mr. Tanimoto had taken on the chairmanship of his local *tonarigumi*, or Neighborhood Association, and to his other duties and concerns this position had added the business of organizing air-raid defense for about twenty families.

Before six o'clock that morning, Mr. Tanimoto started for Mr. Matsuo's house. There he found that their burden was to be a *tansu*, a large Japanese cabinet, full of clothing and household goods. The two men set out. The morning was perfectly clear and so warm that the day promised to be uncomfortable. A few minutes after they started, the air-raid siren went off—a minute-long blast that warned of approaching planes but indicated to the people of Hiroshima only a slight degree of danger, since it sounded every morning at this time, when an American weather plane came over. The two men pulled and pushed the handcart through the city streets. Hiroshima was a fan-shaped city, lying mostly on the six islands formed by the seven estuarial rivers that branch out from the Ota River; its main commercial and residential districts, covering about four square miles in the center of the city, contained three-quarters of its population, which had been reduced by several evacuation programs from a wartime peak of 380,000 to about 245,000. Factories and other residential districts, or suburbs, lay compactly around the edges of the city. To the south were the docks, an airport, and the island-studded Inland Sea. A rim of mountains runs around the other three sides of the delta. Mr. Tanimoto and Mr. Matsuo took their way through the shopping center, already full of people, and across two of the rivers to the sloping streets of Koi, and up them to the outskirts and foothills. As they started up a valley away from the tight-ranked houses, the all-clear sounded. (The Japanese radar operators, detecting only three planes, supposed that they comprised a reconnaissance.) Pushing the handcart up to the rayon man's house was tiring, and the men, after they had maneuvered their load into the driveway and to the front steps, paused to rest awhile. They stood with a wing of the house between them and the city. Like most homes in this part of Japan, the house consisted of a wooden frame and wooden walls supporting a heavy tile roof. Its front hall, packed with rolls of bedding and clothing, looked like a cool cave full of fat cushions. Opposite the house, to the right of the front door, there was a large, finicky rock garden. There was no sound of planes. The morning was still; the place was cool and pleasant.

Then a tremendous flash of light cut across the sky. Mr. Tanimoto has a distinct recollection that it travelled from east to west, from the city toward the hills. It seemed a sheet of sun. Both he and Mr. Matsuo reacted in terror—and both had time to react (for they were 3,500 yards, or two miles, from the center of the explosion). Mr. Matsuo dashed up the front steps into the house and dived among the bedrolls and buried himself there. Mr. Tanimoto took four or five steps and threw himself between two big rocks in the garden. He bellied up very hard against one of them. As his face was against the stone, he did not see what happened. He felt a sudden pressure, and then splinters and pieces of board and fragments of tile fell on him. He heard no roar. (Almost no one in Hiroshima recalls hearing any noise of the bomb. But a fisherman in his sampan on the Inland Sea near Tsuzu, the man with whom Mr. Tanimoto's mother-in-law and sister-in-law were living, saw the flash and heard a tremendous explosion; he was nearly twenty miles from Hiroshima, but the thunder was greater than when the B-29s hit Iwakuni, only five miles away.)

When he dared, Mr. Tanimoto raised his head and saw that the rayon man's house had collapsed. He thought a bomb had fallen directly on it. Such clouds of dust had risen that there was a sort of twilight around. In panic, not thinking for the moment of Mr. Matsuo under the ruins, he dashed out into the street. He noticed as he ran that the concrete wall of the estate had fallen over—toward the house rather than away from it. In the street, the first thing he saw was a squad of soldiers who had been burrowing into the hillside opposite, making one of the thousands of dugouts in which the Japanese apparently intended to resist invasion, hill by hill, life for life; the soldiers were coming out of the hole, where they should have been safe, and blood was running from their heads, chests, and backs. They were silent and dazed.

Under what seemed to be a local dust cloud, the day grew darker and darker.

At nearly midnight, the night before the bomb was dropped, an announcer on the city's radio station said that about two hundred B-29s were approaching southern Honshu and advised the population of Hiroshima to evacuate to their designated "safe areas." Mrs. Hatsuyo Nakamura, the tailor's widow, who lived in the section called Nobori-cho and who had long had a habit of doing as she was told, got her three children—a ten-year-old boy, Toshio, an eight-year-old girl, Yaeko, and a five-year-old girl, Myeko—out of bed and dressed them and walked with them to the military area known as the East Parade Ground, on the northeast edge of the city. There she unrolled some mats and the children lay down on them. They slept until about two, when they were awakened by the roar of the planes going over Hiroshima.

As soon as the planes had passed, Mrs. Nakamura started back with her children. They reached home a little after two-thirty and she immediately turned on the radio, which, to her distress, was just then broadcasting a fresh warning. When she looked at the children and saw how tired they were, and when she thought of the number of trips they had made in past weeks, all to no purpose, to the East Parade Ground, she decided that in spite of the instructions on the radio, she simply could not face starting out all over again. She put the children in their bedrolls on the floor, lay down herself at three o'clock, and fell asleep at once, so soundly that when planes passed over later, she did not waken to their sound.

The siren jarred her awake at about seven. She arose, dressed quickly, and hurried to the house of Mr. Nakamoto, the head of her Neighborhood Association, and asked him what she should do. He said that she should remain at home unless an urgent warning—a series of intermittent blasts of the siren—was sounded. She returned home, lit the stove in the kitchen, set some rice to cook, and sat down to read that morning's Hiroshima *Chugoku*. To her relief, the all-clear sounded at eight o'clock. She heard the children stirring, so she went and gave each of them a handful of peanuts and told them to stay on their bedrolls, because they were tired from the night's walk. She had hoped that they would go back to sleep, but the man in the house directly to the south began to make a terrible hullabaloo of hammering, wedging, ripping, and splitting. The prefectural government, convinced, as everyone in Hiroshima was, that the city would be attacked soon, had begun to press with threats and warnings for the completion of wide fire lanes, which, it was hoped, might act in conjunction with the rivers to localize any fires started by an incendiary raid; and the neighbor was reluctantly sacrificing his home to the city's safety. Just the day before, the prefecture had ordered all able-bodied girls from the secondary schools to spend a few days helping to clear these lanes, and they started work soon after the all-clear sounded.

Mrs. Nakamura went back to the kitchen, looked at the rice, and began watching the man next door. At first, she was annoyed with him for making so much noise, but then she was moved almost to tears by pity. Her emotion was specifically directed toward her neighbor, tearing down his home, board by board, at a time when there was so much unavoidable destruction, but undoubtedly she also felt a generalized, community pity, to say nothing of self-pity. She had not had an easy time. Her husband, Isawa, had gone into the Army just after Myeko was born, and she had heard nothing from or of him for a long time, until, on March 5, 1942, she received a seven-word telegram: "Isawa died an honorable death at Singapore." She learned later that he had died on February 15th, the day Singapore fell, and that he had been a corporal. Isawa had been a not particularly prosperous tailor, and his only capital was a Sankoku sewing machine. After his death, when his allotments stopped coming, Mrs. Nakamura got out the machine and began to take in piecework herself, and since then had supported the children, but poorly, by sewing.

As Mrs. Nakamura stood watching her neighbor, everything flashed whiter than any white she had ever seen. She did not notice what happened to the man next door; the reflex of a mother set her in motion toward her children. She had taken a single step (the house was 1,350 yards, or three-quarters of a mile, from the center of the explosion) when something picked her up and she seemed to fly into the next room over the raised sleeping platform, pursued by parts of her house.

Timbers fell around her as she landed, and a shower of tiles pommelled her; everything became dark, for she was buried. The debris did not cover her deeply. She rose up and freed herself. She heard a child cry, "Mother, help me!," and saw her youngest—Myeko, the five-year-old—buried up to her breast and unable to move. As Mrs. Nakamura started frantically to claw her way toward the baby, she could see or hear nothing of her other children.

In the days right before the bombing, Dr. Masakazu Fujii, being prosperous, hedonistic, and at the time not too busy, had been allowing himself the luxury of sleeping until nine or nine-thirty, but fortunately he had to get up early the morning the bomb was dropped to see a house guest off on a train. He rose at six, and half an hour later walked with his friend to the station, not far away, across two of the rivers. He was back home by seven, just as the siren sounded its sustained warning. He ate breakfast and then, because the morning was already hot, undressed down to his underwear and went out on the porch to read the paper. This porch—in fact, the whole building—was curiously constructed. Dr. Fujii was the proprietor of a peculiarly Japanese institution: a private, single-doctor hospital. This building, perched beside and over the water of the Kyo River, and next to the bridge of the same name, contained thirty rooms for thirty patients and their kinfolk—for, according to Japanese custom, when a person falls sick and goes to a hospital, one or more members of his family go and live there with him, to cook for him, bathe, massage, and read to him, and to offer incessant familial sympathy, without which a Japanese patient would be miserable indeed. Dr. Fujii had no beds—only straw mats—for his patients. He did, however, have all sorts of modern equipment: an X-ray machine, diathermy apparatus, and a fine tiled laboratory. The structure rested two-thirds on the land, one-third on piles over the tidal waters of the Kyo. This overhang, the part of the building where Dr. Fujii lived, was queer-looking, but it was cool in summer and from the porch, which faced away from the center of the city, the prospect of the river, with pleasure boats drifting up and down it, was always refreshing. Dr. Fujii had occasionally had anxious moments when the Ota and its mouth branches rose to flood, but the piling was apparently firm enough and the house had always held.

Dr. Fujii had been relatively idle for about a month because in July, as the number of untouched cities in Japan dwindled and as Hiroshima seemed more and more inevitably a target, he began turning patients away, on the ground that in case of a fire raid he would not be able to evacuate them. Now he had only two patients left—a woman from Yano, injured in the shoulder, and a young man of twenty-five recovering from burns he had suffered when the steel factory near Hiroshima in which he worked had been hit. Dr. Fujii had six nurses to tend his patients. His wife and children were safe; his wife and one son were living outside Osaka, and another son and two daughters were in the country on Kyushu. A niece was living with him, and a maid and a manservant. He had little to do and did not mind, for he had saved some money. At fifty, he was healthy, convivial, and calm, and he was pleased to pass the evenings drinking whiskey with friends, always sensibly and for the sake of conversation. Before the war, he had affected brands imported from Scotland and America; now he was perfectly satisfied with the best Japanese brand, Suntory.

Dr. Fujii sat down cross-legged in his underwear on the spotless matting of the porch, put on his glasses, and started reading the Osaka *Asahi*. He liked to read the Osaka news because his wife was there. He saw the flash. To him—faced away from the center and looking at his paper—it seemed a brilliant yellow. Startled, he began to rise to his feet. In that moment (he was 1,550 yards from the center), the hospital leaned behind his rising and, with a terrible ripping noise, toppled into the river. The Doctor, still in the act of getting to his feet, was thrown forward and around and over; he was buffeted and gripped; he lost track of everything, because things were so speeded up; he felt the water.

Dr. Fujii hardly had time to think that he was dying before he realized that he was alive, squeezed tightly by two long timbers in a V across his chest, like a morsel suspended between two huge chopsticks—held upright, so that he could not move, with his head miraculously above water and his torso and legs in it. The remains of his hospital were all around him in a mad assortment of splintered lumber and materials for the relief of pain. His left shoulder hurt terribly. His glasses were gone.

Father Wilhelm Kleinsorge, of the Society of Jesus, was, on the morning of the explosion, in rather frail condition. The Japanese wartime diet had not sustained him, and he felt the strain of being a foreigner in an increasingly xenophobic Japan; even a German, since the defeat of the Fatherland, was unpopular. Father Kleinsorge had, at thirty-eight, the look of a boy growing too fast—thin in the face, with a prominent Adam's apple, a hollow chest, dangling hands, big feet. He walked clumsily, leaning forward a little. He was tired all the time. To make matters worse, he had suffered for two days, along with Father Cieslik, a fellow-priest, from a rather painful and urgent diarrhea, which they blamed on the beans and black ration bread they were obliged to eat. Two other priests then living in the mission compound, which was in the Nobori-cho section—Father Superior LaSalle and Father Schiffer—had happily escaped this affliction.

Father Kleinsorge woke up about six the morning the bomb was dropped, and half an hour later—he was a bit tardy because of his sickness—he began to read Mass in the mission chapel, a small Japanese-style wooden building which was without pews, since its worshippers knelt on the usual Japanese matted floor, facing an altar graced with splendid silks, brass, silver, and heavy embroideries. This morning, a Monday, the only worshippers were Mr. Takemoto, a theological student living in the mission house; Mr. Fukai, the secretary of the diocese; Mrs. Murata, the mission's devoutly Christian housekeeper; and his fellow-priests. After Mass, while Father Kleinsorge was reading the Prayers of Thanksgiving, the siren sounded. He stopped the service and the missionaries retired across the compound to the bigger building. There, in his room on the ground floor, to the right of the front door, Father Kleinsorge changed into a military uniform which he had acquired when he was teaching at the Rokko Middle School in Kobe and which he wore during air-raid alerts.

After an alarm, Father Kleinsorge always went out and scanned the sky, and in this instance, when he stepped outside, he was glad to see only the single weather plane that flew over Hiroshima each day about this time. Satisfied that nothing would happen, he went in and breakfasted with the other Fathers on substitute coffee and ration bread, which, under the circumstances, was especially repugnant to him. The Fathers sat and talked awhile, until, at eight, they heard the all-clear. They went then to various parts of the building. Father Schiffer retired to his room to do some writing. Father Cieslik sat in his room in a straight chair with a pillow over his stomach to ease his pain, and read. Father Superior LaSalle stood at the window of his room, thinking. Father Kleinsorge went up to a room on the third floor, took off all his clothes except his underwear, and stretched out on his right side on a cot and began reading his *Stimmen der Zeit*.

After the terrible flash—which, Father Kleinsorge later realized, reminded him of something he had read as a boy about a large meteor colliding with the earth—he had time (since he was 1,400 yards from the center) for one thought: A bomb has fallen directly on us. Then, for a few seconds or minutes, he went out of his mind.

Father Kleinsorge never knew how he got out of the house. The next things he was conscious of were that he was wandering around in the mission's vegetable garden in his underwear, bleeding slightly from small cuts along his left flank; that all the buildings round about had fallen down except the Jesuits' mission house, which had long before been braced and double-braced by a priest named Gropper, who was terrified of earthquakes; that the day had turned dark; and that Murata-*san*, the housekeeper, was nearby, crying over and over, "*Shu Jesusu, awaremi tamai!* Our Lord Jesus, have pity on us!"

On the train on the way into Hiroshima from the country, where he lived with his mother, Dr. Terufumi Sasaki, the Red Cross Hospital surgeon, thought over an unpleasant nightmare he had had the night before. His mother's home was in Mukaihara, thirty miles from the city, and it took him two hours by train and tram to reach the hospital. He had slept uneasily all night and had wakened an hour earlier than usual, and, feeling sluggish and slightly feverish, had debated whether to go to the hospital at all; his sense of duty finally forced him to go, and he had started out on an earlier train than he took most mornings. The dream had particularly frightened him because it was so closely associated, on the surface at least, with a disturbing actuality. He was only twenty-five years old and had just completed his training at the Eastern Medical University, in Tsingtao, China. He was something of an idealist and was much distressed by the inadequacy of medical facilities in the country town where his mother lived. Quite on his own, and without a permit, he had begun visiting a few sick people out there in the evenings, after his eight hours at the hospital and four hours' commuting. He had recently learned that the penalty for practicing without a permit was severe; a fellow-doctor whom he had asked about it had given him a serious scolding. Nevertheless, he had continued to practice. In his dream, he had been at the bedside of a country patient when the police and the doctor he had consulted burst into the room, seized him, dragged him outside, and beat him up cruelly. On the train, he just about decided to give up the work in Mukaihara, since he felt it would be impossible to get a permit, because the authorities would hold that it would conflict with his duties at the Red Cross Hospital.

At the terminus, he caught a streetcar at once. (He later calculated that if he had taken his customary train that morning, and if he had had to wait a few minutes for the streetcar, as often happened, he would have been close to the center at the time of the explosion and would surely have perished.) He arrived at the hospital at seven-forty and reported to the chief surgeon. A few minutes later, he went to a room on the first floor and drew blood from the arm of a man in order to perform a Wassermann test. The laboratory containing the incubators for the test was on the third floor. With the blood specimen in his left hand, walking in a kind of distraction he had felt all morning, probably because of the dream and his restless night, he started along the main corridor on his way toward the stairs. He was one step beyond an open window when the light of the bomb was reflected, like a gigantic photographic flash, in the corridor. He ducked down on one knee and said to himself, as only a Japanese would, "Sasaki, *gambare!* Be brave!" Just then (the building was 1,650 yards from the center), the blast ripped through the hospital. The glasses he was wearing flew off his face; the bottle of blood crashed against one wall; his Japanese slippers zipped out from under his feet—but otherwise, thanks to where he stood, he was untouched.

Dr. Sasaki shouted the name of the chief surgeon and rushed around to the man's office and found him terribly cut by glass. The hospital was in horrible confusion: heavy partitions and ceilings had fallen on patients, beds had overturned, windows had blown in and cut people, blood was spattered on the walls and floors, instruments were everywhere, many of the patients were running about screaming, many more lay dead. (A colleague working in the laboratory to which Dr. Sasaki had been walking was dead; Dr. Sasaki's patient, whom he had just left and who a few moments before had been dreadfully afraid of syphilis, was also dead.) Dr. Sasaki found himself the only doctor in the hospital who was unhurt.

Dr. Sasaki, who believed that the enemy had hit only the building he was in, got bandages and began to bind the wounds of those inside the hospital; while outside, all over Hiroshima, maimed and dying citizens turned their unsteady steps toward the Red Cross Hospital to begin an invasion that was to make Dr. Sasaki forget his private nightmare for a long, long time.

Miss Toshiko Sasaki, the East Asia Tin Works clerk, who was not related to Dr. Sasaki, got up at three o'clock in the morning on the day the bomb fell. There was extra housework to do. Her eleven-month-old brother, Akio, had come down the day before with a serious stomach upset; her mother had taken him to the Tamura Pediatric Hospital and was staying there with him. Miss Sasaki, who was about twenty, had to cook breakfast for her father, a brother, a sister, and herself, and—since the hospital, because of the war, was unable to provide food—to prepare a whole day's meals for her mother and the baby, in time for her father, who worked in a factory making rubber earplugs for artillery crews, to take the food by on his way to the plant. When she had finished and had cleaned and put away the cooking things, it was nearly seven. The family lived in Koi, and she had a forty-five-minute trip to the tin works, in the section of town called Kannonmachi. She was in charge of the personnel records in the factory. She left Koi at seven, and as soon as she reached the plant, she went with some of the other girls from the personnel department to the factory auditorium. A prominent local Navy man, a former employee, had committed suicide the day before by throwing himself under a train—a death considered honorable enough to warrant a memorial service, which was to be held at the tin works at ten o'clock that morning. In the large hall, Miss Sasaki and the others made suitable preparations for the meeting. This work took about twenty minutes.

Miss Sasaki went back to her office and sat down at her desk. She was quite far from the windows, which were off to her left, and behind her were a couple of tall bookcases containing all the books of the factory library, which the personnel department had organized. She settled herself at her desk, put some things in a drawer, and shifted papers. She thought that before she began to make entries in her lists of new employees, discharges, and departures for the Army, she would chat for a moment with the girl at her right. Just as she turned her head away from the windows, the room was filled with a blinding light. She was paralyzed by fear, fixed still in her chair for a long moment (the plant was 1,600 yards from the center).

Everything fell, and Miss Sasaki lost consciousness. The ceiling dropped suddenly and the wooden floor above collapsed in splinters and the people up there came down and the roof above them gave way; but principally and first of all, the bookcases right behind her swooped forward and the contents threw her down, with her left leg horribly twisted and breaking underneath her. There, in the tin factory, in the first moment of the atomic age, a human being was crushed by books.

—1945

Learning from Other Writers

1. What is the purpose of the opening paragraph of *Hiroshima*? What is the effect of beginning with Miss Sasaki as opposed to any of the other five characters?
2. Given the information Hersey relates about the Reverend Mr. Tanimoto, do you think Tanimoto survived the bombing because of luck, foresight, or character? What about the other characters?
3. Where and how does Hersey weave in background about the war, the bombing, and the city of Hiroshima?
4. How might Hersey know what Mr. Tanimoto saw, thought, and felt when the bomb hit?
5. What is the effect of including the information about the Japanese soldiers who had been burrowing into the hills above the city?
6. How and when does Hersey cut from character to character?
7. How does Hersey make his subjects seem familiar to American readers? Unfamiliar?
8. What is the effect of ending Chapter One of Hiroshima with Miss Sasaki?

ELWOOD REID

MY BODY, MY WEAPON, MY SHAME

I did bad things for football. Because I could. Because I was 19 years old, weighed 270 pounds, had 5 percent body fat and had muscle to burn. Forget touchdowns, I played football for the chance to hit another man as hard as I could—to fuck him up, move through him like wind through a door. Anybody who tells you different is a liar.

There is the fear that any hit may be your last. That some bigger, stronger, better player will come along—take you down to the turf and end your career with the snap of bone or the pop of an anterior cruciate ligament.

The moment of impact goes like this: You slam helmet-first into another person's back until you can hear the air whoosh out of his lungs. Or better yet—you ram a forearm so hard into his throat that the crunch of cartilage and the fear in his eyes give you pause. Time stops. No pain, only a sucking sound as the physics of the impact sort themselves out—who hit who first, angle, shoulder, mass, helmet, speed, forearm. Silence follows the cruel twist of limbs as the pain rushes in the way oxygen blows through the streets of a firebombed city, leaving flame in its wake. The pain is good. Both of you know it, and for a few precious seconds the world has order. Hitter and hittee. Motherfucker and motherfucked.

I came by football through my father. I played because if you were big, it was what you did in Cleveland. To do anything else was to be soft or queer. As long as I could hit and tackle, nobody made fun of my size. I played football, and that was all you needed to know about me. Then there were the men—the coaches who demanded a single-minded intensity from me each time I strapped on the pads. Even then I knew these were men who kept basements full of plaques and trophies from their glory days, collected beer steins and fell into deep depressions when the Cleveland Browns lost or their wives bore them daughters instead of sons. Their solution to everything was to hit harder. The word was forever on their lips. They scrawled it on chalkboards and spat it in my face: *Hit. Hit. Hit.* They knew how to infect eager minds with the desire to someday play in the pros. And when one of these potbellied men screamed at me to kick ass, act like a man or gut it out, I did, because I wanted to believe that a sport or even life could be boiled down to a few simple maxims. I was big, and I could hit; therefore I had purpose.

In high school, my scrawny body filled out as I moved from junior varsity to varsity and then to captain of a mediocre football team. College scouts came to time me in the forty-yard dash, watch me lift weights and eye me coming out of the shower as if I were a horse they might someday bid for at auction. I can't say I didn't enjoy the attention, but I began to realize that as a potential college-football recruit, I was expected to behave like one. I had to shake hands and look scouts in the eye and thank them for coming to see me. I had to talk sports, tell them who my favorite players were, what team I liked in the Super Bowl. I had to be smart but not too smart. Grades mattered only because colleges like "no risk" players, guys who can be recruited without the worry that they'll flunk out. I couldn't tell them that I didn't care who won the Super Bowl, that what really mattered to me was books. That when I finished *One Flew Over the Cuckoo's Nest* or *Heart of Darkness*, my heart beat faster than it ever had on the football field. I knew that I had to keep this part of me hidden and let the scouts and coaches see the bright-eyed athlete they wanted to see.

Pursuing a football scholarship became a full-time job. Everything I did was for my body. I ate well, went running at night, swallowed handfuls of vitamins, swilled gallons of protein shakes and fell asleep rubbing sore muscles. Everything fell away as I focused on using this body I'd nurtured and cared for, asking it to come back day after day, stronger, better. And it did. Even after the most torturous practices, my body responded by snapping back, fresh and ready to go. If there were limits, I had yet to find them.

On the field, I plugged my heart in, throwing my body at tailbacks with reckless abandon. I went both ways and loved every minute of it—reveling in the sheer exhaustion that came every fourth quarter, when it was all I could do to hunker down into a three-point stance and fire out. To be better than the man lined up across from you was to summon your body to do what it didn't want to do—what it would normally resist doing off the gridiron. Great ballplayers are full of hate and a kind of love for what they are capable of inflicting on another man. And in between whistles, I hated.

When the first recruiting letter arrived, I had this feeling that I was standing on the cusp of what I imagined to be greatness. I saw television, cheerleaders and, I suppose even then, the endgame—the NFL.

"This is a great opportunity," my father said, holding the letter in his hands as if it were alive.

I nodded, knowing that the ante had been raised. I was no longer playing because I liked to hit but for the chance to get out of Cleveland and escape the factory-gray fate that awaited me.

I escaped by signing a letter of intent to play ball for one of those Big Ten colleges, where football is king, the coach is feared and anybody wearing a letterman's jacket is instantly revered. I felt important, my head swirling with the possibilities that seemed to shimmer before me. I had worked hard; my friends had gone out drinking or had sat around watching television, but I'd been running and lifting. Now I felt as if I had been rewarded and everything would be OK.

That was ten years ago, and what I did both on and off the field for football is preserved forever in the aches, pains and injuries that haunt my body, lurking no matter how many aspirins I chew or how early I go to bed.

When I report to freshman summer camp, there are thirty or so other new recruits sitting around a huge indoor practice facility. Some of them are bigger and stronger than me, guys with no necks and triceps that hang off their arms like stapled-on hams. The speedsters and skill guys, mostly thick-legged black dudes with gold chains and shaved heads, pool over into their own corner, staring down at their feet as if the secret of their speed lay somewhere underground. The oddball white guys—quarterbacks, tight ends and a few gangly-looking receivers—find one another and talk like bankers, in slow, measured tones.

I make my way over to the group of big guys who stand, shifting foot to foot, in a loose semicircle, until the coaches walk in and everybody snaps to attention. I am relieved to find that they look like all the other coaches who have ever yelled at me or offered arm-swinging praise. They are the very same gray/white-haired men, swaddled head to toe in loud polyester, I've been trying to impress my whole life.

Nobody says a word. Instead, the coaches stand there looking at us the way a mechanic eyes his socket wrenches, as tools to be picked up, used and thrown aside. There is only this simple equation: As a ballplayer, I am expected to do as I'm told, lay my body on the line or else get out of the way for somebody who will. Everybody in the room knows and understands this and, when asked, will put himself in harm's way with the dim, deluded hope that he will come out the other end a star.

The speech begins, and it's like every other coach's speech, only this time the coach spouting the platitudes owns our bodies and our minds for the next four years, five if we redshirt. He lays down the rules—the same rules I've heard all my life about what I can and can't do—about how we're here to win and anything less is simply unacceptable.

Then his theory of football: "Domination through hard work, men," he says, his short body quivering with anger. "More hard work until we come together as a team of men focused on one thing: *winning*. Am I understood?"

"Yes, sir," we answer.

"Good then," he says. "I'll accept nothing less than smash-mouth, cream-them-in-the-ear-hole football. That is why you are here, and I will not tolerate softness or excuses. You are here because we think each of you will someday become a ballplayer. You are not yet ballplayers, but if you do what we ask, you will become ballplayers, and for that you are lucky."

All thirty of us grunt, "Yes, sir."

Then this no-neck guy, his face swollen with fear and desire, leans into me and says, "I wish we could skip the bullshit, strap on the pads and sort out who's who."

My first inclination is to laugh, to tell him to relax. Instead, I lid my eyes and clench my jaw and tell him that yes, that would be good, that I too like to hit.

Coach finishes his rah-rah speech, and the air is heavy with anticipation as the realization washes over everyone in the room that all of the lifting and running has come down to this—the chance to prove ourselves by putting our bodies on the line with guys who are every bit as strong and as fast.

Then we're marched off to the training room, where a team of doctors pokes and prods us as if we were cattle heading to market. By the time we're through, everybody has a nickname: Fuckhead, Slope, Rope, Sith, Crawdaddy, Pin Dick, Yo Joe, Hernia, Bible Boy, Vic, Napalm, Six-Four, Too Tall, Dead Fuck, Flat-Ass Phil, the Creeper, Revlon. Somebody tags me with Sweet Lou Reid because before every practice I listen to "Coney Island Baby."

On our first day of padded practice, the line coach, a man with steel blue-and-gray hair, cold eyes and a hatchet nose, marches us over to a row of low metal cages. "Get into a three-point," Coach says as he lines us across from one another on opposite sides of the cages.

I hunker down, straddling one of the boards, and look out at the man in front of me.

"*Hit*!" Coach screams.

And with a blast of his whistle, my college football career begins. We hit and fall to the ground, fighting and spitting until he whistles us back to attention. We line up and do it over and over. After ten minutes, I am bleeding from three different places, my arms are numb, and my right thumb hangs from my hand at an angle I know is wrong. But to stop and go to the sideline is to pussy out. So I play through the pain, and after a few more hits I don't care what happens to my thumb.

The rest of practice takes place in five-second bursts, until our pads, wet with blood and sweat, hang on us like second skins. Everything is done harder and faster. Fights break out without warning. Two long-armed D-backs start swinging at each other, and the coaches let it go until the taller one splits his hand on a face mask. Blood flies from his smashed paw as he spins around like some shoulder-padded Tasmanian devil. One of the coaches finally grabs him by the face mask and drags him to the sideline, leaving his opponent alone and bewildered, with nothing to do except join the huddle. Guys suffer knee injuries, pop hamstrings, tear Achilles tendons, while others just go down with silent, allover injuries that are the same as quitting—telling the team you can no longer take it. During the first week, nine walk-ons clear out their lockers and quit.

We learn to live with injuries and spend what little free time we have complaining and scheming about our positions on the depth chart. Hernia has a bruise he can move up and down his forearm. Bible Boy's knee is fucked, and my shoulder slides in and out of place so much that I no longer notice it. All of us have scabbed-over noses and turf burns on our shins that crack and fill our shoes with warm blood the minute practice starts.

After practice and a shower, I stand in front of the mirror and stare at the road map of bruises, cuts and mysterious pink swellings. I touch each bruise, scrape and swelling until I feel something, and I know that my body is still there, capable of doing what I ask of it.

When the upperclassmen report to camp, we become their tackling dummies. Even the coaches forget about us and concentrate on the home opener four weeks off. I'm moved from defense to offense because my feet are too slow and my "opportunities," Coach says, are better on the other side of the ball. He tells me that offense is the thinking man's side of the ball, that it is about forward motion and scoring.

I adjust, and within a week I become an offensive lineman. Every day is the same grind—the same flesh-filled five yards on either side of the ball, where we grunt, shove, kick and gouge at one another. In the trenches, success is measured in feet and inches, not long touchdown runs or head-over-ass catches that bring crowds to their feet.

After three weeks, I begin to root for injuries. Not only do I want the man in front of me on the depth chart to go down but I begin to look for ways to hasten his downfall. I am not the only one. More than once I see guys twisting knees in pileups, lowering helmets into exposed spines, gouging throats and faces with the hope that a few well-placed injuries will move them up the depth chart. The coaches seem to encourage this ballplayer-eat-ballplayer mentality, pitting starter against backup and watching as the two players wrestle and pump padded fists at each other long after the play has been blown dead.

But it is off the field that the real training happens, where I learn about how the team is not really a team. Offensive players hate defensive players. Linemen hate ball handlers because they get all the glory and half the aches and pains. It goes without saying that everybody hates the kickers because of their soft bodies and clean uniforms and the way they run warm-up laps out in front, making the rest of us look bad.

There is also a silent division between blacks and whites. Any white guy who hangs with the brothers and listens to their music is called a "whigger." Black guys who hang with the white guys are called "Oreo-cookie motherfuckers" or sellouts. In the locker room, when there are only white faces around, some guy will call a black guy who fumbles the ball or hits too hard in warm-ups a stupid nigger, and I know that I am supposed to nod in agreement or high-five the racist bastard. And when I don't, there is another line drawn.

But somehow it all comes together, and there are times when black and white, offense and defense and even the kickers seem to be part of the same team, especially when practice is over and we're all glad to be walking off the field, happy to have seen our bodies through another day, united by our aches, pains and fatigue.

I learn that among the linemen there are those who belong and those who don't. To belong means to go about the game of football grim faced, cocksure of your ability to take any hit and keep moving. The guys who zone out on God, refuse the pack or are refused by it end up falling by the wayside, unnoticed by the coaching staff and their fellow players.

Then there are the guys who have already made it—broken out of the pack to start or platoon with another player in a starting position. Among the linemen, they are called "the fellas." Coaches love the fellas because they have proven themselves. But what really distinguishes a fella is not his success on the field but rather his ability to wallow in the easy gratification afforded any athlete at any university that is nuts for football. Everything is permitted—drinking, scoring chicks, fighting off the field—because he has survived the mayhem and the mindless drudgery of practices. I hear the stories over lunch or in the locker room after a workout: how to score with a woman nicknamed "the Dishwasher." How to persuade one of the brains or geeks to cheat for you. How to cop free meals at restaurants or free drinks at a bar. How to wrangle free T-shirts from the equipment manager. How to pass the drug test. And, most important, how to act like you don't give a shit, because you've got it coming to you.

We win our Big Ten opener, and for a few minutes in the locker room the air seems to vibrate with goodwill and camaraderie. Even I who have stood on the sideline getting rained on feel like a player as I listen to reporters question today's heroes. After the coaches leave, word that there will be a party at a fella's house percolates through the sweaty room.

When I enter the party, the room seems to be in some sort of drunken-action overload. Near the keg there is a makeshift wrestling pit, circled by grubby couches full of squealing teased-haired women who look at me briefly, decide that I am not a starter and look away. I am handed a beer and told to drink. My beertender is a huge, smiling defensive tackle named the Wall, who watches as I raise the cup to my lips and sip.

"What's a matter with you?" he says, pointing at the beer. "We've got beer and a roomful of chicks who want to fuck us 'cause we won the game. What more do you want?"

"I'm just a frosh," I tell him.

"Skip the *Leave It to Beaver* bullshit and drink," Wall says.

I nod, drain the cup and follow him to the kitchen, past heavily made-up groupies who stare at me now that I am with Wall. There are others, big guys mostly, and we keep pace with Wall, who tosses back beer as if it's water. After every round, somebody slops an arm around me or smacks me on the shoulder, and for a moment I feel the tug of the fella fraternity.

What happens next is what happens in varying degrees at every subsequent party. Fights erupt over women, favorite teams, etc. There is a girl in an upstairs bedroom handing out blow jobs or an underclassman who is too drunk and vomits before he is stripped naked and thrown out a window or tossed down the stairs.

I down half a bottle of Everclear grain alcohol when it is handed to me and let a sad-eyed chubby girl in tight jeans sit on my lap. As the liquor hits my brain, I realize that there are no victims here, even as I watch this girl get talked into going upstairs with three guys. Later I see her in the front yard, leaning against a lamppost crying, as several players throw empty beer cans at her and call her a whore. Everybody, including the skinny-shouldered engineering student and the jock-sniffing schlub with stars in his eyes whom we occasionally torture and torment, knows the deal and comes back for more. We have something they want, and they'll take anything we have—even the laughter and the cruel pranks—just to be near us, to wear one of our sweatshirts or to talk to us about the game. And it all seems so normal. When our starting defensive tackle rams a frat boy's head into a steel grate, not once but several times, there are no repercussions because he is a star and the team needs him. There are rules on the field and in the locker room when we are around the coaches, but off the field, anything goes.

And I do bad things because I want to belong. I hide the part of me that enjoys classes and reading in my room after practice. I know better, yet I find myself doing the same stupid shit I see others do, and nobody tells me that it's wrong. Nobody blinks when I walk into a party, pick up the first girl I see and pin her to the ceiling until her laughter turns to screams and then finally to tears. I put lit cigarettes out on the back of my hand to prove to the fellas that I don't give a fuck—that I am above pain, above caring what happens to my body, because I am young and I am a ballplayer and my body seems to have no limits.

At another party, I split a frat boy's nose for no particular reason other than that I am drunk and it feels like the right thing to do. He goes down, holding his nose, and I hop up on a thick oak banister, close my eyes and walk, not caring if I fall or if someone pushes me. When I do fall down two flights of stairs, I pop right back up, though my knee doesn't seem to be working, and there are several fraternity brothers closing in on me. Instead of running, I go outside and proceed to kick in the basement windows until I hear police sirens and escape into the snowy backyards. The next day, I am sober and ready to practice, and only at that point do I feel remorse. But then there is the first hit, and my body hurts, my joints crack, and I am absolved.

One night at a party during my sophomore year, I am asked by a fella if I want to help him videotape some girl giving head to a couple of guys in an upstairs room. I nod drunkenly and follow him through the forest of oversize flesh and dull-eyed groupies to the stairs, where he turns around and winks at me. For a moment, I'm not sure if he's joking or not. The music is loud—too loud. There are women playing quarters at a table to my right and guys staring at *Hustler* magazine on a couch in the corner, while several sophomores write their names with a permanent Magic Marker on the body of a passed-out frosh and discuss shaving his balls.

"You ready?" my guide asks. I can tell he's waiting for me to say no so he can call me a pussy or a Boy Scout. I look around at the monster bodies of ballplayers acting like children grabbing at toys, and I realize that I've finally become what the coaches and my fellow players have always expected me to become—a fella, a person living in a world of no consequence. I am not a star or even a starter; still, everything I do is acceptable, allowed and in the end ... empty.

I look at the hulking player as he awaits my response. Part of me wants to go upstairs and rescue the girl, take her away. But I know she'd only be back next week, drunker and more willing, and I would be there, too, and maybe then, a few beers to the better, I'd say yes when asked if I wanted to help with the videotaping, because I could, because it is expected of me and because it is what a fella does.

I turn to go, but before I can get to the door, Fuckhead jumps on my back and screams, "Isn't this great?" I shake him off and toss him to the floor, tell him no and walk outside, feeling cold and hollow. But most of all, I feel simple and stupid, because I can't see a way out. If I quit, I lose my scholarship and go back home to Cleveland having failed. If I choose not to partake in the fun, there will be a line drawn and I will be exiled into the lonely world of those who practice but who will never play or belong. That is my problem, that I want to belong at any cost. I still have the dream that someday I will become a starter, and the pro scouts will come to time me in the forty-yard dash and I will have a chance to go to the next level.

It starts with a tingling in my arm, one of a thousand jolts of pain that have run through my body that I no longer seem to notice. Only this time it doesn't go away.

I hear one of the coaches screaming, "Get up, Reid. Get the fuck up and get your ass back to the huddle."

Without thinking, I roll to my feet and try to shake it off. When I rejoin the huddle, the coach glares at me and another play is called, and I line up, hit and do it again, the pain lingering in my spine. Then one morning I awake unable to raise my arms above my head.

After swallowing a handful of Tylenol Threes and a few anti-inflammatories, I go to practice and hit. My arms dangle from my shoulders, bloodless and weak, forcing me to deliver the blows with my head and helmet. The coaches scream when I am slow to rise after the whistle. And when the pills wear off, the numbness is replaced by a hot poker of pain and a dull, crunching sound in my neck. After I miss a block, Coach sends me to the sideline and motions for the trainers to have a look. I explain and point to my neck as they walk me to the training room. It is the longest walk of my life, and no one even turns a helmet in my direction. In the training room, I am told to lie still while the trainers pull my pads off and wrap ice bags around my neck.

I sit the sideline for a full week. No one except the trainers and the team doctor says a word to me, and it's all right, because for once I am outside looking in at the football machine as it whirs and clicks along without me. But by the end of the week, I want more than anything else to peel the ice bags off my neck and shoulders, strap on pads and prove that I'm still one of them. I think that this time it will be different, that I can hit and go about the game I've played and nursed my body for without acting like one of the fellas off the field.

So when the team doctor works his way up my arm with a safety pin, poking my flesh and asking, "Do you feel this?" I say, "Yes."

"And this?"

Yes, yes and yes. Although I have no idea where or if he is poking me. He plays along with the charade. There are no X rays, only ice and pills that make my head feel like it's stuffed with cotton. After the pain has subsided, I am put on a cycle of cervical steroids and must report to the training room twice a day to have my blood pressure monitored.

In a week, I am back on the field, and everything falls into place. My legs move and my body goes where it's directed, but the pain won't go away. I imagine a rotten spot in my spine, a cancer I want to cut out. My body learns to hit all over again, making small adjustments in some vain hope that the injury will go away and with it the nerve pain that seems to lurk after every collision.

Instead the pain gets worse, and most nights I'm back in the training room with the other gimps, begging for ice and more pills that I hope will somehow allow me to hit again. Nobody questions the toughness of the guys who are hauled off the field with their knees turned inside out or the players who are knocked cold and can't so much as wiggle a toe. But I look healthy. There is no blood, no bone poking through skin, no body cast, no evidence that I am injured. I can walk and talk and smile, and in the eyes of the team the real problem is that I can't stand the pain.

I go another month, practicing when my neck will allow, sitting the sideline when it won't. Finally, I'm referred to a neurologist. This time there are tests: X rays, CAT scans, an MRI and an EMG. When a nurse pumps two needles into each of my arms, telling me my mouth will taste like I have a spoon in it and that I'll feel nauseous, I smile, happy to have the pain and the sickness so controlled.

As I stare into the fluorescent lights with the taste of metal in my mouth, I know that something in my body has given out, that I somehow deserve this for not wanting to be a fella.

When the tests are over, I am not allowed to see the results. "We'll have them sent to the team doctor," the technician tells me.

"Am I OK?" I ask, wanting this guy in a white smock with his needles and nurses to tell me that I'm all right—that I'll have my body back. But I know that I'd only throw it away again, out on the field, to prove that I am one of them.

Instead, there are other tests, more pills and a neck brace. I start going to the parties, watching the fellas go about their fun, envious of what their play and performance has earned them. To prove to the fellas and myself that I still matter, I get drunk, head-butt walls and stick needles into my numb hands, despite rational thoughts that tell me what I am doing is stupid. I am careful to inflict this abuse only on myself, to show them that the injury they can't see is real and I can stand even more pain than they can imagine. So I let someone push a stapler into my biceps over and over until my shirt turns red, and for a few precious minutes the fellas pay attention to me—one even shakes his head and calls me a "sick dog motherfucker." And I'm proud. The pain leaves, and my body feels like it used to—large, powerful and capable of great things.

Then there is the morning, the staples still scabbed into my arms, the cigarette burns on the backs of my hands. But worst of all, there is the silent crunching in my neck and the dead feeling in my fingers. I stand in front of the mirror, staring at the smooth outline of my neck muscles, the slope of my shoulders. I know one thing: I no longer want to play football the way the best of them do—dying between whistles as if you are born to it and there is no other option. Still, when I'm called into the head coach's office and told that I can no longer play, I walk out of the room despising my neck, my body and the fact that it will no longer have the opportunity to hit another man.

Some guys go through life feeding the athlete inside with weekend-warrior games of touch football, season tickets, tailgate parties and war stories about what it was like to play. Athletes don't, as they say, die twice; instead, part of them remains 19 years old forever, with the body ready and willing to prove itself all over again. I had to kill that 19-year-old, the one who enjoyed being able to prove himself to the world with sheer brute force: hitting, taking and not thinking.

After college I headed for Alaska to get away from football. I became a frame carpenter and spent my days pounding nails and lifting twenty-foot sections of wall until my back and neck shivered with pain and my arms went numb. Every time I went home sore, bruised and full of splinters, it felt good—punishment for failing at football and at being a fella. Work helped to kill the jock in me. Falling off buildings and being crushed by two-by-fours dropped by stoned Hi-Lo operators finished what football had started. There were days and even weeks when I couldn't pull myself out of bed. And I liked it, because for once I could see the end—somewhere, sometime I would no longer be able to use my body, and what would be left would be the guy who loved reading and talking about books.

Later I would work as a bouncer, a bartender, a grunt laborer, a truck dispatcher and a handyman. When I needed money, I rented out my body to schizophrenia-drug-testing programs at a VA hospital. The drugs left me with waking aural and visual hallucinations for days. I thought I was Miles Davis and that I could hear ants crawling in the grass. There were other tests with needles and electric current and more drugs. I didn't care. I got paid for all of it and never once questioned why I wanted to do this to myself. But somewhere along the line, the jock in me died.

Now I'm a guy who used to play. I rise out of bed each morning to a symphony of cracks and crunches. I have pain from football injuries I don't remember. My shoulders still slop around in their sockets if I don't sleep in exactly the same position every night. Sometimes my neck and back lock up without warning, and I fall, and I'm reminded that I did bad things for football and it did bad things to me. It left me with this clear-cut of a body, a burned-out village that I sacked for a sport.

—1997

Learning from Other Writers

1. Why did Elwood Reid do "bad things for football"?
2. If you have never played college football, does the essay reveal anything about the sport that surprises you? If you *have* played college football, does anything in the essay surprise you? Either way, do you find Reid's testimony credible? Why or why not?
3. What (if any) larger question is Reid trying to answer by evaluating his own experiences as a member of a Big Ten football team?
4. Who is the audience for this essay?
5. What is Reid's attitude toward the bad things he did for football? The bad things other players, coaches, or fans did for football?
6. Reid is writing about his experiences on the team years after he stopped playing football. What is the effect of this older perspective? What effect does the ending (the final four paragraphs) have on your reaction to the essay as a whole?

WILLIAM FINNEGAN

THE UNWANTED

Film companies used to come to the Antelope Valley, in northern Los Angeles County, to shoot high-desert scenes. It was empty country, a good backdrop for Westerns. Now they come when they need to burn down or blow up a housing tract. In 1992, for the fiery climax of "Lethal Weapon 3," Warner Bros. used a development called the Legends, at Avenue J and Thirtieth Street West, in the city of Lancaster. The Legends had become available after its financing failed, leaving unfinished forty-eight large, Spanish-style homes, each named after a legendary American (Babe Ruth, Marilyn Monroe). Mel Gibson and Danny Glover went on a memorable rampage through the tract. When I drove through its curving streets last year, I found a wasteland (tumbleweeds, shopping carts, graffiti-covered sofas) surrounded by a high brown wall.

The transformation of the Antelope Valley from rural desert into modern suburbia—with neighborhoods, literally, to burn—was very sudden, a historical jump cut. In 1980, the combined population of Lancaster and Palmdale, the Valley's two main cities, was sixty thousand. By 1994, their combined population was two hundred and twenty-two thousand, and today estimates of the Valley's total population range as high as four hundred thousand. This hyper-expansion was first sparked by housing prices in Los Angeles and its nearer suburbs, which soared during the nineteen-eighties, and by white flight from an increasingly Latino and Asian city. The Antelope Valley had been considered too remote for commuters, but the completion of the Antelope Valley Freeway, snaking over the San Gabriel Mountains, helped change that. In the Antelope Valley, one could buy for two hundred thousand dollars a new house that might cost four hundred thousand in the San Fernando Valley. What was more, the air was cleaner and the streets were safer. The commute to jobs in the city was longer—an hour longer, at least, each way—but that was the trade-off. And so it was that the desert brought forth swimming pools and convenience stores beyond number, and wide empty streets as far as the eye could see.

Then, in 1990, the Southern California economy, staggered by cutbacks in the aerospace and defense industries, fell into a deep recession. Los Angeles County alone lost more than half a million jobs, and property values throughout the region collapsed. In the Antelope Valley, abandoned housing tracts began to dot the subdivided desert. Boarded-up shopping centers and bankrupt school districts followed, along with a wave of personal financial disasters so severe that *USA Today* dubbed Palmdale "the foreclosure capital of California."

And yet the Antelope Valley's population has continued to grow. Between 1990 and 1994, Palmdale was the second-fastest-growing city in the United States, Lancaster the sixth-fastest. As a rule, the Valley's newest residents are poorer and darker than their predecessors, live in more crowded lodgings, and are more likely to rent. Still, the Valley remains, in a county where whites are a minority, overwhelmingly white (sixty-eight per cent), home-owning, and politically dominated by conservative Republicans of the pro-growth, antitax stripe. And the reasons most people give for moving out from the city—less crime, less smog, cheaper housing—have not changed. The Valley remains particularly attractive to families with children. Indeed, it has been called "the last great breeding ground of Southern California."

For anyone who has spent time there lately, this is a scary thought—if only because growing up these days in the Antelope Valley seems to be, for many kids, a pretty harrowing, dispiriting affair. This may be true today of growing up in America generally, but the Valley's supersonic growth has led to overcrowded, often chaotic schools; according to the high-school district's superintendent, nearly forty-five per cent of the entering students do not finish with their class. The teen-pregnancy rate is also alarmingly high. Juvenile crime is a major problem, usually attributed to "unsupervised children"—to, that is, the huge number of kids whose parents can't afford after-school care and often don't return from their epic commutes until long after dark. With neighborhoods devoid of adults from early morning to night, the most popular youth crime is, naturally, burglary. A sheriff's-department spokesman in Lancaster estimated that fully half the Valley's children are unsupervised after school. He also said that there are now, not coincidentally, more than two hundred youth gangs represented in the Valley.

I grew up, a generation ago, in Woodland Hills, then an outer suburb of L.A., and when I started spending time with teen-agers in the Antelope Valley I figured I had a head start on understanding their world. As it turned out, my youth might as well have been spent in Kathmandu for all the clues it gave me in this new realm. There was a street war raging in Lancaster between a white-supremacist skinhead gang known as the Nazi Low Riders and a rival gang of antiracist skinheads who called themselves Sharps. This obscure, semi-doctrinal conflict fascinated me long before it escalated to homicide, as it eventually did. And yet no adult, I discovered, could shed any real light on it. I needed a native guide, and I found one in Mindy Turner, who, at seventeen, was already well embarked on the kind of casually terrifying existence I was starting to regard as common.

She was living with her mother, her younger brother, and an older half brother in a four-bedroom white stucco ranch-style house in Lancaster. Her mother, Debbie, worked behind the counter at Thrifty Drugs; she had bought the house with the settlement she got after her husband, a crane operator, was electrocuted on the job in 1989, when Mindy was in elementary school. Mindy recalled, "They came to get me at school and said, 'Your dad's gone to be with your dog and your grandpa in Heaven.' I've never gotten over it. Whenever I get sad, I start thinking about it and just cry."

Debbie remembered Mindy being deeply troubled by the idea that her dad had never been baptized, and thought that that was probably why Mindy later became a Mormon—because she wanted to be baptized herself. Actually, before Mindy became a Mormon she had wanted to become Jewish. But that had turned out to be too much work. Becoming a Mormon was relatively easy. All this was before Mindy got addicted to crystal methamphetamine and became a Nazi, in the ninth grade.

Mindy and her mother shared blond good looks, but Debbie was hearty and outgoing, while Mindy was pale, fashionably thin, moody, intense. Her manner oscillated with unnerving speed—from jaded worldliness to girlish enthusiasm, from precocious grace to gawkiness, from thuggish cynicism to tender vulnerability. She spoke in quick, fluid bursts, as if she had to express each thought before she changed her mind.

In her mother's day, Mindy's looks might have made her a homecoming queen. But Mindy stopped going to school while she was in the tenth grade. "I'm not a people person," she told me. "I didn't like all the little gossip circles that went on there."

Mindy had always been a good student, earning B's, but had slipped academically in junior high (as a disturbingly high number of American girls do). In the seventh and eighth grades, she became first a "hesher"—into heavy-metal music and smoking marijuana—and then a "hippie," into reggae and smoking marijuana. She also became sexually active. Her lovers were mostly older; some were much older. "I was kind of looking for a father," she told me.

Mindy's Nazi period had various sources. Spike Lee had helped get her into it, she said. She and a friend had gone to see "Malcolm X." They found they were the only whites in the audience, and a black guy had asked them sarcastically if they were in the right theatre. "That's why I hate Spike Lee," she told me. "Because he's a racist. And that's when I started thinking, If the black kids can wear 'X' caps, and Malcolm is calling us all 'white devils,' what's wrong with being down with white power?"

Her real political inspiration, though, was methamphetamine, which is also known as crank, crystal, ice, or simply speed. The leading illegal drug in the Valley, methamphetamine is a powerful addictive stimulant whose longtime consumers tend to suffer from paranoia, depression, hallucinations, and violent rages. The Nazi Low Riders were one of Mindy's speed connections. "They're all tweakers," she told me. (Tweakers are speed addicts.) "Speed is just so cheap here. And it makes you feel so powerful, so alert."

The N.L.R.s' hangout was the Malone household, in a run-down neighborhood in downtown Lancaster. Andrea Malone, a single parent, had three teenage boys, all white-supremacist skinheads, and she worked long hours, giving the kids the run of the house. Mindy, who had grown bored with Mormonism, became a regular there, snorting speed, smoking dope, and becoming fast friends with the N.L.R.s. They called her a "skin bitch," but she refused to shave her head. "My dad always said he loved my long blond hair, so I wouldn't cut it off," she told me. She and the other N.L.R. girls ("They called us Property of the N.L.R.s, not members. It's this weird thing") fought with girls from rival gangs, including Sharps. But Mindy claimed she'd never taken part in random attacks on black people—something the N.L.R.s specialized in. "I just used to sit in the car and watch, while they'd get out and be, like, 'Go back to Africa, nigger,' and beat people up."

At first, Mindy's mother had no idea what was going on. "I talked to Mrs. Malone on the phone a few times," Debbie told me. "She seemed really nice. I used to drive Mindy over there, and the Malone kids and some of the others used to come over here. I knew they were prejudiced, but as long as they acted civilized they were welcome. I even took them roller-skating."

The N.L.R.s were into tattoos: swastikas, skulls, Iron Crosses, lightning bolts—though lightning bolts were permitted to be worn only by those who had killed a black person. Mindy got a big swastika on one hip. ("My mom got really mad when she saw it.") Her skinhead friends were also into guns. In early 1995, one of her boyfriends, Jaxon Stines, drove with a group of N.L.R.s by the house of another boy whom Mindy had been seeing, and fired shots through a bedroom window, aiming for the other boy's bed. No one was hurt, but Mindy was picked up by the police for questioning, and Jaxon pleaded guilty to attempted murder.

Debbie was by then deeply alarmed about the company her daughter was keeping. Mindy was severely strung out—a full-tilt tweaker, with a daily habit. She had lost a lot of weight. She rarely slept. Finally, she became so dehydrated that she had to be hospitalized.

While she detoxed, with her mother keeping her skinhead friends away, Mindy seemed to snap out of her gang-girl trance. "I just realized I didn't hate black people," she told me. "Also, I'm totally infatuated with Alicia Silverstone, and she's Jewish. I've seen 'Clueless' like eleven times. So how could I be a Nazi?"

But the N.L.R.s did not take apostasy lightly. "They started calling my house, saying they were going to kick my ass. They started driving by here, throwing bottles at the house." Two N.L.R. girls, Heather Michaels and Angela Jackson, were particularly incensed. "Angela said she was coming over here to kill me. I was scared, but I told her, 'Fine, come over, whatever.' But she never came. Heather, especially, is really, really mad at me. They all say I'm a race traitor."

Debbie Turner took measures. She had an electronic security system installed around the house. "It got really bad after Jaxon went to jail," she told me. "They started coming by here. I was afraid they were going to shoot at the house. It was very scary." Debbie was also paying for a series of painful, expensive laser procedures to remove Mindy's swastika tattoo. The final cost for erasing the tattoo would come to four thousand dollars.

And that was how Debbie and I talked about Mindy's tour with the N.L.R.s during my first visits to the Turners' house—as a nasty accident whose scars were now being, not without cost, erased. Mindy was even back in school, through an independent-study program.

At the same time, we all knew that things were more complicated. For one thing, Jaxon had been released, after just six months in jail, and he and Mindy were seeing each other again. "Me and Jaxon have been through so much together," she told me. For example, a few weeks after her seventeenth birthday, she had had an abortion. "I wanted to keep it," Mindy said. "Because I knew that if Jaxon and I ever broke up I would still have some communication with him, because we would have a kid together. But then we decided we just weren't mentally ready for it. We fight all the time. And I was afraid that if we had a kid and Jaxon stayed friends with those people the kid would be brought up around all that hate."

Jaxon's gang status was actually ambiguous. He hung out with the N.L.R.s, and they considered him one of them, but he didn't publicly "claim" N.L.R. In any event, his association with the N.L.R.s extended no automatic protection to Mindy. She had therefore turned to the antiracist Sharps, her erstwhile enemies, for protection. The Sharps, however, were in no particular hurry to help her—leaving her in an even more vulnerable position.

She and Jaxon did indeed fight all the time, about almost anything. Raves, for example. Mindy indicated a poster on the wall in her bedroom, advertising something called the Insomniac Rave. "That was so great," she said. "It was the first real rave I went to. Dang! It was in Hollywood. Raves are like big parties, with all different races dancing. I took Ecstasy at the Insomniac Rave, and I danced all night." She sighed. "Jaxon can't stand it that I go to raves," she said. "He says I don't act white. But what is acting white? Me and him have been getting drunk almost every night lately, and I ask him, 'What do you think black people do that's so different from whites? They just sit around getting drunk and listening to music. Drive around in cars. Just like us.'"

Kicking around teen-age Lancaster, I sometimes felt as if I had fallen in with a thousand little cultural commissars, young suburban ideologues whose darkest pronouncement on another kid—a kid deviating from, say, the hard-core-punk-anarchist line on some band or arcane point of dress—was, inevitably, "He's confused."

Mindy's own "beliefs," as she called them, were eclectic. Her brave and principled rejection of racism, even her devotion to Alicia Silverstone, did not mean she had embraced enlightened liberalism in all matters. She still had a soft spot for Adolf Hitler—she claimed she was the only N.L.R. to actually study "Mein Kampf"—and her all-time-favorite "leader" was still Charles Manson. "My mom thinks I'm sick, but I think he's cute," she told me. "In a weird, gross way, I think he's attractive. He has the real fuck-you blood. He acts as his own lawyer. He talks for himself. I've read some of 'Helter Skelter.' I wouldn't, like, buy a poster of him and put it up. My mom wouldn't let me do it if I tried. But I don't think it would fit my room, anyway, with all my nice John Lennon and Beatles stuff."

The walls in Mindy's room were indeed adorned with Beatles posters. Her father, she said, had been a big John Lennon fan. But she also loved Trent Reznor, of Nine Inch Nails, whose best-known lyric was "I wanna fuck you like an animal!" I asked about a framed photograph, set next to her bed, of a shirtless, tattooed young man. The picture was obviously taken in prison.

"That's Madness," she said. "He's twenty-three. He says he's in love with me, but he knows I can't get over Jaxon. He's in for armed robbery. I didn't know him too well before he went to jail, but then we started writing letters. He's S.F.V. Peckerwood."

The Peckerwoods are a white gang, known mainly for mindless violence and methamphetamine dealing. They're big in the Antelope Valley but, some say, they're bigger in the San Fernando Valley, or S.F.V. They're biggest of all in prison. "Madness has his beliefs," Mindy said. "He believes whites are better than blacks. But he knows I don't think like that, so we don't talk about it."

Mindy was by no means the only girl I had met in the Valley who had a prisoner boyfriend. I asked her what it was about guys in jail.

"It's sick, I guess," she said. "But I just find it really attractive. I guess it means they're capable of doing something really spontaneous, without regard for the consequences."

"Like shooting somebody."

"Yeah. They're adventurous. And they're tough, usually. There's nothing else to do in there but work out."

Mindy invited me to go with her and some friends to a rave in Hollywood a few days later. "Maybe Darius can come, too," she said. Darius was Darius Houston, one of the Sharps to whom Mindy had turned for protection. Darius is half black, half white, and was probably the N.L.R.s' least favorite skinhead. "I don't think Darius really likes me," Mindy said. "Because when I hung out with the boneheads"—this is a generic term for racist skinheads—"I used to call him a nigger. All the Sharps have good reason to hate me."

I asked Mindy if she might be hoping to become a Sharp herself.

She shook her head, and said, "Most people here say, 'Mindy Turner? Oh, you mean Nazi Mindy.' So I don't want to start being Sharp Mindy. I want to be just Mindy. If somebody asks me what I am now, I just tell them I'm Free Unity. That's not a gang. It's just what I believe."

"Sharp" stands for "skinheads against racial prejudice." It is not, as I first thought, a local Antelope Valley sect. Skinheads claim Sharp throughout the United States, in Europe, and even, reportedly, in Japan. There is no formal organization—just an antiracist ideology, a street-fighting tradition, and a few widely recognized logos, usually worn on jacket patches. Sharp's raison d'être is its evil twin, the better-known white-supremacist and neo-Nazi skinhead movement.

All the Antelope Valley Sharps, I found, were amateur social historians, determined to rescue the skinhead movement—or simply "skinhead," as they call it—from disrepute. In their version, which seemed broadly accurate, the original skinheads emerged in England in the mid-sixties out of other youth cultures—notably the "hard mods" and the Rude Boys, stylish Jamaicans who wore porkpie hats and listened to reggae and ska. Skinheads were clean-cut, working-class, nonracist ("two-tone"), and tough. They loathed hippies, for reasons of both class and hygiene, loved soccer and beer, fighting and ska, scooters and Fred Perry tennis shirts. For a detailed history of skinhead, the Antelope Valley Sharps all urged on me a book, published in 1991, in Scotland, called "Spirit of '69: A Skinhead Bible."

By the seventies, the movement had been hijacked, according to the Sharps, by the anti-immigrant National Front in England. And it was the second wave of British skinhead that crossed over to the United States, in the late seventies, as part of the great punk-rock cultural exchange; by then neo-Nazism and white supremacism were definitely in the mix, and a host of unholy alliances have since been formed between racist skinheads and old-line extremist organizations like the Aryan Nations, White Aryan Resistance, the Church of the Creator, and the Ku Klux Klan. After a decade of hate crimes and racist violence, white-power skinheads have become increasingly familiar figures in the American social landscape, particularly among teen-agers, who tend to know much more about them and their apocalyptic views than adults do.

"The boneheads are looking forward to a race war."

"They're all on some harsh drug."

"Somebody's got to stand up to these guys," Darius Houston said.

Six or seven Sharps were sitting around Jacob Kroeger's mother's house. Jacob, a sardonic eighteen-year-old, still had his hair, but he was about to shave it off and become a full-fledged Sharp—a "fresh cut." His mother was often away with a boyfriend, leaving the house—a modest ranch-style bungalow in a seedy older tract—to become, at least for a while, the Sharps' main hangout. They were a picturesque lot, in boots and braces, extra-short ("flooded") jeans, and Andy Capp–type "snap caps." But the mood that evening was rather grim and besieged. It seemed that a girl from the N.L.R.s had called Christina Fava, Darius's girlfriend, who is white, a "nigger lover" in a hallway at Antelope Valley High School. A black student named Todd Jordan had become involved on Christina's side, and the next day a half-dozen N.L.R.s had jumped Todd on a deserted athletic field, stabbing him five times with a screwdriver. Todd was now in the hospital. Christina, for her part, was transferring to a new school.

Somehow, I said, being a Sharp seemed to mean, more than anything else, a lot of fighting with white-power skinheads.

I was wrong, I was assured.

"It's the music, the fashions, the friendships, the whole life style."

"It's like a big fuckin' family."

"Everybody's got everybody else's back."

"It's all about working class."

This curious, almost un-American class consciousness among the Antelope Valley Sharps turned out, upon examination, to be a very American miscellany. The kids themselves came from a wide range of backgrounds—everything from two-parent middle-class families to drug-addled welfare mothers who had dumped them on the streets as adolescents. For some, "working class" meant simply having a job—any job—as opposed to being a "bum." For others, it was synonymous with "blue collar," and it distinguished them from richer kids, who might decide to be skinheads and buy all the gear but weren't really streetwise and so might just have to be relieved of their new twelve-hole Doc Martens.

There was, in fact, much more to the Sharps than rumbling with the boneheads. For Darius, in particular, Sharp was a godsend. An orphan since his mother died, when he was thirteen, he had been a skateboarder and punk rocker before discovering skinhead. As a half-black kid in a largely white town, being reared by various white relatives, he had always been something of an outsider. Skinhead, as he understood it, was a complete, ready-made aesthetic and way of life. Darius identified, he told me, with its underground energy and its music—he was soon playing bass in a multiracial ska band called the Leisures. Because the idea of a black skinhead drove neo-Nazi skinheads wild, Darius had been fighting on a regular basis for years. He was a skilled fighter, but the backup that the other Sharps provided was still, for Darius, a lifesaver. Going to school had become too dangerous, so he was on independent study. After graduating, he said, he planned to join the Navy and become a medical technician. (Christina, for one, didn't think he was serious.) He was eighteen, beefy, soft-spoken, watchful, with skin the color of light mahogany. When we met, he was homeless and was sleeping on a couch in Jacob's mother's house.

In every gang, the crucial question about any member is "How down is he?" Among the Sharps, one of the most indisputably down was Johnny Suttle. Twenty years old, half Mexican and half Anglo, he was diminutive but super-aggressive. He worked graveyard shifts at a Taco Bell, took classes at the local community college, and, I found, had a great deal to say about skinhead. Skinhead was about loyalty—to your class, home town, soccer team, and nationality, according to Johnny. Thus, if a Japanese or a Chinese skinhead decided to beat up a foreigner, it was O.K. "Because they're just defending their country, and that's good," he said. "The thing is, America is not a white man's country, never mind what the boneheads say. It's a melting pot. And we're about defending that."

Johnny always seemed ready to weigh the moral dimensions of violence. I once heard him deliberate one of the timeless questions: Was it ethically permissible to drop bonehead chicks before taking on the boneheads? The answer, ultimately, was yes. While it was not right to hit females, bonehead chicks were simply too dangerous to leave standing while you fought their boyfriends. They would probably stick a knife in your back. Ergo, they had to be dropped at the outset. Q.E.D.

The Nazi Low Riders, while dedicated skinheads, were not skinhead-history buffs. They were, however, keen on Nazi history. "We believe in Hitler's ways," Tim Malone, a leading member, told me. "But that don't mean we worship him. He was smart, but he was a homosexual. I think what he did with the Jews was right, mainly. They was coming into Germany, buying up the businesses, treating the Germans like slaves."

Chris Runge, another N.L.R., who explained to me that Hitler had actually been working with the Vatican, seemed to be the theorist of the Lancaster clique. He was nineteen, hairless, blue-eyed, pale-skinned, with a worried seriousness that was occasionally interrupted by a big, goofy smile. "I'm basically what you call a political Nazi," he said. "A lot of these Nazis out here are unorganized. They're mostly street skins, doing the dirty work. I want to start getting them organized. Democracy doesn't work. As you can see right now, it's falling apart. But Nazism is about a society with no upper class, no lower class. We'd have equality. We wouldn't have homelessness—because we keep the factories going and everybody has a place. With a Nazi government, we'd just take out all the unwanted and start over again—even whites, if they're doing the same thing as the niggers are." Chris gave me one of his big, blue-eyed smiles.

He grew serious again. "White supremacism just comes from seeing what's happening in society," he said. "We're going down." Though Chris's mother was, by all accounts, a serious tweaker, his grandfather, he said, was an executive with the Xerox Corporation—a point of reference, perhaps, for his bitter assessment. Chris himself had dropped out of school in the tenth grade and had been convicted for participating in the same drive-by shooting that sent Jaxon Stines, who was his best friend, to jail. And Chris had "found the Lord" in his cell, he said—an experience that may have softened some of his judgments. Of Mindy, for instance, Chris merely said, "She's confused. She's young." This was notably gentler than the pronouncements of other N.L.R.s on the subject. Chris even showed some self-awareness when he talked about his life. He told me that his mother's ex-husband used to beat her so badly when he was drunk that she would come lie in bed with Chris in the hope that it would make him stop. It didn't. "And that's a lot of the hate I got inside me now," Chris said quietly.

Though I stopped by the Malones' house many times, I never saw Andrea there. She worked in a plastics factory in Pasadena, more than an hour's drive away, and, according to Tim, she left the house at dawn and got home only late in the evening. When I first met Tim, who was seventeen, he had just spent two months in jail: he had been locked up as an accessory in the Todd Jordan stabbing, but had been released for lack of evidence. He was wiry and well built, with close-cropped dark hair and, tattooed on the back of his neck, an Iron Cross. He described himself as "more of the Gestapo Storm Trooper type than a political Nazi—the type that's ready to go to war over things. There's gonna be a race war around the year 2000."

Tim's father had been a Hell's Angel, he said, so, he told me, his Nazism "was kind of inherited." His dad drank, did speed, and abused his mother—that was why his parents broke up. The family had lived in a predominantly black neighborhood in Montclair, east of Los Angeles, where Tim, at the age of ten, joined a local Crips set for self-protection. He was the middle brother of three, and his joining a black gang did not please his brothers. "Both my brothers was punk rockers, into speed metal, and they used to beat me up, trying to teach me a lesson," he said. "I thank them for it now. You gotta stick with your own race. Now ain't nothing I hate more than a wigger"—white nigger.

Tim and his brothers, Jeff and Steve, became skinheads after moving to the Antelope Valley four years ago and meeting the local neo-Nazis. They were soon a warm little nest of vipers. "We're all family," Tim said. "Even the little kids. Trouble's son, who's only, like, nine months old, already knows how to *Sieg heil.*" Tim imitated an infant giving a Nazi salute, and laughed. (Trouble was the street name of Robert Jones, one of three N.L.R.s charged with firing into a parked car full of black people in Lancaster in 1995. He was recently sentenced to twelve years.)

Among the many kids who were usually around the Malones' house were some who could not have been more than ten. I wondered if their parents had any notion what kinds of things their children were seeing and hearing there. The attractions of the place as a hangout were not mysterious. It was like a child's idea of a pirates' den: scruffy and run by tattooed brigands. I even got the feeling sometimes that a rough, retrograde, neo-communal sort of social experiment was being conducted. A boy would be opening a can of beans to heat up on the stove. Someone would bellow, "Only bitches cook in this house!" The boy would drop the can, while onlookers guffawed. Angela Jackson, one of Mindy' tormentors, would tear herself away from the TV and finish opening the can, declaring herself "a skin bitch, a Featherwood." This giddy, Pleasure Island atmosphere darkened, I thought, after the feud with the Sharps produced its first dead youth.

Darius said he would gladly go to the rave with us, and Mindy seemed pleased. There was some question about whether Mindy herself would be able to go to the rave, however, because her mother had grounded her after finding her passed out, stark naked, on her bed with her head next to a bowl filled with vomit. Too much vodka with Jaxon, Mindy told me. It was now two days later, and still several days before the rave—which we ended up skipping in any case, after Jaxon accused Mindy of really wanting to go to Hollywood to "fuck niggers."

We were now waiting for Jaxon to come over, so that he and I could talk, and Mindy still seemed to be feeling hung over. "I hate light," she said. Her voice was flat and small. "My mom thinks I'm a vampire because I sit in my room with the music on and no lights. I won't even take acid if the sun's out."

Mindy loved LSD. She also liked cocaine. "Because it makes your mouth numb. I like to be numb. Speed lasts longer, but it makes you paranoid, so you end up doing stupid things."

The stupid things she'd done on speed seemed to be legion. "Like, once Heather and Angela and I were tweaking, and we saw two girls holding hands and we were really grossed out. We just said, 'We're going to show them that's not allowed.' We didn't have any weapons, but we really stomped them. One girl had to go to the hospital."

I remarked that I had recently read in a newspaper that "young men use methamphetamine for sexual stimulation." Mindy scoffed: "When Jaxon's tweaking, I could dance naked in front of him with a porno on the TV, and he still wouldn't be interested."

She went outside for a cigarette. Her mother didn't allow smoking in the house. I joined her in the back yard, which had a small swimming pool and a basketball hoop. From where we sat, we could see Mindy's thirteen-year-old brother, Matthew, in the kitchen. "Matthew's one of the reasons I quit the Nazis," Mindy said, her voice suddenly full of feeling. "He's going to play basketball and football in high school, and he's going to have to be able to get along with black people. And it won't work if he gets into something disgusting like I did."

I noticed, not for the first time, a clacking coming from inside Mindy's mouth. I asked about it. She stuck out her tongue. It was pierced with a heavy silver stud. "I've had this for a long time," she said.

She also had a ring through her navel, above which she had her name tattooed in longhand. Her mother absolutely couldn't understand that tattoo. "I mean, your own name? Why?" Debbie asked me. "Is it so that some guy can look down there while you're doing it in case he forgets your name?"

I once asked Mindy what she wanted to be when she grew up.

"Exotic dancer."

Debbie, I felt certain, was unaware of this ambition. She also didn't know that Mindy was not going to school. Her independent-study program required her presence only one hour a week, but I knew she had quietly abandoned it.

"Where is he?"

It looked as if Jaxon might not show, but at last he whipped into the driveway. Mindy jumped up, sat down, jumped up again. Jaxon came into the yard through the chain-link gate, a lean, wary-looking figure in a white T-shirt. He nodded at me, glanced at Mindy.

"We're going camping," he said.

"Can I go?" Mindy asked.

Jaxon didn't reply. He and I went inside and sat at the dining-room table. Mindy followed us in. "Where are you going?" she asked.

"Cottonwood."

"Can I go?"

Again, Jaxon didn't reply. He was a pale, good-looking kid with deep-set eyes and a large, unfortunate silver ring through his nose. ("I hate it. It makes him look like a bull," Mindy said.) His head was shaved except for a small, wispy patch on top. Mindy watched him miserably while we talked.

He had recently turned eighteen, he said. He had been kicked out of school in the ninth grade for fighting and truancy, and since then he had bounced around, living here and there, including a stint with his father, an unsuccessful rock musician who drove a school bus in Northern California. "I've hitchhiked all up and down California," Jaxon told me. "Every place is just as boring as this is." He had a studied jadedness, a cool anger in his eyes. He was plainly intelligent. He had got his high-school diploma by passing an equivalency exam at the age of fifteen. Since getting out of jail, he had been living with his mother and stepfather in Palmdale and working as a repair-line operator for the phone company, where his mother was a computer technician.

Mindy interrupted, pleading and petulant: "Can I go camping with you?"

Jaxon ignored her.

"Have you got sleeping bags?" I asked Jaxon.

"I've only got a mummy bag."

Mindy scurried down the hall in search of camping equipment.

Jaxon's parents divorced when he was three, he said. "My brother was the good little preppie. He never got caught for anything. I was the bad one. I shaved my head when I was, like, nine. They were sending me to shrinks from the fourth grade."

Surprisingly, considering that he had long been warring with the Sharps as part of the N.L.R. cohort, Jaxon said he esteemed Darius's beliefs. "Darius has the right idea," he told me. "We've talked. In fact, he used to be vegetarian straight-edge. That's no drugs, no drinking, no sex—nothing. Not too many people can follow that."

But Jaxon's sympathies were decidedly with the racist side of the skinhead schism. "I'm not, like, Mr. Nazi. And I know some black and Mexican people who are cool. But the majority of them are just welfare-mooching scumballs. I don't want to hear your sob story about how my great-great-grandfather owned your great-great-grandfather." Jaxon's sneer deepened until it severely distorted his face.

He went on, more calmly, "Whether I like it or not, I'm racist. My mom doesn't agree with me. She's not prejudiced. But I like to consider myself less ignorant than most racists. They're all preparing for race war, race war. But it's never going to happen." He shrugged. "I'm just proud of what I am. But being proud of being white doesn't mean I'm proud of every piece of white trash out there snorting speed."

Mindy reappeared, lugging an armful of gear for the camping trip, including an old, square-bottomed sleeping bag, which she displayed proudly. "Where is Cottonwood?" she asked.

Jaxon was right: his mother didn't agree with him. A political liberal with a degree in anthropology, she lived with her second husband and her two sons in a big cathedral-ceilinged house in a gated community. "I don't know why Jaxon holds those racial views," she told me, "I keep hoping it's just a teen-age rebellion, and he'll grow out of it—that it's not how he *is*." Other parents I visited in the Antelope Valley seemed equally mystified by their kids' passionate "beliefs."

Schools failed to provide most parents and children with any common cultural ground. Sheldon Epstein, a high-school principal in Lancaster, who had a cheerleader daughter, told me. "My wife and I are big-time supporters of our daughter's school. But most of the kids are just not bonded with their schools, so for them that school-spirit piece is missing. It's the parents who have school spirit now, not the kids."

The fact was, however, that among the tens of thousands of parents who worked over the mountains, relatively few had the time or energy to involve themselves in their children's schools (or any other community activity). And then there were all those too consumed by their own troubles even to rear their children. I found, that is, a startling number of kids in the Valley being reared not by their parents but by their grandparents. Various explanations were offered for this phenomenon, the commonest being methamphetamine addiction among parents, and particularly mothers. The situation was starkly reminiscent of the better-known syndrome that has left so many African-American grandmothers rearing the children of their crack-addled daughters in the nation's inner cities. In the Antelope Valley, it was white families falling into poverty who were being hit hardest by speed.

Between 1970 and 1995, the poverty rate for children and adolescents in California more than doubled—it is now twenty-eight per cent. And just as crime rates tend to track closely with poverty rates, vast amounts of the state's public spending have been diverted during this period to law enforcement and the penal system. The California prison budget in 1975 was two hundred million dollars. By the year 2000, it will approach five billion dollars. The money for all these jails and prisons has come more or less directly out of the state's higher-education budget. When I graduated from high school, in 1970, California had what was often described as the finest public-university system in the world. That was then. Between 1991 and 1994, the state's higher-education system lost two thousand professors and two hundred thousand students to budget cuts. Meanwhile, University of California tuition in 1995 was, in constant dollars, nearly five times what it was thirty years before. The situation in the schools is no better. When I was in junior high, the state's public schools enjoyed the seventh-highest per-pupil spending in the country; by 1995, California's per-pupil spending ranked forty-seventh nationally.

Nancy Kelso, a middle-aged lawyer in Palmdale who has many juvenile clients, rejects the view, which she says is common among her peers and colleagues, that they grew up in a Golden Age, when children obeyed their parents and ordinary people felt safe and God was in his Heaven. "I remember the Red Scare," she told me. "I remember suffocating pressure to conform. I remember a lot of bad things." She also remembers, however, a radically different opportunity structure. "When I graduated from high school, in 1962, it was like a deal—a contract—between the adults and me," she said. "All I had to do was get a B average and halfway behave myself and I was guaranteed a free education at a top public university, like Berkeley. My four siblings and I all took advantage of it. Our dad was a five-dollar-an-hour nonunion machinist in Los Angeles. We all became productive, responsible citizens. I tell you, I would have a lot more anxiety about what was going to become of me if I were growing up now."

In 1996, Palmdale High School, out of a graduating class of about four hundred, sent exactly six students into the University of California system. Less than ten per cent of the class went on to any four-year college at all.

Listening to Nancy Kelso, I kept thinking of Chris Runge grumbling about "the unwanted." He and his friends look forward to a "Nazi government" whisking this surplus population from sight. Of course, he and his friends undoubtedly feel that they themselves are the real "unwanted." And they are not wrong. But one of the ironies of their predicament is that the withdrawal of resources from education and other social services is fundamentally racist—that is, it is primarily a withdrawal by older whites from the support of those aspects of public welfare, including public education, which seem to benefit a large number of nonwhites. And yet the collapse of educational opportunity caused by this withdrawal is suffered by all nonaffluent children and families. "Affirmative action" is merely the name that many whites give to their sense of disfranchisement.

Issues of race and opportunity are particularly loaded in the Antelope Valley. Esther Gillies, the director of a center for abused children in Lancaster, put it bluntly: "Black families who move to the Valley are often moving up. White families who move to the Valley couldn't make it down below." While I heard many whites complain about lower-class blacks and Latinos settling in the Valley, I often sensed that they were really more concerned about middle-class minority families. Todd Jordan's family lived in a grander house than any of the white-power kids who stabbed him did. I talked with black parents who pronounced themselves delighted with their new, racially integrated neighborhoods (the Valley has developed so fast that the insidious patterns of residential segregation have not taken root), but even they expressed wariness about staying on once their children reach high-school age. In the words of one well-educated black mother of three, "That's when the white-supremacist thing seems to kick in."

I did meet white kids in the Antelope Valley who were college-bound. Natalie Blacker, for instance, was the editor of the school newspaper at Quartz Hill High. Natalie was one of Mindy's idols—"I'm totally in love with her" was how Mindy put it—and was friendly with the Sharps. A feminist, Natalie had started a consciousness-raising group for girls at her school. (*Her* idol was Naomi Wolf.) She nagged her friends not to let their boyfriends treat them badly—Jaxon's cavalier treatment of Mindy was, she told me, a great example of what girls should not put up with—but she cheerfully acknowledged the depth and staying power of the sexism and racism she opposed. She was shocked, she told me, when Mindy fell in with the boneheads, and delighted when Mindy renounced them. "But you really have to be strong to do that, to stay neutral here," she added. "This is a place where everybody feels the need to be in a clique."

An ambitious effort to get teen-agers to channel this need to belong into their school lives was under way at Lancaster High, which opened in the fall of 1995. Students wore uniforms; teachers wore red, white, and blue. The curriculum was demanding and old-fashioned—"fifties style," according to Beverley Louw, the school's dynamic first principal. "Our hope is that we can create the culture, and that way not lose our students to the kinds of fragmented subcultures—the heshers, the skinheads, and so on—that you find kids joining elsewhere."

But after six months at the helm of Lancaster High Ms. Louw already sounded pessimistic. She had too many students whom she couldn't help, she said—kids who arrived at school with too many deficits. Besides that, the Sharps and the neo-Nazis were already fighting at her school.

Antelope Valley officials tend to say that white-supremacist skinheads are less of a problem than they seem. The police say the boneheads are dwarfed in number by the black and Latino gangs who have moved up from Los Angeles. The most obvious gang tension in the Valley, though, was not between the Bloods and the Crips but between the Sharps and the neo-Nazis. If you went to Brunswick Sands Bowl, a bowling alley on the Sierra Highway, in Lancaster, the jacket that caught your eye, worn by a spike-haired teen-age punk, would be the one with a huge patch on the back snarling "NAZI PUNKS FUCK OFF." Or if you went to the only real teen hangout in Lancaster, a coffeehouse called Hang 'n Java, which had a pool table, music, and an Internet connection, you could find a tense conference taking place at the counter between the owner and a group of Sharps. When I went, I found her throwing them out. She supported them, she maintained, but she could not risk their business, because if the boneheads saw them in there they'd come back at night and shoot out her windows. "And I can't pay the insurance," she said tightly.

The police may not have wanted to acknowledge the dimensions of the problem, but for Darius Houston white-supremacist violence seemed inescapable. I once asked him what it felt like to be the target of so much bonehead ire.

Darius looked embarrassed. "Even white powers are people, so you have to respect them," he said. Then he added, "Unless they don't respect me. Which they don't." He shrugged. "Most skinheads fight. It comes with the book. It comes to you."

Once, at a rock concert I attended with the Sharps, I saw just how much of it tended to come to Darius. It was an oi show in San Bernardino. Oi music is a hard form of punk rock, and it appeals to the whole range of skinheads. The headliners at the San Bernardino show were a cult band from Britain called The Business. The Antelope Valley Sharps were deeply thrilled to be seeing them, and when we got to the concert, which was held in an old wrestling arena near the San Bernardino railroad tracks, there were several hundred skinheads inside, most of them white but many of them Latino or Asian. Cliques milled around, exchanging elaborate tribal greetings with other cliques and having their pictures taken together. All was mellow, all was unity, I was assured. No boneheads had come. A couple of punk bands played, and there was some moderate thrashing in the pit, so I retreated to one of the wooden bleachers that rose on three sides of the arena. And that's where I was, looking down on the crowd, when the Orange County Skins arrived. They were in uniform and in formation. Their uniform consisted of black combat boots, white trousers, and the white tank tops known as "wife beaters." Their formation was a sort of flying wedge, which knocked people aside with swift, efficient violence as they swept toward the middle of the pit. There were no more than thirty of them, but their paramilitary coördination overwhelmed each bit of startled resistance. They easily seized the center of the arena, turned to the stunned crowd, and raised their arms in Nazi salutes, bellowing, "White power! White power!"

There was a lengthy pause, during which everyone seemed to consider the boots of the invaders. Whoever approached them first was certain to get his teeth kicked in. Then the crowd rushed the boneheads, and a bloody melee began. It seemed to be all boots and fists. Security at the door had been very tight—a guard had even taken away my pens, tartly demonstrating how someone could jab out my eyes with one of them—so the possibilities for injury presumably had some limits. I caught glimpses of Sharps I knew, flailing away—particularly Darius, who is tall and, as a black skin, seemed to be the focus of a great deal of Nazi fury. But Darius stayed on his feet, blessedly, and seemed to have plenty of help as he spun and kicked and punched. The Nazis were badly outnumbered but preternaturally fierce.

Then I saw Darius running toward the rear bleachers, where I was perched. He was holding one eye—pawing at it frantically—and zigzagging blindly through the crowd. I had a horrible premonition that he had been stabbed in the eye. I ran down the bleachers to meet him, and tripped and twisted my ankle. A security guard had to help us both stagger out through a back door into the rain. Darius, still pawing at his eye, threw himself face first into a puddle. He splashed water into his eye. "Somebody Maced me," he shouted. I felt a rush of relief. Darius rose up, blinking, gasping. "It's O.K.," he said. "It's O.K. I can see." The door behind us flew open, and another casualty came reeling out. Darius sprang to the door, caught it, and, without another word, was gone—back into the roaring fray.

"What the Orange County Skins did at that oi show?" Mindy said. Her tone was petulant, scornful. We were sitting in her room. "These boneheads out here could never think of that. They're just into speed. The original Nazis did no drugs, didn't smoke pot, drink beer—anything. They just trained for war, twenty-four seven. These guys out here have no right to call themselves Nazis. That's why I don't like them."

This, I thought, was new. Mindy had previously disliked the N.L.R.s for a lot of reasons, but not because they failed to emulate Hitler's men properly. And, for the record, many of Hitler's élite troops were in fact tweakers. But Mindy was upset. It seemed she had been jilted by Jaxon for a younger girl, named Casey.

"O.K., I'm not fifteen and six feet tall with two pierced nipples!" she wailed. Casey was apparently all these things. "O.K., I'm immature and selfish! I was spoiled when I was young. But he is so selfish, so conceited, so immature, so arrogant!"

I didn't argue.

"Plus, he won't give me my baby blanket back. My dad gave it to me. It's my security blanket. I'm all 'Give me my blanket.' He's all 'Give me my CD.'"

"I would have gone to jail for Jaxon," she went on bitterly. "For that drive-by. They didn't have anything on me. I had an alibi. But I would have gone."

Debbie was just coming in from work. "You tell him about how you're going back to school or I'm going to send you to live with Grandma?" Debbie asked. She had discovered that Mindy was skipping her independent-study appointments and had grounded her. Mindy carried off the groceries that Debbie had brought home. "My mother still lives in Canyon Country," Debbie told me. Canyon Country, a set of suburbs slightly closer to L.A., was where the Turners lived before they moved to the Antelope Valley. "It's better for kids, I think. Mindy would probably never have got into all this bad stuff there."

"The Antelope Valley sucks!" Mindy called from the kitchen. Debbie and Mindy had been having problems over Debbie's boyfriend, Tom, who, over Mindy's objections, had briefly moved into the Turner household.

Mindy took me to meet her grandparents one evening, in their spotless, triple-wide trailer in Canyon Country. While Mindy darted in and out of the living room, playing on her grandfather's computer—in this house she seemed suddenly about ten years younger, as if she had magically regressed to a calmer, more constrained, less sexualized, less bored self—I talked to Pearl, her grandmother, who was originally from Nebraska. She was decorous and candid as she described her concerns about Mindy's future. Pearl, who used to be a bookkeeper, now does fancy cake decorating and has been married to Jerry, her third husband, for twenty-one years. When he came in, he kissed Mindy and told her the computer she was playing on was going to be hers. He was getting a new one, and all kids needed a computer at home nowadays.

Looking after her as she skipped back to her new toy, he said, "Mindy is probably the biggest frustration I have in my life now. I feel bad that I haven't been more of an influence on her." He told me, in strong language, his feelings about Jaxon and his racist beliefs; I could see how he would have made a very strict guardian. I tried to picture Mindy living with her grandparents, but could picture only a great clash and meltdown.

"The problem is, society requires both parents to work," Pearl said. "Single parents also have to work. So kids are left to raise themselves. That's why they have no respect, no discipline. There's no one to teach them how to care, how to love, how to live. So they form these groups, and, right or wrong, those are their families."

Various Sharps and N.L.R.s had told me the same thing, of course. But it was sadder to hear it from a consummate grandmother in her big, clean, cozy mobile home.

A willowy ice-blond sixteen-year-old girl named Ronda Hardin, who was loosely associated with the Nazi Low Riders, once unnerved me by talking, in a breathy, high, almost reverential voice, about "my hatred." She smiled faintly when she said it, and yet the frame around everything she said, I thought, was a sense of loss—loss of a marginal color-caste privilege that, in her mind, was supposed to keep black people beneath her socially and, in that way, somehow prevent the worst from happening to her. Because she lacked that reassurance, her beloved hatred seemed to be a main prop of her self-respect.

On the night of March 9, 1996, Ronda was in a little brown tract house on East Avenue J-4 in Lancaster. I've heard at least two dozen versions of what happened that night, but a few facts are undisputed. The Sharps were having a party. There were roughly fifty kids there, most of them white, not all of them antiracists. A keg of beer was flowing. Darius, who was drunk, got into a dispute in the kitchen with Ronda, who was wearing a bomber jacket with a Confederate-flag patch on one sleeve. The dispute may have been over the patch. Darius may have choked Ronda. In any case, Ronda fled. After another boy tried to defend her and got beaten up by the Sharps, Ronda, who had gone to the Malones' house and told the N.L.R.s what happened, went back to the party with Tim and Jeff Malone.

The boys went inside. Ronda remained in the car. A confrontation took place almost immediately, not far from the front door. Jeff Malone, a quiet nineteen-year-old whose gang name was Demon, waved a knife at a girl who approached him. She later said she had been trying to warn him to leave. Darius, standing in a knot of his friends, threw a cup of beer at Tim Malone. One of the Malones challenged Darius. The N.L.R.s were standing in close formation, their backs against a living-room wall. Darius ran toward them, a knife in his right hand. With his first thrust, he stabbed Jeff Malone through the heart. Jeff fell. His friends dragged him out the door.

Ronda ran to a neighbor's to phone the police. Jeff's friends drove him to the hospital. On the way, they tried to stop the bleeding. Tim was slapping his brother hard in the face, shouting, "Breathe! Breathe!" To the driver, he yelled, "Run this light! Go! Go!" It was only a few minutes' drive to Antelope Valley Hospital. By the time they got there, Jeff's body was cold. They carried him inside. He was pronounced dead an hour later.

"Homeboy deserved it," Johnny Suttle, the Sharps' ethicist, said. "He shouldn't have come to that party. He wasn't invited."

Johnny himself wasn't at the party. He was at Taco Bell, working. But he heard about the stabbing soon after it happened, and he helped direct the Sharps' flurry of subsequent moves. A group of Sharps had bundled Darius away. They drove first to a cemetery behind Antelope Valley High, and there they all spat on the bloody knife and buried it under a bush. Next, they went to a park and cleaned up Darius, whose clothes and arms were covered with blood. Then, unaware that Jeff was dead, they dispersed for the night.

But the news was soon flying around town. Jacob Kroeger, the fresh-cut Sharp, was lying in bed a couple of hours later when he got a phone call. He jumped up and woke his mother, brother, and sister. Within minutes, they had packed their bags and moved to his grandmother's house. Some of Darius's relatives were also on the move before daybreak. N.L.R. death threats were already in the air.

Johnny called the police in the morning, and he liked what he heard. The police had interviewed a number of witnesses, and to them the killing sounded like self-defense. Johnny, who knew where Darius was hiding, agreed to bring him in for questioning. He did so, and Darius was questioned but not arrested. Darius then went deeper into hiding, with some relatives in Orange County.

The killing became a crossroads of sorts for the Sharps. Johnny took a hard line. "We gotta get more aggressive now," he told me. "You always gotta show the boneheads you're crazier than they are. That's the only way they won't fuck with you. If you punk it and run, you're finished."

Jacob, on the other hand, decided to let his hair grow out—"to hang up my boots and braces," as he put it. When I asked him why, he looked nonplussed. "Why? Death, that's why," he said. "This is just not a win-win situation." His friends understood, he said. He would still back them up. He just wouldn't claim skinhead. Like many Sharps (and ex-Sharps), Jacob was angry at Darius. "Why did he do it? He had no right to play God, to take another man's life. And now we all have to lie low. We can't go out and get drunk, like we used to. We just have to stay in our houses and watch for boneheads."

Jacob's house was actually empty. As the Sharps' old hangout, it was now too dangerous to live in. In fact, less than a week after the killing Jacob's entire family moved to Utah, where his mother's boyfriend had relatives.

The Sharps as a group seemed intent on putting Jeff Malone's death behind them as fast as possible. They joked about "that killer party," and soon began referring glibly to "the time Darius shanked that fool."

Natalie Blacker, the college-bound feminist whom Mindy admired, had been at the fateful party, talking to Darius, just before the trouble started. "It's so terrible," she told me. "Darius has so much potential." She had mixed feelings about her friend Christina's reaction to the tragedy. Christina, who, as Darius's girlfriend, was now in real peril, had chosen not to lie low. She still went to school, still worked in a shop on Lancaster's main drag. She talked to Darius on the phone regularly, and drove down to see him every chance she got. "I mean, it's great that she's so loyal," Natalie said. "But girls around here can be too loyal. Sometimes it's like Christina doesn't realize that he killed someone."

Mindy realized it, and she was devastated. We were sitting in the Hang 'n Java coffeehouse, in Lancaster, a week after the killing, and she could not seem to take her eyes off the floor. "I keep thinking about this one time with Jeff," she said. Her voice was low and dull. "It wasn't that long ago. We were at a party, and he was on a trampoline, just jumping up and down, and he was so happy. We went back to my house, and he was hungry, and all I could find was a can of pork and beans. He wouldn't even let me heat it up for him. He just ate it cold. I can't get that out of my mind."

The Malones were about to bury Jeff, but Mindy was not invited to the funeral. "They should think about what Jeff would want," she said. "Jeff would want me there. But I'm not a Nazi, so I'm not welcome." She sighed. "I think I'll go buy this Danzig CD Jeff liked and listen to it while they're having the funeral. One of his favorite songs is on there. He sang it to me one time when we were lying on his bed. I had such a crush on him. He always had a crush on me, too. I remember one night lying on the roof of his house, just rubbing Jeff's head until we both passed out."

Tears were trickling down Mindy's cheeks. We sat and sipped coffee in silence for a couple of minutes.

"The N.L.R.s will never forgive me for saying Darius was fine," Mindy said suddenly. "It was true, though—he really was good-looking. But I've lost all respect for him now. If I saw him, I wouldn't even talk to him. I would just give him a dirty look."

After a few minutes' reflection, she went on, "I don't want to go back to being a bonehead. I don't want to have a label on me. But Tim says I already have one. He says I'm a 'gang-hopper.'"

It was news to me that Mindy was talking to Tim Malone. As it happened, Tim had just told me that the N.L.R.s were on strict orders to do nothing. The police were watching them, he said, expecting them to retaliate against the Sharps. This ceasefire might mean that Mindy herself was safe, at least temporarily, I thought—a hopeful possibility that I mentioned to her. She thought about it but seemed uncomforted.

Two burly young men had come into the coffeehouse and were standing behind Mindy. Both wore baseball caps, and both had goatees. I watched them idly, wondering if they were boneheads. Then, as they began to walk past us, one of them turned and gave me a startling look right in the face. It was a practiced, frightening, prison-yard challenge. I had never seen the guy before, but I now had no doubt that he was a neo-Nazi. He kept walking. The skin on the back of my neck was crawling. I was so distracted that I suggested we leave, and we did. Mindy, who hadn't noticed a thing, said she wanted to go home and finish a poem she had been working on for Mrs. Malone.

When I asked Tim Malone how his mother was taking Jeff's death, he said, "Like she should. Hard and dry."

That wasn't true, I found, when I talked to her. Mrs. Malone was tearful and despondent, and was wishing aloud that she had never moved her family to the Antelope Valley. "I wanted to get Tim away from the gangs in Montclair," she said. "But there are bad influences here, too, and my boys have gotten under their wing, and I'm hardly ever home to protect them." She knew almost no one in the Valley, she said, and added, "But I've met more people in the last few days—people just calling up to offer condolences—than I'd met in the three years before this happened."

Even Heather Michaels, one of the fiercest N.L.R.s, wasn't "hard and dry" when we spoke. "They didn't want no trouble," she said, meaning, improbably, the N.L.R.s who had rushed to the party that night. "If they wanted trouble, they would've taken guns. They thought there was just five or ten Sharps there. Then they get there, turns out it's like fifty or a hundred Sharps." Heather's eyes welled at the thought. "If one of us had killed this nigger, or even stabbed him, we'd all be locked up."

Tim Malone said the same thing, calling the police treatment of Darius "reverse discrimination." He and Chris Runge and I were standing in the Malones' front yard. It was a sunny afternoon. Both of them were bare-chested and wore boots and jeans.

"Vengeance is mine, saith the Lord, and tenfold," Chris intoned. "Darius will get a lot worse than what Jeff got."

"That's right, brother," Tim said. To me, he said, "You know, we didn't expect Darius to be there. Because he usually runs if he thinks we might be coming."

I asked what had happened.

"We saw him in there, standing with his friends, and when he saw us he started bouncing up and down." Tim demonstrated. I had seen Darius do that fighter's bounce, during the melee at the oi show in San Bernardino. "Then somebody offered me a beer, and when

I went to take it Darius threw a cup of beer at me. I caught it, threw it down, and called him on." Tim demonstrated his quick reactions, his forceful challenge. "'Come on, nigger, let's go! Right now!' Then I spit in his face."

Nobody else had remembered the scene this way.

"Then four guys rushed me, and Darius came in behind them, low, and reached around me and stuck Jeff. I saw it go in. It was a pocketknife, with a black handle. Jeff didn't even know he'd been stuck. Then he looked down at his shirt and saw it. He went, 'Fuck you, nigger!'" Tim imitated Jeff crouching, both middle fingers raised before him like guns. Again, nobody else remembered anything like this. "We dragged him to the car, and we beat the shit out of him on the way to the hospital. 'Wake the fuck up!' But he died before we got there."

We stood and watched the traffic pass. I asked if Jeff had said anything in the car. "No," Tim said. "But I know what he would have said: 'Get that nigger!'"

Tim and Chris looked at each other, their shaved heads slowly nodding.

I found Darius somewhere in the suburban wilderness of Orange County. We met at a Taco Bell. Christina and a Palmdale skinhead named Juan were also there. Juan had been in the group that spirited Darius away from the party after the killing. Darius looked much the same—a little warier, less abashed, slightly exhilarated. We had talked on the phone a few days before, and I had asked how he felt. "I'm going to be more mellow," he had said. "I was sick the first couple of days. I haven't felt that feeling since my parents died. Some people probably get off on it, and some people don't like it. I don't like it. It's weird. You've taken somebody's life, and they're never coming back on this earth. At the same time, you feel happy, because he was, like, your enemy."

I ran Tim Malone's version of the killing past Darius and Juan. When I got to the part about Jeff's noticing he had been stabbed, throwing up his middle fingers in defiance, and bellowing "Fuck you, nigger!" Juan and Darius gaped.

"He did what?" Juan said.

I told them again.

Juan and Darius looked at each other. Darius laughed. Juan shrugged. "O.K.," Juan said. "They want to go out in a blaze of glory. That's cool. They can have their story."

In Darius's version, the boneheads had arrived with two knives. Darius had kicked one of them loose and then picked it up. That was the knife he had used to stab Jeff. None of the other witnesses I interviewed had seen this kick, or anything like it. Darius, I thought, didn't look abashed enough as he told this story.

Sitting in that Taco Bell and talking to the boys, I watched Christina from the corner of my eye. She fidgeted, checked her watch, said nothing. I noticed her studying Darius, her expression both cool and oddly contented. This fugitive skinhead was her main project now, even the center of her life. Other kids in the Antelope Valley were starting to talk about her with awe: her black boyfriend killed a bonehead; he was in hiding; she stuck by him, defying her parents. It was a romantic role, far larger than ordinary Valley teen-age life.

After Christina and Juan set off on the long drive back to the Valley, Darius took me to meet some new friends he had made. "It's a good thing I cliqued up with some other heads," he said. "Because Huntington Beach is just a few miles from here, and that's where the O.C. Skins are from. I need people to watch my back."

Darius's friends lived in a vast low-rise apartment complex. We passed through an empty white brick foyer and were buzzed into a courtyard that seemed to ramble on for blocks—through plots of grass and stands of tattered bamboo, past a lighted swimming pool, around a thousand plastic tricycles and abandoned toys. All the ground-floor apartments had sliding glass doors without curtains. Behind them, virtually in public, people watched TV, ate sushi, and scratched their bellies, oblivious of path traffic like us. There were Asians, Latinos, blacks, whites, bikers, yuppies, buppies, old Samoans, young Cambodians. It was a Free Unity world, I thought. It felt like a vision of the next American century: ramshackle, multiracial, cut-rate. White supremacists, it struck me, fear the future for a reason: it's going to be strange and very complicated.

Darius's friends weren't there, but some other guys were, and they let us in. They looked like skaters. Two were white. One was Asian. They were smoking a bong, listening to music. Darius and I sat on a couch to one side and talked. He was staying with one of his three half brothers, not far away, he said. He was thinking about moving to Germany. First, though, he was going to enroll in the local community college to learn German. Then he thought he might join the Navy. In the meantime, he thought Christina should move down here. It was too dangerous for her in the Antelope Valley now.

The first time I talked to the Lancaster prosecutor in charge of investigating Jeff Malone's death, he shared with me his feelings about gang killings in general. "I say lock 'em all up in a room and prosecute the survivor," he said. I took this to mean that Darius did not have to fear prosecution.

Later, when a decision was officially made not to prosecute, the same assistant district attorney explained his reasoning to me. The victim and his friends had gone to a house where a hostile or opposing gang was having a party. The victim had a knife. He attacked Mr. Houston. Mr. Houston's claim that the knife he used belonged to the victim or to the victim's friends was not credible. But it was not illegal for him to possess that knife inside that house. There were conflicting eyewitness versions of the attack. It was certainly not a particularly vicious attack. The fact that a single knife thrust had killed the victim was simply bad luck. The crucial question for the prosecution was whether a jury could be persuaded that the killing had not been self-defense. That seemed unlikely. The victim was a Nazi skinhead, who would not be viewed sympathetically. Mr. Houston was on his own turf, minding his own business. "I'm not saying Mr. Houston is a great guy," the prosecutor concluded. "He's not. He's a jerk. You need to call me in about six months to see if he is still alive. I do not believe he will be."

To the Malone family's bitter contention that it was really because Jeff was a skinhead from a poor family that no one would be prosecuted for his death, I could think of no rejoinder. It was true.

So families flee the city for far-flung suburbs, but the evils they hope to escape—drugs, gangs, violent crime—flourish wherever they land. Why? I kept recalling Mindy's grandmother's remark about how kids were being left to raise themselves. If most parents must work outside the home, the obvious institution to take up the caretaking slack is the school. There are American communities that have begun to reckon with this imperative, but they are a small minority and the Antelope Valley is decidedly not among them. Beverley Louw's attempt at Lancaster High to replace the baroque array of "fragmented subcultures" that students tend to join with an old-fashioned, school-based culture was the exception. And her frustrations arose from more than just her students' academic deficits.

"Everything is in such flux, which unsettles kids," she told me one afternoon in her office. "The *homelessness* among kids here is just enormous. It's invisible to outsiders, because they don't live on the streets, but they move from place to place, living with friends or relatives or whatever. And lack of supervision is the key, I believe, to most of their problems." Ms. Louw looked out a window onto a windblown parking lot, then went on. "I had a straight-A student commit suicide when I was principal of the continuation school. The kids said she did it on a dare. Her father came to the funeral in a yellow leather suit. I couldn't believe it. *A yellow leather suit.*"

Martha Wengert, a sociologist at Antelope Valley College, said, "This area has grown so fast that neighborhoods are not yet communities. Kids are left with this intense longing for identification." Gangs, race nationalism, and all manner of "beliefs" arose from this longing. I thought of Debbie Turner's inability to comprehend Mindy's enthusiasm for the likes of Charles Manson and Adolf Hitler. "The kids reach out to these historical figures," Dr. Wengert said. "But it's through TV, through comic books, through word-of-mouth. There are no books at home, no ideas, no sense of history." One thing the Valley's young people knew, however, Dr. Wengert said, was that the economic downturn of the nineteen-nineties was not cyclical, that the Cold War was over and the aerospace and defense jobs were not coming back.

—1977

Learning from Other Writers

1. Is William Finnegan an insider in this community? An outsider? What can you surmise about his relationship to the teenagers he interviewed for this essay? His opinions about their behavior and beliefs?
2. Why does Finnegan focus on Mindy rather than one of the other teenagers?
3. Why might Finnegan's readers care about the lives of teenagers they don't know who are living in a place they probably have never visited?
4. What is the effect of including the perspectives of Natalie Blacker and Beverley Louw? The Lancaster prosecutor? Debbie Turner (Mindy's mother)? Jaxon's mother? Nancy Kelso (the lawyer who represents many juvenile clients)?
5. Highlight the passages in which Finnegan provides background about Antelope Valley or the subjects of his group portrait. Does this information fit in smoothly with the rest of the essay? Why or why not?

INSPIRATIONS: TALENTED TAP-DANCERS, SADISTIC BOSSES, AND SAD-SACK STAND-UP COMICS

1. Think of a group of people who have something in common (for example, talented tap-dancers, bosses at fast-food restaurants, immigrants from Taiwan, patients on a pediatric cancer ward, rape victims, deer hunters, or stand-up comics).
2. Think of a question that applies to this group.
3. Write a group portrait, bearing in mind the larger question about the group you are trying to answer. Remember, you might need a secondary structure to help you find an order for the portraits. Is there some action or event in which your group participated (a tryout for a musical? the opening day of a new McDonald's)? If so, you might want to use the chronology of that event to help you figure out when to describe each person in the group. You could structure your essay about the patients on that cancer ward according to the order in which you encountered them, or start with a profile of your worst boss and end with your best boss, or profile those deer hunters according to age, from youngest to most experienced, or introduce us to all the stand-up comics you know, from least funny to most successful.

INSPIRATIONS: MY GANG

1. Choose a community to which you belong (whether as an insider or an insider/outsider).
2. Freewrite about ways in which that community is defined. How are insiders distinguished from outsiders? Do members display special ways of speaking? Dressing? Eating? Telling jokes? Special desires or goals? Are there any rituals or superstitions that insiders follow or believe in?
3. Based on this freewriting, come up with a definition of your community and/or the process by which certain people can become members.
4. Freewrite about the significance of this community and its effect on members, outsiders, or society at large. What does the existence of this community say about some larger aspect of American culture? Should we celebrate or condemn the existence of this community? Work to change it? Abolish it? Preserve or celebrate its existence?
5. Based on personal experience, research, interviews, or a combination of all three, write an essay in which you define your community and explore one of the questions you came up with in your freewriting. Make sure you know whether your audience consists of members of the community, outsiders, or both.

Rituals, Games, Performances, and Events

Writers are always looking for ways to structure the chaos of reality. With so many people in the world, each the starring character in his or her own life and a supporting player in other people's stories, finding a focus and form for a piece of creative nonfiction tends to be a challenge. As we have seen, you can structure an essay around a personal narrative, a journey, a search for answers to a nagging question, a mystery or an experiment, a day on the job (your own or someone else's), an important historical event, or the rituals that define a community.

This last set of structures—the rituals of a group—includes activities that we human beings have created for our own amusement or edification, by which I mean athletic events and other games, concerts and debates, meetings, classes, initiations and inductions, and all variety of religious, social, and family ceremonies, both formal and informal. In writing such a piece, you can focus on one or more performers (as in profiles and group portraits) or on the performance itself (revisit yet again James Agee's poetic re-creation of the rituals that comprised a typical summer evening in Knoxville, Tennessee, in 1915).

John McPhee, one of the modern masters of creative nonfiction, often uses athletic events to structure his pieces, as can be seen in his brilliantly conceived and executed *Levels of the Game*,[1] a book that takes the form of a tennis match between Arthur Ashe and Clark Graebner, with key points in the match interwoven with scenes from the players' very different lives, and "The Search for Marvin Gardens" (reproduced in this chapter), in which McPhee juxtaposes an imaginary Monopoly tournament with a very real journey around the streets of Atlantic City in search of the fabled but hard-to-find Marvin Gardens.

Although academic classes tend to be less physically exciting than athletic matches, the rituals of the schoolroom have served many authors well, among them David Sedaris, whose descriptions of his French classes in *Me Talk Pretty One Day*[2] rank among the funniest humor pieces ever written, and Emily Bernard, whose honest and unexpected meditations on "Teaching the N-Word" can be found in this chapter.

Finally, Lily Tuck shows that structuring an essay around the meetings of a bereavement group can give shape to what otherwise might have been an inchoate mass of grief (not only her own, but that of six other mourners), allowing the author to contemplate how anyone can survive the loss of a beloved spouse and whether the mere act of sharing one's grief with other mourners really might help.

[1] Farrar, Straus & Giroux, 1969.

[2] Little, Brown and Company, 2000.

JOHN MCPHEE

THE SEARCH FOR MARVIN GARDENS

Go. I roll the dice—a six and a two. Through the air I move my token, the flatiron, to Vermont Avenue, where dog packs range.

The dogs are moving (some are limping) through ruins, rubble, fire damage, open garbage. Doorways are gone. Lath is visible in the crumbling walls of the buildings. The street sparkles with shattered glass. I have never seen, anywhere, so many broken windows. A sign—"Slow, Children at Play"—has been bent backward by an automobile. At the lighthouse, the dogs turn up Pacific and disappear. George Meade, Army engineer, built the lighthouse—brick upon brick, six hundred thousand bricks, to reach up high enough to throw a beam twenty miles over the sea. Meade, seven years later, saved the Union at Gettysburg.

I buy Vermont Avenue for $100. My opponent is a tall, shadowy figure, across from me, but I know him well, and I know his game like a favorite tune. If he can, he will always go for the quick kill. And when it is foolish to go for the quick kill he will be foolish. On the whole, though, he is a master assessor of percentages. It is a mistake to underestimate him. His eleven carries his top hat to St. Charles Place, which he buys for $140.

The sidewalks of St. Charles Place have been cracked to shards by through-growing weeds. There are no buildings. Mansions, hotels once stood here. A few street lamps now drop cones of light on broken glass and vacant space behind a chain-link fence that some great machine has in places bent to the ground. Five plane trees—in full summer leaf, flecking the light—are all that live on St. Charles Place.

Block upon block, gradually, we are cancelling each other out—in the blues, the lavenders, the oranges, the greens. My opponent follows a plan of his own devising. I use the Hornblower & Weeks opening and the Zuricher defense. The first game draws tight, will soon finish. In 1971, a group of people in Racine, Wisconsin, played for seven hundred and sixty-eight hours. A game begun a month later in Danville, California, lasted eight hundred and twenty hours. These are official records, and they stun us. We have been playing for eight minutes. It amazes us that Monopoly is thought of as a long game. It is possible to play to a complete, absolute, and final conclusion in less than fifteen minutes, all within the rules as written. My opponent and I have done so thousands of times. No wonder we are sitting across from each other now in this best-of-seven series for the international singles championship of the world.

On Illinois Avenue, three men lean out from second-story windows. A girl is coming down the street. She wears dungarees and a bright-red shirt, has ample breasts and a Hadendoan Afro, a black halo, two feet in diameter. Ice rattles in the glasses in the hands of the men.

"Hey, sister!"

"Come on up!"

She looks up, looks from one to another to the other, looks them flat in the eye.

"What for?" she says, and she walks on.

I buy Illinois for $240. It solidifies my chances, for I already own Kentucky and Indiana. My opponent pales. If he had landed first on Illinois, the game would have been over then and there, for he has houses built on Boardwalk and Park Place, we share the railroads equally, and we have cancelled each other everywhere else. We never trade.

In 1852, R. B. Osborne, an immigrant Englishman, civil engineer, surveyed the route of a railroad line that would run from Camden to Absecon Island, in New Jersey, traversing the state from the Delaware River to the barrier beaches of the sea. He then sketched in the plan of a "bathing village" that would surround the eastern terminus of the line. His pen flew glibly, framing and naming spacious avenues parallel to the shore—Mediterranean, Baltic, Oriental, Ventnor—and narrower transsecting avenues: North Carolina, Pennsylvania, Vermont, Connecticut, States, Virginia, Tennessee, New York, Kentucky, Indiana, Illinois. The place as a whole had no name, so when he had completed the plan Osborne wrote in large letters over the ocean, "Atlantic City." No one ever challenged the name, or the names of Osborne's streets. Monopoly was invented in the early nineteen-thirties by Charles B. Darrow, but Darrow was only transliterating what Osborne had created. The railroads, crucial to any player, were the making of Atlantic City. After the rails were down, houses and hotels burgeoned from Mediterranean and Baltic to New York and Kentucky. Properties—building lots—sold for as little as six dollars apiece and as much as a thousand dollars. The original investors in the railroads and the real estate called themselves the Camden & Atlantic Land Company. Reverently, I repeat their names: Dwight Bell, William Coffin, John DaCosta, Daniel Deal, William Fleming, Andrew Hay, Joseph Porter, Jonathan Pitney, Samuel Richards—founders, fathers, forerunners, archetypical masters of the quick kill.

My opponent and I are now in a deep situation of classical Monopoly. The torsion is almost perfect—Boardwalk and Park Place versus the brilliant reds. His cash position is weak, though, and if I escape him now he may fade. I land on Luxury Tax, contiguous to but in sanctuary from his power. I have four houses on Indiana. He lands there. He concedes.

Indiana Avenue was the address of the Brighton Hotel, gone now. The Brighton was exclusive—a word that no longer has retail value in the city. If you arrived by automobile and tried to register at the Brighton, you were sent away. Brighton-class people came in private railroad cars. Brighton-class people had other private railroad cars for their horses—dawn rides on the firm sand at water's edge, skirts flying. Colonel Anthony J. Drexel Biddle—the sort of name that would constrict throats in Philadelphia—lived, much of the year, in the Brighton.

Colonel Sanders' fried chicken is on Kentucky Avenue. So is Clifton's Club Harlem, with the Sepia Revue and the Sepia Follies, featuring the Honey Bees, the Fashions, and the Lords.

My opponent and I, many years ago, played 2,428 games of Monopoly in a single season. He was then a recent graduate of the Harvard Law School, and he was working for a downtown firm, looking up law. Two people we knew—one from Chase Manhattan, the other from Morgan, Stanley—tried to get into the game, but after a few rounds we found that they were not in the conversation and we sent them home. Monopoly should always be *mano a mano* anyway. My opponent won 1,199 games, and so did I. Thirty were ties. He was called into the Army, and we stopped just there. Now, in Game 2 of the series, I go immediately to jail, and again to jail while my opponent seines property. He is dumbfoundingly lucky. He wins in twelve minutes.

Visiting hours are daily, eleven to two; Sunday, eleven to one; evenings, six to nine. "NO MINORS, NO FOOD, Immediate Family Only Allowed in Jail." All this above a blue steel door in a blue cement wall in the windowless interior of the basement of the city hall. The desk sergeant sits opposite the door to the jail. In a cigar box in front of him are pills in every color, a banquet of fruit salad an inch and a half deep—leapers, co-pilots, footballs, truck drivers, peanuts, blue angels, yellow jackets, redbirds, rainbows. Near the desk are two soldiers, waiting to go through the blue door. They are about eighteen years old. One of them is trying hard to light a cigarette. His wrists are in steel cuffs. A military policeman waits, too. He is a year or so older than the soldiers, taller, studious in appearance, gentle, fat. On a bench against a wall sits a good-looking girl in slacks. The blue door rattles, swings heavily open. A turnkey stands in the doorway. "Don't you guys kill yourselves back there now," says the sergeant to the soldiers.

"One kid, he overdosed himself about ten and a half hours ago," says the M.P.

The M.P., the soldiers, the turnkey, and the girl on the bench are white. The sergeant is black. "If you take off the handcuffs, take off the belts," says the sergeant to the M.P. "I don't want them hanging themselves back there." The door shuts and its tumblers move. When it opens again, five minutes later, a young white man in sandals and dungarees and a blue polo shirt emerges. His hair is in a ponytail. He has no beard. He grins at the good-looking girl. She rises, joins him. The sergeant hands him a manila envelope. From it he removes his belt and a small notebook. He borrows a pencil, makes an entry in the notebook. He is out of jail, free. What did he do? He offended Atlantic City in some way. He spent a night in the jail. In the nineteen-thirties, men visiting Atlantic City went to jail, directly to jail, did not pass Go, for appearing in topless bathing suits on the beach. A city statute requiring all men to wear full-length bathing suits was not seriously challenged until 1937, and the first year in which a man could legally go bare-chested on the beach was 1940.

Game 3. After seventeen minutes, I am ready to begin construction on overpriced and sluggish Pacific, North Carolina, and Pennsylvania. Nothing else being open, opponent concedes.

The physical profile of streets perpendicular to the shore is something like a playground slide. It begins in the high skyline of Boardwalk hotels, plummets into warrens of "side-avenue" motels, crosses Pacific, slopes through church missions, convalescent homes, burlesque houses, rooming houses, and liquor stores, crosses Atlantic, and runs level through the bombed-out ghetto as far—Baltic, Mediterranean—as the eye can see. North Carolina Avenue, for example, is flanked at its beach end by the Chalfonte and the Haddon Hall (908 rooms, air-conditioned), where, according to one biographer, John Philip Sousa (1854–1932) first played when he was twenty-two, insisting, even then, that everyone call him by his entire name. Behind these big hotels, motels—Barbizon, Catalina—crouch. Between Pacific and Atlantic is an occasional house from 1910—wooden porch, wooden mullions, old yellow paint—and two churches, a package store, a strip show, a dealer in fruits and vegetables. Then, beyond Atlantic Avenue, North Carolina moves on into the vast ghetto, the bulk of the city, and it looks like Metz in 1919, Cologne in 1944. Nothing has actually exploded. It is not bomb damage. It is deep and complex decay. Roofs are off. Bricks are scattered in the street. People sit on porches, six deep, at nine on a Monday morning. When they go off to wait in unemployment lines, they wait sometimes two hours. Between Mediterranean and Baltic runs a chain-link fence, enclosing rubble. A patrol car sits idling by the curb. In the back seat is a German shepherd. A sign on the fence says, "Beware of Bad Dogs."

Mediterranean and Baltic are the principal avenues of the ghetto. Dogs are everywhere. A pack of seven passes me. Block after block, there are three-story brick row houses. Whole segments of them are abandoned, a thousand broken windows. Some parts are intact, occupied. A mattress lies in the street, soaking in a pool of water. Wet stuffing is coming out of the mattress. A postman is having a rye and a beer in the Plantation Bar at nine-fifteen in the morning. I ask him idly if he knows where Marvin Gardens is. He does not. "HOOKED AND NEED HELP? CONTACT N.A.R.C.O." "REVIVAL NOW GOING ON, CONDUCTED BY REVEREND H. HENDERSON OF TEXAS." These are signboards on Mediterranean and Baltic. The second one is upside down and leans against a boarded-up window of the Faith Temple Church of God in Christ. There is an old peeling poster on a warehouse wall showing a figure in an electric chair. "The Black Panther Manifesto" is the title of the poster, and its message is, or was, that "the fascists have already decided in advance to murder Chairman Bobby Seale in the electric chair." I pass an old woman who carries a bucket. She wears blue sneakers, worn through. Her feet spill out. She wears red socks, rolled at the knees. A white handkerchief, spread over her head, is knotted at the corners. Does she know where Marvin Gardens is? "I sure don't know," she says, setting down the bucket. "I sure don't know. I've heard of it somewhere, but I just can't say where." I walk on, through a block of shattered glass. The glass crunches underfoot like coarse sand. I remember when I first came here—a long train ride from Trenton, long ago, games of poker in the train—to play basketball against Atlantic City. We were half black, they were all black. We scored forty points, they scored eighty, or something like it. What I remember most is that they had glass backboards—glittering, pendent, expensive glass backboards, a rarity then in high schools, even in colleges, the only ones we played on all year.

I turn on Pennsylvania, and start back toward the sea. The windows of the Hotel Astoria, on Pennsylvania near Baltic, are boarded up. A sheet of unpainted plywood is the door, and in it is a triangular peephole that now frames an eye. The plywood door opens. A man answers my question. Rooms there are six, seven, and ten dollars a week. I thank him for the information and move on, emerging from the ghetto at the Catholic Daughters of America Women's Guest House, between Atlantic and Pacific. Between Pacific and the Boardwalk are the blinking vacancy signs of the Aristocrat and Colton Manor motels. Pennsylvania terminates at the Sheraton-Seaside—thirty-two dollars a day, ocean corner. I take a walk on the Boardwalk and into the Holiday Inn (twenty-three stories). A guest is registering. "You reserved for Wednesday, and this is Monday," the clerk tells him. "But that's all right. We have *plenty* of rooms." The clerk is very young, female, and has soft brown hair that hangs below her waist. Her superior kicks her.

He is a middle-aged man with red spiderwebs in his face. He is jacketed and tied. He takes her aside. "Don't say 'plenty,'" he says. "Say 'You are fortunate, sir. We have rooms available.'"

The face of the young woman turns sour. "We have all the rooms you need," she says to the customer, and, to her superior, "How's that?"

Game 4. My opponent's luck has become abrasive. He has Boardwalk and Park Place, and has sealed the board.

Darrow was a plumber. He was, specifically, a radiator repairman who lived in Germantown, Pennsylvania. His first Monopoly board was a sheet of linoleum. On it he placed houses and hotels that he had carved from blocks of wood. The game he thus invented was brilliantly conceived, for it was an uncannily exact reflection of the business milieu at large. In its depth, range, and subtlety, in its luck-skill ratio, in its sense of infrastructure and socio-economic parameters, in its philosophical characteristics, it reached to the profundity of the financial community. It was as scientific as the stock market. It suggested the manner and means through which an underdeveloped world had been developed. It was chess at Wall Street level. "Advance token to the nearest Railroad and pay owner twice the rental to which he is otherwise entitled. If Railroad is unowned, you may buy it from the Bank. Get out of Jail, free. Advance token to nearest Utility. If unowned, you may buy it from Bank. If owned, throw dice and pay owner a total ten times the amount thrown. You are assessed for street repairs: $40 per house, $115 per hotel. Pay poor tax of $15. Go to Jail. Go directly to Jail. Do not pass Go. Do not collect $200."

The turnkey opens the blue door. The turnkey is known to the inmates as Sidney K. Above his desk are ten closed-circuit-TV screens—assorted viewpoints of the jail. There are three cellblocks—men, women, juvenile boys. Six days is the average stay. Showers twice a week. The steel doors and the equipment that operates them were made in San Antonio. The prisoners sleep on bunks of butcher block. There are no mattresses. There are three prisoners to a cell. In winter, it is cold in here. Prisoners burn newspapers to keep warm. Cell corners are black with smudge. The jail is three years old. The men's block echoes with chatter. The man in the cell nearest Sidney K. is pacing. His shirt is covered with broad stains of blood. The block for juvenile boys is, by contrast, utterly silent—empty corridor, empty cells. There is only one prisoner. He is small and black and appears to be thirteen. He says he is sixteen and that he has been alone in here for three days.

"Why are you here? What did you do?"

"I hit a jitney driver."

The series stands at three all. We have split the fifth and sixth games. We are scrambling for property. Around the board we fairly fly. We move so fast because we do our own banking and search our own deeds. My opponent grows tense.

Ventnor Avenue, a street of delicatessens and doctors' offices, is leafy with plane trees and hydrangeas, the city flower. Water Works is on the mainland. The water comes over in submarine pipes. Electric Company gets power from across the state, on the Delaware River, in Deepwater. States Avenue, now a wasteland like St. Charles, once had gardens running down the middle of the street, a horse-drawn trolley, private homes. States Avenue was as exclusive as the Brighton. Only an apartment house, a small motel, and the All Wars Memorial Building—monadnocks spaced widely apart—stand along States Avenue now. Pawnshops, convalescent homes, and the Paradise Soul Saving Station are on Virginia Avenue. The soul-saving station is pink, orange, and yellow. In the windows flanking the door of the Virginia Money Loan Office are Nikons, Polaroids, Yashicas, Sony TVs, Underwood typewriters, Singer sewing machines, and pictures of Christ. On the far side of town, beside a single track and locked up most of the time, is the new railroad station, a small hut made of glazed firebrick, all that is left of the lines that built the city. An authentic phrenologist works on New York Avenue close to Frank's Extra Dry Bar and a church where the sermon today is "Death in the Pot." The church is of pink brick, has blue and amber windows and two red doors. St. James Place, narrow and twisting, is lined with boarding houses that have wooden porches on each of three stories, suggesting a New Orleans made of salt-bleached pine. In a vacant lot on Tennessee is a white Ford station wagon stripped to the chassis. The windows are smashed. A plastic Clorox bottle sits on the driver's seat. The wind has pressed newspaper against the chain-link fence around the lot. Atlantic Avenue, the city's principal thoroughfare, could be seventeen American Main Streets placed end to end—discount vitamins and Vienna Corset shops, movie theatres, shoe stores, and funeral homes. The Boardwalk is made of yellow pine and Douglas fir, soaked in pentachlorophenol. Downbeach, it reaches far beyond the city. Signs everywhere—on windows, lampposts, trash baskets—proclaim "Bienvenue Canadiens!" The salt air is full of Canadian French. In the Claridge Hotel, on Park Place, I ask a clerk if she knows where Marvin Gardens is. She says, "Is it a floral shop?" I ask a cabdriver, parked outside. He says, "Never heard of it." Park Place is one block long, Pacific to Boardwalk. On the roof of the Claridge is the Solarium, the highest point in town—panoramic view of the ocean, the bay, the salt-water ghetto. I look down at the rooftops of the side-avenue motels and into swimming pools. There are hundreds of people around the rooftop pools, sunbathing, reading—many more people than are on the beach. Walls, windows, and a block of sky are all that is visible from these pools—no sand, no sea. The pools are craters, and with the people around them they are countersunk into the motels.

The seventh, and final, game is ten minutes old and I have hotels on Oriental, Vermont, and Connecticut. I have Tennessee and St. James. I have North Carolina and Pacific. I have Boardwalk, Atlantic, Ventnor, Illinois, Indiana. My fingers are forming a "V." I have mortgaged most of these properties in order to pay for others, and I have mortgaged the others to pay for the hotels. I have seven dollars. I will pay off the mortgages and build my reserves with income from the three hotels. My cash position may be low, but I feel like a rocket in an underground silo. Meanwhile, if I could just go to jail for a time I could pause there, wait there, until my opponent, in his inescapable rounds, pays the rates of my hotels. Jail, at times, is the strategic place to be. I roll boxcars from the Reading and move the flatiron to Community Chest. "Go to Jail. Go directly to Jail."

The prisoners, of course, have no pens and no pencils. They take paper napkins, roll them tight as crayons, char the ends with matches, and write on the walls. The things they write are not entirely idiomatic; for example, "In God We Trust." All is in carbon. Time is required in the writing. "Only humanity could know of such pain." "God So Loved the World." "There is no greater pain than life itself." In the women's block now, there are six blacks, giggling, and a white asleep in red shoes. She is drunk. The others are pushers, prostitutes, an auto thief, a burglar caught with pistol in purse. A sixteen-year-old accused of murder was in here last week. These words are written on the wall of a now empty cell: "Laying here I see two bunks about six inches thick, not counting the one I'm laying on, which is hard as brick. No cushion for my back. No pillow for my head. Just a couple scratchy blankets which is best to use it's said. I wake up in the morning so shivery and cold, waiting and waiting till I am told the food is coming. It's on its way. It's not worth waiting for, but I eat it anyway. I know one thing when they set me free I'm gonna be good if it kills me."

How many years must a game be played to produce an Anthony J. Drexel Biddle and chestnut geldings on the beach? About half a century was the original answer, from the first railroad to Biddle at his peak. Biddle, at his peak, hit an Atlantic City streetcar conductor with his fist, laid him out with one punch. This increased Biddle's legend. He did not go to jail. While John Philip Sousa led his band along the Boardwalk playing "The Stars and Stripes Forever" and Jack Dempsey ran up and down in training for his fight with Gene Tunney, the city crossed the high curve of its parabola. Al Capone held conventions here—

upstairs with his sleeves rolled, apportioning among his lieutenant governors the states of the Eastern seaboard. The natural history of an American resort proceeds from Indians to French Canadians via Biddles and Capones. French Canadians, whatever they may be at home, are Visigoths here. Bienvenue Visigoths!

My opponent plods along incredibly well. He has got his fourth railroad, and patiently, unbelievably, he has picked up my potential winners until he has blocked me everywhere but Marvin Gardens. He has avoided, in the fifty-dollar zoning, my increasingly petty hotels. His cash flow swells. His railroads are costing me two hundred dollars a minute. He is building hotels on States, Virginia, and St. Charles. He has temporarily reversed the current. With the yellow monopolies and my blue monopolies, I could probably defeat his lavenders and his railroads. I have Atlantic and Ventnor. I need Marvin Gardens. My only hope is Marvin Gardens.

There is a plaque at Boardwalk and Park Place, and on it in relief is the leonine profile of a man who looks like an officer in a metropolitan bank—"Charles B. Darrow, 1889–1967, inventor of the game of Monopoly." "Darrow," I address him, aloud. "Where is Marvin Gardens?" There is, of course, no answer. Bronze, impassive, Darrow looks south down the Boardwalk. "Mr. Darrow, please, where is Marvin Gardens?" Nothing. Not a sign. He just looks south down the Boardwalk.

My opponent accepts the trophy with his natural ease, and I make, from notes, remarks that are even less graceful than his.

Marvin Gardens is the one color-block Monopoly property that is not in Atlantic City. It is a suburb within a suburb, secluded. It is a planned compound of seventy-two handsome houses set on curvilinear private streets under yews and cedars, poplars and willows. The compound was built around 1920, in Margate, New Jersey, and consists of solid buildings of stucco, brick, and wood, with slate roofs, tile roofs, multimullioned porches, Giraldic towers, and Spanish grilles. Marvin Gardens, the ultimate outwash of Monopoly, is a citadel and sanctuary of the middle class. "We're heavily patrolled by police here. We don't take no chances. Me? I'm living here nine years. I paid seventeen thousand dollars and I've been offered thirty. Number one, I don't want to move. Number two, I don't need the money. I have four bedrooms, two and a half baths, front den, back den. No basement. The Atlantic is down there. Six feet down and you float. A lot of people have a hard time finding this place. People that lived in Atlantic City all their life don't know how to find it. They don't know where the hell they're going. They just know it's south, down the Boardwalk."

—1972

Learning from Other Writers

1. How does McPhee weave together the two main threads of this essay? Can you find the links that join one section to the next?
2. What recurring patterns or motifs can you find?
3. What larger question about Monopoly, Atlantic City, or America is the author attempting to answer?
4. What is the role of the closing section about Marvin Gardens?

EMILY BERNARD

TEACHING THE N-WORD

Once riding in old Baltimore,
Heart-filled, head-filled with glee,
I saw a Baltimorean
Keep looking straight at me.

Now I was eight and very small,
And he was no whit bigger,
And so I smiled, but he poked out
His tongue, and called me, "Nigger."

I saw the whole of Baltimore
From May until December;
Of all the things that happened there
That's all that I remember.

—COUNTEE CULLEN, "Incident" (1925)

October 2004

Eric is crazy about queer theory. I think it is safe to say that Eve Sedgwick, Judith Butler, and Lee Edelman have changed his life. Every week, he comes to my office to report on the connections he is making between the works of these writers and the books he is reading for the class he is taking with me, African-American autobiography.

I like Eric. So tonight, even though it is well after six and I am eager to go home, I keep our conversation going. I ask him what he thinks about the word "queer," whether or not he believes, independent of the theorists he admires, that epithets can ever really be reclaimed and reinvented.

"'Queer' has important connotations for me," he says. "It's daring, political. I embrace it." He folds his arms across his chest, and then unfolds them.

I am suspicious.

"What about 'nigger'?" I ask. "If we're talking about the importance of transforming hateful language, what about that word?" From my bookshelf I pull down Randall Kennedy's book *Nigger: The Strange Career of a Troublesome Word,* and turn it so its cover faces Eric. "Nigger," in stark white type against a black background, is staring at him, staring at anyone who happens to be walking past the open door behind him.

Over the next thirty minutes or so, Eric and I talk about "nigger." He is uncomfortable; every time he says "nigger," he drops his voice and does not meet my eyes. I know that he does not want to say the word; he is following my lead. He does not want to say it because he is white; he does not want to say it because I am black. I feel my power as his professor, the mentor he has so ardently adopted. I feel the power of Randall Kennedy's book in my hands, its title crude and unambiguous. *Say it,* we both instruct this white student. And he does.

It is late. No one moves through the hallway. I think about my colleagues, some of whom still sit at their own desks. At any minute, they might pass my office on their way out of the building. What would they make of this scene? Most of my colleagues are white.

What would I think if I walked by an office and saw one of them holding up *Nigger* to a white student's face? A black student's face?

"I think I am going to add 'Who Can Say "Nigger"?' to our reading for next week," I say to Eric. "It's an article by Kennedy that covers some of the ideas in this book." I tap *Nigger* with my finger, and then put it down on my desk.

"I really wish there was a black student in our class," Eric says as he gathers his books to leave.

As usual, I have assigned way too much reading. Even though we begin class discussion with references to three essays required for today, our conversation drifts quickly to "Who Can Say 'Nigger'?" and plants itself there. We talk about the word, who can say it, who won't say it, who wants to say it, and why. There are eleven students in the class. All of them are white.

Our discussion is lively and intense; everyone seems impatient to speak. We talk about language, history, and identity. Most students say "the n-word" instead of "nigger." Only one or two students actually use the word in their comments. When they do, they use the phrase "the word 'nigger,'" as if to cushion it. Sometimes they make quotation marks with their fingers. I notice Lauren looking around. Finally she raises her hand.

"I have a question; it's somewhat personal. I don't want to put you on the spot."

"Go ahead, Lauren," I say with relief.

"Okay, so how does it feel for you to hear us say that word?"

I have an answer ready.

"I don't enjoy hearing it. But I don't think that I feel more offended by it than you do. What I mean is, I don't think I have a special place of pain inside of me that the word touches because I am black." *We are both human beings*, I am trying to say. She nods her head, seemingly satisfied. Even inspired, I hope.

I am lying, of course.

I am grateful to Lauren for acknowledging my humanity in our discussion. But I do not want me—my feelings, my experiences, my humanity—to become the center of classroom discussion. Here at the University of Vermont, I routinely teach classrooms full of white students. I want to educate them, transform them. I want to teach them things about race they will never forget. To achieve this, I believe I must give of myself. I want to give to them—but I want to keep much of myself to myself. How much? I have a new answer to this question every week.

I always give my students a lecture at the beginning of every African-American studies course I teach. I tell them, in essence, not to confuse my body with the body of the text. I tell them that while it would be disingenuous for me to suggest that my own racial identity has nothing to do with my love for African-American literature, my race is only one of the many reasons why I stand before them. "I stand here," I say, "because I have a Ph.D., just like all your other professors." I make sure always to tell them that my Ph.D., like my B.A., comes from Yale.

"In order to get this Ph.D.," I continue, "I studied with some of this country's foremost authorities on African-American literature, and a significant number of these people are white.

"I say this to suggest that if you fail to fully appreciate this material, it is a matter of your intellectual laziness, not your race. If you cannot grasp the significance of Frederick Douglass's plight, for instance, you are not trying hard enough, and I will not accept that."

I have another part of this lecture. It goes: "Conversely, this material is not the exclusive property of students of color. This is literature. While these books will speak to us emotionally according to our different experiences, none of us is especially equipped to appreciate the intellectual and aesthetic complexities that characterize African-American literature. This is American literature, American experience, after all."

Sometimes I give this part of my lecture, but not always. Sometimes I give it and then regret it later.

As soon as Lauren asks me how I feel, it is as if the walls of the room soften and collapse slightly, nudging us a little bit closer together. Suddenly, eleven pairs of eyes are beaming sweet messages at me. I want to laugh. I do. "Look at you all, leaning in," I say. "How close we have all become."

I sit at the end of a long narrow table. Lauren usually sits at the other end. The rest of the students flank us on either side. When I make my joke, a few students, all straight men, I notice, abruptly pull themselves back. They shift their eyes away from me, look instead at their notebooks, the table. I have made them ashamed to show that they care about me, I realize. They are following the cues I have been giving them since the beginning of the semester, cues that they should take this class seriously, that I will be offended if they do not. "African-American studies has had to struggle to exist at all," I have said. "You owe it your respect." *Don't be too familiar* is what I am really saying. *Don't be too familiar with me.*

Immediately, I regret having made a joke of their sincere attempt to offer me their care. They want to know me; they see this moment as an opportunity. But I can't stop. I make more jokes, mostly about them, and what they are saying and not saying. I can't seem to help myself.

Eric, who is sitting near me, does not recoil at my jokes; he does not respond to my not-so-subtle efforts to push him and everyone else back. He continues to lean in, his torso flat against the edge of the table. He looks at me. He raises his hand.

"Emily," he says, "would you tell them what you told me the other day in your office? You were talking about how you dress and what it means to you."

"Yes," I begin slowly. "I was telling Eric about how important it is to me that I come to class dressed up."

"And remember what you said about Todd? You said that Todd exercises his white privilege by dressing so casually for class."

Todd is one of my closest friends in the English department. His office is next door to mine. I don't remember talking about Todd's clothing habits with Eric, but I must have. I struggle to come up with a comfortably vague response to stop Eric's prodding. My face grows hot. Everyone is waiting.

"Well, I don't know if I put it exactly like that, but I do believe that Todd's style of dress reflects his ability to move in the world here—everywhere, really—less self-consciously than I do." As I sit here, I grow increasingly more alarmed at what I am revealing: my personal philosophies; my attitudes about my friend's style of dress; my insecurities; my feelings. I quietly will Eric to stop, even as I am impressed by his determination. I meet his eyes again.

"And you. You were saying that the way you dress, it means something too," Eric says. *On with this tug of war,* I think.

I relent, let go of the rope. "Listen, I will say this. I am aware that you guys, all of my students at UVM, have very few black professors. I am aware, in fact, that I may be the first black teacher many of you have ever had. And the way I dress for class reflects my awareness of that possibility." I look sharply at Eric. *That's it. No more.*

September 2004

On the first day of class, Nate asks me what I want to be called.

"Oh, I don't know," I say, fussing with equipment in the room. I know. But I feel embarrassed, as if I have been found out. "What do you think?" I ask them.

They shuffle around, equally embarrassed. We all know that I have to decide, and that whatever I decide will shape our class room dynamic in very important ways.

"What does Gennari ask you to call him?" I have inherited several of these students from my husband, John Gennari, another professor of African-American studies. He is white.

"Oh, we call him John," Nate says with confidence. I am immediately envious of the easy warmth he seems to feel for John. I suspect it has to do with the name thing.

"Well, just call me Emily, then. This is an honors class, after all. And I do know several of you already. And then wouldn't it be strange to call the husband John and the wife Professor?" Okay, I have convinced myself.

Nate says, "Well, John and I play basketball in a pickup game on Wednesdays. So, you know, it would be weird for me to be checking him and calling him Professor Gennari."

We all laugh and move on to other topics. But my mind locks onto an image of my husband and Nate on the basketball court, two white men covered in sweat, body to body, heads down, focused on the ball.

October 2004

"It's not that I can't say it, it's that I don't want to. I will not say it," Sarah says. She wears her copper-red hair in a short, smart style that makes her look older than her years. When she smiles I remember how young she is. She is not smiling now. She looks indignant. She is indignant because I am insinuating that there is a problem with the fact that no one in the class will say "nigger." Her indignation pleases me.

Good.

"I'd just like to remind you all that just because a person refuses to say 'nigger,' that doesn't mean that person is not a racist," I say. They seem to consider this.

"And another thing," Sarah continues. "About dressing for class. I dislike it when my professors come to class in shorts, for instance. This is a profession. They should dress professionally."

Later, I tell my husband, John, about our class discussion. When I get to Sarah's comment about professors in shorts, he says, "Good for her."

I hold up *Nigger* and show its cover to the class. I hand it to the person on my left, gesture for him to pass the book around the room.

"Isn't it strange that when we refer to this book, we keep calling it 'the n-word'?"

Lauren comments on the affect of one student who actually said it. "Colin looked like he was being strangled." Of the effect on the other students, she says, "I saw us all collectively cringing."

"Would you be able to say it if I weren't here?" I blurt. A few students shake their heads. Tyler's hand shoots up. He always sits directly to my right.

"That's just bullshit," he says to the class, and I force myself not to raise an eyebrow at "bullshit." "If Emily weren't here, you all would be able to say that word."

I note that he himself has not said it, but I do not make this observation out loud.

"No." Sarah is firm. "I just don't want to be the kind of person who says that word, period."

"Even in this context?" I ask.

"Regardless of context," Sarah says.

"Even when it's the title of a book?"

I tell the students that I often work with a book called *Nigger Heaven*, written in 1926 by a white man, Carl Van Vechten.

"Look, I don't want to give you the impression that I am somehow longing for you guys to say 'nigger,'" I tell them, "but I do think that something is lost when you don't articulate it, especially if the context almost demands its articulation."

"What do you mean? What exactly is lost?" Sarah insists.

"I don't know," I say. I do know. But right here, in this moment, the last thing I want is to win an argument that winds up with Sarah saying "nigger" out loud.

Throughout our discussion, Nate is the only student who will say "nigger" out loud. He sports a shearling coat and a caesar haircut. He quotes Jay-Z. He makes a case for "nigga." He is that kind of white kid; he is down. "He is so down. he's almost up," Todd will say in December, when I show him the title page of Nate's final paper for this class. The page contains one word, "Nigger," in black type against a white background. It is an autobiographical essay. It is a very good paper.

October 1994

Nate reminds me of a student in the very first class I taught all on my own, a senior seminar called "Race and Representation." I was still in graduate school. It was 1994 and *Pulp Fiction* had just come out. I spent an entire three-hour class session arguing with my students over the way race was represented in the movie. One student in particular passionately resisted my attempts to analyze the way Tarantino used "nigger" in the movie.

"What is his investment in this word? What is he, as the white director, getting out of saying 'nigger' over and over again?" I asked.

After some protracted verbal arm wrestling, the student gave in.

"Okay, okay! I want to be the white guy who can say 'nigger' to black guys and get away with it. I want to be the cool white guy who can say 'nigger.'"

"Thank you! Thank you for admitting it!" I said, and everyone laughed.

He was tall. He wore tie-dyed T-shirts and had messy, curly brown hair. I don't remember his name.

After *Pulp Fiction* came out, I wrote my older brother an earnest, academic e-mail. I wanted to "initiate a dialogue" with him about the "cultural and political implications of the various usages of 'nigger' in popular culture."

His one-sentence reply went something like this: "Nigga, niggoo, niggu, negreaux, negrette, niggrum."

"Do you guys ever read *The Source* magazine?" In 1994, my students knew about *The Source;* some of them had read James Bernard's column, "Doin' the Knowledge."

"He's my brother," I said, not bothering to mask my pride with anything like cool indifference. "He's coming to visit class in a couple of weeks, when we discuss hip-hop culture."

The eyes of the tie-dyed student glistened.

"Quentin Tarantino is a cool-ass white boy!" James said on the day he came to visit my class. "He is one cool white boy."

My students clapped and laughed.

"That's what I said," my tie-dyed student sighed.

James looked at me slyly. I narrowed my eyes at him. *Thanks a lot.*

September 2004

On the way to school in the morning, I park my car in the Allen House lot. Todd was the one who told me about the lot. He said, "Everyone thinks the lot at the library is closer, but the lot behind Allen House is so much better. Plus, there are always spaces, in part because everyone rushes for the library."

It is true that the library lot is nearly always full in the morning. It's also true that the Allen House lot is relatively empty, and much closer to my office. But if it were even just slightly possible for me to find a space in the library lot, I would probably try to park there, for one reason. To get to my office from Allen House, I have to cross a busy street. To get to my office from the library, I do not.

Several months ago, I was crossing the same busy street to get to my office after a class. It was later April, near the end of the semester, and it seemed as if everyone was outside. Parents were visiting, and students were yelling to each other, introducing family members from across the street. People smiled at me—wide, grinning smiles. I smiled back. We were all giddy with the promise of spring, which always comes so late in Vermont, if it comes at all.

Traffic was heavy, I noticed as I walked along the sidewalk, calculating the moment when I would attempt to cross. A car was stopped near me; I heard rough voices. Out of the corner of my eye, I looked into the car: all white. I looked away, but I could feel them surveying the small crowd that was carrying me along. As traffic picked up again, one of the male voices yelled out, "Queers! Fags!" There was laughter. Then the car roared off.

I was stunned. I stopped walking and let the words wash over me. *Queer. Fag.* Annihilating, surely. I remembered my role as a teacher, a mentor, in loco parentis, even though there were real parents everywhere. I looked around to check for the wounds caused by those hateful words. I peered down the street: too late for a license plate. All around me, students and parents marched to their destinations as if they hadn't heard. *Didn't you hear that?* I wanted to shout.

All the while I was thinking, *Not nigger. Not yet.*

October 2004

Nate jumps in.

"Don't you grant a word power by not saying it? Aren't we in some way amplifying its ugliness by avoiding it?" he asks.

"I am afraid of how I will be affected by saying it," Lauren says. "I just don't want that word in my mouth."

Tyler remembers a phrase attributed to Farai Chideya in Randall Kennedy's essay. He finds it and reads it to us. "She says that the n-word is the 'trump card, the nuclear bomb of racial epithets.'"

"Do you agree with that?" I ask.

Eleven heads nod vigorously.

"Nuclear bombs annihilate. What do you imagine will be destroyed if you guys use the word in here?"

Shyly, they look at me, all of them, and I understand. Me. It is my annihilation they imagine.

November 2004

Some of My Best Friends, my anthology of essays about interracial friendship, came out in August, and the publicity department has arranged for various interviews and other promotional events. When I did an on-air interview on a New York radio show, one of the hosts, Janice, a black woman, told me that the reason she could not marry a white man was because she believed if things ever got heated between them, the white man would call her a nigger.

I nodded my head. I had heard this argument before. But strangely I had all but forgotten it. The fact that I had forgotten to fear "nigger" coming from the mouth of my white husband was more interesting to me than her fear, alive and ever-present.

"Are you biracial?"

"No."

"Are you married to a white man?"

"Yes."

These were among the first words exchanged between Janice, the radio host, and me. I could tell—by the way she looked at me, and didn't look at me; by the way she kept her body turned away from me; by her tone—that she had made up her mind about me before I entered the room. I could tell that she didn't like what she had decided about me, and that she had decided I was the wrong kind of black person. Maybe it was what I had written in *Some of My Best Friends*. Maybe it was the fact that I had decided to edit a collection about interracial friendships at all. When we met, she said, "I don't trust white people," as decisively and exactly as if she were handing me her business card. I knew she was telling me that I was foolish to trust them, to marry one. I was relieved to look inside myself and see that I was okay, I was still standing. A few years ago, her silent judgment—this silent judgment from any black person—would have crushed me.

When she said she could "tell" I was married to a white man, I asked her how. She said, "Because you are so friendly," and did a little dance with her shoulders. I laughed.

But Janice couldn't help it; she liked me in spite of herself. As the interview progressed, she let the corners of her mouth turn up in a smile. She admitted that she had a few white friends, even if they sometimes drove her crazy. At a commercial break, she said, "Maybe I ought to try a white man." She was teasing me, of course. She hadn't changed her mind about white people, or dating a white man, but she had changed her mind about me. It mattered to me. I took what she was offering. But when the interview was over, I left it behind.

My husband thought my story about the interview was hilarious. When I got home, he listened to the tape they gave me at the station. He said he wanted to use the interview in one of his classes.

A few days later, I told him what Janice had said about dating a white man, that she won't because she is afraid he will call her a nigger. As I told him, I felt an unfamiliar shyness creep up on me.

"That's just so far out of ... it's not in my head at all." He was having difficulty coming up with the words he wanted, I could tell. But that was okay. I knew what he meant. I looked at him sitting in his chair, the chair his mother gave us. I can usually find him in that chair when I come home. He is John, I told myself. And he is white. No more or less John and no more or less white than he was before the interview, and Janice's reminder of the fear that I had forgotten to feel.

I tell my students in the African-American autobiography class about Janice. I say, "You would not believe the indignities I have suffered in my humble attempts to 'move this product,' as they say in publishing." I say, "I have been surrounded by morons, and now I gratefully return to the land of the intellectually agile." They laugh.

I flatter them, in part because I feel guilty that I have missed so many classes in order to do publicity for my book. But I cringe, thinking of how I have called Janice, another black woman, a "moron" in front of these white students. I do not tell my students she is black.

"Here is a story for your students," John tells me. We are in the car, on our way to Cambridge for the weekend. "The only time I ever heard 'nigger' in my home growing up was when my father's cousin was over for a visit. It was 1988, I remember. Jesse Jackson was running for president. My father's cousin was sitting in the kitchen, talking to my parents about the election. 'I'm going to vote for the nigger,' my father's cousin said. 'He's the only one who cares about the workingman.'"

John laughs. He often laughs when he hears something extraordinary, whether it's good or bad.

"That's fascinating," I say.

The next time class meets, I tell my students this story.

"So what do we care about in this sentence?" I say. "The fact that John's father's cousin used a racial epithet, or the fact that his voting for Jackson conveys a kind of ultimate respect for him? Isn't his voting for Jackson more important for black progress than how his father's cousin *feels*?"

I don't remember what the students said. What I remember is that I tried to project for them a sense that I was untroubled by saying "nigger," by my husband's saying "nigger," by his father's cousin's having said "nigger," by his parents'—my in-laws'—tolerance of "nigger" in their home, years ago, long before I came along. What I remember is that I leaned on the word "feels" with a near sneer in my voice. *It's an intellectual issue,* I beamed at them, and then I directed it back at myself. *It has nothing to do with how it makes me feel.*

After my interview with Janice, I look at the white people around me differently, as if from a distance. I do this, from time to time, almost as an exercise. I even do it to my friends, particularly my friends. Which of them has "nigger" in the back of her throat?

I go out for drinks with David, my senior colleague. It is a ritual. We go on Thursdays after class, always to the same place. I know that he will order, in succession, two draft beers, and that he will ask the waitress to help him choose the second. "What do you have on draft that is interesting tonight?" he will say. I order red wine, and I, too, always ask the waitress's advice. Then we order a selection of cheeses, again soliciting assistance. We have our favorite waitresses. We like the ones who indulge us.

Tonight David orders a cosmopolitan.

We never say it, but I suspect we both like the waitresses who appreciate the odd figure we cut. He is white, sixty-something, male. I am black, thirty-something, female. Not such an odd pairing elsewhere, perhaps, but uncommon in Burlington, insofar as black people are uncommon in Burlington.

Something you can't see is that we are both from the South. Different Souths, perhaps, thirty years apart, black and white. I am often surprised by how much I like his company.

All the way up here, I sometimes think when I am with him, *and I am sitting with the South, the white South that, all of my childhood, I longed to escape.* I once had a white boyfriend from New Orleans. "A white southerner, Emily?" my mother asked, and sighed with worry. I understood. We broke up.

David and I catch up. We talk about the writing we have been doing. We talk each other out of bad feelings we are harboring against this and that person. (Like most southerners, like the South in general, David and I have long memories.) We talk about classes. I describe to him the conversation I have been having with my students about "nigger." He laughs at my anecdotes.

I am on my second glass of wine. I try to remember to keep my voice down. It's a very nice restaurant. *People in Burlington do not want to hear "nigger" while they are eating a nice dinner,* I say, chastising myself. I am tipsy.

As we leave, I accidentally knock my leg against a chair. *You are drunk,* I tell myself. *You are drunk and black in a restaurant in Burlington. What were you thinking?* I feel eyes on me as I walk out of the restaurant, eyes that may have been focused elsewhere, as far as I know, because I do not allow myself to look.

Later that evening, I am alone. I remember that David recently gave me a poem of his to read, a poem about his racist grandmother, now dead, whom he remembers using the word "nigger" often and with relish. I lie in bed and reconstruct the scene of David and me in the restaurant, our conversation about "nigger." Was his grandmother at the table with us all along?

The next day, I see David in his office, which is next to mine, on the other side from Todd. I knock on the door. He invites me in. I sit in a chair, the chair I always sit in when I come to talk to him. He tells me how much he enjoyed our conversation the night before.

"Me too," I say. "But today it's as if I'm looking at you across from something," I say. "It has to do with race." I blame a book I am reading, a book for my African-American autobiography class, Toi Derricotte's *The Black Notebooks.*

"Have you read it?" David is a poet, like Derricotte.

"No, but I know Toi and enjoy her poetry. Everything I know about her and her work would lead me to believe that I would enjoy that book." He is leaning back in his chair, his arms folded behind his head.

"Well, it's making me think about things, remember the ways that you and I will always be different," I say abruptly.

David laughs. "I hope not." He looks puzzled.

"It's probably just temporary." I don't ask him my question about his grandmother, whether or not she is always somewhere with him, in him, in the back of his throat.

John is at an African-American studies conference in New York. Usually I am thrilled to have the house to myself for a few days. But this time I mope. I sit at the dining room table, write this essay, gaze out the window.

Today, when John calls, he describes the activity at the conference. He tells me delicious and predictable gossip about people we know, and the divas that we know of. The personalities, the infighting—greedily we sift over details on the phone.

"Did you enjoy your evening with David last night?" he asks.

"I did, very much," I say. "But give me more of the who-said-what." I know he's in a hurry. In fact, he's talking on a cell phone (my cell phone; he refuses to get one of his own) as he walks down a New York street.

"Oh, you know these Negroes." His voice jounces as he walks.

"Yeah," I say, laughing. I wonder who else can hear him.

Todd is married to Hilary, another of my close friends in the department. She is white. Like John, Todd is out of town this weekend. Since their two boys were born, our godsons, John and I see them less frequently than we used to. But Hilary and I are determined to spend some time together this weekend, with our husbands away.

Burlington traffic keeps me from her and the boys for an hour, even though she lives only blocks away from me. When I get there, the boys are ready for their baths, one more feeding, and then bed. Finally they are down, and we settle into grown-up conversation. I tell her about my class, our discussions about "nigger," and my worries about David.

"That's the thing about the South," Hilary says. I agree, but then start to wonder about her grandmother. I decide I do not want to know, not tonight.

I do tell her, however, about the fear I have every day in Burlington, crossing that street to get back and forth from my office, what I do to guard myself against the fear.

"Did you grow up hearing that?" she asks. Even though we are close, and alone, she does not say the word.

I start to tell her a story I have never told anyone. It is a story about the only time I remember being called a nigger to my face.

"I was a teenager, maybe sixteen. I was standing on a sidewalk, trying to cross a busy street after school, to get to the mall and meet my friends. I happened to make eye contact with a white man in a car that was sort of stopped—traffic was heavy. Anyway, he just said it, kind of spit it up at me.

"Oh, that's why," I say, stunned, remembering the daily ritual I have just confessed to her. She looks at me, just as surprised.

December 2004

I am walking down a Burlington street with my friend Anh. My former quilting teacher, Anh is several years younger than I am. She has lived in Vermont her whole life. She is Vietnamese; her parents are white. Early in our friendship, she told me her father was a logger, as were most of the men in her family. *Generations of Vietnamese loggers in Vermont,* I mused. It wasn't until I started to describe her to someone else that I realized she must be adopted.

Anh and I talk about race, about being minorities in Burlington, but we usually do it indirectly. In quilting class, we would give each other looks sometimes that said, *You are not alone,* or *Oh, brother,* when the subject of race came up in our class, which was made up entirely of white women, aside from the two of us.

There was the time, for instance, when a student explained why black men found her so attractive. "I have a black girl's butt," she said. Anh and I looked at each other: *Oh, brother.* We bent our heads back over our sewing machines.

As we walk, I tell Anh about my African-American autobiography class, the discussions my students and I have been having about "nigger." She listens, and then describes to me the latest development in her on-again, off-again relationship with her fifty-year-old boyfriend, another native Vermonter, a blond scuba instructor.

"He says everything has changed," she tells me. "He's going to clean up the messes in his life." She laughs.

Once, Anh introduced me to the boyfriend she had before the scuba instructor when I ran into them at a restaurant. He is also white.

"I've heard a lot about you," I said, and put out my hand.

"I've never slept with a black woman," he said, and shook my hand. There was wonder in his voice. I excused myself and went back to my table. Later, when I looked over at them, they were sitting side by side, not speaking.

Even though Anh and I exchanged our usual glances that night, I doubted that we would be able to recover our growing friendship.

Who could she be, dating someone like that? The next time I heard from her, months later, she had broken up with him.

I am rooting for the scuba instructor.

"He told me he's a new person," she says.

"Well, what did you say?" I ask her.

"In the immortal words of Jay-Z, I told him, 'Nigga, please.'"

I look at her and we laugh.

In lieu of a final class, my students come over for dinner. One by one, they file in. John takes coats while I pretend to look for things in the refrigerator. I can't stop smiling.

"The books of your life" is the topic for tonight. I have asked them to bring a book, a poem, a passage, some art that has affected them. Hazel has brought a children's book. Tyler talks about *Saved by the Bell*. Nate talks about Freud. Dave has a photograph. Eric reads "The Seacoast of Despair" from *Slouching Towards Bethlehem*.

I read from *Annie John* by Jamaica Kincaid. Later I will wonder why I did not read "Incident" by Countee Cullen, the poem that has been circulating in my head ever since we began our discussion about "nigger." *What held me back from bringing "Incident" to class?* The question will stay with me for months.

The night of our dinner is an emotional one. I tell my students that they are the kind of class a professor dreams about. They give me a gift certificate to the restaurant that David and I frequent. I give them copies of *Some of My Best Friends* and inscribe each one. Eric demands a hug, and then they all do; I happily comply. We talk about meeting again as a class, maybe once or twice in the spring. The two students who will be abroad promise to keep in touch through our listserv, which we all agree to keep going until the end of the school year, at least. After they leave, the house is quiet and empty.

Weeks later, I post "Incident" on our listserv and ask them to respond with their reactions. Days go by, then weeks. Silence. After more prodding, finally Lauren posts an analysis of the poem, and then her personal reactions to it. I thank her online and ask for more responses. Silence.

I get e-mails and visits from these students about other matters, some of them race-related. Eric still comes by my office regularly. Once he brings his mother to meet me, a kind and engaging woman who gives me a redolent candle she purchased in France, and tells me her son enjoyed the African-American autobiography class. Eric and I smile at each other.

A few days later, I see Eric outside the campus bookstore.

"What did you think about 'Incident'?"

"I've been meaning to write you about it. I promise I will."

In the meantime, *Nigger* is back in its special place on my bookshelf. It is tucked away so that only I can see the title on its spine, and then only with some effort.

—2005

Learning from Other Writers

1. What is the effect of Emily Bernard's choice to place Countee Cullen's poem at the start of her essay?
2. What is the central question that Bernard is exploring in this essay? Is this the same question she urges her students to explore in her course?

3. What is the effect of placing the "October 2004" section *before* the "September 2004" section? Of skipping from there back to "October 1994"? And then back to September 2004? If you had been Emily Bernard's editor, would you have advised her to put her sections in simple chronological order? Why or why not?
4. Does anything surprise you about this professor's view of her students? Her class? Her subject? Her experiences outside the classroom?
5. What do you learn or see in a new way from reading this essay? Could you have learned this more effectively from a more traditional essay or academic paper? Why or why not?

LILY TUCK

GROUP GRIEF

In the elevator going down from the seventeenth floor, everyone is crying. My bereavement support group has just let out. The Visiting Nurse Service of New York runs two groups: one is for adults whose parents have died, the other is for adults whose life partner or spouse has died. My group meets one evening a week for an hour and a half. It lasts eight weeks and is free. According to an article in this December's *Harvard Women's Health Watch* newsletter, I am among the one million Americans who have lost a spouse this year.

I. Sharing Our Stories

There are seven of us in the group—five women, two men, plus the bereavement counselor, Sally. Each session has a theme. The first thing Sally asks us to do is write our spouse's name on a little stone with a felt marker. I write *Edward,* but the last *d* does not quite fit on the stone: *Edwar.* Then Sally tells us to shut our eyes, put our feet flat on the floor (we are sitting) and our hands palms-up on our thighs, and breathe deeply. I do yoga and I know about breathing exercises, but instead of making me relax, they make me anxious—most of the time I can't tell whether I am inhaling or exhaling—nevertheless I try to inhale deeply through my nose and exhale through my mouth. Afterward we go around the table and each one of us has a chance to tell his or her story.

Fred, who is a dapper, chatty, white-haired man in, I guess, his mid-seventies, and who sits on my right, begins. Fred was married for fifty-four years, and one of the hardest things for him now, he says, is having to shop and cook for himself. He starts to say that something else is hard, but he starts to cry and cannot go on.

Amy goes next. She is an African American in her late forties, the youngest in the group. She wears large gold hoop earrings, which she touches and twirls nervously. Amy tells how her husband, Johnny, was on dialysis and sick for a long time. She says that although she knew Johnny was going to die, she was not prepared for how she felt after he did. She has panic attacks, she cannot sleep or eat, her heart beats too fast; only her daughter, whom she looks after, keeps her from jumping out of the window.

Next is Florence, an older, heavyset woman, also an African American. Florence has a quiet dignity. She tells how she was cooking supper for her husband the way she always did, only that night it happened to be his favorite meal—fish cakes, sweet potatoes, and green beans—and how her husband, also called Johnny, told her he was just going to run to the corner for a minute and buy a lotto ticket, and then she tells how she waited and waited for him, supper getting cold and getting spoilt, and after an hour and a half had gone by, the telephone rang, and it was a call from Bellevue Hospital saying her husband had been hit by a bicycle and was in the emergency room. Her husband underwent several operations but he never fully recovered. Her husband, who was six foot five inches, a big man, deteriorated horribly, Florence said; he no longer looked or acted like himself, nor was he able to care for himself. After her husband died, Florence, like Amy, could not eat or sleep. Eventually she had to take antidepressants, and although she feels calmer now, the feelings of grief and loss remain.

Sue, a Korean-American woman, starts out by saying how all their lives she and her husband worked hard; how they saved their money in order to give their three children an education; and how this year, finally, their youngest son, who is twenty-three years old, got a job, and Sue and her husband could stop sending him money. Sue and her husband were looking forward to spending the money on themselves, giving themselves some small—small, she repeats the word—pleasures, like ballroom dancing lessons. Sue is a tidy-looking woman with short dark hair. I guess she is in her late fifties or early sixties, about my age. (I am sixty-four.) Then her husband got sick, Sue says. A tumor on his kidney was removed, he had chemotherapy, the cancer did not appear to have spread—Sue speaks matter-of-factly; she and her husband were able to resume the ballroom dancing lessons. After a few months, however, her husband began to have digestion problems (without any sign of embarrassment. Sue describes in detail his bowel movements, or lack of them, and having to administer enemas), and he had to go back to the hospital. A larger tumor was found. This time the tumor was inoperable. Sue says that she too is on antidepressant medication, but yesterday, Sunday, she could not get out of bed all day. Also, her whole body aches. Sue raises her arms in the air and starts to cry.

Robert, a gray-haired man in his fifties, who was married for thirty-one years and whose wife, Marjorie, died four months ago of lung cancer, shakes his head. The only thing he says is that he sometimes thinks that Marjorie never existed.

Teresa is the loose cannon; I don't trust her. The first thing she says is that she suffered from child abuse. She speaks with a thick middle European accent, and she is difficult to understand. Teresa's brown hair is cut short, in bangs, a girlish hairstyle that does not suit her. She frowns when she speaks (maybe she is nearsighted, I don't know). William, Teresa's husband, had a lovely singing voice, she says. He also played the trumpet, but then he got throat cancer. For two years William had to be fed through a tube in his stomach. Teresa shows how she opened the cans of Ensure and poured them into the tube. Twice the tube broke and had to be replaced. One day William could not get out of bed; when he tried, he fell to the floor. He was foaming at the mouth, Teresa says. She called 911, and in her panic she could not remember her street address, whether it was 325 or 235—she had to look it up in the phone book. By the time the paramedics arrived it was too late. Nevertheless, they spent an hour trying to resuscitate William. To show how hard they tried, Teresa grabs and squeezes the arm of the man sitting next to her, Robert, Marjorie's husband.

My turn, but I cannot speak.

2. *The Journey of Grief*

What shall I do about my wife's clothes? Fred asks right away. He says he does not know whether to keep the clothes or give them away. (Earlier, as we were coming in, Fred seemed cheerful enough: he commented on the cold weather, asked each one of us how our week had been, joked with Sally.) Now his face crumples and he starts to cry. Sally makes soothing noises and tells him that it is probably too soon. She also says it is best to give clothes away to someone one knows. Fred says his wife was very petite, very slender; he does not know anyone who would fit into her clothes. She had a lot of beautiful clothes, he adds. Sue, the Korean-American woman, says that she got rid of all her husband's clothes right away, that she could not bear the sight of them. She asked her children to dispose of them and they did. Now she regrets that she did not keep something, a sweater. Sally tells how someone once told her about finding a candy in one of her husband's pockets and she ate it. The candy was a comfort. (What, I think, if she had found a condom? a woman's phone number? But I don't say anything. Am I the only one who has these dark thoughts?)

One of my problems, I realize, is that I tend to feel superior to other people—smarter and, years ago, probably prettier too—and that has always been my problem. Why can't I act like everyone else? Why can't I just fit into the group? Why must I be so judgmental? I remember how once a writing teacher told me I had an "attitude," and I could never write until I got rid of it. He was probably right. Another time, in another group, we were asked to write down the quality we liked best about ourselves, and everyone wrote down things like loyalty, honesty, a sense of humor, and I, to show off (and to disrupt), wrote: my slender ankles.

Tonight there are only six of us—no Robert.

In the printout we have been given, grief is defined as "the realization that life will no longer be lived in the way we expected. We grieve not only the past history we've shared with our loved one, but also our hopes and dreams for the future." This realization will affect us on a number of different levels: physical, emotional, cognitive, and spiritual. Under the cognitive level it says: "Inability to concentrate, preoccupation with thoughts of your loved one or the days and events leading up to the death."

My husband, Edward, who was seventy-five, died within ten days of when he was diagnosed with cholangiocarcinoma, which is cancer of the gallbladder. When I telephoned the doctor to tell him that Edward had died, even he could not hide his surprise. "Oh, my," he said. A friend, who is also a doctor, said, "Edward might as well have been run over by a truck, it happened so fast." All I can think about now is those last days of his life.

In August, while we were vacationing in our house on an island in Maine, Edward said he had a pain in his chest, on the right side; it hurt him to take a deep breath, cough, or sneeze. Earlier, he had slipped on rocks on the beach while swimming, and we assumed he had broken or cracked a rib, and we also both knew that nothing could be done about that. However, the pain did not go away, it got worse. Mid-August, we went by boat to the neighboring, larger island, where there was a physician's assistant. The PA examined Edward and found nothing amiss. She did, however, suggest that he have blood work done at Penobscot Bay Medical Center, the nearest hospital on the mainland, but with two more weeks of vacation left and houseguests arriving, Edward decided to wait until we returned to the city. By this time, we had discarded the broken-rib theory and had adopted the gallstones theory.

On September 5, home again, Edward had a thorough physical checkup, the first in many years (Edward was the sort of person who shunned both doctors and dentists). The physician, whom Edward liked, found nothing much wrong except when he did an ultrasound of Edward's liver, but even so, he did not seem particularly alarmed. Edward then underwent a number of procedures (a hateful word): a colonoscopy, a CAT scan, an endoscopy, and finally a biopsy of his liver. All this took time. During that time, Edward, who was a lawyer, continued to go to the office, although he went in later and came home earlier than usual. He was tired and his skin had turned yellow. He had lost his appetite and no longer drank alcohol, not even a glass or two of red wine, which he had always enjoyed. In addition, he had trouble sleeping. One night—temporarily, I hoped, I had moved to the guest room—I was woken by Edward opening the front door. "Where have you been?" He had frightened me. "I could not sleep. I went walking around the block," Edward answered. "But it's three o'clock in the morning!" I said. Finally a tentative diagnosis was made (it still was not 100 percent clear where the cancer had originated, also there was a slight possibility that the cancer was lymphoma, which is treatable), and Edward made an appointment to see an oncologist at Memorial Sloan-Kettering Cancer Center.

The appointment was on Friday, September 27. Edward and I went together. By this time, Edward's stomach was very bloated and he was in severe discomfort. After the oncologist, Dr. Carlton (not his real name, and all names but Edward's have been changed), had examined Edward and studied the pathologist's report, he told Edward that in his case, since the cancer had spread so invasively to the liver, neither chemotherapy nor radiation was an option. Edward then asked Dr. Carlton how long he thought he still had to live. Dr. Carlton answered: "Oh, I would say between two to six months" (which makes me think of the article by Dr. Jerome Groopman in *The New Yorker* not too long ago about how ill equipped doctors are at predicting their patients' life expectancy). Edward got dressed and we went home; he died five days later.

Sally hands out paper and crayons and says we are going to do a visualization exercise. Sally tells us to shut our eyes and breathe deeply and try to relax as she reads aloud a description of a bridge. She then asks us to draw that bridge from the place where we are now to the place where we hope to be in the future. I draw a blue line straight across the page, and around the line I draw blue and green tsunamis. Gradually the waves diminish in size and become a tranquil pool—wishful thinking, I think.

Fred says he could not draw anything.

Amy drew a window with rain outside. She says she cannot see beyond that.

Florence says she could not see the bridge. She drew a smudgy black line across the paper.

Sue drew mountains and a little figure at the bottom. She says she cannot picture herself getting to the top. As a matter of fact, she cannot picture any kind of life for herself at all, and she starts to cry.

Perhaps, Sally tells Sue, they should talk privately.

Teresa drew a house and a tree and a figure running away. Ever since she was seven years old, she says, her mother would grab her by the hair and beat her head against a wall. Her mother, Teresa says, wanted to kill her.

I am the only one who drew the damn bridge.

3. Asking for Help

Again Fred starts out by talking about his wife's clothes. Again Sally says that it may be too soon to give them away. Maybe, she suggests, Fred should put the clothes in a box, a first step. Fred says all right. He also says that he feels he is slipping backward. Three months since his wife died, and he seemed to be coping better before. For example, he says, he goes into the kitchen and can't remember what he went in there for. This happens all the time now; he can't concentrate.

Frowning, Teresa says the same thing happens to her. Teresa, I notice, is wearing the same clothes, a plaid suit, she wore last week and the week before. I too, I realize, wear the same thing every day—a long, gray wool cardigan. The cardigan is a small comfort.

No Florence and still no Robert this week.

Amy is going to visit her in-laws for the holidays. Reaching for the box of tissues on the table, she says she is afraid that her mother-in-law is going to disapprove of her grieving and crying all the time.

Fred says he likes to go out so long as he doesn't have to talk about his wife.

I say I feel just the opposite. I want to talk about Edward when I go out. I don't want to hear people talk about trivia or laugh or tell jokes. I want them to honor my grief, I say dramatically. I am not fine, I add, and I am not going to "have a nice day."

Sally hands out a sheet with a list of the dos and don'ts of what you say to a grieving person. Some of the don'ts are:

"I know you will be okay ..."

"At least you have your children ..."

"It's God's will ..."

"Time heals all wounds ..."

Wiping her eyes with the tissue, Amy says that on the day of her husband's funeral, her brother came up to her and said: Amy, I don't want you to be lonely—when are you going to find someone else? We agree that was the dumbest thing in the world he could say.

Apropos of nothing. Teresa tells about a dream she had in which her husband asked her to write a letter to his mother, who died a long time ago. She tells the group that her husband fled the Communists and went to Siberia, where his father and his three brothers were killed, and also that he never saw his mother again.

Sally asks her how she feels about the dream.

Teresa says the dream frightened her.

I do not tell the group that last night I again dreamt about Edward. In my dream, I am walking somewhere and I am going to throw away a garlic clove (this summer, in Maine, I was given a garlic clove, red garlic, by a friend who grew it in his garden, and I have the clove in my kitchen now, only in the dream the garlic clove is larger and far heavier; inexplicably, it is the size of a rabbit) and Edward is with me. When we stop walking, he kisses me. The kiss is hard to describe: it is passionate but not sexual, our mouths are pressed together. Afterward, in the dream, Edward tells me to write him a letter—a one-page letter, he specifies. In the morning, first thing, I write:

> Dear Edward,
>
> I wish we could have had more time together. I wish we could have driven through Tuscany and Umbria together. I wish we could have gone to Burma, the way we had talked about, and watched as the "dawn comes up like thunder outer China 'crost the Bay!" I wish we could have gone to Paris again and had dinner at the Voltaire, the restaurant we liked so much, and drunk a lot of good wine and eaten white asparagus to start with and veal kidneys cooked in a mustard sauce and fraises des bois for dessert; I wish we could have walked hand in hand around the reservoir in Central Park just one more time. I love you very much. I don't think I knew how much I loved you until you died. I miss you more than I can ever say or write, you gave me a marvelous life.
>
> Lily

4. Taking Care of Ourselves

I went away Christmas week and missed this session (only two people came to it, Fred and Florence). Over the holidays, my daughter-in-law gave me *A Grief Observed* by C. S. Lewis. (Earlier, someone had given me *When Things Fall Apart: Heart Advice for Difficult Times* by Pema Chödrön, a Buddhist nun. I tried to read it but nothing she said stayed with me—that my grief can also be my source of wisdom sounds good but is too abstract and not practical.) In *A Grief Observed*, Lewis begins by writing: "No one ever told me that grief felt so like fear. I am not afraid, but the sensation is like being afraid."

And speaking of being afraid, normally I am afraid to fly. This time, as I flew to California for the holidays, I almost wished for turbulence or for worse—what did I care? To make matters still worse, last year Edward and I had also spent the holidays in California, and I would be at the same hotel we had stayed in together, and that, more than anything else, made me afraid. "At first," C. S. Lewis also writes, "I was afraid of going to places where H. [his wife] and I were happy—our favourite pub, our favourite wood. But I decided to do it at once—like sending a pilot up again as soon as possible after he's had a crash. Unexpectedly, it makes no difference. Her absence is no more emphatic in those places than anywhere else. It's not local at all ... Her absence is like the sky, spread over everything."

5. Using Rituals to Heal Our Grief

Tonight there are only four of us: Teresa, Fred, Florence, and myself. Hard to believe but true, once more Fred speaks about his wife's clothes. This time, however, he says that he feels much better about the clothes because, urged by his sons, he has made up his mind to give the clothes away. Sally nods her approval.

Teresa says that she has thirteen cases of Ensure (everyone understands her to say "booze") and does not know what to do with them. There are various tentative suggestions before it becomes clear what the cases in fact contain.

Florence says she stayed home alone for Christmas. For the first time since her husband died, she cooked herself a proper dinner (Florence was the one cooking dinner when her husband went out to buy a lotto ticket and was run over by a bicycle). She describes how she stuffed a chicken, bought cranberry sauce, and cooked string beans. Everyone agrees that cooking is a therapeutic activity.

Sally begins by listing certain rituals that could be helpful: lighting a candle, planting a tree—not so easy in the city—going to a homeless shelter to help out, giving money to charity, wearing the spouse's ring or making it into another piece of jewelry.

I say that, to me, rituals smack of superstition and I am superstitious enough as it is.

Fred says he is taking care of his wife's hibiscus plants, and for him that is like a ritual.

I say, "What if the plants should die?"

"The plants have never done better," Fred answers me.

Edward and I were married six weeks after we met, we were so certain of each other. Afterward we took our combined children, six teenagers, to Europe on our honeymoon. In a rented Volkswagen bus, we drove from Paris to Venice. During those two weeks, the children made it clear how much they disliked us—one of us—and each other. Whenever Edward and I looked back on that time, we would marvel at our naive optimism and laugh out loud.

Next Sally says that we are going to do a visualization exercise. She reads from a piece she calls "The Wise Guide." (I understand her to say "Wise Guy.") In the piece, we are walking through a pretty wood, gentle breezes are blowing, birds are chirping. Then we get to a moss-covered clearing where there is a fire burning and the Wise Guide is waiting for us. We sit down next to the Wise Guide and we are allowed to ask him a question. After he answers it he gives us a present that we can take back home with us.

Tonight everyone strikes me as particularly stupid and uninteresting, and Teresa, I have decided unkindly, is certifiably mad. To make matters worse, the Wise Guide in the story makes me think of a hunchbacked dwarf with a long white beard in a fairy tale. We are supposed to draw what comes to mind. I don't draw anything. Nevertheless, the question that comes to my mind, the one I would ask the Wise Guide, is:

"Where is Edward?"

6. Spirituality for Healing Grief

There are six of us—Robert, Sally tells us, wrote her a letter saying he was not coming back, but he did not state a reason. I keep thinking about his wife, Marjorie, and his saying that sometimes he thought Marjorie never existed. I too am afraid, not that I will think Edward never existed, but that his memory will fade. Already, it has a bit. The physical part I remember best about Edward is his head, a big heavy head, and his hair, thick curly blondish-white hair. Edward had a wonderful leonine look, with robust legs. Like C. S. Lewis writing about his wife, I fear that "slowly, quietly, like snow-flakes—like the small flakes that come when it is going to snow all night—little flakes of me, my impressions, my selections, are settling down on the image of her. The real shape will be quite hidden in the end. Ten minutes—ten seconds of the real H. would correct all this. And yet, even if those ten seconds were allowed me, one second later the little flakes would begin to fall again. The rough, sharp, cleansing tang of her otherness is gone. What pitiable cant to say, 'She will live forever in my memory!' *Live?* That is exactly what she won't do."

We begin with another visualization exercise. After handing out the paper and crayons, Sally reads a piece describing how one can put all one's anxieties and troubles into a box and send the box—there could be several boxes—across a smooth surface. We are to draw what we see. I am reminded of the Isaac Bashevis Singer story about how if everyone was told to put all his troubles inside a sack and put the sack in the center of the room and then everyone could choose any sack to take away, how everyone would choose his own sack of troubles. Familiarity breeds what? acceptance? resignation? more familiarity?

I see a bomb exploding in the box I draw in my head.

Sally asks me what I felt when she read, and I say I did not feel anything. In spite of myself, I go on to tell her that I feel infantilized by these stories (why can't I just keep quiet? why must I sound so angry?) and that my grief is being trivialized by having to draw pictures. I compare this to our way of thinking about 9/11 (with a big nod to Joan Didion)—why must we feel okay? Sally looks both hurt and pleased—pleased that I have spoken out. She says she worried about me and about my body language. *Body language!* (I hate Sally all of a sudden, and I hate her clothes—a clown outfit—at each session she has worn the same odd-looking overalls that require suspenders.) And what, I think, if I were to slap or kick her? Would she still consider that body language? Unruffled, Sally goes on to say that drawing can bring one in touch with some other level of feeling. I say I feel very much in touch with my feelings—too much, in fact. Sally then says that counseling is not like therapy. Counseling is meant to be educational and to leave one with more positive feelings.

Turning on me and sounding smug, Fred asks: What is it that you are looking for?

I say I don't know. Something more. Words of comfort. Words of wisdom.

Fred says, Wisdom does not exist. Only experience.

Fuck you, Fred, I want to tell him.

Florence says that she has tried the ritual of lighting a candle in front of a picture of her husband and speaking to him for fifteen minutes each day. She says that this has made her feel better.

Sue says that all of a sudden, she does not know why, she feels a bit better too. During the holidays, her children and friends gave her many gifts, more gifts than she had ever received in her life, and for the first time she realized how loved she was. Her daughter who had always appeared cold is now very affectionate. She feels she must go on for her children's sake. She has made a plan for her life. No more tears, she says; she has to be strong. Not looking at me—no one but Teresa, who is frowning, looks at me—Sue says that everyone has to find their own way to deal with their grief.

Sally says that since the theme of this session is spirituality, does anyone have anything to say about that?

Florence says that her sister keeps calling and telling her to read the Bible, but her sister, she says, has a husband.

Afraid of offending again, I don't say how a few friends, who are religious, have sent me cards saying that they have arranged for special Masses to be said for Edward's soul. Likewise, a Buddhist priest friend wrote that he asked his brother monks in a faraway monastery in India to pray for Edward. For some reason, instead of comforting me, this irritates me. Neither Edward nor I was particularly religious. To me, although I know better and I know that prayers cannot hurt, this feels like an intrusion and as if those people have in some way appropriated Edward's soul and had no business doing it.

Teresa says she goes to church to pray, but also because it is quiet there. Then, again, she goes off on a tangent, this time about her neighbor who, Teresa says, has lost five family members, beginning with her husband, who had a heart attack last year, and a daughter who died of colon cancer. (I look over at Sally—why doesn't she stop Teresa's crazy rant? Instead, Sally is nodding encouragement at Teresa.) The neighbor drinks, Teresa continues. The neighbor is seventy-six and she began drinking when she was thirteen. She smokes, too, Teresa says. Teresa and her husband tried to help the neighbor, they gave her money, bought her groceries, but the neighbor was not grateful (who can blame her?). Teresa says she's tried to get the neighbor to come to church with her, but the neighbor refuses to.

Amy says that for her daughter's sake she has to be careful and she no longer drinks. She starts to fiddle with her gold hoop earrings. She also says that all the things that once made her happy, like Christmas and parties, make her unhappy now.

Sally says, Your life has changed.

Florence says a friend asked her to a wedding next month. The friend insists that Florence go to the wedding, but Florence does not want to go. She won't have an escort, she says, and who, she asks, would dance with her?

A week or so before he died, Edward, who loved to dance, took me in his arms and we did a brief little fox trot down the hall of the apartment.

7. Creating Your Own Inner Sanctuary

Yes! Fred starts in on how, this week, he chose some of his wife's best clothes, some of the clothes he says were custom made, and offered them to his neighbor, and as a result he feels that he has made progress and is coping better.

Shaking her head, Amy says she still feels lonely. She says that at night she sleeps in her daughter's bed instead of in her own and Johnny's bed.

Sally says that grief is a very isolating experience. One can be in a room full of people and still feel alone.

Sue says that she has always slept in her and her husband's bed, and in fact, after her husband died—in that bed—she did not change the sheets for a week. She could still smell him, she says, and there were urine stains on the sheets.

I don't say that I, too, sleep in our bed, and that while Edward was alive I used to change the sheets on the bed once a week, on Tuesday. Now the sheets don't get dirty, and only one side of the bed is slept on and the other stays fresh and clean. Sometimes two or three weeks go by before I bother to change the sheets on the bed.

Sally then asks if there is something someone wants to talk about.

Remorse and regret, I suggest.

I say I regret that I was not more tender or affectionate with Edward during the last few weeks of his life. Part of the reason for this, I say, was that I wanted to put on a brave face, I wanted to protect Edward from my own fear and grief. Also I did not want him to have to worry about me. As a result, I acted too much like an efficient nurse: Did you take your meds? Did you have a bowel movement? Did you drink enough water? I never once said: Edward, I love you.

Florence says she knows just what I mean. Two days before her husband, Johnny, died, he told her that he was tired, and although she knew perfectly well what he meant, that he was tired of living, she pretended not to, and she acted as if what he meant was that he was tired of the hospital routine, of the procedures. She said that she and her husband had always understood each other and they had never played games with each other; and this time she did play a game by pretending not to understand what he had meant by "tired," and she deeply regrets that, and that she did not confront him honestly.

Amy says that her husband was the affectionate one. He was the one to rub her back and tell her how much he loved her or how she meant the whole world to him, while she never told him how much she loved him. She hopes and prays that he knows now.

Again Teresa tells how her husband tried to get out of bed and how instead he fell and began to foam at the mouth. I cannot look at her as she speaks. Teresa says she regrets that she did not know how ill William must have been and that she did not take him to the hospital. The paramedics, when they finally arrived, told her it would not have made a difference.

One time, a week or so before Edward died and while I was helping him get dressed, buttoning his shirt, Edward said he was not afraid to die. He was afraid of being a burden and of losing his dignity. He also told me, "I don't know what I would do without you," which is when I could have said "I love you."

(During this session we never mention creating your own inner sanctuary—whatever that is.)

8. Remembering and Honoring

This week, for this our final session, we were asked to bring photos of our loved ones.

Fred has made a collage of his wife when she was young. His wife is surprisingly beautiful and fashionable—she looks like a young Katharine Hepburn—and everyone remarks on it. "She looks like a movie star," says Florence. We all agree. I show my photo of Edward taken in Bermuda this past summer, where we went as a family (seventeen of us, including six grandchildren and one more on the way) to celebrate his seventy-fifth birthday. In the photo, Edward looks strong and healthy; there is absolutely no sign in his face that he will be dead in less than three months. Florence hands around a framed picture of Johnny. A big man, Johnny is wearing his security guard uniform. He is smiling, laughing almost. Sue has brought two photos of her husband: before and after he got sick, to show the difference, she explains. In the first, her husband is standing between his two sons-in-law, who are much taller and not Asian. He has his arms around his sons-in-law's shoulders and he is smiling. In the second photo, he is sitting in a chair in what looks like his underwear, his bony knees jutting out. His family stands behind him. Bald and skeletal, he looks like someone in a prison camp. Teresa has brought a bunch of photos: William playing the trumpet; William with his brother (one of the brothers, she says, who died in Siberia); William and Teresa all dressed up in evening clothes—Teresa's hair is done up in a beehive—at a formal dinner, an older woman standing behind them, her hands resting possessively on both their shoulders (Teresa's mother!).

Amy has the flu and could not come, Sally says.

Sally then takes out the "bridge" drawings we did in an earlier session and hands them back to us. Do we perceive ourselves on the bridge differently now? she asks.

Sue says that she does. She sees herself climbing a little way up the mountain. She says that the group has helped her. In fact, she says she is doing pretty well. She sounds almost cheerful and she laughs, embarrassed at herself. What has helped? she asks, and answers her own question: a combination of family, her job, her own efforts to keep busy. It is true, today, when she was walking to work, she remembered something her husband had said to her and she started to cry. Fortunately she was wearing a hat and no one could see her tears, but she is determined to be strong. She also says that she wants to survive. (Funny how people, even if you expect them to, surprise you. At the beginning of our group counseling I felt certain that Sue was by far the most vulnerable among us, I even thought she might commit suicide, yet now she appears to be the strongest and the one who is handling her grief and bereavement with the most aplomb and equanimity.)

I say that the tsunamis' waves are still huge but there are not as many of them.

Fred, who did not draw a bridge, says he has a surprise. He sounds pleased. What kind of surprise? Sally asks. Fred says that against the advice of everyone—his friends, his sons—he put a notice in D'Agostino, the grocery store, saying that he was looking for a roommate. And guess what? he asks us, smiling. The roommate he found is a woman! Sue giggles. No, Fred says, it is not like that. He has a big two-bedroom apartment, and the woman is a teacher and she is serious. Fred says he knows he is taking a risk, but it will do him good because he has gotten into the habit, as he puts it, of "going native," of wandering around his apartment in his underwear. Now he will have to get dressed. For the first time, Fred looks happy (he has not mentioned his wife's clothes once).

All of a sudden, I like Fred a lot.

Even though she is still on medication, Florence says, she is grateful to the group. It has helped her, she says, to know that we all feel the same.

Teresa starts on another story about someone she knows who has lost her entire family, but this time I do not even try to listen.

As a parting gift, I have brought everyone in the group a copy of Auden's poem "Funeral Blues." I say that although it is not a cheerful poem, it is the poem that captures best how I feel. Sally asks me to read it out loud. When I get to the lines "He was my North, my South, my East and West, / my working week and Sunday rest," my voice breaks and I think I will not be able to read on. When I finish, I look at Florence, who is sitting next to me. Tears are streaming down her face.

The night before Edward died, I asked my son and Edward's son, my stepson, to spend the night with me in the apartment, since I had not gotten much sleep the night before and I was afraid I would not be able to manage Edward alone—I was afraid he would try to get out of bed and fall, he had become so weak. We each sat with Edward in two-hour shifts, and at about four o'clock in the morning, when it was my turn, I walked into our bedroom and found both my son and stepson, dressed in only their boxer shorts, sitting next to Edward's bed, talking softly about Carly Simon and the songs Edward liked to listen to. Edward was asleep.

Sally then hands out a sheet with a list of our names and telephone numbers. She says that we could have a reunion at some later date if we wanted to. We all say yes, we want to. (I want to, too.) All of a sudden, I know that I will miss everyone (except for Teresa).

Florence and I hug, I shake Fred's hand and wish him luck. When Sue and I say goodbye, she smiles and tells me to call her: I work in the city, she says, and I say that I will. I wave to Teresa, and Sally promises me that she will stay in touch.

Before we leave, we each take back our stones with our spouses' names written on them. I am surprised at how little the stone is—I had remembered it as being a lot bigger. Also, I had fantasized about picking up my stone and hurling it through the room's plate-glass window and having the stone fall seventeen stories to the street below—what then? Instead, I slip the stone into my purse—*Edwar*.

—2005

Learning from Other Writers

1. What scheme does Lily Tuck use to divide her essay into sections? From what does she derive the titles of those sections? How does she structure the material *within* each section?
2. Which people's names does the author change and why? What effect does this have on your willingness to believe what she writes about the other people in her group? About herself?
3. What is her initial attitude toward attending a bereavement group? Toward the other members of this group? Do these attitudes change over time?
4. Sally, the leader of the group, hands around "a list of the dos and don'ts of what you say to a grieving person." Using these and other platitudes, write a column in which the cliché expert testifies about grief and loss. (For help, see Mr. Arbuthnot's testimony on the nuclear age in Chapter 2.)
5. What, if anything, does Tuck learn about bereavement from attending this group? What do *you* learn about bereavement from reading Tuck's essay?
6. Do you find the ending of "Group Grief" satisfying? Why or why not?

INSPIRATIONS: THEY'VE GOT GAME

1. Think of a public performance, an athletic event or some other contest or competition, a class (or a series of classes), a tournament, or a religious or social ritual. This might be an event in which you participated or an event you merely watched.
2. Use this event to structure your meditation on a question that seems related to that event.

Codes (and Their Unraveling)

As is apparent from the previous two chapters, structuring an essay or a book according to the rituals of a community often leads to a discussion of what's going on beneath the surface, what values might be encoded in the group's decisions as to what clothes to wear, what foods to eat, what actions are required, permissible, or forbidden. Such an analysis might be informal, as in Lily Tuck's meditations on the behavior of people who have lost a spouse, or more overt and systematic, as in Tom Wolfe's attempt to define the values that underlie the attitudes and conduct of test pilots who have the Right Stuff (or think they do).

In this chapter, we focus less on the people who wear these clothes, eat these foods, or carry out these rituals than on the underlying meaning of the clothes, foods, and rituals themselves; in other words, we turn our attention to essays that take as their goal explicating the deeper significance of some code of dressing, eating, speaking, praying, telling jokes, buying and displaying possessions, or building and decorating a place to live. This might seem to entail a shift toward studying an essay's subject rather than its structure, but this is another case in which subject and structure interact in a helpful way. Usually, the system of behaviors or signs you are trying to decode will contain within itself the best structure for your essay. If you think back to Ann Hodgman's "No Wonder They Call Me a Bitch" in Chapter 8, you can see that she is explicating the connotations of the labels on cans and packets of pet food . . . as she consumes their contents. Similarly, you might decode the vocabulary of a certain group by translating for your readers a real or imagined encounter in which one speaker creatively insults another speaker's mother or tries to convince someone to leave a party with him or her. You might interpret the significance of the articles that make up a certain style of dress by describing each item as it appears in the J. Crew catalogue or as the articles might be worn, from head to foot; you might explain the significance of the figurines in your mother's china cabinet as you move from the bottom shelf to the top; you might translate the cultural connotations of the dishes that make up a certain cuisine as these appear on a typical menu, from appetizers to dessert; or you might decode the items that make up the décor in a sorority as you move around the house. (Again, the categories in this textbook sometimes overlap; an essay in which you analyze the types of people who are drawn to various characters on a cable TV series might look structurally similar to a group portrait, while you might use a game structure to guide your readers through an analysis of the various personalities of people who play a computer game like *World of Warcraft* or *The Sims.*)

You might even structure your essay according to the steps by which you first encountered the set of signs you are trying to decode and figured out what they meant. In his classic essay "The Art of Donald McGill," George Orwell describes how he came to collect a certain type of bawdy

English postcard, then divided his cards according to the subject of their humor (sex, home life, drunkenness, bathroom jokes, class snobbery, stereotypes, and politics), then analyzed the deeper values of the working-class British people who buy and send such cards . . . and those government officials and aristocrats who might want to ban the cards as obscene.[1]

In Paul Fussell's "Notes on Class," which is included in this chapter, the author takes as his project unraveling the system of signs by which Americans advertise their social class, consciously or not, and the ways in which we tend to read other people's class behavior. Whatever your reactions to Fussell's claims, you must admit that many aspects of our culture remain to be analyzed. What kind of boots or shoes are your classmates wearing this year—and why? What necessities are in their backpacks? Were these "necessities" in students' backpacks a year ago? Five years ago? How many of your classmates visit a house of worship in a given week? What kinds of cars do they drive—if any? What greeting cards do they send to their loved ones on their birthdays?

Once you get the idea as to how such systems can be decoded, you will find inspirations all around you: witness Meghan Daum's bitterly funny and perceptive treatise on the paraphernalia that amateur musicians accumulate and show off in "Music Is My Bag" and David Sedaris's hysterical dissection of holiday traditions in foreign lands in "Six to Eight Black Men."

---

[1] "The Art of Donald McGill" first appeared in *Horizon Magazine* in London in September 1941 and can be found in any major collection of Orwell's essays, including the Penguin edition published in 1994.

PAUL FUSSELL

NOTES ON CLASS

If the dirty little secret used to be sex, now it is the facts about social class. No subject today is more likely to offend. Over thirty years ago Dr. Kinsey generated considerable alarm by disclosing that despite appearances one-quarter of the male population had enjoyed at least one homosexual orgasm. A similar alarm can be occasioned today by asserting that despite the much-discussed mechanism of "social mobility" and the constant redistribution of income in this country, it is virtually impossible to break out of the social class in which one has been nurtured. Bad news for the ambitious as well as the bogus, but there it is.

Defining class is difficult, as sociologists and anthropologists have learned. The more data we feed into the machines, the less likely it is that significant formulations will emerge. What follows here is based not on interviews, questionnaires, or any kind of quantitative technique but on perhaps a more trustworthy method—perception. Theory may inform us that there are three classes in America, high, middle, and low. Perception will tell us that there are at least nine, which I would designate and arrange like this:

Top Out-of-Sight
Upper
Upper Middle

Middle
High-Proletarian
Mid-Proletarian
Low-Proletarian

Destitute
Bottom Out-of-Sight

In addition, there is a floating class with no permanent location in this hierarchy. We can call it Class X. It consists of well-to-do hippies, "artists," "writers" (who write nothing), floating bohemians, politicians out of office, disgraced athletic coaches, residers abroad, rock stars, "celebrities," and the shrewder sort of spies.

The quasi-official division of the population into three economic classes called high-, middle-, and low-income groups rather misses the point, because as a class indicator the amount of money is not as important as the source. Important distinctions at both the top and bottom of the class scale arise less from degree of affluence than from the people or institutions to whom one is beholden for support. For example, the main thing distinguishing the top three classes from each other is the amount of money inherited in relation to the amount currently earned. The Top Out-of-Sight Class (Rockefellers, du Ponts, Mellons, Fords, Whitneys) lives on inherited capital entirely. Its money is like the hats of the Boston ladies who, asked where they got them, answer, "Oh, we *have* our hats." No one whose money, no matter how ample, comes from his own work, like film stars, can be a member of the Top Out-of-Sights, even if the size of his income and the extravagance of his expenditure permit him temporary social access to it.

Since we expect extremes to meet, we are not surprised to find the very lowest class, Bottom Out-of-Sight, similiar to the highest in one crucial respect: it is given its money and kept sort of afloat not by its own efforts but by the welfare machinery or the prison system. Members of the Top Out-of-Sight Class sometimes earn some money, as directors or board members of philanthropic or even profitable enterprises, but the amount earned is laughable in relation to the amount already possessed. Membership in the Top Out-of-Sight Class depends on the ability to flourish without working at all, and it is this that suggests a curious brotherhood between those at the top and the bottom of the scale.

It is this also that distinguishes the Upper Class from its betters. It lives on both inherited money and a salary from attractive, if usually slight, work, without which, even if it could survive and even flourish, it would feel bored and a little ashamed. The next class down, the Upper Middle, may possess virtually as much as the two above it. The difference is that it has earned most of it, in law, medicine, oil, real-estate, or even the more honorific forms of trade. The Upper Middles are afflicted with a bourgeois sense of shame, a conviction that to live on the earnings of others, even forebears, is not entirely nice.

The Out-of-Sight Classes at top and bottom have something else in common: they are literally all but invisible (hence their name). The façades of Top Out-of-Sight houses are never seen from the street, and such residences (like Rockefeller's upstate New York premises) are often hidden away deep in the hills, safe from envy and its ultimate attendants, confiscatory taxation and finally expropriation. The Bottom Out-of-Sight Class is equally invisible. When not hidden away in institutions or claustrated in monasteries, lamaseries, or communes, it is hiding from creditors, deceived bail-bondsmen, and merchants intent on repossessing cars and furniture. (This class is visible briefly in one place, in the spring on the streets of New York City, but after this ritual yearly show of itself it disappears again.) When you pass a house with a would-be impressive façade addressing the street, you know it is occupied by a mere member of the Upper or Upper Middle Class. The White House is an example. Its residents, even on those occasions when they are Kennedys, can never be classified as Top Out-of-Sight but only Upper Class. The house is simply too conspicuous, and temporary residence there usually constitutes a come-down for most of its occupants. It is a hopelessly Upper- or Upper-Middle-Class place.

Another feature of both Top and Bottom Out-of-Sight Classes is their anxiety to keep their names out of the papers, and this too suggests that socially the President is always rather vulgar. All the classes in between Top and Bottom Out-of-Sight slaver for personal publicity (monograms on shirts, inscribing one's name on lawn-mowers and power tools, etc.), and it is this lust to be known almost as much as income that distinguishes them from their Top and Bottom neighbors. The High- and Mid-Prole Classes can be recognized immediately by their pride in advertising their physical presence, a way of saying, "Look! We pay our bills and have a known place in the community, and you can find us there any time." Thus hypertrophied house-numbers on the front, or house numbers written "Two Hundred Five" ("Two Hundred and Five" is worse) instead of 205, or flamboyant house or family names blazoned on façades, like "The Willows" or "The Polnickis."

(If you go behind the façade into the house itself, you will find a fairly trustworthy class indicator in the kind of wood visible there. The top three classes invariably go in for hardwoods for doors and panelling; the Middle and High-Prole Classes, pine, either plain or "knotty." The knotty-pine "den" is an absolute stigma of the Middle Class, one never to be overcome or disguised by temporarily affected higher usages. Below knotty pine there is plywood.)

Façade study is a badly neglected anthropological field. As we work down from the (largely white-painted) bank-like façades of the Upper and Upper Middle Classes, we encounter such Middle and Prole conventions as these, which I rank in order of social status:

Middle 1. A potted tree on either side of the front door, and the more pointy and symmetrical the better.

2. A large rectangular picture-window in a split-level "ranch" house, displaying a table-lamp between two side curtains. The cellophane on the lampshade must be visibly inviolate.

3. Two chairs, usually metal with pipe arms, disposed on the front porch as a "conversation group," in stubborn defiance of the traffic thundering past

High-Prole 4. Religious shrines in the garden, which if small and understated, are slightly higher class than

Mid-Prole 5. Plaster gnomes and flamingos, and blue or lavender shiny spheres supported by fluted cast-concrete pedestals.

Low-Prole 6. Defunct truck tires painted white and enclosing flower beds. (Auto tires are a grade higher.)

7. Flower-bed designs worked in dead light bulbs or the butts of disused beer bottles.

The Destitute have no façades to decorate, and of course the Bottom Out-of-Sights, being invisible, have none either, although both these classes can occasionally help others decorate theirs—painting tires white on an hourly basis, for example, or even watering and fertilizing the potted trees of the Middle Class. Class X also does not decorate its façades, hoping to stay loose and unidentifiable, ready to re-locate and shape-change the moment it sees that its cover has been penetrated.

In this list of façade conventions an important principle emerges. Organic materials have higher status than metal or plastic. We should take warning from Sophie Portnoy's aluminum venetian blinds, which are also lower than wood because the slats are curved, as if "improved," instead of classically flat. The same principle applies, as *The Preppy Handbook* has shown so effectively, to clothing fabrics, which must be cotton or wool, never Dacron or anything of that prole kind. In the same way, yachts with wood hulls, because they must be repaired or replaced (at high cost) more often, are classier than yachts with fiberglass hulls, no matter how shrewdly merchandised. Plastic hulls are cheaper and more practical, which is precisely why they lack class.

As we move down the scale, income of course decreases, but income is less important to class than other seldom-invoked measurements: for example, the degree to which one's work is supervised by an omnipresent immediate superior. The more free from supervision, the higher the class, which is why a dentist ranks higher than a mechanic working under a foreman in a large auto shop, even if he makes considerably more money than the dentist. The two trades may be thought equally dirty: it is the dentist's freedom from supervision that helps confer class upon him. Likewise, a high-school teacher obliged to file weekly "lesson plans" with a principal or "curriculum co-ordinator" thereby occupies a class position lower than a tenured professor, who reports to no one, even though the high-school teacher may be richer, smarter, and nicer. (Supervisors and Inspectors are titles that go with public schools, post offices, and police departments: the student of class will need to know no more.) It is largely because they must report that even the highest members of the naval and military services lack social status: they all have designated supervisors—even the Chairman of the Joint Chiefs of Staff has to report to the President.

Class is thus defined less by bare income than by constraints and insecurities. It is defined also by habits and attitudes. Take television watching. The Top Out-of-Sight Class doesn't watch at all. It owns the companies and pays others to monitor the thing. It is also entirely devoid of intellectual or even emotional curiosity: it *has* its ideas the way it has its money. The Upper Class does look at television but it prefers Camp offerings, like the films of Jean Harlow or Jon Hall. The Upper Middle Class regards TV as vulgar except for the highminded emissions of National Educational Television, which it watches avidly, especially when, like the Shakespeare series, they are the most incompetently directed and boring. Upper Middles make a point of forbidding children to watch more than an hour a day and worry a lot about violence in society and sugar in cereal. The Middle Class watches, preferring the more "beautiful" kinds of non-body-contact sports like tennis or gymnastics or figure-skating (the music is a redeeming feature here). With High-, Mid-, and Low-Proles we find heavy viewing of the soaps in the daytime and rugged body-contact sports (football, hockey, boxing) in the evening. The lower one is located in the Prole classes the more likely one is to watch "Bowling for Dollars" and "Wonder Woman" and "The Hulk" and when choosing a game show to prefer "Joker's Wild" to "The Family Feud," whose jokes are sometimes incomprehensible. Destitutes and Bottom Out-of-Sights have in common a problem involving choice. Destitutes usually "own" about three color sets, and the problem is which three programs to run at once. Bottom Out-of-Sights exercise no choice at all, the decisions being made for them by correctional or institutional personnel.

The time when the evening meal is consumed defines class better than, say, the presence or absence on the table of ketchup bottles and ashtrays shaped like little toilets enjoining the diners to "Put Your Butts Here." Destitutes and Bottom Out-of-Sights eat dinner at 5:30, for the Prole staff on which they depend must clean up and be out roller-skating or bowling early in the evening. Thus Proles eat at 6:00 or 6:30. The Middles eat at 7:00, the Upper Middles at 7:30 or, if very ambitious, at 8:00. The Uppers and Top Out-of-Sights dine at 8:30 or 9:00 or even later, after nightly protracted "cocktail" sessions lasting usually around two hours. Sometimes they forget to eat at all.

Similarly, the physical appearance of the various classes defines them fairly accurately. Among the top four classes thin is good, and the bottom two classes appear to ape this usage, although down there thin is seldom a matter of choice. It is the three Prole classes that tend to fat, partly as a result of their use of convenience foods and plenty of beer. These are the classes too where anxiety about slipping down a rung causes nervous overeating, resulting in fat that can be rationalized as advertising the security of steady wages and the ability to "eat out" often. Even "Going Out for Breakfast" is not unthinkable for Proles, if we are to believe that they respond to the McDonald's TV ads as they're supposed to. A recent magazine ad for a diet book aimed at Proles stigmatizes a number of erroneous assumptions about body weight, proclaiming with some inelegance that "They're all a crock." Among such vulgar errors is the proposition that "All Social Classes Are Equally Overweight." This the ad rejects by noting quite accurately:

> Your weight is an advertisement of your social standing. A century ago, corpulence was a sign of success. But no more. Today it is the badge of the lower-middle-class, where obesity is *four times* more prevalent than it is among the upper-middle and middle classes.

It is not just four times more prevalent. It is at least four times more visible, as any observer can testify who has witnessed Prole women perambulating shopping malls in their bright, very tight jersey trousers. Not just obesity but the flaunting of obesity is the Prole sign, as if the object were to give maximum aesthetic offense to the higher classes and thus achieve a form of revenge.

Another physical feature with powerful class meaning is the wearing of plaster casts on legs and ankles by members of the top three classes. These casts, a sort of white badge of honor, betoken stylish mishaps with frivolous but costly toys like horses, skis, snowmobiles, and mopeds. They signify a high level of conspicuous waste in a social world where questions of unpayable medical bills or missed working days do not apply. But in the matter of clothes, the Top Out-of-Sight is different from both Upper and Upper Middle Classes. It prefers to appear in new clothes, whereas the class just below it prefers old clothes. Likewise, all three Prole classes make much of new garments, with the highest possible polyester content. The question does not arise in the same form with Destitutes and Bottom Out-of-Sights. They wear used clothes, the thrift shop and prison supply room serving as their Bonwit's and Korvette's.

This American class system is very hard for foreigners to master, partly because most foreigners imagine that since America was founded by the British it must retain something of British institutions. But our class system is more subtle than the British, more a matter of gradations than of blunt divisions, like the binary distinction between a gentleman and a cad. This seems to lack plausibility here. One seldom encounters in the United States the sort of absolute prohibitions which (half-comically, to be sure) one is asked to believe define the gentleman in England. Like these:

A gentleman never wears brown shoes in the city, or
A gentleman never wears a green suit, or
A gentleman never has soup at lunch, or
A gentleman never uses a comb, or
A gentleman never smells of anything but tar, or
"No gentleman can fail to admire Bellini"—W. H. Auden.

In America it seems to matter much less the way you present yourself—green, brown, neat, sloppy, scented—than what your backing is—that is, where your money comes from. What the upper orders display here is no special uniform but the kind of psychological security they derive from knowing that others recognize their freedom from petty anxieties and trivial prohibitions.

"Language most shows a man," Ben Jonson used to say. "Speak, that I may see thee." As all acute conservatives like Jonson know, dictional behavior is a powerful signal of a firm class line. Nancy Mitford so indicated in her hilarious essay of 1955, "The English Aristocracy," based in part on Professor Alan S. C. Ross's more sober study "Linguistic Class-Indicators in Present-Day English." Both Mitford and Ross were interested in only one class demarcation, the one dividing the English Upper Class ("U," in their shorthand) from all below it ("non-U"). Their main finding was that euphemism and genteelism are vulgar. People who are socially secure risk nothing by calling a spade a spade, and indicate their top-dog status by doing so as frequently as possible. Thus the U-word is *rich*, the non-U *wealthy*. What U-speakers call *false teeth* non-U's call *dentures*. The same with *wigs* and *hairpieces*, *dying* and *passing away* (or *over*).

For Mitford, linguistic assaults from below are sometimes so shocking that the only kind reaction of a U-person is silence. It is "the only possible U-response," she notes, "to many embarrassing modern situations: the ejaculation of 'cheers' before drinking, for example, or 'It was so nice seeing you' after saying goodbye. In silence, too, one must endure the use of the Christian name by comparative strangers...." In America, although there are more classes distinguishable here, a linguistic polarity is as visible as in England. Here U-speech (or our equivalent of it) characterizes some Top Out-of-Sights, Uppers, Upper Middles, and Class X's. All below is a waste land of genteelism and jargon and pretentious mispronunciation, pathetic evidence of the upward social scramble and its hazards. Down below, the ear is bad and no one has been trained to listen. Culture words especially are the downfall of the aspiring. Sometimes it is diphthongs that invite disgrace, as in *be-yóu-ti-ful.* Sometimes the aspirant rushes full-face into disaster by flourishing those secret class indicators, the words *exquisite* and *despicable,* which, like another secret sign, *patina,* he (and of course she as often) stresses on the middle syllable instead of the first. High-class names from cultural history are a frequent cause of betrayal, especially if they are British, like Henry Purcell. In America non-U speakers are fond of usages like "Between he and I." Recalling vaguely that mentioning oneself last, as in "He and I were there," is thought gentlemanly, they apply that principle uniformly, to the entire destruction of the objective case. There's also a problem with *like.* They remember something about the dangers of illiteracy its use invites, and hope to stay out of trouble by always using *as* instead, finally saying things like "He looks as his father." These contortions are common among young (usually insurance or computer) trainees, raised on Leon Uris and *Playboy,* most of them Mid- or High-Proles pounding on the firmly shut door of the Middle Class. They are the careful, dark-suited first-generation aspirants to American respectability and (hopefully, as they would put it) power. Together with their deployment of the anomalous nominative case on all occasions goes their preference for jargon (you can hear them going at it on airplanes) like *parameters* and *guidelines* and *bottom lines* and *funding, dialogue, interface,* and *lifestyles.* Their world of language is one containing little more than smokescreens and knowing innovations. "Do we gift the Johnsons, dear?" the corporate wife will ask the corporate husband at Christmas time.

Just below these people, down among the Mid- and Low-Proles, the complex sentence gives trouble. It is here that we get sentences beginning with elaborate pseudo-genteel participles like "Being that it was a cold day, the furnace was on." All classes below those peopled by U-speakers find the gerund out of reach and are thus forced to multiply words and say, "The people in front of him at the theater got mad due to the fact that he talked so much" instead of "His talking at the theater annoyed the people in front." (But *people* is not really right: *individuals* is the preferred term with non-U speakers. Grander, somehow.) It is also in the domain of the Mid- and Low-Prole that the double negative comes into its own as well as the superstitious avoidance of *lying* because it may be taken to imply telling untruths. People are thus depicted as always *laying* on the beach, the bed, the grass, the sidewalk, and without the slightest suggestion of their performing sexual exhibitions. A similar unconscious inhibition determines that *set* replace *sit* on all occasions, lest low excremental implications be inferred. The ease with which *sit* can be interchanged with the impolite word is suggested in a Second World War anecdote told by General Matthew Ridgway. Coming upon an unidentifiable head and shoulders peeping out of a ditch near the German border, he shouted, "Put up your hands, you son of a bitch!", to be answered, so he reports, "Aaah, go sit in your hat."

All this is evidence of a sad fact. A deep class gulf opens between two current generations: the older one that had some Latin at school or college and was taught rigorous skeptical "English," complete with the diagramming of sentences; and the younger one taught to read by the optimistic look-say method and encouraged to express itself—as the saying goes—so that its sincerity and well of ideas suffer no violation. This new generation is unable to perceive the number of syllables in a word and cannot spell and is baffled by all questions of etymology (it thinks *chauvinism* has something to do with gender aggressions). It cannot write either, for it has never been subjected to tuition in the sort of English sentence structure which resembles the sonata in being not natural but artificial, not innate but mastered. Because of its misspent, victimized youth, this generation is already destined to fill permanently the middle-to-low slots in the corporate society without ever quite understanding what devilish mechanism has prevented it from ascending. The disappearance of Latin as an adjunct to the mastery of English can be measured by the rapid replacement of words like *continuing* by solecisms like *ongoing*. A serious moment in cultural history occurred a few years ago when gasoline trucks changed the warning word on the rear from *Inflammable* to *Flammable*. Public education had apparently produced a population which no longer knew *In-* as an intensifier. That this happened at about the moment when every city was rapidly running up a "Cultural Center" might make us laugh, if we don't cry first. In another few generations Latinate words will be found only in learned writing, and the spoken language will have returned to the state it was in before the revival of learning. Words like *intellect* and *curiosity* and *devotion* and *study* will have withered away together with the things they denote.

There's another linguistic class-line, dividing those who persist in honoring the nineteenth-century convention that advertising, if not commerce itself, is reprehensible and not at all to be cooperated with, and those proud to think of themselves not as skeptics but as happy consumers, fulfilled when they can image themselves as functioning members of a system by responding to advertisements. For U-persons a word's succeeding in an ad is a compelling reason never to use it. But possessing no other source of idiom and no extra-local means of criticizing it, the subordinate classes are pleased to appropriate the language of advertising for personal use, dropping brand names all the time and saying things like "They have some lovely fashions in that store." In the same way they embrace all sub-professional euphemisms gladly and employ them proudly, adverting without irony to hair stylists, sanitary engineers, and funeral directors in complicity with the consumer world which cynically casts them as its main victims. They see nothing funny in paying a high price for an article and then, after a solemn pause, receiving part of it back in the form of a "rebate." Trapped in a world wholly defined by the language of consumption and the hype, they harbor restively, defending themselves against actuality by calling habitual drunkards *people with alcohol problems*, madness *mental illness*, drug use *drug abuse*, building lots *homesites*, houses *homes* ("They live in a lovely $250,000 home"), and drinks *beverages*.

Those delighted to employ the vacuous commercial "Have a nice day" and those who wouldn't think of saying it belong manifestly to different classes, no matter how we define them, and it is unthinkable that those classes will ever melt. Calvin Coolidge said that the business of America is business. Now apparently the business of America is having a nice day. Tragedy? Don't need it. Irony? Take it away. Have a nice day. Have a nice day. A visiting Englishman of my acquaintance, a U-speaker if there ever was one, has devised the perfect U-response to "Have a nice day": "Thank you," he says, "but I have other plans." The same ultimate divide separates the two classes who say respectively when introduced, "How do you do?" and "Pleased to meet you." There may be comity between those who think *prestigious* a classy word and those who don't, but it won't survive much strain, like relations between those who think *momentarily* means in a moment (airline captain over loudspeaker: "We'll be taking off momentarily, folks") and those who know it means for a moment. Members of these two classes can sit in adjoining seats on the plane and get along fine (although there's a further division between those who talk to their neighbors in planes and elevators and those who don't), but once the plane has emptied, they will proceed toward different destinations. It's the same with those who conceive that *type* is an adjective ("He's a very classy type person") and those who know it's only a noun or verb.

EXERCISE

To what class would you assign each of the following?

1. A fifty-five-year-old pilot for a feeder airline who cuts his own grass, watches wrestling on TV, and has a knotty-pine den?
2. A small-town podiatrist who says "Have a nice day" and whose wife is getting very fat?
3. A young woman trust officer in a large New York bank who loves to watch Channel 13, WNET, and likes to be taken out to restaurants said to serve "gourmet" food?
4. A periodontist in a rich suburb? Is his class higher than that of an exodontist in a large mid-western city who earns more?
5. A man in a rich Northeastern suburb who, invited to a dinner party on Tuesday night, appears in a quiet suit with a white shirt but at a similar, apparently more formal dinner party on Saturday night shows up in a bright green linen jacket, red trousers, no tie, and no socks?
6. Students of all kinds?

ANSWERS

1. Pilots have roughly the same class as field-grade Army officers, that is, High Prole. Feeder airline pilots have less status than national airline pilots, and those who work for the longest established international airlines like Pan Am and TWA have the highest status of all. The Middle-Class den and the Mid-Prole TV wrestling addiction cancel each other out.
2. At the moment, High Prole. If his wife gets much fatter, he will sink to Mid-Prole.
3. Middle, with hopeless fantasies about being Upper-Middle.
4. The periodontist is Middle. Because he is not a "professional specialist," the exodontist is slightly lower, regardless of where he lives or what he earns.
5. He is from the Upper-Middle Class, but he'd like to be taken for a member of the Upper. The suit on Tuesday night is to give the impression that he's just returned from the city, where he "works." The weekend get-up validates his identity as a suburbanite, devoting his weekend to much-needed unbuttoning and frivolity. The difference between Tuesday and Saturday is supposed to be significant. But I don't trust this man. He pays too much attention to his clothes to be really Upper Class.
6. All students, regardless of age or institution attended, are Mid-Proles, as their large consumption of beer and convenience foods suggests. Sometimes they affect the used clothing of the Destitute, but we should not be fooled.

The pretence that either person can feel at ease in the presence of the other is an essential element of the presiding American fiction. Despite the lowness of the metaphor, the idea of the melting pot is high-minded and noble enough, but empirically it will be found increasingly unconvincing. It is our different language habits as much as anything that make us, as the title of Richard Polenberg's book puts it, *One Nation Divisible*.

Some people invite constant class trouble because they believe the official American publicity about these matters. The official theory, which experience is constantly disproving, is that one can earn one's way out of his original class. Richard Nixon's behavior indicates dramatically that this is not so. The sign of the Upper Class to which he aspired is total psychological security, expressed in loose carriage, saying what one likes, and imperviousness to what others think. Nixon's vast income from law and politics—his San Clemente property aped the style of the Upper but not the Top Out-of-Sight Class, for everyone knew where it was, and he wanted them to know—could not alleviate his original awkwardness and meanness of soul or his nervousness about the impression he was making, an affliction allied to his instinct for cunning and duplicity. Hammacher Schlemmer might have had him specifically in mind as the consumer of their recently advertised "Champagne Recork": "This unusual stopper keeps 'bubbly' sprightly, sparkling after uncorking ceremony is over. Gold electro-plated." I suspect that it is some of these same characteristics that make Edward Kennedy often seem so inauthentic a member of the Upper Class. (He's not Top Out-of-Sight because he chooses to augment his inheritance by attractive work.)

What, then, marks the higher classes? Primarily a desire for privacy, if not invisibility, and a powerful if eccentric desire for freedom. It is this instinct for freedom that may persuade us that inquiring into the American class system this way is an enterprise not entirely facetious. Perhaps after all the whole thing has something, just something, to do with ethics and aesthetics. Perhaps a term like *gentleman* still retains some meanings which are not just sartorial and mannerly. Freedom and grace and independence: it would be nice to believe those words still mean something, and it would be interesting if the reality of the class system—and everyone, after all, hopes to rise—should turn out to be a way we pay those notions a due if unwitting respect.

—1980

Learning from Other Writers

1. In the first paragraph, the author states that "it is virtually impossible to break out of the social class in which one has been nurtured." Is the rest of the essay designed to prove this assertion? If so, does the author succeed? If not, what (if anything) allows him to get away with making that assertion? If you don't think that proving this statement is Fussell's goal, what *is* the purpose of his essay?
2. In paragraph two, Fussell admits that his analysis doesn't depend on "interviews, questionnaires, or any kind of quantitative technique but on perhaps a more trustworthy method—perception." Do you agree that "perception" is a trustworthy method for performing the sort of analysis Fussell performs in this essay? Or is that the author's excuse for airing his prejudices and opinions? Who should or shouldn't be allowed to perform an analysis based on "perception" rather than quantitative research?
3. How would you describe the author's tone? Is this a humor piece, or a serious attempt to define class in America?
4. What is your reaction to the "Exercise" that Fussell includes in his essay?
5. How does Fussell structure his analysis? Can you think of other possible organizational schemes for an essay on class distinctions?
6. What is the function of the final paragraph? How does this conclusion affect your reading (or rereading) of all that's come before?
7. Fussell's essay was first published (under a different title) in *The New Republic* in 1980. Do you think his analysis is still relevant?

MEGHAN DAUM

MUSIC IS MY BAG

The image I want to get across is that of the fifteen-year-old boy with the beginning traces of a mustache who hangs out in the band room after school playing the opening bars of a Billy Joel song on the piano. This is the kid who, in the interests of adopting some semblance of personal style, wears a fedora hat and a scarf with a black-and-white design of a piano keyboard. This is the kid who, in addition to having taught himself some tunes from the *Songs from the Attic* sheet music he bought at the local Sam Ash, probably also plays the trombone in the marching band, and experienced a seminal moment one afternoon as he vaguely flirted with a not-yet-kissed, clarinet-playing girl, a girl who is none too popular but whose propensity for leaning on the piano as the boy plays the opening chords of "Captain Jack" give him a clue as to the social possibilities that might be afforded him via the marching band.

If the clarinet-playing girl is an average student musician, she carries her plastic Selmer in the standard-issue black plastic case. If she has demonstrated any kind of proficiency, she carries her Selmer in a tote bag that reads "Music Is My Bag." The boy in the piano-key scarf definitely has music as his bag. He may not yet have the tote bag, but the hat, the Billy Joel, the tacit euphoria brought on by a sexual awakening that, for him, centers entirely around band, is all he needs to be delivered into the unmistakable realm that is Music Is My Bagdom.

I grew up in Music Is My Bag culture. The walls of my parents' house were covered with framed art posters from musical events: The San Francisco Symphony's 1982 production of St. Matthew's Passion, The Metropolitan Opera's 1976 production of Aida, the original Broadway production of Sweeney Todd. Ninety percent of the books on the shelves were about music, if not actual musical scores. Childhood ceramics projects made by my brother and me were painted with eighth notes and treble clef signs. We owned a deck of cards with portraits of the great composers on the back. A baby grand piano overtook the room that would have been the dining room if my parents hadn't forgone a table and renamed it "the music room." This room also contained an imposing hi-fi system and a $300 wooden music stand. Music played at all times: Brahms, Mendelssohn, cast recordings of Sondheim musicals, a cappella Christmas albums. When my father sat down with a book, he read musical scores, humming quietly and tapping his foot. When I was ten, my mother decided we needed to implement a before-dinner ritual akin to saying grace, so she composed a short song, asking us all to contribute a lyric, and we held hands and sang it before eating. My lyric was, "There's a smile on our face and it seems to say all the wonderful things we've all done today." My mother insisted on harmonizing at the end. She also did this when singing "Happy Birthday."

Harmonizing on songs like "Happy Birthday" is a clear indication of the Music Is My Bag personality. If one does not have an actual bag that reads "Music Is My Bag"—as did the violist in the chamber music trio my mother set up with some women from the Unitarian Church—a $300 music stand and musical-note coasters will more than suffice. To avoid confusion, let me also say that there are many different Bags in life. Some friends of my parents have a $300 dictionary stand, a collection of silver bookmarks, and once threw a dinner party wherein the guests had to dress up as members of the Bloomsbury Group. These people are Literature Is My Bag. I know people who are Movies Are My Bag (detectable by key chains shaped like projectors, outdated copies of *Halliwell's Film Guide,* and one too many T-shirts from things like the San Jose Film Festival), people who are Cats Are My Bag (self-explanatory), and, perhaps most annoyingly, Where I Went To College Is My Bag (Yale running shorts, plastic Yale tumblers, Yale Platinum Plus MasterCard, and, yes, even Yale screensavers—all this in someone aged forty or more, the perennial contributor to the class notes).

Having a Bag connotes the state of being overly interested in something, and yet, in a certain way, not interested enough. It has a hobbyish quality to it, a sense that the enthusiasm developed at a time when the enthusiast was lacking in some significant area of social or intellectual life. Music Is My Bag is the mother of all Bags, not just because in the early 1980s some consumer force of the public radio fund-drive variety distributed a line of tote bags that displayed that slogan, but because its adherents, or, as they tend to call themselves, "music lovers," give off an aura that distinguishes them from the rest of the population. It's an aura that has to do with a sort of benign cluelessness, a condition that, even in middle age, smacks of that phase between prepubescence and real adolescence. Music Is My Bag people have a sexlessness to them. There is a pastiness to them. They can never seem to find a good pair of jeans. You can spot them on the street, the female French horn player in concert dress hailing a cab to Lincoln Center around seven o'clock in the evening, her earrings too big, her hairstyle unchanged since 1986. The fifty-something recording engineer with the running shoes and the shoulder bag. The Indiana marching band kids in town for the Macy's Thanksgiving Day Parade, snapping photos of each other in front of the Hard Rock Cafe, having sung their parts from the band arrangement of *Hello, Dolly!* the whole way on the bus, thinking, knowing, that it won't get better than this. Like all Music Is My Bag people, they are a little too in love with the trappings. They know what their boundaries are and load up their allotted space with memorabilia, saving the certificates of participation from regional festivals, the composer-a-month calendars, the Mostly Mozart posters. Their sincerity trumps attempts at snideness. The boys' sarcasm only goes a fraction of the way there, the girls will never be great seducers. They grow up to look like high school band directors even if they're not. They give their pets names like Wolfgang and Gershwin. Their hemlines are never quite right.

I played the oboe. This is not an instrument to be taken lightly. The oboist runs a high risk of veering into Music Is My Bag culture, mostly because to get beyond the entry level is to give oneself over to an absorption with technique that can make a person vulnerable to certain vagaries of a subcategory, the oboe phylum. This inevitably leads to the genus of wind ensemble culture, which concerns itself with the socio-political infrastructure of the woodwind section, the disproportionate number of solo passages, a narcissistic pride in sounding the A that tunes the orchestra. Not many people play the oboe. It's a difficult instrument, beautiful when played well, horrifying when played poorly. I was self-conscious about playing the oboe, mostly because so many people confuse it with the bassoon, its much larger, ganglier cousin in the double-reed family. The act of playing the oboe, unlike the graceful arm positions of the flute or the violin, is not a photogenic one. The embouchure puckers the face into a grimace; my childhood and adolescence is documented by photos that make me look slightly deformed—the lipless girl. It's not an instrument for the vain. Oboe playing revolves almost entirely around saliva. Spit gets caught in the keys and the joints and must be blown out using cigarette rolling paper as a blotter (a scandalous drugstore purchase for a twelve-year-old). Spit can accumulate on the floor if you play for too long. Spit must constantly be sucked out from both sides of the reed. The fragile, temperamental reed is the player's chronic medical condition. It must be tended to constantly. It must be wet but never too wet, hard enough to emit a decent sound, but soft enough to blow air through. The oboist must never stray far from moisture; the reed is forever in her mouth, in a paper cup of water that teeters on the music stand, being doused at a drinking fountain in Parsippany High School at the North Jersey Regional Band and Orchestra Audition. After a certain age, the student oboist must learn to make her own reeds, build them from bamboo using knives and shavers. Most people don't realize this. Reed-making is an eighteenth-century exercise, something that would seem to require an apprenticeship before undertaking solo. But oboists, occupying a firm, albeit wet, patch of ground under the tattered umbrella of Music Is My Bag, never quite live in the same era as everyone else.

Though I did, at one point, hold the title of second-best high school player in the state of New Jersey, I was a mediocre oboist. My discipline was lacking, my enthusiasm virtually nil, and my comprehension of rhythm (in keeping with a lifelong math phobia) held me back considerably. But being without an aptitude for music was, in my family, tantamount to being a Kennedy who knows nothing of politics. Aptitude was something, perhaps even the only thing, I possessed. As indifferent to the oboe as I was—and I once began an orchestra rehearsal without noticing that I had neglected to screw the bell, which is the entire bottom portion, onto the rest of my instrument—I managed to be good enough to play in the New Jersey All-State High School Orchestra as well as a local adult symphony. I even gained acceptance into a music conservatory. These aren't staggering accomplishments unless you consider the fact that I rarely practiced. If I had practiced with any amount of regularity, I could have been, as my parents would have liked me to be, one of those kids who was schlepped to Juilliard on Saturdays. If I had practiced slightly more than that, I could have gone to Juilliard for college. If I had practiced a lot I could have ended up in the New York Philharmonic. This is not an exaggeration, merely a moot point. I didn't practice. I haven't picked up the oboe since my junior year in college, where, incidentally, I sat first chair in the orchestra even though I did not practice once the entire time.

I never practiced and yet I always practiced. My memory is always of being unprepared, yet I was forced to sit in the chair for so many hours that I suspect something else must have been at work, a lack of consciousness about it, an inability to practice on my own. "Practice" was probably among the top five words spoken in our family, the other four probably being the names of our family members. Today, almost ten years since I've practiced, the word has lost the resonance of our usage. I now think of practice in terms of law or medicine. There is a television show called *The Practice,* and it seems odd to me that I never associate the word sprawled across the screen with the word that wove relentlessly throughout our family discourse. For my entire childhood and adolescence, practicing was an ongoing condition. It was both a given and a punishment. When we were bad, we practiced. When we were idle, we practiced. Before dinner and TV and friends coming over and bedtime and a thousand other things that beckoned with the possibility of taking place without all that harrowing noise, we practiced. "You have practicing and homework," my mother said every day. In that order. My father said the same thing without the homework part.

Much of the reason I could never quite get with the oboe-playing program was that I developed, at a very young age, a deep contempt for the Music Is My Bag world. Instead of religion, my family had music, and it was the church against which I rebelled. I had clergy for parents. My father: professional composer and arranger, keyboard player and trombonist, brother of a high school band director in Illinois. My mother: pianist and music educator of the high school production of *Carousel* genre. My own brother was a reluctant Christ figure. A typically restless second child in youth (he quit piano lessons but later discovered he could play entirely by ear), my brother recently completed the final mix of a demo CD of songs he wrote and performed—mid-eighties pop, late Doobie Brothers groove. His house is littered with Billy Joel and Bruce Hornsby sheet music, back issues of *Stereo Review,* the liner notes to the digital remastering of John Williams's score for Star Wars. Music is the Bag.

I compose songs in my sleep. I can't do it awake. I'll dream of songwriters singing onstage. I'll hear them perform new songs, songs I've never heard, songs I therefore must have written. In childhood I never put one thought toward composing a song. It would have been like composing air, creating more of something of which there was already quite enough. Wind players like flutists and saxophonists need as much air as they can get. Oboists are always trying to get rid of air. They calibrate what they need to get the reed to vibrate, end up using even less, and dispense with the rest out the corners of their mouths. It's all about exhaling. On an eighth rest, they're as likely to blow air out as they are to steal a breath. There's always too much air for oboists, too much of everything, too many bars when they're not playing and too many bars where there's hardly anyone playing but them, too many percussion players dropping triangles on the floor, too many violinists playing "Eleanor Rigby" before the rehearsal starts. Orchestras have only two oboists, first chair and second chair, pilot and copilot, though the "co" in this case is, like all "co's," a misnomer. The second oboist is the perpetual backup system, the one on call, the one who jumps in and saves the other when his reed dries up in the middle of a solo, when he misses his cue, when he freezes in panic before trying to hit a high D. I've been first oboist and I've been second oboist and, let me tell you, first is better, but not by much. It's still the oboe. Unlike the gregarious violinist or the congenial cellist, the oboist is a lone wolf. To play the oboe in an orchestra is to complete an obstacle course of solos and duets with the first flutist who, if she is hard-core Music Is My Bag, will refer to herself as a "flautist." Oboe solos dot the great symphonies like land mines, the pizzicati that precede them are drumrolls, the conductor's pointing finger an arrow for the whole audience to see: Here comes the oboe, two bars until the oboe, now, *now.* It's got to be nailed, one flubbed arpeggio, one flat half note, one misplaced pinky in the middle of a run of sixteenth notes, and *everyone* will hear, everyone.

My parents' presence at a high school orchestra concert turned what should have been a routine event into something akin to the finals of the Olympic women's figure skating long program. Even from the blinding, floodlit stage I could practically see them in the audience, clucking at every error, grimacing at anything even slightly out of tune. Afterwards, when the other parents—musically illiterate chumps—were patting their kids on the head and loading the tuba into the station wagon, I would receive my critique. "You were hesitating in the second movement of the Haydn Variations." "You over-anticipated in the berceuse section of the Stravinsky." "Your tone was excellent in the first movement but then your chops ran out." My brother, who was forced for a number of years to play the French horn, was reduced to a screaming fight with our father in the school parking lot, the kind of fight only possible between fathers and sons. He'd bumbled too many notes, played out of tune, committed some treasonous infraction against the family reputation. My father gave him the business on the way out to the car, eliciting the alto curses of a fourteen-year-old, pages of music everywhere, an instrument case slammed on the pavement.

This sort of rebellion was not my style. I cried instead. I cried in the seventh grade when the letter telling me I'd been accepted to the North Jersey regional orchestra arrived three days late. I cried in the tenth grade, when I ended up in the All-State Band instead of the orchestra. I cried when I thought I'd given a poor recital (never mind that the audience thought I was brilliant—all morons), cried before lessons (under-prepared), cried after lessons (sentenced to a week of reviewing the loathsome F-sharp étude). Mostly I cried during practice drills supervised by my father. These were torture sessions wherein some innocent tooting would send my father racing downstairs from his attic study, screaming, "Count, count, you're not counting! Jesus Christ!" Out would come a pencil—if not an actual conductor's baton—hitting the music stand, forcing me to repeat the tricky fingerings again and again, speeding up the tempo so I'd be sure to hit each note when we took it back down to real time. These sessions would last for hours, my mouth muscles shaking from atrophy, tears welling up from fatigue and exasperation. If we had a copy of the piano part, my mother would play the accompaniment, and together my parents would bark commands. "Articulate the eighth notes more. More staccato on the tonguing. Don't tap your foot, tap your toe inside your shoe." The postman heard a lot of this. The neighbors heard all of it. After practicing we'd eat dinner, but not before that song—"There's a smile on our face, and it seems to say all the wonderful things ..." "Good practice session today," my mother would say, dishing out the casserole, WQXR's *Symphony Hall* playing over the kitchen speakers. "Yup, sounding pretty good," my father would say. "How about one more go at it before bed?"

My mother called my oboe a "horn." This infuriated me. "Do you have your horn?" she'd ask every single morning. "Do you need your horn for school today?" She maintained that this terminology was technically correct, that among musicians, a "horn" was anything into which air was blown. My oboe was a $4,000 instrument, high-grade black grenadilla with sterling silver keys. It was no horn. But such semantics are a staple of Music Is My Bag, the overfamiliar stance that reveals a desperate need for subcultural affiliation, the musical equivalent of people in the magazine business who refer to publications like *Glamour* and *Forbes* as "books." As is indicated by the use of "horn," there's a subtly macho quality to Music Is My Bag. The persistent insecurity of musicians, especially classical musicians, fosters a kind of jargon that would be better confined to the military or major league baseball. Cellists talk about rock stops and rosin as though they were comparing canteen belts or brands of glove grease. They have their in-jokes and aphorisms, "The rock stops here," "Eliminate Violins In Our Schools."

I grew up surrounded by phrases like "rattle off that solo," "nail that lick," and "build up your chops." Like acid-washed jeans, "chops" is a word that should only be invoked by rock-and-roll guitarists but is more often uttered with the flailing, badly timed anti-authority of the high school clarinet player. Like the violinist who plays "Eleanor Rigby" before rehearsal, the clarinet player's relationship to rock and roll maintains its distance. Rock and roll is about sex. It is something unloved by parents and therefore unloved by Music Is My Bag people, who make a vocation of pleasing their parents, of studying trig and volunteering at the hospital and making a run for the student government even though they're well aware they have no chance of winning. Rock and roll is careless and unstudied. It might possibly involve drinking. It most certainly involves dancing. It flies in the face of the central identity of Music Is My Baggers, who chose as their role models those painfully introverted characters from young adult novels—"the klutz," "the bookworm," "the late bloomer." When given a classroom assignment to write about someone who inspires her, Music Is My Bag will write about her grandfather or perhaps Jean-Pierre Rampal. If the bad-attitude kid in the back row writes about AC/DC's Angus Young, Music Is My Bag will believe in her heart that this student should receive a failing grade. Rock and roll is not, as her parents would say when the junior high drama club puts on a production of *Grease,* "appropriate for this age group." Even in the throes of adolescence, Music Is My Bag will deny adolescence. Even at age sixteen, she will hold her ears when the rock and roll gets loud, saying it ruins her sense of overtones, saying she has sensitive ears. Like a retiree, she will classify the whole genre as nothing but a bunch of noise, though it is likely she is a fan of Yes.

During the years that I was a member of the New Jersey All-State Orchestra I would carpool to rehearsals with the four or so other kids from my town who made All State every year. This involved spending as much as two hours each way in station wagons driven by people's parents and, inevitably, the issue would arise of what music would be played in the car. Among the most talented musicians in school was a freshman who, in addition to being hired by the Boston Symphony Orchestra at age twenty-two, possessed, as a fifteen-year-old, a ripe enthusiasm for the singer Amy Grant. This was back in the mid-1980s when Amy Grant's hits were still relegated to the Christian charts. Our flute-playing carpool-mate loved Amy Grant. Next to Prokofiev and the Hindemith Flute Sonata, Amy Grant occupied the number one spot in this girl's studious, late-blooming heart. Since her mother, like many parents of Baggers, was devoted solely to her daughter's musical and academic career, she did most of the driving to these boony spots—Upper Chatham High School, Monmouth Regional, Long Branch Middle School. Mile after New Jersey Turnpike mile, we were serenaded by the wholesome synthesizers of songs like "Saved By Love" and "Wait for the Healing," only to spill out of the car and take no small relief in the sound of twenty-five of New Jersey's best student violinists playing "Eleanor Rigby" before the six-hour rehearsal.

To participate in a six-hour rehearsal of the New Jersey All-State Band or Orchestra is to enter a world so permeated by Music Is My Bagdom that it becomes possible to confuse the subculture with an entire species, as if Baggers, like lobsters or ferns, require special conditions in order to thrive. Their ecosystem is the auditorium and the adjacent band room, any space that makes use of risers. To eat lunch and dinner in these venues is to see the accessories of Badgom tumble from purses, knapsacks, and totes; here more than anyplace are the real McCoys, actual Music Is My Bag bags, canvas satchels filled with stereo Walkmen and A.P. math homework and Trapper Keeper notebooks featuring the piano-playing Schroeder from the *Peanuts* comic strip. The dinner break is when I would embark on oboe maintenance, putting the reed in water, swabbing the instrument dry, removing the wads of wax that, during my orthodontic years, I placed over my front teeth to keep the inside of my mouth from bleeding. Just as I had hated the entropy of recess back in my grade-school years, I loathed the dinner breaks at All-State rehearsals. To maximize rehearsal time, the wind section often ate separately from the strings, which left me alone with the band types. They'd wolf down their sandwiches and commence with their jam session, a cacophonous white noise of scales, finger exercises, and memorized excerpts from their hometown marching band numbers. During these dinner breaks I'd generally hang with the other oboist. For some reason, this was almost always a tall girl who wore sneakers with corduroy pants and a turtleneck with nothing over it. This is fairly typical Music Is My Bag garb, though oboists have a particular spin on it, a spin characterized more than anything by lack of spin. Given the absence in most classical musicians of a style gene, this is probably a good thing. Oboists don't accessorize. They don't wear buttons on their jackets that say "Oboe Power" or "Who Are You Going to Tune To?"

There's high-end Bagdom and low-end Bagdom, with a lot of room in between. Despite my parents' paramilitary practice regimes, I have to give them credit for being fairly high-end Baggers. There were no piano-key scarves in our house, no "World's Greatest Trombonist" figurines, no plastic tumblers left over from my father's days as director of the Stanford University Marching Band. Such accessories are the mandate of the lowest tier of Music Is My Bag, a stratum whose mascot is P.D.Q. Bach, whose theme song is "Piano Man," and whose regional representative is the kid in high school who plays not only the trumpet but the piano, saxophone, flute, string bass, accordion, and wood block. This kid, considered a wunderkind by his parents and the rest of the band community, plays none of these instruments well, but the fact that he knows so many different sets of fingerings, the fact that he has the potential to earn some college money by performing as a one-man band at the annual state teacher's conference, makes him a hometown hero. He may not be a football player. He may not even gain access to the Ivy League. But in the realm of Music Is My Bag, the kid who plays every instrument, particularly when he can play Billy Joel songs on every instrument, is the Alpha Male.

The flip side of the one-man-band kid are those Music Is My Baggers who are not musicians at all. These are the kids who twirl flags or rifles in the marching band, kids who blast music in their rooms and play not air guitar but air keyboards, their hands fluttering out in front of them, the hand positions not nearly as important as the attendant head motions.

This is the essence of Bagdom. It is to take greater pleasure in the reverb than the melody, to love the lunch break more than the rehearsal, the rehearsal more than the performance, the clarinet case more than the clarinet. It is to think nothing of sending away for the deluxe packet of limited-edition memorabilia that is being sold for the low, low price of one's entire personality. It is to let the trinkets do the talking.

I was twenty-one when I stopped playing the oboe. I wish I could come up with a big, dramatic reason why. I wish I could say that I sustained some kind of injury that prevented me from playing (it's hard to imagine what kind of injury could sideline an oboist—a lip strain? carpal tunnel?) or that I was forced to sell my oboe in order to help a family member in crisis or, better yet, that I suffered a violent attack in which my oboe was used as a weapon against me before being stolen and melted down for artillery. But the truth, I'm ashamed to say, has more to do with what in college I considered to be an exceptionally long walk from my dormitory to the music building, and the fact that I was wrapped up in a lot of stuff that, from my perspective at the time, precluded the nailing of Rachmaninoff licks. Without the prodding of my parents or the structure of a state-run music education program, my oboe career had to run on self-motivation alone—not an abundant resource—and when my senior year started I neither registered for private lessons nor signed up for the orchestra, dodging countless calls from the director imploring me to reassume my chair.

Since then, I haven't set foot in a rehearsal room, put together a folding music stand, fussed with a reed, marked up music, practiced scales, tuned an orchestra or performed any of the countless activities that had dominated my existence up until that point. There are moments every now and then when I'll hear the oboe-dominated tenth movement of the Bach Mass in B Minor or the berceuse section of Stravinsky's *Firebird* and long to find a workable reed and pick up the instrument again. But then I imagine how terrible I'll sound after eight dormant years and put the whole idea out of my mind before I start to feel sad about it. I can still smell the musty odor of the inside of my oboe case, the old-ladyish whiff of the velvet lining and the tubes of cork grease and the damp fabric of the key pads. Unlike the computer on which I now work, my oboe had the sense of being an ancient thing. Brittle and creaky, it was vulnerable when handled by strangers. It needed to be packed up tight, dried out in just the right places, kept away from the heat and the cold and from anyone stupid enough to confuse it with a clarinet.

What I really miss about the oboe is having my hands on it. I could come at that instrument from any direction or any angle and know every indentation on every key, every spot that leaked air, every nick on every square inch of wood. When enough years go by, the corporeal qualities of an instrument become as familiar to its player as, I imagine, those of a longstanding lover. Knowing precisely how the weight of the oboe was distributed between my right thumb and left wrist, knowing, above all, that the weight would feel the same way every time, every day, for every year that I played, was a feeling akin to having ten years of knowledge about the curve of someone's back. But I put my oboe down, and I never picked it back up. I could have been a pretty good oboist if I had practiced, if I had ignored the set design and just played the instrument. But I didn't and I wasn't. When I look back I hardly recognize myself, that person who could play a Mozart sonata by memory, whose fingers could move three times faster than I now type—a person who was given a gift, but who walked away from it because of piano-key scarves and fedora hats and all those secondary melodies that eventually became the only thing I could hear.

—2000

Learning from Other Writers

1. In the first four paragraphs of her essay, Daum attempts to familiarize her readers with the system of signs she is trying to decode. How does she structure her presentation of these objects and behaviors?
2. What is the function of the fifth paragraph?
3. In "Music Is My Bag," is Daum writing for an audience of outsiders, insiders, both, or neither? Does she position herself inside this culture, outside it, both, or neither? What is the larger significance of Daum's analysis (i.e., to readers who aren't necessarily musicians)?
4. What aspects of "Music Is My Bag" culture does Daum decode for her readers?
5. The essay's structure shifts in paragraph six; what basic shape does it assume from there until the end?

DAVID SEDARIS

SIX TO EIGHT BLACK MEN

I've never been much for guidebooks, so when trying to get my bearings in a strange American city, I normally start by asking the cabdriver or hotel clerk some silly question regarding the latest census figures. I say silly because I don't really *care* how many people live in Olympia, Washington, or Columbus, Ohio. They're nice enough places, but the numbers mean nothing to me. My second question might have to do with average annual rainfall, which, again, doesn't tell me anything about the people who have chosen to call this place home.

What really interests me are the local gun laws. Can I carry a concealed weapon, and if so, under what circumstances? What's the waiting period for a tommy gun? Could I buy a Glock 17 if I were recently divorced or fired from my job? I've learned from experience that it's best to lead into this subject as delicately as possible, especially if you and the local citizen are alone and enclosed in a relatively small space. Bide your time, though, and you can walk away with some excellent stories. I've heard, for example, that the blind can legally hunt in both Texas and Michigan. They must be accompanied by a sighted companion, but still, it seems a bit risky. You wouldn't want a blind person driving a car or piloting a plane, so why hand him a rifle? What sense does that make? I ask about guns not because I want one of my own but because the answers vary so widely from state to state. In a country that's become so homogenous, I'm reassured by these last touches of regionalism.

Guns aren't really an issue in Europe, so when I'm traveling abroad, my first question usually relates to barnyard animals. "What do your roosters say?" is a good icebreaker, as every country has its own unique interpretation. In Germany, where dogs bark "vow vow" and both the frog and the duck say "quack," the rooster greets the dawn with a hearty "kik-a-ricki." Greek roosters crow "kiri-a-kee," and in France they scream "coco-rico," which sounds like one of those horrible premixed cocktails with a pirate on the label. When told that an American rooster says "cock-a-doodle-doo," my hosts look at me with disbelief and pity.

"When do you open your Christmas presents?" is another good conversation starter, as it explains a lot about national character. People who traditionally open gifts on Christmas Eve seem a bit more pious and family oriented than those who wait until Christmas morning. They go to mass, open presents, eat a late meal, return to church the following morning, and devote the rest of the day to eating another big meal. Gifts are generally reserved for children, and the parents tend not to go overboard. It's nothing I'd want for myself, but I suppose it's fine for those who prefer food and family to things of real value.

In France and Germany, gifts are exchanged on Christmas Eve, while in Holland the children receive presents on December 5, in celebration of Saint Nicholas Day. It sounded sort of quaint until I spoke to a man named Oscar, who filled me in on a few of the details as we walked from my hotel to the Amsterdam train station.

Unlike the jolly, obese American Santa, Saint Nicholas is painfully thin and dresses not unlike the pope, topping his robes with a tall hat resembling an embroidered tea cozy. The outfit, I was told, is a carryover from his former career, when he served as a bishop in Turkey.

One doesn't want to be too much of a cultural chauvinist, but this seemed completely wrong to me. For starters, Santa didn't *use to do* anything. He's not retired, and, more important, he has nothing to do with Turkey. The climate's all wrong, and people wouldn't appreciate him. When asked how he got from Turkey to the North Pole, Oscar told me with complete conviction that Saint Nicholas currently resides in Spain, which again is simply not true. While he could probably live wherever he wanted, Santa chose the North Pole specifically because it is harsh and isolated. No one can spy on him, and he doesn't have to worry about people coming to the door. Anyone can come to the door in Spain, and in that outfit, he'd most certainly be recognized. On top of that, aside from a few pleasantries, Santa doesn't speak Spanish. He knows enough to get by, but he's not fluent, and he certainly doesn't eat tapas.

While our Santa flies on a sled, Saint Nicholas arrives by boat and then transfers to a white horse. The event is televised, and great crowds gather at the waterfront to greet him. I'm not sure if there's a set date, but he generally docks in late November and spends a few weeks hanging out and asking people what they want.

"Is it just him alone?" I asked. "Or does he come with some backup?"

Oscar's English was close to perfect, but he seemed thrown by a term normally reserved for police reinforcement.

"Helpers," I said. "Does he have any elves?"

Maybe I'm just overly sensitive, but I couldn't help but feel personally insulted when Oscar denounced the very idea as grotesque and unrealistic. "Elves," he said. "They're just so silly."

The words *silly* and *unrealistic* were redefined when I learned that Saint Nicholas travels with what was consistently described as "six to eight black men." I asked several Dutch people to narrow it down, but none of them could give me an exact number. It was always "six to eight," which seems strange, seeing as they've had hundreds of years to get a decent count.

The six to eight black men were characterized as personal slaves until the mid-fifties, when the political climate changed and it was decided that instead of being slaves they were just good friends. I think history has proven that something usually comes *between* slavery and friendship, a period of time marked not by cookies and quiet times beside the fire but by bloodshed and mutual hostility. They have such violence in Holland, but rather than duking it out among themselves, Santa and his former slaves decided to take it out on the public. In the early years, if a child was naughty, Saint Nicholas and the six to eight black men would beat him with what Oscar described as "the small branch of a tree."

"A switch?"

"Yes," he said. "That's it. They'd kick him and beat him with a switch. Then, if the youngster was really bad, they'd put him in a sack and take him back to Spain."

"Saint Nicholas would *kick* you?"

"Well, not anymore," Oscar said. "Now he just *pretends* to kick you."

"And the six to eight black men?"

"Them, too."

He considered this to be progressive, but in a way I think it's almost more perverse than the original punishment. "I'm going to hurt you, but not really." How many times have we fallen for that line? The fake slap invariably makes contact, adding the elements of shock and betrayal to what had previously been plain, old-fashioned fear. What kind of Santa spends his time pretending to kick people before stuffing them into a canvas sack? Then, of course, you've got the six to eight former slaves who could potentially go off at any moment. This, I think, is the greatest difference between us and the Dutch. While a certain segment of our population might be perfectly happy with the arrangement, if you told the average white American that six to eight nameless black men would be sneaking into his house in the middle of the night, he would barricade the doors and arm himself with whatever he could get his hands on.

"*Six to eight*, did you say?"

In the years before central heating, Dutch children would leave their shoes by the fireplace, the promise being that unless they planned to beat you, kick you, or stuff you into a sack, Saint Nicholas and the six to eight black men would fill your clogs with presents. Aside from the threats of violence and kidnapping, it's not much different from hanging your stockings from the mantel. Now that so few people have a working fireplace, Dutch children are instructed to leave their shoes beside the radiator, furnace, or space heater. Saint Nicholas and the six to eight black men arrive on horses, which jump from the yard onto the roof. At this point, I guess, they either jump back down and use the door, or they stay put and vaporize through the pipes and electrical wires. Oscar wasn't too clear about the particulars, but, really, who can blame him? We have the same problem with our Santa. He's supposed to use the chimney, but if you don't have one, he still manages to come through. It's best not to think about it too hard.

While eight flying reindeer are a hard pill to swallow, our Christmas story remains relatively simple. Santa lives with his wife in a remote polar village and spends one night a year traveling around the world. If you're bad, he leaves you coal. If you're good and live in America, he'll give you just about anything you want. We tell our children to be good and send them off to bed, where they lie awake, anticipating their great bounty. A Dutch parent has a decidedly hairier story to relate, telling his children, "Listen, you might want to pack a few of your things together before you go to bed. The former bishop from Turkey will be coming along with six to eight black men. They might put some candy in your shoes, they might stuff you in a sack and take you to Spain, or they might just pretend to kick you. We don't know for sure, but we want you to be prepared."

This is the reward for living in Holland. As a child you get to hear this story, and as an adult you get to turn around and repeat it. As an added bonus, the government has thrown in legalized drugs and prostitution—so what's not to love about being Dutch?

Oscar finished his story just as we arrived at the station. He was a polite and interesting guy—very good company—but when he offered to wait until my train arrived, I begged off, saying I had some calls to make. Sitting alone in the vast terminal, surrounded by other polite, seemingly interesting Dutch people, I couldn't help but feel second-rate. Yes, it was a small country, but it had six to eight black men and a really good bedtime story. Being a fairly competitive person, I felt jealous, then bitter, and was edging toward hostile when I remembered the blind hunter tramping off into the Michigan forest. He might bag a deer, or he might happily shoot his sighted companion in the stomach. He may find his way back to the car, or he may wander around for a week or two before stumbling through your front door. We don't know for sure, but in pinning that license to his chest, he inspires the sort of narrative that ultimately makes me proud to be an American.

—2002

Learning from Other Writers

1. Obviously, one of the author's main purposes is to make you laugh. But is making you laugh his *only* purpose?
2. What is the function of the opening three paragraphs? What is your judgment as to the seriousness or the validity of the sort of research Sedaris describes?
3. We've all been taught not to make fun of other people's cultures or religions. Is Sedaris making fun of Dutch customs? If not, why did you laugh so hard when you read the essay? If so, where is the line between laughing at someone's holiday customs and showing intolerance or mean-spiritedness?
4. Go back through the essay and find the lines that made you laugh. Can you pinpoint the source of the humor? Are you laughing solely at the content (i.e., the notion that Saint Nicholas travels with "six to eight black men"), or does Sedaris do something to the content (via style, organization, tone, the use of dialogue) that heightens the humor? We noticed that E. B. White gets many of his laughs from conflating high and low diction and high and low culture. Does Sedaris use this trick? What other tricks does he use to make us laugh?
5. What is the effect of Sedaris's decision to end by returning to the Michigan law that allows blind people to hunt?

INSPIRATIONS: CRYPTOGRAPHY

1. Select an interesting set of signs or behaviors (i.e., a style of dress, a group of objects that people buy and/or display, a set of ritualized behaviors or ways of communicating).
2. Decipher the code you've selected, helping an audience of outsiders to understand the significance of the code or what's going on at a deeper level. (To defamiliarize the code and help your audience see it in a new light, you might pretend that you're explaining a set of human behaviors to an alien from another planet or to a time traveler from the future or the past.) Structure your essay according to the way in which you or someone else might encounter these signs or behaviors in everyday life. If that seems too complicated, you can structure your essay according to a list of the signs or behaviors you are decoding.

13 Spatial Forms

Some of the most original examples of creative nonfiction rely more heavily on movements through space than movements through time. To understand what this means, imagine an author meditating on a question about his mother's life while leafing through her favorite cookbook, inspecting the sailboat she designed and built and sailed around the world, fiddling with the pedalboard, keys, and drawbars of the electric organ she loved to play, or wandering the village in Cambodia where she lived as a little girl. As you will see from the examples in this chapter, essays and books whose structures mimic the structures of objects, documents, or places comprise one of the most exciting and important segments of the genre.

Although I've always referred to such structures as spatial (or found) forms, I also like the term coined by Brenda Miller and Suzanne Paola in their textbook *Tell It Slant*. In honor of the hermit crab, which steals and inhabits the shells cast off by other creatures, Miller and Paola use the term "hermit-crab essay" to describe an "essay that appropriates other forms as an outer covering to protect its soft, vulnerable underbelly.... The 'shells' come from wherever you can find them, anywhere in the world. They may borrow from fiction and poetry, but they also don't hesitate to armor themselves in more mundane structures: the descriptions in a mail order catalog, for example, or the entries in a checkbook register." As Miller and Paola point out, such forms allow writers who might otherwise feel overwhelmed by the emotional intensity of their subject to gain not only structural but psychological mastery over their material. My only objection to Miller and Paola's analysis is that the forms they describe are far more central to the craft of creative nonfiction than the authors seem to think.[1]

OBJECTS

As we all know, certain objects can serve as the repositories of our memories and emotions. Like Hamlet discoursing on vanity while cradling the skull of the jester Yorick, who once carried him on his back, sang to him, kissed him, and told him jokes, any of us might pick up a basketball, a dancing shoe, a G.I. Joe, or a senior yearbook and use it as a catalyst to contemplate our past. With a larger or more complex object, we might even structure our reminiscences according to its parts, moving from the glove compartment of a Jaguar to the monitors along its dash, to the back seat and the trunk, to the hubcaps, then the fenders, then the ornament on the hood.

Illustrations of the spatial form are easiest to see in poetry. In Book Eighteen of *The Iliad* (an example I owe to John Hersey), Homer moves us around the scenes painted by Hephaistos on

[1] For the full text of Miller and Paola's discussion of this form, see *Tell It Slant*, McGraw-Hill, 2005, pp. 111–113.

the five-folded shield of Achilles, using the images on the shield to spur his reflections on life in Greece and Troy. In a gesture that might have been inspired by these same Homeric lines, Keats holds in his hand that famous Grecian urn and uses the images along its sides—men pursuing women beneath an arbor of leafy trees, pipers piping timbrels, priests sacrificing a heifer at an altar—to structure his ruminations on beauty, youth, and art.

We don't usually think of ourselves as objects, but in "Portrait of My Body," Philip Lopate structures his autobiography—and an analysis of the effects of our bodies on our selves—along his own frame, moving upward from feet to head. And even though James Agee's nonfiction masterpiece *Let Us Now Praise Famous Men* is basically a group portrait of a community of sharecroppers in the deep South in the 1930s, within that group portrait Agee structures one lengthy meditation according to the table of contents of a child's geography book, while another section takes its shape from the parts of a pair of overalls.

LISTS AND OTHER DOCUMENTS

In a similar way, you can structure an essay or a book by moving spatially around the images or words on a painting, map, photograph, or other document (this form has grown more familiar as we have become accustomed to the layout of a Web page). Each month, the authors of the Annotation feature in *Harper's Magazine* create a visual essay by commenting on the various parts of an object or a document (i.e., a baseball bat, a bouquet of flowers, a sheet of ballet notations) splayed like a butterfly on a dish. At the end of this chapter, we've included an example of this feature in which Jon Mooallem decodes the significance of the parts of a can of Campbell's Soup at Hand; the essay is structured around the physical object—the can of soup—although the label itself qualifies as a document.

Primo Levi's use of the periodic table to structure his memoir of life before, during, and after his internment at Auschwitz has to rank among the most inventive possibilities of the document form ("Chromium," in Chapter 7, is an "element" from Levi's *The Periodic Table*). But I once taught an undergraduate who displayed a similar ingenuity when he chose to structure his reflections on his peripatetic childhood by considering the child-custody clauses in his parents' divorce decree.

One of the documents that writers routinely cannibalize to provide the structure for an essay is the instruction manual or how-to guide. In fact, two examples of this structure, Katha Pollitt's "Learning to Drive" and Atul Gawande's "The Learning Curve," were chosen to appear in the 2003 edition of *The Best American Essays*. Like Philip Weiss, whose "How to Get Out of a Locked Trunk" we discussed in Chapter 8, Pollitt relies on a parodic appropriation of the how-to form not only to make us laugh, but also to explore the deeper truth about her relationship to a former lover, while Gawande recounts the nerve-wracking process by which he learned to perform various medical procedures and guides us through the deathly important debate about how best to train our surgeons.

Thankfully, not many of us can follow Brent Staples's example and use a coroner's report to mediate our response to our brother's life and death as a drug dealer, but we all use documents to order our experiences, the To-Do list being a case in point. Some of the most successful contemporary short stories borrow their structure from the list, among them "Girl" by Jamaica Kincaid (a list of rules and admonitions from a mother to a daughter), "In the Fifties" by Leonard Michaels (a list of the narrator's activities during that surprisingly turbulent decade), "Lust" by Susan Minot (a list of the narrator's sexual encounters with boys and men), and "The Things They Carried" by Tim O'Brien (a list of the tangible and intangible burdens carried by a group of soldiers in Vietnam).[2] The same is true for poems, whether Walt Whitman's "I Hear America Singing" (which can be found in any edition of *Leaves of Grass* or on the Web) or the following list-poem by Raymond Carver (from *All of Us: The Collected Poems*):

FEAR

Fear of seeing a police car pull into the drive.
Fear of falling asleep at night.
Fear of not falling asleep.
Fear of the past rising up.
Fear of the present taking flight.
Fear of the telephone that rings in the dead of night.
Fear of electrical storms.
Fear of the cleaning woman who has a spot on her cheek!
Fear of dogs I've been told won't bite.
Fear of anxiety!
Fear of having to identify the body of a dead friend.
Fear of running out of money.
Fear of having too much, though people will not believe this.
Fear of psychological profiles.
Fear of being late and fear of arriving before anyone else.
Fear of my children's handwriting on envelopes.
Fear they'll die before I do, and I'll feel guilty.
Fear of having to live with my mother in her old age, and mine.
Fear of confusion.
Fear this day will end on an unhappy note.
Fear of waking up to find you gone.
Fear of not loving and fear of not loving enough.
Fear that what I love will prove lethal to those I love.
Fear of death.
Fear of living too long.
Fear of death.

I've said that.

So, too, many essayists have taken to ordering their meditations according to lists. In a famous example of this form, aptly named "The Car," the novelist Harry Crews uses a list of the first three vehicles he owned (and the separate parts of one of those cars, a 1938 Ford coupe) to reconsider the young man he used to be and to ponder the possibility that Americans "have found God in cars, or if not the true God, one so satisfying, so powerful and awe-inspiring that the distinction is too fine to matter."[3] And in "*Memoria ex Machina*," which appears in this chapter (and in the 2003 edition of *Best American Essays*), Marshall Jon Fisher inventories the

[2] "Girl" appeared in *The New Yorker* on June 26, 1976, and was reprinted in *At the Bottom of the River*, published by Farrar, Straus & Giroux in 1983; "In the Fifties" can be found in *I Would Have Saved Them If I Could*, Farrar, Straus & Giroux, 1975; Minot's "Lust and Other Stories" was published in 1989 by Houghton Mifflin; "The Things They Carried" appeared in *Esquire's* August 1986 edition before re-appearing as part of O'Brien's book by the same title, published in 1990 by Houghton Mifflin.

[3] "The Car" first appeared in the December 1975 issue of Esquire and has been reprinted in three of Crews's essay collections: *Florida Frenzy*, *Blood and Grits*, and *Classic Crews: A Harry Crews Reader*.

mechanical and digital objects—the stainless-steel analog watch he received for his bar mitzvah, the primitive clock radio with burnt-amber numerals, the Sony Walkman, the 1985 Kaypro computer—whose lingering presence in his memory comprise his understanding of his past.

PLACES

Nor does the object that a writer uses to structure an essay need to be as manageable or compact as a clock radio, as evidenced by Joan Didion's melancholy reflections on why she can't stop thinking about the Hoover Dam. At this size, the spatial structure of the essay begins to resemble a tour (which differs from a journey or a pilgrimage in that the writer is already *there* when the essay starts). Lawrence Weschler, in his bizarre and brilliant book *Mr. Wilson's Cabinet of Wonder* (Vintage, 1996), takes his readers on a tour of the exhibits they would encounter if they were fortunate enough to visit the mind-bending Museum of Jurassic Technology in Los Angeles (one of whose "exhibits" is its sly and elfish curator, David Wilson). In a similar way, William Zinsser structures his search for the fundamental ideals that America represents—in our imaginations if not reality—around a series of visits to such iconographic sites as Mount Rushmore, the Alamo, Appomattox, Disneyland, and Montgomery (see *American Places*, Paul Dry Books, 2007). And in his frequently anthologized essay "Where Worlds Collide," which first appeared in the August 1995 issue of *Harper's*, Pico Iyer ponders the ironies and complexities of our multiracial nation, meditating on his hypothesis that airports are "the new epicenters and paradigms of our dawning post-national age—not just the bus terminals of the global village but the prototypes, in some sense, for our polyglot, multicolored, user-friendly future," while wandering the vast interior spaces of the weirdly outdated LAX airport in Los Angeles.

PHILLIP LOPATE

PORTRAIT OF MY BODY

I am a man who tilts. When I am sitting, my head slants to the right; when walking, the upper part of my body reaches forward to catch a sneak preview of the street. One way or another, I seem to be off-center—or "uncentered," to use the jargon of holism. My lousy posture, a tendency to slump or put myself into lazy, contorted misalignments, undoubtedly contributes to lower back pain. For a while I correct my bad habits, do morning exercises, sit straight, breathe deeply, but always an inner demon that insists on approaching the world askew resists perpendicularity.

I think if I had broader shoulders I would be more squarely anchored. But my shoulders are narrow, barely wider than my hips. This has always made shopping for suits an embarrassing business. (Françoise Gilot's *Life with Picasso* tells how Picasso was so touchy about his disproportionate body—in his case all shoulders, no legs—that he insisted the tailor fit him at home.) When I was growing up in Brooklyn, my hero was Sandy Koufax, the Dodgers' Jewish pitcher. In the doldrums of Hebrew choir practice at Feigenbaum's Mansion & Catering Hall, I would fantasize striking out the side, even whiffing twenty-seven batters in a row. Lack of shoulder development put an end to this identification; I became a writer instead of a Koufax.

It occurs to me that the restless angling of my head is an attempt to distract viewers' attention from its paltry base. I want people to look at my head, partly because I live in my head most of the time. My sister, a trained masseuse, often warns me of the penalties, like neck tension, that may arise from failing to integrate body and mind. Once, about ten years ago, she and I were at the beach and she was scrutinizing my body with a sister's critical eye. "You're getting flabby," she said. "You should exercise every day. I do—look at me, not an ounce of fat." She pulled at her midriff, celebrating (as is her wont) her physical attributes with the third-person enthusiasm of a carnival barker.

"But"—she threw me a bone—"you do have a powerful head. There's an intensity..." A graduate student of mine (who was slightly loony) told someone that she regularly saw an aura around my head in class. One reason I like to teach is that it focuses fifteen or so dependent gazes on me with such paranoiac intensity as cannot help but generate an aura in my behalf.

I also have a commanding stare, large sad brown eyes that can be read as either gentle or severe. Once I watched several hours of myself on videotape. I discovered to my horror that my face moved at different rates: sometimes my mouth would be laughing, eyebrows circumflexed in mirth, while my eyes coolly gauged the interviewer to see what effect I was making. I am something of an actor. And, as with many performers, the mood I sense most in myself is that of energy-conserving watchfulness; but this expression is often mistaken (perhaps because of the way brown eyes are read in our culture) for sympathy. I see myself as determined to the point of stubbornness, selfish, even a bit cruel—in any case, I am all too aware of the limits of my compassion, so that it puzzles me when people report a first impression of me as gentle, kind, solicitous. In my youth I felt obliged to come across as dynamic, arrogant, intimidating, the life of the party; now, surer of myself, I hold back some energy, thereby winning time to gather information and make better judgments. This results sometimes in a misimpression of my being mildly depressed. Of course, the simple truth is that I have less energy than I once did, and that accumulated experiences have made me, almost against my will, kinder and sadder.

Sometimes I can feel my mouth arching downward in an ironic smile, which, at its best, reassures others that we need not take everything so seriously—because we are all in the same comedy together—and, at its worst, expresses a superior skepticism. This smile, which can be charming when not supercilious, has elements of the bashful that mesh with the worldly—the shyness, let us say, of a cultivated man who is often embarrassed for others by their willful shallowness or self-deception. Many times, however, my ironic smile is nothing more than a neutral stall among people who do not seem to appreciate my "contribution." I hate that pain-in-the-ass half-smile of mine; I want to jump in, participate, be loud, thoughtless, vulgar.

Often I give off a sort of psychic stench to myself, I do not like myself at all, but out of stubborn pride I act like a man who does. I appear for all the world poised, contented, sanguine when inside I may be feeling self-revulsion bordering on the suicidal. What a wonder to be so misread! Of course, if in the beginning I had thought I was coming across accurately, I never would have bothered to become a writer. And the truth is I am not misread, because another part of me is never less than fully contented with myself.

I am vain about these parts of my body: my eyes, my fingers, my legs. It is true that my legs are long and not unshapely, but my vanity about them has less to do with their comeliness than with their contribution to my height. Montaigne, a man who was himself on the short side, wrote that "the beauty of stature is the only beauty of men." But even if Montaigne had never said it, I would continue to attribute a good deal of my self-worth and benevolent liberalism to being tall. When I go out into the street, I feel well-disposed toward the (mostly shorter) swarms of humanity; crowds not only do not dismay, they enliven me; and I am tempted to think that my passion for urbanism is linked to my height. By no means am I suggesting that only tall people love cities; merely that, in my case, part of the pleasure I derive from walking in crowded streets issues from a confidence that I can see above the heads of others, and cut a fairly impressive, elevated figure as I saunter along the sidewalk.

Some of my best friends have been—short. Brilliant men, brimming with poetic and worldly ideas, they deserved all of my and the world's respect. Yet at times I have had to master an impulse to rumple their heads; and I suspect they have developed manners of a more formal, *noli me tangere* nature, largely in response to this petting impulse of taller others.

The accident of my tallness has inclined me to both a seemingly egalitarian informality and a desire to lead. Had I not been a writer, I would surely have become a politician; I was even headed in that direction in my teens. Ever since I shot up to a little over six feet, I have had at my command what feels like a natural, Gregory Peck authority when addressing an audience. Far from experiencing stage fright, I have actually sought out situations in which I could make speeches, give readings, sit on panel discussions, and generally tower over everyone else onstage. To be tall is to look down on the world and meet its eyes on your terms. But this topic, the noblesse oblige of tall men, is a dangerously provoking one, and so let us say no more about it.

The mental image of one's body changes slower than one's body. Mine was for a long while arrested in my early twenties, when I was tall and thin (165 pounds) and gobbled down whatever I felt like. I ate food that was cheap and filling, cheeseburgers, pizza, without any thought to putting on weight. But a young person's metabolism is more dietetically forgiving. To compound the problem, the older you get, the more cultivated your palate grows—and the more life's setbacks make you inclined to fill the hollowness of disappointment with the pleasures of the table.

Between the age of thirty and forty I put on ten pounds, mostly around the midsection. Since then my gut has suffered another expansion, and I tip the scales at over 180. That I took a while to notice the change may be shown by my continuing to purchase clothes at my primordial adult size (33 waist, 15 1/2 collar), until a girlfriend started pointing out that all my clothes were too tight. I rationalized this circumstance as the result of changing fashions (thinking myself still subconsciously loyal to the sixties' penchant for skintight fits) and laundry shrinkage rather than anything to do with my own body. She began buying me larger replacements for birthdays or holidays, and I found I enjoyed this "baggier" style, which allowed me to button my trousers comfortably, or to wear a tie and, for the first time in years, close my top shirt button. But it took even longer before I was able to enter a clothing store myself and give the salesman realistically enlarged size numbers.

Clothes can disguise the defects of one's body, up to a point. I get dressed with great optimism, adding one color to another, mixing my favorite Japanese and Italian designers, matching the patterns and textures, selecting ties, then proceed to the bathroom mirror to judge the result. There is an ideal in my mind of the effect I am essaying by wearing a particular choice of garments, based, no doubt, on male models in fashion ads—and I fall so far short of this insouciant gigolo handsomeness that I cannot help but be a little disappointed when I turn up so depressingly myself, narrow-shouldered, Talmudic, that grim, set mouth, that long, narrow face, those appraising eyes, the Semitic hooked nose, all of which express both the strain of intellectual overachieving and the tabula rasa of immaturity ... for it is still, underneath, a boy in the mirror. A boy with a rapidly receding hairline.

How is it that I've remained a boy all this time, into my late forties? I remember, at seventeen, drawing a self-portrait of myself as I looked in the mirror. I was so appalled at the weak chin and pleading eyes that I ended up focusing on the neckline of the cotton T-shirt. Ever since then I have tried to toughen myself up, but I still encounter in the glass that haunted uncertainty—shielded by a bluffing shell of cynicism, perhaps, but untouched by wisdom. So I approach the mirror warily, without lighting up as much as I would for the least of my acquaintances; I go one-on-one with that frowning schmuck.

And yet, it would be insulting to those who labor under the burden of true ugliness to palm myself off as an unattractive man. I'm at times almost handsome, if you squinted your eyes and rounded me off to the nearest *beau idéal*. I lack even a shred of cowboy virility, true, but I believe I fall into a category of adorable nerd or absentminded professor that awakens the amorous curiosity of some women. "Cute" is a word often applied to me by those I've been fortunate enough to attract. Then again, I attract only women of a certain lopsided prettiness: the head-turning, professional beauties never fall for me. They seem to look right through me, in fact. Their utter lack of interest in my appeal has always fascinated me. Can it be so simple an explanation as that beauty calls to beauty, as wealth to wealth?

I think of poor (though not in his writing gifts) Cesare Pavese, who kept chasing after starlets, models, and ballerinas—exquisite lovelies who couldn't appreciate his morose coffeehouse charm. Before he killed himself, he wrote a poem addressed to one of them, "Death Will Come Bearing Your Eyes"—thereby unfairly promoting her from rejecting lover to unwitting executioner. Perhaps he believed that only beautiful women (not literary critics, who kept awarding him prestigious prizes) saw him clearly, with twenty-twenty vision, and had the right to judge him. Had I been more headstrong, if masochistic, I might have followed his path and chased some beauty until she was forced to tell me, like an oracle, what it was about me, physically, that so failed to excite her. Then I might know something crucial about my body, before I passed into my next reincarnation.

Jung says somewhere that we pay dearly over many years to learn about ourselves what a stranger can see at a glance. This is the way I feel about my back. Fitting rooms aside, we none of us know what we look like from the back. It is the area of ourselves whose presentation we can least control, and which therefore may be the most honest part of us.

I divide backs into two kinds: my own and everyone else's. The others' backs are often mysterious, exquisite, and uncannily sympathetic. I have always loved backs. To walk behind a pretty woman in a backless dress and savor how a good pair of shoulder blades, heightened by shadow, has the same power to pierce the heart as chiseled cheekbones! ... I wonder what it says about me that I worship a part of the body that signals a turning away. Does it mean I'm a glutton for being abandoned, or a timid voyeur who prefers a surreptitious gaze that will not be met and challenged? I only know I have often felt the deepest love at just that moment when the beloved turns her back to me to get some sleep.

I have no autoerotic feelings about my own back. I cannot even picture it; visually it is a stranger to me. I know it only as an annoyance, which came into my consciousness twenty years ago, when I started getting lower back pain. Yes, we all know that homo sapiens is constructed incorrectly; our erect posture puts too much pressure on the base of the spine; more workdays are lost because of lower back pain than any other cause. Being a writer, I sit all day, compounding the problem. My back is the enemy of my writing life: if I don't do exercises daily, I immediately ache; and if I do, I am still not spared. I could say more, but there is nothing duller than lower back pain. So common, mundane an ailment brings no credit to the sufferer. One has to dramatize it somehow, as in the phrase "I threw my back out."

Here is a gossip column about my body: My eyebrows grow quite bushy across my forehead, and whenever I get my hair cut, the barber asks me diplomatically if I want them trimmed or not. (I generally say no, associating bushy eyebrows with Balzackian virility, *élan vital*; but sometimes I acquiesce, to soothe his fastidiousness). . . . My belly button is a modest, embedded slit, not a jaunty swirl like my father's. Still, I like to sniff the odor that comes from jabbing my finger in it: a very ripe, underground smell, impossible to describe, but let us say a combination of old gym socks and stuffed derma (the Yiddish word for this oniony dish of ground intestines is, fittingly, *kishkas*). . . . I have a scar on my tongue from childhood, which I can only surmise I received by landing it on a sharp object, somehow. Or perhaps I bit it hard. I have the habit of sticking my tongue out like a dog when exerting myself physically, as though to urge my muscles on; and maybe I accidentally chomped into it at such a moment. . . . I gnash my teeth, sleeping or waking. Awake, the sensation makes me feel alert and in contact with the world when I start to drift off in a daydream. Another way of grounding myself is to pinch my cheek—drawing a pocket of flesh downward and squeezing it—as I once saw JFK do in a filmed motorcade. I do this cheek-pinching especially when I am trying to keep mentally focused during teaching or other public situations. I also scratch the nape of my neck under public stress, so much so that I raise welts or sores which then eventually grow scabs; and I take great delight in secretly picking the scabs off. . . . My nose itches whenever I think about it, and I scratch it often, especially lying in bed trying to fall asleep (maybe because I am conscious of my breathing then). I also pick my nose with formidable thoroughness when no one, I hope, is looking. . . . There is a white scar about the size of a quarter on the juicy part of my knee; I got it as a boy running into a car fender, and I can still remember staring with detached calm at the blood that gushed from it like a pretty, half-eaten peach. Otherwise, the sight of my own blood makes me awfully nervous. I used to faint dead away when a blood sample was taken, and now I can control the impulse to do so only by biting the insides of my cheeks while steadfastly looking away from the needle's action. . . . I like to clean out my ear wax as often as possible (the smell is curiously sulfurous; I associate it with the bodies of dead insects). I refuse to listen to warnings that it is dangerous to stick cleaning objects into your ears. I love Q-Tips immoderately; I buy them in huge quantities and store them the way a former refugee will stock canned foodstuffs. . . . My toes are long and apelike; I have very little fellow feeling for them; they are so far away, they may as well belong to someone else. . . . My flattish buttocks are not offensively large, but neither do they have the "dream" configuration one sees in jeans ads. Perhaps for this reason, it disturbed me puritanically when asses started to be treated by Madison Avenue, around the seventies, as crucial sexual equipment, and I began to receive compositions from teenage girl students declaring that they liked some boy because he had "a cute butt." It confused me; I had thought the action was elsewhere.

About my penis there is nothing, I think, unusual. It has a brown stem, and a pink mushroom head where the foreskin is pulled back. Like most heterosexual males, I have little comparative knowledge to go by, so that I always feel like an outsider when I am around women or gay men who talk zestfully about differences in penises. I am afraid that they might judge me harshly, ridicule me like the boys who stripped me of my bathing suit in summer camp when I was ten. But perhaps they would simply declare it an ordinary penis, which changes size with the stimulus or weather or time of day. Actually, my penis does have a peculiarity: it has two peeing holes. They are very close to each other, so that usually only one stream of urine issues, but sometimes a hair gets caught across them, or some such contretemps, and they squirt out in two directions at once.

This part of me, which is so synecdochically identified with the male body (as the term "male member" indicates), has given me both too little, and too much, information about what it means to be a man. It has a personality like a cat's. I have prayed to it to behave better, to be less frisky, or more; I have followed its nose in matters of love, ignoring good sense, and paid the price; but I have also come to appreciate that it has its own specialized form of intelligence which must be listened to, or another price will be extracted.

Even to say the word "impotence" aloud makes me nervous. I used to tremble when I saw it in print, and its close relation, "importance," if hastily scanned, had the same effect, as if they were publishing a secret about me. But why should it be my secret, when my penis has regularly given me erections lo these many years—except for about a dozen times, mostly when I was younger? Because, even if it has not been that big a problem for me, it has dominated my thinking as an adult male. I've no sooner to go to bed with a woman than I'm in suspense. The power of the flaccid penis's statement, "I don't want you," is so stark, so cruelly direct, that it continues to exert a fascination out of all proportion to its actual incidence. Those few times when I was unable to function were like a wall forcing me to take another path—just as, after I tried to kill myself at seventeen, I was obliged to give up pessimism for a time. Each had instructed me by its too painful manner that I could not handle the world as I had previously construed it, that my confusion and rage were being found out. I would have to get more wily or else grow up.

Yet for the very reason that I was compelled to leave them behind, these two options of my youth, impotence and suicide, continue to command an underground loyalty, as though they were more "honest" than the devious strategies of potency and survival which I adopted. Put it this way: sometimes we encounter a person who has had a nervous breakdown years before and who seems cemented over sloppily, his vulnerability ruthlessly guarded against as dangerous; we sense he left a crucial part of himself back in the chaos of breakdown, and has since grown rigidly jovial. So suicide and impotence became for me "the roads not taken," the paths I had repressed.

Whenever I hear an anecdote about impotence—a woman who successfully coaxed an ex-priest who had been celibate and unable to make love, first by lying next to him for six months without any touching, then by cuddling for six more months, then by easing him slowly into a sexual embrace—I think they are talking about me. I identify completely: this, in spite of the fact, which I promise not to repeat again, that I have generally been able to do it whenever called upon. Believe it or not, I am not boasting when I say that: a part of me is contemptuous of this virility, as though it were merely a mechanical trick that violated my true nature, that of an impotent man absolutely frightened of women, absolutely secluded, cut off.

I now see the way I have idealized impotence: I've connected it with pushing the world away, as a kind of integrity, as in Molière's *The Misanthrope*—connected it with that part of me which, gregarious socializer that I am, continues to insist that I am a recluse, too good for this life. Of course, it is not true that I am terrified of women. I exaggerate my terror of them for dramatic effect, or for the purposes of a good scare.

My final word about impotence: Once, in a period when I was going out with many women, as though purposely trying to ignore my hypersensitive side and force it to grow callous by thrusting myself into foreign situations (not only sexual) and seeing if I was able to "rise to the occasion," I dated a woman who was attractive, tall and blond, named Susan. She had something to do with the pop music business, was a follower of the visionary religious futurist Teilhard de Chardin, and considered herself a religious pacifist. In fact, she told me her telephone number in the form of the anagram, N-O-T-O-W-A-R. I thought she was joking and laughed aloud, but she gave me a solemn look. In passing, I should say that all the women with whom I was impotent or close to it had solemn natures. The sex act has always seemed to me in many ways ridiculous, and I am most comfortable when a woman who enters the sheets with me shares that sense of the comic pomposity behind such a grandiloquently rhetorical use of the flesh. It is as though the prose of the body were being drastically squeezed into metrical verse. I would not have known how to stop guffawing had I been D. H. Lawrence's lover, and I am sure he would have been pretty annoyed at me. But a smile saying "All this will pass" has an erotic effect on me like nothing else.

They claim that men who have long, long fingers also have lengthy penises. I can tell you with a surety that my fingers are long and sensitive, the most perfect, elegant, handsome part of my anatomy. They are not entirely perfect—the last knuckle of my right middle finger is twisted permanently, broken in a softball game when I was trying to block the plate—but even this slight disfigurement, harbinger of mortality, adds to the pleasure I take in my hands' rugged beauty. My penis does not excite in me nearly the same contemplative delight when I look at it as do my fingers. Pianists' hands, I have been told often; and though I do not play the piano, I derive an aesthetic satisfaction from them that is as pure and Apollonian as any I am capable of. I can stare at my fingers for hours. No wonder I have them so often in my mouth, biting my fingernails to bring them closer. When I write, I almost feel that they, and not my intellect, are the clever progenitors of the text. Whatever narcissism, fetishism, and proud sense of masculinity I possess about my body must begin and end with my fingers.

—1993

Learning from Other Writers

1. Nothing could be more narcissistic than writing about one's own body (down to the odor of one's navel). Is there any larger thematic significance to this essay?
2. Does Lopate's portrait of his body cause you to think about your own body? If you had to write an essay about one of your own body parts, which would you choose and why? Could you structure that essay around the smaller divisions of that body part (i.e., each feature on your face or each finger on your hand)?
3. If you had to reconstruct Lopate's autobiography in chronological order, what would be the major events in his life? If you had to list his virtues (or flaws), what might be the items on that list?
4. What is the function of the final paragraph of the essay? The final sentence?

BRENT STAPLES

THE CORONER'S PHOTOGRAPHS

My brother's body lies dead and naked on a stainless steel slab. At his head stands a tall arched spigot that, with tap handles mimicking wings, easily suggests a swan in mourning. His head is squarish and overlarge. (This, when he was a toddler, made him seem top-heavy and unsteady on his feet.) His widow's peak is common among the men in my family, though this one is more dramatic than most. An inverted pyramid, it begins high above the temples and falls steeply to an apex in the boxy forehead, over the heart-shaped face. A triangle into a box over a heart. His eyes (closed here) were big and dark and glittery; they drew you into his sadness when he cried. The lips are ajar as always, but the picture is taken from such an angle that it misses a crucial detail: the left front tooth tucked partly beyond the right one. I need this detail to see my brother full. I paint it in from memory.

A horrendous wound runs the length of the abdomen, from the sternum all the way to the pubic mound. The wound resembles a mouth whose lips are pouting and bloody. Massive staplelike clamps are gouged into these lips at regular intervals along the abdomen. This is a surgeon's incision. The surgeon was presented with a patient shot six times with a large-caliber handgun. Sensing the carnage that lay within, he achieved the largest possible opening and worked frantically trying to save my brother's life. He tied off shattered vessels, resectioned the small intestine, repaired a bullet track on the liver, then backed out. The closing would have required two pairs of hands. An assistant would have gripped the two sides of the wound and drawn them together while a second person cut in the clamps. The pulling together has made my brother's skin into a corset that crushes in on the abdomen from all sides. The pelvic bones jut up through the skin. The back is abnormally arched from the tension. The wound strains at the clamps, threatening to rip itself open. The surgeon worked all night and emerged from surgery gaunt, his greens darkened with sweat. "I tied off everything I could," he said, and then he wept at the savagery and the waste.

This is the body of Blake Melvin Staples, the seventh of my family's nine children, the third of my four brothers, born ten years after me. I know his contours well. I bathed and diapered him when he was a baby and studied his features as he grew. He is the smallest of the brothers, but is built in the same manner: short torso but long arms and legs; a more than ample behind set high on the back; knocking knees; big feet that tend to flat. The second toe is also a signature. It curls softly in an extended arc and rises above the others in a way that's unique to us. His feelings are mine as well. Cold: The sensation moves from my eyes to my shoulder blades to my bare ass as I feel him naked on the steel. I envision the reflex that would run through his body, hear the sharp breath he would draw when steel met his skin. Below the familiar feet a drain awaits the blood that will flow from this autopsy.

The medical examiner took this picture and several on February 13, 1984, at 9:45 B/N. The camera's flash is visible everywhere: on the pale-green tiles of the surrounding walls, on the gleaming neck of the spigot, on the stainless steel of the slab, on the bloody lips of the wound.

The coroner's report begins with a terse narrative summary: "The deceased, twenty-two-year-old Negro male, was allegedly shot by another person on the premises of a night club as a result of a 'long standing quarrel.' He sustained multiple gunshot wounds of the abdomen and legs and expired during surgery."

Blake was a drug dealer; he was known for carrying guns and for using them. His killer, Mark McGeorge, was a former customer and cocaine addict. At the trial Mark's lawyer described the shooting as a gunfight in which Blake was beaten to the draw. This was doubtful. Blake was shot six times: three times in the back. No weapon was found on or near his body. Blake's gunbearer testified that my brother was unarmed when Mark ambushed and gunned him down. But a gunbearer is not a plausible witness. A drug dealer known for shooting a rival in plain public view gets no sympathy from a jury. The jury turned back the prosecution's request for a conviction of murder in the first degree. Mark was found guilty of second-degree murder and sentenced to seven years in jail. Five years for the murder. Two years for using the gun.

Blake is said to have cried out for his life as he lay on the ground. "Please don't shoot me no more. I don't want to die." "*Please don't shoot me no more. I don't want to die.*" His voice had a touch of that dullness one hears from the deaf, a result of ear infections he suffered as a child. The ear openings had narrowed to the size of pinholes. He tilted his head woefully from side to side trying to pour out the pain. His vowels were locked high in his throat, behind his nose. This voice kept him a baby to me. This is the voice in which he would have pleaded for his life.

The coroner dissects the body, organ by organ:

HEART:	300 grams. No valve or chamber lesions. Coronary arteries show no pathologic changes.
LUNGS:	900 grams combined. Moderate congestion. Tracheobronchial and arterial systems are not remarkable.
LIVER:	1950 grams. There is a sutured bullet track at the interlobar sulcus and anterior portion of the right hepatic lobe. There has been moderate subcapsular and intraparenchymal hemorrhage.
SPLEEN:	150 grams. No pathologic changes.
KIDNEYS:	300 grams combined. No pathologic changes.
ADRENALS:	No pathologic changes

PANCREAS:	No pathologic changes
GI TRACT:	The stomach is empty. Portions of the small bowel have been resected, along with portions of the omentum. The bowel surface is dusky reddish-brown, but does not appear gangrenous.
URINARY BLADDER:	Empty.
NECK ORGANS:	Intact. No airway obstructions.
BRAIN:	1490 grams. Sagittal and serial coronal sections show no discrete lesions or evidence of injury
SKULL:	Intact.
VERTEBRAE:	Intact.
RIBS	Intact.
PELVIS:	There is a chip fracture of the left public ramus, and there is also fracturing of the right pubic ramus. There is extensive fracturing of the left femur, and there is a through-and-through bullet wound of the right femur just below the hip joint.

The coroner describes the wounds in detail. The surgical incision and its grisly clamps are dismissed in a single sentence. The six bullet holes receive one full paragraph each. The coroner records the angle that each bullet traveled through the body, the organs it passed through along the way, and where it finally came to rest. With all this to occupy him, the coroner fails to note the scar on Blake's left hand. The scar lies in the webbing between the thumb and index finger and is the result of a gun accident. A shotgun recoiled when Blake fired it and drove the hammer deep into the web, opening a wound that took several stitches to close.

I saw the wound when it was fresh, six weeks before Blake was murdered. I was visiting Roanoke from Chicago, where I then lived. I sought Blake out to tell him that it was time to get out of the business and leave Roanoke. The signs of death were everywhere; his name was hot in the street. Blake and I were making small talk when we slapped each other five. Blake clutched his hand at the wrist and cried out in pain. Then he showed me the stitches. This ended the small talk. I told him that he was in danger of being killed if he didn't leave town.

Staples men have been monolinguists for generations. We love our own voices too much. Blake responded to my alarm by telling me stories. He told me about the awesome power of the shotgun that had injured him. He told me about making asses of the police when they raided his apartment looking for drugs. The door of his apartment was steel, he said; they'd sent for a tow truck to pull it from its frame. Inside they found him twiddling his thumbs in the bathroom. He'd flushed the cocaine down the toilet. The night he told me these stories was the last time I saw him alive.

Six weeks later my brother Bruce called me with the news. "Brent, Blake is dead," he said. "Some guy pulled up in a car and emptied out on him with a magnum. Blake is dead." I told myself to feel nothing. I had already mourned Blake and buried him and was determined not to suffer his death a second time. I skipped the funeral and avoided Roanoke for the next three years. The next time I visited my family I went to see the Roanoke Commonwealth Attorney and questioned him about the case. He was polite and impatient. For him, everything about the killing had been said. This, after all, had been an ordinary death.

I asked to see the files. A secretary brought a manila pouch and handed it to the Commonwealth Attorney, who handed it to me and excused himself from the room. The pouch contained a summary of the trial, the medical examiner's report, and a separate inner pouch wrapped in twine and shaped like photographs. I opened the pouch; there was Blake dead and on the slab, photographed from several angles. The floor gave way, and I fell down and down for miles.

—1994

Learning from Other Writers

1. Given what Staples tells us about his brother, why do you think he chose to structure his essay according to the coroner's report? What thematic role does the report and its contents play in this essay?
2. What question about his brother's life and death is Staples asking us to consider?
3. How would you describe the author's tone for most of the essay? His attitude toward his subject? Does his tone or attitude change at the end?
4. How would you describe the intended audience for this essay?
5. Imagine if Staples had decided to tell us the story of his brother's life in chronological order, followed by an account of his murderer's trial and the author's visit to the Roanoke Commonwealth Attorney. How might that essay differ in tone or theme from the essay Staples actually wrote?

MARSHALL JON FISHER

MEMORIA EX MACHINA

It was a silver Seiko watch with a clasp that folded like a map and snapped shut. The stainless-steel casing was a three-dimensional octagon with distinct edges, too thick and ponderous, it seems now, for a thirteen-year-old. Four hands—hour, minute, second, and alarm—swept around a numberless metallic-blue face. I received it for my bar mitzvah; a quarter century later I can, in my mind, fingernail the button just one click to set the alarm hand—not too far, or I'll change the time—and pull out the other, obliquely positioned button to turn on the alarm. When the hour hand finally overcame the angle between itself and the alarm hand, a soft, deep mechanical buzzing would ensue—a pleasant hum long since obliterated by hordes of digital beeps. I haven't seen my watch for twenty years, but I can still hear that buzz, feel its vibrations in my wrist.

What I cannot remember is the timbre or inflection of my sister's voice from that time. She flitted in and out of view, appearing in the gaps between high school, club meetings, and dates. I can't even recall her at the dinner table with my parents, my brother, and me, though she must have been there most of the time.

After she and my brother left for college, when I was in high school, I spent countless hours lying in bed listening to my clock radio. I can still see the burnt-amber numerals and the way their discrete line segments would metamorphose each minute. The tuning knob on the right-hand side, and the way it resisted torque as you approached either end of the dial, remain as clear to me as the remote controls of my new DVD player. I was listening in the dark to a Monday-night Miami Dolphins game (home, against the New England Patriots) when the radio broadcast broke to the announcement that John Lennon had been shot. I heard Bruce Springsteen singing "Racing in the Street" for the first time on that radio, along with other songs I'd rather forget, like Queen's "We Are the Champions," dedicated one night by a local disc jockey to some high school basketball team. I remember the golden light from within illuminating the frequency band, and I remember tuning by sound for years after that light burned out.

Yet I can't remember what time I went to bed as an adolescent, or anything else about my nocturnal ritual. Did I say goodnight and then go off to my room, or did my parents come in to say goodnight after I was in bed? I don't know. But I do know, decades after it found oblivion, exactly how to set that radio to play for half an hour and then shut off.

The memory of my quotidian habits of those years has been washed away by a thousand new habits, just as my sister's teenage presence has given way to her succeeding selves. In his novel *Vertigo*, W. G. Sebald paraphrases Stendahl's advice "not to purchase engravings of fine views and prospects seen on one's travels, since before very long they will displace our memories completely, indeed one might say they destroy them." "For instance," Sebald continues, "[Stendahl] could no longer recall the wonderful *Sistine Madonna* he had seen in Dresden, try as he might, because Müller's engraving after it had become superimposed in his mind." In the same way, as the people in our lives grow older, their new faces, voices, and demeanors replace those of their former selves in our memory. Yet the new technology that continually replaces old machines fails to have the same effect, because the individuals—the radios, wristwatches, and automobiles that inhabited our lives—never change. That chrome "sleep knob" on my clock radio still looks exactly the same, wherever it may now rest in the center of some unknowable mountainous landfill.

"The past," wrote Proust, "is hidden somewhere outside the realm, beyond the reach, of intellect, in some material object (in the sensation which that material object will give us) which we do not suspect." And just as the taste of the famous *petite madeleine* awakens in Proust's narrator an entire vanished world—the memories of his childhood vacations in Combray—the thought of my old Walkman resurrects my postcollegiate existence. It was a red and black 1985 model, and I've never seen another just like it. The tendency of Sony to constantly bring out new designs lent an air of individuality to one's Walkman, but it also caused successful designs to get lost in the shuffle. Mine was a particularly pleasing construction—sleek, rounded, with an analog radio dial and push buttons that made you feel that you were *doing* something. Unlike many other models, it also worked properly for years, providing the soundtrack to a decade of my life. I can summon the physical memory of squeezing the Play button, the middle of three oblong pieces of silver metal, and suddenly I am back in Munich in 1986, listening to the new Bob Dylan album on a brown threadbare corduroy sofa in my Goethestrasse apartment. Or I'm driving eight hours down I-95 to visit a girlfriend, listening to tapes on the Walkman because my Rabbit's stereo has been stolen. Or I'm riding the Amtrak between New York and Boston, listening to Indigo Girls while the autumn leaves blow by the window. I can even tell you the album and track that unwound on the tape, visible through the tape player's window, in that specific recollection. I have no idea why that moment should survive in my mind, but the red and black Walkman is as much a part of that moment as the music itself, and the leaves, and the dark, sheltering train.

Another machine still lingering in the afterlife: the 1973 Datsun 1200 my dad handed down to me to run into the ground, which I eventually did. A bottom-of-the-line economy model, "the Green Machine," as my friends called it, looked like a vehicle out of Dr. Seuss, but it always started and got forty miles to the gallon—a cause for nostalgia, indeed, in these simmering, gas-guzzling days. I can still see the schematic four-gear diagram on the head of the stick shift and feel the knob—and the worn transmission of the gears—in my right hand. The radio had five black cuboid push buttons for preset stations: the two on the left each sported BN in white indentations, and the other three said GN. It took almost the entire ten-minute ride to school for the anemic defogger to rid the windshield of its early-morning dew. One day that teary outward view was replaced, at forty miles an hour, by green. A rusted latch had finally given out, and the wind had opened the hood and slapped it all the way back against the glass. Luckily, the glass didn't break, and I could see enough through the rust holes to avoid a collision as I braked. Whenever the friend I drove to school was not ready to go, her father would come out and wait with me, looking the Green Machine up and down and shaking his head.

What does it mean that some of my fondest memories are of technology? Have we begun our slide toward the ineluctable merging of man and machine? Are Walkman headphones in the ears the first step toward a computer chip implanted in the brain? Or is it merely that inanimate objects, whether Citizen Kane's wooden "Rosebud" or my handheld electronic circuitry, by virtue of their obliviousness to the passage of time, seize our longing? As photographs do, these objects capture particular periods of our lives. The sense memory of turning that clock-radio knob, or shifting that gear stick, fixes the moment in time as well as any photograph. Just as we painstakingly fit photos into albums or, in the new age, organize them into computer folders and make digital copies for safekeeping, so I hang on to the impression of a stainless-steel wristwatch that once applied a familiar force of weight to my left wrist.

(Where have they gone, these mechanisms of my youth? The Datsun was hauled off for parts. The clock radio and the Walkman no doubt were tossed without a second thought when they no longer functioned properly. But the Seiko? Who would throw out a fine watch that, to my recollection, never broke? My mother swears she wouldn't have. Spring cleaning is not exactly my father's pastime. Could a watch, along with its deep blue case with the silvery embossed square border, vanish into time itself?)

Of course, my memory of these objects may be inaccurate. Were I to come upon my old clock radio, wrapped in old T-shirts inside a threadbare leather overnight bag in the attic, the sensation might be like that felt on entering a high school reunion and being jolted by the discrepancy between the memory of old friends and their current reality. In this case the object has not aged, but the memory has. In his wonderful book-length essay *U and I*, Nicholson Baker practices what he calls "memory criticism": he records his impressions of John Updike's works without allowing himself to reread them. When he does go back to the texts to check, Baker finds that his memories of many passages, so emblazoned upon his mind, are imperfect. He fashions an argument around a remembered line from a poem, discovers that the actual poem does not support the argument, and finishes off the argument anyway. A story remembered fondly for its metaphor likening a character's sick stomach to "an unprepossessing tuber" turns out not to contain the treasured trope. Baker remembers Updike making a brilliant comparison between "a strange interruption in his act of signature, between the *p* and the *d*," and his verbal stuttering—a comparison that had never in fact been made.

Even Nabokov, that grand master of recollection, with a self-ascribed "almost pathological keenness of the retrospective faculty," is fallible. In the first version of his autobiography, *Speak, Memory*, he describes his family coat of arms as depicting two bears holding up a chessboard. Later, the chess-loving author is chagrined to discover that the bears are lions, and that they support a knight's shield comprising "only one sixteenth of a checkerboard."

So perhaps the clock radio is better off in oblivion. Unearthed, it might strike me as simply a cheap J. C. Penney's item from the 1970s—hardly a golden age for design. Now, for better or worse, holding the object in my hands might remind me of the bored loneliness of the years I spent steering its tuning knob, just as Baker feared being "disappointed by the immediate context of a phrase [of Updike's he] loved, when the context was now hazy and irrelevant."

Once, these humanly flawed recollections were the only means we had of reconstructing the past. And even though our selective memory may have been salubrious, we yearned to possess the past more completely. Now we have created the technology to satisfy our longing. Only machines—tape recorders, cameras, video cameras—can accurately preserve the details of our former selves, of our loved ones' younger faces, of our long-gone possessions. Nostalgia, even for machines, is bolstered by machines of nostalgia.

I am typing this on a Macintosh G4 Powerbook. Will the thought of this laptop someday conjure up such piquant memories? As much as the recollection of my first computer, a 1985 Kaypro I received for college graduation? It was the first "portable" computer—a thirty-pound metal box the size of a small suitcase, with a keyboard that detached from one end. I can still feel the power switch on the right side of the back, where I reached to flick it on thousands of times. The green glow of the characters on screen, the five-and-a-half-inch floppy disks that had to be inserted in order to boot up or run Wordstar, even the control-K commands that brought up various menus—they all seem like the markings of a bygone era, even as they retain an intimate immediacy.

Yet computers, while they have probably replaced the automobile and the television as the most dominating technological feature of our daily lives, seem to have reached a uniformity—as well as a dismayingly short lifespan—that may weaken their nostalgic potential. This laptop isn't very different from past laptops, and I've gone through a succession of desktop computers with almost identical exteriors. I feel little nostalgia for my PCs of the early 1990s. It's hard to get choked up about the fact that a particular box packed only twenty megabytes.

Perhaps, though, this very act of typing is what will linger one day in my mind's reliquary. Voice-recognition software is pounding at the gates; videomail seems every day more feasible. How much longer will our computers even have keyboards? Typing may someday survive only as another sense memory. A writer, while composing with his voice, will still tap his fingers on the desk like an amputee scratching a wooden leg. Rather than the ghost of a particular machine, it will be this metacarpal tapdance, an apparition of the way we used to express language, that will haunt him.

—2002

Learning from Other Writers

1. List the objects whose descriptions comprise the basic structure of this essay.
2. At the start of paragraph six, Fisher quotes Proust to the effect that "The past is hidden somewhere outside the realm, beyond the reach, of intellect, in some material object (in the sensation which that material object will give us) which we do not suspect." Is this the theme of "*Memoria ex Machina*"? If so, does that diminish the originality of Fisher's essay?

3. Look at the set of questions that introduce the next section of the essay (paragraph eight). Do you think Fisher's central theme is the quote from Proust, or one or more of these questions? Are the quote and the questions related?
4. What is the effect of Fisher's decision to conclude his list with a discussion of various computers he has owned? What secondary structure has he used to order the objects he discusses in his essay?

JOAN DIDION

AT THE DAM

Since the afternoon in 1967 when I first saw Hoover Dam, its image has never been entirely absent from my inner eye. I will be talking to someone in Los Angeles, say, or New York, and suddenly the dam will materialize, its pristine concave face gleaming white against the harsh rusts and taupes and mauves of that rock canyon hundreds or thousands of miles from where I am. I will be driving down Sunset Boulevard, or about to enter a freeway, and abruptly those power transmission towers will appear before me, canted vertiginously over the tailrace. Sometimes I am confronted by the intakes and sometimes by the shadow of the heavy cable that spans the canyon and sometimes by the ominous outlets to unused spillways, black in the lunar clarity of the desert light. Quite often I hear the turbines. Frequently I wonder what is happening at the dam this instant, at this precise intersection of time and space, how much water is being released to fill downstream orders and what lights are flashing and which generators are in full use and which just spinning free.

I used to wonder what it was about the dam that made me think of it at times and in places where I once thought of the Mindanao Trench, or of the stars wheeling in their courses, or of the words *As it was in the beginning, is now and ever shall be, world without end, amen.* Dams, after all, are commonplace: we have all seen one. This particular dam had existed as an idea in the world's mind for almost forty years before I saw it. Hoover Dam, showpiece of the Boulder Canyon project, the several million tons of concrete that made the Southwest plausible, the *fait accompli* that was to convey, in the innocent time of its construction, the notion that mankind's brightest promise lay in American engineering.

Of course the dam derives some of its emotional effect from precisely that aspect, that sense of being a monument to a faith since misplaced. "They died to make the desert bloom," reads a plaque dedicated to the 96 men who died building this first of the great high dams, and in context the worn phrase touches, suggests all of that trust in harnessing resources, in the melliorative power of the dynamo, so central to the early Thirties. Boulder City, built in 1931 as the construction town for the dam, retains the ambience of a model city, a new town, a toy triangular grid of green lawns and trim bungalows, all fanning out from the Reclamation building. The bronze sculptures at the dam itself evoke muscular citizens of a tomorrow that never came, sheaves of wheat clutched heavenward, thunderbolts defied. Winged Victories guard the flagpole. The flag whips in the canyon wind. An empty Pepsi-Cola can clatters across the terrazzo. The place is perfectly frozen in time.

But history does not explain it all, does not entirely suggest what makes that dam so affecting. Nor, even, does energy, the massive involvement with power and pressure and the transparent sexual overtones to that involvement. Once when I revisited the dam I walked through it with a man from the Bureau of Reclamation. For a while we trailed behind a guided tour, and then we went on, went into parts of the dam where visitors do not generally go. Once in a while he would explain something, usually in that recondite language having to do with "peaking power," with "outages" and "dewatering," but on the whole we spent the afternoon in a world so alien, so complete and so beautiful unto itself that it was scarcely necessary to speak at all. We saw almost no one. Cranes moved above us as if under their own volition. Generators roared. Transformers hummed. The gratings on which we stood vibrated. We watched a hundred-ton steel shaft plunging down to that place where the water was. And finally we got down to that place where the water was, where the water sucked out of Lake Mead roared through thirty-foot penstocks and then into thirteen-foot penstocks and finally into the turbines themselves. "Touch it," the Reclamation said, and I did, and for a long time I just stood there with my hands on the turbine. It was a peculiar moment, but so explicit as to suggest nothing beyond itself.

There was something beyond all that, something beyond energy, beyond history, something I could not fix in my mind. When I came up from the dam that day the wind was blowing harder, through the canyon and all across the Mojave. Later, toward Henderson and Las Vegas, there would be dust blowing, blowing past the Country-Western Casino FRI & SAT NITES and blowing past the Shrine of Our Lady of Safe Journey STOP & PRAY, but out at the dam there was no dust, only the rock and the dam and a little greasewood and a few garbage cans, their tops chained, banging against a fence. I walked across the marble star map that traces a sidereal revolution of the equinox and fixes forever, the Reclamation man had told me, for all time and for all people who can read the stars, the date the dam was dedicated. The star map was, he had said, for when we were all gone and the dam was left. I had not thought much of it when he said it, but I thought of it then, with the wind whining and the sun dropping behind a mesa with the finality of a sunset in space. Of course that was the image I had seen always, seen it without quite realizing what I saw, a dynamo finally free of man, splendid at last in its absolute isolation, transmitting power and releasing water to a world where no one is.

—1970

Learning from Other Writers

1. What is Didion's central question about the Hoover Dam? Why does she expect her readers to care about her question?
2. What is the source of the quote in paragraph two ("As it was in the beginning, is now and ever shall be, world without end, amen")? What is the function of this quote in the essay as a whole?
3. How does each part of the Hoover Dam contribute to the author's meditation on her central thematic question?
4. In the first part of the essay, Didion presents an image of the Hoover Dam as reflected in her mind's eye. In the second part, she takes us on a tour of the actual dam. What is her strategy in the final paragraph? What is the effect of this strategy on your understanding of the essay's central thematic question?
5. Locate a copy of the poem "Ozymandias" by Percy Bysshe Shelley. Discuss the ways in which Didion's essay alludes to or borrows from Shelley's poem in terms of style, tone, theme, and/or structure. Should Didion have made her allusions and borrowings more explicit?

THE LAST

Living by one-handed food

Since the Neolithic era, when the first soups were prepared and eaten communally in shells or emptied animal stomachs, soup has served as the archetypal food to be eaten in fellowship with others. Yet the venerable place of soup—and of food more generally—as a focal point for human culture has slowly been eroded by our drive toward increasingly convenient eating. In the nineteenth century, soup was reduced to a desiccated cube, then compressed to a gelatinous clot. By 1961, when Andy Warhol began painting Campbell's soup cans, the product had come condensed and canned for six decades. The next frontier is this microwaveable, drinkable, fully-portable Soup at Hand, along with an array of other ultra-convenience foods that require no silverware and only one appendage to eat. Whereas eating once united us, "one-handed food" sanctions a solipsistic withdrawal to places where we feed alone.

Here Campbell has tweaked its nearly seventy-five-year-old slogan "M'm! M'm! Good" to read "M'm! M'm! Good! to Go"—clambering, as CEO Douglas Conant puts it, "to make the 'C' in Campbell synonymous with convenience." Americans are now willing to pay two to three times as much for revved-up versions of previously table-bound products, from cereal bars with baked-in milk to individually wrapped, American cheese-like slices of conjoined peanut butter and jelly, which are simply peeled off and slapped on bread. A one-serving Soup at Hand retails for $1.69; a two-and-a-half-serving can of the condensed stuff costs $0.89. It's part of a multibillion-dollar industry in which intensely processed, single-portion foods yielding higher profit margins are marketed not to families but to individuals, who are empowered to gulp them down wherever and whenever possible.

With its seventy-millimeter diameter, Soup at Hand fits snugly in most car cup holders. The emergence of so-called cup-holder cuisine has opened up countless miles of new eating occasions for otherwise time-strapped consumers. Research by Culinary Institute of America food historian John Nihoff shows that 19 percent of meals in this country are currently guzzled in cars, a trend reflected both in the variety of foods being shaped into cup holder-friendly packages and in the demand for vehicles that accommodate such expedited eating. A recent study found that a new car buyer is less likely to care about a vehicle's gas mileage than about the versatility of its cup holders, which in only two decades have added twenty millimeters in diameter. Luxury car brands like Saab offer refrigerated glove compartments; a backseat microwave, according to Aaron Brody, a food-packaging executive and columnist, is "not only feasible, it's inevitable."

SUPPER

alone, by Jon Mooallem.

Notice how, in this Matisse-like illustration, the figure drinks soup from an open, steaming cup, not through Soup at Hand's friction-fit sip-top. Curiously, the drawing reflects our more traditional understanding of soup—as a warm expression of kindness, a curative to be savored—rather than soup as redefined here; that is, as an aseptic, multilaminate snack canister to be chugged in the left lane of the expressway. Food companies, by colonizing cars, cubicles, and gym bags, have been kind enough to free us not merely from tables and utensils but also from one another. And with no one else around to see, we are much more willing to put the objectionably un-foodlike in our mouths. Thus, one-handed food de-emphasizes food altogether, as the nuisance of eating is dispatched via increasingly pill-like "meal solutions." "Your whole life is fast, portable, wireless," reads one Soup at Hand tag line. "Shouldn't your soup be, too?"

Making eating this effortless requires exhaustive engineering. This slight undulation in Soup at Hand's container produces an ergonomically grip-able cylinder and increases surface area, allowing more of the loving microwave radiation to penetrate and heat the soup. Like StarKist's un-refrigerated, ready-to-eat-anywhere pouch of tuna, the container's five separate layers of resins, each with a distinct function, reflect a decades-long evolution of sterilization technology and packaging. Last year food scientists in North Carolina made macaroni and cheese fully handheld by congealing it in an edible coating; other flavorless sealants now prevent pre-cut apple slices from browning or losing their crunch for twenty-one days. Parents once had to specially prepare a child's favorite food, serving it just so or wrapping it for a lunch so as not to get soggy. Today lab technicians can implant that tender handiwork directly into our food.

In this flavor, "Pizza," Campbell essentially has created a portable soup and a portable pizza in one. Soup at Hand "Mexican Fiesta"—that is, taco soup—operates by a similar logic. Pizza and tacos are already one-handed foods in their own right, albeit in a prediluvian, naive way; translating them into soups both challenges our conception of soup and blurs the familiar characteristics of these foods. (In fact, the pizza and taco flavors each include pasta.) The Italian Futurists, enamored with swiftness and motion, believed food would one day be broadcast directly into our bodies via radio waves. No longer does this fantastic idea seem such an improbability. As meals rapidly accelerate to serve our ever-quickening lives, a kind of centripetal force is acting upon our foods. All food is being sucked inward, collapsing into a muddled amalgam—a soup—as we are being sucked farther and farther apart.

—2005

INSPIRATIONS: OBJECTS OF MY AFFECTION

1. Choose an object that has at least three parts.
2. Use the parts of that object to structure a meditation on a question that interests you and seems somehow linked to your object.
3. Alternatively, think of a document (i.e., a school planner, a recipe file, a list of things to take to college, your birth certificate, the prenuptial agreement you've just signed with your fiancé, your family's mass-mailed holiday newsletter) and use its structure to guide you through an essay.

INSPIRATIONS: WELCOME TO MY HOMETOWN

1. Take your readers on an actual or remembered tour of your hometown or neighborhood while meditating on some aspect of your childhood or your town's or neighborhood's history, economy, or sociology.
2. Alternatively, take your readers on a tour of one building (or other well-defined site) in your hometown or neighborhood.

The Collage

Just as the profile of a single character extends naturally to the profile of a group, so, too, an essay structured around a single object leads gracefully to an essay structured around a collage or a group of objects. In creating a collage, the author relies on intuition to come up with a set of objects (or images or vignettes) that seem related to each other, then tries to figure out what thematic question unites them all. Finally, the writer uses his or her aesthetic sense to come up with a pleasing order for the fragments.

Now, you might wonder how you can acquire this type of intuition or "aesthetic sense," but you probably already have one; think of all the photographs you've arranged in albums, the clippings and mementoes you've pasted in your scrapbook, the mix tapes, CDs, and playlists you've created for your iPod or your dance parties, or the physical collages you used to cut and paste in your art class in elementary school. As is true with a photo album, scrapbook, mix tape, or third-grade art project, exercising your artistic intuition usually means alternating the items in your collection according to length and tone (i.e., you probably won't want to clump together five long, slow, serious songs, then follow them with ten short, wild, goofy numbers), allowing neighboring elements to communicate with each other visually, aurally, or thematically, and creating resonances or echoes between sections that are spaced farther apart.

Technically, a true collage is an essay whose segments are arranged according to a purely aesthetic or thematic scheme rather than a linear movement through time or space. But if you order the segments of your essay according to a faintly chronological or spatial scheme, with a good deal of artistic and thematic intuition thrown in, no one is going to criticize your piece because it doesn't fit neatly into Chapter 14 of this anthology. As is usual when you try to divide a genre into categories, the categories overlap, with the confusion exacerbated by the variety of terms that writers have applied to describe this form (in this case, the lyric, the mosaic, the montage, the segmented essay). If you present a series of vignettes in the order in which they presented themselves to you, doesn't the resulting essay also qualify as a personal narrative? "The Search for Marvin Gardens" (in Chapter 11) is structured according to a Monopoly game, but its jerky, fragmented style certainly gives it the feel of a segmented essay.

Still more confusing (confusion in this case being a good thing), consider what happens when you add photographs or drawings to your collage. If you arrange the images and text in a nonlinear order, you still have a collage. The same is true if you insert the text *into* the images and present your readers with a disjointed array of cartoon panels. Imagine a graphic artist arranging five panels in random order: one panel shows the artist as a young boy, standing in the outfield waiting hopelessly for a ball to be hit his way; another panel shows him at an even younger age, rolling a gutter ball at a bowling party; another shows him in his twenties, swinging a golf club and missing the ball; yet another shows him in junior high, grabbing a football as five enormous guys prepare to pile on top of him; while the fifth panel shows the artist in middle age, sitting at a computer blasting aliens to bits. The panels would qualify as a graphic collage, but if you were to rearrange them in chronological order, you would be back to a personal narrative, although now in graphic form (with Art Spiegelman's *Maus* and Marjane Satrapi's *Persepolis* representing the highest levels of this genre).

To help make sense of this potentially confusing form, I offer an essay that not only makes use of the collage for its structure, but also discusses the lyric or collage as a genre of artistic expression. The essay, Charles Simic's "The Little Venus of the Eskimos," comes from his wonderful collection *The Unemployed Fortune-Teller,* in which you can find such erudite, playful, and evocative prose pieces as "Food and Happiness," "Elegy in a Spider's Web," "No Cure for the Blues," "The Necessity of Poetry," "Luneville Diary (December 1, 1962—March 1, 1963)," and "The Minotaur Loves His Labyrinth," any one of which is likely to inspire you to attempt the form. Nowhere will you find a better discussion of the ways in which a writer's unconscious, in conjunction with random chance and the exercise of his or her intellectual will and artistic intuition, collaborate to create a poem or lyric essay.[1]

After "The Little Venus of the Eskimos," which I offer with no questions for discussion because its author leaves me nothing to add, you will find collages that are less about the form itself than the author's life. In "Three Pokes of a Thistle," Naomi Shihab Nye prods us to consider what it takes to be a good Arab girl, while Wayne Koestenbaum (in the opening fragments of *The Queen's Throat*) uses the segmented form to ponder why so many gay men love opera. Finally, Thomas Lynch, who is an undertaker and a poet as well as an essayist, looks at caskets and coffins from a multiplicity of perspectives and in so doing asks some sobering questions about our attitudes toward death and the trappings that surround it.

---

[1] See also "Collage, Montage, Mosaic, Vignette, Episode, Segment" by Robert L. Root, Jr., in *The Fourth Genre: Contemporary Writers of/on Creative Nonfiction,* by Robert L. Root, Jr. and Michael Steinberg, Allyn and Bacon, 1999.

CHARLES SIMIC

THE LITTLE VENUS OF THE ESKIMOS

You just go on your nerve

—Frank O'Hara

In India, I remember reading as a child, there once lived people who were called Sciapodes. They had a single large foot on which they moved with great speed and which they also employed as an umbrella against the burning sun. The rest of their marvelous lives was up to the reader to imagine. The book was full of such creatures. I kept turning its pages, reading the brief descriptions and carefully examining the drawings. There was Cerberus, the dog with three heads, the Centaur, the Chinese Dragon, the Manticora, which has the face of a man, the body of a lion, and a tail like the sting of a scorpion, and many other wonders. They resembled, I realized years later, the creations of Cadavre Exquis, the surrealist game of chance. I was also reminded of Max Ernst's surrealist novels in collage where bird wings sprout from people's backs and rooster-headed men carry off naked women.

The history of these fabulous beings is dateless. They are found in the oldest mythologies and in all cultures. Their origins vary. Some are very probably symbolic representations of theological ideas by long forgotten sects and alchemist schools for whom the marriage of opposite elements was the guiding idea. Others, I'd like to believe, are the products of sheer fantasy, the liar's art, and our fascination with the grotesque image of the body. In both cases, they are the earliest instances of the collage aesthetic. Mythological zoos testify to our curiosity about the outcome of the sexual embrace of different species. They are the earliest examples of the collaboration of dream and intellect for the sake of putting appearances into doubt.

Were these visual oxymorons of ancient bestiaries first imagined and then drawn, or was it the other way around? Did one start drawing a head and the hand took off on its own, as it does in automatic writing? It's possible, although I don't have a lot of faith in automatic writing, with its aping of mediums and their trances. All my attempts at opening the floodgates of my psyche were unimpressive. "You need a certain state of vacancy for the marvelous to condescend to visit you," said Benjamin Peret. Very well and thanks for the advice, but I have my doubts. The reputation of the unconscious as the endless source of poetry is over-rated. The first rule for a poet must be, cheat on your unconscious and your dreams.

It was Octavio Paz, I believe, who told me the story about going to visit André Breton in Paris after the War. He was admitted and told to wait because the poet was engaged. Indeed, from the living room where he was seated, he could see Breton writing furiously in his study. After a while he came out, and they greeted each other and set out to have lunch in a nearby restaurant.

"What were you working on, maître?" Paz inquired as they were strolling to their destination.

"I was doing some automatic writing," Breton replied.

"But," Paz exclaimed in astonishment, "I saw you erase repeatedly!"

"It wasn't automatic enough," Breton assured the young poet.

I must admit to being shocked, too, when I heard the story. I thought I was the only one who did that. There have always been two opposite and contradictory approaches to chance operations. In the first, one devises systems to take words at random out of a dictionary or writes poems with scissors, old newspapers, and paste. The words found in either manner are not tampered with. The poem is truly the product of blind chance. All mechanical chance operations, from Dada's picking words out of a hat to the compositions of John Cage and the poems of Jackson Mac Low, work something like that. There is no cheating. These people are as honest and as scrupulous as the practitioners of photo realism. I mean, they are both suspicious of the imagination. They handle chance with a Buddhist's disinterestedness of mind and do not allow it to be contaminated by the impurities of desire.

My entire practice, on the other hand, consists of submitting to chance only to cheat on it. I agree with Vincent Huidobro who said long ago: "Chance is fine when you're dealt five aces or at least four queens. Otherwise, forget it." I, for example, may pull a book from my bookshelf and, opening it anywhere, take out a word or a phrase. Then, to find another bit of language to go along with my first find, I may grab another book or peek into one of my notebooks and get something like this:

he rips some papers
forest
whispers
telephone book
a child's heart
the mouse has a nest
concert piano
lost innocence
my mother's mourning dress

Once the words are on the page, however, I let them play off each other. In the house of correction called sense, where language and art serve their sentences, the words are making whoopee.

Innocence

Someone rips a telephone book in half.
The mouse has a nest in a concert piano.

In a forest of whispers,
A child's heart,
The mother's mourning dress.

This is more interesting. I'm beginning to feel that there are real possibilities here. To see what comes next, I'll call on chance for help again. My premise in this activity is that the poet finds poetry in what comes by accident. It's a complete revision of what we usually mean by creativity.

Twenty years ago, James Tate and I collaborated on some poems in the following manner: We'd take a word or a phrase and then we'd turn ourselves into a "pinball machine of associations," as Paul Auster would say. For example, the word "match" and the word "jail" would become "matchstick jail." At some point we'd stop and see what we had. We'd even do a bit of literary analysis. We'd revise, free associate again, and watch an unknown poem begin to take shape. At some moments we felt as if we were one person; at others, one of us was the inspired poet and the other the cold-blooded critic.

Russell Edson, who with James Tate and John Ashbery is one of our greatest believers in lucky finds, says, "This kind of creation needs to be done as rapidly as possible. Any hesitation causes it to lose its believability, its special reality." I have the same experience. One doesn't come up with phrases like Tate's "the wheelchair butterfly" or Bill Knott's "razorblade choir" by way of a leisurely Cartesian meditation. They are as much a surprise to the poet as they will be to the future reader.

I open myself to chance in order to invite the unknown. I'm not sure whether it's fate or chance that dogs me, but something does. I'm like a reader of tea leaves in that store on the corner. In Madame Esmeralda's metaphysics, there is a recognition scene, too. Clairvoyants believe that there are lucky days, moments when one's divinatory abilities are especially acute. Today, one says to oneself, I'm the waking dream, the source of the magical river! I see the hand that guides fate. The miraculous thing is that the tea leaves and the poem always end up by resembling me. Here is a near-portrait, the story of my life, and I've no idea how they got there.

If you worship in the Church of Art with a Message, stay away. Chance operations make trouble, promote ambiguity, spit on dogmatism of any kind. Everything from our ideas of identity to our ideas of cause and effect are cheerfully undermined. Surrealist games are the greatest blasphemy yet conceived by the arts against the arts. In them, the disordering of the senses is given ontological status. Chance brings a funhouse mirror to reality. They used to burn people at the stake for far less.

There has never been a poet who didn't believe in a stroke of luck. What is an occasional poem but a quick convergence of unforeseen bits of language? That's what Catullus and Frank O'Hara are all about. Only literary critics do not know that poems mostly write themselves. Metaphors and similes owe everything to chance. A poet cannot will a memorable comparison. These things just pop into somebody's head. In the past one thanked the gods or the Muse for it, but all along chance has been passing out freebies. Pierce claimed that only by granting the occurrence of chance events can one account for the diversity of the universe. The same is true of art and literature.

How does one recognize that blind accident has given one poetry? This is what puzzles me. What is it that guides the eye or the ear to accept what appears at first ugly or nonsensical? One says to oneself many times while writing, what I have here I do not understand at all, but I'm going to keep it no matter what.

Painter of doll faces
Here's a window where my soul
Used to peek out at night
At the quickly improvised gallows

If there's no such a thing as an aesthetic sense, how does one pick and choose among the various products of chance and decide some are worthless and some are not? Obviously, the history of modern art and literature has accustomed the eye and ear to the unexpected. We are happy, or so we believe, to reorient our vision, to accept any outrage. Is it still our old fascination with freak shows that drives us, or are formal aesthetic considerations just as important?

No doubt both. Successful chance operations stress the ambiguous origin and complex nature of any work of art or literature. The art object is always a collaboration of will and chance, but like our sense of humor, it eludes analysis. There has never been an adequate definition of why something is funny or why something is beautiful, and yet we often laugh and make poems and paintings that reassemble reality in new and unpredictably pleasing ways.

What shocks us more in the end, what we see or what we hear? Is the ear more avant-garde or the eye? Surrealist art has found more admirers than surrealist poetry, so it must be the eye. It's the new image that both painters and poets have dreamed of in this century, an image that would be ahead of our ideas and our desires, an image magnificent in its shock and its irreverence. Perhaps some new Temptation of Saint Anthony, in which the holy martyr praying in the desert would be surrounded by the rioting menagerie of exquisite corpses instead of traditional demons?

Surrealists intuited that the creation of the world is not yet finished. The Chaos spoken of in ancient creation myths has not said its last word. Chance continues to be one of the manifestations of cosmic mystery. The other one is mathematics. We are crucified in awe between freedom and necessity. The future is the forever unfolding game of Cadavre Exquis.

In the meantime, like the song says, "I've got my mojo working."

—1993

NAOMI SHIHAB NYE

THREE POKES OF A THISTLE

Hiding inside the Good Girl

"She has the devil inside her," said my first report card from first grade. I walked home slowly, holding it out from my body, a thistle, a thorn, to my mother, who read the inside, then the note on the back. She cried mightily, heaves of underground rivers, we stood looking deep into the earth as water rushed by.

I didn't know who he was.

One day I'd smashed John's nose on the pencil sharpener and broken it. Stood in the cloakroom smelling the rust of coats. I said No. No thank you. I already read that and it's not a very good story. Jane doesn't do much. I want the spider who talks. The family of little women and their thousand days. No. What I had for breakfast is a secret. I didn't want to tell them I ate dried apricots. I listened to their lineage of eggs. I listened to the bacon crackle in everyone else's pail. Thank you.

What shall we do, what shall we do? Please, I beg you. Our pajamas were flying from the line, waists pinned, their legs fat with fabulous air. My mother peeled beets, her fingers stained deep red. She was bleeding dinner for us. She was getting up and lying down.

Once I came home from school in the middle of the day in a taxi. School gave me a stomachache. I rode in the front passenger seat. It would be expensive. My mother stood at the screen door peering out, my baby brother perched on her hip. She wore an apron. The taxi pulled up in front of the blue mailbox I viewed as an animal across from our house—his opening mouth. Right before I climbed out, another car hit the taxi hard from behind so my mother saw me fly from the front seat to the back. Her mouth wide open, the baby dangling from her like fringe. She came toward us running. I climbed up onto the ledge inside the back window to examine the wreckage. The taxi driver's visored cap had blown out the window. He was shaking his head side to side as if he had water in his ears.

You, you, look what a stomachache gets you. Whiplash.

The doctor felt my neck.

Later I sat on the front steps staring at the spot where it had happened. What about that other driver? He cried when the policeman arrived. He was an old man coming to mail a letter. I was incidental to the scene, but it couldn't have happened without me. *If you had just stayed where you belonged....* My classmates sealed into their desks laboring over pages of subtraction, while out in the world, cars were banging together. Yellow roses opened slowly on a bush beside my step. I was thinking how everything looked from far away.

Then I was old. A hundred years before I found it, Mark Twain inscribed the front of his first-edition leatherbound book, "BE GOOD—AND YOU WILL BE LONESOME." In black ink, with a flourish. He signed his name. My friend had the book in a box in her attic and did not know. It was from her mother's collection. I carried it down the stairs, trembling. My friend said, "Do you think it is valuable?"

Language Barrier

Basically our father spoke English perfectly, though he still got his bs and ps mixed up. He had a gentle, deliberate way of choosing words. I could feel him reaching up into the air to find them. At night, he told us whimsical, curling "Joha" stories which hypnotized us to sleep. I especially liked the big cooking pan that gave birth to the little pan. My friend Marcia's father who grew up in the United States hardly talked. He built airplanes. I didn't think I would want to fly in anything he made. When Marcia asked him a question, he grunted a kind of pig sound. He sank his face into the paper. My father spilled out musical lines, a horizon of graceful buildings standing beside one another in a distant city. You could imagine people living inside one of my father's words.

He said a few things to us in Arabic—fragrant syllables after we ate, blessings when he hugged us. He hugged us all the time. He said, "I love you" all the time. But I didn't learn how to say "Thank you" in Arabic till I was fourteen, which struck me, even then, as a preposterous omission.

Marcia's father seemed tired. He had seven children because he was a Catholic, Marcia said. I didn't get it. Marcia's mother threw away the leftovers from their table after dinner. My mother carefully wrapped the last little mound of mashed potato inside waxed paper. We'd eat it later.

I felt comfortable in the world of so many different people. Their voices floated around the neighborhood like pollen. On the next block, French-Canadians made blueberry pie. I wanted a slice. It is true that a girl knocked on our door one day and asked to "see the Arab," but I was not insulted. I was mystified. Who?

Sometimes Marcia and I slept together on our screened-in back porch, or in a big green tent in her yard. She was easy to scare. I said the giant harvest moon was coming to eat her and she hid under her pillow. She told me spider stories. We had fun trading little terrors.

When I was almost ready to move away, Marcia and I stood in Dade Park together one last time. I said good-bye to the swings and benches and wooden seesaws with chipped red paint. Two bigger boys rode up on bicycles and circled us. We'd never seen them before. One of them asked if we knew how to do the F-word. I had no idea what they were talking about. Marcia said she knew, but wouldn't tell me. The boys circled the basketball courts, eyeing us strangely. Walking home with Marcia, I felt almost glad to be moving away from her. She stuck her chest out. She said, "Did you ever wish someone would touch you in a private place?"

I looked in the big dictionary at home. Hundreds of F-words I didn't know reached their hands out so it took a long time. And I asked my mother, whose face was so smooth and beautiful and filled with sadness because nothing was quite as good as it could be.

She didn't know either.

Bra Strap

It felt like a taunt, the elastic strap of Karen's bra visible beneath her white blouse in front of me in fifth grade. I saw it even before Douglas snapped it. Who did she think she was, growing older without me?

I spent the night with her one Saturday. In the bathtub together, we splashed and soaped, jingling our talk of teachers, boys, and holidays. But my eyes were on her chest, the great pale fruits growing there. Already they mounded toward stems.

She caught me looking and said, "So?" Sighing, as if she were already tired. Said, "In my family they grow early." Downstairs her bosomy mother stacked cups in a high old cabinet that smelled of grandmother's hair. I could hear her clinking. In my family they barely grew at all. I had been proud of my mother's boyishness, her lithe trunk and straight legs.

Now I couldn't stop thinking about it: what was there, what wasn't there. The mounds on the fronts of certain dolls with candy-coated names. One by one, watching the backs of my friends' blouses, I saw them all fall under the spell. I begged my mother, who said, "For what? Just to be like everybody else?"

Pausing near the underwear displays at Famous and Barr, I asked to be measured, sizing up boxes. "Training Bra"—what were we in training for?

When Louise fell off her front porch and a stake went all the way through her, I heard teachers whispering, "Hope this doesn't ruin her for the future." We discussed the word "impaled." What future? The mysteries of ovaries had not yet been explained. Little factories for eggs. Little secret nests. On the day we saw the film, I didn't like it. If that was what the future meant, I didn't want it anymore. As I was staring out the window afterwards, my mouth tasted like pennies, my throat closed up. The leaves on the trees blurred together so they could carry me.

I sat on a swivel chair practicing handwritings. The backwards slant, the loopy up-and-down. Who would I ever be? My mother was inside the lawyer's office signing papers about the business. That waiting room, with its dull wooden side tables and gloomy magazines, had absolutely nothing to do with me. Never for a second was I drawn toward the world of the dreary professional. I would be a violinist with the Zurich symphony. I would play percussion in a traveling band. I would bake zucchini muffins in Yarmouth, Nova Scotia.

In the car traveling slowly home under a thick gray sky, I worked up courage. Rain, rain, the intimacy of cars. At a stoplight, staring hard at my mother, I asked, "What really happens between men and women to make babies?"

She jumped as if I'd thrown ice at her.

"Not *that!* Not *now!*" From red to green, the light, the light. "There is *oh so much you do not know.*"

It was all she ever told me. The weight of my ignorance pressed upon us both.

Later she slipped me a book, *Little Me, Big Me.* One of the more incomprehensible documents of any childhood: "When a man and a woman love one another enough, he puts his arms around her and part of him goes into part of her and the greatness of their love for one another causes this to feel pleasurable."

On my twelfth birthday, my father came home with our first tape recorder. My mother produced a bouquet of shiny boxes, including a long, slim one. My Lutheran grandparents sat neatly on the couch as the heavy reels wound up our words. "Do you like it? Is it just what you've been waiting for?"

They wanted me to hold it up to my body, the way I would when I put it on. My mother shushing, "Oh, I guess it's private!"

Later the tape would play someone's giggles in the background. My brother? Or the gangs of little girl angels that congregate around our heads, chanting, "Don't grow up, don't grow up!"

I never liked wearing it as much as I did thinking about it.

—1995

Learning from Other Writers

1. List the discrete objects, images, and vignettes that comprise the first section of Nye's essay ("Hiding inside the Good Girl"). Are all the items in your list connected thematically by the title of that section? Make a similar list for each of the other sections.
2. In what way does the title of the essay as a whole unite its separate sections?
3. Are the essay's three sections placed in chronological order? If not, can you speculate as to why the author placed them in the order she chose?
4. What role (if any) does the author's ethnicity play in this essay?
5. Find the book that is mentioned in each of the essay's three major segments. What role does each book play in its own segment? In the essay as a whole?
6. Should the author have spent more time meditating on the thematic connections that unite the segments of her collage? Why or why not?

WAYNE KOESTENBAUM

FROM: *THE QUEEN'S THROAT*

OPERA QUEENS

1

The first opera I ever saw: *Aida*. San Francisco War Memorial Opera House, 1969. I was eleven. By the last act I was exhausted, bored. All I remember now is the color of the sky above the Nile—beyond midnight blue, a shade redolent of witchcraft and spice.

In childhood, I stored all my programs in a crate. Recently I found that first opera program: the Radames was Jon Vickers. Only now do I appreciate the name's weight and valor. A house's foundation, even if invisible, exists—has once, long ago, without witnesses, been poured. And so as I try to compose this fragmented history, I must begin with my first *Aida*, unremembered except for the high blue sky.

2

Am I an opera queen? My proudly gay friend David—eight years my senior, and infinitely more sophisticated in matters sexual and cultural—first told me about opera queens. (We were riding a bus in Baltimore. It was 1980. I was trying to convince him I was bisexual, not gay.) The opera queen seemed the victim of a severe, pleasureless affliction. The opera queen seemed to have given up more reasonable pastimes. I, at twenty-one, could not recognize myself as an opera queen. I told David, "I still have crushes on women." And he said, "Stop kidding yourself."

Opera queens, according to David, went to the opera on Monday nights. I couldn't afford to go to the opera at all. How could I be an opera queen? I owned only four complete operas, and they were budget recordings. Didn't opera queens put on airs? I wasn't a queen. I was delicately built, and wore black pegged trousers, and listened to *Rigoletto* at night with the lights out, and no one in years had called me "femme."

3

Even before my first *Aida,* I saw a student performance of *Hänsel und Gretel,* from which I recall only the scalloped shape of the auditorium, and the sensation of riding in a car, over mountains, toward a townlet unfamiliar and obtuse, where opera grew among grapevines and a heat more lancing than in our development.

4

My first three opera sets, talismanic, purchased by my grandparents for my tenth birthday:

Carmen, the Richmond/London budget set, called by a contemporary guide to recorded opera "perhaps the worst *Carmen* on records";

Aida, the Toscanini version, with Herva Nelli and Richard Tucker;

Madama Butterfly, with Anna Moffo, to which I listened only once—and I stopped midway, because I couldn't find the melodies.

But I made it far enough through the first act to be struck, when Anna Moffo, entered, with a sensation I've tried to describe before, and may never adequately name. Her timbre was separate from its surroundings. Her voice wasn't the canopy, the column, the architrave; gravely self-sufficient, it seemed not a copy of life, but life itself, and, like a breathing property, it entered my system with a vector so naïve, unadulterated, and elemental, so unpolluted by the names I would later impose on the experience, that my drab bedroom shifted on its axis.

And yet, after that initiation, I waited eleven years to listen again to the *Butterfly* recording. Taking up the opera at twenty-one, I knew the ability to respond was stationed in my body, waiting for reveille.

5

The voices of Barbra Streisand, Shirley Jones, and Julie Andrews prepared me for opera and for homosexuality. Barbra, because in *Funny Girl* she sang "I'm the Greatest Star"; Shirley, because her pitch was pure, classical, her soprano not a belter's, but a virgin's; Julie, because she was a nanny in *Mary Poppins* and a governess in *The Sound of Music,* because her haircut was short and mannish, like my mother's, and because her voice, like my idea of opera, confidently checkered the air with summary, silver, emotionless bellicosity.

The voice of Marni Nixon, ghosting for Audrey Hepburn in *My Fair Lady* and for Deborah Kerr in *The King and I,* told me everything about singing in the dark, singing without a body, singing from an erased, invisible place in the universe. No one saw Marni Nixon's body; invisibility made her voice operatic, characterless. Audrey Hepburn lip-synched "I Could Have Danced All Night": like Eliza, I listened but didn't sing. I opened my mouth, in a wide, vapid O of awe and shame, while women's voices streamed from my green Magnavox record player, vibrato so quick it was nearly undetectable.

Vibrato was best when it gave the note elasticity, length, and vigor—discreetly. On the cornet I was embarrassed to use vibrato (to tremble the hand over the three valves). Vibrato was a kind of limpness, like a wrist.

6

Predictive sign: a fondness for musical comedy. I worried, listening to records of *Darling Lili, Oklahoma!, The Music Man, Company,* and *No, No, Nanette,* that I would end up gay: I didn't know the word "gay," I knew about homosexuality only from *Time* feature stories about liberation, but I had a clear impression (picked up where?) that gays liked musical comedy. My mother told my father, "Isn't it time that we buy the boys some original-cast albums?" I cowered as I overheard this question, because I *already* loved original-cast albums, and yet my mother bizarrely thought my predilection was still a future event she had to foster, and she thought, even more irrationally, that a taste for show tunes was a necessary rite of passage for teenage boys: *all boys of a certain age must pass through the purging fire of original-cast albums.*

Adriana Caselotti, operatic-style soprano, with a timbre that, like Jeanette MacDonald's, must have seemed fashionable in the 1930s, dubbed for Snow White in the Disney film. I owned the *Snow White* soundtrack, and wanted a photograph of the invisible Adriana Caselotti. I stared at the calves of Helen Gallagher in the photo spread of the original-cast album of *No, No, Nanette,* and connected the calf muscle's swell (unnaturally developed from wearing high heels?) with her capable voice, and knew I'd have neither those calves nor that voice, and therefore my position on the bedroom carpet, admiring the liner-note photo, was not normal, would get me in trouble someday: why was I staring in solitude at Helen Gallagher's calves, and was this passion sexual?

7

Bart, a fourth-grader, sang "People" ("People who need people are the luckiest people in the world") at the school assembly. He wanted to be a star and claimed already to be a semistar. But he was a laughingstock.

I wondered why the boy put himself through this martyrdom, and why he thought an appearance at the school assembly would advance his career.

I also felt a grudging respect for him, and seeds of an affinity. But I pretended to be dumbstruck by his conduct.

8

How, from musical comedy, did I make the transition to opera? The idea of opera coagulated with most density in the cover photograph of my mother's Joan Sutherland album—"Operatic Arias," 1959: Joan's face blanched and huge against a sky-blue backdrop. But here is the strange and resonant part: Joan's lipstick was the result of retouching. The lipstick didn't match the lips, but hung askew. Before I listened to her coloratura, I knew Joan Sutherland and opera as errors in makeup: I enjoyed the spectacle of lipstick separate from the lips on which it was supposed to rest.

My mother kept her records in the closet. Why? Fear of dust. She rarely played them. And so this image of female vocalism remains separate from sound: Renata Tebaldi's torso, on the *Aida* highlights album, put under considerable pressure by a too-tight costume, so an ampleness makes itself known.

9

I never heard my spinster aunt play her records; and yet because of her old Victor set of *La Forza del Destino*, I will always associate Verdi with my aunt's maiden destiny. I don't know if she was a lesbian, but I know she traveled with women in Germany, lived with women in Venezuela, and, in old age, wore a ring given her by a San Francisco lady friend. In the backseat of my parents' car, she hummed Papageno's aria and tapped its downbeats with her fingers on my leg, and told me about the choirs she'd heard in Munich before the war.

In the late 1960s, I was in my bedroom practicing Papageno's aria, transcribed for trumpet. (At the time, I thought of it as sheer exercise. I didn't know it was an operatic excerpt.) My aunt entered the room and listened to me play the aria. Some recognition passed between us, on the back of the Mozart melody: the understanding that I, like my aunt, would live apart from marriage (bachelor, spinster), and that a fondness for Papageno's tune and *La Forza del Destino* were secret signs of a destiny we never described to each other in words.

10

My piano teacher, who had no evident sexual life, who lived, a maiden, with her aged father, couldn't carry a tune, but when she wanted to demonstrate how to shape a phrase, she would falteringly, expressively sing it, off-pitch. I, a virgin who couldn't sing, understood this peculiar paralysis of the throat, and connected it to a life apart from marriage, a life of secrets and containment.

11

When I speak too much or too loudly, I lose my voice: and at all times I speak from my throat, not my diaphragm. Faulty speaking means I'm perennially hoarse. Too much talking on the phone puts pressure on my throat, and it starts to ache. Though my voice is relatively high-pitched, I speak huskily, like Harvey Fierstein. I don't lisp, though I used to stutter. I've always admired the voice placement of actors, even if my actor friends are embarrassed, in casual conversation, to speak as they were trained (from the diaphragm): it sounds pretentious, oratorical, and nervously earnest.

The last time I tried to sing in public was in fourth grade when I auditioned for *Oliver!*, a children's light-opera production. All auditioning boys stood in a line and sang "Consider Yourself" together; then, one by one, we stepped out of line and sang a phrase, and continued to sing until told to stop. "Consider yourself at home, consider yourself one of the family...." Doubtless I flubbed: I remember that sensation of vulnerability in the throat, of exposure, of sacrifice.

When Walt Whitman wrote so extensively and rhapsodically about the throat (*"O throat! O trembling throat!"*) he was urging us to liberate our throats, to imitate the wide-mouthed opera singer: "A tenor large and fresh as the creation fills me, / The orbic flex of his mouth is pouring and filling me full." We drink sound through our throats: our throats are activated, brought to life, by what we hear. Listening is a reciprocation: grateful for what the ear receives, the throat responds by opening.

12

Cultural folklore convinces us that we can tell someone is gay by voice alone. Decadent novelist J.-K. Huysmans wrote in a letter to Marc-André Raffalovich that "sodomy changes the voice, which becomes almost identical in all of them. After several days' study in that world, from nothing but the sound of the voice of people I did not know, I could infallibly predict their tastes. Do you not think there would be research to be done on the influence of one organ on another?"

And Earl Lind, the remarkable author of *Autobiography of an Androgyne* (1918), believed that "the voice is one of the chief criteria by which to determine abnormal sexuality. I fancy that I can diagnose a man sexually simply by hearing him sing." This same Earl Lind, whose drag names were "Jennie June," "Baby," and "Pussie," daydreamed of becoming a prima donna. "At the opera I would imagine myself as identified with the leading soprano—that I was she. As is usual with professional fairies, I sought to cultivate a soprano singing voice, though singing a baritone when in my every-day circle."

Calling information (411) in Manhattan, I'm pleased by the sound of a distinctly gay-voiced male operator. Finding such an operator, I try to make my request more flamboyant and femmy: I insert an extra "please," and I push against the "please," to stretch the vowel into a diphthong. Even on the phone, voice-to-voice, I want to make my affiliation clear. (Why? No chance to meet the operator. Flirting for its own sake.)

13

Opening my mouth wide for tonsillectomy (I can't remember the operation, but, occurring before the age of school, before I learned to read, it foreshadows my commitment to the throat), I sucked ether and courted loss of consciousness.

First French kisses with women: slow ballet of tongues.

First fellatio: surprise at the mouth's flexibility and tolerance for foreign objects.

The same year I discovered gay 69, I formed an opera club with a girl I loved (we were eighteen), and we listened to *The Marriage of Figaro* together on her couch; she sang "Voi, che sapete" down an echoing dormitory stairwell.

We planned to move on to *Norma* but we discontinued the club before making that progress.

14

In Marcia Davenport's novel *Of Lena Geyer* (1936), drab Elsie deHaven has a crush on soprano Lena Geyer. Elsie sends the diva a huge box of yellow roses after each performance, with a note disguising her gender (E. deH.). Clearly this is queer behavior: Elsie says, "Call me a freak if you like."

Why does Elsie follow Lena around Europe and eventually become her companion? Because the diva's voice, says Elsie, "meant as much to me as parents, a husband, children, or anything most women attach themselves to"; because when she first heard Lena sing, "I was too thrilled to breathe; I remember how the pulse in my throat choked me"; because the sensation of hearing Geyer was like "fresh water pouring into the throat of someone nearly dead of thirst," a physical thrill that "gripped me and made something inside me leap into my ears and throat." Throat, throat, throat! Elsie confesses: "It was exactly like the unlocking of a prison door. The voice poured into me, and from that moment it became the one thing I cared to live for. The whole identity that my parents had so carefully created melted in the force of the singing I heard that night. All the barriers built up by convention and habit seemed to shrivel, and I felt in those few moments a free and purposeful individual. I did not even know I was repressed, or inarticulate, yet once I felt freed, I knew that I had never lived before."

Elsie comes out—her parched self watered by the geyser of another woman's voice. Elsie knows she is excited and in love because she can't breathe and because the pulse in her throat chokes her. The throat, not the ears, receives the diva: the throat, organ from which "I" speak.

The grandiosity of operatic utterance is a wild compensation for the listener's silence. Our ability to speak of ourselves has been foreshortened; we turn to opera because we need to breathe, to regain a right we imagine is godgiven—the right to open.

15

Nuns in the Middle Ages believed they were pregnant because Jesus had *thought* of them; no wonder, then, that opera queens, nuns of an unnamed order, believe that voices entering through the ear are forms of the Holy Ghost. Freud's disciple and biographer Ernest Jones, in his provocative essay "The Madonna's Conception through the Ear," speculates on the ear's erotic significances. To hear is metaphorically to be impregnated—with thought, tone, and sensation.

How loudly do you play your opera? Loud enough to hurt the ear? In the opera house, I distinguish between two kinds of sound: the baritone, mezzo, and bass, in whose presence I remain Subject, knowing the heard voice as Object; and the soprano and tenor, which, as they ascend in volume and pitch, become Subject, incapable of remaining the distant Object. Thus opera interrupts and reverses our ground. I can't remain separate from the tenor or soprano at the height of their ranges, because high notes enter my ear, assault, make a demand. In Family Circle, listening to Cheryl Studer sing Donna Anna in *Don Giovanni*, I can't remain detached and analytical, because her voice makes incursions on my sense of volition. Listen to Rosa Ponselle. Her tones are rounded, median, warm; but then they renounce plum-thickness and become sabers. Moments of being pierced, being surrounded by sound, being called, are worth collecting.

16

And so the opera queen keeps lists. Experiences are accreted, because none can be exhaustively explained. If, once, you could describe the summons a voice sends out, maybe you could stop listening, stop looking to opera for satisfaction and consummation.

Would Proust have written his *A la Recherche du Temps Perdu* if a single enigmatic phrase from a violin had not "opened and expanded his soul" and made him wish to move linearly and at length, ramification upon ramification, room after room, through one instant? And would he have felt compelled to sip recollection from the cup of one phrase if his eroticism hadn't seemed troublingly asocial and wretched, needing to be transformed into a colossus and a labyrinth? "But while I was humming softly to myself the notes of this tune and returning its kiss, the pleasure peculiar to itself which it made me feel became so dear to me that I would have left my father and mother to follow it through the singular world which it constructed in the invisible...."

James McCourt's implicitly gay novel of the diva and her fan, *Mawrdew Czgowchwz* (1975), opens with "The List"—a list of characters. A diva leaves a list of fans and friends with the stage-door guard: only those on the list are admitted. In McCourt's fan-fantasy, every character is allowed backstage; McCourt (novelist as diva) opens stardom's private recesses to all gawkers.

I keep a tiny "Opera Journal" in which I list every opera performance I attend. (I rarely include recitals.) I list the opera, the house, the principal singers, the date. But there's no room for evaluation or criticism. The purpose of a list is not to refine or browbeat, but to include, and to move toward a future moment when accumulation stops and the list-keeper can cull, recollect, and rest on the prior amplitude.

Opera queens catalogue their highs; they don't categorize or explain. Memoirs of operagoing take the form of laterally spreading reminiscences, one after another, with no sequence except chronology. Richard Edgcumbe's *Musical Reminiscences of an Old Amateur for Fifty Years, from 1773 to 1823* is a mnemonic project that leads to no conclusion—just a list of what has been heard. He recalls nothing of diva Caterina Gabrielli's voice—only an image of her judicious, antinaturalistic way with costume: "I can remember seeing her once in the opera of Didone, but can say nothing of her performance, all I can recollect of it being the care with which she tucked up her great hoop as she sidled into the flames of Carthage."

List-making is a prophylaxis against loss. Lists perform sympathetic magic: we want names (of operas, theaters, divas, roles) to be corporeal. A fan writes of Elisabeth Rethberg (in a 1939 *Opera News*): "As to the number of her roles, the other day I sat down and wrote the names of twenty-six operas in which she has sung." In such a fashion I used to keep a list (abandoned in 1969) of every movie I had seen, beginning with *Mary Poppins*, traveling through *I Confess*, and ending with—I can't recall where the list ended, which movie persuaded me it was pointless to keep a list of beloved properties.

17

Only in 1979, at the end of college, did I begin openly to listen to opera: that same year I went to the Napoleon Club in Boston's Beacon Hill and stared, youthful and muddled behind my wire-rimmed glasses, at peacock men, gays I'd never seen in such number.

A more logical narrative of my life would have had me embrace disco, for disco was the theme music of gay sexuality in the late 1970s. But I never went dancing; I preferred furtive cruising; my desires were ruminative, oblivious to beat.

Opera has always suited those who have failed at love. I entered sexuality assuming that I would fail at it and that it had failed me, that I, by virtue of my lust for men, was where sexuality broke down, where the system stopped working, where a mistake materialized.

I remember the girl who sang the lead in our high school's production of *Guys and Dolls* (a flamboyant redhead with a large bosom). Did I love her? Or did I envy her? I spent much of childhood trying to distinguish identification from desire, asking myself, "Am I in love with Julie Andrews, or do I think I *am* Julie Andrews?" I knew that to love Julie Andrews placed me, however vaguely, in heterosexuality's domain; but to identify with Julie Andrews, to want to be the star of *Star!*, placed me under suspicion.

When I left behind my original-cast albums and began to listen, again and again, in 1980, to the four operas I owned, I had by that time acquired a boyfriend, a sexuality, and a hunger (I still can't explain the urge, I can only point to it, and surround it with anecdote, reflection, and context) to have opera take over my reason, as if opera were the antithesis of reason.

—1993

Learning from Other Writers

1. If you were to apply a one- or two-word label or heading to each of these segments, what would each label be? Look at each label and ask if it describes an object, an image, an anecdote, a person, a question, or an idea. Do certain types of labels occur in your list more frequently than others?
2. Are these segments arranged in chronological order? If not, can you find some other pattern that governs which segment follows which segment?
3. Is there anything about Koestenbaum's material that makes it especially well or ill suited to a nonlinear form?
4. What connections does the author draw between the human body and opera? The gay male body and opera?
5. What discoveries did you make while reading these excerpts from Koestenbaum's book? Does he prove these discoveries or merely assert them to be true? If he proves them, how does he prove them? If he doesn't prove them, do you believe his assertions anyway?

THOMAS LYNCH

JESSICA, THE HOUND AND THE CASKET TRADE

This would normally be the place to say (as critics of the American funeral trade invariably do), "I am not, of course, speaking of the vast majority of ethical funeral directors." But the vast majority of ethical funeral directors is precisely the subject of this book.

—JESSICA MITFORD, *THE AMERICAN WAY OF DEATH,* FOREWORD, P. VIII

She went to a long-established, "reputable" undertaker. Seeking to save the widow expense, she chose the cheapest redwood casket in the establishment and was quoted a low price. Later, the salesman called her back to say the brother-in-law was too tall to fit into this casket, she would have to take the one that cost $100 more. When my friend objected, the salesman said, "Oh, all right, we'll use the redwood one, but we'll have to cut off his feet."

—*IBID.* CHAPTER TWO, P. 24

The same mortician who once said he'd rather give away caskets than take advantage of someone in grief later hung billboards out by the interstate—a bosomy teenager in a white bikini over which it read *Better Bodies by Bixby* (not the real name) and the phone numbers for his several metro locations.

I offer this in support of the claim that there are good days and there are bad ones.

No less could be said for many of the greats.

I'm thinking of Hemingway's take on Pound when he said, "Ezra was right half the time, and when he was wrong, he was so wrong you were never in any doubt of it." But ought we be kept from "The River-Merchant's Wife" by his mistaken politics? Should outrage silence the sublime?

The same may be asked of Mr. Bixby's two memorable utterances.

Or, as a priest I've long admired once said, "Prophesy, like poetry, is a part-time job—the rest of the time they were only trying to keep their feet out their mouths." I suppose he was trying to tell me something.

Indeed, mine is an occupation that requires two feet firmly on the ground, less for balance, I often think, than to keep one or the other from angling toward its true home in my craw.

I sell caskets and embalm bodies and direct funerals.

Pollsters find among the general public a huge ambivalence about funeral directors. "I hope you'll understand it if I never want to see you again," the most satisfied among my customers will say. I understand.

And most of the citizenry, stopped on the street, would agree that funeral directors are mainly crooks, "except for mine ...," they just as predictably add. "The one who did my (*insert primary relation*) was really helpful, really cared, treated us like family."

This tendency, to abhor the general class while approving of the particular member is among the great human prerogatives—as true of clergy and senators as it is of teachers and physicians. Much the same could be said of Time: "Life sucks," we say, "but there was this moment ...," or of racial groups: "Some of my best friends are (*insert minority*) ...," or of gender. "(*Insert sex*)! You can't live with them and you can't live without them!"

Of course, there are certain members of the subspecies—I'm thinking lawyers, politicians, revenue agents—who are, in general and in particular, beyond redemption and we like it that way. "The devil you know's better than the one you don't ..." is the best we can say about politicians. And who among us wants a "nice" divorce attorney or has even one fond memory involving the tax man? Really, now.

But back to caskets and bodies and funerals.

When it comes to caskets I'm very careful. I don't tell folks what they should or shouldn't do. It's bad form and worse for business. I tell them I don't have any that will get them into heaven or keep them out. There's none that turns a prince into a frog or, regrettably, vice-versa. There isn't a casket that compensates for neglect nor one that hides true love, honorable conduct, or affection.

If worth can be measured by what they do, it might help to figure out what caskets "do" in the inanimate object sense of the verb.

How many here are thinking "handles"? When someone dies, we try to get a handle on it. This is because dead folks don't move. I'm not making this part up. Next time someone in your house quits breathing, ask them to get up and answer the phone or maybe get you some ice water or let the cat out. He won't budge. It's because he's dead.

There was a time when it was easier to change caves than to drag the dead guy out. Now it's not so easy. There's the post office, the utilities, the closing costs. Now we have to remove the dead. The sooner the better is the rule of thumb, though it's not the thumb that will make this known.

This was a dour and awful chore, moving the dead from place to place. And like most chores, it was left to women to do. Later, it was discovered to be a high honor—to *bear the pall* as a liturgical role required a special place in the procession, special conduct, and often a really special outfit. When hauling the dead hither and yon became less a chore and more an honor, men took it over with enthusiasm.

In this it resembles the history of the universe. Much the same happened with protecting against the marauding hordes, the provision of meaty protein sources, and more recently, in certain highly specialized and intricate evolutions of food preparation and child care.

If you think women were at least participant and perhaps instrumental in the discovery of these honors, you might better keep such suspicions to yourself. These are not good days to think such thoughts.

But I stray again. Back to business.

Another thing you'll see most every casket doing is being horizontal. This is because the folks that make them have taken seriously the demonstrated preference of our species to do it on the level. Oh, sure—it can be done standing up or in a car or even upside down. But most everyone goes looking for something flat. Probably this can be attributed to gravity or physics or fatigue.

So horizontal things that can be carried—to these basic properties, we could add a third: it should be sturdy enough for a few hundred pounds. I'm glad that it's not from personal experience that I say that nothing takes the steam out of a good funeral so much as the bottom falling out.

And how many of you haven't heard of this happening?

A word on the words we're most familiar with.

Coffins are the narrow, octagonal fellows—mostly wooden, nicely corresponding to the shape of the human form before the advent of the junk food era. There are top and bottom, and the screws that fasten the one to the other are often ornamental. Some have handles, some do not, but all can be carried. The lids can be opened and closed at will.

Caskets are more rectangular and the lids are hinged and the body can be both carried and laid out in them. Other than shape, coffins and caskets are pretty much the same. They've been made of wood and metal and glass and ceramics and plastics and cement and the dear knows what else. Both are made in a range of prices.

But *casket* suggests something beyond basic utility, something about the contents of the box. The implication is that it contains something precious: heirlooms, jewels, old love letters, remnants and icons of something dear.

So casket is to coffin as tomb is to cave, grave is to hole in the ground, pyre is to bonfire. You get the drift? Or as, for example, eulogy is to speech, elegy to poem, home is to house, or husband to man. (I love this part, I get carried away.)

But the point is a *casket* presumes something about what goes in it. It presumes the dead body is important to someone. For some this will seem like stating the obvious. For others, I'm guessing, maybe not.

But when buildings are bombed or planes fall from the sky, or wars are won or lost, the bodies of the dead are really important. We want them back to let them go again—on our terms, at our pace, to say you may not leave without permission, forgiveness, our respects—to say we want our chance to say goodbye.

Both coffins and caskets are boxes for the dead. Both are utterly suitable to the task. Both cost more than most other boxes.

It's because of the bodies we put inside them. The bodies of mothers and fathers and sons, daughters and sisters and brothers and friends, the ones we knew and loved or knew and hated, or hardly knew at all, but know someone who knew them and who is left to grieve.

In 1906, John Hillenbrand, the son of a German immigrant bought the failing Batesville Coffin Company in the southeastern Indiana town of the same name. Following the form of the transportation industry, he moved from a primarily wooden product to products of metal that would seal against the elements. *Permanence* and *protection* were concepts that Batesville marketed successfully during and after a pair of World Wars in which men were being sent home in government boxes. The same wars taught different lessons to the British, for whom the sight of their burial grounds desecrated by bombs at intervals throughout the first half century suggested permanence and protection were courtesies they could no longer guarantee to the dead. Hence, the near total preference for cremation there.

Earth burial is practiced by "safe" societies and by settled ones. It presumes the dead will be left their little acre and that the living will be around to tend the graves. In such climates the fantasies of permanence and protection thrive. And the cremation rate in North America has risen in direct relation to the demographics and geographics of mobility and fear and the ever more efficient technologies of destruction.

The idea that a casket should be sealed against air and moisture is important to many families. To others it means nothing. They are both right. No one need to explain why it doesn't matter. No one need explain why it does. But Batesville, thinking that it might, engineered the first "sealed" casket with a gasket in the 1940s and made it available in metal caskets in every price range from the .20 gauge steels to the coppers and bronzes. One of the things they learned is that ninety-six percent of the human race would fit in a casket with interior dimensions of six feet six by two feet high by two feet wide—give or take.

Once they had the size figured out and what it was that people wanted in a casket—protection and permanence—then the rest was more or less the history of how the Hillenbrand brothers managed to make more and sell more than any of their competition. And they have. You see them in the movies, on the evening news being carried in and out of churches, at gravesides, being taken from hearses. If someone's in a casket in North America chances are better than even it's a Batesville.

We show twenty-some caskets to pick from. They're samples only. There are plenty more we can get within a matter of hours. What I carry in blue, my brother Tim, in the next town, carries in pink. What I carry tailored, Tim carries shirred. He carries one with the Last Supper on it. I've got one with the Pietà. One of his has roses on the handles. One of mine has sheaves of wheat.

You name it, we've got it. We aim to please.

We have a cardboard box (of a kind used for larger appliances) for seventy-nine dollars. We also have a mahogany box (of a kind used for Kennedys and Nixons and Onassises) for nearly eight grand. Both can be carried and buried and burned. Both will accommodate all but the tallest or widest citizens, for whom, alas, as in life, the selection narrows. And both are available to any customer who can pay the price.

Because a lot of us tend to avoid the extremes, regardless of how we elect to define them, we show a wide range of caskets in between and it would look on a chart like one of those bell curves: with the most in the middle and the least at either end. Thus, we show three oak caskets and only one mahogany, a bronze, a copper, a stainless steel, and six or seven regular steels of various gauges or thicknesses. We show a cherry, a maple, two poplars, an ash, a pine, a particle board, and the cardboard box. The linings are velvet or crepe or linen or satin, in all different colors, tufted or ruffled or tailored plain. You get pretty much what you pay for here.

I should probably fess up that we buy these caskets for less than we sell them for—a fact uncovered by one of our local TV news personalities, who called himself the News Hound, and who was, apparently, untutored in the economic intrigues of wholesale and retail. It was this same News Hound who did an expose on Girl Scout Cookie sales—how some of the money doesn't go to the girls at all, but to the national office where it was used to pay the salaries of "staff."

It was a well-worn trail the News Hound was sniffing—a trail blazed most profitably by Jessica Mitford who came to the best-selling if not exactly original conclusion that the bereaved consumer is in a bad bargaining position. When you've got a dead body on your hands it's hard to shop around. It's hard to shop lawyers when you're on the lam, or doctors when your appendix is inflamed. It's not the kind of thing you let out to bids.

Lately there has been a great push toward "pre-arrangement." Everyone who's anyone seems to approve. The funeral directors figure it's money in the bank. The insurance people love it since most of the funding is done through insurance. The late Jessica, the former News Hound, the anti-extravagance crowd—they all reckon it is all for the best to make such decisions when heads are cool and hearts are unencumbered by grief and guilt. There's this hopeful fantasy that by pre-arranging the funeral, one might be able to pre-feel the feelings, you know, get a jump on the anger and the fear and the helplessness. It's as modern as planned parenthood and prenuptial agreements and as useless, however tidy it may be about the finances, when it comes to the feelings involved.

And we are uniformly advised "not to be a burden to our children." This is the other oft-cited *bonne raison* for making your final arrangements in advance—to spare them the horror and pain of having to do business with someone like me.

But if we are not to be a burden to our children, then to whom? The government? The church? The taxpayers? Whom? Were they not a burden to us—our children? And didn't the management of that burden make us feel alive and loved and helpful and capable?

And if the planning of a funeral is so horribly burdensome, so fraught with possible abuses and gloom, why should an arthritic septuagenarian with blurred vision and some hearing loss be sent to the front to do battle with the undertaker instead of the forty-something heirs-apparent with their power suits and web browsers and cellular phones? Are they not far better outfitted to the task? Is it not their inheritance we're spending here? Are these not decisions they will be living with?

Maybe their parents do not trust them to do the job properly.

Maybe they shouldn't.

Maybe they should.

The day I came to Milford, Russ Reader started pre-arranging his funeral. I was getting my hair cut when I first met him. He was a massive man still, in his fifties, six-foot-something and four hundred pounds. He'd had, in his youth, a spectacular career playing college and professional football. His reputation had preceded him. He was a "character"—known in these parts for outrageous and libertine behavior. Like the Sunday he sold a Ford coupe off the used car lot uptown, taking a cash deposit of a thousand dollars and telling the poor customer to "come by in the morning when the office is open" for the keys and paperwork. That Russ was not employed by the car dealer—a devout Methodist who kept holy his Sabbaths—did not come to light before the money had been spent on sirloins and cigars and round after round of drinks for the patrons of Ye Olde Hotel—visiting matrons from the Eastern Star, in town with their husbands for a regional confab. Or the time a neighbor's yelping poodle—a dog disliked by everyone in earshot—was found shot one afternoon during Russ's nap time. The neighbor started screaming at one of Russ's boys over the back fence, "When I get my hands on your father!" Awakened by the fracas, Russ appeared at the upstairs window and calmly promised, "I'll be right down, Ben." He came down in his paisley dressing gown, decked the neighbor with a swift left hook, instructed his son to bury "that dead mutt," and went back upstairs to finish his nap. Halloween was Russ's favorite holiday, and he celebrated in more or less pre-Christian fashion, dressing himself up like a Celtic warrior, with an antlered helmet and mighty sword that, along with his ponderous bulk and black beard and booming voice, would scare the bejaysus out of the wee trick-or-treaters who nonetheless were drawn to his porch by stories of full-sized candy bars sometimes wrapped in five-dollar bills. Russ Reader was, in all ways, bigger than life, so that the hyperbole that attended the gossip about him was like the talk of heros in the ancient Hibernian epics—Cuchulainn and Deirdre and Queen Maeve, who were given to warp-spasms, wild couplings, and wondrous appetites.

When he first confronted me in the barber's chair, he all but blotted out the sun behind him.

"You're the new Digger O'Dell I take it."

It was the black suit, the wing rips, the gray striped tie.

"Well, you're never getting your mitts on my body!" he challenged.

The barber stepped back to busy himself among the talcums and clippers, uncertain of the direction the conversation might take.

I considered the size of the man before me—the ponderous bulk of him, the breathtaking mass of him—and tried to imagine him horizontal and uncooperative. A sympathetic pain ran down my back. I winced.

"What makes you think I'd want anything to do with your body?" I countered in a tone that emphasized my indignation.

Russ and I were always friends after that.

He told me he intended to have his body donated to "medical science." He wanted to be given to the anatomy department of his alma mater, so that fledgling doctors could practice on him.

"Won't cost my people a penny."

When I told him they probably wouldn't take him, on account of his size, he seemed utterly crestfallen. The supply of cadavers for medical and dental schools in this land of plenty was shamefully but abundantly provided for by the homeless and helpless, who were, for the most part, more "fit" than Russ was.

"But I was an all-American there!" Russ pleaded.

"Don't take my word for it," I advised. "Go ask for yourself."

Months later I was watering impatiens around the funeral home when Russ screeched to a halt on Liberty Street.

"OK, listen. Just cremate me and have the ashes scattered over town from one of those hot-air balloons." I could see he had given this careful thought. "How much will it cost me, bottom line?"

I told him the fees for our minimum services—livery and paperwork and a box.

"I don't want a casket," he hollered from the front seat of his Cadillac, idling at curbside now.

I explained we wouldn't be using a casket as such, still he would have to be *in* something. The crematory people wouldn't accept his body unless it was *in* something. They didn't *handle* dead bodies without some kind of handles. This made tolerable sense to Russ. In my mind I was thinking of a shipping case—a kind of covered pallet compatible with fork-lifts and freight handlers—that would be sufficient to the task.

"I can only guess at what the balloon ride will cost, Russ. It's likely to be the priciest part. And, of course, you'd have to figure on inflation. Are you planning to do this very soon?"

"Don't get cute with me, Digger," he shouted. "Whadayasay? Can I count on you?"

I told him it wasn't me he'd have to count on. He'd have to convince his wife and kids—the nine of them. They were the ones I'd be working for.

"But it's *my* funeral! *My* money."

Here is where I explained to Russ the subtle but important difference between the "adjectival" and "possessive" applications of the first-person singular pronoun for ownership—a difference measured by one's last breath. I explained that it was really *theirs* to do—his survivors, his family. It was really, listen closely, "the heirs"—the money, the funeral, what was or wasn't done with his body.

"I'll pay you now," he protested. "In cash—I'll pre-arrange it all. Put it in my Will. They'll have to do it the way I want it."

I encouraged Russ to ponder the worst-case scenario: his wife and his family take me to court. I come armed with his Last Will and pre-need documents insisting that his body get burned and tossed from a balloon hovering over the heart of town during Sidewalk Sale Days. His wife Mary, glistening with real tears, his seven beautiful daughters with hankies in hand, his two fine sons, bearing up manfully, petition the court for permission to lay him out, have the preacher in, bury him up on the hill where they can visit his grave whenever the spirit moves them to.

"Who do you think wins that one, Russ? Go home and make your case with them."

I don't know if he ever had that conversation with them all. Maybe he just gave up. Maybe it had all been for my consumption. I don't know. That was years ago.

When Russ died last year in his easy chair, a cigar smoldering in the ashtray, one of those evening game shows flickering on the TV, his son came to my house to summon me. His wife and his daughters were weeping around him. His children's children watched and listened. We brought the hearse and waited while each of the women kissed him and left. We brought the stretcher in and, with his sons' help, moved him from the chair, then out the door and to the funeral home where we embalmed him, gave him a clean shave, and laid him out, all of us amazed at how age and infirmity had reduced him so. He actually fit easily into a Batesville casket—I think it was cherry, I don't remember.

But I remember how his vast heroics continued to grow over two days of wake. The stories were told and told again. Folks wept and laughed outloud at his wild antics. And after the minister, a woman who'd known Russ all her life and had braved his stoop on Halloween, had had her say about God's mercy and the size of Heaven, she invited some of us to share our stories about Russ. After that we followed a brass band, holding forth with "When the Saints Go Marching In," to the grave. And after everything had been said that could be said, and done that could be done, Mary and her daughters went home to the embraces of neighbors and the casseroles and condolences, and Russ's sons remained to bury him. They took off their jackets, undid their ties, broke out a bottle and dark cigars and buried their father's body in the ground that none of us thought it would ever fit into. I gave the permit to the sexton and left them to it.

And though I know his body is buried there, something of Russ remains among us now. Whenever I see hot-air balloons—fat flaming birds adrift in the evening air—I sense his legendary excesses raining down on us, old friends and family—his blessed and elect—who duck our heads or raise our faces to the sky and laugh or catch our breath or cry.

In even the best of caskets, it never all fits—all that we'd like to bury in them: the hurt and forgiveness, the anger and pain, the praise and thanksgiving, the emptiness and exaltations, the untidy feelings when someone dies. So I conduct this business very carefully because, in the years since I've been here, when someone dies, they never call Jessica or the News Hound.

They call me.

—1997

Learning from Other Writers

1. In what way does the essay's title prepare you for its structure? What expectations do the epigraphs set up?
2. What is the thematic relevance of the opening six paragraphs to the essay that follows?
3. What is the object, image, or word that provides the focus for the second segment of this essay? The third segment? The fourth?
4. How would you describe the author's tone? Does it strike you as off-putting? Appropriate? Both?
5. What complaint do the News Hound, Jessica Mitford, and "the anti-extravagance crowd" hold against undertakers as a group? What is Lynch's answer to this complaint? Whose side are you on (and why)?
6. What role does the long section about Russ Reader play in the essay as a whole? What can you say about the internal structure of that segment?
7. Read Marcie Hershman's essay about being a pallbearer at her grandmother's funeral (in Chapter 5) and compare that essay to this in terms of structure, tone, and central question.

INSPIRATIONS: WHY THESE FIVE THINGS GO TOGETHER

1. Choose a period of your life that strikes you as important (seventh grade, a parent's illness, a term in the Peace Corps).
2. List five objects that pop into your mind as important to that period.
3. Describe each object on an index card, then lay the cards on a table so all five can be seen at once.
4. Freewrite to figure out what question or discovery connects all five descriptions.
5. After moving the index cards around on the table, settle on an order that makes sense to you.
6. Using the five descriptions on the cards and the meditations suggested by the freewriting part of the assignment, write a collage. If you need to add or subtract objects or meditations, feel free to do so.
7. Optional: Think of a sixth object from the same period of your life . . . but pick an object that seems completely *un*related to your original five. Freewrite a meditation about the way(s) in which this object doesn't fit with the other five. Then write a segment about how (despite everything) this object *does* fit with the other five. Add this segment to your essay.

Dominoes

This chapter was inspired by an exercise from that old (but still wise and extremely useful) standby for composition courses, Ken Macrorie's *The I-Search Paper.*[1] To combat the sorts of boring assignments that used to lead students to go to the encyclopedia (I told you the book was old) and look up whatever information the teacher told them to go look up, then write down that information (being careful to change the wording) and turn in the resulting hash of quotes (thereby proving that they could re-search and re-find what superior beings known as experts already had searched and found), Macrorie advised instructors to nudge their students toward coming up with questions that genuinely intrigued them, then going out in the world and discovering their own answers to those questions.

In one assignment, Macrorie prompted students to visit the library and peruse newspapers and periodicals from the day or week they were born, with instructions that they find an interesting invention, cultural artifact, or event that had exerted a significant effect on their lives (and/or the lives of other members of their generation). Because I decided early in my teaching career that I would never ask students to do anything that I wouldn't enjoy doing myself, I quickly adopted Macrorie's exercise. (I defy anyone—of any age—to look through periodicals from the week of his or her birth and *not* come up with an exciting topic for a cause-and-effect essay.)

Over the years, my students have responded to Macrorie's assignment by incorporating into their essays the excitement of the search, how one item jumped out from the mass of print, how this article or that advertisement prompted them to consider the effects of the invention of the digital watch on their perception of time, or the effect of the *Star Wars* series on the fantasies and moral values of millions of young men their age, or the effect of the Kent State riots on their family members' lives. Honestly, I can't recall a single dud among the bunch. (I once had a student who could have passed for white but was in fact the son of a black mother and a white father; while reading magazines from the week of his birth, this student discovered that his parents' marriage—an act of miscegenation—had been illegal in the state they lived in, a discovery that shocked him into a lengthy reconsideration of how much braver and more rebellious they must have been than he previously had understood.)

Not only did this assignment provide students with a motive to go to the library and conduct research that seemed exciting rather than dreary, something about Macrorie's exercise inspired my students to *think*. At some point, the structure of the essay pushed its writer right up to the brink of a cliff and said: Okay, now you must consider the effects of the

[1] *The I-Search Paper* (Boynton/Cook, 1988) is a revised and expanded version of Macrorie's *Searching Writing*, which came out in 1980.

microwave oven on the way your family ate its meals, or the effects of the first Gulf War on your aunt Jane and uncle Mark, or the effects of video games on the lives of girls your age. And most of my students took that leap ... only to discover that they were indeed able to think original thoughts, and that thinking such thoughts could be exhilarating.

Until now, I haven't put too much emphasis on the thinking part of your essays. When most people are *told* to think, their brains freeze up and they become too nervous or self-conscious to remember what they ate for breakfast, let alone to think great thoughts. And many of the finest examples of creative nonfiction, especially personal narratives, achieve their thematic coherence and depth indirectly, if for no other reason than telling a story or going on a journey with a question simmering in the back of your mind will lead you to notice or select the details that relate to that question. As we've seen, if you know what question you're supposed to be thinking about, and you care about that question, and you come up with a structure that pulls you naturally along the path toward answering that question, your mind usually will generate at least a few original thoughts, which you can supplement by talking to other people or performing various types of research.

But in this chapter—and the chapter that follows—we are going to pay a bit more attention to the meditative or analytic aspects of creative nonfiction. This isn't to say that the more meditation you put in an essay the better it will be, only that the basic elements of creative nonfiction are the same, whether you are writing a narrative about the death of your pig or an analysis of the effects of a toxic-waste dump in your neighborhood.

Certainly, your language needn't change (Macrorie uses the wonderful term "Engfish" for the sort of fake, fishy prose that many people—including professors—slip into when they write academic or analytical papers[2]). You should feel free to use the same creative, cliché- and jargon-free prose no matter what you write. If you read "The Clan of One-Breasted Women" at the end of this chapter, you won't find much difference between the language Terry Tempest Williams uses in her analysis of the effects of nuclear testing on the incidence of breast cancer in her family—and, by extension, other families living in Utah in the 1950s—and the language used by the authors of the personal narratives earlier in this book. Jane Brox's subtle evocation of the causes and effects of the influenza epidemic of 1918 on her hometown of Lawrence, Massachusetts, is nothing if not lyrical. And even a self-proclaimed geek like Adam Rogers manages to avoid computer jargon and instead turns the terminology of online gaming into its own kind of poetry as he tries to convince his readers that the role-playing aspects of the game Dungeons and Dragons spawned not only later online games but also social networks such as Facebook and our entire culture's way of viewing and constructing our identities, both online and off.

You may find Rogers's final claim hard to accept, but you have to give the guy credit for creating a fairly plausible chain of cause-and-effect relationships that carries you from start to finish, especially within the confines of a thousand-word *New York Times* op-ed piece. Not only does "Geek Love" prove that computer experts can avoid jargon when they write, it is a striking example of the relationship between content and structure in a cause-and-effect essay. If you imagine your initial cause as the first domino in a row of dominoes standing on their ends, all you need to do to get your essay moving is to push that first domino and see where it lands; then push *that* domino and see what secondary effect it produces, and so on until the last domino has hit the table.

You might also take heart from Rogers's essay and its promise that even if you've never taken a direct role in an historical event, the mere fact that you were born into an age in which

[2] See Macrorie's *Telling Writing*, Boynton/Cook, 1985.

technological innovations keep changing the way we experience reality qualifies you to write a cause-and-effect essay. After all, who is more of an expert than you on the psychological and sociological changes wrought by e-mail and instant-messaging systems, cell phones, iPods, computer gambling and computer porn, cable TV, antidepressants, safe and effective birth control, treatments for AIDS and other medical conditions, global warming, genetic testing, and ... well, you get the point.

TERRY TEMPEST WILLIAMS

THE CLAN OF ONE-BREASTED WOMEN

I belong to a Clan of One-Breasted Women. My mother, my grandmothers, and six aunts have all had mastectomies. Seven are dead. The two who survive have just completed rounds of chemotherapy and radiation.

I've had my own problems: two biopsies for breast cancer and a small tumor between my ribs diagnosed as a "borderline malignancy."

This is my family history.

Most statistics tell us breast cancer is genetic, hereditary, with rising percentages attached to fatty diets, childlessness, or becoming pregnant after thirty. What they don't say is living in Utah may be the greatest hazard of all.

We are a Mormon family with roots in Utah since 1847. The "word of wisdom" in my family aligned us with good foods—no coffee, no tea, tobacco, or alcohol. For the most part, our women were finished having their babies by the time they were thirty. And only one faced breast cancer prior to 1960. Traditionally, as a group of people, Mormons have a low rate of cancer.

Is our family a cultural anomaly? The truth is, we didn't think about it. Those who did, usually the men, simply said, "bad genes." The women's attitude was stoic. Cancer was part of life. On February 16, 1971, the eve of my mother's surgery, I accidentally picked up the telephone and overheard her ask my grandmother what she could expect.

"Diane, it is one of the most spiritual experiences you will ever encounter."

I quietly put down the receiver.

Two days later, my father took my brothers and me to the hospital to visit her. She met us in the lobby in a wheelchair. No bandages were visible. I'll never forget her radiance, the way she held herself in a purple velvet robe, and how she gathered us around her.

"Children, I am fine. I want you to know I felt the arms of God around me."

We believed her. My father cried. Our mother, his wife, was thirty-eight years old.

A little over a year after Mother's death, Dad and I were having dinner together. He had just returned from St. George, where the Tempest Company was completing the gas lines that would service southern Utah. He spoke of his love for the country, the sandstoned landscape, bare-boned and beautiful. He had just finished hiking the Kolob trail in Zion National Park. We got caught up in reminiscing, recalling with fondness our walk up Angel's Landing on his fiftieth birthday and the years our family had vacationed there.

Over dessert, I shared a recurring dream of mine. I told my father that for years, as long as I could remember, I saw this flash of light in the night in the desert—that this image had so permeated my being that I could not venture south without seeing it again, on the horizon, illuminating buttes and mesas.

"You did see it," he said.

"Saw what?"

"The bomb. The cloud. We were driving home from Riverside, California. You were sitting on Diane's lap. She was pregnant. In fact, I remember the day, September 7, 1957. We had just gotten out of the Service. We were driving north, past Las Vegas. It was an hour or so before dawn, when this explosion went off. We not only heard it, but felt it. I thought the oil tanker in front of us had blown up. We pulled over and suddenly, rising from the desert floor, we saw it, clearly, this golden-stemmed cloud, the mushroom. The sky seemed to vibrate with an eerie pink glow. Within a few minutes, a light ash was raining on the car."

I stared at my father.

"I thought you knew that," he said. "It was a common occurrence in the fifties."

It was at this moment that I realized the deceit I had been living under. Children growing up in the American Southwest, drinking contaminated milk from contaminated cows, even from the contaminated breasts of their mothers, my mother—members, years later, of the Clan of One-Breasted Women.

It is a well-known story in the Desert West, "The Day We Bombed Utah," or more accurately, the years we bombed Utah: above ground atomic testing in Nevada took place from January 27, 1951 through July 11, 1962. Not only were the winds blowing north covering "low-use segments of the population" with fallout and leaving sheep dead in their tracks, but the climate was right. The United States of the 1950s was red, white, and blue. The Korean War was raging. McCarthyism was rampant. Ike was it, and the cold war was hot. If you were against nuclear testing, you were for a communist regime.

Much has been written about this "American nuclear tragedy." Public health was secondary to national security. The Atomic Energy Commissioner, Thomas Murray, said, "Gentlemen, we must not let anything interfere with this series of tests, nothing."

Again and again, the American public was told by its government, in spite of burns, blisters, and nausea, "It has been found that the tests may be conducted with adequate assurance of safety under conditions prevailing at the bombing reservations." Assuaging public fears was simply a matter of public relations. "Your best action," an Atomic Energy Commission booklet read, "is not to be worried about fallout." A news release typical of the times stated, "We find no basis for concluding that harm to any individual has resulted from radioactive fallout."

On August 30, 1979, during Jimmy Carter's presidency, a suit was filed, *Irene Allen v. The United States of America*. Mrs. Allen's case was the first on an alphabetical list of twenty-four test cases, representative of nearly twelve hundred plaintiffs seeking compensation from the United States government for cancers caused by nuclear testing in Nevada.

Irene Allen lived in Hurricane, Utah. She was the mother of five children and had been widowed twice. Her first husband, with their two oldest boys, had watched the tests from the roof of the local high school. He died of leukemia in 1956. Her second husband died of pancreatic cancer in 1978.

In a town meeting conducted by Utah Senator Orrin Hatch, shortly before the suit was filed, Mrs. Allen said, "I am not blaming the government, I want you to know that, Senator Hatch. But I thought if my testimony could help in any way so this wouldn't happen again to any of the generations coming up after us ... I am happy to be here this day to bear testimony of this."

God-fearing people. This is just one story in an anthology of thousands.

On May 10, 1984, Judge Bruce S. Jenkins handed down his opinion. Ten of the plaintiffs were awarded damages. It was the first time a federal court had determined that nuclear tests had been the cause of cancers. For the remaining fourteen test cases, the proof of causation was not sufficient. In spite of the split decision, it was considered a landmark ruling. It was not to remain so for long.

In April 1987, the Tenth Circuit Court of Appeals overturned Judge Jenkins's ruling on the ground that the United States was protected from suit by the legal doctrine of sovereign immunity, a centuries-old idea from England in the days of absolute monarchs.

In January 1988, the Supreme Court refused to review the Appeals Court decision. To our court system it does not matter whether the United States government was irresponsible, whether it lied to its citizens, or even that citizens died from the fallout of nuclear testing. What matters is that our government is immune: "The King can do no wrong."

In Mormon culture, authority is respected, obedience is revered, and independent thinking is not. I was taught as a young girl not to "make waves" or "rock the boat."

"Just let it go," Mother would say. "You know how you feel, that's what counts."

For many years, I have done just that—listened, observed, and quietly formed my own opinions, in a culture that rarely asks questions because it has all the answers. But one by one, I have watched the women in my family die common, heroic deaths. We sat in waiting rooms hoping for good news, but always receiving the bad. I cared for them, bathed their scarred bodies, and kept their secrets. I watched beautiful women become bald as Cytoxan, cisplatin, and Adriamycin were injected into their veins. I held their foreheads as they vomited green-black bile, and I shot them with morphine when the pain became inhuman. In the end, I witnessed their last peaceful breaths, becoming a midwife to the rebirth of their souls.

The price of obedience has become too high.

The fear and inability to question authority that ultimately killed rural communities in Utah during atmospheric testing of atomic weapons is the same fear I saw in my mother's body. Sheep. Dead sheep. The evidence is buried.

I cannot prove that my mother, Diane Dixon Tempest, or my grandmothers, Lettie Romney Dixon and Kathryn Blackett Tempest, along with my aunts developed cancer from nuclear fallout in Utah. But I can't prove they didn't.

My father's memory was correct. The September blast we drove through in 1957 was part of Operation Plumbbob, one of the most intensive series of bomb tests to be initiated. The flash of light in the night in the desert, which I had always thought was a dream, developed into a family nightmare. It took fourteen years, from 1957 to 1971, for cancer to manifest in my mother—the same time, Howard L. Andrews, an authority in radioactive fallout at the National Institutes of Health, says radiation cancer requires to become evident. The more I learn about what it means to be a "downwinder," the more questions I drown in.

What I do know, however, is that as a Mormon woman of the fifth generation of Latter-day Saints, I must question everything, even if it means losing my faith, even if it means becoming a member of a border tribe among my own people. Tolerating blind obedience in the name of patriotism or religion ultimately takes our lives.

When the Atomic Energy Commission described the country north of the Nevada Test Site as "virtually uninhabited desert terrain," my family and the birds at Great Salt Lake were some of the "virtual uninhabitants."

One night, I dreamed women from all over the world circled a blazing fire in the desert. They spoke of change, how they hold the moon in their bellies and wax and wane with its phases. They mocked the presumption of even-tempered beings and made promises that they would never fear the witch inside themselves. The women danced wildly as sparks broke away from the flames and entered the night sky as stars.

And they sang a song given to them by Shoshone grandmothers:

Ah ne nah, nah	Consider the rabbits
nin nah nah—	How gently they walk on the earth—
ah ne nah, nah	Consider the rabbits
nin nah nah—	How gently they walk on the earth—
Nyaga mutzi	We remember them
oh ne nay—	We can walk gently also—
Nyaga mutzi	We remember them
oh ne nay—	We can walk gently also—

The women danced and drummed and sang for weeks, preparing themselves for what was to come. They would reclaim the desert for the sake of their children, for the sake of the land.

A few miles downwind from the fire circle, bombs were being tested. Rabbits felt the tremors. Their soft leather pads on paws and feet recognized the shaking sands, while the roots of mesquite and sage were smoldering. Rocks were hot from the inside out and dust devils hummed unnaturally. And each time there was another nuclear test, ravens watched the desert heave. Stretch marks appeared. The land was losing its muscle.

The women couldn't bear it any longer. They were mothers. They had suffered labor pains but always under the promise of birth. The red hot pains beneath the desert promised death only, as each bomb became a stillborn. A contract had been made and broken between human beings and the land. A new contract was being drawn by the women, who understood the fate of the earth as their own.

Under the cover of darkness, ten women slipped under a barbed-wire fence and entered the contaminated country. They were trespassing. They walked toward the town of Mercury, in moonlight, taking their cues from coyote, kit fox, antelope squirrel, and quail. They moved quietly and deliberately through the maze of Joshua trees. When a hint of daylight appeared they rested, drinking tea and sharing their rations of food. The women closed their eyes. The time had come to protest with the heart, that to deny one's genealogy with the earth was to commit treason against one's soul.

At dawn, the women draped themselves in mylar, wrapping long streamers of silver plastic around their arms to blow in the breeze. They wore clear masks, that became the faces of humanity. And when they arrived at the edge of Mercury, they carried all the butterflies of a summer day in their wombs. They paused to allow their courage to settle.

The town that forbids pregnant women and children to enter because of radiation risks was asleep. The women moved through the streets as winged messengers, twirling around each other in slow motion, peeking inside homes and watching the easy sleep of men and women. They were astonished by each stillness and periodically would utter a shrill note or low cry just to verify life.

The residents finally awoke to these strange apparitions. Some simply stared. Others called authorities, and in time the women were apprehended by wary soldiers dressed in desert fatigues. They were taken to a white, square building on the other edge of Mercury. When asked who they were and why they were there, the women replied, "We are mothers and we have come to reclaim the desert for our children."

The soldiers arrested them. As the ten women were blindfolded and handcuffed, they began singing:

You can't forbid us everything
You can't forbid us to think—
You can't forbid our tears to flow
And you can't stop the songs that we sing.

The women continued to sing louder and louder, until they heard the voices of their sisters moving across the mess:

Ah ne nah, nah
nin nah nah—

Ah ne nah, nah
nin nah nah—
Nyaga mutzi
oh ne nay—
Nyaga mutzi
oh ne nay—

"Call for reinforcements," one soldier said.

"We have," interrupted one woman, "we have—and you have no idea of our numbers."

I crossed the line at the Nevada Test Site and was arrested with nine other Utahns for trespassing on military lands. They are still conducting nuclear tests in the desert. Ours was an act of civil disobedience. But as I walked toward the town of Mercury, it was more than a gesture of peace. It was a gesture on behalf of the Clan of One-Breasted Women.

As one officer cinched the handcuffs around my wrists, another frisked my body. She found a pen and a pad of paper tucked inside my left boot.

"And these?" she asked sternly.

"Weapons," I replied.

Our eyes met. I smiled. She pulled the leg of my trousers back over my boot.

"Step forward, please," she said as she took my arm.

We were booked under an afternoon sun and bused to Tonopah, Nevada. It was a two-hour ride. This was familiar country. The Joshua trees standing their ground had been named by my ancestors, who believed they looked like prophets pointing west to the Promised Land. These were the same trees that bloomed each spring, flowers appearing like white flames in the Mojave. And I recalled a full moon in May, when Mother and I had walked among them, flushing out mourning doves and owls.

The bus stopped short of town. We were released.

The officials thought it was a cruel joke to leave us stranded in the desert with no way to get home. What they didn't realize was that we were home, soul-centered and strong, women who recognized the sweet smell of sage as fuel for our spirits.

—1991

Learning from Other Writers

1. What chain of events leads the author to suspect that the aboveground atomic testing that took place in Nevada from January 27, 1951, through July 11, 1962, caused a higher than normal incidence of cancer in her family? Whom else does she seem to think was affected by these atomic tests?
2. What research did William carry out to investigate her theory? Where and how does she work these findings into her essay?
3. In the middle of the essay, Williams admits that she can't prove that her mother, grandmothers, or aunts "developed cancer from nuclear fallout in Utah." In what way does that affect the validity or usefulness of her essay?
4. What do you make of the dream sequence? Do you think that Williams actually dreamed this dream, or did she make the whole thing up?
5. How does the final section relate to the cause-and-effect structure at the core of "The Clan of One-Breasted Women"?

JANE BROX

INFLUENZA 1918

In ordinary times, the bankers, lawyers, and mill owners who lived on Tower Hill opened their doors to a quiet broken only by the jostle of a laden milk wagon, the first stirrings of a wind in the elms, or the quavering notes of a sparrow. It was the height of country; the air, sweet and clear. Looking east from their porches they could survey miles of red-brick textile mills that banked the canals and the sluggish Merrimack, as well as the broad central plain mazed with tenements. To their west was a patchwork of small dairy holdings giving over to the blue distance. But for the thirty-one mornings of October 1918 those men adjusted gauze masks over their mouths and noses as they set out for work in the cold-tinged dawn, and they kept their eyes to the ground so as not to see what they couldn't help but hear: the clatter of motorcars and horse-drawn wagons over the paving stones, as day and night without ceasing the ambulances ran up the hill bringing sufferers from the heart of the city and the hearses carried them away.

It had started as a seemingly common thing—what the line-storm season always brings, born on its wind and on our breath, something that would run its course in the comfort of camphor and bed rest. At first there had been no more than six or eight or ten cases a day reported in the city, and such news hardly took up a side column in the papers, which were full of soldiers' obituaries and reports of a weakening Germany. As September wore on, however, the death notices of victims of the flu began to outnumber the casualties of war. Finally it laid low so many the Lawrence Board of Health set aside its usual work of granting permits to keep roosters, charting the milk supply, and inspecting tenements. The flu took up all its talk—how it was to be treated, how contained, how to stay ahead of the dead. The sufferers needed fresh air and isolation, and their care had to be consolidated to make the most of the scarce nurses and orderlies. So the board took a page from other stricken cities and voted to construct a makeshift tent hospital on their highest, most open land that offered the best air, which was the leeward side of Tower Hill where a farm still spread across the slope.

Lawrence, Massachusetts, in 1918 was largely a city of immigrants who had come for work in the textile mills. Most had been in the city for only a short time and still spoke Polish, Arabic, French, Italian, German—forty-five different languages and dialects within the few square miles of the central district. They made worsteds and woolens; they were dyers, cutters, and weavers. They fixed the looms, rigged the warps, and felt along the yardage for slubs, working more than fifty hours a week, breathing in air white with cloth dust. At home they breathed in the smells of rubbish and night soil that drifted up from the alleyways between tenements. Where they lived was low-lying, so such smells, together with smoke and ash, hung in the air. Their heat was sparse. They were crowded into their rooms. The flu cut right through, spreading ahead of its own rumors, passing on a handshake and on the wind and with the lightest kiss. No spitting. No sharing food. Keep your hands clean. Avoid crowds. Walk everywhere. Sleep with your windows open.

They slept to the sound of rain—rain pouring from their gutterless roofs turning the alleyways into thick mud, rain on the wandering hens pecking at stones in the streets, rain on the silenced pigeons puffed and caged in their coops. At times it was hard, driven from the north like mare's hooves on their roofs, drowning the parsley and oregano set in enamel basins on the window ledges. Other times it fell soft and fine out of a pale gray sky, making circles fragile as wrists on the surfaces of the canals before being lost to the brown, frothy water there. And sometimes it was no more than a mist that settled in the low places, obscuring the bottoms of the stairwells and the barrels and the piles of sawdust, only to shift and reveal the same world as always. Then the rain would gather its strength again, seeming to rake their lives all that much harder. Scrap coal couldn't keep away its chill.

A doctor may as well have gone house to house down Common, Haverhill, and Jackson streets, so numerous were the cases. Often his knock would go unanswered, since it wasn't the family who had sought him out. More likely the sickness had been reported by their landlord or neighbor—afraid that the influenza would spread—so the doctor heard a sudden silence within and a face at the window disappearing into shadow. What kept the families from responding wasn't a lack of a common language so much as the fear that the doctor would tack a card to the door warning of the infection within, and the greater fear that their sick children would be ordered to the tent hospital. Once there, they wouldn't be seen again until they were dead or cured.

When the doctor finally gained entrance—at times with the help of the police—he could find whole families had been laid low, with the sick tending those who were sicker. They had sacks of camphor around their necks, or mustard spread on their chests, a cup of chamomile by the cot. Whiskey. Garlic and onions weighed in the air. Some sufferers lay in windowless rooms where the damp had kept in the smoke from a low coal fire, and what light there was wavered from a kerosene lamp. Almost always the disease had gone beyond a cough and aches and a runny nose. There was blood mixed in with their phlegm, and they couldn't move from their beds. In the worst cases their skin was tinted blue.

One doctor could see hundreds of cases a day, and in his haste to complete his records, he sometimes left out the ages of the victims and often the names. They come down now in the *Influenza Journal* distinguished only by their address or their nationality: *four Cases, 384 Common Street (downstairs)*. Or: *Mother and Child. Baby Rossano. Father and Son. A Syrian fellow. Polish man.* When the rain finally let up and days of mist lifted to bring on clear dry air, the number of influenza cases still didn't slow. Every woman who gave birth, it seems, died. The elderly, schoolchildren, and infants, yes—but strangest of all was how it took the young and healthy who had never been sick in their lives. Just yesterday they had worked a full day.

The entrance to the tent hospital on Tower Hill was clotted with ambulances arriving with patients and standing ambulances awaiting their dispatch orders. Many were still horse drawn, and the mares stood uneasy in the confusion. The motorized cars idled and choked the air with gasoline, the tang of which overlay the warm, familiar smells of hay and animal sweat. Everyone wore gauze masks, and there was no talk but orders. *Don't back up. Bring that one over here.* Nurses checked the pulse and color of patients and listened to their lungs. *We need more masks. Find me a doctor. Help me with this one.* The gate was patrolled by a military guard to assure that only the sufferers and those who tended them went beyond. Waiting black hacks stood three deep.

Every day at 5 A.M. a soldier blew reveille. The quick, bright notes parted the confusion at the entrance and gleamed above the hospital grounds—a far call from a country those patients no longer came from. The general din at the gate may as well have been the sound of a market day in a port city, and they, drowsing on a ship that had pulled away. They didn't stir. It was no concern of theirs, each in his or her own tent, the tent flap open to the back of a neighboring tent. Tents were arranged in rows, in wards, and in precincts, making a grid of the old hayfield. Its crickets were silent. Its summer birds had flown. Electrical wires hung on makeshift poles, and you could hear them swaying in the storms. The soaked canvas flanks of the tents ballooned in a wind and settled back on their frames. Boardwalks had been laid down between the tents, and footfalls, softened by the drenched wood, came near and receded. The nuns' habits swished. What country was this? A cough. A groan. The stricken tossed in their fevers. Their muscles ached. One moment they had the sweats; the next, chills. In forty-five different languages and dialects they called for water and warmth.

Many were cared for in words they couldn't understand. The student nurses and sisters of Saint Jeanne d'Arc spoke both English and French, but to the Germans and Italians and Syrians their voices may just as well have been more soft rain. A face half covered with gauze leaned near their own. They were given water to drink. Cool cloths were placed on their brows. They were wrapped in blankets and wheeled outside for more air. Someone listened to their hearts and then to their bogged-down lungs. A spoonful of thick serum was lifted to their lips. Their toes and fingertips turned blue from a lack of oxygen. In many pneumonia set in.

It was the same suffering in each tent, in each ward, in each precinct of the hospital. And the same in the surrounding country, in all cities, in all the known nations of the world. It struck those already stricken with war in the military camps, the troop ships, the trenches, in the besieged villages along the Meuse, in the devastated plain called the Somme, in the Argonne woods. It struck those who knew nothing of the war—all the Eskimos in a remote outpost, villagers in China. Some died without having given it a name. Others called it "the grippe," the flu—influenza—meaning "under the influence of the stars," under Orion and the Southern Cross, under the Bear, the Pole Star, and the Pleiades.

When care failed in the Tower Hill hospital, the sisters of Saint Jeanne d'Arc closed the eyes of the dead, blessed the body in the language that they knew, blessed themselves, and closed the tent flap. The sisters on the next shift said a last prayer in front of each closed tent and turned to the living.

In the central city those who were spared became captive to a strange, altered music. All the sounds of their streets—voices and songs, teams hauling loads over paving stones, elm whips cracking the air and animals, bottles nudging one another in the back of a truck, the deliberate tread of the iceman on their stairs—all these were no longer heard. Or they weren't heard as usual. Survivors strained at the absence, as if they were listening for flowing water after a cold snap, water now trapped and nearly silenced by clear ice. Schools and movie houses had been ordered closed and bolted shut; public gatherings were curtailed. Workers, their numbers halved, walked down Essex Street to the mills in a slackened ribbon. Their tamped-down gossip touched only on who had been stricken, who had died in the night. They traded preventions and cures, some wearing masks, others with garlic hung around their necks. More pronounced than the usual smells of the fouled canals or lanolin or grease were the head-clearing scents of camphor and carbolic soap.

The flow of supply wagons slowed as well. There was no commerce in bolts of velvet, silk puffs, worsted suits, or pianos. Bakers who used to shape one hundred granary loaves a day—split and seeded and washed with a glaze of milk—took to preparing fifty or sixty unadorned loaves. In the corner groceries, scab spread on the early apple crop, grapes softened then soured, and pears turned overripe in their crates.

The absence filled with uncommon sounds. Children with nowhere to go played in the streets and in the parks as if it were another kind of summer. They sang their jump-rope songs and called out sides in the letups between rains. The pharmacies swarmed with customers looking for Vaporub, germicide, and ice. And all the carpenters—whether they had formerly spent their days roughing out tenements or carving details into table legs—had turned to making pine boxes. Their sawing and the sound of bright nails driving into soft wood could be heard long into the night. Even so, coffins remained scarce and expensive.

The streets running up to Tower Hill rushed with ambulances, police cars, and fire engines. The alleyways and side streets were clogged with passing funerals. Meager corteges were everywhere—there, out of the corner of an eye, or coming straight on. In hopes of slowing the spread of the epidemic, the board of health had limited the size of the funerals to one carriage. They prohibited church services for the dead, and forbade anyone other than the immediate family to accompany the coffin. So, a black hack or a utility wagon with a loose knot of mourners following on foot behind was all. Some of the grieving were sick themselves, some barely recovered, and they had trouble keeping up if the hack driver was proceeding faster than he should—there were so many, had been so many, and someone else was waiting for his services. The processions appeared to be blown by a directionless wind down home streets past the millworks and across the bridge to the burial grounds on the outskirts of the city.

The mourners entered a place starred with freshly closed graves and open graves with piles of earth next to them—clay, sea-worn gravel, sodden sandy loam. The gravediggers kept on shoveling—they had long stopped looking up from their work. Even so, they couldn't stay ahead, and most of the coffins had to be escorted to the yard and left near the entrance along with others to await a later burial. Few of the processions were accompanied by ministers or priests. The parents or children or sisters of the deceased bowed their heads and said their own prayers. Perhaps they threw a handful of earth on the set-aside box. Maybe they lay a clutch of asters on the top. So plain and unsacred, it may just as well have been a death in the wilderness. Small. A winter spider crawling across an old white wall.

"We knew it was serious, but we didn't know how serious," my father says. The farm is less than five miles to the west of Lawrence, but by the time news reached here, it was muted and slowed—no more than a rumor on the sea winds biting in from Cape Ann. Their eastward view was open then, and they could see the leeward slope of Tower Hill, though it was far enough away to appear plainly blue. On the first of October 1918 they woke to see the flanks of those white canvas tents set in columns and rows across the hill. And that night the horizon was so crowded with lights that it must have seemed as if the heart of the city had grown closer.

As in the city, whole families on some farms were stricken, others spared. His family was spared—all he knew of the flu then was white chips of camphor in an old sock around his neck, and his mother whispering to his father in the evenings: "You'll bring it here...." His aunt and uncle, who had a nearby farm, and his cousins all came down with it in turn. It had begun when his uncle, for all his old strength, just couldn't get up. His aunt cared for him, until the whole household was confined to their beds. No doctor came. My grandfather, after he had tended his own herd, saw to theirs—to their water and grain, as well as the milking. He drew water for the house and brought them bread. He'd light the fires and bring in a day's supply of wood. Even so, with the windows open the rooms felt as cold as quarried granite.

The last to contract it, the youngest boy, died. The parents, still weak, were slow to perform the offices of the strong. They washed the body and had to rest. It seemed to take most of a day to make a respectable, small pine coffin. They cleaned the front room, set the coffin in the bay window, and took their turns sitting beside it. Not even small things were the same. Not the rust-colored chrysanthemums blooming against the kitchen door. Not the lingering fragrance of thyme and mint in the yard.

And the large things to be done—the work that had waited all through their sickness—waited still and weighed heavier. It was late enough in the year so that the weeding didn't matter anymore. But carrots, potatoes, and cabbages had to be harvested and stored. Wood to be gotten in. The late apple tree was laden with fruit—Ben Davis apples would cling to the branches all winter if you let them. Enough work to fill their days for as long as they could foresee.

There are two small, walled-in graveyards in the middle of our farm. They seem odd and adrift now among our fields and woods, though in the early part of this century there had been a Protestant church adjoining them. It was pulled down for salvage sometime in the forties, and its granite steps are now my parents' doorstone. My father sits on one of the pews when he pulls off his work boots. He will be buried among those graves, just up the hill behind a white birch. But in those years only the names of the settlers—Richardson, Coburn, Clough—had been chiseled into the stones. It wasn't a place for recent immigrants to be buried, so his uncle's family walked behind the coffin to Lawrence and set their child beside all the recent victims in the city. The mounds of earth beside the open graves were composed of heavier and stonier soils than any they had cultivated in the arid land they had been born to. Impossible to return to that country now, though they said their words in Arabic before turning west out of the gate.

For another week after the funeral they could still see the tents, white in the new days, just like yesterday. Then at the end of October the epidemic broke, the fires were banked. The tent hospital was taken down in a driving rain, and the stricken were moved to winter quarters at the General Hospital. At night Tower Hill once again appeared darker than the night sky. Predictable quiet returned to the neighborhood of mill owners, bankers, lawyers. The schools opened again, then the theaters. The policemen and firemen took off their gauze masks. On the twelfth of November, even the Red Cross workers marched in the Victory Day parade. When the city looked up, they counted more dead of the flu than of the war.

The winter of 1918 was so cold that the water over the Lawrence dam froze and had to be dynamited. The following spring, the field where the tent hospital had stood was seeded in hay. It was mown three times that summer and winds swept the timothy and redtop. Here, after the child had become bone, a liturgy was said for him. A child whose life is no longer given a name or a length, so short it is remembered by the one fact of his death.

It is a summer evening, and my father sits on his porch, looking at our own horizon. The long simple line of the hill is gone. Pine and maple have grown up and buildings square off against the sky. Out of nowhere he mentions the lights of the tent hospital, as if he could still see them, strange and clear.

Author's Note

I am indebted to the Immigrant City Archives Historical Society of Lawrence, Massachusetts, where I was able to consult the *Records of the Board of Health, January 1918–April 1931,* and the *Board of Health Influenza Journal,* 1918–1920. In addition, the Archives house recordings of oral histories. Listening to these voices was invaluable to my understanding of the atmosphere of the time. The recordings made of the recollections of Daniel Murphy and Sister Jeanne d'Arc were particularly helpful. I am also indebted to Alfred Crosby's *America's Forgotten Pandemic: The Influenza of 1918* (Cambridge: Cambridge University Press, 1989) and to two local newspapers, the *Lawrence Telegram* and the *Lawrence Sun American* (September–November 1918).

—1995

Learning from Other Writers

1. Why does Brox interrupt her narrative of the unfolding epidemic to insert a sociological description of Lawrence?
2. How does the author know that the mill workers "slept to the sound of rain," let alone that the rain fell on the "wandering hens pecking at stones in the streets" or that at times the rain fell "soft and fine out of a pale gray sky, making circles fragile as wrists on the surfaces

of the canals before being lost to the brown, frothy water there"? Find Brox's reference to a "winter spider crawling across an old white wall." Is that a real spider? If not, what is it doing in the essay?

3. In paragraphs five, six, and seven, is Brox describing the activities of a specific (real) doctor or a made-up (invented/composite) doctor? How does your answer to this question influence your willingness to believe the scenes she describes?
4. What is the effect of Brox's decision to wait so long to insert her father's quote ("We knew it was serious, but we didn't know how serious") and inform us that he lived on a farm less than five miles from Lawrence and that his uncle's family came down with the flu and his youngest cousin died?
5. What conditions affected the way the influenza epidemic of 1918 unfolded in Lawrence? What short- and long-term effects does Brox attribute to the epidemic? In each case, does she prove that these causes and effects are linked, or does she merely suggest that such relationships are plausible?

ADAM ROGERS

GEEK LOVE

Gary Gygax died last week and the universe did not collapse. This surprises me a little bit, because he built it.

I'm not talking about the cosmological, Big Bang part. Everyone who reads blogs knows that a flying spaghetti monster made all that. But Mr. Gygax co-created the game Dungeons & Dragons, and on that foundation of role-playing and polyhedral dice he constructed the social and intellectual structure of our world.

Dungeons & Dragons was a brilliant pastiche, mashing together tabletop war games, the Conan-the-Barbarian tales of Robert E. Howard and a magic trick from the fantasy writer Jack Vance with a dash of Bulfinch's mythology, a bit of the Bible and a heaping helping of J. R. R. Tolkien.

Mr. Gygax's genius was to give players a way to inhabit the characters inside their games, rather than to merely command faceless hordes, as you did in, say, the board game Risk. Roll the dice and you generated a character who was quantified by personal attributes like strength or intelligence.

You also got to pick your moral alignment, like whether you were "lawful good" or "chaotic evil." And you could buy swords and fight dragons. It was cool.

Yes, I played a little. In junior high and even later. Lawful good paladin. Had a flaming sword. It did not make me popular with the ladies, or indeed with anyone. Neither did my affinity for geometry, nor my ability to recite all of *Star Wars* from memory.

Yet on the strength of those skills and others like them, I now find myself on top of the world. Not wealthy or in charge or even particularly popular, but in instead of out. The stuff I know, the geeky stuff, is the stuff you and everyone else has to know now, too.

We live in Gary Gygax's world. The most popular books on earth are fantasy novels about wizards and magic swords. The most popular movies are about characters from superhero comic books.

The most popular TV shows look like elaborate role-playing games: intricate, hidden-clue-laden science fiction stories connected to impossibly mathematical games that live both online and in the real world. And you, the viewer, can play only if you've sufficiently mastered your home-entertainment command center so that it can download a snippet of audio to your iPhone, process it backward with beluga whale harmonic sequences and then podcast the results to the members of your Yahoo group.

Even in the heyday of Dungeons & Dragons, when his company was selling millions of copies and parents feared that the game was somehow related to Satan worship, Mr. Gygax's creation seemed like a niche product. Kids played it in basements instead of socializing. (To be fair, you needed at least three people to play—two adventurers and one Dungeon Master to guide the game—so Dungeons & Dragons was social. Demented and sad, but social.) Nevertheless, the game taught the right lessons to the right people.

Geeks like algorithms. We like sets of rules that guide future behavior. But people, normal people, consistently act outside rule sets. People are messy and unpredictable, until you have something like the Dungeons & Dragons character sheet. Once you've broken down the elements of an invented personality into numbers generated from dice, paper and pencil, you can do the same for your real self.

For us, the character sheet and the rules for adventuring in an imaginary world became a manual for how people are put together. Life could be lived as a kind of vast, always-on role-playing campaign.

Don't give me that look. I know I'm not a paladin, and I know I don't live in the Matrix. But the realization that everyone else was engaged in role-playing all the time gave my universe rules and order.

We geeks might not be able to intuit the subtext of a facial expression or a casual phrase, but give us a behavioral algorithm and human interactions become a data stream. We can process what's going on in the heads of the people around us. Through careful observation of body language and awkward silences, we can even learn to detect when we are bringing the party down with our analysis of how loop quantum gravity helps explain the time travel in that new *Terminator* TV show. I mean, so I hear.

Mr. Gygax's game allowed geeks to venture out of our dungeons, blinking against the light, just in time to create the present age of electronic miracles.

Dungeons & Dragons begat one of the first computer games, a swords-and-sorcery dungeon crawl called Adventure. In the late 1970s, the two games provided the narrative framework for the first fantasy-based computer worlds played by multiple, remotely connected users. They were called multi-user dungeons back then, and they were mostly the province of students at the Massachusetts Institute of Technology. But they required the same careful construction of virtual identities that Mr. Gygax had introduced to gaming.

Today millions of people are slaves to Gary Gygax. They play EverQuest and World of Warcraft, and someone must still be hanging out in Second Life. (That "massively multiplayer" computer traffic, by the way, also helped drive the development of the sort of huge server clouds that power Google.)

But that's just gaming culture, more pervasive than it was in 1974 when Dungeons & Dragons was created and certainly more profitable—today it's estimated to be a $40 billion-a-year business—but still a little bit nerdy. Delete the dragon-slaying, though, and you're left with something much more mainstream: Facebook, a vast, interconnected universe populated by avatars.

Facebook and other social networks ask people to create a character—one based on the user, sure, but still a distinct entity. Your character then builds relationships by connecting to other characters. Like Dungeons & Dragons, this is not a competitive game. There's no way to win. You just play.

This diverse evolution from Mr. Gygax's 1970s dungeon goes much further. Every Gmail login, every instant-messaging screen name, every public photo collection on Flickr, every blog-commenting alias is a newly manifested identity, a character playing the real world.

We don't have to say goodbye to Gary Gygax, the architect of the now. Every time I make a practical move (like when I suggest to my wife this summer that we should see *Iron Man* instead of *The Dark Knight*), I'm counting my experience points, hoping I have enough dexterity and rolling the dice. And every time, Mr. Gygax is there—quasi-mystical, glowing in blue and bearing a simple game that was an elegant weapon from a more civilized age.

That was a reference to *Star Wars*. Cool, right?

—2008

Learning from Other Writers

1. In the first two paragraphs of "Geek Love," the author makes intentionally grandiose claims for various cause-and-effect relationships. How does this strategy influence your reading of the essay that follows?
2. Is Rogers writing for an audience of gamers? A more general audience? Both?
3. How satisfying do you find his explanations of Gary Gygax's contributions to our culture?
4. If we take Gygax's "genius" in giving players "a way to inhabit characters inside their games" as the primary cause in the chain of cause-and-effect relationships that structure Rogers's essay, what effect does Rogers claim was produced by that initial cause? What effect does Rogers claim *that* effect produces? Can you label the entire chain of causes and effects that structure this essay?
5. What, if anything, qualifies Rogers to write this essay? Does he offer any proof for his arguments? Do you find his claims for the existence of this chain of causes and effects to be convincing?

INSPIRATIONS: ON THE DAY I WAS BORN ...

1. You guessed it: the idea here is to make a trip to the periodicals room of your favorite library and search through newspapers or magazines from the day (or week) of your birth until you find an event or an invention, a book, movie, an article of clothing, or other product that affected your life and the lives of some larger segment of the population, then write an essay in which you make a case for the existence of this cause-and-effect relationship and explain its larger significance.
2. Be careful to distinguish between a *causal* relationship, in which one event can be proved to have caused another event, and a *noncausal* relationship, in which two events happen at the same time or in sequence but don't necessarily affect one another (i.e., unless you are writing a humor piece, you probably won't want to blame your propensity to fall in love with the wrong people on the satellite that landed on Venus the day you were born). Like Terry Tempest Williams, you needn't prove beyond a doubt that a causal relationship exists, but you should be able to convince your readers that a causal link is possible or plausible or (best of all) highly likely.
3. If the effects of the phenomenon you've chosen seem too small to warrant an essay or if you're finding it difficult to prove the existence of a link between the invention or historical event you've chosen and the fairly major effect on society you're claiming it produced, try structuring your essay as a series of smaller cause-and-effect relationships (i.e., one domino falls and hits another domino, which hits another domino, which hits another), as Adam Rogers does when proving his claims in "Geek Love."

Variations and Inventions

MEDITATIVE ESSAYS

The meditative essay is not a separate form, but rather a stylistic variation on the forms we've already discussed. Any nonfiction structure can lend itself to a heavier or lighter dose of meditation, according to the writer's taste. An analogy to fiction might help to make this clear. Minimalists such as Raymond Carver or Amy Hempel convey the meaning of a scene by selection and indirection rather than by overt thematic exposition, while maximalists such as John Updike, Philip Roth, Susan Sontag, and Milan Kundera layer their scenes with trowelfuls of philosophizing. So, too, nonfiction minimalists such as Joseph Mitchell, Primo Levi, John Hersey, or Jane Brox rely mostly on the objective presentation of scenes to get across their points, as opposed to Annie Dillard's injection of her own elaborate meditations into her profile of Dave Rahm in "The Stunt Pilot" or Terry Tempest Williams's direct revelation of her suspicions that radiation from nuclear testing in the 1950s made her family ill.

As discussed in Part I, most of us find it difficult to engage in abstract reasoning without our essays floating off into vague, clichéd prose and empty rhetoric, circling around a general topic for two or three pages, then dying a leaden death. As we've also seen, the interplay between your essay's central question and a natural, organic form can help to *generate* your meditation. You start with your central question, then move a step ahead in time or space as suggested by your form, which leads you to ponder your question in a more specific way, after which you move another step along the path. At one end of the spectrum, the essay's meaning is created by selection or hinted at by indirection, with little if any analysis on the page. At the other end of that same spectrum, the formal seeds of the meditation may be compressed so tightly that the reader barely recognizes the structure's presence or the ways in which a personal experience or a journey, an experiment or an interview or a visit to a museum might have served to generate the meditation; the writer compresses the essay's structure down to its barest kernel and allows his or her meditations to explode outward, popcorn-wise, from there.

In Charles Baxter's "Dysfunctional Narratives: or: 'Mistakes Were Made,'" we can reconstruct the ways in which the author's meditations were occasioned by a reading of Richard Nixon's autobiography *RN*, which led him to ruminate on Nixon's infamous nonadmission of wrongdoing in the Watergate scandal and the way this exerted a pall of moral passivity over the generations that followed, in literary as well as political terms. Taken as a whole, the essay's brilliance is daunting, not least because Baxter's meditations seem to spring full-blown from his brain. And with all due respect to the advantages of youth, when you're hoping to produce a sustained meditation on what's gone wrong with your society, it helps to have lived a long time and read a lot of books and thought a great deal about what's going on in the world.

But if you take it step by step, you can see that Baxter has simply knocked over the first domino in his chain of causes and effects, then carried us along as he meditates on what effect each domino produced. Starting with the notion that Nixon's tendency to shun responsibility for his mistakes affected the tenor of succeeding administrations, Baxter notes that this led to a "climate in which social narratives are designed to be deliberately incoherent and misleading," which caused (or went hand-in-hand with) our national tendency to fall prey to conspiracy theories, which caused ... which caused ... and so on.

Rather than feel daunted by the prospect of giving birth to a lengthy and erudite meditation the way Zeus gave birth to Athena full-grown from his brow, you can start with a question that strikes you as important, couple it with one of the basic structures in this book (in Baxter's case, the dominoes form we discussed in the previous chapter), and see where your question leads you. Some writers will find that their meditations grow slowly, one paragraph here, another sentence there, over the course of an essay. Other writers find that the friction between a specific question and a form, catalyzed by a spark of intellectual confidence, ignites a firestorm of meditation that consumes most of the resulting essay. Neither method is necessarily superior to the other. No matter your temperament, no matter your question or your form, the basic process is the same.

ARGUMENTATIVE ESSAYS

You can see the same principles at work if you consider the argumentative essay, a type of writing that generally is regarded as outside the realm of creative nonfiction. At first glance, this division makes sense, given that argumentative essays aren't usually noted for their creative or poetic language, often concern themselves with proving a thesis rather than exploring a central question, tend to rely on exposition, evidence, and logic rather than on narrative or scene to support that thesis, and in many cases follow the basic five-paragraph structure we learned in elementary school rather than any of the organic forms we have considered in this book.

But these distinctions are artificial. Just because argumentative essays often are written in wooden or pseudoacademic prose doesn't mean that they *must* be. At the very least, people who write argumentative essays can strive to keep their language natural, specific, and jargon free. And even though an argumentative essay, by definition, must prove a thesis to be true, the give-and-take between the writer's position and whatever possible counterarguments a reader might present allows us to view any thesis as a question. The orator in a rant like Jamaica Kincaid's "On Seeing England for the First Time" (which is included in this chapter) isn't merely hammering us over the head with an argument that she already has settled in her mind; if you listen carefully, you can hear Kincaid arguing with any readers who might accuse her of being mean-spirited or unfair in presenting such a view (if you listen even more carefully, you can hear her argue with herself).

Argumentative essays usually rely more on exposition than scenic writing, but nothing precludes the writer from using scenes and anecdotes to prove a point. Nor is there any reason that an essay's arguments can't be structured according to a narrative, journey, profile, group portrait, or collage; in each case, the writer of an argumentative essay simply arrives at a more definitive answer to his or her question than might be true for other examples of the form. To see what I mean, consider such powerful yet artistic examples as Leslie Marmon Silko's "In the Combat Zone" (reproduced in this chapter) and Richard Rodriguez's frequently reprinted (and much debated) "Aria: A Memoir of a Bilingual Childhood,"[1] in which the authors use the personal narrative to structure and support their arguments (Silko is in favor of women carrying concealed weapons, while Rodriguez argues against the necessity of providing bilingual education in public schools), as well as Kincaid's listlike tirade against the emphasis that her teachers and parents placed on the wonders and glories of England when she was growing up in the West Indies.

---

[1] "Aria" can be found in *Hunger of Memory: The Education of Richard Rodriguez*, which was originally published by David R. Godine in 1982 and is available in several more recent paperback editions.

CHARLES BAXTER

DYSFUNCTIONAL NARRATIVES: OR: "MISTAKES WERE MADE"

Here are some sentences of distinctive American prose from our era:

> From a combination of hypersensitivity and a desire not to know the truth in case it turned out to be unpleasant, I had spent the last ten months putting off a confrontation with John Mitchell.... I listened to more tapes.... I heard Haldeman tell me that Dean and Mitchell had come up with a plan to handle the problem of the investigation's going into areas we didn't want it to go. The plan was to call in Helms and Walters of the CIA and have them restrain the FBI.... Haldeman and I discussed [on the "smoking gun" tape] having the CIA limit the FBI investigation for political rather than the national security reasons I had given in my public statements.... On June 13, while I was in Egypt, Fred Buzhardt had suffered a heart attack. Once I was assured that he was going to pull through, I tried to assess the impact his illness would have on our legal situation.

These sentences are almost enough to make one nostalgic for an adversary with a claim upon our attention. There he is, the lawyer-president setting forth the brief for the defense, practicing the dogged art of the disclaimer in *RN: The Memoirs of Richard Nixon*. I've done some cut-and-pasting, but the sentences I've quoted are the sentences he wrote. And what sentences! Leaden and dulling, juridical-minded to the last, impersonal but not without savor—the hapless Buzhardt and his heart attack factored into the "legal situation," and that wonderful "hypersensitivity" combined with a desire "not to know the truth" that makes one think of Henry James's Lambert Strether or an epicene character in Huysmans—they present the reader with camouflage masked as objective thought.

The author of the memoir does not admit that he lied, exactly, or that he betrayed his oath of office. In his "public statements," he did a bit of false accounting, that was all. One should expect this, he suggests, from heads of state.

Indeed, the only surprise this reader had, trudging gamely through *RN* looking for clues to a badly defined mystery, was the author's report of a sentence uttered by Jacqueline Kennedy. Touring the White House after RN's election, she said, "I always live in a dream world." Funny that she would say so; funny that he would notice, and remember.

Lately I've been possessed of a singularly unhappy idea: The greatest influence on American fiction for the last twenty years may have been the author of *RN*, not in the writing but in the public character. He is the inventor, for our purposes and for our time, of the concept of *deniability*. Deniability is the almost complete disavowal of intention in relation to bad consequences. A made-up word, it reeks of the landfill-scented landscape of lawyers and litigation and high school. Following Richard Nixon in influence on recent fiction would be two runners-up, Ronald Reagan and George Bush. Their administrations put the passive voice, politically, on the rhetorical map. In their efforts to attain deniability on the arms-for-hostages deal with Iran, their administrations managed to achieve considerable notoriety for self-righteousness, public befuddlement about facts, forgetfulness under oath, and constant disavowals of political error and criminality, culminating in the quasi-confessional passive-voice-mode sentence, "Mistakes were made."

Contrast this with Robert E. Lee's statement the third day after the battle of Gettysburg and the calamity of Pickett's Charge: "All this has been my fault," Lee said. "I asked more of men than should have been asked of them."

Lee's sentences have a slightly antique ring. People just don't say such things anymore.

What difference does it make to writers of stories if public figures are denying their responsibility for their own actions? So what if they are, in effect, refusing to tell their own stories accurately? So what if the President of the United States is making himself out to be, of all things, a *victim*? Well, to make an obvious point, they create a climate in which social narratives are designed to be deliberately incoherent and misleading. Such narratives humiliate the act of storytelling. You can argue that only a coherent narrative can manage to explain public events, and you can reconstruct a story if someone says, "I made a mistake," or "We did that." You can't reconstruct a story—you can't even know what the story *is*—if everyone is saying, "Mistakes were made." Who made them? Everybody made them and no one did, and it's history anyway, so let's forget about it. Every story is a history, however, and when there is no comprehensible story, there is no history. The past, under these circumstances, becomes an unreadable mess. When we hear words like "deniability," we are in the presence of narrative dysfunction, a phrase employed by the poet C. K. Williams to describe the process by which we lose track of the story of ourselves, the story that tells us who we are supposed to be and how we are supposed to act.

The spiritual godfather of the contemporary disavowal movement, the author of *RN*, set the tenor for the times and reflected the times as well in his lifelong denial of responsibility for the Watergate break-in and cover-up. He has claimed that misjudgments were made, although not necessarily by him. Mistakes were made, although they were by no means his own, and the crimes that were committed were only crimes if you define "crime" in a certain way, in the way, for example, that his enemies like to define the word, in a manner that would be unfavorable to him, that would give him, to use a word derived from the Latin, some culpability. It wasn't the law, he claimed. It was all just politics.

A curious parallel: The Kennedy assassination may be *the* narratively dysfunctional event of our era. No one really knows who's responsible for it. One of the signs of a dysfunctional narrative is that we cannot leave it behind, and we cannot put it to rest, because it does not, finally, give us the explanation we need to enclose it. We don't know who the agent of the action is. We don't even know why it was done. Instead of achieving closure, the story spreads over the landscape like a stain as we struggle to find a source of responsibility. In our time, responsibility without narratives has been consistently displaced by its enigmatic counterpart, conspiracy. Conspiracy works in tandem with narrative repression, the repression of who-has-done-what. We go back over the Kennedy assassination second by second, frame by frame, but there is a truth to it that we cannot get at because we can't be sure who really did it or what the motivations were. Everyone who claims to have closed the case simply establishes that the case will stay open. The result of dysfunctional narrative, as the poet Lawrence Joseph has suggested to me, is sorrow; I would argue that it is sorrow mixed with depression or rage, the condition of the abject, but in any case we are talking about the psychic landscape of trauma and paralysis, the landscape of, for example, two outwardly different writers, Don DeLillo (in most of *Libra*) and Jane Smiley (in the last one hundred pages of *A Thousand Acres*).

Jane Smiley's novel has been compared to *King Lear*, and its plot invites the comparison, but its real ancestors in fiction are the novels of Émile Zola. *A Thousand Acres* is Zola on the plains. Like Zola, Jane Smiley assembles precisely and carefully a collection of facts, a naturalistic pileup of details about—in this case—farming and land use. As for characters, the reader encounters articulate women (including the narrator, Rose) and mostly frustrated inarticulate men driven by blank desires, like Larry, the Lear figure. Lear, however, is articulate. Larry is not. He is like one of Zola's male characters, driven by urges he does not understand or even acknowledge.

Somewhat in the manner of other naturalistic narratives, *A Thousand Acres* causes its characters to behave like mechanisms, under obscure orders. Wry but humorless, shorn of poetry or any lyric outburst, and brilliantly observant and relentless, the novel at first seems to be about 1980s greed and the destruction of resources that we now associate with Reaganism, a literally exploitative husbandry. Such a story would reveal clear if deplorable motives in its various characters. But no: The book is about the essential criminality of furtive male desire. With the revelation of Larry's sexual abuse of his daughters, in a recovered memory scene not so much out of Zola as *Geraldo*, it shifts direction toward an account of conspiracy and memory, sorrow and depression, in which several of the major characters are acting out rather than acting, and doing their best to find someone to blame.

The characters' emotions are thus preordained, and the narrator gathers around herself a cloak of unreliability as the novel goes on. It is a moody novel, but the mood itself often seems impenetrable, because the characters, including the men, are not acting upon events in present narrative time but are reacting obscurely to harms done to them in the psychic past from unthinkable impulses that will go forever unexplained. Enacting greed at least involves making some decisions, but in this novel, the urge to enact incest upon one's daughter is beyond thought, if not the judicial system, and, in turn, creates consequences that are beyond thought. Rose herself lives in the shadow of thought. Throughout much of the book she is unaccountable, even to herself, by virtue of having been molested by her father. This is dysfunctional narrative as literary art, a novel that is also very much an artifact of *this* American era.

Watergate itself would have remained narratively dysfunctional if the tapes hadn't turned up, and, with them, the "smoking gun"—notice, by the way, the metaphors that we employ to designate narrative responsibility, the naming and placing of the phallically inopportune protagonist at the center. The arms-for-hostages deal is still a muddled narrative because various political functionaries are taking the fall for what the commander in chief is supposed to have decided himself. However, the commander in chief was not told; or he forgot; or he was out of the loop; or he didn't understand what was said to him. The buck stops here? In recent history, the buck doesn't stop anywhere. The buck keeps moving, endlessly. Perhaps we are in the era of the endlessly recirculating buck, the buck seeking a place to stop, like a story that cannot find its own ending.

We have been living in a political culture of disavowals. Disavowals follow from crimes for which no one is capable of claiming responsibility. Mistakes and crimes tend to create narratives, however, and they have done so from the time of the Greek tragedies. How can the contemporary disavowal movement not affect those of us who tell stories? We begin to move away from fiction of protagonists and antagonists into another mode, another model. It is hard to describe this model but I think it might be called the fiction of finger-pointing, the fiction of the quest for blame. It often culminates with a scene in a court of law.

In such fiction, people and events are often accused of turning the protagonist into the kind of person the protagonist is, usually an unhappy person. That's the whole story. When blame has been assigned, the story is over. In writing workshops, this kind of story is often the rule rather than the exception. Probably this model of storytelling has arisen because sizable population groups in our time feel confused and powerless, as they often do in mass societies when the mechanisms of power are carefully masked. For people with irregular employment and mounting debts and faithless partners and abusive parents, the most interesting feature of life is its unhappiness, its dull constant weight. But in a commodity culture, people are *supposed* to be happy. It's the one myth of advertising. You start to feel cheated if you're not happy. In such a consumerist climate, the perplexed and unhappy don't know what their lives are telling them, and they don't feel as if they are in charge of their own existence. No action they have ever taken is half as interesting to them as the consistency of their unhappiness.

Natural disasters, by contrast—earthquakes and floods—are narratively satisfying. We know what caused the misery, and we usually know what we can do to repair the damage, no matter how long it takes.

But corporate and social power, any power carefully masked and made conspiratorial, puts its victims into a state of frenzy, a result of narrative dysfunction. Somebody must be responsible for my pain. Someone *will* be found. Someone, usually close to home, *will* be blamed. TV loves dysfunctional families. Dysfunctional S&Ls and banks and corporate structures are not loved quite so much. They're harder to figure out. They like it that way. In this sense we have moved away from the naturalism of Zola or Frank Norris or Dreiser. Like them, we believe that people are often helpless, but we don't blame the corporations anymore. We blame the family, and we do it on afternoon TV talk shows, like *Oprah*.

Afternoon talk shows have only apparent antagonists. Their sparring partners are not real antagonists because the bad guys usually confess and then immediately disavow. The trouble with narratives without antagonists or a counterpoint to the central character—stories in which no one ever seems to be deciding anything or acting upon any motive except the search for a source of discontent—is that they tend formally to mirror the protagonists' unhappiness and confusion. Stories about being put-upon almost literally do not know what to look at. The visual details are muddled or indifferently described or excessively specific in nonpertinent situations. In any particular scene, everything is significant, and nothing is. The story is trying to find a source of meaning, but in the story everyone is disclaiming responsibility. Things have just happened.

When I hear the adjective "dysfunctional" now, I cringe. But I have to use it here to describe a structural unit (like the banking system, or the family, or narrative) whose outward appearance is intact but whose structural integrity has been compromised or has collapsed. No one is answerable from within it. Every event, every calamity, is unanswered, from the S&L collapse to the Exxon Valdez oil spill.

So we have created for ourselves a paradise of lawyers: We have an orgy of blame-finding on the one hand and disavowals of responsibility on the other.

All the recent debates and quarrels about taking responsibility as opposed to being a victim reflect bewilderment about whether in real life protagonists still exist or whether we are all minor characters, the objects of terrible forces. Of course, we are often both. But look at *Montel Williams*, or *Oprah*. (I have, I do, I can't help it.) For all the variety of the situations, the unwritten scripts are often similar. Someone is testifying because s/he's been hurt by someone else. The pain-inflicter is invariably present and accounted for onstage, and sometimes this person admits, abashedly, to inflicting the ruin: cheating, leaving, abusing, or murdering. Usually, however, there's no remorse or shame. Some other factor caused it: bad genes, alcoholism, drugs, or—the cause of last resort—Satan. For intellectuals it may be the patriarchy: some devil or other, but at least an *abstract* devil. In any case, the malefactor may be secretly pleased: s/he's on television and will be famous for fifteen minutes.

The audience's role is to comment on what the story means and to make a judgment about the players. Usually the audience members disagree and get into fights. The audience's judgment is required because the dramatis personae are incapable of judging themselves.

They generally will not say that they did what they did because they wanted to, or because they had *decided* to do it. The story is shocking. You hear gasps. But the participants are as baffled and as bewildered as everyone else. So we have the spectacle of utterly perplexed villains deprived of their villainy. Villainy, properly understood, gives someone a largeness, a sense of scale. It seems to me that this sense of scale has probably abandoned us.

What we have instead is not exactly drama and not exactly therapy. It exists in that twilight world between the two, very much of our time, where deniability reigns. Call it therapeutic narration. No verdict ever comes in. Every verdict is appealed. No one is in a position to judge. The spectacle makes the mind itch as if from an ideological rash. Hour after hour, week after week, these dysfunctional narratives are interrupted by commercials (on the Detroit affiliates) for lawyers.

But wait: Isn't there something deeply interesting and moving and sometimes even beautiful when a character acknowledges an error? And isn't this narrative mode becoming something of a rarity?

Most young writers have this experience: They create characters who are imaginative projections of themselves, minus the flaws. They put this character into a fictional world, wanting that character to be successful and—to use that word from high school—*popular*. They don't want these imaginative projections of themselves to make any mistakes, wittingly or, even better, unwittingly, or to demonstrate what Aristotle thought was the core of stories, flaws of character that produce intelligent misjudgments for which someone must take the responsibility.

What's an unwitting action? It's what we do when we have to act so quickly, or under so much pressure that we can't stop to take thought. It's not the same as an urge, which may well have a brooding and inscrutable quality. For some reason, such moments of unwitting action in life and in fiction feel enormously charged with energy and meaning.

It's difficult for fictional characters to acknowledge their mistakes, because then they become definitive: They *are* that person who did *that* thing. The only people who like to see characters performing such actions are readers. They love to see characters getting themselves into interesting trouble and defining themselves.

Lately, thinking about the nature of drama and our resistance to certain forms of it, I have been reading Aristotle's *Poetics* again and mulling over his definition of what makes a poet. A poet, Aristotle says, is first and foremost a maker, not of verses, but of plots. The poet creates an imitation, and what he imitates is an action.

It might be useful to make a distinction here between what I might call "me" protagonists and "I" protagonists. "Me" protagonists are largely objects—objects of impersonal forces or the actions of other people. They are central characters to whom things happen. They do not initiate action so much as receive it. They are largely reactionary, in the old sense of that term, and passive. They are figures of fate and destiny, and they tend to appear during periods of accelerated social change, such as the American 1880s and 1890s, and again in the 1980s.

The "I" protagonist, by contrast, makes certain decisions and takes some responsibility for them and for the actions that follow from them. This does not make the "I" protagonist admirable by any means. It's this kind of protagonist that Aristotle is talking about. Such a person, Aristotle says, is not outstanding for virtue or justice, and s/he arrives at ill fortune not because of any wickedness or vice, but because of some mistake that s/he makes. There's that word again, "mistake."

Sometimes—if we are writers—we have to talk to our characters. We have to try to persuade them to do what they've only imagined doing. We have to nudge but not force them toward situations where they will get into interesting trouble, where they will make interesting mistakes that they may take responsibility for. When we allow our characters to make mistakes, we release them from the grip of our own authorial narcissism. That's wonderful for them, it's wonderful for us, but it's best of all for the story.

A few instances: I once had a friend in graduate school who gave long, loud, and unpleasantly exciting parties in the middle of winter. He and his girlfriend usually considered these parties unsuccessful unless someone did something shocking or embarrassing or both—something you could talk about later. He lived on the third floor of an old house in Buffalo, New York, and his acquaintances regularly fell down the front and back stairs.

I thought of him recently when I was reading about Mary Butts, an English writer of short fiction who lived from 1890 to 1937. Her stories have now been reissued in a collection called *From Altar to Chimneypiece*. Virgil Thomson, who was gay, once proposed marriage to her, and says the following about her in his autobiography:

> I used to call her the "storm goddess," because she was at her best surrounded by cataclysm. She could stir up others with drink and drugs and magic incantations, and then when the cyclone was at its most intense, sit down at calm center and glow. All of her stories are of moments when the persons observed are caught up by something, inner or outer, so irresistible that their highest powers and all their lowest conditionings are exposed. The resulting action therefore is definitive, an ultimate clarification arrived at through ecstasy.

As it happens, I do not think that this is an accurate representation of Mary Butts's stories, which tend to be about crossing thresholds and stumbling into very strange spiritual dimensions. But I am interested in Thomson's thought concerning definitive action because I think the whole concept of definitive action is meeting up with considerable cultural resistance these days.

Thomson, describing his storm goddess, shows us a temptress, a joyful, worldly woman, quite possibly brilliant and bad to the bone. In real life people like this can be insufferable. Marriage to such a person would be a relentless adventure. They're constantly pushing their friends and acquaintances to lower their defenses and drop their masks and do something for which they will probably be sorry later. They like it when anyone blurts out a sudden admission, or acts on an impulse and messes up conventional arrangements. They like to see people squirm. They're *gleeful*. They prefer Bizet to Wagner; they're more Carmen than Sieglinde. They like it when people lunge at a desired object, and cacophony and wreckage are the result.

The morning after, you can say, "Mistakes were made," but with the people I've known, a phrase like "Mistakes were made" won't even buy you a cup of coffee. There is such a thing as the poetry of a mistake, and when you say, "Mistakes were made," you deprive an action of its poetry, and you sound like a weasel. When you say, "I fucked up," the action retains its meaning, its sordid origin, its obscenity, and its poetry. Poetry is quite compatible with obscenity.

Chekhov says in two of his letters, "... shun all descriptions of the characters' spiritual state. You must try to have that state emerge from their actions.... The artist must be only an impartial witness of his characters and what they said, not their judge." In Chekhov's view, a writer must try to release the story's characters from the aura of judgment that they've acquired simply because they're fictional.

In an atmosphere of constant moral judgment, characters are not often permitted to make interesting and intelligent mistakes and then to acknowledge them. The whole idea of the "intelligent mistake," the importance of the mistake made on an impulse, has gone out the window. Or, if fictional characters do make such mistakes, they're judged immediately and without appeal. One thinks of the attitudes of the aging Tolstoy and of his hatred of Shakespeare's and Chekhov's plays, and of his obsessive moralizing. He especially hated *King Lear*. He called it stupid, verbose, and incredible, and thought the craze for Shakespeare was like the tulip craze, a matter of mass hypnosis and "epidemic suggestion."

In the absence of any clear moral vision, we get moralizing instead. Moralizing in the 1990s has been inhibiting writers and making them nervous and irritable. Here is Mary Gaitskill, commenting on one of her own short stories, "The Girl on the Plane," in a recent *Best American Short Stories*. An account of a gang rape, the story apparently upset quite a few readers.

> In my opinion, most of us have not been taught how to be responsible for our thoughts and feelings. I see this strongly in the widespread tendency to read books and stories as if they exist to confirm how we are supposed to be, think, and feel. I'm not talking wacky political correctness. I'm talking mainstream.... Ladies and gentlemen, please. Stop asking "What am I supposed to feel?" Why would an adult look to me or to any other writer to tell him or her what to feel? You're not *supposed* to feel anything. You feel what you feel.

Behind the writer's loss of patience one can just manage to make out a literary culture begging for an authority figure, the same sort of figure that Chekhov refused for himself. Mary Gaitskill's interest in bad behavior and adulthood is that of the observer, not the judge. Unhappy readers want her to be both, as if stories should come prepackaged with discursive authorial opinions about her own characters. Her exasperation is a reflection of C. K. Williams's observation that in a period of dysfunctional narratives, the illogic of feeling erodes the logic of stories. When people can't make any narrative sense of their own feelings, readers start to ask writers to tell them what they are supposed to feel. They want moralizing polemics. Reading begins to be understood as a form of personal therapy or political action. In such an atmosphere, already moralized stories are more comforting than stories in which characters are making complex or unwitting mistakes. In such a setup, *Uncle Tom's Cabin* starts to look better than any other nineteenth-century American novel.

Marilynne Robinson, in her essay "Hearing Silence: Western Myth Reconsidered," calls the already moralized story, the therapeutic narrative, part of a "mean little myth" of our time. She notes, however, that "we have ceased to encode our myths in narrative as that word is traditionally understood. Now they shield themselves from our skepticism by taking on the appearance of scientific or political or economic discourse...." And what is this "mean little myth"?

> One is born and in passage through childhood suffers some grave harm. Subsequent good fortune is meaningless because of this injury, while subsequent misfortune is highly significant as the consequence of this injury. The work of one's life is to discover and name the harm one has suffered.

This is, as it happens, a fairly accurate representation of the mythic armature of *A Thousand Acres*.

As long as this myth is operational, one cannot act, in stories or anywhere else, in a meaningful way. The injury takes for itself all the meaning. The injury *is* the meaning, although it is, itself, opaque. All achievements, and all mistakes, are finessed. There is no free will. There is only acting out, the acting out of one's destiny. But acting out is not the same as acting. Acting out is behavior that proceeds according to a predetermined, invisible pattern created by the injury. The injury becomes the unmoved mover, the replacement for the mind's capacity to judge and to decide. One thinks of Nixon here: the obscure wounds, the vindictiveness, the obsession with enemies, the acting out.

It has a feeling of Calvinism to it, of predetermination, this myth of injury and predestination. In its kingdom, sorrow and depression rule. Marilynne Robinson calls this mode of thought "bungled Freudianism." It's both that and something else: an effort to make pain acquire some comprehensibility so that those who feel helpless can at least be illuminated. But unlike Freudianism it asserts that the source of the pain can never be expunged. There is no working through of the injury. It has no tragic joy because, within it, all personal decisions have been made meaningless, deniable. It is a life fate, like a character disorder. Its politics cannot get much further than gender injury. It cannot take on the corporate state.

Confronted with this mode, I feel like an Old Leftist. I want to say: The Bosses are happy when *you* feel helpless. They're pleased when you think the source of your trouble is your family. They're delighted when you give up the idea that you should band together for political action. They'd rather have you feel helpless. They even like addicts, as long as they're mostly out of sight. After all, addiction is just the last stage of consumerism.

And I suppose I am nostalgic—as a writer, of course—for stories with mindful villainy, villainy with clear motives that any adult would understand, bad behavior with a sense of scale that would give back to us our imaginative grip on the despicable and the admirable and our capacity to have some opinions about the two. Most of us are interested in characters who willingly give up their innocence and start to act like adults, with complex and worldly motivations. I am fascinated when they do so, when they admit that they did what they did for good and sufficient reasons. At such moments the moral life becomes intelligible. It also becomes legibly political. If this is the liberal fallacy, this sense of choice, then so be it. (I know that people *do* get caught inside systems of harm and cannot maneuver themselves out—I have written about such situations myself—but that story is hardly the only one worth telling.)

It does seem curious that in contemporary America—a place of considerable good fortune and privilege—one of the most favored narrative modes from high to low has to do with disavowals, passivity, and the disarmed protagonist. Possibly we have never gotten over our American romance with innocence. We would rather be innocent than worldly and unshockable. Innocence is continually shocked and disarmed. But there is something wrong with this. No one can go through life perpetually shocked. It's disingenuous. Writing in his journals, Thornton Wilder notes, "I think that it can be assumed that no adults are ever really 'shocked'—that being shocked is always a pose." If Wilder's claim is even half true, then there is some failure of adulthood in contemporary American life. Our interest in victims and victimization has finally to do with our constant ambivalence about power, about being powerful, about wanting to be powerful but not having to acknowledge the buck stopping at our desk.

Romantic victims and disavowing perpetrators land us in a peculiar territory, a sort of neo-Puritanism without the backbone of theology and philosophy. After all, *The Scarlet Letter* is about disavowals, specifically Dimmesdale's, and the supposed "shock" of a minister of God being guilty of adultery. Dimmesdale's inability to admit publicly what he's done has something to do with the community—i.e., a culture of "shock"—and something to do with his own pusillanimous character.

The dialectics of innocence and worldliness have a different emotional coloration in British literature, or perhaps I am simply unable to get Elizabeth Bowen's *The Death of the Heart* out of my mind in this context. Portia, the perpetual innocent and stepchild, sixteen years old, in love with Eddie, twenty-three, has been writing a diary, and her guardian, Anna, has been reading it. Anna tells St. Quentin, her novelist friend, that she has been reading it. St. Quentin tells Portia what Anna has been doing. As it happens, Portia has been writing poisonously accurate observations about Anna and her husband, Thomas, in the diary. Anna is a bit pained to find herself so neatly skewered.

Bowen's portrait of Portia is beautifully managed, but it's her portrayal of Anna that fascinates me. Anna cannot be shocked. A great character you would never think of describing as "nice" or "likable," she is only what fictional characters should be—interesting. Everything she has done, she admits to. In the sixth chapter of the novel's final section, she really blossoms: Worldly, witty, rather mean, and absolutely clear about her own faults, she recognizes the situation and her own complicity in it. She may be sorry, but she doesn't promise to do better. Portia is the one who is innocent, who commands the superior virtues. Speaking of reading private diaries, Anna says, "It's the sort of thing I do do. Her diary's very good—you see, she has got us taped.... I don't say it has changed the course of my life, but it's given me a rather more disagreeable feeling about being alive—or, at least, about being me."

That "disagreeable feeling" seems to arise not only from the diary but from Anna's wish to read it, to violate it. Anna may feel disagreeable about being the person she is, but she does not say that she could be otherwise. She is honorable about her faults. She is the person who does what she admits to. As a result, there is a clarity, a functionality to Bowen's narrative that becomes apparent because everybody admits to everything in it and then gives their reasons for doing what they've done. Their actions have found a frame, a size, a scale. As bad as Anna may be, she is honest.

Anna defines herself, not in the American way of reciting inward virtues, but in a rather prideful litany of mistakes. In her view, we define ourselves at least as much by our mistakes as by our achievements. In fictional stories, mistakes are every bit as interesting as achievements are. They have an equal claim upon truth. Perhaps they have a greater one, because they are harder to show, harder to hear, harder to say. For that reason, they are rare, which causes their value to go up.

Speaking of a library book that is eighteen years overdue, but which she has just returned, the narrator of Grace Paley's story "Wants" says, "I didn't deny anything." She pays the thirty-two-dollar fine, and that's it. One of the pleasures of Paley's stories derives from their freedom from denial and subterfuge. Their characters explain themselves but don't bother to excuse themselves. City dwellers, they don't particularly like innocence, and they don't expect to be shocked. When there's blame, they take it. When they fall, they have reasons. They don't rise. They just get back on their feet, and when they think about reform, it's typically political rather than personal. For one of her characters, this is the "powerful last-half-of-the-century way." Well, it's nice to think so. Free of the therapeutic impulse, and of the recovery movement, and of Protestantism generally, her characters nevertheless *like* to imagine various social improvements in the lives of the members of their community.

Dysfunctional narratives tend to begin in solitude and they tend to resist their own forms of communication. They don't have communities so much as audiences of fellow victims. There is no polite way for their narratives to end. Richard Nixon, disgraced, resigned, still flashing the V-for-victory from the helicopter on the White House lawn, cognitively dissonant to the end, went off to his enforced retirement, where, tirelessly, year after year, in solitude, he wrote his accounts, every one of them meant to justify and to excuse. The title of his last book was apt: *Beyond Peace.*

—1994

Learning from Other Writers

1. In support of his thesis, Baxter invites us to compare Nixon's statement "Mistakes were made" with Robert E. Lee's "All this has been my fault," asserting that "People just don't say such things anymore." What (if anything) entitles Baxter to make such a sweeping generalization?
2. The structure of Baxter's essay is a chain of cause-and-effect arguments: A caused B, B caused C, C caused D, and so on, with a discussion of the harms caused by the fall of each domino. For each domino, list the examples or arguments that Baxter offers to support that part of his argument.
3. What is the difference between "blame" and "responsibility"? Between "victims" and "protagonists"? Between "me" protagonists and "I" protagonists?
4. What suggestions does Baxter offer to writers as an antidote to the literary malaise he describes in the first half of his essay?
5. Does Baxter offer proof of his arguments, or does he merely invite you to check each assertion against your knowledge and experience? Can you see this method being used to advance arguments that *feel* true—but are, in fact, false? Is this a dangerous basis for an essay? Why or why not?

LESLIE MARMON SILKO

IN THE COMBAT ZONE

Women seldom discuss our wariness or the precautions we take after dark each time we leave the apartment, car, or office to go on the most brief errand. We take for granted that we are targeted as easy prey by muggers, rapists, and serial killers. This is our lot as women in the United States. We try to avoid going anywhere alone after dark, although economic necessity sends women out night after night. We do what must be done, but always we are alert, on guard and ready. We have to be aware of persons walking on the sidewalk behind us; we have to pay attention to others who board an elevator we're on. We try to avoid all staircases and deserted parking garages when we are alone. Constant vigilance requires considerable energy and concentration seldom required of men.

I used to assume that most men were aware of this fact of women's lives, but I was wrong. They may notice our reluctance to drive at night to the convenience store alone, but they don't know or don't want to know the experience of a woman out alone at night. Men who have been in combat know the feeling of being a predator's target, but it is difficult for men to admit that we women live our entire lives in a combat zone. Men have the power to end violence against women in the home, but they feel helpless to protect women from violent strangers. Because men feel guilt and anger at their inability to shoulder responsibility for the safety of their wives, sisters, and daughters, we don't often discuss random acts of violence against women.

When we were children, my sisters and I used to go to Albuquerque with my father. Sometimes strangers would tell my father it was too bad that he had three girls and no sons. My father, who has always preferred the company of women, used to reply that he was glad to have girls and not boys, because he might not get along as well with boys. Furthermore, he'd say, "My girls can do anything your boys can do, and my girls can do it better." He had in mind, of course, shooting and hunting.

When I was six years old, my father took me along as he hunted deer; he showed me how to walk quietly, to move along and then to stop and listen carefully before taking another step. A year later, he traded a pistol for a little single shot .22 rifle just my size.

He took me and my younger sisters down to the dump by the river and taught us how to shoot. We rummaged through the trash for bottles and glass jars; it was great fun to take aim at a pickle jar and watch it shatter. If the Rio San Jose had water running in it, we threw bottles for moving targets in the muddy current. My father told us that a .22 bullet can travel a mile, so we had to be careful where we aimed. The river was a good place because it was below the villages and away from the houses; the high clay riverbanks wouldn't let any bullets stray. Gun safety was drilled into us. We were cautioned about other children whose parents might not teach them properly; if we ever saw another child with a gun, we knew to get away. Guns were not toys. My father did not approve of BB guns because they were classified as toys. I had a .22 rifle when I was seven years old. If I felt like shooting, all I had to do was tell my parents where I was going, take my rifle and a box of 12 shells and go. I was never tempted to shoot at birds or animals because whatever was killed had to be eaten. Now, I realize how odd this must seem; a seven-year-old with a little .22 rifle and a box of ammunition, target shooting alone at the river. But that was how people lived at Laguna when I was growing up; children were given responsibility from an early age.

Laguna Pueblo people hunted deer for winter meat. When I was thirteen I carried George Pearl's saddle carbine, a .30–30, and hunted deer for the first time. When I was fourteen, I killed my first mule deer buck with one shot through the heart.

Guns were for target shooting and guns were for hunting, but also I knew that Grandma Lily carried a little purse gun with her whenever she drove alone to Albuquerque or Los Lunas. One night my mother and my grandmother were driving the fifty miles from Albuquerque to Laguna down Route 66 when three men in a car tried to force my grandmother's car off the highway. Route 66 was not so heavily traveled as Interstate 40 is now, and there were many long stretches of highway where no other car passed for minutes on end. Payrolls at the Jackpile Uranium Mine were large in the 1950s, and my mother or my grandmother had to bring home thousands from the bank in Albuquerque to cash the miners' checks on paydays.

After that night, my father bought my mother a pink nickel-plated snubnose .22 revolver with a white bone grip. Grandma Lily carried a tiny Beretta as black as her prayer book. As my sisters and I got older, my father taught us to handle and shoot handguns, revolvers mostly, because back then, semiautomatic pistols were not as reliable—they frequently jammed. I will never forget the day my father told us three girls that we never had to let a man hit us or terrorize us because no matter how big and strong the man was, a gun in our hand equalized all differences of size and strength.

Much has been written about violence in the home and spousal abuse. I wish to focus instead on violence from strangers toward women because this form of violence terrifies women more, despite the fact that most women are murdered by a spouse, relative, fellow employee, or next-door neighbor, not a stranger. Domestic violence kills many more women and children than strangers kill, but domestic violence also follows more predictable patterns and is more familiar—he comes home drunk and she knows what comes next. A good deal of the terror of a stranger's attack comes from its suddenness and unexpectedness.

Attacks by strangers occur with enough frequency that battered women and children often cite their fears of such attacks as reasons for remaining in abusive domestic situations. They fear the violence they imagine strangers will inflict upon them more than they fear the abusive home. More than one feminist has pointed out that rapists and serial killers help keep the patriarchy in place.

An individual woman may be terrorized by her spouse, but women are not sufficiently terrorized that we avoid marriage. Yet many women I know, including myself, try to avoid going outside of their homes alone after dark. Big deal, you say; well yes, it is a big deal since most lectures, performances, and films are presented at night; so are dinners and other social events. Women out alone at night who are assaulted by strangers are put on trial by public opinion: Any woman out alone after dark is asking for trouble. Presently, for millions of women of all socioeconomic backgrounds, sundown is lockdown. We are prisoners of violent strangers.

Daylight doesn't neccessarily make the streets safe for women. In the early 1980s, a rapist operated in Tucson in the afternoon near the University of Arizona campus. He often accosted two women at once, forced them into residential alleys, then raped each one with a knife to her throat and forced the other to watch. Afterward the women said that part of the horror of their attack was that all around them, everything appeared normal. They could see people inside their houses and cars going down the street—all around them life was going on as usual while their lives were being changed forever.

The afternoon rapist was not the only rapist in Tucson at that time; there was the prime-time rapist, the potbellied rapist, and the apologetic rapist all operating in Tucson in the 1980s. The prime-time rapist was actually two men who invaded comfortable foothills homes during television prime time when residents were preoccupied with television and eating dinner. The prime-time rapists terrorized entire families; they raped the women and sometimes they raped the men. Family members were forced to go to automatic bank machines, to bring back cash to end the ordeal. Potbelly rapist and apologetic rapist need little comment, except to note that the apologetic rapist was good looking, well educated, and smart enough to break out of jail for one last rape followed by profuse apologies and his capture in the University of Arizona library. Local papers recounted details about Tucson's last notorious rapist, the red bandanna rapist. In the late 1970s this rapist attacked more than twenty women over a three-year period, and Tucson police were powerless to stop him. Then one night, the rapist broke into a midtown home where the lone resident, a woman, shot him four times in the chest with a .38 caliber revolver.

In midtown Tucson, on a weekday afternoon, I was driving down Campbell Avenue to the pet store. Suddenly the vehicle behind me began to weave into my lane, so I beeped the horn politely. The vehicle swerved back to its lane, but then in my rearview mirror I saw the small late-model truck change lanes and begin to follow my car very closely. I drove a few blocks without looking in the rearview mirror, but in my sideview mirror I saw the compact truck was right behind me. OK. Some motorists stay upset for two or three blocks, some require ten blocks or more to recover their senses. Stoplight after stoplight, when I glanced into the rearview mirror I saw the man—in his early thirties, tall, white, brown hair, and dark glasses. This guy must not have a job if he has the time to follow me for miles—oh, ohhh! No beast more dangerous in the U.S.A. than an unemployed white man.

At this point I had to make a decision: do I forget about the trip to the pet store and head for the police station downtown, four miles away? Why should I have to let this stranger dictate my schedule for the afternoon? The man might dare to follow me to the police station, but by the time I reach the front door of the station, he'd be gone. No crime was committed; no Arizona law forbids tailgating someone for miles or for turning into a parking lot behind them. What could the police do? I had no license plate number to report because Arizona requires only one license plate, on the rear bumper of the vehicle. Anyway, I was within a block of the pet store where I knew I could get help from the pet store owners. I would feel better about this incident if it was not allowed to ruin my trip to the pet store.

The guy was right on my rear bumper; if I'd had to stop suddenly for any reason, there'd have been a collision. I decide I will not stop even if he does ram into the rear of my car. I study this guy's face in my rearview mirror, six feet two inches tall, 175 pounds, medium complexion, short hair, trimmed moustache. He thinks he can intimidate me because I am a woman, five feet five inches tall, 140 pounds. But I am not afraid, I am furious. I refuse to be intimidated. I won't play his game. I can tell by the face I see in the mirror this guy has done this before; he enjoys using his truck to menace lone women.

I keep thinking he will quit, or he will figure that he's scared me enough; but he seems to sense that I am not afraid. It's true. I am not afraid because years ago my father taught my sisters and me that we did not have to be afraid. He'll give up when I turn into the parking lot outside the Pet Store, I think. But I watch in my rearview mirror; he's right on my rear bumper. As his truck turns into the parking lot behind my car, I reach over and open the glove compartment. I take out the holster with my .38 special and lay it on the car seat beside me.

I turned my car into a parking spot so quickly that I was facing my stalker who had momentarily stopped his truck and was watching me. I slid the .38 out of its holster onto my lap, I watched the stranger's face, trying to determine whether he would jump out of his truck with a baseball bat or gun and come after me. I felt calm. No pounding heart or rapid breathing. My early experience deer hunting had prepared me well. I did not panic because I felt I could stop him if he tried to harm me. I was in no hurry. I sat in the car and waited to see what choice my stalker would make. I looked directly at him without fear because I had my .38 and I was ready to use it. The expression on my face must have been unfamiliar to him; he was used to seeing terror in the eyes of the women he followed. The expression on my face communicated a warning: if he approached the car window, I'd kill him.

He took a last look at me then sped away. I stayed in my car until his truck disappeared in the traffic of Campbell Avenue.

I walked into the pet store shaken. I had felt able to protect myself throughout the incident, but it left me emotionally drained and exhausted. The stranger had only pursued me—how much worse to be battered or raped.

Years before, I was unarmed the afternoon that two drunken deer hunters threatened to shoot me off my horse with razor-edged hunting crossbows. I was riding a colt on a national park trail near my home in the Tucson Mountains. These young white men in their late twenties were complete strangers who might have shot me if the colt had not galloped away erratically bucking and leaping—a moving target too difficult for the drunken bow hunters to aim at. The colt brought me to my ranch house where I called the county sheriff's office and the park ranger. I live in a sparsely populated area where my nearest neighbor is a quarter-mile away. I was afraid the men might have followed me back to my house so I took the .44 magnum out from under my pillow and strapped it around my waist until the sheriff or park ranger arrived. Forty-five minutes later, the park ranger arrived—the deputy sheriff arrived fifteen minutes after him. The drunken bow hunters were apprehended on the national park and arrested for illegally hunting; their bows and arrows were seized as evidence for the duration of bow hunting season. In southern Arizona that is enough punishment; I didn't want to take a chance of stirring up additional animosity with these men because I lived alone then; I chose not to make a complaint about their threatening words and gestures. I did not feel that I backed away by not pressing charges; I feared that if I pressed assault charges against these men, they would feel that I was challenging them to all-out war. I did not want to have to kill either of them if they came after me, as I thought they might. With my marksmanship and my .243 caliber hunting rifle from the old days, I am confident that I could stop idiots like these. But to have to take the life of another person is a terrible experience I will always try to avoid.

It isn't height or weight or strength that make women easy targets; from infancy women are taught to be self-sacrificing, passive victims. I was taught differently. Women have the right to protect themselves from death or bodily harm. By becoming strong and potentially lethal individuals, women destroy the fantasy that we are sitting ducks for predatory strangers.

In a great many cultures, women are taught to depend upon others, not themselves, for protection from bodily harm. Women are not taught to defend themselves from strangers because fathers and husbands fear the consequences themselves. In the United States, women depend upon the courts and the police; but as many women have learned the hard way, the police cannot be outside your house twenty-four hours a day. I don't want more police. More police on the street will not protect women. A few policemen are rapists and killers of women themselves; their uniforms and squad cars give them an advantage. No, I will be responsible for my own safety, thank you.

Women need to decide who has the primary responsibility for the health and safety of their bodies. We don't trust the State to manage our reproductive organs, yet most of us blindly trust that the State will protect us (and our reproductive organs) from predatory strangers. One look at the rape and murder statistics for women (excluding domestic incidents) and it is clear that the government FAILS to protect women from the violence of strangers. Some may cry out for a "stronger" State, more police, mandatory sentences, and swifter executions. Over the years we have seen the U.S. prison population become the largest in the world, executions take place every week now, inner-city communities are occupied by the National Guard, and people of color are harassed by police, but guess what? A woman out alone, night or day, is confronted with more danger of random violence from strangers than ever before. As the U.S. economy continues "to downsize," and the good jobs disappear forever, our urban and rural landscapes will include more desperate, angry men with nothing to lose.

Only women can put a stop to the "open season" on women by strangers. Women are TAUGHT to be easy targets by their mothers, aunts, and grandmothers who themselves were taught that "a women doesn't kill" or "a woman doesn't learn how to use a weapon." Women must learn how to take aggressive action individually, apart from the police and the courts.

Presently twenty-one states issue permits to carry concealed weapons; most states require lengthy gun safety courses and a police security check before issuing a permit. Inexpensive but excellent gun safety and self-defense courses designed for women are also available from every quality gun dealer who hopes to sell you a handgun at the end of the course. Those who object to firearms need trained companion dogs or collectives of six or more women to escort one another day and night. We must destroy the myth that women are born to be easy targets.

—1995

Learning from Other Writers

1. Do you believe the sweeping assertions that Silko makes in her opening two paragraphs? What, if anything, gives her the right to use "we" and speak for all women? Do you think she has the right to speak about "men" as a group? Why or why not?
2. What functions do the third and fourth paragraphs in Silko's essay play? What leads from the end of the first major section (before the space break) to the second major section ("Laguna Pueblo people hunted deer ...")? What leads from the second major section to the third?
3. What (if any) evidence does Silko offer about the frequency and nature of domestic violence?
4. What leads from the third section of the essay to the fourth? What is the purpose of her description of the rapists who terrorized Tucson in the 1980s? Of the personal narrative that follows the paragraph about the Tucson rapists?
5. Why does Silko follow the incident at the pet store with her encounter years earlier with the drunken hunters? What leads from the section about the deer hunters to the final section? What gives Silko the right to claim that women aren't victims because of a lack of height, weight, or strength but because they're conditioned to be passive?
6. By the time you reach the final paragraph, in which the author states her argument, do you find yourself agreeing or disagreeing? In what ways, if any, does she anticipate and head off possible objections?
7. If you had to state the focus of this essay as a question rather than an argument, what would the question be? What answer does Silko supply in her conclusion?

JAMAICA KINCAID

ON SEEING ENGLAND FOR THE FIRST TIME

When I saw England for the first time, I was a child in school sitting at a desk. The England I was looking at was laid out on a map gently, beautifully, delicately, a very special jewel; it lay on a bed of sky blue—the background of the map—its yellow form mysterious, because though it looked like a leg of mutton, it could not really look like anything so familiar as a leg of mutton because it was England—with shadings of pink and green, unlike any shadings of pink and green I had seen before, squiggly veins of red running in every direction. England was a special jewel all right, and only special people got to wear it. The people who got to wear England were English people. They wore it well and they wore it everywhere: in jungles, in deserts, on plains, on top of the highest mountains, on all the oceans, on all the seas, in places where they were not welcome, in places they should not have been. When my teacher had pinned this map up on the blackboard, she said, "This is England"—and she said it with authority, seriousness, and adoration, and we all sat up. It was as if she had said, "This is Jerusalem, the place you will go to when you die but only if you have been good." We understood then—we were meant to understand then—that England was to be our source of myth and the source from which we got our sense of reality, our sense of what was meaningful, our sense of what was meaningless—and much about our own lives and much about the very idea of us headed that last list.

At the time I was a child sitting at my desk seeing England for the first time, I was already very familiar with the greatness of it. Each morning before I left for school, I ate a breakfast of half a grapefruit, an egg, bread and butter and a slice of cheese, and a cup of cocoa; or half a grapefruit, a bowl of oat porridge, bread and butter and a slice of cheese, and a cup of cocoa. The can of cocoa was often left on the table in front of me. It had written on it the name of the company, the year the company was established, and the words "Made in England." Those words, "Made in England," were written on the box the oats came in too. They would also have been written on the box the shoes I was wearing came in; a bolt of gray linen cloth lying on the shelf of a store from which my mother had bought three yards to make the uniform that I was wearing had written along its edge those three words. The shoes I wore were made in England; so were my socks and cotton undergarments and the satin ribbons I wore tied at the end of two plaits of my hair. My father, who might have sat next to me at breakfast, was a carpenter and cabinet maker. The shoes he wore to work would have been made in England, as were his khaki shirt and trousers, his underpants and undershirt, his socks and brown felt hat. Felt was not the proper material from which a hat that was expected to provide shade from the hot sun should be made, but my father must have seen and admired a picture of an Englishman wearing such a hat in England, and this picture that he saw must have been so compelling that it caused him to wear the wrong hat for a hot climate most of his long life. And this hat—a brown felt hat—became so central to his character that it was the first thing he put on in the morning as he stepped out of bed and the last thing he took off before he stepped back into bed at night. As we sat at breakfast a car might go by. The car, a Hillman or a Zephyr, was made in England. The very idea of the meal itself, breakfast, and its substantial quality and quantity was an idea from England; we somehow knew that in England they began the day with this meal called breakfast and a proper breakfast was a big breakfast. No one I knew liked eating so much food so early in the day; it made us feel sleepy, tired. But this breakfast business was Made in England like almost everything else that surrounded us, the exceptions being the sea, the sky, and the air we breathed.

At the time I saw this map—seeing England for the first time—I did not say to myself, "Ah, so that's what it looks like," because there was no longing in me to put a shape to those three words that ran through every part of my life, no matter how small; for me to have had such a longing would have meant that I lived in a certain atmosphere, an atmosphere in which those three words were felt as a burden. But I did not live in such an atmosphere. My father's brown felt hat would develop a hole in its crown, the lining would separate from the hat itself, and six weeks before he thought that he could not be seen wearing it—he was a very vain man—he would order another hat from England. And my mother taught me to eat my food in the English way: the knife in the right hand, the fork in the left, my elbows held still close to my side, the food carefully balanced on my fork and then brought up to my mouth. When I had finally mastered it, I overheard her saying to a friend, "Did you see how nicely she can eat?" But I knew then that I enjoyed my food more when I ate it with my bare hands, and I continued to do so when she wasn't looking. And when my teacher showed us the map, she asked us to study it carefully, because no test we would ever take would be complete without this statement: "Draw a map of England."

I did not know then that the statement "Draw a map of England" was something far worse than a declaration of war, for in fact a flat-out declaration of war would have put me on alert, and again in fact, there was no need for war—I had long ago been conquered. I did not know then that this statement was part of a process that would result in my erasure, not my physical erasure, but my erasure all the same. I did not know then that this statement was meant to make me feel in awe and small whenever I heard the word "England": awe at its existence, small because I was not from it. I did not know very much of anything then—certainly not what a blessing it was that I was unable to draw a map of England correctly.

After that there were many times of seeing England for the first time. I saw England in history. I knew the names of all the kings of England. I knew the names of their children, their wives, their disappointments, their triumphs, the names of people who betrayed them, I knew the dates on which they were born and the dates they died. I knew their conquests and was made to feel glad if I figured in them; I knew their defeats. I knew the details of the year 1066 (the Battle of Hastings, the end of the reign of the Anglo-Saxon kings) before I knew the details of the year 1832 (the year slavery was abolished). It wasn't as bad as I make it sound now; it was worse. I did like so much hearing again and again how Alfred the Great, traveling in disguise, had been left to watch cakes, and because he wasn't used to this the cakes got burned, and Alfred burned his hands pulling them out of the fire, and the woman who had left him to watch the cakes screamed at him. I loved King Alfred. My grandfather was named after him; his son, my uncle, was named after King Alfred; my brother is named after King Alfred. And so there are three people in my family named after a man they have never met, a man who died over ten centuries ago. The first view I got of England then was not unlike the first view received by the person who named my grandfather.

This view, though—the naming of the kings, their deeds, their disappointments—was the vivid view, the forceful view. There were other views, subtler ones, softer, almost not there—but these were the ones that made the most lasting impression on me, these were the ones that made me really feel like nothing. "When morning touched the sky" was one phrase, for no morning touched the sky where I lived. The mornings where I lived came on abruptly, with a shock of heat and loud noises. "Evening approaches" was another, but the evenings where I lived did not approach; in fact, I had no evening—I had night and I had day and they came and went in a mechanical way: on, off; on, off. And then there were gentle mountains and low blue skies and moors over which people took walks for nothing but pleasure, when where I lived a walk was an act of labor, a burden, something only death or the automobile could relieve. And there were things that a small turn of a head could convey—entire worlds, whole lives would depend on this thing, a certain turn of a head. Everyday life could be quite tiring, more tiring than anything I was told not to do. I was told not to gossip, but they did that all the time. And they ate so much food, violating another of those rules they taught me: do not indulge in gluttony. And the foods they ate actually: if only sometime I could eat cold cuts after theater, cold cuts of lamb and mint sauce, and Yorkshire pudding and scones, and clotted cream, and sausages that came from upcountry (imagine, "up-country"). And having troubling thoughts at twilight, a good time to have troubling thoughts, apparently; and servants who stole and left in the middle of a crisis, who were born with a limp or some other kind of deformity, not nourished properly in their mother's womb (that last part I figured out for myself; the point was, oh to have an untrustworthy servant); and wonderful cobbled streets onto which solid front doors opened; and people whose eyes were blue and who had fair skins and who smelled only of lavender, or sometimes sweet pea or primrose. And those flowers with those names: delphiniums, foxgloves, tulips, daffodils, floribunda, peonies; in bloom, a striking display, being cut and placed in large glass bowls, crystal, decorating rooms so large twenty families the size of mine could fit in comfortably but used only for passing through. And the weather was so remarkable because the rain fell gently always, only occasionally in deep gusts, and it colored the air various shades of gray, each an appealing shade for a dress to be worn when a portrait was being painted; and when it rained at twilight, wonderful things happened: people bumped into each other unexpectedly and that would lead to all sorts of turns of events—a plot, the mere weather caused plots. I saw that people rushed: they rushed to catch trains, they rushed toward each other and away from each other; they rushed and rushed and rushed. That word: rushed! I did not know what it was to do that. It was too hot to do that, and so I came to envy people who would rush, even though it had no meaning to me to do such a thing. But there they are again. They loved their children; their children were sent to their own rooms as a punishment, rooms larger than my entire house. They were special, everything about them said so, even their clothes; their clothes rustled, swished, soothed. The world was theirs, not mine; everything told me so.

If now as I speak of all this I give the impression of someone on the outside looking in, nose pressed up against a glass window, that is wrong. My nose was pressed up against a glass window all right, but there was an iron vise at the back of my neck forcing my head to stay in place. To avert my gaze was to fall back into something from which I had been rescued, a hole filled with nothing, and that was the word for everything about me, nothing. The reality of my life was conquests, subjugation, humiliation, enforced amnesia. I was forced to forget. Just for instance, this: I lived in a part of St. John's, Antigua, called Ovals. Ovals was made up of five streets, each of them named after a famous English seaman—to be quite frank, an officially sanctioned criminal: Rodney Street (after George Rodney), Nelson Street (after Horatio Nelson), Drake Street (after Francis Drake), Hood Street, and Hawkins Street (after John Hawkins). But John Hawkins was knighted after a trip he made to Africa, opening up a new trade, the slave trade. He was then entitled to wear as his crest a Negro bound with a cord. Every single person living on Hawkins Street was descended from a slave. John Hawkins's ship, the one in which he transported the people he had bought and kidnapped, was called *The Jesus*. He later became the treasurer of the Royal Navy and rear admiral.

Again, the reality of my life, the life I led at the time I was being shown these views of England for the first time, for the second time, for the one-hundred-millionth time, was this: the sun shone with what sometimes seemed to be a deliberate cruelty; we must have done something to deserve that. My dresses did not rustle in the evening air as I strolled to the theater (I had no evening, I had no theater; my dresses were made of a cheap cotton, the weave of which would give way after not too many washings). I got up in the morning, I did my chores (fetched water from the public pipe for my mother, swept the yard), I washed myself, I went to a woman to have my hair combed freshly every day (because before we were allowed into our classroom our teachers would inspect us, and children who had not bathed that day, or had dirt under their fingernails, or whose hair had not been combed anew that day, might not be allowed to attend class). I ate that breakfast. I walked to school. At school we gathered in an auditorium and sang a hymn, "All Things Bright and Beautiful," and looking down on us as we sang were portraits of the Queen of England and her husband; they wore jewels and medals and they smiled. I was a Brownie. At each meeting we would form a little group around a flagpole, and after raising the Union Jack, we would say, "I promise to do my best, to do my duty to God and the Queen, to help other people every day and obey the scouts' law."

Who were these people and why had I never seen them, I mean really seen them, in the place where they lived? I had never been to England. No one I knew had ever been to England, or I should say, no one I knew had ever been and returned to tell me about it. All the people I knew who had gone to England had stayed there. Sometimes they left behind them their small children, never to see them again. England! I had seen England's representatives. I had seen the governor general at the public grounds at a ceremony celebrating the Queen's birthday. I had seen an old princess and I had seen a young princess. They had both been extremely not beautiful, but who of us would have told them that? I had never seen England, really seen it, I had only met a representative, seen a picture, read books, memorized its history. I had never set foot, my own foot, in it.

The space between the idea of something and its reality is always wide and deep and dark. The longer they are kept apart—idea of thing, reality of thing—the wider the width, the deeper the depth, the thicker and darker the darkness. This space starts out empty, there is nothing in it, but it rapidly becomes filled up with obsession or desire or hatred or love—sometimes all of these things, sometimes some of these things, sometimes only one of these things. The existence of the world as I came to know it was a result of this: idea of thing over here, reality of thing way, way over there. There was Christopher Columbus, an unlikable man, an unpleasant man, a liar (and so, of course, a thief) surrounded by maps and schemes and plans, and there was the reality on the other side of that width, that depth, that darkness. He became obsessed, he became filled with desire, the hatred came later, love was never a part of it. Eventually, his idea met the longed-for reality. That the idea of something and its reality are often two completely different things is something no one ever remembers; and so when they meet and find that they are not compatible, the weaker of the two, idea or reality, dies. That idea Christopher Columbus had was more powerful than the reality he met, and so the reality he met died.

And so finally, when I was a grown-up woman, the mother of two children, the wife of someone, a person who resides in a powerful country that takes up more than its fair share of a continent, the owner of a house with many rooms in it and of two automobiles, with the desire and will (which I very much act upon) to take from the world more than I give back to it, more than I deserve, more than I need, finally then, I saw England, the real England, not a picture, not a painting, not through a story in a book, but England, for the first time. In me, the space between the idea of it and its reality had become filled with hatred, and so when at last I saw it I wanted to take it into my hands and tear it into little pieces and then crumble it up as if it were clay, child's clay. That was impossible, and so I could only indulge in not-favorable opinions.

There were monuments everywhere; they commemorated victories, battles fought between them and the people who lived across the sea from them, all vile people, fought over which of them would have dominion over the people who looked like me. The monuments were useless to them now, people sat on them and ate their lunch. They were like markers on an old useless trail, like a piece of old string tied to a finger to jog the memory, like old decoration in an old house, dirty, useless, in the way. Their skins were so pale, it made them look so fragile, so weak, so ugly. What if I had the power to simply banish them from their land, send boat after boatload of them on a voyage that in fact had no destination, force them to live in a place where the sun's presence was a constant? This would rid them of their pale complexion and make them look more like me, make them look more like the people I love and treasure and hold dear, and more like the people who occupy the near and far reaches of my imagination, my history, my geography, and reduce them and everything they have ever known to figurines as evidence that I was in divine favor, what if all this was in my power? Could I resist it? No one ever has.

And they were rude, they were rude to each other. They didn't like each other very much. They didn't like each other in the way they didn't like me, and it occurred to me that their dislike for me was one of the few things they agreed on.

I was on a train in England with a friend, an English woman. Before we were in England she liked me very much. In England she didn't like me at all. She didn't like the claim I said I had on England, she didn't like the views I had of England. I didn't like England, she didn't like England, but she didn't like me not liking it too. She said, "I want to show you my England, I want to show you the England that I know and love." I had told her many times before that I knew England and I didn't want to love it anyway. She no longer lived in England; it was her own country, but it had not been kind to her, so she left. On the train, the conductor was rude to her; she asked something, and he responded in a rude way. She became ashamed. She was ashamed at the way he treated her; she was ashamed at the way he behaved. "This is the new England," she said. But I liked the conductor being rude; his behavior seemed quite appropriate. Earlier this had happened: we had gone to a store to buy a shirt for my husband; it was meant to be a special present, a special shirt to wear on special occasions. This was a store where the Prince of Wales has his shirts made, but the shirts sold in this store are beautiful all the same. I found a shirt I thought my husband would like and I wanted to buy him a tie to go with it. When I couldn't decide which one to choose, the salesman showed me a new set. He was very pleased with these, he said, because they bore the crest of the Prince of Wales, and the Prince of Wales had never allowed his crest to decorate an article of clothing before. There was something in the way he said it; his tone was slavish, reverential, awed. It made me feel angry; I wanted to hit him. I didn't do that. I said, my husband and I hate princes, my husband would never wear anything that had a prince's anything on it. My friend stiffened. The salesman stiffened. They both drew themselves in, away from me. My friend told me that the prince was a symbol of her Englishness, and I could see that I had caused offense. I looked at her. She was an English person, the sort of English person I used to know at home, the sort who was nobody in England but somebody when they came to live among the people like me. There were many people I could have seen England with; that I was seeing it with this particular person, a person who reminded me of the people who showed me England long ago as I sat in church or at my desk, made me feel silent and afraid, for I wondered if, all these years of our friendship, I had had a friend or had been in the thrall of a racial memory.

I went to Bath—we, my friend and I, did this, but though we were together, I was no longer with her. The landscape was almost as familiar as my own hand, but I had never been in this place before, so how could that be again? And the streets of Bath were familiar, too, but I had never walked on them before. It was all those years of reading, starting with Roman Britain. Why did I have to know about Roman Britain? It was of no real use to me, a person living on a hot, drought-ridden island, and it is of no use to me now, and yet my head is filled with this nonsense, Roman Britain. In Bath, I drank tea in a room I had read about in a novel written in the eighteenth century. In this very same room, young women wearing those dresses that rustled and so on danced and flirted and sometimes disgraced themselves with young men, soldiers, sailors, who were on their way to Bristol or someplace like that, so many places like that where so many adventures, the outcome of which was not good for me, began. Bristol, England. A sentence that began "That night the ship sailed from Bristol, England" would end not so good for me. And then I was driving through the countryside in an English motorcar, on narrow winding roads, and they were so familiar, though I had never been on them before; and through little villages the names of which I somehow knew so well though I had never been there before. And the countryside did have all those hedges and hedges, fields hedged in. I was marveling at all the toil of it, the planting of the hedges to begin with and then the care of it, all that clipping, year after year of clipping, and I wondered at the lives of the people who would have to do this, because wherever I see and feel the hands that hold up the world, I see and feel myself and all the people who look like me. And I said, "Those hedges" and my friend said that someone, a woman named Mrs. Rothchild, worried that the hedges weren't being taken care of properly; the farmers couldn't afford or find the help to keep up the hedges, and often they replaced them with wire fencing. I might have said to that, well if Mrs. Rothchild doesn't like the wire fencing, why doesn't she take care of the hedges herself, but I didn't. And then in those fields that were now hemmed in by wire fencing that a privileged woman didn't like was planted a vile yellow flowering bush that produced an oil, and my friend said that Mrs. Rothchild didn't like this either; it ruined the English countryside, it ruined the traditional look of the English countryside.

It was not at that moment that I wished every sentence, everything I knew, that began with England would end with "and then it all died; we don't know how, it just all died." At that moment, I was thinking, who are these people who forced me to think of them all the time, who forced me to think that the world I knew was incomplete, or without substance, or did not measure up because it was not England; that I was incomplete, or without substance, and did not measure up because I was not English. Who were these people? The person sitting next to me couldn't give me a clue; no one person could. In any case, if I had said to her, I find England ugly, I hate England; the weather is like a jail sentence, the English are a very ugly people, the food in England is like a jail sentence, the hair of English people is so straight, so dead looking, the English have an unbearable smell so different from the smell of people I know, real people of course, she would have said that I was a person full of prejudice. Apart from the fact that it is I—that is, the people who look like me—who made her aware of the unpleasantness of such a thing, the idea of such a thing, prejudice, she would have been only partly right, sort of right: I may be capable of prejudice, but my prejudices have no weight to them, my prejudices have no force behind them, my prejudices remain opinions, my prejudices remain my personal opinion. And a great feeling of rage and disappointment came over me as I looked at England, my head full of personal opinions that could not have public, my public, approval. The people I come from are powerless to do evil on grand scale.

The moment I wished every sentence, everything I knew, that began with England would end with "and then it all died, we don't know how, it just all died" was when I saw the white cliffs of Dover. I had sung hymns and recited poems that were about a longing to see the white cliffs of Dover again. At the time I sang the hymns and recited the poems, I could really long to see them again because I had never seen them at all, nor had anyone around me at the time. But there we were, groups of people longing for something we had never seen. And so there they were, the white cliffs, but they were not that pearly majestic thing I used to sing about, that thing that created such a feeling in these people that when they died in the place where I lived they had themselves buried facing a direction that would allow them to see the white cliffs of Dover when they were resurrected, as surely they would be. The white cliffs of Dover, when finally I saw them, were cliffs, but they were not white; you would only call them that if the word "white" meant something special to you; they were dirty and they were steep; they were so steep, the correct height from which all my views of England, starting with the map before me in my classroom and ending with the trip I had just taken, should jump and die and disappear forever.

—1991

Learning from Other Writers

1. A rant is generally defined as an angry and unstructured venting of unpopular beliefs, prejudices, or opinions, unsupported by evidence or logic. Certainly, Kincaid's tone in this essay is angry. How well does this essay fit the other criteria for a rant?
2. If you think of the structure of this essay as a list of the "first times" that the author "saw England," what are the items on that list?
3. Is it possible to view this essay as an argument? If so, what is Kincaid arguing for or against?
4. Does the author take into account the possible objections of her critics or opposing points of view? Does she anticipate efforts by her readers to soften her rage? If not, why not? If so, how does she respond to those critics or voices?
5. Is it possible to view this essay as an exploration of a question rather than as an argument or a rant? If so, what would that question be? What, if any, answers does Kincaid come up with?
6. Reread the final long sentence of the essay. What is the essay really saying here? Given all that's come before, is this what you expected the author to conclude? How would you

describe the author's tone at the very end of the essay compared to her tone elsewhere in the piece?

7. When, if ever, is it permissible to offend your readers?

INSPIRATIONS: TESTING YOUR EDUCATION

1. Think of some aspect of your education that puzzles you. Examples might include: Can bullying ever be stopped? What are the advantages and disadvantages of attending a single-sex high school? What is the value of a certain method of teaching math or reading?
2. Choose any of the forms we have studied so far (narration, journey, experiment, profile, group portrait, etc.) and use that form to structure a meditation centered on your question.
3. Alternatively, set forth an argument about some aspect of your education and use a collage or list to convince us that you're right.

COMPLEX AND COMPOUND FORMS

Some writers rely on more than one form as they write, whether by juggling two or more forms simultaneously or embedding one form within another (I call both of these options *complex forms*) or by combining two or more forms in sequence (*compound forms*). In earlier chapters, we've seen essays in which the author juggles two or more structures simultaneously: John McPhee combines a journey around Atlantic City with an imaginary Monopoly game; John Hersey orders the profiles in his group according to a third-person narrative of the atomic blast at Hiroshima. An example of the slightly simpler approach of embedding one or more forms within a larger structural framework would be Bernard Cooper's "A Clack of Tiny Sparks," in which he embeds his memory of an experiment—to kiss a girl and enjoy it—within the larger personal narrative of his social life in ninth grade.

As you might imagine, attempting to juggle several forms at the same time or to embed one form within another can cause you to lose track of what you're doing and end up with a disorganized mess. But when the technique works, it can help a writer handle an otherwise overwhelming topic or assignment. Professionals like McPhee, who have been working in the genre for many years, writing magazine-length essays and nonfiction books, become masters of combining—and inventing—whatever forms they need to accomplish their thematic goals.

But a slightly simpler tactic is to combine two or more forms in sequence rather than simultaneously, starting with one form, then switching to another as the subject demands. You might start out on a journey, only to realize that you need to take your readers on a tour of the historical site at which you've now arrived, followed by a group portrait of the soldiers and commanding officers who fought a battle at that site, followed by an experiment in which you try to experience how difficult it must have been to charge up a hill in full uniform, carrying a heavy pack, having marched for nine days without sleep or food or water. Using a series of forms can provide the flexibility of approach you need to organize the wealth of material you want or need to cover in a particularly ambitious project, the downside being that switching forms in the middle of an essay or a book might make the finished product resemble a creature with the hind parts of a horse and the front quarters of a cow.

The more advanced writer who seeks to combine two or more forms sequentially might consult Julian Barnes's marvelous piece of nonfiction "Shipwreck,"[2] in which he sets out to solve the

[2] "Shipwreck" initially was published in the June 12, 1989, issue of *The New Yorker* and later appeared as a chapter in Barnes's *A History of the World in 10 ½ Chapters*.

mystery of why the painter Théodore Géricault painted his masterpiece "Scene of Shipwreck" the way he finally painted it and not some other way, thereby helping us understand how catastrophes inspire art. Barnes begins with a lengthy third-person narrative (which, like Sebastian Junger's *The Perfect Storm*, recounts a disaster at sea), followed by a how-to guide, with an embedded substructure of a list of possibilities for the painting that Gericault might have considered and discarded, followed by an analysis of the composition of the painting he *did* paint, structured spatially along the lines of the painting itself, after which we resume the how-to guide, followed by an attempt to solve the mystery of why Noah's Ark is so rarely portrayed in great art, with a conclusion in which the author picks up his how-to narrative and carries it forward to the showing of the painting at the salon, the artist's deathbed denunciation of his masterpiece as a mere vignette, and the painting's deterioration and decay through the centuries that followed.

If you feel overwhelmed by these categories and distinctions, don't worry. What's important is that you come away with the understanding that the structures I've described in this book can be varied and combined at will, that they are meant to serve your essay-writing needs rather than to strangle or confine your creativity, and that you can find pleasure in combining and inventing forms to meet your needs.

To leave you with a sense of play and possibility, I end this chapter with John D'Agata's "Round Trip," a compound-complex essay in which the author meditates on the human propensity to categorize and visit the wonders of the world while he travels on a bus to and from the Hoover Dam. In the course of this journey, D'Agata employs the following additional forms: the list, the collage, the group portrait, the tour, the game, the experiment, the document, the personal narrative, and the profile. I hope you also will have fun in noting that D'Agata dedicates his essay to Joan Didion's earlier meditation on the same dam, an allusion that ought to make you realize you now possess a certain familiarity with the classics of the genre. You might also notice that I present D'Agata's essay with no further commentary. At this point, you have all the tools you need to enable you to learn from other writers and improvise or invent your own nonfiction forms. As you read further in the field and discover essays and books whose content, form, or style excites you, or as you come up with ideas that might inspire the rest of us to write our own essays and books, we hope you will e-mail us at www.creativenonfiction@cengage.com and share with us what you've found.

JOHN D'AGATA

ROUND TRIP

I

Isaac, who is twelve, has come involuntarily.

"We insist he grow up cultured," his mother says, leaning over our headrests from the seat behind. "My father brought me to Hoover Dam on a bus. There is just no other way to see it."

Hours ago, before the bus, I found the tour among the dozens of brochures in my hotel lobby. It had been typed and Xeroxed, folded three times into the form of a leaflet, and crammed into the back of a countertop rack on the bellhop's "What To Do" desk in Vegas.

Nearby my tour in the brochure rack were announcements for Colorado River raft rides that would paddle visitors upstream into the great gleaming basin of the dam.

There were ads, too, for helicopter rides—offering to fly "FOUR friends and YOU" over "CROWDS, TRAFFIC, this RIVER & MAN's MOST BEAUTIFUL structure—all YOURS to be PHOTOGRAPHED at 10,000 FEET!"

Hot-air balloon tours.

Rides on mountain bikes.

Jaunts on donkeys through the desert, along the river, and up the dam's canyon wall.

There was even something called the Hoover Dam Shopper's Coach, whose brochure guaranteed the best mall bargains in Nevada, yet failed to mention anywhere on its itinerary Hoover Dam.

Brochure in hand, I stood in line at the tour's ticket booth behind a man haggling with a woman behind the glass. He wanted a one-way ticket to Hoover Dam.

"Impossible," the woman said. "We sell The Eleven-Dollar Tour. One tour, one price."

The one-way man went on about important business he had at the dam, things he had to see to, how the tour's schedule just wasn't time enough.

"Sir," she said, through security glass, "I'm telling you, you'll have to come back. They're not gonna let you stay out there."

He bought a ticket, moved on.

We boarded.

Like the ad said, The Eleven-Dollar Tour comes with a seat on the bus, a free hot-dog coupon, and a six-hour narrative, there and back.

Our bus is silver, round, a short, chubby thing. It is shaped like a bread box. Like a bullet. "Like they used to make them," says Isaac's mom.

I turn to Isaac, my seatmate, say, "Hi, my name is John," and he says he doesn't care, and proceeds to pluck the long blond lashes from his eyelids, one by one, standing them on his wrist, stuck there by their follicles.

It is at this point that Isaac's mom leans over our headrests and tells me that Isaac is a good boy, "talkative, really," that he just happens to be grumpy today because "Mother and Father" have insisted that he accompany them on this "educational tour." Isaac's mother tells me that to keep Isaac entertained in Las Vegas they are staying in a new hotel—the largest in the world, in fact—with 5,000 guest rooms, 4 casinos, 17 restaurants, a mega-musical amphitheater, a boxing ring, a monorail, and a 33-acre amusement park, all inside an emerald building. She presents the brochure.

I say, "Wow."

Then Isaac's dad, looking up from another brochure he holds in his lap, says, "You know, kiddo, this Hoover Dam looks pretty special!" And then come statistics from the paragraph he's reading.

The feet high.

The feet thick.

The cubic yards of concrete.

Of water.

The 3 million kilowatts.

And the plaque.

"Let me see that." Isaac's mom takes the brochure and reads the plaque's inscription to herself. She shakes her head.

"Do you believe that? Isaac, honey, listen."

Isaac's eyes roll far away. His mother's voice climbs up a stage.

She is just loud enough to be overhead. Just hushed enough to silence all of us.

It is her voice, and the quiet, and the words on the plaque that I think might have made the whole trip worth it even then, even before we left the tour company's parking lot and learned there'd be no air-conditioning on the six-hour ride; even before we stood in line for two hours at the dam; before the snack bar ran out of hot dogs and the tour guide of his jokes; before the plaque was laid in 1955 by Ike; before the dam was dedicated in 1935 by FDR; before the ninety-six men died "to make the desert bloom"; or before the Colorado first flooded, before it leaked down from mountains, carved the Grand Canyon, and emptied into the ocean. Even before this plaque was cast by a father and his son in their Utah blacksmith shop, there was the anticipation of the plaque, its gold letters riding on the backs of all creators. And Isaac's mother's voice, even then, I believe, was ringing circles somewhere in the air: "... the American Society of Civil Engineers voted this one of the Seven Modern Wonders of the World!"

> *These are the seven wonders of the world: a beacon, a statue, gardens, pyramids, a temple, another statue, and a tomb. I have set eyes on them all—this Lofty fire of Pharos, and the statue of Zeus by Alpheus, and the Hanging Gardens, and the Colossus of the Sun, and the Huge Labor of the High Pyramids, and the Vast tomb of Mausolus, and the House of Artemis mounted to the Clouds—and I tell you, as a scholar and as a wanderer and as a man devoted to the gods, they are and always will be the Seven Greatest Liberties man will ever take with Nature.*
>
> (Antipater of Sidon, from his lost guidebook, c. 120 B.C.)

2

Our driver maneuvers lithely through the streets filled with rental cars. I tilt my head into the aisle. There is his green-sleeved arm, his pale, pudgy hand that is dancing on the gear stick rising out of the floor. His head, bobbing above the rows of seats in front of me, seems to bounce in rhythm with his horn. He honks to *let* pedestrians cross.

He rearranges his hair.

Leans a little forward.

Fluffs a cushion at his back.

We are idling at a crosswalk. We are there seven minutes, when suddenly, out of the air, our driver's voice comes coiling.

On the right side of us is the Flamingo Hotel where Elvis Presley owned a floor of that hotel on our right side.

On the left side of us is the Mirage Hotel where Michael Jackson owns a floor of that hotel on our left side.

His words emit circles, whip bubbles around our heads. His sentences wrap around the bus and greet themselves in midair. All the way to the dam the bus rumbles inside this cloud, the date slips steadily away, the tour transforms into a silent scratchy film that is slowly flitting backward through frames of older dreams.

We sit among neo-Gothic images heaping up from the pages of a souvenir borrowed from Isaac's grandfather, a 1935 photographic essay entitled "The Last Wonder of the World: The Glory of Hoover Dam." On its brittle pages machines still throb, light still beams from the book's center spread.

A full, glossy, long-shot view of the generator room reveals round, sleek, plastic bodies lined up like an army, surrounded by looming concrete walls adorned with pipes of gleaming chrome. Everything stands at attention. Nothing but light is stirring. The whole scene is poised forever to strike against an enemy that never breached the river's shore.

Gambling wasn't legalized in our state until 1935 is when they legalized gambling in Nevada.

The patterns in these pictures are like wax dripping from candles, islands coagulating from spurts of lava, liquid steel pouring out of kettles into rifle molds, Buick frames, the skyscrapers of Chicago. The round machines spin their energy like spools, all of it rolling off their bodies, through the pages, over the slick, curved surface of the next machine, which is identical to the last: which is blinking the same, rounded the same, parodying his sentences revolving around our heads, and shielding our tour from starts and stops, from *In the beginning*, from *Ever after*, from *Now* and from *Then*, and from any time—from all time—in which this vacuous progression cannot fit, because its round body is nowhere near the right shape for the boxy borders of dates.

Just to let you know, folks, our tour company's been on the road since 1945 is how long we've been traveling this road.

I mention to Isaac that the machines resemble something I once saw in *Doctor Who*, and he says, "No they don't"—which is the first thing he has said to me in an hour.

"It's more like *Star Trek's* Plasma Generator," he says. But when I tell him I don't quite follow him, we decide that something from *Batman* suits our conflicting descriptions best.

What we do not know at this moment, however, is that in 1935, when the dam was opened, Batman was about to make his debut in comic strips. So was Superman, and other superheroes—summoned from Krypton or Gotham City to defend our country against impending evils—their bodies toned flawlessly as turbines. They came with tales of an ideal Tomorrow. They came jostled between two wars, buffering our borders against enemies on every side, encircling the country with an impenetrable force field, and introducing at home a new architecture of resistance: round, sleek, something the old clunky world slipped off.

A lot of these trees and most of this grass is brought in from out of state.

A lot of these trees and most of this grass is brought in from Arizona.

These are the same curves I once found in my grandmother's basement. Toasters so streamlined they're liable to skid off the kitchen counter. A hair dryer filched from Frankenstein's brain-wave lab. A Philharmonic radio taller than my ten-year-old body, and reeking of Swing—leaking tinny voices, platinum songs, and the catch-me-if-you-can whorls from Benny Goodman's silvery tube.

My grandmother's is the world that dropped the bomb—itself a slick object—so elegantly smooth it managed to slip past American consciousness, past enemy lines.

Afterward, in her world, "Atomic" was a prefix attached to the coming world and all the baubles to be found there. But in that present, at the opening of Hoover Dam, the designers of the future could only have guessed what atoms looked like.

And still their imaginations leaped instantly to *round*, to *fast*, to *heralds of the future.*

3

> *During the sixth century, St. Gregory of Tours compiled a list of the seven wonders of the medieval world which demonstrates an inaccurate knowledge of history. He retained four wonders from the original list, but made three additions of his own: Noah's Ark, Solomon's Temple, and the Original Tree of Life—which, he claimed, had been discovered in the underground archives of a church in his native France. But St. Gregory, of course, was wrong. The remains of the Tree of Life were used to construct the Crucifix on which our Saviour died—now housed, of course, in the Holy Cross Church in Rome.*
>
> (from my grandmother's library, G. B. Smith's *Remembering the Saints*)

4

"There's this computer game I like so I guess that counts right? It's not the real world but it lets you do really awesome stuff that's pretty cool so you can call that a wonder I bet. But I gotta go to my friend's house to play it though 'cause my parents won't get it for me 'cause they think it's too violent. Hey you can't write this down or I'm not talking man. It's called *Civilization.*

You start with two guys—a guy and a girl—and they're like at the start of the world or something. But after all the animals are made and stuff. And then—um—you have to make babies because the whole point is to you know start the civilization. So the computer keeps asking you what you want to do. Like if you want to have babies at a certain time or if you wanna be a hunter and gatherer or start farming and all that. So at the same time the computer has its own family that it's starting and you have to be in competition with them. So you start your family and all that and you become a village and ... that's all the boring stuff. But you have to do it to start up the game. So before you know it you're like the leader and everything and people start gods and that kind of stuff and there's laws that you get to make up like if you want people to steal or how many wives you can have. And all of a sudden the computer calls war on you and you have to fight them 'cause if you don't then the game ends 'cause the computer can kill all your people. So there's whole long parts when you gotta learn how to do battle and you decide if you wanna use your metal to make weapons or not and how many people you'll make fight 'cause after you play a long time you learn that if you keep some people in the village during the war you can make them keep making weapons and stuff and help the fighters who are hurt. And usually if you make it through the war with some people left then the computer won't kill you off 'cause it'll let you try to start the village again. So all that happens and—um—every now and then the computer lets you know that someone in the village makes an invention. Like if they use the well to try to make a clock or they build a building with stones that has a roof so you can put more floors on top of it and—you know—then cities start. Then people start sailing down the river and they find other places to live and there are like whole new civilizations that the computer controls that you get to find. Now it all depends on how you act with the new people that tells whether or not you start a war or something or if you join their village and team up your forces. When that happens the computer gives you a lot more technology. So all that goes on and like thousands of years go by and pretty soon it starts looking like the modern world and you're controlling a whole country. Then your goal is to get control of the whole world which only one of my friends has done but then there's always this little place you don't know about that starts a revolution and then the whole world starts fighting and everyone ends up dead. I've never gotten that far though. I've controlled a couple countries before and I usually make them all start a colony in space and what's great is that if you tell them to fly to a planet in the solar system then the computer isn't programmed that far and it lets you do whatever you want for a little while until it just ends the game 'cause it doesn't know how to continue 'cause it can't compete with you if you just keep inventing new stuff it hasn't heard of. So sometimes I get like three countries to go up there and they start this whole new civilization and there are new animals and just the right amount of people and all the buildings are beautiful and built with this river that turns hard when you pick up the water and you can shape it how you want. So there's all this glass around and it's awesome but it only lasts like a year because the computer gets freaked out and ends up stopping the game. The game always ends up destroying the world."

5

> *When the Canal was being completed, the renowned sculptor Daniel Chester French and the best-known landscape architect of the day, Frederick Law Olmsted, were hired to decorate it. After a careful survey, the two artists refused the commission. So impressed were they by the beauty which the engineers had created that they declared, "For we artists to add to it now would be an impertinence."*
>
> 1. The Panama Canal, 1914

My List

"Hello, Joe Miller here."

"Hi, sir. I'm wondering if maybe you could help me out. I'm trying to find the American Society of Civil Engineers' list of the Seven Modern Wonders of the World. Are you the right person to talk to?"

"Yeah, yeah that's me. I think the list you're talking about is pretty old, though. We just announced a new list you might be interested in."

"A new list?"

"The 1999 Modern Wonders of the World."

"Oh. Well, actually I guess I'm interested in the old Modern list."

"Well that's forty years old! This new one we have is a lot more impressive. I think this is what you're looking for."

"Well, could you maybe tell me about the first list anyway? I can't find it mentioned anywhere in my library. I kind of need it."

"Well, that'll take some time.... Let me get back to you ..."

A common witticism on that bleak Depression day when this spectacular skyscraper opened its doors was, "The only way the landlords will ever fill that thing is if they tow it out to sea." But such pessimistic sentiments were wrong, as pessimists always have been in America. The population of the building now is that of a small city!

2. The Empire State Building, 1931

My Grandfather's List

"Just put down the Statue of Liberty.
That's all I want you to put down."

How do you dig a hole deeper than anyone has ever dug, fill it with more concrete and steel than has been used in any other public works campaign, and do it all in the middle of California's busiest harbor, swiftest current, most stormy shore? No, no! it would be sheer folly to try—but they did it anyway!

3. The San Francisco–Oakland Bay Bridge, 1936

My Mother's List

1. The Twin Towers
2. The Apollo Space Program
3. PCs
4. Cannabis
5. Picasso
6. August 9, 1974 (Richard Nixon's resignation)
7. Cape Cod

Then the fun begins. The aqueduct's route crosses two hundred forty-two miles of terrain that looks as if it had been dropped intact from the moon: a landscape of mountainous sands, dry washes, empty basins—one of the hottest, deadliest wastelands in the civilized world.... And this conduit, man's longest, spans it all!

4. The Colorado River Aqueduct, 1938

Isaac's Mother's List

"Oh, I know these. One must be the Brooklyn Bridge. I practically grew up on that thing! The Eiffel Tower has to be on there. Probably the Sears Tower, too. The Washington Monument. Niagara Falls. What about the Pentagon? And the Hoover Dam, of course."

Flying over the city, below the left wing of the plane, you will see Chicago's Southwest Works, one of the largest and most advanced sewage treatment facilities in the world. It is a veritable modern city, as spanking-looking as if sealed in a fresh-washed bottle, and as motionless and silent as a hospital at night.

5. The Chicago Sewage Disposal System, 1939

Guy-in-a-bar's List

1. A rapid development in our fine and visual arts
2. With all of our technological advancements, a continued sadness among the people
3. Our ignorance of environmental problems
4. Magic
5. The Internet
6. Alaska
7. Hoover Dam

A certain stopper was the fact that the Coulee could only rise to 550 feet. At that height it backed up the Columbia River into a 150-mile-long lake. Any higher and it would have flooded Canada.

6. The Grand Coulee Dam, 1941

Joe Miller's List

"Yeah, this is a message for John D'Agata. I have that information you requested. This is the 1999 list of Modern Wonders of the World:
one is The Golden Gate Bridge;
two, The World Trade Center;
three, The U.S. Interstate Highway System;
four, The Kennedy Space Center;
five, The Panama Canal;
six, The Trans-Alaskan Pipeline;
and seven is Hoover Dam."

It lofts up with the majesty of Beauty itself, and you marvel at what manner of men could have conceived the possibility of building such a wonder.

7. The Hoover Dam, 1935 (from *America the Beautiful: An Introduction to Our Seven Wonders*)

6

Perhaps the Book of Genesis is the first and most famous list of wonders. Today, however, such rosters of remarkable things are common in America.

Whenever I visit a city for the first time, I always notice the gold stars on storefronts—"Voted Best Barbershop," "... Mexican Food," "... Auto Repair." My brother, who prides himself on his ability to spot "quality trends," as he calls them, has sworn for years by *Boston Magazine's* annual "Best Of" issue.

He says that living by the list is like living in a perfect world. And the list has grown so comprehensive each year that, these days, my brother seldom has to live without perfection. He has found, for example, a "professional scalper" with the best last-minute Bruins ticket deals, a launderer known for having the best-pressed cuffs, and a sportsman's lodge with the best range for skeet shooting—a sport my brother has taken up simply out of awe of it being listed.

Another purveyor of perfection has gone so far as to publish a book-length list, entitled *The Best of Everything*, which includes the Best Sexy Animal (the female giraffe), the Best Labor-Saving Device (the guillotine), the Best Vending Machine (a mashed-potato dispenser in Nottingham, England), and the Best Souvenir (a shrunken head from Quito, Ecuador).

Not to be outdone, proponents of the worst things in the world have published *The Worst of Everything*. On this list can be found the Worst Nobel Peace Prize Recipient (Henry Kissinger), the Worst Item Ever Auctioned (Napoleon's dried penis), the Worst Poem Ever Written ("The Child" by Friedreich Hebbel), and the Worst Celebrity Endorsement for a Car (Hitler, for the Volkswagen Bug: "This streamlined fourseater is a mechanical marvel. It can be bought on an installment plan for six Reichsmarks a week—including insurance!")

Now Isaac's mother leans over our seats and shows us both another brochure.

"Just think how happy they all must have been," she says, unfolding an artist's rendition of the future across our laps. "I sure wish I lived back then. You know?"

1939. Queens, New York.

She, Isaac, and I have just paid our fifty cents, and before us—miles wide—are promenades, sculptures, buildings, and glittery things, all laid out in perfect grids. "So bright and lovely," she says, "it makes me want to close my eyes." Even the people around us shine, sweaty inside their wool suits and skirts. There are thousands of them, Isaac decides—just like the people who walk around EPCOT.

"You know," he says. "The kind who you can't really tell are real or not."

We buy frankfurters, a guidebook, little silver spoons at every exhibition. We are here because—even as far west as Nevada, even as far into the future as 1999—we have heard that this is the greatest fair ever orchestrated on earth.

We start with Isaac's mom's list: the Gardens on Parade, the Town of Tomorrow, the House of Jewels, the Plaza of Light, Democracity.

Then we visit Isaac's list: the Futurama, the Academy of Sports, the Court of Power, the Lagoon of Nations, the Dome of the Heinz Corp.

And by the time we visit my list we have stumbled smack into the middle of the fair, inches from its epicenter, squinting back up at those dazzling fair trademarks known in our guidebook as *Trylon* and *Perisphere*. The obelisk and the globe stand like silence behind the roaring and spurting of ten giant fountains.

The two of them are like fountains behind the silence of our gaze.

One of them is stretched so high it scrapes the color from the sky. The other is arched playfully on its own curved back.

The obelisk, we read, is 610 feet tall ("That's 50 feet taller than the Washington Monument!" our guidebook claims). The sphere is 180 feet in diameter ("The largest globe in the state of New York!").

Both objects are words that never before existed. And despite all the euphoria surrounding them in '39, all the family photos posed in front of them, the silverware and shaving kits and Bissell Carpet Sweepers that bore their images, *Trylon* and *Perisphere* never made it into our lexicon.

At the foot of them, I can't see why.

One is like a list, the other is like a wonder. But I don't say this aloud.

"An arrow and a bull's-eye!" one of us blurts out. And so they are. Perfectly.

Or one is like an ancient scroll unrolled; the other is an orb of indecipherable glyphs. One is how we describe a fantasy; the other is what we've secretly dreamt.

Shoulder to shoulder, we three look them up, then down. Our mouths hang wide—with *awe*—filled with them.

I remember the first list of wonders that I ever knew. One year, an old man on our street told my mother that he had once been a college professor, a master of Latin and Greek. Within days I was studying classics with him. I had just turned eight.

My tutor, Mr. Newcomb, lived alone among statuary and plaster casts of temple friezes. Tapestries padded his walls. I met with him each day in the barest room of his house: a desk, two chairs, a lamp, a rug, and seven hanging woodcuts of the seven ancient wonders.

Some days, instead of reading, Mr. Newcomb beguiled me with trivia about the hanging wonders on his walls. And some days, strewn over the years, he divulged their secrets. Why, for instance, the curse of the Pyramids in fact is real; where, in Turkey, the Colossus' body parts are actually hidden; what, according to Vatican documents, which Mr. Newcomb alone had read in Rome, Napoleon "felt" as he pissed on the charred remains of Diana's great temple.

Later, Mr. Newcomb's woodcuts of the seven ancient wonders became mine once he had died. At that point, however, I had only managed to grasp the first conjugation in Latin, so for years after, until I could return to Latin in school, the ancient wonders lived beside me in a parallel present tense.

I have them still. They hang around—dark, worn—reminding me of the last wonderful secret my tutor left: that he had never studied Latin, never read the classics. That he had never traveled to Rome, nor much farther beyond our town.

He had never actually liked school.

Yet what he had was curiosity. Crustiness. An air of scholastic formality. He had a dustiness that was reliable. A home adorned tastefully, lessons always prepared for me, cookies, milk, stories that kept me rapt. He had a knack, which was his lure, for both the mundane and fantastic.

The black-breasted roadrunner, my favorite bird, is that black-breasted roadrunner there.

The bird hurries past our bus, darting up the mountain pass as we slowly descend its peak. I am awakened by our driver's voice and my ears popping as we slide into the valley. Everyone else, everyone except for Isaac and the one-way man, is asleep. They chat across the center aisle.

"I'm gonna live there," says the one-way man, when Isaac asks what he'll do when we arrive at the dam.

"You can live there?" Isaac asks.

"Well, I'm gonna," says the man.

Isaac's mom, I know, would want me to intervene here, tell Isaac the man's just joking with him. Tell Isaac the one-way man is crazy.

But when Isaac starts talking about his computer game, and the one-way man explains how the concave wall of the Hoover Dam would be awesome for skateboarding, it is they who stop, mutually—nowhere conclusive and without any care.

They sit back in their seats, stare forward awhile, and fall asleep.

7

continents, days per week, Deadly Sins, Epochs of Man according to Shakespeare, hills of Rome, liberal arts, perfect shapes, planets in the Ptolemaic system, Pleiades in Greek myth, Sacraments, seas, Sleepers of Ephesus, wives of Bluebeard, wonders of Yemen, Years War

Notes

Doors Number One, Two, Three, Four, Five, Six, and *Seven*: All are taken from the results of a catalogue search in the Library of Congress, Washington, D.C., under the title heading "wonders and of."

*

Round Trip: To date, the best essay to capture the aspirations of the generation that built Hoover Dam is, in my opinion, Joan Didion's elegant "At the Dam" (*The White Album*, 1979). This essay is dedicated to that one.

—2003

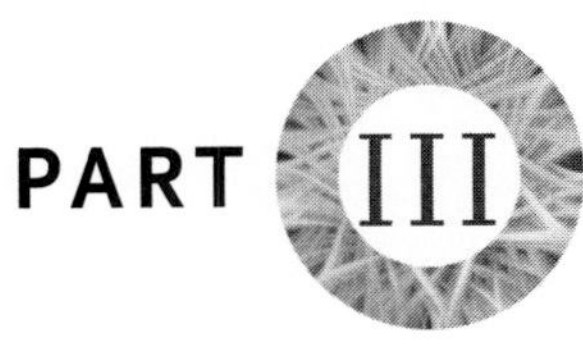

PART III

Notes on Revision

Revising on Your Own

1. After you've completed an initial draft of an essay, ask yourself whether anyone but your immediate family and friends might be interested in the question you are trying to answer. If not, can you rephrase your question so it might interest a larger group of readers? (If your question is: "Why did my parents wait until I was sixteen to tell me that I was adopted?," you might broaden it to: "When is the best time to tell a child that he's adopted?" or: "What are the pros and cons of waiting to tell a child that she is adopted until she is a teenager?")
2. At what moment does your material heat up and get exciting? Is that where you actually chose to start your essay? If not, why not?
3. Many essays (especially personal narratives) begin with a scene to grab the reader's attention, then pause for an expository passage in which the writer provides a bit of background and conveys the central question he or she will attempt to answer, after which the writer picks up where he or she left off and presents a second major scene, image, or vignette. Ask yourself if this might be a useful strategy for your essay or whether you might want to use a different approach.
4. Where have you used scenic writing to re-create events or actions for your readers? Where have you chosen to summarize events with exposition? Are you happy with these choices? Should some of the expository passages be turned into scenes? Should some of the scenes be summed up or compressed via exposition? In either case, have you used enough details and dialogue to bring your material alive? Too many details or too much dialogue?
5. To whom are you telling your story? What would that audience know or not know about you and your subject? What expectations, prejudices, or preconceived notions would that audience bring to your material? What would be the appropriate vocabulary and tone to use when speaking to this audience? Would your readers need any background information to help clarify or contextualize what you're telling them? Might your essay cause some readers to become squeamish? Combative? Despairing? Do you want to head off any of these reactions?
6. Go over what you've written and highlight the passages in which you meditate on your question. Are there any places in your essay where additional meditations seem called for by the importance of what's just happened—or what's about to happen? In real life, when do we stop and think about what's happening to us or the people around us? What are the advantages and disadvantages of waiting to meditate on your central question until the very end of your narrative?
7. Ask yourself what you know now about your original question that you didn't know when you started to write. Freewrite and get these new thoughts on paper. Is your initial

question the question you still want to explore, or do you want to radically change or slightly tweak that question?

8. What have you discovered since you began thinking and writing about this material? Is your conclusion obvious (i.e., "Don't disobey your parents" or "Don't start off on a wilderness hike without a compass")? Have you simply re-proved a moral we already accept as true (i.e., "Don't judge a book by its cover" or "What doesn't kill you makes you stronger")? Is there some less obvious discovery you might make based on your actual experience, research, or discussions with other people?
9. Do you believe your conclusion? Does your essay *demonstrate* that it's true? Is there anything you need to add to support your assertions? Who might disagree with your interpretation of events? How might you convince such skeptics that you're right?
10. Is there some final image or scene that expresses your discovery? Were there consequences to the events (or journey, experiment, or encounter) you've just described? Are other people's responses to your experience relevant or important? Or do you want to end with your own thoughts on whatever happened?
11. If possible, let your draft sit for a week (or, at the very least, twenty-four hours), then reread what you've written with fresh eyes and revise as needed. Once you've done all you can do on your own, see Chapter 18 for hints on how to share your work with other readers.

Sharing Your Work with Others

A SENSE OF WHAT YOU'VE ALREADY ACCOMPLISHED

1. When you've done everything you can do on your own, show your essay or book to at least one other person (or to everyone in your class as part of a workshop). Ask your readers to start by telling you what works. Can your readers pinpoint the most interesting or vivid scenes? Which characters are engaging? Which details, lines of dialogue, or passages of meditation or analysis add the most to your essay? Even if your readers can come up with only one or two effective details, lines, or scenes, take their praise to heart. Can you do more of whatever is working in this draft when you write the next draft?
2. Next, ask your readers to restate the central question you're exploring, the discovery you are trying to make, or the argument you are attempting to convince your readers is true. If they are unable to do so, ask them to help you clarify what that question, discovery, or argument might become in your next draft.
3. Ask your readers if the manuscript's structure or form is clear. Are you telling a story? Taking your readers on a journey? Conducting an experiment? Profiling one or more subjects?
4. Can your readers follow what's going on? Is the pacing too fast or too slow? Do you use too many details, or too few? Too much dialogue, or not enough? Does the dialogue seem natural and believable? Can your readers see the locations where the events in your essay or book take place?
5. Do your readers need any backstory or other information to make the essay comprehensible?
6. Ask if they can trace the process by which you develop at least a partial answer to your question or prove your discovery or argument to be valid. Are your assertions believable? Supported by your experience? By logic? By evidence or research?
7. Is your discovery interesting and believable? Are your meditations and conclusions clearly worded? Satisfying? Does your essay sound preachy? Are your conclusions obvious or surprising in any way?

SUGGESTIONS FOR IMPROVEMENT

8. Now ask your readers if they can suggest anything specific you might do to make your essay even better than it is. Ask them to be specific (and tactful) in describing your essay's flaws and to provide at least one concrete way in which you might overcome each flaw when you write the next draft.
9. Try not to get defensive. Usually, it helps to simply write down everything you hear, whether praise or constructive criticism. Sitting through a workshop is like listening to a doctor

talk about an upcoming operation: you think you're taking in everything the doctor says, but you tend to forget most of it because your heart is pounding too loudly. In the case of workshop, surprisingly, most people tend to forget their readers' praise!

10. After the workshop, ask yourself which suggestions ring true or echo your own fears about your essay. Which suggestions make you excited to return to your computer? Which suggestions seem beside the point or wrongheaded? Which suggestions would turn your essay into an essay you never intended to write? Might these new intentions be better than your old ones? Might you want to change your intentions and start over?

Final Drafts

MAKING THE BIG CHANGES

1. Go back to your essay and make the improvements you decided to make in the previous two chapters. If feedback from your readers has significantly changed your understanding of your essay's central question or the form that will best allow you to explore it, then you will probably find it easiest to start over from scratch. Otherwise, make a list of all the changes you want to make, then set yourself the goal of accomplishing each improvement one by one rather than trying to make all the improvements at the same time, in one huge revision. Try not to feel overwhelmed. Know that everyone feels lost at some point in the revision of an essay (let alone a book). If you do get lost, try to freewrite until you've found your way past your confusion, or give your draft to another reader and ask him or her to help you figure out the answer to your problem. Let this new draft sit for as long as possible. Come back to it. Rinse. Repeat.
2. When you've figured out all the large and medium-sized questions as regards content, form, and style and you feel satisfied with your essay (or as satisfied as any of us ever feels with an essay), go through your essay and ask yourself if there are any sections or scenes that don't relate to your central question or don't add anything important to your essay. Then force yourself to cut them.
3. Now go through your essay paragraph by paragraph and ask yourself whether each paragraph is vital to your essay. If it isn't, force yourself to cut it. If you consider a given paragraph vital to your essay, go through it sentence by sentence and ask yourself whether each sentence is vital to that paragraph, and if it isn't, force yourself to cut it.

POLISHING YOUR PROSE

4. Once you've gotten your essay down to its essential sentences, go through each sentence word by word and ask yourself if each word is vital to that sentence, and if it isn't, force yourself to cut it. Rather than seeing this as a chore, you can see it as a game, awarding yourself a point for every word you can cut from the original length of your essay. Here are some hints to help you recognize and delete excess verbiage and strengthen the prose that's left:
   a) An empty noun is a noun that's so vague or abstract it doesn't lead your readers to see anything in their mind's eye or experience an emotion. The most common examples of vague nouns tend to be "it" and "thing," but "situation," "problem," "process," "type," "sort," and "kind" are ubiquitous as well. You would be surprised

how powerful and vivid a passage can become simply by changing most of the empty nouns and pronouns to concrete nouns and names. (And don't be worried about repeating nouns. Readers would rather see the word "dog" recur three times in a paragraph than see the word "it" three times.)

b) Beware vague phrases. Remember in the Introduction, when we tried to guess what various writers meant when they talked about dealing with their parents' problems with alcohol or the situations in their homes? If a parent has "a problem with alcohol," he or she is an alcoholic or a drunk (or, in milder cases, a drinker), a "domestic violence situation" is a case of wife beating or child abuse, and if someone "is engaged in a decision-making process to determine whether to quit a dysfunctional football team situation," he is deciding whether to quit a team because the coach forces kids to play even when they're injured.

c) As you might guess, an empty verb is a verb that doesn't convey a vivid action. At this point in your writing life, you've probably heard teachers say not to use the passive voice, so I'll just offer a brief reminder that "the ball was hit" is almost always less vivid than "the girl hit the ball," while "the pie was eaten" leaves out the vital information that "the old lady ate the pie." But even experienced writers need frequent nagging to prod them to purge their sentences of "is/was" verbs. "There was blood on the floor" rarely can compete with "Blood pooled on the floor."

d) Be wary of unnecessary qualifiers, not only because they add empty words to your essay, but also because they weaken the force of your opinions. Save the qualifiers for occasions when you really *aren't* sure of what you're saying—or when you might be sued for making too strong an argument, especially with insufficient evidence to back it up. You might want to write "I think the principal was afraid to suspend me because my mother is our city's chief of police and he didn't want to get pulled over for going a mile over the speed limit on Main Street," but you probably won't want to write "I think I might have broken up with John because there might have been a chance that he probably might have been fooling around with someone who might have been my best friend."

e) Remember the cliché expert and make sure he isn't testifying anywhere in your essay. Root out what Ken Macrorie calls "Engfish"—that is, fishy English that comes from an attempt to mimic jargon or diction you don't normally use. If you don't tend to say "thereupon" or "whereby" or "veritable plethora of deconstructed postmodern postcolonial hermeneutic strategies" in your everyday life, why would you write such pretentious phrases in an essay? Erudition and elegance are often to be admired, but if your prose strikes you as unnecessarily verbose, convoluted, or pretentious, ask yourself: "If I were explaining this to my best friend from home, my mother, or my little brother, what wording would I use?"

f) Hunt out redundancies. All of us write drafts that contain sentences such as: "After my father divorced my mother, he left the marriage and went to live in an utterly dingy, completely empty apartment that wasn't furnished on the outskirts of town." The trick is to catch such a sentence before the final draft and compress it to: "My father divorced my mother and went to live in a dingy, unfurnished apartment on the outskirts of town." Other redundancies require that you believe that your verbs actually do their jobs. Consider these examples:
I thought to myself;
I shrugged my shoulders;
I sat down;
I stood up;
I whispered softly;
I walked in a jerky motion.

g) If your paragraphs follow each other in an orderly way dictated by the organic structure of your essay, you won't need to use elaborate transitions or topic sentences to lead us from one paragraph to the next. Rather than repeating what you told us in the previous paragraph and/or telling us what you're about to tell us in the coming paragraph, just let the paragraphs do their jobs. In a similar way, you don't need to tell us what someone is going to tell us in a quote; just let the quotation convey what it's meant to convey.
h) In the old days, before computers, writers would cut apart the sections of a rough draft, rearrange them on a table or on the floor, then paste or tape them to the pages of a legal pad in a new and better order. Or we would cut out the salvageable parts of an early draft, paste or tape them to a pad, then write the new version of the essay in and around those sections. Although cumbersome, this method allowed the writer to see the entire essay at a glance, move around various sections, and try this or that structural possibility without losing track of what he or she was doing. With computers, the writer can see only one or two sections of the essay at a time and therefore can become confused when moving large chunks of text back and forth through hyperspace. As retro as this sounds, don't be afraid to take a pair of scissors and cut a hard copy of your essay into sections, then rearrange the sections and tape them to a pad before returning to your computer and keying in the changes.

TWO PARTING CAVEATS

First, please know that most writers end up disliking what they've written. If you find yourself ready to hit the delete button and cut your entire draft, go back and look at your notes from workshop and remind yourself of everything your readers praised.

Second, know that some writers work according to an entirely different method than the process I've outlined here. Rather than beginning with a disorganized, poorly written, and barely thought-out first draft, these writers agonize over the first sentence of an essay and can't or won't move on to the second sentence until the first sentence strikes them as perfect and they've solved whatever thematic, structural, or stylistic problems the second sentence presents. Such writers take forever to produce a preliminary draft, but that draft usually doesn't need much revision. If your method works for you, use it. Either way, don't let the need to revise an essay dampen the passion or the poetry that inspired you to write it in the first place.[1]

---

[1] See also Donald M. Murray's *The Craft of Revision*, fifth edition, Thomson/Wadsworth, 2004.

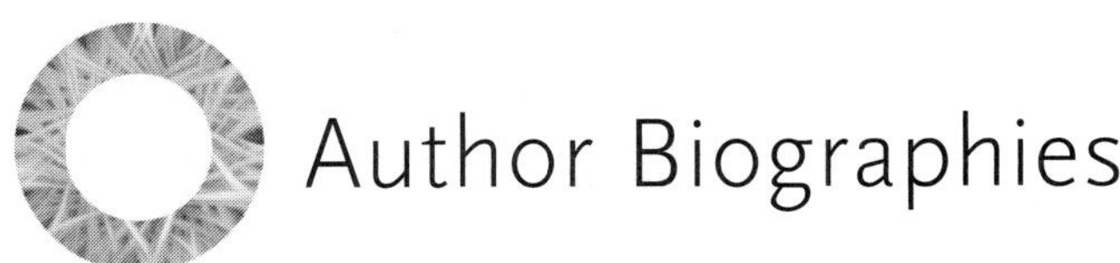

Author Biographies

James Agee (1909–1955) was born in Knoxville, Tennessee, and lost his father to an automobile accident when he was six. Though Agee would go on to write poetry, essays, film criticism, and the journalistic classic *Let Us Now Praise Famous Men* (1941), his masterpiece was the novel shaped by his early loss. *A Death in the Family* was published posthumously in 1957 and received a Pulitzer Prize. "Knoxville: Summer of 1915" (1935) is a prose poem that takes place the year before Agee's father died. In 1947, Samuel Barber set the poem to music, to be sung by a solo soprano and accompanied by an orchestra; if you're interested, you can download several versions of it on iTunes.

Charles Baxter (1947–) is the author of five novels, four collections of short stories, three collections of poems, and a collection of essays on fiction, *Burning Down the House* (1997). "Dysfunctional Narratives, or: 'Mistakes Were Made'" appeared originally in a 1994 issue of *Ploughshares* and is the first chapter in Baxter's collection. His novel *The Feast of Love* was a fiction finalist for the 2001 National Book Award and became a major motion picture in 2007. From 1989 to 2002, Baxter was a member of the MFA faculty at the University of Michigan. He now teaches at the University of Minnesota in Minneapolis, his hometown.

Emily Bernard (1967–) received both her B.A. and her Ph.D. in American Studies at Yale. She is the editor of *Remember Me to Harlem: The Letters of Langston Hughes and Carl Van Vechten* (2001) and *Some of My Best Friends: Writers on Interracial Friendship* (2004). "Teaching the N-Word" first appeared in the October 2004 issue of *The American Scholar* and was selected for *The Best American Essays* of 2006; it is based on her experience at the University of Vermont, where she still teaches.

Jane Brox (1956–) received the 1996 L. L. Winship/PEN New England Award for her first book, *Here and Nowhere Else* (1995). Her second book, *Five Thousand Days Like This One,* was a 1999 finalist for the National Book Critics Circle Award in nonfiction; its essays trace the history of the Merrimack Valley of Massachusetts, where Brox makes her home and where her family has lived for generations. "Influenza 1918," part of that collection, has since appeared in *One Hundred Great Essays* (Penguin, 2001) and *Best American Essays* of 1996. Brox teaches nonfiction writing in the MFA program at Lesley College in Cambridge, Massachusetts.

Raymond Carver (1938–1988) is one of the first names that comes up when people talk about the American short story. In the 1970s and '80s, with his ear for dialogue and trademark minimalism, he revitalized interest in this form. His stories, now widely anthologized, originally appeared in four collections: *Put Yourself in My Shoes* (1974), *Will You Please Be Quiet, Please?* (1976), *What We Talk About When We Talk About Love* (1981), and *Where I'm Calling From* (published posthumously in 1988). You can find his poetry in *All of Us: The Collected Poems*, which was published by Knopf in 1998.

Bernard Cooper (1951–) is an O. Henry Prize–winning fiction writer, also known for his memoirs: *Maps to Anywhere*, which won the PEN/Ernest Hemingway Award in 1990; *Truth Serum* (1996); and *The Bill From My Father: A Memoir* (2006). As a boy discovering his sexuality in the 1950s and a gay man in the age of AIDS, Cooper tells important American stories by telling us his own story. He has taught at Antioch/Los Angeles and at the UCLA Writer's Program. Currently, he is an art critic for *Los Angeles Magazine*.

John D'Agata (1974–) specializes in the lyric essay, so it should be no surprise that he holds two MFA degrees, one in nonfiction and one in poetry, both from the Iowa Writers' Workshop. In 2002, he applied his poetic sensibility to editing the innovative anthology *The Next American Essay*. D'Agata is now the editor of lyric essays for *The Seneca Review*, and he teaches nonfiction at the University of Iowa. "Round Trip" appears in his 2001 collection *Halls of Fame*.

Meghan Daum (1970–) is the author of a novel, *The Quality of Life Report* (a *New York Times* Notable Book of 2003), and a collection of essays, *My Misspent Youth* (2001), in which you can find "Music Is My Bag" (which originally appeared in *Harper's*). Born in California in 1970, Daum grew up on the East Coast, earning her undergraduate degree from Vassar and an MFA in creative writing from Columbia before moving west again, first to Nebraska and then to Los Angeles. In addition to writing a column for the *Los Angeles Times* and contributing nonfiction pieces to *The New Yorker*, *Harper's*, *GQ*, and *Vogue*, she also can be heard on National Public Radio's *Morning Edition* and *This American Life*.

Joan Didion (1934–) is the mother of the personal, political essay. Since she appeared on the literary scene in the 1960s, she has been a nonfiction powerhouse, pumping out precise, elegant prose on everything from '60s counterculture to Central American politics to her own private grief. As of 2006, all seven of Didion's nonfiction books—including the National Book Award winner, *The Year of Magical Thinking* (2005)—are available in the single volume *We Tell Ourselves Stories in Order to Live*. Didion also has written five novels and, with her late husband, worked on a number of screenplays for Hollywood feature films. A sixth-generation Californian, she now lives in New York.

Annie Dillard (1945–) finds God and natural beauty in unexpected places. The product of a comfortable upbringing in Pittsburgh, Dillard attended Hollins University, where she met and married her writing teacher, the poet R.H. Dillard. In 1974, she emerged onto the literary scene with her Pulitzer Prize–winning book *Pilgrim at Tinker Creek*, and since then has received just about every honor available to a writer (the intimidating list of honors is available on her website, www.anniedillard.com). Throughout the 1970s and '80s, she served as a Contributing Editor at *Harper's Magazine*, and she has continued to work on her own writing. Her publications include an autobiography, a book of poetry, a novel, and other forms of hard-to-classify narrative nonfiction.

Andre Dubus III (1959–) began school at Bradford College, where his father, the late author Andre Dubus, taught. He later dropped out of a Ph.D. program at the University of Wisconsin and worked a series of odd jobs—as an actor, a carpenter, a private investigator, a bartender, and a bounty hunter—while he wrote on the side. Now a successful novelist and short-story writer, Dubus teaches at the University of Massachusetts Lowell. He is best known for his novel *House of Sand and Fog*, which was a 1999 National Book Award Finalist and is now a motion picture.

Barbara Ehrenreich (1941–) sees no conflict between her roles as journalist and activist. In addition to being a full-time journalist and author, she fights for peace, women's rights, fair health-care, and economic justice. You can find her essays and opinion pieces in *The New York Times*, *Harper's*, and *Time* (where she is a contributing writer), and at her blog, www.barbaraehrenreich.com. The essay in this anthology began as a feature for *Harper's* on the effects of the 1996 Welfare Reform Act and became the bestselling book *Nickl-and-Dimed: On (Not) Getting By in America* (2001). Ehrenreich is also the author of a follow-up book, *Bait and Switch: The (Futile) Pursuit of the American Dream.*

Richard Feynman (1918–1988) was not your average essayist. He helped develop the atomic bomb during World War II, is credited with introducing the concept of nanotechnology, and in 1965 won a Nobel Prize in physics. Yet he was an unusually public figure for a scientist, due in part to his semi-autobiographical books, *Surely You're Joking, Mr. Feynman!* (1985) and *What Do You Care What Other People Think?* (1988). Feynman also reached students through his years of teaching at Cornell and at the California Institute of Technology; he lectured until two weeks before his death, when he succumbed to an eight-year battle with cancer.

William Finnegan (1952–) is the author of *A Complicated War: The Harrowing of Mozambique* (1992), *Dateline Soweto: Travels with Black South African Reporters* (1988), and *Crossing the Line: A Year in the Land of Apartheid* (1986), which was named one of the ten best nonfiction books of 1986 by *The New York Times*. Finnegan was a National Magazine Award finalist in both 1990 and 1995, and he has been a staff writer at *The New Yorker* since 1987. "The Unwanted" is part of his most recent book, *Cold New World: Growing Up in a Harder Country*, a *New York Times* Notable Book of the Year and a *Los Angeles Times* Best Nonfiction of 1998 selection.

Marshall Jon Fisher (1963–) is a freelance writer who contributes frequently to *The Atlantic Monthly*. He has co-authored all three of his books with his father, David E. Fisher. Together, they are responsible for *Tube: The Invention of Television* (1996), *Strangers in the Night: A Brief History of Life on Other Worlds* (1998), and *Mysteries of Lost Empires* (2000).

Paul Fussell (1924–) is a graduate of Pomona College and Harvard University, a cultural and literary historian known best for his anti-war stance and for his observations on class in America. As a young man, Fussell was drafted into World War II, an experience that left him enraged at the way war is romanticized in U.S. culture. Fussell's 1975 literary study *The Great War and Modern Memory* won the National Book Award for Arts and Letters, the National Book Critics Circle Award for Criticism, and the Ralph Waldo Emerson Award of

Phi Beta Kappa. If you enjoy his essay "Notes on Class," you may want to track down his book on the subject, *Class: A Guide Through the American Status System* (1983).

John Hersey (1914–1993) was born in China and moved to the United States when he was ten. After graduating from Yale and Cambridge, he became the Far East correspondent for *Time,* and during World War II, he also wrote for *Life* and *The New Yorker.* As a war journalist, Hersey accompanied the U.S. Army on the invasions of Italy and Sicily. The novel inspired by his experiences there, *A Bell for Adano* (1944), won a Pulitzer Prize. After the U.S. dropped the atomic bomb in Hiroshima, Hersey was commissioned by *The New Yorker* to write a series of articles about the decimated city. He chose to demonstrate the effects of the atomic explosion by following six survivors, and the resulting pieces were so powerful that *The New Yorker* dedicated an entire issue to printing them (August 31, 1946). The material was published as the book *Hiroshima* later that year.

Marcie Hershman (1951–) is a fiction writer and journalist, author of the novels *Safe in America* (1995) and *Tales of the Master Race* (1991). After her brother's death, she wrote the meditative memoir *Speak To Me: Grief, Love, and What Endures* (2001). Currently, Hershman is a lecturer in creative writing at Tufts University.

Ann Hodgman (1956–) is the author of humor books, cookbooks, and more than forty children's books. Her work has also appeared in *The Atlantic Monthly, The New Yorker,* and *Salon.* "No Wonder They Call Me a Bitch" did not appear in her regular food column but was first published in *Spy* magazine, where Hodgman was a Contributing Editor; later it was selected for *The Best American Essays* of 1990. Hodgman lives and writes in Connecticut with her husband, two children, and twenty pets.

Sue Hubbell (1935–) is the author of *A Country Year: Living the Questions* (1986) and *A Book of Bees: And How to Keep Them* (1998), both selected by *The New York Times* Book Review as Notable Books of the Year. Originally from Kalamazoo, Michigan, Hubbell is a self-taught naturalist. For more than thirty years, she has made her home in the Ozarks, where she writes and keeps bees.

Sebastian Junger (1962–) knows how to make an entrance: his first novel *The Perfect Storm* (1997) was a *New York Times* Bestseller in hardcopy for one year and in paperback for two years before becoming a motion picture, starring George Clooney and Mark Wahlberg. His other books include the collection *Fire* (2001) and the historically based novel *A Death in Belmont* (2006). Now a journalist, Junger writes for *Outside, American Heritage,* and *Men's Journal.* He lives in New York City.

Jamaica Kincaid (1949–) was born Elaine Potter Richardson and raised on the island of Antigua, a British colony until 1967. At seventeen, Richardson was sent to New York to work as an au pair—or a "servant," in her terms. After three years of nannying, she quit the job, began school, dropped out, and started freelance writing for a teen magazine. In 1973, she changed her name to write anonymously. Three years later, William Shawn, then the editor of *The New Yorker,* discovered Kincaid and hired her as a staff writer. She went on to marry Shawn's son, a composer and professor at Bennington

College. They live together in Vermont. "On Seeing England for the First Time" appeared in *Harper's* in 1991.

Wayne Koestenbaum (1958–) is a poet, a novelist, and a critic of art and culture, best known for his book *The Queen's Throat: Opera, Homosexuality, and the Mystery of Desire* (1993). The opening of the book, an autobiographical meditation on gay males' affinity for opera, is excerpted here. Koestenbaum is currently a Distinguished Professor of English at City University of New York Graduate Center and writes frequently for *The New York Times Magazine* and the *London Review of Books.*

Robert Kurson (1963–) earned a B.A. in philosophy from the University of Wisconsin and a J.D. from Harvard Law School. "My Favorite Teacher," which appeared in *Esquire* in 2000, was his first magazine story and a finalist for the National Magazine Award. Since then, his stories have appeared in *Rolling Stone, The New York Times Magazine,* and *Esquire,* where he is a contributing editor.

Primo Levi (1919–1987) was a chemist by training and a Holocaust survivor by ancestry, history, and chance. Born into a family of assimilated Italian Jews, he received his degree from the University of Turin and worked as a chemist until 1941, when the Germans invaded Northern Italy. In 1943, Levi was apprehended as a part of the anti-Fascist resistance and deported to Auschwitz. By working at a synthetic rubber factory in the camp, he was spared the gas chamber, but his guilt over surviving haunted him until his controversial death. *If This Is a Man* (1947), Levi's famous memoir, was the first of his many attempts to make sense of what he and Europe had endured. "Chromium" appears in *The Periodic Table* (1975), a collection of twenty-one short works, each named for an element.

Li-Young Lee (1957–) has lived in Chicago since 1964, but he carries the burden of his family's history and writes as an intimate of loss. His father served as a physician to Mao Zedong until exile forced the family to Indonesia, where Lee was born. Two years later, due to anti-Chinese sentiment, his family fled again, first to Hong Kong and finally to the United States. Lee is the author of four books of poetry: *Rose* (1986), *The City in Which I Love You* (1991), *Book of My Nights* (2001), and most recently, *Behind My Eyes* (2008). His memoir, *The Winged Seed: A Remembrance* (1995), traces not only his life, but the lives of his parents and grandparents through histories, dreams, and reconstructed remembrances.

Phillip Lopate (1943–) has written novels, collections of poetry, and book-length works of film criticism, but his forte seems to be the personal essay, as evinced by the following collections: *Being With Children* (1975), *Bachelorhood* (1981), *Against Joie de Vivre* (1989), and *Portrait of My Body* (1996). Lopate also served as editor of the anthology *The Art of the Personal Essay* (1994) and has written the Phillip Lopate reader, *Getting Personal* (2003). He holds the John Cranford Adams Chair at Hofstra University, and teaches in the M.F.A. programs at Columbia, the New School, and Bennington.

Thomas Lynch (1948–) is quite likely the only essayist and poet who also is a funeral director, his family having buried three generations' of the dead in Milford, Michigan. Lynch's earliest volumes of poetry (*Skating with Heather Grace,* 1986 , *Grimalkin & Other*

Poems, 1994, and *Still Life in Milford*, 1998) were followed by his first collection of essays, *The Undertaking* (1997), which not only was a finalist for the National Book Award and won the American Book Award but also served as the inspiration for the HBO series *Six Feet Under*. Lynch's second collection of prose pieces, *Bodies in Motion and at Rest* (2001), won the Great Lakes Book Award; his most recent nonfiction book, *Booking Passage: We Irish and Americans*, appeared in 2005. He was the subject of a *Frontline* profile on PBS and occasionally teaches creative nonfiction at the University of Michigan.

John McPhee (1931–) has been a staff writer at *The New Yorker* since 1965 and somehow also has managed to put out 27 books of nonfiction. One of the founding fathers of the New Journalism, he is famous for rendering complex, specialized material in readable and literary ways. *Annals of the Former World*, McPhee's tetralogy on geology, was published in a single volume in 1998 and was awarded the Pulitzer Prize in 1999. Today, he teaches nonfiction at Princeton University, his alma mater.

James Alan McPherson (1943–) made his literary debut in 1965, when his short story "Gold Coast" won a writing contest at *The Atlantic Monthly*; John Updike would later select that story to be anthologized in *The Best American Short Stories of the Century* (2000). McPherson's second collection, *Elbow Room* (1977), made him the first African American to win a Pulitzer Prize in fiction. He also has been the recipient of a Guggenheim Fellowship, a MacArthur Fellowship, and a number of Pushcart Prizes. The essay "Umbilicus" appears in the story-like memoir *Crabcakes* (1998) and in a Pushcart Prize anthology (1998). McPherson teaches at the University of Iowa, from which he earned an M.F.A. in 1971.

Joseph Mitchell (1908–1996) was born, raised, and educated in North Carolina, but after he moved to New York City in 1929, he remained there for the rest of his life. He began as a journalist for *The World-Telegram* and *The Herald-Tribune*, then joined *The New Yorker* staff in 1938. There, he became famous for doing "Talk of the Town" pieces and portraits of eccentrics living on the City's fringe. *McSorley's Wonderful Saloon* (1943) is based on the customers at New York's oldest saloon and has been called the *Dubliners* of Manhattan. In 1996, Mitchell died, having written for *The New Yorker* for 58 years.

Jon Mooallem (1978–) used to be a kosher butcher in New Jersey. No, really. In 2006, he graduated from UC Berkeley Graduate School of Journalism, and now he is a journalist whose articles and essays have appeared in *The Believer, Harper's, The Nation, The New Yorker*, and *Salon.com*, and he is a contributing writer to *The New York Times Magazine*.

Naomi Shihab Nye (1952–) is a Palestinian-American poet who has lived in St. Louis and Jerusalem and now makes her home in San Antonio. Known for her poetry, lyric essays, and anthologies on the Middle East, she is the winner of four Pushcart Prizes, a Guggenheim Fellowship, and a Lavan Award from the American Academy of Poets. Her poetry collection *19 Varieties of Gazelle* was a finalist for a 2002 National Book Award. Nye is also an award-winning writer of poetry and essays for young adults.

Judith Ortiz Cofer (1952–) was born in Hormigueros in Puerto Rico, but soon after her birth, her father, who was in the U.S. Navy, was transferred to New Jersey. Though the family often traveled back and forth to Puerto Rico, Ortiz Cofer attended school in Paterson and later in Augusta, Georgia. She holds a B.A. in English from Augusta College and an M.A. from Florida Atlantic University. A poet and fiction writer as well as an essayist, Ortiz Cofer has been honored with a long list of awards, including a nomination for the Pulitzer Prize for her early novel *The Line of the Sun*. She is currently the Franklin Professor of English and Creative Writing at the University of Georgia.

George Orwell (1903–1950), christened Eric Arthur Blair, was born in British India and moved to England in 1904. When it came time to attend university, Blair was unable to pay or to win a scholarship, so he joined the Indian Imperial Police in Burma, where he learned to hate imperialism. Blair returned to England, resigned from the service, and struggled for many years to support himself before changing his name and earning a reputation as a journalist. Today, we remember Orwell as one of the finest essayists of the twentieth century and as the author of the acclaimed novels *Animal Farm* (1945) and *Nineteen Eighty-Four* (1949).

Grace Paley (1922–2007) described herself as a "somewhat combative pacifist and cooperative anarchist." During Vietnam, she was jailed repeatedly for protesting the war, and in later years, she lobbied for women's rights and against the war in Iraq. When not advocating liberal causes, she wrote poignantly about the daily lives of women—New Yorkers, Jews, and single mothers in particular. From 1986–1988, she was New York's first official state author. Her *Collected Stories* was a finalist for both the Pulitzer Prize and the National Book Award in 1994.

Elwood Reid (1966–) played football for the Wolverines as an undergraduate, then went on to earn his M.F.A. from the University of Michigan in 1996. His first novel, *If I Don't Six* (1998), describes the daily life of a Big Ten football player in scandalizing detail. Reid is also the author of the story collection *What Salmon Know* (1999) and the novels *Midnight Sun* (2000) and *D.B.* (2004). He and his wife and their four daughters divide their time between Montana and California, where Reid works as a scriptwriter.

Daniel Rivas (1978–) was born in Washington State and graduated with an MFA in creative writing from the University of Michigan. He won a Hopwood Award from the University for his essay "The Master of Machines," and the piece later appeared in the literary journal *Brick*. Rivas now teaches writing at American University and works at Politics and Prose Bookstore in Washington, D.C.

Adam Rogers (1970–) was born in Los Angeles, earned his undergraduate degree from Pomona College, and has a master's in science writing from Boston University. He put his knowledge and proclivities as a geek to work covering science, technology, medicine and the emerging Internet revolution for *Newsweek* for eight years before moving to WIRED Magazine in San Francisco, where he is a Senior Editor. As a Knight Science Journalism Fellow at the Massachusetts Institute of Technology (2002–2003), Rogers studied the intersection of urban theory, ecology, and public health.

Oliver Sacks, M.D. (1933–) was born into a British family of physicians and scientists. He earned his medical degree at Oxford University and published his first book, *Awakenings*, in 1973. Since 1965, he has lived in New York, where he is a practicing neurologist and a prolific writer. Sacks is best known for his collections of case histories, *The Man Who Mistook His Wife for a Hat* (1985) and *An Anthropologist on Mars* (1995), the latter documenting extreme and peculiar examples of neurological dysfunction. His work appears regularly in *The New Yorker,* as well as in medical journals. In July 2007, he was appointed a Professor of Clinical Neurology and Clinical Psychiatry at Columbia University Medical Center and was designated that university's first Columbia Artist.

David Sedaris (1956–) has been famously funny since 1992, when National Public Radio broadcast his "SantaLand Diaries" about working as a Macy's Christmas elf. Since then, Sedaris' humorous essays have appeared regularly in *The New Yorker* and are often broadcast on NPR. All four of his essay collections have been *New York Times* Bestsellers: *Naked* (1997), *Holidays on Ice* (1997), *Me Talk Pretty One Day* (2000), and *Dress Your Family in Corduroy and Denim* (2004). He lives and works in Paris with his partner, Hugh Hamrick.

Leslie Marmon Silko (1948–) grew up on the fringe of the Laguna Pueblo reservation, geographically and figuratively. Because she is of mixed ancestry—part white, part Mexican—she was not fully able to participate in reservation life, but her grandmother raised her in the storytelling tradition of the Laguna. She has become one of the most acclaimed Native American writers—a novelist, poet, and essayist, and the recipient of a 1981 MacArthur Foundation "genius" grant. Her novels include *Ceremony* (1977), *Storyteller* (1981), and *Almanac of the Dead* (1991). Although she no longer teaches at the University of Arizona, Silko continues to live in Tucson.

Charles Simic (1938–), born in Yugoslavia, has won just about every honor an American poet can win. In 1990, he received a Pulitzer Prize for his book of prose poems, *The World Doesn't End* (1989); his 1996 collection, *Walking the Black Cat,* was a finalist for the National Book Award for Poetry. He has been awarded fellowships from the MacArthur Foundation, the Guggenheim Foundation, and the National Endowment for the Arts. On the day that he was appointed the fifteenth Poet Laureate Consultant by the Librarian of Congress, Simic also won the Wallace Stevens Award from the Academy of American Poets. He is an essayist, a translator, an editor, and an Emeritus Professor at the University of New Hampshire, where he has taught since 1973.

Brent Staples (1951–) grew up in Chester, Pennsylvania, and earned his Ph.D. in psychology from the University of Chicago. His memoir, *Parallel Time: Growing up in Black and White,* was the winner of the Anisfield Wolff Book Award in 1995. "The Coroner's Photographs," included here, serves as the memoir's first chapter. In the late 1970s, Staples worked as a reporter for the *Chicago Sun-Times,* and since 1983 he has been an editorial writer for *The New York Times.*

Susan Allen Toth (1940–) graduated from Smith College and Berkeley and received a Ph.D. in English literature from the University of Minnesota in 1969. She has been a contributor to periodicals such as *Harper's, Cosmopolitan,* and *Ms.* In addition to essays and stories, Toth has written two book-length memoirs and a series of books on England, where she travels regularly. "Going to the Movies" was originally published in *Harper's* in 1980.

Lily Tuck (1938–) was born in Paris and now lives in the United States, dividing her time between New York City and Maine. She is the author of four novels, including *Siam, or the Woman Who Shot a Man* (1999), a finalist for a PEN/Faulkner Award, and *The News From Paraguay,* which won a National Book Award in 2004. Her short stories have appeared in *The New Yorker* and *Paris Review,* in addition to the collection *Limbo, or Other Places I've Lived* (2000). "Group Grief" appeared in a 2005 issue of *The Hudson Review* before being chosen for *The Best American Essays* of 2006.

Alice Walker (1944–) received a Pulitzer in 1983 for her novel *The Color Purple,* making her the first African American woman to receive that prize. She won a National Book Award for the same novel, which became a motion picture in 1985 and a Tony Award–nominated musical in 2005. *The Color Purple* is Walker's best-known work, but she is also a poet, an essayist, and an activist. The 1975 article "Looking For Zora" was largely responsible for a renewal of interest in Zora Neale Hurston, one of the authors whose work inspired Walker's own.

Philip Weiss (1956–) does not actually spend much time in locked trunks. He is a New York journalist and essayist who has written extensively on the Clinton administration, American Jewish life, and American-Israeli relations. He is also the author of *American Taboo: A Murder in the Peace Corps* (2004) and the blog "Mondo Weiss" at www.philipweiss.org.

E.B. White (1899–1985) once said of Thoreau's *Walden*: "Every man, I think, reads one book in his life, and this one is mine." White's commemorative essay "Walden" (August 1939) first appeared in "One Man's Meat," the regular column he wrote for *Harper's Magazine* from 1938 to 1943. Throughout his career, White also wrote for *The New Yorker* and *The Atlantic Monthly,* where "Death of a Pig" was first published in 1948. White was one of America's greatest literary stylists, a master of the essay form, and also the author of the children's classics *Stuart Little* (1945) and *Charlotte's Web* (1952). His 1959 revision of William Strunk's writing guide, *The Elements of Style,* is still widely used in composition courses. In 1978, White received a special Pulitzer citation for his letters, essays, and his body of work as a whole.

Terry Tempest Williams (1955–) is celebrated as both a writer and an advocate for the American West. She is a Utah native and a sixth-generation Mormon, whose worldview is deeply informed by the landscape she loves. "The Clan of One-Breasted Women" appears as the epilogue to her sixth book, *Refuge: An Unnatural History of Family and Place* (1991). Now a classic of environmental literature, the book shows how Williams' family history intersects with the history of the Great Salt Lake region, where Williams still makes her home.

Credits

This page constitutes an extension of the copyright page. We have made every effort to trace the ownership of all copyrighted material and to secure permission from copyright holders. In the event of any question arising as to the use of any material, we will be pleased to make the necessary corrections in future printings. Thanks are due to the following authors, publishers, and agents for permission to use the material indicated.

Chapter 2. 9: Frank Sullivan, "The Cliche Expert Testifies on the Atom," in *New Yorker*, November 17, 1945, p. 27. **15:** *The Partisan Review*, no. 5, 1938 for "Knoxville: Summer of 1915" by James Agee. First published in *The Partisan Review*, May 1938. Copyright © 1938 by James Agee. Reprinted with permission of The Wylie Agency, Inc. **19:** Cofer, Judith Ortiz. From *Prairie Schooner*. 1989. Copyright © 1989 by the University of Nebraska Press. All rights reserved. Reproduced by permission of the University of Nebraska Press.

Chapter 3. 23: Barbara Ehrenreich, "Nickel-and-Dimed: On (Not) Getting By in America," in *Harper's*, January, 1999. Reproduced by permission.

Chapter 5. 43: "Shooting an Elephant" from *Shooting an Elephant and Other Essays by George Orwell*, copyright 1950 by Sonia Brownwell Orwell and renewed 1978 by Sonia Pitt-Rivers, reprinted by permission of Houghton Mifflin Harcourt Publishing Company. **47:** Bernard Cooper, "A Clack of Tiny Sparks: Remembrance of a Gay Boyhood," in *Harper's*, January, 1991, pp. 64–69. Reproduced by permission. **53:** Andre Dubus III, "Tracks and Ties," in *Epoch*, no. 422, 1995. Reproduced by permission of the author, conveyed through the Phillip G. Spitzer Literary Agency. **57:** Marcie Hershman, "No Burden to Bear," in *New York Times*, October 4, 1992. Reprinted by permission of the New York Times Company. **60:** *Atlantic Monthly*, January, 1948 for "Death of a Pig" by E. B. White. Reproduced with permission. **65:** Grace Paley, "Six Days: Some Rememberings," in *Alaska Quarterly Review*, Fall/Winter 1994. Reproduced by permission.

Chapter 6. 77: "Once More to the Lake" from *One Man's Meat*, text copyright © 1941 by E. B. White. Copyright renewed. Reprinted by permission of Tilbury House, Publishers, Gardiner, Maine and the author's estate. **81:** Walker, Alice. From *Ms. Magazine*. 1975. Copyright © 1975 by Verso. Reproduced by permission of the author. **92:** James Alan McPherson, "Umbilicus," in *Doubletake*, 1998. Reproduced by permission of the author, conveyed through the Faith Childs Literary Agency. **95:** Sue Hubbell, "The Vicksburg Ghost," in *The New Yorker*, September 25, 1989, p. 106.

Chapter 7. 109: Kurson, Robert. From *Esquire*. March 1, 2000. Reproduced by permission of the author. **118:** Reprinted with the permission of Simon & Schuster Adult Publishing Group and the author, from *The Man Who Mistook His Wife for a Hat and Other*

Clinical Tales by Oliver Sacks. Copyright © 1970, 1981, 1983, 1984, 1985 by Oliver Sacks. All rights reserved. **127:** From *The Periodic Table* by Primo Levi, translated by Raymond Rosenthal, translation copyright © 1984 by Shocken Books, a division of Random House, Inc. Used by permission of Shocken Books, a division of Random House, Inc.

Chapter 8. 139: *Spy Magazine,* 1989 for "No Wonder They Call Me a Bitch" by Ann Hodgman. Reproduced by permission. **142:** From *"Surely You're Joking, Mr. Feynman!": Adventures of a Curious Character* by Richard Feynman as Told to Ralph Leighton. Copyright © 1985 by Richard P. Feynman and Ralph Leighton. Used by permission of W. W. Norton & Company, Inc. and Random House Group, Ltd. **143:** Copyright © 1992 by *Harper's Magazine.* All rights reserved. Reproduced from the June issue by special permission. **147:** Barbara Ehrenreich, "Nickel-and-Dimed: On (Not) Getting By in America," in *Harper's,* January, 1999. Reproduced by permission.

Chapter 9. 168: From *The Perfect Storm* by Sebastien Junger. Copyright © 1997 by Sebastien Junger. Used by permission of W. W. Norton & Company, Inc. and the author. **172:** Reprinted with the permission of Simon & Schuster and Darhansoff, Verrill, Feldman Literary Agency. From *THE WINGED SEED: A REMEMBRANCE* by Li-Young Lee. Copyright © 1995 by Li-Young Lee. **176:** Dillard, Annie. From *Esquire.* 1989. Reproduced by permission of the author. **184:** Daniel Rivas, "Master of Machines," in *Brick: A Literary Journal,* summer, 2004, pp. 33–39. Reprinted by permission of the author. **189:** Mitchell, Joseph. From *New Yorker.* 1940. Reproduced by permission.

Chapter 10. 204: Susan Allen Toth, "Cinematypes: Going to the Movies," in *Harper's,* May, 1980, pp. 99–100. Reprinted by permission of the author. **206:** John Hersey, "Chapter One," in *Hiroshima,* 1989, pp. 1–16. Reprinted by permission of Random House, Inc. **214:** Reid, Elwood. From *GQ.* 1997. Reproduced by permission. **222:** William Finnegan, "The Unwanted," *New Yorker,* December 1, 1977. Reproduced by permission of the author.

Chapter 11. 244: "The Search for Marvin Gardens" from *PIECES OF THE FRAME* by John McPhee. Copyright © 1975, renewed 2003 by John McPhee. Reprinted by permission of Farrar, Straus and Giroux, LLC. **251:** Emily Bernard, "Teaching the N-Word," in *The American Scholar,* Autumn 2005. Reprinted by permission of the author. **262:** *The Hudson Review,* winter, 2005 for "Group Grief" by Lily Tuck. Copyright © 2005 by Lily Tuck. Reprinted by permission of Georges Borchardt, Inc., on behalf of the author.

Chapter 12. 275: Paul Fussell, *The Boy Scout Handbook and Other Observations,* Oxford: Oxford University Press, 1982. Reproduced by permission of Oxford University Press, Inc. **283:** Meghan Daum, "Music Is My Bag," in *Harper's,* March, 2000, pp. 64–69. Reproduced by permission. **291:** Sedaris, David. From *Esquire.* 2002. Reproduced by permission.

Chapter 13. 297: "Fear," from *ALL OF US: THE COLLECTED POEMS* by Raymond Carver, copyright © 1996 by Tess Gallagher. Used by permission of Alfred A. Knopf, a division of Random House, Inc. **299:** "Portrait of My Body," copyright © 1996 by Philip Lopate. First appeared in the *Michigan Quarterly,* from *PORTRAIT OF MY BODY* by Philip Lopate. Used by permission of Doubleday, a division of Random House, Inc. and the author, conveyed through Wendy Weil Agency. **305:** From *Parallel Time* by Brent Staples, copyright © 1994 by Brent Staples. Used by permission of Pantheon Books, a division of Random House, Inc. and International Creative Management. **308:** Marshall Fischer, "*Memoria ex Machina*," *Harper's*, December, 2002, pp. 22–26. Reproduced by permission of the author, conveyed through the Albert LaFarge Literary Agency. **312:** Joan Didion, "At the Dam," in *The White Album*, Simon & Schuster, 1979. Reproduced by permission of Farrar, Straus & Giroux, LLC. **314:** Jon Mooallem, "The Last Supper: Living by One-Handed Food Alone," *Harper's*, July, 2005. Copyright © 2005 by *Harper's Magazine*. All rights reserved. Reproduced from the July issue by special permission.

Chapter 14. 319: Charles Simic, "The Little Venus of the Eskimos," in *The Unemployed Fortune-Teller*, University of Michigan Press, pp. 13–18. Reproduced by permission. **322:** Nye, Naomi Shihab. From "Three Pokes of a Thistle," in *Never in a Hurry: Essays on People and Places*. University of South Carolina Press. Reproduced by permission. **325:** Copyright © 1993 by Wayne Koestenbaum. **332:** From *The Undertaking: Life Studies From the Dismal Trade* by Thomas Lynch. Copyright © 1997 by Thomas Lynch. Used by permission of W. W. Norton & Company, Inc. and Richard P. McDonough.

Chapter 15. 344: "The Clan of One-Breasted Women," from *REFUGE: AN UNNATURAL HISTORY OF FAMILY AND PLACE* by Terry Tempest Williams, copyright ©1991 by Terry Tempest Williams. Used by permission of Pantheon Books, a division of Random House, Inc. and by Brandt & Hochman Literary Agents, Inc. **349:** Jane Brox, "Influenza: 1918," in *GEORGIA REVIEW*, fall, 1995, p. 687 ff. Reproduced by permission. **354:** *The New York Times*, March 9, 2008 for "Geek Love" by Adam Rogers. Copyright © 2008 *The New York Times*. All rights reserved. Used by permission and protected by the Copyright Laws of the United States. The printing, copying, redistribution or retransmission of the Material without express written permission is prohibited. www.nytimes.com.

Chapter 16. 360: Charles Baxter, "Dysfunctional Narratives: or: 'Mistakes Were Made'," in *Burning Down the House*, Graywolf Press, 1998, pp. 1–26. **369:** First published in *Hungry Mind Review* Fall 1995. Copyright © 1995 by Leslie Marmon Silko, reprinted with permission of The Wylie Agency, Inc. **374:** First published in *Harper's*, August 1991. Copyright © 1991 by Jamaica Kincaid, reprinted with permission of The Wylie Agency, LLC. **382:** John D'Agata, "Round Trip," in *Halls of Fame*, 2003, pp. 3–22, 239.

Index

F

G

H

I

M

N

O

T